THE POLITICS OF POVERTY REDUCTION

The Politics of Poverty Reduction

PAUL MOSLEY

with assistance from Blessing Chiripanhura, Jean Grugel, and Ben Thirkell-White

OXFORD
UNIVERSITY PRESS

OXFORD
UNIVERSITY PRESS

Great Clarendon Street, Oxford, OX2 6DP,
United Kingdom

Oxford University Press is a department of the University of Oxford.
It furthers the University's objective of excellence in research, scholarship,
and education by publishing worldwide. Oxford is a registered trade mark of
Oxford University Press in the UK and in certain other countries

First published 2012
First published in paperback 2015

Published in the United States of America by Oxford University Press
198 Madison Avenue, New York, NY 10016, United States of America

British Library Cataloguing in Publication Data
Data available

Library of Congress Cataloging in Publication Data
Data available

ISBN 978–0–19–969212–5 (Hbk.)
ISBN 978–0–19–874375–0 (Pbk.)

Preface to the Paperback Edition

Since the first appearance of this book in 2012, global poverty has continued to fall at a rate never previously experienced. Most countries have this year achieved their primary Millennium Development Goal target of halving headcount poverty over the quarter-century between 1990 and 2015, and across the world as a whole, poverty has more than halved. In only two widely contrasting regions did the poverty trend fail to conform to this astonishing performance, and continued to increase: Russia (always hampered by deindustrialization and the natural resource curse, as described in chapter 12 of this book, and now wrestling with falling oil prices and the Ukrainian conflict as well)[1] and, a more serious case because it was so poor in the first place, sub-Saharan Africa. Not, of course, the whole of Africa, and some of the success stories, such as Ghana and Uganda, are celebrated in chapter 13; but most of the large African countries, and in particular South Africa, Nigeria, and the Democratic Republic of the Congo. In the midst of the hype about 'Africa's growth miracle' and 'African cheetahs' who are now expected to rival the 'Asian tigers' (Sala-i-Martin and Pinkovskiy, 2010; Martins, 2013), the failure of more than half of Africa to reduce poverty rates at all over the last twenty-five years, not to mention the failure of the international community to draw attention to this, is very worrying. These large, populous countries of Africa, most of whose people are still locked in a poverty trap, represent the principal challenge for development in the twenty-first century.

The development policy discourse, however, has notably changed in the last few years. Some of the euphoria associated with 'making poverty history' has dissipated, and the main reason for this is that a number of developing-country governments have become keen, in the interests of national autonomy, to distance themselves from dependence on aid donors and their agendas—including the poverty reduction cause. Rather, they are seeking to implement 'transformational' strategies based on national development plans (Hickey, 2013), the language of which harks back to the development thinking of half a century ago as well as indicating a desire to finally break the shackles of dependence on former colonial powers. Emerging countries such as China, South Korea, Brazil, and the Gulf states have emerged as growth poles, and in many cases as alternative aid donors also (Gore, 2015), in support of this desire for greater autonomy on the part of several poor countries. These changing political realities inevitably condition all dimensions of the development process, including the possibilities for global poverty reduction.

However, political economy research of recent years continues to confirm the persistence of a miraculous paradox: even though the poor are politically weak, poverty continues to fall in a majority of places. What have we learned in recent

[1] In 2014, the Russian national headcount poverty rate was 13%, the same as in 2007; in other words poverty had not gone down in seven years, a period during which there had been considerable growth in the national economy. See 'Divide between rich and poor increases in Russia', www.telegraph.co.uk/rbth/society, 9 March 2015.

years that explains this—and, even more important, helps us understand what can be done in the countries that provide the exception to the rule?

In the first instance, we have learned that a number of the old enemies of pro-poor development, from urban bias to the natural resource curse, no longer hold the sway that they did. A number of recent contributions, from Hertog (2010) writing about the Gulf states, to Booth and Golooba-Mutebi (2012) in Rwanda, to Ayo (2014) in Bolivia, have shown that, even outside the Far East, it is perfectly possible for state enterprises to challenge rent-seekers and promote transformation and an increase in productivity rather than becoming captured by special interests. These findings have particular relevance for natural-resource intensive countries, such as the three African states (South Africa, Nigeria, and the Democratic Republic of Congo), where poverty reduction performance is generally worst.

Second, social protection in developing countries continues to evolve in ways which go beyond the description given in chapters 5 and 6 of this book. The significance of conditional cash transfers, the main modality by which social protection is provided in developing countries, is that they transfer to low-income households not only money but an asset—most typically health or education—and thereby help prevent the transmission of poverty from the parents of one generation to the children of the next (Barrientos, 2013). The idea of asset-based welfare, like microfinance which is one aspect of it, has now made its way from South to North, into the thinking of welfare systems in industrialized countries (Sherraden, 1991; Emmerson and Wakefield, 2001). Recent extensions of this idea into fiscal systems—such as the financing of social protection expenditure out of taxes on natural resources, as is common in Latin America and is now spreading to Africa—not only reduce poverty but send a signal that the politics of development are no longer dictated by the interests of powerful multinationals; a signal which, we have argued, is relevant for political stability as well as for growth and poverty reduction (Hudson et al. 2011). For these reasons, the World Bank authors Fiszbein, Kanbur, and Yemtsov (2014: figure 3) have argued that social protection provided by these means is strongly correlated with poverty reduction, and for this reason needs to be given an enhanced role in the post-2015 poverty agenda.

Finally, this book probably, with hindsight, places too much emphasis on fiscal and institutional tools as instruments of poverty reduction, in relation to the framework of civil and political rights in which they are located. The contributions made by improvements in rights are hard to quantify, and where they are quantified the findings are often so mutually contradictory that it is hard to assemble a coherent story out of them. Nonetheless an attempt of this task has been made by Fedderke and Klitgaard (2013) who find that there is a trend over the last thirty years towards improved human and political rights, and that their effect is non-linear: their positive impact 'is particularly strong at low rights levels, is either absent or negative in an intermediate rights range; and returns to a moderate positive impact at high levels of rights' (Fedderke and Klitgaard 2013: 187). Looking ahead, in 2015, the expiry date of the Millennium Development Goals, there has been a wave of proposals to improve on 'the world's biggest promise' (Hulme 2010). These include suggestions to include rights within an expanded set of post-millennium objectives, as well as greater emphasis on social protection (as recommended by Fiszbein et al.) and a greater use of multidimensional measures of poverty (Alkire and Seth, 2015; Lingnau and Lang, 2015; Tiwari, 2015), going even beyond the seven indicators contained in the current Millennium Development Goals.

Several of these authors, in particular Lingnau and Lang, emphasize that it would be good for the public understanding of the poverty debate to have clearer public health warnings about what indicators are being used. The good news that global poverty has fallen so much is muddled by the fact that the Millennium Development Goals reports of this news (UNDP 2014) are based on a mish-mash of 'World Bank' type measures, based on an international poverty line of $1.25 a day, national poverty lines, and sometimes other deprivation measures. The public deserves better guidance about what is going on.

Preface

The origins of this book lie in the global economic crisis of the late 1990s, which is often known as the 'East Asian crisis' but spread to Russia and the southern cone of Latin America after 1998. Many people including ourselves were disturbed to see how severe was the increase in global poverty which followed from this shock, but also interested to observe that this increase was very uneven between countries, apparently because of differences in the policies followed in the different countries affected. Pursuing this idea, we sought from ESRC, and in early 2005 were awarded, a grant of about £200,000 through the Council's World Economy and Finance Programme to study the political economy of pro-poor adjustment, mainly in middle-income countries. The grant provided for country case studies of Indonesia, Malaysia, Argentina, Bolivia, and Russia as well as for broader comparative analytical work, and these country case studies were executed between 2005 and 2007. Our gratitude goes to the ESRC and to the World Economy and Finance Programme's director, John Driffill, for supporting our initial idea and setting us on the road.

Our theme was clearly intimately related with the work of the international financial institutions, and at the mid-point of our project, in 2007, we discussed our early findings with several of these institutions, including representatives of the IMF and the World Bank in Washington. This was a time when global crisis was not seen as a threat, a view which was disproved within the year. However, interest in global poverty reduction and in the achievement of the Millennium Development Goals continued to be intense. It so happened that in that year the World Bank, with support from several bilateral donors, had recently concluded a comparative study of pro-poor growth which explicitly suggested the need for a 'political economy dimension' to work of this sort. In this context, it was suggested to us that it would be interesting to see how well our ideas about the political economy of *short-term* poverty reduction, as they were beginning to emerge from our country case studies, stood up in the context of longer-term growth and poverty reduction processes.

We decided to take up this challenge, and the study became an inquiry into the politics of poverty reduction in the medium term as well as in the short term. In the process, two pairs of low-income African countries, similar in income but very contrasted in their historical origins and experience of poverty, were added to the case-study sample—Kenya and Zimbabwe, which in the twentieth century developed originally as colonies of European settlement, and Ghana and Uganda, which developed on the basis of African smallholder exports. Case studies of poverty dynamics in these four countries, together with the five middle-income countries from which we had begun, make up Part 2 of this book.

Part 1 of the book carries our main argument, which seeks to explain, on the basis of both our country case studies and a broader global sample, what political interests may support actions to reduce poverty and suffering and what policies and institutions can effectively complement those political forces. Although, as

I argue in Chapter 1, there have been few empirical studies of this question in recent times, the broader issue of how to achieve an equitable outcome when markets are imperfect has been a preoccupation of scholars for two hundred years and more, and my intellectual debt to Arthur Lewis and, behind him, John Stuart Mill will be very clear.

The writing of this book has been a hugely rewarding experience and it is a great pleasure to thank those who helped me put it together. My Sheffield colleagues, Jean Grugel and Ben Thirkell-White (now at the University of Wellington, New Zealand) were the co-authors of the initial grant application to ESRC, and gave very generously of their political science skills; they are also the authors, respectively, of Chapter 9 on Argentina and Chapter 11 on Malaysia and Indonesia. Blessing Chiripanhura, after completing his PhD in economics at Sheffield, embarked on the massive task of tidying up and strengthening the database, and I cannot speak highly enough of the care and patience which he put into this enormous task; his skills as an analyst of the Zimbabwean economy will also be evident. Norbert Fiess lent us his analytical skills during a period when he was working at the University of Glasgow on leave from the World Bank, and his influence is particularly evident in Chapter 4 on conflict. Pia Riggirozzi and Altay Mussurov were appointed as research associates in politics and in economics, respectively, on the ESRC project, and our case studies of Argentina in Chapter 9 and Russia in Chapter 12 are heavily indebted to them.

We conducted in-country fieldwork in the IMF, in the World Bank, in several bilateral donor agencies, and in eight of our nine case-study countries, and it is a great pleasure to acknowledge the support and stimulus so willingly provided by so many people in those countries. Many of these are thanked at the beginning of the case-study chapters, Chapters 9 through 13, but there are some whose influence is more general. The study could scarcely have begun without the stimulus and steadying hand of Alexandros Mourmouras, chief of the European Division at the IMF Institute. It is not every economist in the Fund who shares our interest, as Alex does, in marrying political science tools with economic analysis, but surely there are fewer still who have experience of good-naturedly debating with a student and practitioner audience, as Alex did in March 2009 at our dissemination seminar in Sheffield, exactly what the Fund's role was in coping with the current global economic crisis. We would also like to acknowledge Ajay Sharma and Tim Williams, respectively Senior Economist and Senior Governance Adviser in the Department of International Development (DFID), especially for their role in stimulating some of the ideas in Chapters 6 and 7. Lindsay Whitfield also provided valuable criticism of several chapters from a political science angle. And the support I have received from the editorial staff at Oxford University Press, in particular from Aimee Wright, Rachel Platt, and three of their anonymous reviewers, has been first-rate.

Several of my friends, finally, have had a crucial role in this book. John Toye was kind enough to pass on transcripts of interviews with Robert MacNamara and Hollis Chenery from the World Bank's oral history, which have been very important in compiling the short history of anti-poverty policy provided in Chapter 2; and it was to the work on bargaining between donors and recipients which John and I, with Jane Harrigan, jointly did in the 1980s that I turned to in search of inspiration for Chapter 7 on the global politics of poverty reduction.

David Hulme, like me, has been racing to finish a book on global poverty—now published as Hulme (2010), and it has been a privilege to exchange ideas with him throughout the writing of this book, most particularly when his own book was being discussed in draft at the Johan Skytte Seminar at Uppsala University in May 2009. Paul Whiteley's influence has been important, first in showing me how to do political-economic modelling more than twenty years ago, and more recently in discussing its application to some of the ideas in this book. John Hudson has also been a source of inspiration, and of econometric rigour, to me for many years; so more recently has Pamela Lenton, and both of them have contributed heavily to the ideas of 'pro-poor expenditure' and the 'social efficiency wage' to be found in Chapters 4 and 5. Still more recently it is a pleasure to acknowledge the support of my son Nicholas Mosley, who in early 2008 accomplished a great deal of the fieldwork, with Altay Mussurov, for Chapter 12 on Russia, and of Helena and Francesca Mosley at all times.

Paul Mosley
February 2011

List of Contents

List of Figures

List of Tables

List of Contributors

Blessing Chiripanhura is Lecturer in Economics, Polytechnic of Namibia, Windhoek.

Sue Bowden is Professor of Economic History, University of York.

Jean Grugel is Professor of Global Politics and Development, Open University.

Altay Mussurov is Senior Lecturer in Economics, Kazakhstan Institute of Management, Almaty.

Pia Riggirozzi is Senior Lecturer (Associate Professor) in Politics, University of Southampton.

Ben Thirkell-White is Senior Lecturer in Politics, Victoria University of Wellington, New Zealand.

Part 1

Analysis and policy recommendations

1

Introduction

1.1 THE PROBLEM

During the 1990s, poverty returned to its rightful place as the key objective for global development policy. Poverty reduction, we now realize, will not happen simply if the economy is growing. And policymakers are now aware that having 'the right policies' is not enough, since pro-poor policies will only occur if the dominant political structures and processes favour their introduction. This book explores those structures and processes.

We argue that policies that actively address problems of interpersonal fairness and equity are vital to political stability. In the short term, they help to secure government legitimacy by sending clear signals to the population that government has their interests at heart. Over the medium term, success in creating political stability can boost state legitimacy and popularity, and increase the political constituency in favour of further pro-poor strategies, enhancing the elite's incentives to continue on the path towards pro-poor growth. The obvious difficulty is that the poor tend to be politically weak in the first place, creating an opposite vicious circle in which the interests of the poor are ignored and policies embed and enhance social cleavages. But we argue here that, in some circumstances at least, that problem can be overcome.

In establishing the Millennium Development Goals, the various interests which make up the development lobby made to the billion or so people who live below the poverty line has been called 'the world's biggest promise':[1] to halve extreme poverty within the seven years to 2015. Much of that promise, as we shall see, has been met. And yet, in many regions of the developing world, in particular in most parts of Africa, poverty is still growing (Table 1.1).

As we can see from the table, it is in the poorest developing countries, which also have the most fragile environments[2] and are the most conflict-prone, that poverty trends are still worst: the problem referred to in Jeffrey Sachs' recent Reith lectures (2007) as the 'challenge of the weakest links'. Thus since the 1980s, especially, there has been a tendency for the living standards of the richer and the poorer developing countries to diverge, and for a gap to emerge between the poorer group—the 'bottom billion', as Paul Collier (2007) calls them—and the

[1] The phrase is from David Hulme (2010), who explains in his book the driving forces behind the establishment of the Millennium Goals.

[2] For example, it is African countries that are most vulnerable to global warming: see the map at Stern (2006), Figure 3.8, page 88.

Table 1.1 Industrialized and developing countries: comparative growth and poverty performance, 1965–2008.

	GDP per capita						Poverty levels (headcount, numbers below $1/day)				
	Level (US$)		per cent annual growth								
	1969	2008	1965–80	1980–90	1990–2000	2000–8	1970*	1990	1999	2005	2008**
Industrialized countries	9,764	39,345	3.8	2.1	2.4	1.6	small#	small	small	small	small
Developing countries	417	15,683	2.7	4.3	5.1	4.4	1,815	1,276.4	1145.6	876.0	810.0
East Asia and Pacific	159	2,631	4.5	5.8	7.1	8.3	1,196	623.4	420.8	175.6	142.6
South Asia	218	986	0.7	3.3	3.2	5.8		381.2	359.5	350.5	311.5
Russia and Eastern Europe	NA	9,620	NA	NA	−3.1	6.3	NA	13.2	24.0	25.0	19.0
Latin America and Caribbean	2,568	6,780	6.0	3.0	3.4	2.7	260	29.0	37.8	30.7	28.0
Sub-Saharan Africa	521	1,082	1.4	−0.9	−0.4	2.7	345	245.2	308.4	304.2	310.5
'Bottom billion'$	309	524	0.7	−1.2	−0.2	2.1	110	185.0	211.5	204.5	206.5

Notes: * World Bank measure of those below the $75 per annum poverty line: not strictly comparable with data for other years.
** Poverty data for 2008 are adapted from World Bank's World Development Report for 2010, which uses a poverty line of $1.25 a day.
#'Small' denotes less than 10 million.
$ Highly indebted (HIPC) poor countries, as defined by *World Development Indicators*, 2008.

Source: World Bank, *World Development Reports,* 1990, 2000, 2010 (Appendix, Table 1), also (1970 income data), H. Chenery et al., *Redistribution with Growth* (OUP 1975), Tables 1.1 and 1.2.

Figure 1.1 Short-term poverty in relation to growth.
(a) Our calculation—period 1996–2003.

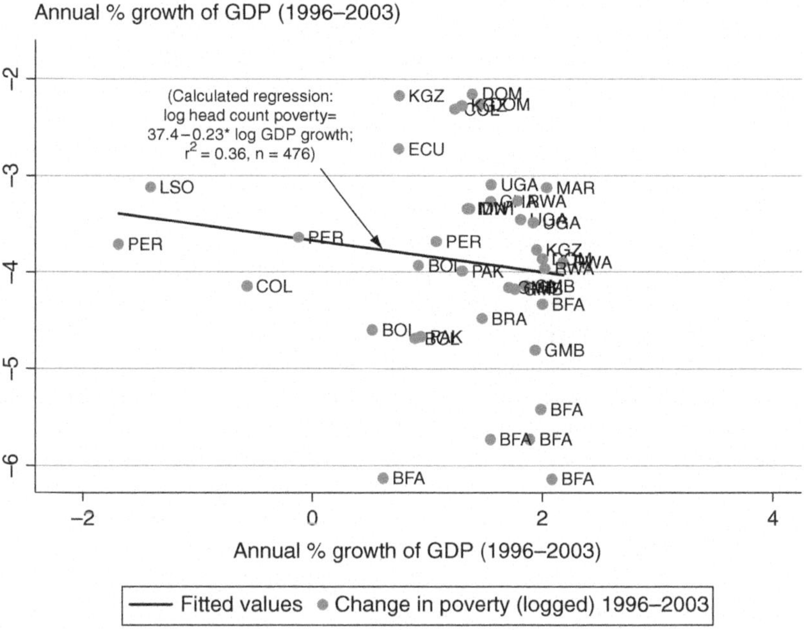

(b) World Bank calculation—various periods between 1990 and 2005.

Source: International Bank for Reconstruction and Development/The World Bank: *World Development Report 2006*. Authors' calculations.

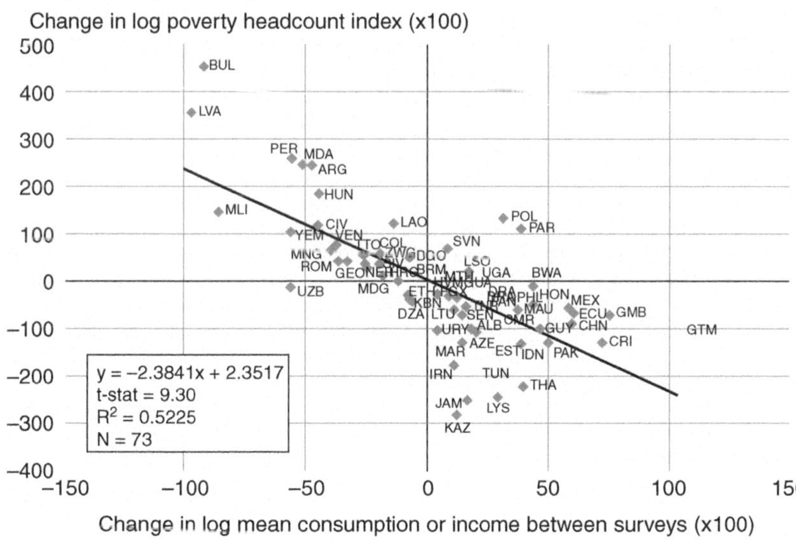

richer and more self-sufficient six billion. This split, between those developing countries which are converging on the living standards of industrialized countries and those who are not, is the central problem of global development.

A common starting point for all investigators seeking to reduce poverty is policies to boost the growth rate of income, on the grounds that if growth is increased, poverty will reliably fall. This approach is typically supported by evidence such as that portrayed in Figure 1.1, a scatterplot from the most recent *World Development Report* of growth and poverty outcomes for all available countries over the quarter of a century to 2005. This study suggests that 'without controlling for any characteristics of the country, 1 percentage point growth in a country's mean income can be expected to reduce the incidence of poverty in that country by about 2.4 percentage points' (World Bank 2006a, page 85).[3] The Bank further argues that 'on average, growth is distribution-neutral', meaning that within growing economies, poor groups gain at least as much as rich groups. This is certainly true in a number of countries, notably in the Far East, such as Indonesia[4] and Malaysia, featured as case studies in the second part of this book; and where it is the case, a part of the political problem has gone away, since a tide which is rising fast enough will lift all boats, even those of the poor.

However, this proposition is emphatically not true everywhere, or at all times. Although, *on average*, higher rates of growth do tend to be associated with reduction of poverty, this is not true in every environment—for example it is not true of the group of countries in the top right-hand quadrant of Figure 1.1. For many reasons, one of the most important of which is inequality in the distribution of income, assets and power,[5] many countries which are growing

[3] In one early and famous World Bank contribution on the growth-poverty relationship (Dollar and Kraay 2003) the poverty elasticity was exactly one, in other words a one per cent increase in growth would lead to a one per cent reduction in poverty (rather idiosyncratically defined as the income share of the bottom twenty per cent of the population). As discussed below, estimates of the poverty elasticity vary greatly around this average, and for some periods and regions they are positive, i.e. perverse.

[4] See also Timmer (2007) for the case of Indonesia.

[5] There are various reasons for expecting inequality to be a barrier to poverty reduction:

1. In income-unequal countries the poverty of the mass of the population leads to low demand for labour-intensive, non-traded services and manufactures. As a consequence the local market for these manufactures and services cannot breach the 'economies of scale barrier' and local industries serving this market fail to materialize, thereby aggravating poverty.
2. Because the local market for manufactures and services is depressed, the local labour market is depressed also. The poorest people have nothing to sell except their labour, and being by the previous argument unable to do this, are caught in a low-level equilibrium trap in which the one thing which needs to expand cannot be expanded because of the structure of demand.
3. In income-unequal countries there is a higher risk of civil conflict (riots, industrial disputes, and roadblocks, sometimes escalating into broader conflict) which deters investment and thereby increases poverty levels (Haggard and Kaufman 2008; Mussurov 2007; see also Chapter 5 below).
4. Conflict over resources arising from income inequality may delay stabilization and cause macro-economic disequilibrium (Alesina and Drazen 1991), which will depress investment and increase poverty.

The World Bank has repeatedly identified income inequality as a cause of poor poverty reduction performance, and supported this claim, especially in its *2006 World Development Report*, with findings suggesting that greater inequality reduces the power of growth to reduce poverty. These are confirmed by our more recent data (Figure 2.2(b) below).

fast are not reducing poverty. The problem extends much further than is indicated on the diagram, as it applies within countries as well as between countries. South Africa, Russia, Mexico, and India are all rapidly-developing economies, apparently far removed from the stagnation of the bottom billion, but within those economies the Northern Province of South Africa, Chechnya Autonomous Region, and the states of Chiapas and Bihar have experienced both the near-subsistence living standards (and as it happens also the social conflict) associated with the marginalized group. The problem of chronic poverty transcends national boundaries.

This is not at all a recent problem. The very first period of sustained growth in history, in Britain from the late eighteenth through to the middle of the nineteenth century, increased per capita gross domestic product by over fifty per cent but, although the evidence is disputed, it is far from clear that living standards (e.g. in the sense of real wages) increased at all during that time;[6] in today's language, the growth pattern of that time was not at all pro-poor, since it excluded most women, most unskilled workers, and farm labourers from the gains from growth. The dramatic industrial growth of Russia during the second half of the nineteenth century allowed few rights to workers and peasants and very little scope for social mobility; a fact from which all subsequent history follows. But when, in the wake of the turbulent and dismal performance of the capitalist economies during the inter-war period, a successful attempt was made to establish a New International Economic Order through the new Bretton Woods institutions, the focus of the new financial institutions was on growth, driven by the World Bank, facilitated by liberalization, driven by the General Agreement on Tariffs and Trade (GATT—now the World Trade Organization, WTO) and stabilization, driven by the International Monetary Fund (IMF). It was not influenced by distributional considerations. The logic behind this is that of the Lewis model (Lewis 1954), which visualizes that equity would come *through* growth as the modernizing abilities of the high-technology sector spread through, and increased the productivity of, the traditional sector. This vision is also apparent in the first ever global development policy manifesto, the UN's *Measures for the Economic Development of Underdeveloped Countries* (United Nations 1951). In several industrialized countries, some of this vision was achieved[7] through the establishment of welfare states, building on the national insurance and pensions systems established half a century beforehand. But in developing

[6] National-level data on poverty were not available at that time, and so economic historians have needed to use surrogate measures of well-being, especially real wages and mortality but more recently also anthropomorphic data, especially on people's heights and weights. The evidence is disputed but several recent views suggest no increase in the average real wage in Great Britain between the 1780s and the 1840s (Feinstein 1998; for other views see Crafts 1997). Other commentators have tried to shed light on the trend of the standard of living by disaggregating it between groups. For an essay which examines the trend of real wages separately for men and women (and documents the increase in the Gini coefficient of inequality for each group) see Horrell and Humphries (1992).

[7] Seebohm Rowntree (1901), who had carried out the pioneering study of poverty in York in 1899, returned to that city in 1936 and again, towards the end of his life, in 1950. He found that the overall poverty rate, which had been around ten per cent in 1899 but had risen to thirty-one per cent during the interwar depression, had fallen to 4.6 per cent by 1951. See Hatton and Bailey (2000).

countries, these instruments of social protection were not established, except sporadically in urban areas; nor was their absence seen by the international institutions of the time as a threat to economic or political stability in poor countries, but rather as simple realism.[8] The route to reducing poverty and inequality was seen purely in terms of the creation of new jobs: equity would be achieved through growth, rather than through independent policies. In terms of strict short-term economics, this might appear to make sense; but politically it was a costly error, as we shall illustrate.

The first evidence of this, as we discuss in Chapter 2, arrived at the end of the 1960s, and it resulted in many valuable anti-poverty initiatives during the 1970s. These, however, were then submerged under the waves of readjustment to market forces known as 'structural adjustment', which followed the global economic crisis of the 1980s that in developing countries was deeper than the inter-war depression (Figure 1.2), and provoked fears of unilateral default by a third world debtors' cartel, and even, amongst some authoritative observers, of a Third World War between North and South (Clark 1984).[9]

In the midst of these panics, concerns about poverty were soon demoted to priority zero in relation to the serious business of preventing a global economic meltdown. Not until ten years later, as we shall see in Chapter 2, did a poverty focus re-emerge; and even when it did, as we have seen, 'growth first' continued to be the dominant prescription for dealing with it. The idea that policies additional to those which maximize short-term growth are necessary for development in the fuller sense continues to be a precarious claim.

What are these additional policies? This question has recently been addressed, in particular, by a multinational task-force chaired by the World Bank (see World Bank 2006, published as Besley and Cord 2007). Examining a sample of fourteen countries, eventually trimmed down to eight in the Besley and Cord study, the authors of the constituent studies provide a range of answers, listed in Table 1.2

[8] 'Rapid economic development is . . . the greatest cure for technological unemployment, and also the only fundamental remedy for disguised unemployment.' United Nations, *Measures for the Economic Development of Less Developed Countries* (1951, page 7). In this report there is no discussion of social protection measures (although there is discussion of investment in health and education) and little discussion of the political costs of inequality, except this:

> (To increase savings) taxation is not enough; it is necessary also to use controls which ration luxury consumption, such as import controls, and special taxes on luxuries. Possibly, the total sum released in this way will not be large. But, on the other hand, attempts to control the consumption of the rich have real political value if the government is trying to win the confidence and the cooperation of the low and middle income groups for its development programme.
>
> (UN 1951, page 39)

This is the first glimmer of a political insight more fully developed twenty years later in the World Bank *Redistribution with Growth* study (see Chapter 2 below) and drawn on throughout this book.

[9] This extraordinary book, a best-selling paperback in 1985, is well worth revisiting. It begins with a coordinated default on debt by members of a developing-world cartel called Solidarity of the Poor, with Mexico and Nigeria prominent. The defaulters are expelled from the international financial institutions, and retaliate by means of various terrorist acts, some of them quite high-tech, for example the British Chancellor of the Exchequer, one of the 'hawks' on the creditor side, has his heart pacemaker immobilized through computer hacking machinated by Solidarity of the Poor. All attempts at peacemaking are abortive, and the conflict proceeds to a *Götterdämmerung* in which Israel and (pre-Mandela) South Africa are obliterated. Do not miss.

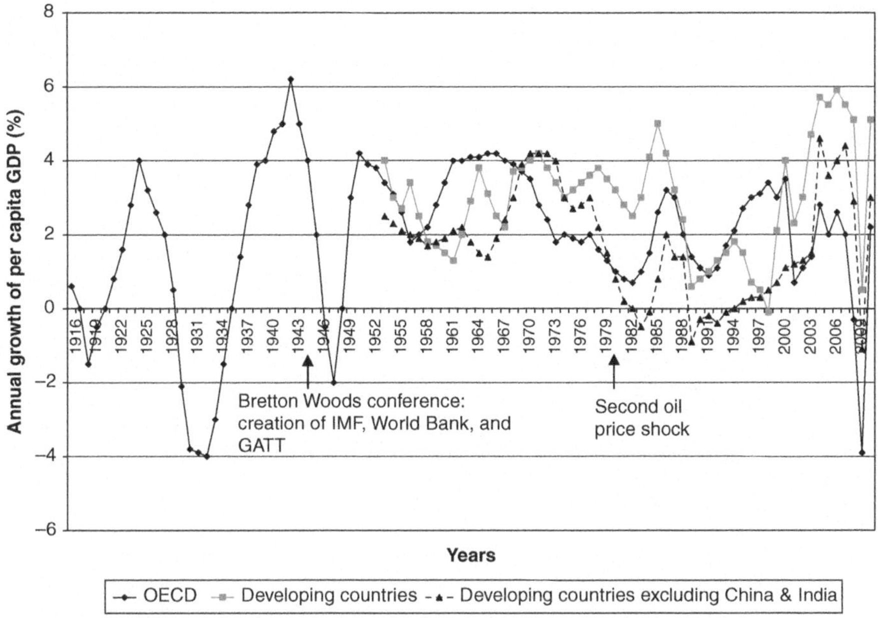

Figure 1.2 Comparative economic development 1915–2010: panoramic view.

alongside other ideas discussed above. Some of Besley and Cord's proposals, such as 'improving the investment climate' and 'expanding access to secondary and girls' education'(both on page 17 of their book) rehearse ideas which have been in the Bank domain for more than thirty years. But others, especially the large range of recommendations devoted to agriculture (on page 13), are new. And what is not in the Bank's list is as interesting as what is. Apart from the ritualized urgings in support of 'improving the investment climate', there is now very little insistence on the free-market principles of the 'Washington Consensus'. The analysis takes us into a post-Washington Consensus world, many additional illustrations of which we shall encounter in the course of this book.

In Table 1.2, these ideas are divided into three groups, *macro* (policies which operate at the level of the whole economy), *meso* (policies which operate at the level of individual sectors), and *micro* (policies which operate at the level of individual markets or factors of production, such as land or finance). Table 1.2 lists some of the anti-poverty ideas so far encountered, together with illustrations of where they have worked, biased towards countries for which our own case studies (Chapters 9 through 13 below) provide illustrations.

But why should anyone adopt these or any other pro-poor policies? As the Besley and Cord study points out, this is a gap: 'Political economy considerations often affect the distributional outcomes of structural and investment policies, at times at the expense of poor households. Public policies to enhance the ability of the poor to participate in and influence government processes is another area for further exploration' (Besley and Cord 2007, page 21).

That further exploration is exactly what is attempted here. We know that the policies recommended against poverty (in particular the ones listed in the final

Table 1.2 A typology of anti-poverty policies.

	Options	Source	Illustration of successful implementation
Macro-adjustment options	1. Maintain competitive real exchange rate, with, in aid-recipient countries, occasional aggressive devaluations to combat 'Dutch disease'	Bourguignon and Morrisson 1992	Most East Asian countries; see Chapters 3 and 11 below
	2. Avoid tax increases (especially indirect tax increases) during recession periods		
	3. Improving the investment climate	Besley and Cord 2007, page 17	
Meso (sectoral-level) options	4. 'Poverty-conscious restructuring of public expenditures' (especially reduction of military spending)	Sachs 2007 (especially health)	Uganda 1994; see Chapter 5 below
	5. Pro-agriculture policies	Sachs 2007	Most east Asian countries in 1970s; Uganda, Ghana, and Ethiopia in 1990s, see Besley and Cord 2007, page 12; Mosley and Suleiman 2006 See Chapter 5 below
	6. Conflict avoidance (including lowering of military expenditure)	Collier, 2007	
Micro-(individual market-level) options	7. Primary education (especially for girls)	Besley and Cord 2007, page 17	Bangladesh; Uganda, see Chapter 13 below
	8. Micro-credit, micro-insurance	Besley and Cord 2007, page 17 (represented there as 'helping poorer and smaller producers deal with risk')	Bolivia, see Chapter 10 below
	9. Expanding the technology available to smallholder producers	Besley and Cord 2007, page 12	East Asia, see Chapter 11 below Uganda, Ghana, Ethiopia, see Chapters 5 and 13 below
	10. Labour intensity; designing labour market regulations to create attractive employment opportunities	Besley and Cord 2007, page 17	East Asia, see Chapter 11 below; counter-examples, Bolivia, Chapter 10 and Russia, Chapter 12 below

column) work in some countries and at some times, but not at others, but we do not know why this variation occurs. This book argues that a fundamental element missing from the anti-poverty literature, and hence from the global anti-poverty effort, is not just the policies considered above, but rather the political motivation to deploy them in support of the poor. For all that it has been acknowledged since Machiavelli that without political motivation the interests of none can be advanced, there has been little discussion in the recent wave of anti-poverty literature of the political process by which the interests of poor people can be promoted. It is the purpose of this book to supply it.

Once the problem is confronted, it is easy to feel defeated by it, because if each follows their own self-interest, and the rich control the levers of power, then that will cause and perpetuate a process in which policymaking is dominated by the interests of the rich and the middle class rather than the poor. As a recent OECD publication has put it, 'the politically most active groups are not usually the poorest' (Haggard et al. 1995, page 120). The poor are nowhere a class with the ability to organize in their own interest, and have little leverage in their own right. But as shown in the table above, many cases exist where it has suited the interests of the elite to make alliances either with the poor or of indirect benefit to the poor, and the central question of this book is, 'when and why is this likely to happen?'

1.2 THE APPROACH

In this book we present five kinds of answers:

1. Poverty reduction is more likely to happen if opportunities, for example rifts within the elite, arise which make the elite vulnerable, and if the elite has the breadth of vision to make *strategic alliances with the poor* in face of this threat.
2. However, no vision can be sustained unless there is also *political stability*, backed up by institutional capacity.
3. Poverty reduction is more likely to happen if the *underlying technology* of the economy is geared towards producing livelihoods for low-income people. Since the poorest, usually can sell nothing but labour, this implies *labour intensity* (e.g. Ghana, Uganda, Indonesia, and indeed most Far Eastern countries). Most pro-poor growth has been along a labour-intensive production function.
4. Often, both political stability and the adoption of a labour-intensive production function depend on a *pro-poor fiscal policy* being adopted. Often, as we shall show in Chapters 5 and 13, the political roots of a pro-poor fiscal policy lie a long way back in time, even back in the colonial period.
5. In an increasingly open economy, relationships with *donors and international financial institutions* are clearly critical to the poverty outcome. Against the conventional wisdom, we argue that in poor countries donors do have leverage to reduce poverty; but to our surprise, it is *not* the case that pro-poor initiatives are always strongest in aid-supported countries, and we present several examples of pro-poor initiatives in middle-income countries which are not dependent on aid.

In addition to these five key elements in pro-poor chemistry, we find, finally, that *spin-offs* are often critical determinants of poverty dynamics. Often poverty falls for completely unintended reasons. Thus, in Russia during the 2000s, poverty fell most in countries which presented a high security risk, having rebelled against federal authority in the 1990s, because federal subsidies for social expenditure were pumped into those regions. This was not because of compassionate motives; and yet the objective of reducing severe poverty was achieved.

Much of our job of this book consists of trying to categorize these cases and thereby to understand the political scope for reducing poverty. We begin, in Chapter 2, by taking a historical approach to these problems. The proposition that 'the poor you have always with you' is neither a recent cliché, although since the 1990s it has often felt like one, nor one confined to any specific country. In search of the widest possible range of ideas about exit routes from poverty, we examine the experience of pro-poor interventions in the developing world from the 1960s onward, showing how the first wave of anti-poverty strategies, in the following decade, was broken on the rocks of the global economic crisis of the 1980s, but then reasserted itself in the 1990s. At this stage the approach is mainly descriptive—to trace broad trends in the recent history of poverty in relation to the strategies deployed against it—and to give an initial idea of what works, in different environments, to convert growth into poverty reduction and what does not. We treat the list of 'promising pro-poor options' in Table 1.2 as a point of departure for this initial investigation, and seek to build on it through examination of general tendencies and case studies. What emerges from this historical examination is that there seem to be three key elements in the chemistry by which these coalitions happen: a *trigger* which provides the impulse for pro-poor action, a *critical mass of partners* in the coalition to make the action happen, and a *vehicle*, or institutional framework, to spread and sustain it. The role of conflict itself in this process is complex, as the threat of conflict acts as a stimulant to pro-poor action, but actual conflict, as we observe in Chapter 4, is disastrous for the poor. The inheritance of economic structure, especially in the sense of capital-intensive technologies and associated inequality of income distribution, acts as an important constraint upon this process.

In Chapter 3, we blend the five factors mentioned above: pro-poor alliances, political stability, expenditure in support of pro-poor sectors and institutions, labour intensity, and the international context, into a composite theoretical story. This yields hypotheses which are tested in subsequent chapters.

In Chapter 4, we bring a conflict perspective into the story. We ask whether a specific factor acting as a constraint on policy consists of the risk of conflict, and more conventionally whether conflict impacts on investment and growth, focusing, however, not only on conflict in the sense of civil war, as most of the literature has done, but rather on conflict in the sense of riots, public demonstrations, and industrial strife, which might be expected to be aggravated by economic misfortune but where the linkages have not hitherto been traced. We seek to define the linkages not only between policy and this 'narrow' concept of conflict, but also the circumstances under which 'narrow' conflict in the sense of riots may broaden outwards into civil war, or alternatively act as an early warning indicator, and shrink back into narrow conflict, or peace. We find that conflict in this sense is produced not only by shocks to personal consumption and by horizontal and vertical inequalities, but also by economic instability, both of revenue and expenditure.

In Chapter 5, we move to a longer-term focus, and build on our earlier analysis of pro-poor coalitions to examine how such coalitions can be sustained. We examine the politics of how, in East Asia and other regions, labour-intensive manufacturing, the spread of the green revolution, and other policies have enabled poverty to be brought down over the long term. We use a 'supply and demand' approach, in which the supply of pro-poor actions is dependent on the ability of elites to assemble and sustain pro-poor coalitions, but constrained by the 'demand' for such actions from within the broader political system, on which equality of income distribution, in particular, is a powerful influence.

Within this approach, we examine what policy instruments are alterable in a pro-poor direction. We focus especially on fiscal instruments, public expenditure, and taxation, as they are the most readily alterable in the short term, but also briefly examine the asset-transfer instruments discussed in Chapter 2. We develop the idea of the 'social efficiency wage', in which the 'social wage'—the targetable benefits provided by public expenditure—is used to signal to the electorate which interests it identifies with and what policies it will follow in order to attract loyalty, just as within the labour market some employers pursue high-wage policies to attract loyalty and thereby enhance the stability and productivity of the labour force. Within this framework, we revisit the proposition originally put forward by Haggard et al. (1996, page 120) to the effect that 'a focus on social equity is not necessarily relevant to understanding the politics of adjustment', and ask in the light of our evidence whether and in what context a pro-poor policy, in particular a pro-poor expenditure pattern and a pro-poor tax policy, will be politically productive. Our results are more optimistic than Haggard's towards the idea of there being a political dividend to pro-poor policy, suggesting that the global political climate may have evolved in a pro-poor direction in recent years. Whether pro-poor coalitions once established can be sustained, however, depends on whether pro-poor policy initiatives are embedded in an inadequate institutional framework, without which no long-term development strategy is possible.

The elaboration of this framework is the task of Chapter 6. Here we focus on the determinants of state capacity and their relationship to the poverty objective. We examine what improved governance has contributed to growth, and find that only two of the current 'official' indicators of governance, political stability and law and order, are in fact significantly associated with growth rates. Drawing on our country case studies, we argue that a broader set of indicators is needed to understand the impact of institutions on growth and poverty, incorporating measures of tax-generating capacity, access to labour and capital markets, and social capital and state-business relations, in addition to the standard governance indicators, and devise a new 'pro-poor institutions index' to incorporate their impact. We show that initial conditions (in particular the distribution of income and wealth) and policies (in particular towards the allocation of public expenditure) impact on the effectiveness of institutions; many institutions, and political characteristics premised on them, such as legitimacy, are not rigid, but responsive to the influence of policy instruments. We identify a 'political poverty trap', into which poor countries may fall if the influences of conflict, institutional decline and poverty on one another are mutually reinforcing rather than mutually offsetting.

Some of the factors confining countries within the poverty trap—as illustrated by our studies of Africa, Bolivia, and some parts of Russia—are globally rather than locally induced, and overseas aid in particular has often been accused of causing institutional damage, a threat which our analysis confirms is real, but suggests is sensitive to choice of policies.

Chapter 7 presents the international framework within which the rest of the analysis is set. This brings us to the influence of international financial institutions—the International Monetary Fund (IMF), the World Bank, and aid donors. Our focus is on the process by which the level of international financial flows is determined, and on its effectiveness in reducing poverty. We develop our model of the bargaining process between developing countries and international financial institutions, and show that under certain circumstances that process may mutate into what we call a *trust game,* in which mutual confidence coalesces around a core of agreed strategy; under such circumstances the financial flow is larger and more stable, and under the umbrella of trust there is wide scope for deviations from the 'Washington Consensus'. Whether prospects for poverty reduction improve as a result of such increases in aid flows depends on institutions as well as short-term policies; but we find that aid flows do not necessarily undermine institutional capacity in developing countries, as much of the literature has argued.

The concluding chapter in Part 1, Chapter 8, summarizes our findings in relation to possible pro-poor policy options. As we write, the world has once again been hit by a global crisis, and we discuss the lessons which have been learned for crisis management in the interests of poor people.

Our country case studies, discussed in the final five chapters, are chosen with two objectives in mind: in the first place, to compare successful and unsuccessful exit strategies from the 'East Asian crisis' of 1997–2002, and in the second place to compare successful and unsuccessful long-term poverty strategies. Thus, within East Asia, Malaysia and Indonesia (Chapter 11) can be seen as cases where the short-term effects of the global crisis on poverty were relatively mild and relatively severe respectively, as can Argentina and Bolivia in Latin America (Chapters 9 and 10), and so within the following pages there are a good many comparisons between these bilateral country pairs. Africa (Chapter 13), although extremely severely hit by the global recession of the 1980s, was bypassed by the 1997–8 global crisis, and the shocks with which its economies have to cope have more to do with drought, war, and commodity price collapse than with a financial crash. Within Africa, we examine, within the same spirit of comparing between good and bad experiences, Uganda and Ghana—two countries which have experienced impressive levels of pro-poor growth for most of the 1990–2007 period, with Kenya, which performed well until the 1980s but since then has been hit by a wave of governance problems, and Zimbabwe, an example to the whole of Africa in the 1980s,[10] which has now become one of the world's most spectacular cases of macro-economic meltdown. Our analysis of poverty in these four chapters covers a longer historical period than the others, going back to the beginning of the twentieth century.

[10] Notably in the areas of industrial development and smallholder agriculture development—both of them key elements in the achievement of competitiveness and broad-based growth.

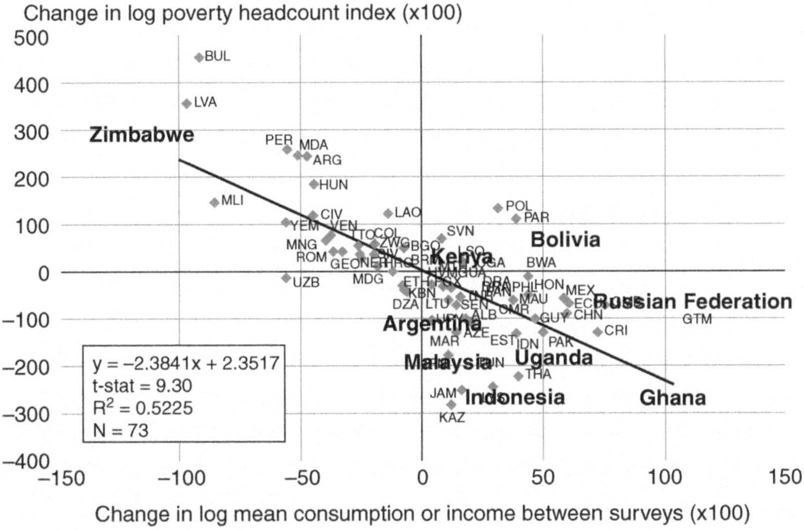

Figure 1.3 Growth and poverty: all developing countries, with case-study countries superimposed.

Sources: main scatter and associated regression from World Bank 2006a, Figure 4.3, drawing on Chen and Ravallion 2004. Data for our nine case-study countries from our own computations (see www.poverty.group.shef.ac.uk), drawing on World Bank's *World Development Indicators.*

To these eight contrasted cases we add Russia (Chapter 12), the only global power, in the sense of membership of the G8, within our sample, and the only former member of the communist bloc. Russia is also a country where the social impact of the initial global crisis of the 1980s and 90s was perhaps the gravest in the world, where the social costs of adjustment during that decade were so severe that they involved increases in mortality and in suicide, and helped to bring about a long-term decline in population (Brainerd 2001), which still continues. In Russia, in common with other large countries such as India (Besley, Burgess, and Esteve-Volart 2007) we find that the poverty-growth relationship varied across different parts of the country, in response to the characteristics and policies of individual regions.

In Figure 1.3, we display the nine case-study countries in terms of their performance in growth and poverty reduction: it is a major part of our task to understand why this relationship diverged across the nine countries of the sample, and in the wider world.

The vision is, therefore, to discover whether a look through the lens of political rationality can produce policies and institutions which will reduce global poverty more effectively. In his concluding Reith lecture, Jeffrey Sachs called for a 'new politics for a new age' (Sachs 2007, lecture 5) and we hope that, by bringing together the currently rather separated literatures on adjustment, conflict, and poverty reduction around the five themes mentioned above, we have made a contribution to these politics.

2

A short history of 'pro-poor policy' 1970–2010

> It is now clear that little more than a decade of rapid growth in underdeveloped countries has been of little benefit to perhaps a third of their population. Although the average per capita income of the Third World has increased by fifty per cent since 1960, this growth has been very unequally distributed between countries, regions within countries, and socio-economic groups. Paradoxically, while growth policies have succeeded beyond the expectations of the first development decade, the very idea of aggregate growth as a social objective has increasingly been called into question
>
> (Chenery et al. 1974, page xiii).

2.1 INTRODUCTION

With these words, written in the early 1970s, the World Bank's vice-president for Development Policy, Hollis Chenery, signalled the derailment of what we in the previous chapter called the 'equity-through-growth project' of the capitalist economic powers. For a significant part of the developing world, growth, it was now clear, was not at all pro-poor. As discussed in the previous chapter, this is not remotely the first time this had been illustrated, or indeed acted upon, but it was the first time that it had been demonstrated with statistical data for the developing world, and the first time that it led to a programme of action for the developing world as a whole. We shall, therefore, use the Bank's diagnosis of the 1970s, the programme of action which it subsequently led, and the consequences of this plan of action as an initial springboard with which to derive insights about pro-poor action. We shall then show how, in the crisis of the 1980s, the donors' poverty focus disappeared. But, of course, it reappeared in the 1990s, and in the final section we draw on the experience of, especially, our case-study countries since that time to derive a picture of the mainsprings of pro-poor political action, which is then developed across the subsequent chapters.

2.2 REDISTRIBUTION WITH GROWTH AND THE MACNAMARA PLAN OF ACTION

The triggers for pro-poor action

Much of Chenery's alarm about the performance of the pro-poor project derived from Latin America. At the beginning of the 1970s Albert Fishlow had published a paper on Brazil showing that, in spite of GDP growth rates averaging over seven per cent during the 1960s, the standard of living of the lowest deciles had not improved, and that the already high level of inequality was deteriorating (Fishlow 1972, pages 391, 399). This inconvenient fact destroyed the simple linkage between investment, labour market expansion, and poverty reduction underlying the Lewis model and replaced it with a vision of polarization of wealth between haves and have-nots, putting at risk the stability of both north and south, consistent with the grimmer vision of Chenery's opening statement.

Subsequent controversy on income distribution in Latin America (e.g. Bacha and Taylor 1978; Wells 1974) did not alter this basic insight, and indeed subsequent research, much of it by Chenery's team based at the Bank, extended the insight into much of the rest of Latin America, notably the parts where enormous capitalist landholdings, originally established by Spanish or Portuguese colonists, coexisted with tiny subsistence plots belonging to peasant farmers. The more the economic structure was dominated by this structural contrast between *latifundios* and *minifundios* (as, for example, in Bolivia, Peru, and Colombia, but also, outside Latin America, in South Africa, Zimbabwe, and Kenya, and indeed much of North India also), and hence by an unequal income distribution, the more implausible it was to expect that the poor would be able to escape from poverty in large numbers. As shown by Table 2.1, Brazil, Colombia, and other high-inequality countries in Latin America[1] have higher incomes and growth rates than South Korea, Malaysia, and comparable countries in South-East Asia, but much more unequal income distributions and higher capital intensity, and as a consequence of this, higher poverty rates.

A second, and even more emotive, post-war expectation that also fell short of realization was the promise of a world without famine. Both India and Africa had been vulnerable to famine throughout the nineteenth and the first half of the twentieth century, and in 1943, as the tide began to turn in the Second World War and the work of post-war institution-building began to get under way, notably at Bretton Woods, the worst famine to have hit the world up to that point killed three million people in the densely populated region of Bengal, on the borders of India and what is now Bangladesh. Much of Indian post-war policy was dominated by the determination to prevent a recurrence, and in most of the developing world food security appeared, by the end of the 1960s, to have been achieved for good (the appalling suffering of the Chinese famine of 1958–62, which killed between thirty and sixty million people, was suppressed by the Chinese media of the time). The news that thousands of people had died of starvation, first in Ethiopia in 1972, and

[1] Note that Argentina, not conforming to the latifundios–minifundios dichotomy, is an outlier from this Latin American high-inequality pattern.

Table 2.1 Early 1970s: income distribution, capital-intensity, and growth; sample countries.

	Per capita GDP ($, 1969)	Growth rate of GDP (per cent, 1960–81)	Inequality: share of income in hands of top 20 per cent (per cent, 1970)	Capital-intensity measure (energy consumption per capita, kg coal equivalent 1960)	Poverty data (per cent below $75p.a. in 1969, 1971 prices)
Brazil	347	5.1	61.6	375	20.0
Argentina	1,054	1.9	47.4	1,057	—
Bolivia	—	2.1	—	177	—
Colombia	347	3.2	65.0	494	20.0
Comparators					
Kenya (1969)	—	2.9	68.0	144	—
Zimbabwe (1968)	274	1.0	69.0		37.4
Uganda	128	-0.6	47.1	39	49.8
Indonesia	247	4.0	..	125	..
Malaysia	323	4.3	56.0	239	15.5
South Korea	224	6.9	45.0	208	17.0

Source: *Inequality Measures and Poverty Rates*: Chenery et al. (1974), Tables 1.1, page 8, and 1.2, page 12. (A summary of original sources for these data is given at pages 30 through 37 of the same table.) *Capital-intensity measure*: energy consumption per capita from World Bank, *World Development Report 1982*, Table 7.

then in a newly independent Bangladesh in 1974, therefore came as a massive shock. Famine is the most severe form of poverty, and in the early 1980s A.K. Sen, in his study of *Poverty and Famines* (Sen 1982) was to show that famine could be caused, not only by deficient food production (there had been a bumper harvest during the great Bengal famine of 1943) but by inequality in the distribution of resources, and specifically by the inability of casually-paid landless workers to control any assets which could protect them against the rocketing price of rice, their main food. Thus, in two separate contexts, it had become clear that the developing world was more vulnerable than headline statistics gave reason to believe—and vulnerable, in each case, for the same basic reason.

Behind these two obvious failings of post-war economic development in the capitalist world, in the 1970s, lay the awareness that the world was politically unstable, and that a failure to cope with the two challenges just mentioned might tilt the balance of advantage in the cold war. Across the entire developing world, and especially in the those countries where current policies were unable to achieve food security (e.g. India, Malaysia, Indonesia in the 1960s) it was an ever-present fear of the capitalist elites running those countries that if this situation persisted 'the communist bloc', either the Russian part or the apparently better-adapted-to-small-farm-agriculture Chinese part, might be able to pose a credible threat to those elites on the basis of its ability to feed the hungry.

With whom did the responsibility lie for dealing with these failures of the developmental process to deliver? The answer was not clear, as it was the first time that the conventional wisdom underlying the New International Economic Order had been tested. The most obvious guess, however, was somewhere between the World Bank and the UN, with an emphasis towards the latter. In the environment of the early 1970s, the financial centre of gravity lay with the Bank, but many of the key ideas were with the UN system.[2] Within the Bretton Woods system of international financial governance, the responsibility for supporting long-term economic development clearly lay with the World Bank; but the World Bank, in those days, was much more of a bank (for the finance of infrastructural projects such as roads and power stations) than the ideas factory it now is.[3] The United Nations system, with its own economic commissions in Africa, Asia, and Latin America, was arguably better equipped and motivated to launch initiatives on behalf of the developing world; it was, as we saw in the previous chapter, the Economic and Social Council of the UN which in 1951 had launched the first global development manifesto, *Measures for the Economic Development of Underdeveloped Countries* (United Nations 1951) and one of the staff of the Economic Commission for Latin America, Raul Prebisch, had been credited with the discovery of one of the fundamental asymmetries between North and South, the 'Prebisch-Singer thesis' of the early 1950s, which provided a rationale for the tendency of the terms of trade of developing countries to deteriorate over the long term.[4] The World Bank of the 1950s and 1960s had no such discoveries of global scope to its credit.[5] Nonetheless, it was the Bank, its president from 1968 to 1980, Robert MacNamara, and its vice-president for development policy, Hollis Chenery—a Harvard academic whose previous work had been principally in the territory of input–output analysis and the explanation of patterns of industrial growth[6] (Chenery 1960) who were first to appreciate the need for an initiative in the uncharted waters of poverty research.

The MacNamara programme and the redistribution with growth prescription

In their attempt to piece together what had gone wrong, the World Bank team took aim at two targets in particular: capital-intensive industrialization and poverty-inducing market imperfections.

Capital-intensive production is a menace to the poor because they are labour-dependent, indeed the poorest people of all have nothing but labour to sell. The pressure towards capital intensity, however, has long been embedded in the

[2] For a history of these ideas and their application within the UN system, see the book by John and Richard Toye (Toye and Toye 2004).

[3] When President MacNamara arrived at the World Bank in the late 1960s 'research on development was not a major, on-going activity of the World Bank' (World Bank/IFC Oral History Program: transcript of interview by Robert Asher with Hollis Chenery, 27 January 1983).

[4] Recent research by Richard Toye suggests that Singer played a larger part than Prebisch in the discovery of this mechanism (Toye and Toye 2004, Chapters 5 and 9).

[5] 'The World Bank, for example, began by merely defending the doctrine of sound finance and had little use for its few economists' (Toye and Toye 2004, page 9).

[6] Most of this work followed up the research of Simon Kuznets in establishing databases and analyses of comparative growth patterns, not least in the field of income distribution, where the 'Kuznets hypothesis' (Kuznets 1955) illustrated the tendency of income inequality to first increase and then fall as development proceeds. Chenery had used this idea to show that industrial development tends to be less in countries 'such as South Africa, Kenya, and Peru, in which predominantly European communities have much higher per capita incomes than the layer native communities' (Chenery 1960, page 646).

development process of industrializing countries. Nineteenth-century Germany, Italy, and most of all Russia used huge industrial complexes for the manufacture of capital goods as battering-rams with which to force their way into world markets, prompting the economic historian Alexander Gerschenkron to suggest the general principle that, the later industrialization occurred, the faster, the more large-scale, the more oligopolistic and, crucially, the more capital-intensive the process would be (Gerschenkron 1959, Chapters 1, 6, and 7). During the inter-war period, in the 1920s and 30s, the Russian success at sustaining and expanding industrial production in the teeth of the global depression[7] was envied and emulated by a number of developing countries anxious to develop their own economic self-sufficiency. Notable amongst these was Brazil, the original trigger for the Bank's anxieties. Under President Getulio Vargas from 1930 to 1945, the capital-intensive industrial complexes, and the planning structures, characteristic of the Russian Five-Year Plans were used as the basis for a leap out of under-development.[8] Argentina launched its own import-substituting industrialization drive at this time, which was less successful, in the sense that unlike Brazil it did not lead to the emergence of any export-based industries. After the Second World War, the capital-intensive industrialization approach to economic strategy was also adopted by South Korea, India, and China, whose attempts to decentralize industrial production into farmers' backyards under the Great Leap Forward, coupled with collectivization of agricultural production, led directly to the hideous famine of 1958–1962,[9] and also by a small cluster of African countries, including South Africa, Nigeria, and Ghana.[10]

For all these countries except South Korea, and to a limited extent Brazil, these experiments in forced industrialization were a failure. Nonetheless, the conventional wisdoms of the time did not acknowledge this. The UN system's main report on economic development of the time (United Nations 1951), as we have seen, accepted, even if it did not glorify, state-sponsored industrialization as the way forward.[11] World Bank lending operations of the time were mainly infrastructure-focused; and a number of planning models of the time, including one by A.K. Sen (1957), favoured the maximization of capital-intensity, on the premise that the higher the level of capital-intensity, the higher the 'reinvestible surplus' left after consumption requirements are satisfied. (This assumes, quite inaccurately, that workers and peasants are incapable of saving—a standard assumption going back to the classical economists that it took the 'microfinance revolution' of the 1990s to finally overturn.) It therefore required some courage for the Bank, at

[7] Between 1921 and 1939 the average annual rate of growth of GDP was around seven per cent in Russia, and six per cent in Brazil by comparison with around one per cent in USA and most European countries.

[8] See the account of Vargas's administration by Hilton (1975).

[9] For excellent accounts of the Chinese famine and its consequences, see Lin (1990) and Chang and Wen (1997).

[10] The best-documented of these cases are those of Ghana, which has been chronicled by Lewis (1953)—an early and during that period rare critic of state-sponsored industrialization—and by Killick (1978). For a discussion of Nigeria see also Lewis (1967).

[11] Chapters 8 and 9 of *Measures for the Economic Development of Underdeveloped Countries* (United Nations 1951, pages 49–70) are devoted to a discussion of 'Development Planning: Techniques' and 'Development Planning: Priorities'.

this point, to reject the conventional wisdoms and declare that labour intensity was the way forward and the small-scale agricultural sector the main instrument through which it should be achieved. What turned the tide was a confrontation with the data. The conventional wisdom of the time stated that only with capital-intensive projects and large-scale agriculture could Bank-financed projects operate profitably. Chenery, acting on MacNamara's instructions, discovered that this was not so, and that a pro-poor strategy therefore did not have to be at the expense of a high rate of return for the Bank or its shareholders. He described the breakthrough in this way:

> I think it was no coincidence that about this time the Director of the Agriculture Department was changed. The former Director was retiring and Monty [Montague] Yudelman was brought in from the OECD. He had a much broader approach, a broader understanding of development and an interest in rural development and in income distribution which his predecessor had not had.
>
> Some of the early debates were about how rapidly we could move in the direction of supporting small farmers and shifting towards poverty-focused agricultural programmes . . . One of the early assertions made was that there was a large trade-off, that if you tried to lend money to small farmers it would be much less productive. I think one of the real contributions made by MacNamara and Yudelman in this area was to push technicians to really find out. On the whole the results of our research were that under controlled conditions, small farmers were as productive as large farmers . . . It was not necessary to change the Bank's evaluation criteria in order to accommodate a shift in emphasis in helping the rural poor.[12]

In advocating the opening up of markets to give the poor access—the second major plank of their strategy—the Bank required less intellectual radicalism, because it was political rather than intellectual vested interests against which they were arrayed. In particular, they worried about unequal access to land, credit, and education (Chenery et al. 1974, page xiv): 'While we advocate maximum use of instruments that operate through factor and product markets, this will often not be sufficient' (ibid, xvii). One particular implication of this was that frequently rural poverty and low agricultural poverty were caused not by poor skills and management by farmers, but rather by the absence or underperformance of the inputs which they required to make them competitive—fertilizers, skilled extension advice, financial services including savings, credit, and insurance, irrigation water, and most of all, infrastructure. The implication was that the Bank, especially in the poorest countries, could not expect to reduce rural poverty simply by

[12] Hollis Chenery, transcript of evidence given to Robert Asher, 27 January 1983, World Bank/IFC Archives, Oral History Program. For further evidence on agriculture in Asia see, in particular, the book by Singh (1990); on Africa see case-study material from Chapter 13 below. But, certainly in the Bank, projects in Africa turned out on average worse than elsewhere. 'What [this] proved to me,' MacNamara subsequently said, 'was not that the approach was wrong, but that the institutional fabric in Africa was so much weaker than, say, in Latin America or India that we could not achieve as much by poverty-oriented projects without greater strengthening of the institutional fabric, than we undertook, and that was a serious error, I think, on our part.' Robert MacNamara: transcript of interview with John Lewis, Richard Webb, and Devesh Kapur, 3 October 1991; World Bank/IFC Archives, Bank Oral History Program.

putting resources into agriculture, and needed to invest, not just in infrastructure as per its Articles of Agreement, but specifically in the rural infrastructure needed to connect the smallholder with the market.

Finally, at precisely the time that the severity of *rural* poverty was perceived, a very large component of *urban* poverty—the huge shantytowns around the periphery of third world cities, now christened 'the informal sector'—was acknowledged for the first time. From Soweto to El Alto (La Paz) and from Calcutta to Nairobi, scores of millions of people owed their existence to activities every element in which—the land which they occupied, the cardboard-and-corrugated-iron huts which they erected on them, and the businesses which they ran from that base—were technically illegal, and which the municipal authorities were doing their utmost to frustrate, if not burn down.[13] Because the informal sector was illegal, no data on it existed, and because there were no data, there was no research on which the Bank could base recommendations. Eventually, especially through the agency of an anthropologist (Hart 1973), an economist (Weeks 1973), and an ILO mission (International Labour Organization 1973) this major potential asset in the fight against poverty was spotted and, for the first time, supported by official agencies in the teeth of the fact that no data on it were available and that in law it had no right to exist. The strategy, as in the rural economy, was to increase labour intensity, for example by engineering a shift from high-specification housing for lower income groups towards simpler site-and-service schemes.

In building up its research programme on pro-poor growth, the Bank did not just rely on internal advice, but looked outwards. Notably, Chenery took the lead in co-organizing, with the newly-established Institute for Development Studies at the University of Sussex, a conference which sought to assimilate some of the radical policy messages deriving from the income distribution research of Fishlow and others, including the Institute's director, Dudley Seers.[14] The proceedings of this conference, later published as *Redistribution with Growth* (Chenery et al. 1974) became the keystone of the World Bank's new poverty focus, given formal Bank support at the Annual Meeting of the Bank's Board of Governors in 1973. The main elements of the strategy (Ayres 1982; van der Laar 1980; MacNamara 1973; World Bank 1983) are described below.

[13] In Nairobi in 1969–71, where I was an assistant economist, informal-sector shanties illegally erected on state land were destroyed most weeks. When I returned in 1997, the process was still going on.

[14] The Bank caused something of a stir even by soliciting Seers' advice, since his approach to development, which saw political power as a key determinant of the allocation of resources and measures to change that allocation of power, for example land reform in Latin America, as an important factor underlying the distribution of income, ran counter to the Bank's approach of treating only the rate of return on capital as relevant to lending decisions, and would never have been asked for prior to the MacNamara/Chenery period. 'There was one quite crucial debate,' Chenery reported, 'between Gus Ranis of Yale who was advocating a fairly orthodox view of how development functions, and Dudley Seers of IDS, who was advocating a much more radical view . . . At the end of the seminar I asked [MacNamara] "Who do you think had the better of it?" and he said "I think Seers had the better of the argument." It was interesting that, without great exposure to the less orthodox views, he was attracted by a more activist approach to development problems.' Hollis Chenery, transcript of interview with Robert Asher, 27 January 1983, World Bank/IFC Archives, Oral History Program.

Table 2.2 Sectoral distribution of World Bank/IDA lending (in per cent).

	Through 1963	1964–8	1975–8
Agriculture	8.6	12.3	32.4
Education	0.1	3.1	4.2
Development finance corporations	3.9	9.6	10.5
Energy/power	34.5	29.0	13.4
Population and nutrition	—	—	0.6
Infrastructure*	39.4	34.5	25.5
Project lending sub-total	**86.5**	**88.5**	**86.0**
Technical assistance	—	—	0.2
Programme lending	3.3	9.0	4.7

Notes: *'Infrastructure' is telecommunications, tourism, transportation, urbanization, plus water supply and sewerage.
Sources: World Bank Group *Annual Reports*, various; some of these data adapted from van der Laar (1980, Table 3.6).

First, there was a shift of Bank resources, in every low income country, into agriculture, especially smallholder agriculture and rural development to deal with the capital-intensity problem, as illustrated in Table 2.2.

Second, within rural areas there were 'integrated rural development programmes' (IRDPs), which in poor countries' most backward regions (for example northern Ghana, north and east Kenya, southern Tanzania, the Nepalese hills, central-southern Sri Lanka, and northern Peru) sought to extract those regions from a poverty trap caused by interlocking failures in input markets (infrastructure, credit, extension, health, and education) by acting on each of those bottlenecks simultaneously.

Third there was support for the urban sector, biased towards the bottom end of the market, through site-and-service and low-cost housing schemes.

Fourth, policy initiatives were designed to redirect assets into the hands of the worse off—land reform, deregulation of urban housing markets, investments in education and agriculture, including green revolution-type measures[15] aimed at directly increasing food security and providing a rationale for reduced population growth among the worse off. 'Our major conclusion as to the choice of strategy', the *Redistribution with Growth* team reported, 'is that there is considerable potential for raising income in low-income groups through a policy of "investment transfers" (so as to) achieve substantial improvements in patterns of asset transfers over time' (Chenery et al. 1974, page 235). By the end of the 1970s cuts in military expenditure, sponsored by the IMF, had joined this list—an unexpected example of the Fund outflanking the donors, not to mention the World Bank, on the left, which gave the Fund a great deal of *schadenfreude* at the time.[16]

[15] 'Since low incomes result from the lack of physical capital, access to infrastructure, and a wide range of complementary inputs, government policy should be directed to providing these inputs over time. Rural development programs aimed at providing a balanced addition to (and improvement of) rural infrastructure in the form of land improvement, drainage, small irrigation, feeder roads, credit, and marketing institutions, and so on, provide one example of this approach' (Chenery et al. 1974, page 81).

[16] MacNamara at the time was compromised by his past as the US Secretary for Defence and thereby as the promoter of the Vietnam war. He subsequently became a defender of cuts in military spending ('a cut of fifty per cent in the third world as a percentage of GNP devoted to the military

No programme of this type had ever previously been announced by an international financial institution. The MacNamara initiative was quickly copied by a number of bilateral donors, which by 1975 included all the Scandinavian countries, the Netherlands, Switzerland, the USA, and the United Kingdom (Mosley 1981).

It is worth exploring in a little more detail the political economy by which the *Redistribution with Growth* team hoped to bring pro-poor policies into being in the 1970s, as a preparation for our own discussion of the same issue in later periods. This was drafted by a Bank staff member and core member of the *Redistribution with Growth* team, C.L.G. Bell, and is exposited in more detail in Bell (1974).

As discussed in Chapter 1, the poor are typically scattered, politically weak, and politically uncohesive. Bell argues that there may be two reasons why, in spite of this, action by the non-poor in the interests of the poor may be nonetheless be politically rational:

1. *Individual self-interest.* As Bell argued, 'The elite may fear that the revolutionary potential of the poor will be realized [as it was, of course, in Russia in 1905 and 1917] unless the burden of their poverty is eased. The rich who subscribe to this view may be prepared to give up something so as not to lose all in a total revolution' (Bell 1974, page 54). More positively, Bell showed that investments in the poor by the rich, such as health and education, might play an important part in raising productivity, and reducing the likelihood of rebellion.[17] A further illustration of this a quarter of a century later was 'the spectre of mass migration to urban areas, with attendant problems of growing slums and rising demands on already overburdened urban services' (World Bank 2000, page 109). The basic insight is that it may be appropriate to see poverty reduction as a public rather than a private good, on the grounds that those who pursue it achieve benefits for people other than just themselves;[18] these benefits, of course, include self-protection.

would be a major advance, and the Bank can help lead the way') but this was not a part of his development strategy whilst at the Bank. He defended this approach as follows: 'You couldn't convince Pakistan or Egypt to reduce their military expenditures when the US as part of the cold war was seeking to line up Pakistan as an offset to India and seeking to line up Egypt as an offset to the Soviet Union... At certain times there are rigidities you can't go beyond, and the cold war was one such rigidity', Robert MacNamara, interviewed by John Lewis, Richard Webb, and Devesh Kapur, 10 May 1991, World Bank/IFC Archives, Oral History Program.

[17] The first of these ideas underlies the 'efficiency wage' idea of microeconomics—the employer deliberately pays a wage higher than the equilibrium in order to increase productivity and thus profit. A historical illustration of the second idea is provided by the following quotation related to Zimbabwe, one of the most unequal of all developing countries, in the 1940s: 'The persistence of this low standard of health must necessarily retard an increased effort by the Natives to improve their social and economic conditions... Tuberculosis is increasing to an extent which in the medical view is ominous. Owing to want of suitable accommodation, Natives with this disease are being sent to the Reserves [African rural areas] where they are likely to share a windowless hut with several others. Drastic and immediate action is not only humane, *it is mere self-protection*' (emphasis added) (from Southern Rhodesia, *Report of the Native Production and Trade Commission 1944*, page 19). In Chapter 5 below, we develop this idea into the notion of a 'social efficiency wage'—productivity, on this view, is determined by the risk of conflict, which in turn is determined by the level of the social, rather than the private, wage.

[18] See the World Bank's 2000 *World Development Report* (World Bank 2000, page 109).

2. *Self-protection through the formation of a coalition*. Some of the constituent groups of the elite may have conflicts serious enough for them to need a measure of support from groups outside the elite—and to the extent that the membership of these outsider-groups is poor or vulnerable, the act of forming a coalition with them will bring them above the poverty line, and keep them there for as long as the coalition holds and its instruments are effective.[19] For example, since all urban groups have an interest in cheap food—an interest which will be resisted by rich landlords—they may side with workers, many of whom are poor, against those rich landlords.

The underlying political strategy of *Redistribution with Growth* is therefore to identify fault-lines of this sort, and then reinforce the possibilities for pro-poor political action by either compensating powerful losers, or inflicting the losses on them in a sufficiently unobvious way that they do not hit back. Analysis of this sort provides the rationale for many of the MacNamara proposals, for example the recommendation to implement *land reform* (of the kind encouraged by the Bank in Kenya, Taiwan, Thailand, Philippines, Peru, Bolivia, and Brazil, *inter alia*, at this time)[20] takes advantage of the idea that employers, in order to achieve cheaper food and lower labour costs, might support the idea of achieving that via land reforms, against the opposition of landed interests, who could be bought off with the help of Bank or aid finance. Many of the Bank's expenditure proposals have the same attraction: for example education[21] and integrated rural development proposals financed not out of taxation, whose welfare cost is obvious, but out of borrowing,[22] which looks cost free (and for poor (IDA) countries with income below $1000 very nearly is, since they pay only a service charge of 0.75 per cent). And in Indonesia, one of the Bank's greatest success stories of the 1970s and 80s, the elite was very happy to follow the Bank's prescribed rural development-led strategy, not only to head off splits of the kind described above but more fundamentally to decentralize the control of the ruling party into the rural areas and to prevent a recurrence of the chaos of the 1960s.

The MacNamara programme thus achieved a substantial switch of expenditure towards 'poverty groups' and a substantial fall in poverty levels during the 1970s (Tables 1.1 and 2.2); at the same time, it achieved a more than satisfactory return on capital, including on its poverty-focused programmes. And yet by 1980 the Bank's inaugural poverty initiative, and that of nearly all its development partners, had been dismantled. Before we can begin to understand the right way to construct pro-poor programmes in the present, we need to understand this occurrence and its causes.

[19] For example, 'In nineteenth-century Britain, landed interests supported the reformers over the issue of industrial working conditions, and the capitalists fought successfully to have the Corn Laws repealed' (footnote taken from Bell 1974, page 54).

[20] Land reform had, of course, been an important element in Latin American redistributive policy ever since the Zapata revolution of 1911 in Mexico.

[21] Increasingly the Bank became aware of a tension between the form of education which was most pro-poor (i.e. primary education, especially of girls) and the form which was most politically attractive to LDC elites (i.e. secondary and tertiary education). Resolving this tension was to be a major theme of Bank policy in the 1980s.

[22] Bell (1974, page 56) correctly argues that 'intervention which alters the distribution to the increment to the overall capital stock will arouse less hostility than transfers which bite into their existing assets and reserves': always redistribute out of planned investment, not out of expected income.

2.3 DEATH AND TRANSFIGURATION OF THE MACNAMARA INITIATIVE (1980–96)

Death (1980–7)

In 1979 the World Bank's first poverty initiative, and that of its main development partners, was terminated. The poverty objective ceased to be a formal goal of donor strategies, and some of the most high-profile elements in the MacNamara redistribution-through-growth strategy, such as land reform, integrated rural development programmes, and urban slum-upgrading programmes, were brought to an end.

Much of this change, of course, occurred as a consequence of a transformation of the economic and political environment. The early 1970s, the time of the MacNamara initiative, marked the peak of a global boom (Figure 1.2), which turned out too powerful to be manageable through the standard Keynesian techniques of fiscal and monetary restraint, especially when the oil price increases of the mid-1970s were imposed on top of it. In the industrialized countries, the consequence of trying to control this boom was not just recession but 'stagflation'—the hitherto unprecedented combination of rising inflation and rising unemployment. On both sides of the North-South divide, the consequence was a change in the rules of the game. In industrialized countries, the administrations elected at the turn of the decade abandoned the balancing act that they had been trying to maintain between unemployment and inflation, and opted for the simpler strategy of trying to control inflation over the medium term. One way of doing this was a traditional (quantity theory of money) one: severe restraints on the level of monetary demand, imposed, however, not in stop-go fashion, but in the form of a gradual and continuous suffocation until inflation was, as Margaret Thatcher put it, 'squeezed out of the system'. But the other approach was quite new: this was to stimulate the supply side of the system by removing monopolies, trade union privileges, subsidized public enterprises and other 'price distortions', as the World Bank was to call them: devices designed to increase the incomes of specific interest groups at the expense of the mass.[23]

Developing countries, caught between the upper millstone of this collapsing demand for their exports and the nether millstone of shrinking availability of finance,[24] were forced increasingly to default on their debts—leading some lurid imaginations, as we recall (Chapter 1 above) to fear a financial and geo-political meltdown. This was not an easy environment in which to sustain the long-term perspective, never mind the idealism, needed to support a global anti-poverty programme.

The MacNamara poverty initiative could have been sustained, however, if two further difficulties had not got in the way. One of these was the uncomfortable fact that poverty programmes, or more precisely the form in which some forms of

[23] Collectively, these are known to economists as 'rents', by analogy with the household meaning of rents on land or property, which like the privileges described above are resources whose supply cannot be varied in the short term.

[24] International private financial flows—bank lending, bond lending, and foreign direct investment—shrank from $75bn in 1980 to around $20bn in 1985. See World Bank, *Global Financial Flows*, 1981 and 1986 issues.

them were administered within the MacNamara programme, were deeply unpopular. They increased workload, they increased the costs of coordination, they multiplied the opportunities for corruption, and because of this they eliminated all hope of achieving the first requirement of any effective development administrator—spend the budget. Trying to make any project work in a hot, poor, and mosquito-ridden developing country is bad enough, but trying to, in addition, coordinate the transport budget and the livestock development budget and the crop extension budget and the water development budget and the training budget and the rural credit budget and the road budget and the power supply budget, and to find that none of these add up or can be spent because of feuds up the road between provincial administrators over whom you have no control, is to invite not loyalty at a time when poverty focus was under threat, but voice, and quite savage voice at that. As one of the best commentaries on the integrated rural development programmes of the 1970s pithily remarked, 'Concern for the rural poor evaporates quite fast when hard-pressed administrators are still emptying their in-trays at 7 pm on Friday evening.'[25]

At this point the second and clinching objection to poverty focus enters the argument. This was the precipitous ascent in the popularity of supply-side economics, previously described, from being an interesting footnote, at the time of the MacNamara programme, to all of a sudden the *sine qua non* of economic recovery, without which a revival of global growth could not be expected. Since without growth there is nothing to redistribute from, it came to be put about that continuing with poverty strategies amidst the current predicament amounted to rearranging the deckchairs on the *Titanic*. This view is, in our judgement, quite wrong, but it corresponds quite accurately[26] to the approach to poverty dominant in the donor community at this time.

In industrialized countries, the main elements in the supply-side economics programme consisted of tax cuts, privatization of loss-making public enterprises, and legislation to reduce the power and privileges of trade unions, brought in with enthusiasm, even moral fervour,[27] by the newly-elected right-wing administrations of Reagan (in the United States), Thatcher (in Britain), and Kohl (in Germany). In developing countries, even though the loss-making public enterprises were conspicuously present, there was by contrast very little spontaneous enthusiasm for measures of this sort—the only developing country actively undertaking such measures during the early 1980s being General Pinochet's Chile. Thus, the supply-side revolution in developing countries, to the extent that it took place at all, was not

[25] Wiggins (1985, page 105).

[26] In 1981 a group including the present author formed the Independent Group on British Aid (IGBA 1981), a pressure group formed to argue for the maintenance of improvement in the quality of aid (in particular through poverty focus, abolition of aid as export subsidy, untying of aid, and greater devolution of the aid budget to NGOs) at a time when the real value of the aid budget was under pressure for macro-economic reasons. The reception in DFID (ODA as it then was) was at that time hostile, but all of its recommendations have now been implemented.

[27] Cf. Andrew Marr's remark: Margaret Thatcher 'did not believe in privatizing industries or defeating inflation for merely economic reasons. She wanted to re-moralize society, creating a nation whose Victorian values were expressed through secure marriages, self-reliance and savings, restraint, good neighbourliness, hard work. Though much attacked by church leaders she talked of God and morality a lot: "I am in politics because of the conflict between good and evil"' (Marr 2007, page 381).

spontaneous, but imposed, and like the MacNamara poverty programme, the degree of its implementation was patchy, depending on the relative vulnerability of different recipient countries to external pressure and the relative extent to which local elites could be persuaded of the applicability of the 'new economics', as we discuss further in Chapter 7.

The main agent of change within the developing countries in the early 1980s, was therefore the Bretton Woods institutions, not, however, in the shape of the harmonious interaction between its three elements which the founding fathers had envisaged, but rather in the form of an undignified power struggle, with the World Bank taking advantage of the global crisis in order to make up lost ground on the IMF. In essence, what happened was that the severity and depth of the global crisis exposed a gaping hole in the international financial structure, which the Bank won the race to fill. The Bretton Woods structure, as it stood between 1945 and 1980, provided for a division of labour between an IMF which would deal with short-term balance of payments emergencies, a World Bank which would provide longer-term support for investment and growth (initially, as we have seen, mostly in the form of infrastructure), and a GATT[28] (now WTO), which would build and sustain the free flows of trade and investment needed to underpin these institutions. But the viability of this structure depended on macro-economic crises being short term, and therefore resolvable by means of the short-term conditional support which the IMF offered. This description applied, indeed, to most of the crises which hit the world between the 1940s and the 1970s; but not to the crisis of the 1980s, which was much longer term in nature, and indeed hit many of the poorer parts of the developing world much worse than the inter-war depression of the 1920s and 1930s.[29] What the 1980s crisis required was medium-term, not short-term, adjustment finance, and that form of finance, at the beginning of the crisis, was not being offered by anyone.[30] The IMF, which had never seen itself as a development institution, and was only just awakening to the fact that its main business was now irrevocably in the developing world, had tried to offer this sort of finance, through its Extended Facility (Helleiner 1983; Killick 1984a); but this was not nearly enough, and for want of long-term budgetary support, many poor countries were being rapidly carried towards the waterfall labelled 'default'. This was the 'hole in the system' which the World Bank in the early 1980s identified.

The plaster which the Bretton Woods system applied to fill this hole was a mixture of supply-side components adapted for developing-country use, of which the main new World Bank element became known as *Structural Adjustment Loans* (SALs). 'Structural adjustment' was the Bank's name for supply-side measures, such as liberalization of agricultural prices, import tariffs, public

[28] General Agreement on Tariffs and Trade, as it was known for the first fifty years of its life. It changed its name to World Trade Organization (WTO) in 1995.

[29] Most of Africa, for example the poorest part of the world, experienced negative per capita GDP growth for fifteen years after 1980, but scarcely shrank at all during the inter-war recession, in particular because peasant exports such as Ghanaian cocoa, Ugandan cotton, and Kenyan coffee were very resilient to that recession; for detailed illustration see in particular Chapter 13 below.

[30] The 'poverty focus' measures of the MacNamara programme were particularly unhelpful from the point of view of macro-economic recovery, as they were slow-disbursing and inflexible.

enterprises, and most of all exchange rates and exports, which in many countries had been heavily taxed with devastatingly negative developmental impact ever since the 1940s.[31] By means of these modern varieties of neo-liberalism, rather different from the supply-side measures of America and western Europe, where the emphasis was much more on the labour market and cuts in direct taxes,[32] the Bank hoped to achieve a long-term opening-up of the economy and a shift from protected low-productivity (or 'non-tradable') activities into activities which were competitive on international markets. This shift, it was hoped, would make possible a resumption of growth, from which redistribution, if developing countries so chose, would eventually be possible.

Structural adjustment loans (otherwise known, in many countries, as sector adjustment loans, economic recovery loans, reconstruction loans, policy-based loans, and eventually as budget support operations) quickly became a large element in the Bank's portfolio, as illustrated by Table 2.5. They went from zero to nearly a quarter of the Bank's lending in the course of the 1980s, for many of the poorer countries the share was as much as half,[33] and were very different from any kind of operation which the Bank had previously done. They were not capital development projects, as envisaged in the Bank's 1945 Articles of Agreement, indeed they were not projects at all; they were import support operations designed to deal with the mega-balance of payments crisis in which the developing world had found itself enmeshed. Also, by contrast with previous Bank operations, quite elaborate conditionality was attached to them, in some cases more than a hundred conditions attached to a single loan.[34] In both respects, there was, however, a big overlap with the kind of work which the Fund had previously done, and the 1980s were characterized by recurrent 'turf wars' between the Bank and the Fund concerning which of those institutions should lead on tax reform, or exchange rate reform, or arrangements for privatization: all of them had fiscal implications, traditionally the Fund's territory, and also resource-allocation implications, increasingly a territory which the Bank was trying to take over.

Conditionality applied to overseas financial flows such as SALs, at this time, was seen as the international financial community's great hope for improving the quality of investment in developing countries. Of its nature, it created conflicts of political interest, which no amount of euphemism or diplomacy such as describing conditionality as 'policy dialogue' could conceal. Indeed, if there had been no internal political opposition to conditions, there would have been no point in imposing them, since by hypothesis they would have been implemented anyway.

[31] For African countries, see Bates (1981). There had been earlier critics of commodity taxation, notably Bauer (1954), based mainly on the grounds that it was economically inefficient. But since it taxed poor farmers to yield a benefit for rich trading companies and governments, it was also inequitable, a theme taken up both by Bates in Africa and in Asia by Lipton (1977).

[32] For a listing of the instruments of liberalization used as conditionality on Bank structural adjustment loans in the 1980s, see Mosley (1987). In essence the choice of which elements to liberalize in each country was partly an economic judgement, related to which sectors and activities were seen as most heavily distorted, and partly a political judgement, related to which sectors and activities were seen as easiest to reform.

[33] See Mosley, Harrigan, and Toye (1995, Chapters 3 and 4).

[34] These multi-condition loans became known as 'Christmas trees', offering presents for everyone. See Mosley, Harrigan, and Toye (1995, Chapters 2 and 3).

However, the extent to which these internal conflicts of interest became serious depended on the extent to which, with the global crisis, governments had come to depend on the Bank and Fund for finance. In most of Asia, with the exception of Indonesia, Pakistan, and Bangladesh, the need to depend on international sources of development finance was only transient. South Korea resorted to a Structural Adjustment Loan in 1981, Thailand in 1981 and 1983, and India, after an unexpected but frightening leakage of reserves, in 1991; but all of these parties thought it unnecessary to become involved in elaborate conditionality negotiations, paid back their loans rapidly, and never went back to the Bank again. Latin America (including Argentina and Brazil), and eventually also Russia and Eastern Europe when they embarked on reform in the 1990s, became much more deeply entrapped in debt problems, and for this reason were obliged to take on large SALs, but in none of these cases did the Bank and Fund see fit to argue with them about how the money was used, as they were 'too big to fail'. There was no point in making an issue about breaches of conditionality, since the enforcement of conditionality would have meant breaking off lending, and that would have put the client's ability to repay debt at risk, and potential default was a much bigger problem than failure to privatize this or that company, or to set right this or that interference with the market mechanism.[35] This of course created a moral hazard problem, since the Bank's conditionality in such cases was not credible, and this was transparent to all parties, enabling large and powerful LDC clients to breach whatever policy conditions they wished. The only region of the developing world where this was not the case was, of course, Africa; as we shall see, this fact eventually was to lead to some very pleasing results in, amongst other fields, poverty reduction.

But all this was to come. Supply-side conditionality was an experiment, and a very precarious one. Most of Asia recovered its economic momentum by the mid-1980s, and Latin America also began to do so by the end of the decade, but the whole of Africa remained stuck on a continuous downward path throughout this period, and, globally, the investment rate fell and fell (Mosley, Harrigan, and Toye 1995, Chapter 4), provoking fears about whether the promised shift from non-tradables to tradables, which structural adjustment was supposed to deliver, was ever going to happen in the real world.

There were other worries. One of them was that poverty was now clearly on an increasing long-term trend,[36] and could no longer be dismissed as a blip which the resumption of growth, via structural adjustment, would automatically set right. The UNICEF study, *Adjustment with a Human Face* (Cornia, Jolly, and Stewart 1987),[37] was the first to document the human costs of the global recession, and to show that even though the recession itself had formally ended, poverty was still

[35] For the large Latin America cases see Mosley, Harrigan, and Toye (1995), Vol. 1, Chapters 3 and 4; also Chapter 9 below (for Argentina); for Russia and eastern Europe, Mosley (2006), also Chapter 12 below.

[36] This also happened in industrialized countries (e.g. Britain), where poverty continuously increased between 1979 and 1996. See, for example, Hills and Stewart (2005), Chapter 1, Table 1.1.

[37] Richard Jolly is the element of continuity between this study and *Redistribution with Growth*, having been a co-author of both studies. The allusion in the title of this study is to the 'socialism with a human face' which the Czech leader, Alexander Dubcek, attempted to implant into a weakening communist system before the Russian invasion of the country in 1968.

rising (recall Table 1.1). The study discovered evidence, of particular concern to UNICEF, that structural adjustment-induced expenditure cuts might have fallen particularly hard on the most vulnerable groups, and specifically on investment in the social sectors (agriculture, health, education, and social protection), which were particularly crucial for the well-being of the poorest, and notably of poor children. One particular contribution of *Adjustment with a Human Face* was to identify a category of 'new poor', in other words people made poor not by innate lack of land, skills, or labour power, but by collapse of demand for their skills in the global recession.

The World Bank, not amused by the fact that the UNICEF initiative, having emerged from a UN institution, had put it on the back foot,[38] at first reacted in an improvisatory manner, by inserting a miscellany of 'measures to reduce the social costs of adjustment' into its structural adjustment programmes. Three examples of such programmes, treated in more detail in our case-study chapters, are PAMSCAD (Programme to Mitigate the Social Costs of Adjustment, Ghana, 1988), PAPSCA (Programme against Poverty and the Social Costs of Adjustment, Uganda, 1989) and FSE/FIS *(Fondo Social de Emergencia and Fondo Social de Inversion*/Emergency Social Fund and Social Investment Fund, Bolivia, 1988). PAMSCAD and PAPSCA were purely compensatory programmes, handing out dollops of cash support to people experiencing financial loss as a result of adjustment programmes (typically government employees retrenched as a consequence of cutbacks in public expenditure). FSE/FIS was more ambitious, achieving such compensation not by means of consumption support but rather by labour-intensive investment projects, typically in the health and education sectors, for which private entrepreneurs were invited to bid.[39] It is one of the pioneer projects supporting the theme of 'investing in the human resources of the poor', prefigured in a very public-sector-oriented way in *Redistribution with Growth*, which through to the present has been a major theme of the new poverty strategies.

At this stage, in the late 1980s, it was far from clear that a new poverty strategy would emerge out of the ashes of the old one. Everything which was being done at that time in relation to poverty was short-term, improvisatory, and ad hoc, and not embedded in any longer-term plan. The long-term and overriding objective continued to be supply-side reform, which notably in Russia and Eastern Europe was only just beginning (over the course of the next ten years the liberalizing Russian and Eastern European economies were to revisit almost every one of the Latin American traumas of the 1970s—hyperinflation, natural resources boom and curse,

[38] There was much informal contact between the Bank and UNICEF during the run-up to *Adjustment with a Human Face*, in which an initially contemptuous Bank was somewhat won over from its insistence on non-interference in the free-market mechanism by an awareness that it was itself intervening in that mechanism. The ice was finally broken, as one member of the *Adjustment with a Human Face* team relates, at a World Bank (not-quite-free) lunch. 'I looked at the menu and read: "Lobster Thermidor, $5, Tournedos Rossini, $4 . . . and so on. And I said to our host at the Bank, you evidently think it is OK to subsidize the meals in the Bank canteen. So why then do you oppose food subsidies in the Third World, if it is OK to apply them here?"' Giovanni Andrea Cornia, personal communication.

[39] For a description of the FSE scheme, and an analysis of its effects on employment and poverty, see the paper by Newman, Pradhan, and Jorgensen (1990).

capital-intensity problems, and, most of all, a highly unequal income distribution, which in a few years went from one of the most equal in the world to 'more unequal than the United States' (Brainerd 1998, page 1094)). The transition from poverty reduction as short-term improvisation to poverty reduction as long-term institutional structure was made very gradually, with the first thrust occurring through the World Bank's *World Development Report* (WDR) of 1990, which its authors clearly saw as the first step in a campaign. At that time, however, few people saw it as having a long-term significance going beyond that normally accorded to such a report.

The analysis of the 1990 report was based on three simple propositions. First, because the poorest and most vulnerable people in any country are those who have nothing to sell but their labour, the first step in a pro-poor strategy is to make the pattern of development as labour intensive as possible (the emerging experience of the Far East was an inspiration in this regard), not a principle formally emphasized in *Redistribution with Growth*, although it is entirely consistent with that report's emphasis on equalizing the income distribution. Second, to build up the productivity of the poor, they need both physical and human assets; of these, human assets have higher productivity, since they themselves generate technical progress, and so the second plank of the 1990 strategy is investment in the human capital of the poor, reminiscent of *Redistribution with Growth*'s 'promotion of education so as to develop a more equal pattern of human capital'.[40] Finally, for those who have access neither to labour nor capital, such as the retired and disabled, the third plank in the strategy was 'social safety nets', not a concept precisely defined in the WDR, but with a presumption that the key thing, especially in rural areas, is informal sources of social protection—savings, insurance, and other mutual support networks—rather than the formal state- and employer-based welfare systems found in industrialized countries.[41]

Not having visited this territory for a decade, the Bank concentrated, in its report, on reorienting priorities for policy and institution-building, and did not write down detailed numbers on what it expected those priorities to deliver. Simply in trying to establish the basic benchmark of how many people were poor, it encountered major difficulties: the main table in which it portrays the changes in poverty since the 1970s, for example, contains no information on Africa.[42] Even for Asia and Latin America, the poverty data used by the Bank rely on national poverty lines based on different estimates of what constitutes deprivation, and therefore not commensurable. It was only in the course of the 1990s, as the poverty reduction commitment became entrenched, that the Bank embarked on the *Living Standards Measurement Surveys* exercise, which for the first time provided internationally comparable data on poverty levels. These are the data used in the first table of this book, Table 1.1 above. But for most countries it is only in the last fifteen years, since the 1990s, that we can make international comparisons of even the simplest

[40] *Redistribution with Growth* (Chenery et al. 1974), page 81.

[41] There are some exceptions to this principle, for example the state pensions schemes found in South Africa.

[42] World Bank 1990, Table 3.2, page 41. The Bank comments: 'A weakness in this assessment is the lack of reliable data for Sub-Saharan Africa. [The evidence of stagnant consumption per capita suggests] that progress in reducing poverty has probably been slowest in that region.' This data problem was also a difficulty in *Redistribution with Growth*.

poverty measure, the headcount index. Thus, all long-period analyses of poverty are vitiated: this is a major limitation which afflicts all studies including this one.[43] There is at this stage, it hardly needs to be added, no attempt to differentiate even conceptually between all the different meanings which can be attached to the idea of poverty, in the way which is now commonplace.

In deriving its diagnosis and its prescriptions, the Bank uses certain key exemplars, especially the entire Far East region, which illustrated several of the principles on which the Bank's three-cornered strategy drew: realization of the growth-with-equity potential of productivity increases in smallholder agriculture (and of the need for heavy state intervention to bring these increases about),[44] practical application of technical flexibility in industry, heavy investment in education at all levels, and an early realization of the uses of aggressive devaluation in achieving macro-adjustment in a progressive manner. Many of the Far Eastern countries had already graduated a long way out of poverty by 1990, but one which had not, and from which the Bank (and, in their wake, the Besley and Cord report) drew particular inspiration is Indonesia, which 'took less than a generation in the 1970s and 80s to reduce the incidence of poverty from almost sixty per cent of the population to less than twenty per cent' (World Bank 1990, page 1). We discuss the Indonesian case, of which MacNamara was particularly proud because he took the risk of reinitiating a large lending programme when the Indonesian economy was on its uppers in 1968,[45] further in Chapters 5, 6, and 11 below.

From the time of the 1990 WDR onwards, then, the poverty idea was locked back into the list of criteria which had to be considered in development policy, but how they should be considered was still for discussion. From that point on we see a gradual traverse from 'growth but not forgetting the poor' to 'reduction of many poverties, achieved principally through pro-growth policies'.

Transfiguration (1990–6)

Through the early 1990s international institutions trod gingerly across the thin ice of pro-poor reform, emboldened and distracted by the huge windfall of *perestroika* in the former communist bloc (and the fall of the Soviet Union), which is discussed in detail in Chapter 11, but uneasily aware that the core problems described in the first chapter—namely the failure of Africa and the rest of the 'bottom billion' either to increase investment and growth in response to structural adjustment or to reduce poverty levels—were failing to come good after more than a decade. In response to this challenge, there was a three-way split of opinion. Washington fundamentalists urged that the reform agenda should be widened and deepened (e.g. World Bank 1994), anti-Washington fundamentalists, mostly

[43] For an attempt to finesse the problem for six African countries by using anthropomorphic wage and, especially mortality, data, see Chapter 13 below.

[44] The essay by Birgegard in Djurfeldt et al. (2004) most usefully describes the historical antecedents of these green revolution programmes in Japan, South Korea, and (especially) Taiwan.

[45] For MacNamara's anecdote of this episode, in which he explained his instinctive decision to take a gamble on Indonesia, see Chapter 7 below, page 212.

in the NGO movement, argued that it should be abandoned, but very many people realized that some of the problems associated with both poverty and reform were much deeper than could be dealt with by getting prices right, or even by redistributing from growth (if any growth there was), or even by investing in human resources. Three problems associated with this schism surfaced in the 1990s, and they remain unsolved: conflict, governance, and the protection of the poor against risk. We now venture into the politics of these issues.

Conflict and political violence

Conflict in a small way has always been part of development policy, since the adjustment programmes of the IMF require people to be hurt (for example through increases in food prices resulting from expenditure cuts) in ways which weak and vulnerable states find impossible to manage in a non-conflictual way. Since the 1950s it had been clear that political violence resulting from public anger at the consequences of economic measures was a frequent occurrence in developing countries, and that it had not only human costs but developmental ones also, since such violence would deter investment and aggravate the brain drain, and other elements in the capital flight, of developing countries. The stock response of the IMF to this anger was that adjustment of expenditure was inescapable, and that the issue of how to adjust was one for the recipient developing country to determine.

During the 1980s, the level of this violence and instability escalated, especially in Africa, and in a number of cases it was becoming clear that often apparently minor riot-type incidents could escalate into full-scale civil war. Two of the clearest cases of this are Sierra Leone, where the grievances resulting from a series of failed adjustment operations in the 1980s were picked up on by a political opposition which gradually moved into guerrilla war against the government,[46] and Yugoslavia (incidentally something of a darling of the *Redistribution with Growth* team in the 1970s)[47] which in an attempt to stabilize a runaway inflation in 1989–90 applied meat-axe methods (including a forty per cent cut in the money supply in one year) to the macro-economy of the entire federation, in a manner which contributed enormously to the secession of Slovenia and Croatia and, by the early nineties, also to the outbreak of civil war in Bosnia-Herzegovina and in Kosovo. At the same time, civil war itself could be clearly seen as the reason why much of Africa was failing to respond to the supply-side medicine offered by the structural adjustment teams (Mosley, Subasat, and Weeks 1995). Not only Sierra Leone, but also Angola, Algeria, Burundi, Chad, Congo-Kinshasa, Ethiopia, Eritrea, Liberia, Mozambique, Nigeria, Rwanda, Somalia, Sudan, Zimbabwe, and even for a time South Africa[48]—all the largest economies in Africa, in fact—were

[46] On the disastrous failed adjustment in Sierra Leone in the 1980s, and the consequent drift towards civil war, see Weeks (1992).

[47] See, for example, Table 1.1 of Chenery et al. (1974) and the discussion surrounding this, which shows income inequality in Yugoslavia as being relatively low.

[48] In response to the disturbances in South Africa during the early 1990s, and in particular the grievances over the inequity in the distribution of land which underlay them, one policy instrument central to *Redistribution with Growth*, but dormant since the 1970s, land reform, was brought back. However,

clearly experiencing a level of civil conflict which no amount of exchange-rate liberalization, devaluation, tariff liberalization or export promotion could hope to counteract by purely economic measures. And at this same time, the economics profession, which for over a century had stood aloof from the debate on the causes of war, now entered the civil-war debate (Collier and Hoeffler 1998, 2004; Nafziger and Auvinen 2002; Stewart 1993). Although controversy continues to be intense, the one thing about which there is now consensus is that an anti-poverty policy which does not help to contain conflict, whether long term or short term, is an inadequate policy. Our Chapter 4 examines the conflict-poverty linkage, with an emphasis on short-term policy and localized, riot-type conflict, where the literature is thinner.

One thing which the 'new' adjustment literature of the 1990s has found it necessary to emphasize is that (contrary to Margaret Thatcher's famous dictum of 1980) 'there is an alternative' (to stabilization through the control of the money supply alone). There was, for example, an alternative to stabilizing the Yugoslav economy in 1990 by cutting the Yugoslav money supply by forty per cent per annum, and it consisted of (1) cutting it by less, (2) using a range of alternative technologies of deflation, possibly less hostile to the poor, (3) stimulating supply as well as cutting demand, and (4) explaining the need for stabilization and the rationale for the technologies used more eloquently to the Yugoslav electorate. It was the merit of the OECD in the early 1990s (Bourguignon and Morrisson 1992) to explain what alternative technologies of adjustment might have a more human face. They concluded in particular (Bourguignon and Morrisson 1992; Morrisson 1992, case study of Morocco) that:

1. Devaluation might be the most progressive way to achieve adjustment to a macro-economic deficit, especially in the context of an economy where exports were intensive in poor people's labour.
2. Increases in tax rates might be a very unprogressive way to achieve adjustment to a macro-economic deficit, especially increases in indirect taxes, which to be fiscally effective must be imposed on essential commodities, which *ipso facto* will tend to be a larger share of the consumption of the poor than of the rich.

Thus, pro-poor, and almost certainly conflict-reducing, alternatives exist; but if pro-poor political interests are unable to achieve any leverage within the resource-allocation process this will be only an academic finding, rather than a measure of direct help to the poor. The OECD team duly initiated a follow-up study (Haggard et al. 1995) to investigate the circumstances under which pro-poor adjustment was feasible, and, as we have seen, opined rather pessimistically that 'the politically most active groups are not usually the poorest' (Haggard et al. 1995, page 120). This led them to despair of achieving poverty reduction through completely open and democratic politics and inclined them towards policy instruments which can be adjusted in a more technocratic way—a classic example being the exchange rate, which can be changed in an afternoon by a unilateral decision of the

the amount of land so far transferred is still less than five per cent of the amount originally aimed at, and even for this five per cent it is not possible to show that food security or other dimensions of poverty have improved (Valente 2008).

governor of the central bank and his advisory group, possibly in consultation with the finance ministry and possibly not. The Haggard study also emphasized the importance of presentational style, spin, and *glasnost* in explaining the strategy underlying adjustment processes, reiterating the principle that for government staff to be seen sharing the burden of adjustment could be a hugely effective instrument for pacifying the anger caused by its costs—a principle which Bolivia and Indonesia, in particular, were to disregard to their cost a few years later during the East Asian crisis (Chapters 10 and 11 below). In the next section, we argue that the OECD team's view is over-pessimistic, and that changes in the composition of elites, in particular the rise of progressive rural elites in Africa, have created a scope for democratic pro-poor initiatives that was not available to those who launched the 'first poverty wave'.

Governance

Economists have always cherished a feeling that if only they could rule the world alone, it would be a better and a fairer place. Distinguished examples of this persuasion include Paul Collier, who in Collier and Hoeffler (2004) argues that the only factors which have a significant influence on the outbreak of war are political and not economic,[49] and Arthur Lewis, who in the early 1960s, wounded by his failure at persuading the government of a newly independent Ghana to adopt sensible economic policies, concluded that the primary problem was Nkrumah's advice to 'seek ye first the political kingdom'.[50] But the greatest illustration of the principle was the World Bank's attempt, during the years of structural adjustment, to get rid of rent-seekers by invoking the laws of free-market economics. If only the Mobutus and the Marcoses and the Mois ('politics', in the mind of the econocrats) could be got rid of, ran the reasoning (Krueger 1974),[51] that would expand the supply side of the economy as nothing else could, and the proper working of the price mechanism would pull the world out of recession. As we have seen, this mechanism simply did not work in many parts of the world, Africa in particular, and thus the search began for keys to making the poorer economies of the world behave. If the first of these was conflict reduction, the second was 'governance'—the cluster of capacities which enable, or do not enable, a state to function.

Thus was reopened, at this very same time (the World Bank's World Development Report on this theme came out in 1997), one of the oldest questions in politics, 'what holds a state together?' The question was about to be given a new twist by the East Asian crisis—two of our case-study countries, Indonesia and Bolivia, experienced attempts at secession during the post-crisis period, and a

[49] For an extended discussion of this view see Chapter 4 below.

[50] Nkrumah, against Lewis's insistent advice, sought to create an industrial complex in Ghana, by means of import-substituting industrialization, and thereby to achieve greater self-sufficiency for the newly independent colony. For a discussion of Lewis's attempts at persuasion, see Tignor (2005), Chapter 5.

[51] Anne Krueger, whose paper on the political economy of the rent-seeking society (Krueger 1974) had helped to explain the rationale for states to engage in protectionist policies, became World Bank chief economist in 1979, and thus was put in a strong position to dismantle protectionist structures in developing countries.

third traditionally seen as one of the strongest of all, Russia, suddenly stood on the precipice of state collapse after the storming of its parliament in 1993. One of the most knee-jerk answers conventionally given to the question in a developmental context—freedom from corruption[52]—was clearly questionable in a developmental context, since many of the countries which at the end of the twentieth century had the best performance overall and specifically in poverty reduction—South Korea, China, Indonesia, indeed some regions of Russia also since perestroika—also have some of the highest levels of corruption.[53] The long-term effectiveness of old-style short-term solutions, strengthening the centrality of the army and the police, is also obviously context-specific, and still subject to debate. One absolutely fundamental correlate of state capacity was clearly the fiscal capacity to support the expansion of expenditure by levying taxes and user charges. The difference in fiscal capacity between Asia and Africa was clearly influential in enabling most parts of Asia, during the 1970s and 80s, to experience a sustained green revolution leading to average cereal yields of between three and four tons per hectare by the millennium, whilst Africa's attempts to replicate the same process were constantly aborted by fiscal weakness[54]—possibly the biggest of all the reasons for the divergence between the continents. There is no doubt at all that successful institutions have been key in development, and that de-institutionalization has been a crucial component of institutional decline—for the Bolivian case see Chapter 9 below. However, how to make bad institutions into good ones, and even how to overcome some of the systemic problems associated with the international financial system, for example the fact that it will always be politically more attractive in a weak state to increase revenue by increasing aid receipts than by raising taxes,[55] are not problems which have been satisfactorily resolved. Huge problems of measurement remain; for example we do not even now properly know what a pro-poor institution is. This is one of the frontiers of work on pro-poor growth, and the Bank's *Delivering on the Promise* team (Besley and Cord 2007), as we saw in Table 1.3, rightly devoted considerable space to institutional deficiencies. The whole of our Chapter 6 is concerned with these issues.

Risk and risk management

The process of reducing poverty requires assets—land, equipment, and ideas—to be put in the hands of poor people and productively used by them. But very poor people, because they are poor, face much grimmer consequences from others if things go wrong. If comfortably-off people are hit by a shock and run short of money, they borrow, or draw on a savings account, or ask their friends. If poor

[52] Duly repeated and demonstrated by the authors of the *1997 World Development Report.*

[53] Hudson and Mosley (2009) find that corruption as measured by the World Bank's quality of government index is positively and not negatively related to the rate of economic growth.

[54] African cereal yields are still only just over one ton per hectare. On this see, in particular, Mosley (2002), Gebre-Madhin and Haggblade (2004), and Djurfeldt et al. (2005).

[55] On this see Moore (1997) and other outputs from the IDS Centre for the Future State, see further Chapter 6 below. There is some cross-sectional evidence that high aid flows depress tax effort, for example Brautigam and Knack (2004); however, this is not an iron law. Several countries, notably Uganda and Ghana within our sample, have been successful in raising tax revenue within an environment of high dependence on aid flows.

people run out of money, they may be unable to do any of these things, and so they may be forced to pawn or sell their only assets, and if these strategies do not work or are compounded by other shocks such as conflict or repeated drought, they may go short of food or even starve. In such a predicament, where the consequences of doing the wrong thing are so grave, 'progressive' steps such as acquisition of equipment, and even the laying-out of money on children's school fees, may be foregone because they carry a risk of having to sell one's only assets if things go wrong—the problem of risk-aversion. Inability, or a completely rational unwillingness, to acquire these assets thus leaves many of the poorest people trapped at first base, and in no position to respond to supply-side type stimuli.

These problems had defeated the sponsors of the first 'poverty wave', whose only recourse for those lacking the good fortune to benefit from land reform had been the expansion of agricultural and industrial development finance schemes, measures which require collateral which the very poor do not have. The devising of 'substitutes for collateral' which might relieve the very poor of the risks associated with productive investment was not even much more than a gleam in the eye of those who composed the World Bank's first (1990) *World Development Report* on poverty. However, such substitutes—microfinance, savings development, and microinsurance, alongside complementary measures which fulfil an insurance function such as investment in rural roads and water supplies, and social protection measures generally—were developed with great creativity in the 1990s. By 1995 a new NGO, the *Microcredit Summit,* was promising to take 75 million families, half the world's poor, out of poverty by means of microfinance alone within ten years (see Rogaly 1996). The promise, of course, proved to be overblown, like many made in the run-up to the millennium, but a new, and to some extent a financially sustainable,[56] vehicle for empowering and delivering protection against risk to low-income rural people had been found. The availability of this new instrument substantially altered the balance of power in favour of those seeking to deliver pro-poor services—as we shall see, a good proportion of the success of Bolivia, Indonesia, and Uganda, as well as outside our sample Bangladesh, can be ascribed to it.

The emergence of a development 'third sector'

During the early 1990s, therefore, as the anti-poverty snowball slowly started to re-gather momentum, those seeking to encourage this tendency found themselves needing to wrestle with fundamental features of the landscape of underdevelopment that had not unduly influenced their predecessors of the 1970s—in particular, the prevalence of conflict, of weak governance, and of risk-aversion.

It might seem too good to be true that there was an institution-in-waiting offering to deal with all these problems, but apparently there was. One of the main things that had changed between the 1970s and the 1990s was the rise of

[56] By the mid-1990s several microfinance NGOs were financially viable without subsidy, and one, BancoSol of Bolivia, was the most profitable bank in the country at the time (Hulme and Mosley 1996). However, viability is only one of many objectives, and several leading microfinance organizations including the Grameen Bank of Bangladesh never attempted to become fully viable. On the Grameen Bank see Morduch (1999).

non-governmental organizations (NGOs). Four of the most important dimensions of this expansion were the following.

First, the Northern NGOs, in multiple, had contributed heavily to documenting the costs of structural adjustment for the poor, in particular by providing evidence concerning the social costs of adjustment,[57] and heavily lobbied the Bank (in particular) to get them mitigated, through debt relief, through a softening of policy conditionality, and by standing out against the expenditure cuts imposed by the IMF, which they saw as their main adversary. NGOs' 'advocacy function', hitherto a small and questioned part of their operations, now moved to centre stage, and in the process, not by accident, they found themselves more and more at the top negotiating table.

Second, as we have seen, all kinds of government developmental services had been cut under the stress of structural adjustment. Southern NGOs picked up this mantle and took over a number of state functions, in some cases to the point where the poor looked more to them than to government for service delivery. Within our sample, two important examples are Bolivia, where large parts of health, education, and agricultural services and nearly all of microfinance, were picked up by the NGO sector during the 1980s and early 1990s, and Uganda, where the NGO sector plays a key role in all of those sectors and agricultural extension also.

Third, this process was welcomed from the 1980s on by international financial institutions and aid donors seeking, as part of the structural adjustment process, an 'exit route' in the shape of competition for inefficient and corrupt government services. But services for the poor are not at all easy to privatize in the conventional way, no private company will find it lucrative to take them on. This left the door open for the entry of local and international NGOs with a charitable, pro-poor, not-for-profit function. The role played by NGOs is further examined in Chapters 6 and 7.

Fourth, more recently, even the relief component of NGO operations became the object of additional patronage by international financial organizations, as a route towards internal security, the securing of fragile states, and the reduction of conflict. In Africa and the Balkans in the 1990s, and of course in Iraq and Afghanistan now, NGOs are routinely entrusted with helping to provide the kind of social and economic framework which will make future conflict less likely.

Thus, one crucial element of the structural adjustment process was that NGOs, in its aftermath, found themselves entrusted not only with more money and more power in replacement of government functions but, in return, were expected to wrestle with three of the problems which over the last thirty years have caused a split between the top six billion and the bottom billion: risk, state fragility, and war. A new political force has emerged within the developing world, to which, however, the conventional working assumptions of profit maximization and power maximization do not apply. We shall examine its significance in the forming of pro-poor coalitions in later chapters.

All of this was reflected in the procedures and the resource allocation of the international financial institutions. The changes in this resource allocation since

57 See the evidence provided by Save the Children, etc. to the *Adjustment with a Human Face* report (Cornia, Jolly, and Stewart 1987).

Table 2.3 Compositional shifts within the budgets of international finance organizations, 1980–2006.

Percentages of total budget	1973	1980	1983	1996	2007
(a) ODA/DFID					
Project aid	38		17	8	0
Programme aid (including budget support and debt relief)	0		9	7	24
Technical cooperation	33		42	51	33
Private sector (CDC) and civil society organizations	9		8	15	18
Emergency and humanitarian	0		2	9	15
Other	20		22	10	10
(b) World Bank group					
Project aid		82		48	
Programme aid ('adjustment lending')	0	2		23	
Private sector (IFC)		15		27	
Other		1		2	

Sources: DFID, *British Aid Statistics* (for recent years available on www.dfid.gov.uk); World Bank, *Annual Reports*.

the 1970s are depicted in Table 2.3 for two of these institutions: the World Bank and the UK Department for International Development. Many of the transformations which had occurred in development thinking since the 1970s are visible here: the decline of capital-intensive solutions to development as reflected in the eclipse of 'heavy project' aid; the rise of conditional budget-support policies; the rise of human capital through technical assistance budgets; the decline of the state sector in favour of private-sector operations; and finally the rise of the third (NGO) sector, now expected to deal somehow or other with nearly all of the roles in which states had failed, including war and peace. In Chapters 5 and 6, we illustrate how the changing structure of global relationships, of which these financial changes are only a part, impinged on the politics of poverty reduction.

By the middle of the decade, the global poverty objective had come in sufficiently from the cold to be incorporated in a new process of indicative planning, only a few years after the demise of the previous phase. In 1996 the OECD, prompted by a range of international organizations and NGOs,[58] announced a new set of International Development Targets. The main target was a promise to halve extreme poverty by 2015, now defined in terms of the World Bank's new global standard of a dollar a day (for the poorest countries) at 1990 purchasing power parity. However, awareness that the poor were not at all a homogeneous group had gained ground, and there were separate targets for poverty defined in terms of health, education, women's well-being, and environment. David Hulme (2008a) argues that this multiple-target approach represents a fusion between the human development approach and the 'results-based management' method routinely employed by public and private corporations to achieve targets.

The year 1996 was one of widespread hope and consolidation globally, and it was widely foreseen by all the international forecasting organizations that the global economy would have a smooth and equitable run-up to the millennium.

[58] For the politics of this process, see Hulme (2008b, 2010).

Things of course turned out otherwise, and the 'East Asian crisis', beginning in the following year, was one of the most severe, and certainly the most unexpected, to hit the global economy since the establishment of the Bretton Woods system. We examine the consequences of this shock in the next chapter. As a prelude to that we can usefully explore what had happened since the 1970s, in each of the affected countries, to their 'initial conditions': the political and economic factors which made them more or less vulnerable to a descent into poverty. In Table 2.4 we set out these data, arrayed according to their success in poverty reduction, as discussed in the previous chapter.

This table shows how political alignments, and the manner in which they impact on poverty outcomes, had changed since the period of the MacNamara anti-poverty initiative. In the MacNamara period the main 'target' for equity-orientated reforms was the landowners, and the strategy in response to this was to organize workers' representatives against them in the interests of cheap food by means of devices such as land reform. In the 1990s the main target was 'rent-seekers'—inefficient, protected fat-cat capitalists in both urban and rural sectors, and new instruments of intervention, including supply-side reforms and the NGO form of organization, had emerged as vehicles which anti-poverty coalitions could deploy in support of their cause. As a pro-poor strategy, the transfer of *land* had been replaced by an attempt to liberalize *privileges*, such as access to foreign exchange, loan capital, and other scarce inputs; however, this strategy could only yield pro-poor outcomes if the initial conditions (inherited equality in their income distributions, labour-intensive production functions) were satisfied and built on by the political process. As is already apparent from the table, the developing countries towards the top of the table were able (often with the help of aid donors, in the poor countries), to create fragile coalitions to advance these causes, with help from pro-poor institutions in the fields of, especially, finance, access to infrastructure, legal rights, health, and education. As we shall see throughout the book, the allocation of public expenditure and taxation were to prove, in many cases, very important tools in support of these processes.

2.4 THE IDEA OF POVERTY REBORN (1997–2007)

Poverty reduction—in the Bank's 1990 *World Development Report*, only a theme of the moment, with very insecure tenure—had by the end of the decade, as we saw, become a focus for the International Development Targets, and indeed the focus for a new idea of poverty, used as an international consensus-building instrument. Gertrude Himmelfarb's excellent book, *The Idea of Poverty* (Himmelfarb 1984) shows how, although poverty had always and everywhere been present, the *idea* of poverty was created and underwent mutations during the early nineteenth century in England which defined the shape of future anti-poverty actions. In England, the distinction which came to be made at that time, not on moralistic grounds but on practical principles of wealth-maximization, between those whose poverty arose in spite of their efforts (because of low wages, or disablement, or old age) and those

Table 2.4 On the eve of the East Asian crisis: political conditions and poverty outcomes in the case-study countries to 1996.

	Initial conditions:		Nature of structural adjustment response:		Stimuli to pro-poor adjustment:				Outcome to 1997:
	(1) Inequality (Gini coefficient), 1990	(2) Democracy as of 1996	(3) Sachs-Warner 'narrow' openness indicator	(4) CPIA 'broad' policy quality index	(5) Capital-intensity, 1990 (km railway per 1,000 labour force)	(6) 'Trigger' to include the poor	(7) Effective pro-poor coalitions	(8) Institutional forces to sustain adjustment	(9) Poverty elasticity (level (1990–2006)
Poverty-reducing countries (pov. elasticity in column 9):									
Indonesia	0.32	Regular elections, but always controlled by dominant GOLKAR party	Always open	1999: 4 (poor) 2003: 2 (good)	0.5	Sustained political violence 1961–7	Small businesses + capitalist farmers + exporting interests	Strong and diversified microfinance institutions, many of them working at local level	–1.36 (1993–2002)
Malaysia	0.50	Multi-party democracy, but elections always won by dominant coalition	Always open		0.1		Agro-exporters, small high-tech businesses	Controls on capital exports, 1997	–2.49 (1990–2004)
Ghana	0.33	Multi-party democracy	Open after mid-1980s	1999: 1 (very good) 2003: 2 (good)	0.1	1992: multiparty democracy	*Especially in NDC:* urban workers, northern ethnic groups, some cocoa farmers *Especially in NPP:* cocoa farmers, small businesses	Increasingly open party-political climate after 1992; rural infrastructural investment	–0.3 (1991–9)

Uganda	0.37	One-party democracy, limitations on press freedom	Open after late 1980s	1999, 2003: 1 (very good)	0.1	1986: end of guerrilla war; appointment of new NRM regime, basically a coalition of southern and central rural interests	Central and southwestern rural interests; large business, in particular foreign-owned businesses invited back to Uganda after 1986	Microfinance institutions, mainly in rural areas, and rural-oriented banks; rapid spread of service-delivery NGOs	−0.8 (1992–2006)
Intermediate countries (trend in poverty elasticity not clear or disputed)									
Bolivia	0.63	Multi-party democracy	Open 1985–	1999: 1 (very good) 2003: 2 (good)	1.3	1999: beginning of severe recession and rise in unemployment, 2000: beginning of riot-type violence in Cochabamba, 2003: violent action by Bolivian army in suppression of riot-type violence in El Alto 2005: election of first Aymara president	Within west of country, Aymara-Quechua workers and urban middle class	Microfinance institutions, mainly in urban areas	1.04 (1990–2002)

Continued

Table 2.4 Continued

	Initial conditions:		Nature of structural adjustment response:		Stimuli to pro-poor adjustment:				Outcome to 1997:
	(1) Inequality (Gini coefficient), 1990	(2) Democracy as of 1996	(3) Sachs-Warner 'narrow' openness indicator	(4) CPIA 'broad' policy quality index	(5) Capital-intensity, 1990 (km railway per 1,000 labour force)	(6) 'Trigger' to include the poor	(7) Effective pro-poor coalitions	(8) Institutional forces to sustain adjustment	(9) Poverty elasticity (level (1990–2006)
Poverty-increasing countries									
Argentina	0.50	Multi-party democracy	Open 1980–		2.5	1999–2001: economic collapse, followed by roadblocks organized by the newly unemployed	Disaffected workers previously allied to Peronists and 'new poor' made unemployed by economic collapse of 2001–03	Conciliation forums (*mesas de dialogo*)	0.57 (1990–2003)
Russia	0.39	Multi-party democracy (as of 1992)	'Always closed'		1.1	1992–5: political instability and rebellion against federal authority by Chechnya and thirteen other republics and autonomous regions	Coalitions between foreign investors and workforce in some cities in European Russia	Subsidies within each region directly related to level of civil disturbance	–0.47 (1992–2005)
Zimbabwe	0.50	Multi-party democracy, with limitations on press freedom		1999: 4 (poor) 2003: 5 (very poor)	0.5		*De facto* none (attempt to make coalition between ruling ZANU-PF party and landless war veterans)		–6.7 (1995–2004)

Sources: col. *1 poverty elasticities*—from Table 1.1, col. 2 Gini inequality coefficient—World Development Indicators, col. 3 Sachs-Warner openness indicator from Sachs and Warner 1995, col. 4 CPIA index from World Bank, as reproduced in Eifert and Gelb, Chapter 12 in Koeberle, Stavreski, and Walliser (2006), col. 5 capital-intensity measure from World Bank, *World Development Indicators*, cols 6–8 measures of political orientation from Chapter 5 below, col. 9 poverty elasticities from Table 5.1 below.

whose poverty could be directly ascribed to their lack of effort,[59] led directly to the New Poor Law of 1834, and 150 years later, after grand experiments with universalistic welfare states, to the apparatus of welfare-into-work schemes and means-testing standardly used as poverty reduction instruments by the governments of both industrialized and, now, developing countries. The International Development Targets (soon to be rechristened the Millennium Development Goals) trod the same path: of course, they defined a broader range of targets, but, even as they broadened their conception of the ultimate goal, they clung at the level of means to the New Poor Law idea that eligibility for anti-poverty benefits should be need-related. Most pro-poor expansions of public expenditure in the 2000s have adhered to this principle, as we show in Chapter 5.

In the millennium year the World Bank issued a second *World Development Report* on poverty. This, ambitiously, attempted to grapple with all of the challenges which had caused the Bank's reform programmes in Africa to fail in the 1980s and 90s: war, governance, and risk. Like its 1990 predecessor, the new report employed a three-part diagnosis and prescription for global poverty, with the original 'three-legged stool' of labour-intensity, investment in the human capital of the poor, and social safety nets now supplanted by the three new pillars of opportunity, empowerment, and security (Table 2.5). Security and opportunity derive directly from the 1990 concepts of 'social safety nets' and 'investment in the human capital of the poor' respectively, but the security idea has now been immensely broadened to encompass personal security, protection against political and military as well as economic shocks,[60] and protection against the risks to which the developing-country poor are vulnerable (drought, illness, asset damage, and political violence) for which conventional insurance is typically unavailable. The empowerment theme is new to the 2000 report, again broadening the concept of poverty—from lack of income and assets to lack of power. We may return to one of A.K. Sen's insights related to the Bengal famine of 1943: that those who starved in that famine died not because of an overall shortage of food, but because they had no control over the food which was available.

Empowerment in this sense can indeed be pursued by the strategies which we have examined so far in this chapter, in other words the assembling of pro-poor coalitions. Relevant to this objective, however, are not only the relationships between elements in the elite which have the ability to reduce poverty, but also the social relationships, or trust-relationships, between individuals at every level from the governing elite to the shantytown and the poorest village. It had recently been emphasized by Robert Putnam (1993) that these relationships could be seen as *social capital*, an asset on which, by analogy with physical capital, a return could be earned in terms of support in time of trouble. Putnam had shown that the denser social ties of northern, by contrast with southern, Italy could be used to explain the greater economic progress of northern Italy, and the Bank, with particular support from its employees Deepa Narayan and Michael Woolcock (see Narayan and Pritchett 1999; Woolcock and Narayan 2000) now used the new *World Development Report* to disseminate the social capital concept within the

59 See Himmelfarb (1984), especially Chapter 8.
60 See World Bank (2000), especially Chapter 8.

Table 2.5 Poverty waves, 1970–2000.

	First wave 1973–9	Second wave 1987–	
Key references	Redistribution with growth	WDR 1990 and related literature.	WDR 2000 and related literature.
Concept of poverty	Income and assets	Income (explicitly headcount) and assets.	Multiple: income, assets, and vulnerability. All of these assessed not only in terms of objective measurements but also in terms of perceptions of the poor.
Macro-policies		*Not formally in WDR 1990 but alluded to in text*: pro-poor adjustment (especially through exchange rate). Avoid indirect tax increases during recessions.	Examination of 'socially responsible macroeconomics' (e.g. early warning systems, and more radically, capital controls) in the wake of the East Asian crisis.
Meso-policies (sectoral)	Redirection of fiscal resources to support of agriculture	Social safety nets—mechanisms of cash income support, usually informal and village level. Measures to promote labour-intensive sectors e.g. agriculture and informal-sector construction.	Security theme; social funds, workfare programmes (see also Haggard on roles for social expenditure).
Micro-policies (individual markets):			
Labour	Mechanisms against overt discrimination (both gender and ethnic-based)	Labour-intensity: measures to promote employment of low-income labour.	
Education	'Promote education so as to develop a more equal distribution of human capital' (RwG, 81)	'Investment in human resources of the poor': expansion of education, especially of girls and especially at primary level.	Opportunity: expansion of education, especially of girls and especially at primary level.
Capital markets	Land reform and other forms of asset transfer (e.g. water rights)	Support for microfinance loans.	Risk minimization and effective response to shocks (hence within microfinance, emphasis on savings and insurance functions within microfinance).
Infrastructure and other	Expansion of supply of services to poor people in rural areas through 'integrated rural development projects'		General: aim at increasing empowerment/ bargaining power of poor and promotion of mutual social protection arrangements ('social capital').

developing world. This adds a new dimension to the politics of poverty reduction, by illustrating that pro-poor action could be induced through social relationships at the grass-roots level, for example by direct political action, such as that carried through the Argentinian *piqueteros* and the Bolivian radical parties, the MAS and the MIP, or through advocacy and supply of services by NGOs, such as that carried out by such as the Self-Employed Women's Association (SEWA) in Gujerat, and the Bangladesh Rural Advancement Committee (BRAC) in Bangladesh,[61] as well as by top-down actions by the elite (World Bank 2000, pages 108–12).

Table 2.5 portrays these waves of global anti-poverty action: MacNamara, 'World Bank I', and 'World Bank II' side by side. These are merely convenient labels for phases of anti-poverty thought and action, and do not of course indicate a World Bank monopoly, or even dominance, of such action, which by 2000 the Bank itself, as we have seen, was itself anxious to disavow.

Trends since 2000

The global macro-economic crisis of the end-1990s receded quite quickly, and the worst of it was over, except in Latin America, by the time that the 2000 *World Development Report* was drafted. As the shock-waves from the 'East Asian' crisis have receded, so all countries affected have done what they can to minimize the risks of a repetition, including the risks of exposure to the IMF—Russia, Argentina, Brazil, Indonesia, and all the other large countries exposed to the crisis having paid back their stand-by credits. Not only the World Bank but even the IMF (Buira 2006) feared, until the global recession of 2008–9, having their portfolio reduced to the basket cases, the countries unable to secure finance on world markets—Collier's bottom billion—the problem known to the insurance world as adverse selection. Thus, in the first decade of the twenty-first century, the trends of the last quarter of the twentieth have accelerated, with the divergence between the rich and the poorest increasing. However, within the hard core of the 'bottom billion', there has been some improvement in Africa, and a majority of African countries, for the first time since the 1970s, can now report positive per capita GDP growth for at least the last five years in succession (Ndulu 2008). But by contrast with the Asian situation, it is the small countries on the periphery—Mauritius, Tanzania, Mozambique, Ghana—which are the stars, and the large countries in the interior (Sudan, Nigeria, DRC Congo, and arguably Ethiopia) which are still the 'sick men of Africa'. These large, populous, conflict-vulnerable, and poor countries represent the most notable challenge for world development in the twenty-first century.

These new fault-lines have had their own impacts on the politics of pro-poor action; in particular, as the split between the 'bottom billion' and the rest has widened, so has a gap opened between the political economy of the former and the latter group, with aid donors and, to a lesser extent, NGOs being much more salient and influential in the poorer and more externally dependent group (Table 2.4 above). In addition, and obviously connected with this, overt violations of the Washington

[61] For discussion of the achievements of BRAC in poverty alleviation, see Chapter 6 below.

Consensus such as export taxes, price controls, minimum wage legislation, and capital export controls are, within our sample, much commoner in the richer and more powerful 'BRIC-type countries'[62] than in their poorer neighbours. The end of history has itself come to an end (Kanbur 2001; Simmons and Elkins 2004), and policy divergence is proceeding apace. So far as poverty is concerned, the small-sample evidence of our little group of countries (Table 2.4 above) is that it is the poorer, still aid-dependent countries (Indonesia, Uganda, Ghana, and since 2006 Bolivia also) which are reducing poverty significantly faster than the middle-income countries (Argentina, Russia), by virtue of their more open-economy, pro-agriculture, and small-business policies. The 2008–9 global crisis hit Russia especially hard, and accentuated this trend. But inference from a sample of six is not sensible, and more rigorous evidence is provided in Chapters 5 and 6 below.

For their part, many of the aid donors have embarked since 2002 on an expansionary phase (somewhat curtailed since the global crisis of 2008), proposing a scaling-up of aid volumes in support of the Millennium Development Goals, and in particular trying to fend off the prediction that, especially in Africa, those Goals, in particular the promise to cut extreme poverty in half, will fall short of realization (Hanmer and Naschold 2000). Optimists will take heart from the tentative finding just reported, and conclude that the evidence of poverty reduction potential being higher in poorer countries makes this gamble a worthwhile one. Pessimists will invoke 'Dutch disease' and diminishing returns, and predict that if the focus of aid really is going to be on Sudan, Nigeria, Ethiopia, and Congo DRC, as true poverty targeting would require, the aid optimists are sure to be disappointed.

2.5 POLITICAL ECONOMY LESSONS OF THE TWO 'POVERTY WAVES'

At this point we can return to the 'promising pro-poor ideas' put forward at the end of Chapter 1. In the light of what we have discovered, do they have any chance of being implemented, and if they are implemented will they work?

A preliminary answer to the feasibility question would be 'yes in the poorer countries, if the state structure holds together'. In several poorer countries, Indonesia being in the lead in the 1980s, but now including several African countries such as Ghana, Uganda, Tanzania, and Mozambique, an alliance between aid donors, NGOs, and the rural elite has caused growth to cohere around a labour-intensive production function, and a range of the pro-agriculture, open-economy, flexible exchange-rate policies advocated in Table 1.3 have already come into being. All of these are 'governance states' (Harrison 2004), in which donors dictate terms quite heavily, and which have even managed to buck some of the most common negative institutional consequences of this, such as the tendency for tax effort to be depressed by high aid flows. Where governance is still fragile and riot-type conflict or worse persists, as in Zimbabwe, Bolivia, and a number of African countries such as Sudan, DRC, Angola, and Burundi, the hope of such

[62] BRICs = Brazil, Russia, India, China. Russia is the only BRIC studied in depth in this book.

policy improvements is implausible, and it is unlikely that the ingenious ideas that have recently been proposed to improve aid effectiveness, such as the 'aid for results' scheme recently proposed by the Centre for Global Development[63] (Barder and Birdsall 2006; Birdsall 2010) can alter this outcome.

Both agriculturally and institutionally, we are in some respects barely at the beginning of the road. In Africa, yields are still around one ton per hectare by contrast with three to four in Asian countries (see Chapter 5 below) and especially in Africa, but more broadly in bottom billion countries 'there are almost no insurance markets in developing countries because of problems of contract enforcement and asymmetric information' (World Bank, *World Development Report 2000*, page 143); hence the poor and weak can only protect themselves against shocks by informal means. This suggests that there is a great deal of elementary institutional work still to be done. Indeed, in terms of agricultural emphasis there has been less policy effort visible in raising the productivity of subsistence agriculture during the 1990s and 2000s than in the MacNamara period in the 1970s. Since the 1970s, however, there have been a number of transformations in the politics which determine what efforts are made on behalf of, and what resources are available to, poor people.

The task of the rest of this book is to see how, in the wake of all the transformations reported above, it is possible to understand the basic elements we have identified in the politics of development—the possibilities for forming and sustaining pro-poor coalitions, and the limitations on these imposed by technology and income distribution—in the interests of poverty reduction. We begin by putting our promising pro-poor ideas from Chapter 1 together with the historical lessons from this one into a framework for pro-poor action. This yields a set of hypotheses which are then put to the test in the rest of the book.

[63] In this scheme, aid commitments are exchanged for poverty-reducing 'outputs', such as children enrolled in primary school; see Chapter 5 below.

3

Building blocks in a poverty strategy

3.1 INTRODUCTION

At the end of Chapter 1 we presented five elements of an answer to the question 'what are the factors which make poverty reduction likely to happen?' and our discussion in Chapter 2 has begun to explain how those causal influences have varied over time. The five factors which we identified in a pro-poor chemistry were:

1. A sustained poverty reduction effort is more likely to happen if the elite, in seeking to maintain power, perceives a *partnership with a low-income group* as being useful to it. This is more likely to occur if events occur (such as conflict or the threat of it) which make the elite vulnerable, as in Indonesia in the late 1960s, and if the elite has the breadth of vision to make strategic alliances with the poor, which, we shall show, was achieved within our case studies in Argentina, Bolivia, Ghana, and Uganda in the course of the 1990s and 2000s, as well as earlier in Indonesia.
2. *Political stability* is important for the maintenance of a growth impulse and hence for the reduction of poverty over the long term, and the realization of this, as we saw in Chapter 2, was one of the key factors differentiating the donors' approach to poverty in the 2000s from what it was in the 1970s. However, as noted above, the threat or recent experience of conflict may act as a potent impulse, motivating elites to make new forms of alliance and to construct new policies to help stabilize the state and prevent future conflict.
3. Poverty reduction is more likely to happen if the underlying technology of the economy is geared towards producing livelihoods for low-income people. Since the poorest can sell nothing but their labour, this implies that a pro-poor programme needs to operate along a *labour-intensive production function*, as emphasized in the World Bank's 1990 *World Development Report*. The ability to implement and, where necessary, invent policies and institutions which make this possible is a crux.
4. Often, both political stability and the adoption of a labour-intensive production function depend on a *pro-poor fiscal policy* being adopted. Fiscal policy has unique advantages as a progressive policy instrument because, unlike other forms of policy, it can be varied between different inputs, sectors, and interest groups. Often, as we shall show in Chapters 5 and 13, the political roots of a pro-poor fiscal policy and of pro-poor institutions lie a long way back in time, even back in the colonial period.

5. In an increasingly open global economy, relationships with *donors* and *international financial institutions* are clearly critical to the poverty outcome. Against the conventional wisdom, we argue that in poor countries donors do have leverage to reduce poverty; in Chapter 2 we illustrated the instruments with which this was attempted in the two 'global poverty waves' of the 1970s and the 1990s, and the politics which caused these particular instruments to be used. However, to our surprise, it is *not* the case that pro-poor initiatives are always strongest in poor countries, and we present several examples of pro-poor initiatives in middle-income countries which are not dependent on aid.

We now develop these five propositions as building blocks in our argument. The first two define a political environment, and the last three define actions, the combination of which may be important for achieving a sustained fall in poverty. Thus, rather crudely, we can sum up our story as:

Pro-poor environment	+	**pro-poor actions**	→	**pro-poor outcomes**
(building blocks 1 and 2: existence of pro-poor coalitions and political stability)		(building blocks 3, 4, and 5: labour-intensive growth, pro-poor fiscal policy and institutions, positive influence of IFIs)		(likelihood of a sustained fall in poverty)

Together with the historical insights from the last chapter and from our country case studies (Chapters 9–12), we use them here to derive a map of the political pathways towards long-term poverty reduction. At this stage, however, all that our map does is to identify particular questions as being crucial for poverty outcomes. The task of the remaining chapters is to give as good an answer to these questions as can be done with the available evidence.

3.2 THE FORMATION OF PRO-POOR COALITIONS

We begin by asking how governments select between policy packages, and what might motivate them to use policy instruments with a pro-poor impact within such a package. On this point, we have observed the pessimistic conclusion of the OECD team that a pro-poor bias to policy may not be helpful because 'the politically most active groups are not usually the poorest' (Haggard et al. 1995, page 120). However, there are reasons for arguing otherwise. One is forward-looking self-interest: it is wise to make concessions to the poor if that can protect the incumbent against being ousted, as many members of the Russian landowning and industrial elite attempted to do prior to the revolutions of 1905 and 1917.[1] It may for

[1] As argued by Bell, 'The elite may fear that the revolutionary potential of the poor will be realized [as it was, of course, in Russia in 1905 and 1917] unless the burden of their poverty is eased. The rich who subscribe to this view may be prepared to give up something so as not to lose all in a total revolution' (Bell 1974, page 54). More positively, Bell showed that investments in the poor by the rich,

this reason be appropriate to see poverty reduction as a public, rather than a private, good, on the grounds that those who pursue it achieve benefits for people other than just themselves.[2] However, a second reason is self-protectional: a constituent group within the elite may be sufficiently insecure or fragmented for them to need a measure of support from groups outside the elite, and to the extent that the membership of these outsider groups is poor or vulnerable, the act of forming a coalition with them will bring them above the poverty line, and keep them there for as long as the coalition holds and its instruments are effective.[3] For example, since all urban groups have an interest in cheap food, an interest which will be resisted by rich landlords, they may side with workers, many of whom are poor, against those rich landlords.

Against this background, we can now revisit the question 'why do some countries pursue pro-poor policies and not others?' We suggest that, for the reasons given above, it may be in the political interest of a government to offer a *policy signal* to a low-income interest-group such as higher social expenditure, higher agricultural expenditure, or a faster devaluation of the real exchange rate. Such a signal is an implicit bargain: it offers anti-poverty action now in return for increased support and a diminished threat of opposition and possible violence in the future. Such signals are often ambiguous and therefore not always trusted, and if trusted they do not always reduce poverty; but our thesis is that an effective pro-poor politics depends on the elite thinking it worth offering such signals. The 'decision tree' of possible actions is portrayed in Figure 3.1.

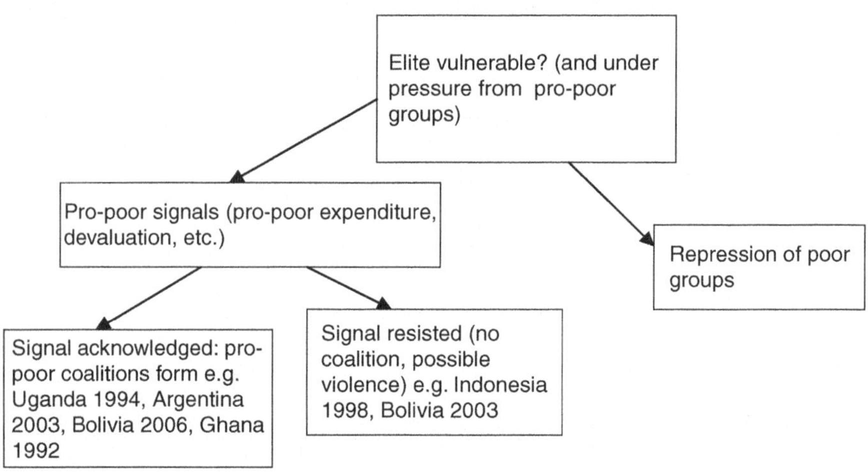

Figure 3.1 To be or not to be (pro-poor): the beginning of the decision tree.

such as health and education, might play an important part in raising productivity, and reducing the likelihood of rebellion.

[2] See the World Bank's 2000 *World Development Report* (World Bank 2000, page 109).

[3] For example, 'In nineteenth-century Britain, landed interests supported the reformers over the issue of industrial working conditions, and the capitalists fought successfully to have the Corn Laws repealed' (Bell 1974, page 54).

We now compare, across six of our case-study countries (Bolivia, Argentina, Indonesia, Russia, Uganda, and Ghana), the tendency of pro-poor coalitions to form or weaken during the 1990s and 2000s, and the role of pro-poor signals in this process. These countries are discussed in much more detail in Chapters 9–13 below. The underlying poverty dynamics (see Tables 5.1 and 5.2 below) are that in Uganda and Ghana the poverty trend has been sharply downwards throughout the period; in Indonesia mainly downwards with an upward blip in the late 1990s; and in the other three countries fluctuating, with a tendency for poverty to fall after the early to middle 2000s.

Bolivia is the poorest country in South America, and since independence in 1825, one of the most politically unstable and also one of the most unequal, with a Gini coefficient of fifty-eight per cent in 1999. The ethnic and regional dimensions of the inequality are important, between the lighter-skinned minority, principally located in the east and south of the country, where the country's oil and gas reserves are mainly to be found, and the darker-skinned Quechua/Aymara ethnic majority. Prevailing levels of poverty, political instability, and, in a small way, also income inequality diminished somewhat during a period of liberalizing economic reform between 1985 and 1999—that is, until the onset of the global crisis of the early 2000s.

During the 1999–2003 global crisis, by contrast with all the other affected countries except Russia, macro-economic discipline was lost, and the fiscal deficit rose to a peak of 8.5 per cent in 2003; unemployment and inequality grew also at this time (see Chapter 10). One of the dimensions of this growing inequality is particularly significant, which is the increasing tendency of utilities and oil and gas industries privatized during the economic reform period to be corruptly excused payment of corporation tax.[4] Other symptoms of institutional debility also occurred at this time, including a weakening rule of law, rising rates of default in the financial system and also deteriorating standards of justice.[5]

At the turn of the millennium, the white governmental oligarchy (the MIR, MNR, and ADN)[6] encountered for the first time an effective parliamentary challenge from two indigenous political parties (MIP and MAS),[7] representing principally the interests of low-income groups, which by 2002 had twenty-five per cent of the national

[4] Rolando Morales, *La Prensa,* 12 February 2003, page 6. 'The Confederacion de Empresarios Privados de Bolivia', Morales adds, 'indicated that the fall in the country's fiscal revenues [between end-2001 and end-2002, which had caused a shortfall in revenues and required the IMF to be called in] was 7.3 per cent, and that the principal reason for that was a fall of 25.4 per cent over the same period in tax revenues due from the hydrocarbons (oil and gas) sector.'

[5] See *La Prensa,* 23 December 2003, and also the interview with Ana Maria Romero de Campero, the recently-dismissed *Defensora del Pueblo* (or ombudsman) in *Pulso,* issue 218, 10–16 October 2003, in which she describes Bolivia as a 'democradura' (half democracy, half dictatorship).

[6] Respectively: *Movimiento Izquierdista Revolucionario* (Revolutionary Left Movement), *Movimiento Nacional Revolucionario* (National Revolutionary Movement), and *Alianza Democratica Nacional* (National Democratic Alliance). The first two titles are misleading, and reflect the mood of 1952, a time of widespread land reforms and mining nationalization, not the 1990s.
Between 1986 and 2002 the MNR, the MIR, and the ADN simply rotated power between themselves 'like good lovers, sometimes with one partner on top and sometimes the other' as depicted by the columnist and former independent MP Cayetano Llobet (Llobet 2005).

[7] Respectively: *Movimiento Indigena Pachacuti* (Pachacuti Indigenous Movement) and *Movimiento al Socialismo* (Movement to Socialism).

vote between them. Thus, not only was the government highly vulnerable in relation to prevailing expectations, inequality having deteriorated,[8] but the effective demands of the poor had risen. Confronted by this first fork in the decision tree, the government of the MNR party under its veteran President, Gonzalo Sanchez de Losada, a mining millionaire who had also been the leader of a reformist government from 1989 to 1997, emitted mixed signals. Macro-policies continued to be progressive in their thrust: real health and education expenditures, explicitly in Aymara/Quechua areas, continued to rise during this crisis period, and the exchange rate—one of the OECD's test cases for progressivity of macro-economic reform[9]—remained flexible. But at three crucial points in 2003, the government's behaviour was confrontational rather than conciliatory: it shot thirteen coca growers in January who were refusing to accept production quotas;[10] the following month it fired on police who were on strike in protest against an extension of the income tax net, recommended as part of an IMF (ESAF) package to deal with the country's fiscal dilemma;[11] and in October 2003, it attempted to break by force a general strike called ostensibly in protest against the routing of a gas pipeline through Chile (in practice against privatization and job losses in the industry as a whole), resulting in some 60 deaths among the Aymara/Quechua population, and in the fall of the government a few days later.[12] The effect of these actions, over the period 2002–5, was to wreck all possibility of a revival of investment, to cause the poverty rate to rise further, even in the middle of an oil boom,[13] and

[8] Asked to comment on the violence which followed in February 2003, the Governor of the Central Bank of Bolivia blamed it almost entirely on this factor:

> [The increases in] Bolivia's external debt and the external aid aimed at reducing poverty benefited mainly the middle class. Even if improvements were achieved in the Human Development Index and poverty fell, the distribution of income deteriorated, as it did across the whole of Latin America. The deterioration of income distribution in a poor and supremely politicized country is perhaps among the main causes of the tragedy of [last] February. Juan Antonio Morales, 'Que le ha pasado a Bolivia?' (What has happened to Bolivia?), *Pulso*, 14–20 March 2003, page 7.

[9] Bourguignon and Morrisson (1992) show that where adjustment is carried out principally through exchange-rate reform, the impact is more progressive than with any other form of adjustment, because by contrast with other forms of adjustment such as expenditure cuts and tax increases, some poor people gain—mainly low-income employees in export industries.

[10] Throughout the period of extreme crisis from January to October 2003, the elite refused to negotiate or even talk informally to the rival Aymara-Quechua parties, the MAS, and the MIP, preferring rather to characterize the leader of the MAS, Evo Morales, as a *narcotraficante* (drug-dealer) (Chapter 10 below).

[11] It was insisted by the IMF at the time (and maintained also by those donors to whom the Bolivian government went for advice) that no alternative to these income tax increases existed as a response to the Bolivian government's fiscal predicament (a fiscal deficit of 8.5 per cent). We argue, however, in Mosley (2007) that with more imagination a whole range of fiscally equivalent and politically less disastrous options could have been explored, including a broadening of small business taxation, a freeze on new hiring and the creation of new ministries in the civil service, and the reform of the pensions scheme which was largely responsible for the fiscal deficit (see further Chapter 10 below). The theme of the breadth of the government's field of vision is further explored in our discussion of Indonesia below, and also in the model of the next section.

[12] All of these events are described in more detail in Mosley (2007) and in Chapter 10 below.

[13] It might have been hoped that the donors, or at any rate some or all of the 'gang of four' who deal with all the budgetary support and macro-policy advice given to Bolivia, would warn the Sanchez de Losada government of the danger associated with its chosen instrument of fiscal adjustment. They did not. Indeed, the president of one of them appeared on national television to defend the need for a downward extension of the income tax network on 11 February, the night before first the police and

to bring about a return to political instability, with four new governments trying and failing to retain power over that three-year period. An opportunity to adapt the elite in a pro-poor direction had, at considerable human and economic cost, been wasted.

After eighteen months of interim government, however, the MAS achieved a decisive breakthrough in the elections of December 2005, which in effect saw the installation of a pro-poor coalition: Evo Morales, the Aymara leader of the coca growers' union, was elected President with the support of a high proportion of the western middle class, representing professional as distinct from industrial (oil/gas) and agribusiness interests. For the first time since the 1950s, Bolivia is run by a pro-poor coalition, and for the first time ever this coalition is dominated by the historically subordinate and oppressed group. In spite of the somewhat bloodthirsty, anti-capitalistic rhetoric of the MAS government, Bolivian macro-policies have continued to respect the Washington Consensus line of exchange rate flexibility and achievement of redistribution through the expenditure mix, and by contrast with Argentina (see below) have avoided a wholesale attack on the Washington Consensus in the form of price controls, capital controls and agricultural export taxes, none of which exist in Bolivia. There have however been taxes on oil and gas exports whose proceeds are allocated to increases in the basic state pension (*Renta Dignidad*), a partial renationalization of the oil and gas industry, and a constitutional reform (*Asemblea Constituyente*) designed to correct the ethnic bias of the legislative and judicial system, which allocates additional seats to poor indigenous areas. Since 2005 there has been tentative evidence of a fall in poverty (Chapter 10 below), but the Morales government's ability to carry through a pro-poor programme continues to be fragile, menaced not only by separatist threats in the east and south but also by fragmentation of the Aymara/Quechua dominant coalition, with some thirty people having been killed since the beginning of 2008 in internecine riots within this group.

Like Bolivia, *Argentina*, our other Latin American case, experienced its initial financial crisis later than East Asia and Russia. In Argentina, like Bolivia, but quite unlike East Asia, the budgetary deficit refused to respond to corrective measures and continued to get worse after 1999. When this deficit exploded into a political crisis in early 2002—involving the collapse of the peso/dollar parity, the dismissal of the central bank governor, a temporary freeze on savings accounts, widespread rioting in Buenos Aires and three new governments in the course of 2002/3—the Argentinian state was indeed very vulnerable, but the cause of, and the nature of the challenges to, that vulnerability were quite different from the case of Bolivia. Argentina, unlike Bolivia, was a semi-industrialized economy with a globally competitive commercial agriculture and historically strong trade unions, damaged but not broken by the structural adjustments of the late 1980s and 1990s. As a

then the whole of La Paz rioted against the injustice (Lazarte Rojas 2005, page 18). The World Bank's representative very uncharacteristically claimed that it did not see fiscal policy and other short-term policy issues as a Bank, much more a Fund, responsibility, and the Corporacion Andina de Fomento (CAF) argued that it saw its role at the time as to achieve implementation of expenditure projects on which money was unspent and development thereby delayed, not tax reform. Interviews, Carlos Mollinedo and Oscar Bonifaz Paz, La Paz, 14 and 22 September 2005.

consequence of this, prevailing economic inequalities were a good deal lower in Argentina than in Bolivia and most of Latin America,[14] and the inter-ethnic inequality which provided the mainspring of Bolivian politics in the early 2000s was absent. As in Russia, examined below, and as in many industrialized countries, the anger of the poor consisted not of a revolt of the socially excluded who had never had a secure place in the system, but was caused by job losses among (mainly low-skill) urban workers who had had such a place for up to fifty years. The resultant unemployment loosened the bonds which made the working class loyal to Peronism and, in substantial measure, casualized the labour force, creating a 'vast pool of low-paid workers organically disconnected from union activities and whose interests were not easily articulable with those of wage workers' (Grugel and Riggirozzi 2009a, page 14, quoting Villareal 1987, page 85).

Even more than in Russia at this time, the dynamics of pro-poor politics were a mainly in-house affair and had little to do with the Washington institutions; there were no significant aid donors or external NGOs to placate. Positioned at the same fork in the road as Bolivia in the early 2000s, what pro-poor signals did the Argentinian government offer? One of the responses of the new Kirchner government in 2003 was very reminiscent of the approach of the Morales government in Bolivia, namely to offer to tackle inequity, not only through the standard apparatus of tax, expenditure, and exchange rate policies, but by constitutional and process reforms, including the *piqueteros*, the unemployed protesters who had led the extra-legal opposition to previous governments, and by seeking to lay a longer-term basis for political and juridical inequity, including reform of the constitution. However, there was a sharp divide between the two countries in terms of macro-economic policies. Argentinian policies since 2003 have featured heavy use of capital controls, export taxes, and price controls, policy instruments not used in Bolivia since the dictatorships of the 1980s and, indeed, complete anathema to the 'Washington Consensus' but reminiscent rather of the import-substitution policies used through much of the developing world between the 1950s and the 1970s. The adjective *desarollista* ('developmentalist') applied to Latin American policies at that time was now taken off the shelf and converted by the Kirchner government into the consensus-building instrument, *neodesarrollismo* (Grugel and Riggirozzi 2007), a combination of a new and attractive democratic revival with price controls and macro-economic austerity. Crucially, the groups with whom government sought to make alliance in this second phase went beyond the organized labour which had formed Peronism's centre of gravity, incorporating businesses (especially those orientated towards the home market), professionals (some of them 'newly poor'), NGOs, and consumer groups, all of them containing a good representation among lower-income groups. Strains in this alliance, however, became apparent by the end of the 2000s, notably among agro-exporting interests, who were paying many of the new export taxes.[15]

[14] The Gini coefficient of inequality did deteriorate somewhat in the 1990s; but never to a level approaching that in Bolivia, or even to the Latin American average.

[15] For example, in early 2008 President Fernandez de Kirchner was forced by agro-exporters to rescind a planned increase in export taxes.

Indonesia, one of the most successful economies in the world in terms of its achievement in overcoming poverty in the last quarter of the twentieth century,[16] is comparable with Bolivia in terms of some of its vulnerabilities: its per capita income level is similar to Bolivia's at around $1,000 and like Bolivia, it has been vulnerable to fluctuations in the price of oil and gas and also to secessionist pressures in East Timor, now independent, and elsewhere. But some of its initial conditions were more favourable. In particular, and in common with the rest of East Asia, Indonesia had no budget deficit, but rather a surplus. Second, levels of inequality were still low by world standards (Table 5.2 below), a circumstance heavily related to state support for smallholder agriculture,[17] but by the 1990s were on an upward trend:[18] any previous perception that authoritarianism might be a necessary 'firm hand' to deliver national unity and consistent economic policy was rapidly being replaced by a vision of the New Order as a centre of authoritarian patronage, governing for the few. Finally, institutions were much stronger than in Bolivia, in particular the local government institutions which in the 1970s were used to transfer inputs and credit to smallholders, and which over the course of the reforms became converted into financially self-sustaining regional development banks both at head office level and in the regions, where Central Java, East Java, Bali, and most of the other provinces, uniquely for this period, all had their own regional microfinance bank. Thus, whereas institutional discipline crumbled during the 1990s crisis in Bolivia, in Indonesia it did not do so on anything like the same scale.[19]

Nonetheless, when the crisis hit Indonesia at the end of 1997, the government was taken by surprise, because of its good fiscal record. The authorities responded with an immediate devaluation (avoiding the mistakes of the Thai and Korean authorities, who had used up reserves in a futile attempt to defend their currencies). As pressures continued to grow during the autumn, the IMF was called in and it appears that President Suharto simply expected a 'seal of approval' on existing policy to resolve the crisis, as it had in previous episodes in Indonesia. However, the Fund, and some of Suharto's long-standing technical advisors used the opportunity to press for action on 17 Indonesian banks with weak balance sheets and also suggested scaling back on infrastructure projects that would benefit well-connected conglomerates. The bank closures were doubly mismanaged. The technical advice Suharto was given paid insufficient attention to deposit insurance, so bank closures started to create runs across the Indonesian banking

[16] As noted in Chapter 2 above, poverty fell from around sixty per cent to around fifteen per cent between 1970 and 1990, and as a result of this discovery Indonesia became the Bank's main exemplar for poverty reduction in Asia, if not the world (World Bank, *World Development Report 1990*, page 1).

[17] Until the 1980s these were mediated through BIMAS (*Bimbingan Massal*), an agency which provided highly subsidized loans linked to extension support for all small farmers.

[18] Economic liberalization during the 1980s, and particularly privatization of public infrastructure and liberalization of the financial system, also contributed to the rise of a group of politically well-connected domestic conglomerates mostly operating in the domestic sector. During the 1990s, poverty reduction slowed and state resources were increasingly diverted into these large conglomerates, leading to growing political opposition and widespread popular perceptions of elite corruption, particularly as economic success had led to a growing concentration of better educated and potentially more politically active Indonesians in the cities.

[19] On the microfinance aspect of this, see essay by Patten and Rosengard (1991).

system. Equally, Suharto vacillated over the infrastructure projects and allowed two of the banks with particularly strong political connections to re-open. That undermined market confidence in his willingness to take tough measures to resolve the crisis, playing into a growing perception that 'crony capitalism' was key to the crisis across the region. It also sent a message to ordinary Indonesians that Suharto put his elite allies above the popular interest. In the second round of negotiations in early 1998, the IMF pushed for a much fuller list of reforms, notably withdrawal of subsidies on agricultural inputs, hoping that the result would be enhanced market confidence in reform momentum and a return of capital. Thus, as in Bolivia in early 2003, a mixed and inadequate signal of support to the poor was being sent by an old guard (both Suharto and Sanchez de Losada were over seventy-five at their moments of crisis), unable to see that the kind of top-down pro-poor gestures which had worked in the past were unable to do so now, and through its failure leading to the disintegration of the existing pro-poor coalition;[20] the reform programme agreed with the Fund did ring-fence social expenditure but did little else to enhance Suharto's political popularity. Reforms cut to the heart of Indonesian patronage but did little, directly, to address the corporate debt issue. As a last desperate manoeuvre, Suharto tried to scapegoat the Chinese traders, seeking to persuade the increasingly restive urban poor that increases in the price of rice were due to their speculative activity, rather than exchange rate depreciation.[21] Finally, in (May 1998), Suharto gambled, and removed fuel and food subsidies in one swift burst (when the IMF programme had suggested phased reductions). That triggered riots in Jakarta and the downfall of his regime. Why Suharto decided to do something so provocative in a tense political climate remains something of a mystery. One possibility is that he was genuinely trying to convince the markets he was prepared to take 'painful' measures in the interests of reform. His mistake, like Sanchez de Losada's in Bolivia five years later, was to see hurting the masses as more politically expedient than hurting his elite support. Another, more Machiavellian, explanation is that he hoped violent responses to price rises would separate middle class support from working class animosity, renewing political support for the military enforced *status quo*. Support here comes from the evidence that radical Muslim elements in the Indonesian military were responsible for fanning the flames of the riots[22] (Hefner 2000b). A key and widely relevant question is what workable alternatives

[20] Both in Indonesia in 1998 and in Bolivia in 2003, the phrase 'coalition' should be seen not as an explicit agreement, but rather as an implicit contract, in which the government offered broad-based growth in return for a continuance of dictatorship and patronage.

[21] See Rodrik 1999, page 93. Attempts to pass the blame for falling rice prices onto Chinese distributors during this period were supposed to redirect popular animosity and send signals to more radical elements of Indonesian political Islam, particularly within the military, that support for him would deliver a more Muslim-friendly form of politics.

[22] Overall, both the Indonesian and the Bolivian crises demonstrate very clearly the ways in which policies that play into pre-existing political grievances produce political instability, with dramatic consequences for investment flows. Can one accuse either leader of irrationality? Yes, in the sense that they both threw away a lifebelt; but the cases differ somewhat, since competition between elites in Indonesia was an established fact, whereas in Bolivia it was a contested fact concerning which the President was in denial, insisting that Evo Morales, whom he always styled as a *narcotraficante* (drug-dealer) was not a figure with whom he could negotiate or treat as an equal.

were perceived: how wide the field of vision was. Some have suggested that a more interventionist approach to debt reorganization, earlier in the crisis, would have resolved matters without the need for drastic governance reform. However, the international political climate would have been extremely unfavourable to such a course, which would have had to be attempted very early in the crisis as the debt situation, particularly in the corporate sector, rapidly became extremely complex and difficult to resolve. Large debt write-downs would probably not have been acceptable, particularly when they would inevitably have protected corrupt business and an autocratic regime. Another possibility is that greater attention to safety nets earlier in the programme would have headed off popular unrest. Certainly fuel price subsidies were eventually removed in 2005 without any political unrest, in conjunction with a compensation programme for those worst affected. However, that was done in more stable economic circumstances and after a transition to democracy. Additionally, the administrative machinery for compensatory social policy in Indonesia was barely present; considerable improvisation was needed to implement the new social programmes that eventually emerged from crisis and there were significant concerns that funds would be diverted to local-level patronage.

Following a transition to democracy, massive exchange rate devaluation helped to cushion the impact on the poorest, fuel and rice price policies were reversed, and the mix of public expenditures was reconfigured so as to strengthen the social safety net (Chapter 5 below). The protective thicket of capital controls was also strengthened, although not as powerfully as in Malaysia where in September 1997, as a pre-emptive measure against capital flight, a ban on capital exports had been introduced which was highly successful in stabilizing the rate of investment and growth, in reducing inequality in the late 1990s and early 2000s,[23] and in general in achieving a softer landing than Indonesia achieved from its crisis.[24] The

[23] The inspiration behind these controls, imposed in September 1997, was that they would allow reflationary macro-economic policy without triggering further capital flight. However, it should be acknowledged that Malaysian banking regulation was better prior to the crisis and it may be that Malaysian financial imbalances were just less severe than elsewhere in the region.

The politics of the capital controls are also important, though. Although some were keen to interpret them as a cynical attempt to protect 'crony' conglomerates, their implementation suggests a more complex picture in which they provided more of a compromise between big business and broader social interests. Although the balance had shifted during the 1990s, Malaysian industrial policy always contained more genuine business promotion and less patronage than in Indonesia. The capital controls were not simply a shield for struggling corporate groups, they also allowed a broader reflation of the Malaysian economy. The controls were accompanied by significant corporate sector restructuring, revisions to prudential and corporate governance regulation, and a high profile (if not terribly effective) campaign against corruption. IMF econometric work shows that market expectations of favouritism for politically connected business following the crisis turned out to be inaccurate. Finally, the capital controls and earlier public attacks on 'speculation', whatever their economic merit, sent positive signals to the population that their government was doing something to protect them. For a general review of capital controls comparing the Malaysian case with other countries, see Duasa and Mosley (2006) and for discussion of their longer-term impact see Chapter 5 below.

[24] This is not only due to the foresight of the Malaysian government in introducing capital controls. Although Malaysia's institutions are only partially democratic, they are well designed, certainly better than Indonesia's or Bolivia's, for dealing with inter-ethnic grievance. They also allow public debate over economic policy and a sanctioned outlet for the expression of disapproval, together with a history of at least moderate responsiveness to popular demands.

political transition itself also diverted attention from economic woes and focused it on creating a new political settlement. The establishment of relative political stability coincided with a gradual turnaround in the economy. However, such a dramatic political change inevitably also creates further political uncertainty and instability. There were distinct economic jitters in the run up to the first constitutional elections, in 1999. Although the electoral process has worked quite smoothly, communal violence and institutional weaknesses, particularly in the judicial system, have helped to keep investment well below pre-crisis levels. In Indonesia, then, it is easier to see how our model accounts for crisis than it is to see how the ill-effects could have been avoided. Political systems are not simply places in which technocratic decisions are made. They are also power structures that provide incentives to behave in particular ways and that has a tendency to create path-dependence, or a vicious circle of destabilizing action, so that regimes play into their political weaknesses, rather than compensating for them. That is one reason why Rodrik (1999), amongst others, has argued that democracies may be better in a crisis as they provide for much smoother changes in government, facilitating both a symbolic break with the past and a change in the political constituencies represented by government:

> (The) sense of shared sacrifice and compromise (evident in South Korea and Thailand) has been conspicuous in Indonesia by its absence. The financial difficulties spawned by the economic crisis were exacerbated by President Suharto's unwillingness to relinquish power, the lack of voice mechanisms (such as independent parties and free trade unions) and a generalized sense that the crisis would be passed on to the workers and the poor ... To divert blame from the government, some officials apparently incited ethnic tensions. According to one human rights group, some 'senior officials ... have tried to deflect blame for the economic crisis on to prominent members of the ethnic Chinese community' ... The conventional view among economists and many political scientists is that ... democracy, even when not hostile to reform, complicates it. The systematic evidence from the 1970s and 1980s, as well as the more recent Asian experience, suggests that the opposite is closer to the truth.
>
> (Rodrik 1999, pages 93–4)

That point of view certainly has some merit in Indonesia. However, as we will see, it assumes that democratic procedures can deliver sufficiently radical political change to satisfy highly volatile political populations. As our Latin American cases illustrated, this need not necessarily be the case.

Russia, in 1998, was exposed to a larger shock than any other country within our sample (see Figure 12.2 and Table 12.4 below), because its capital-account crisis of that year was grafted on to a structural adjustment process which, by contrast with other adjusting countries, had involved the liberalization not of a mixed economy but of a structure of universal state ownership, in which all private enterprise except household subsistence plots, from 1924 to 1992, was illegal. Having moved further than any other country in insulating government from the market through most of the twentieth century, Russia, in common with the rest of the former Soviet Union and other centrally planned economies, had much further to fall than most countries. When, in the early 1990s, the insulation was removed and the economy was suddenly exposed to the pressures of globalization, much of the country's industrial base was wiped out. Russia's initial conditions, purely in terms of income inequality, were thus different from any other adjusting economy outside of the former communist bloc: the Gini coefficient of inequality went from one of the lowest levels in the world to being worse than that of the United States (Brainerd 1998), much of this associated with the conversion of old communist governance structures into new capitalist oligarchies. However, its vulnerabilities were not only economic, and not confined to the states on the Muslim periphery. During the 1990s, not only Chechnya but fifteen of the other eight-five 'federal subject' regions (oblasts, autonomous regions, and autonomous republics) took advantage of the weakness of the new Russian federation to refuse to comply with federal instructions, ranging from payment of taxes to provision of data and compliance with police directives. During the early to mid-1990s Russia was 'on the precipice of state collapse' (Giuliano 2006) and, in its attempts to try and reconstruct a constituency of support, was constrained by the consequences of deindustrialization, and by the fact that when economic recovery came, it was in the oil and gas sector, which was far more capital intensive than the country's traditional heavy industrial base.

Hence the pro-poor signals which the federal Russian government was able to send were highly selective, both geographically and in terms of instruments of adjustment. In seeking to understand its political response, Argentina is not an inappropriate point of departure, as Russia like Argentina was an industrialized middle-income country trying to propitiate the anger and despair of a suddenly insecure, fairly unionized (and even more educated) working class. The Communist party, in its newly competitive environment, briefly mounted a serious challenge to restore the old order, but never mustered more than twenty per cent of the vote. In reconfiguring its macro-economy, Russia took advice from the former Argentinian finance minister, Domingo Cavallo, and, like Argentina, it expanded the role of the state and employed the standard heterodox instruments of *neodesarollismo* (subsidies, minimum wages, and export taxes)[25] as instruments to bend the direction of recovery towards its favoured clients, in addition to improvisations of its own, such as leaving salaries and wages unpaid.[26] The Prime Minister's party, Russia's Choice (later United Russia), was from the 1998 crisis onward successful in co-opting those able to do political damage, in particular the communists, and at the same time in providing a focus for the aspirations of much of the urban middle-class. But it did not contain within it any groups committed to enhancing the welfare of the under-privileged, and when such a group did briefly emerge, during the Pensioners' Party campaign in 2005, it was quickly assimilated and emasculated by United Russia. Within the Russian federal system, this co-option of local dissent was during the 1990s devolved to the most dangerous and disaffected regions, through the imposition of subsidies, minimum wages, and export taxes at *oblast* (regional) as well as national level,[27] before being recentralized during the 2000s. It took a considerable time for the benefits to materialize: in terms of per capita income, the recovery for the federation as a whole began in 1999 but in terms of mortality, not until 2004, and some regions are still declining (Tables 12.4 and 12.5 below).

[25] For a development of this comparison, see Chapter 9 below.

[26] The determinants of wage arrears by region are discussed in Mussurov (2007).

[27] At this regional level, controls in restraint of local price rises appear to have been a particularly powerful way of buying local political support (Mussurov and Mosley 2008).

Finally, we consider two African cases which are far poorer than any of our Asian and Latin American examples, with per capita incomes under $500. Both were 'peasant export economies' whose growth impulse derived from a labour-intensive export crop (coffee in Uganda, cocoa in Ghana) which in the 1980s emerged from a long period of political instability. In Uganda, the three crucial gateways to pro-poor policy were the rural smallholder orientation of the post-1986 elite, the incentive to pull together provided by fear of renewed conflict, and the avoidance of ultimatum conditionality by aid donors. Like Indonesia, Malaysia, and Ghana, *Uganda* is historically a 'peasant export economy', capable as world trade grows of producing an improvement in livelihoods for a large number of low-income, small-scale growers of coffee and cotton and their employees, and tending to generate a relatively equitable income distribution. This kind of productive structure is relatively resilient to economic shocks: during the global depression of the 1930s, peasant exports from Uganda fell only briefly and insignificantly, and from this resilience and from the investments in human capital made by the colonial state in the inter-war period derives much of the progress made by Uganda in relation to other African countries up to the 1960s, as illustrated in Chapter 13 below. This progress was dismantled by a period of political chaos lasting from 1972 to 1986, during which per capita income fell by more than forty per cent (Reinikka and Collier 2001).

The core of the coffee export economy since the beginning of the twentieth century has been based on the ancient kingdom of Buganda in the centre of the country, to whose traditional authorities there was considerable devolution of power by the colonial authorities. The pattern of Ugandan politics since colonial times has been set by other ethnic groups' resentment of Buganda, and the political chaos of 1972–86 derived from attempts by two presidents from northern tribes: Idi Amin, a Kakwa, and Milton Obote, a Lango, to establish control by force and plunder over the resources of the centre of the country. In 1991 Yoweri Museveni, the son of cattle-herders from the southwest of the country and a political science graduate of the University of Dar es Salaam, initiated a revolt against Obote's presidency with twenty-seven rifles acquired from the Tanzanian government,[28] the springboard for which was a successful bid for control of the 'Luwero triangle', in essence the smallholder coffee, banana, and maize producers of Buganda, who had been looking since 1972 to throw off the control of the northern tribes. Once control over Buganda was established, the rebels of Museveni's National Resistance Movement (NRM) spread into his own home region of western and southwestern Uganda, and upon this alliance (smallholder agriculture in the west and centre of Uganda) the pro-poor initiatives of the next twenty-five years were based. Museveni, the first guerrilla leader ever to take over an African post-colonial state, was sworn in as president in August 1986. His diagnosis of Uganda's fourteen years of chaos ran in terms of what subsequent growth theorists were to call 'ethno-linguistic fragmentation':

[28] These weapons were supplied during the late 1970s as part of a Tanzanian bid, eventually successful in 1979, to oust Amin from power. From 1981 to 1985 the Tanzanians lent support to the Obote government, so for a time Museveni could get no further support from this source; his long-standing friendship with Tanzania has, however, now resumed. For a description of the guerrilla war see Museveni (1997) or Ondoga (1998).

> The basis of political affiliation at the very beginning of Uganda's Independence [in 1962] was ... opportunistic and sectarian, with divisions along ethnic and tribal lines ... The interests and needs of the people were, therefore, not made a focal point because opportunistic, ideologically and politically backward politicians had so fragmented society that common interests were lost sight of. The peasant in Lango, northern Uganda, did not regard the peasant in Buganda as his ally: he was persuaded to believe that the Baganda were 'arrogant' while the Baganda were told that the Langi were 'primitive and cruel'. This atomisation of the masses into sectarian groups served the interests of the politicians who divided and ruled the people. Sectarianism gave them an automatic and cheap, exploitative political base. It was what philosophers call 'ideological obscurantism', which means obscuring the truth in order to serve the interests of a clique.
>
> (Museveni 1997, page 36)

In other words, the sectarian social structures of Uganda were in Museveni's view politically incapable of expressing the general will of the people for economic development, or even its wish for peace. This is not an uncommon diagnosis of the African predicament, but the fact of its being made by the man responsible for implementing the prescription more successfully than anywhere else in low-income Africa commands attention. The prescription was to reconstitute the NRM as a one-party, or rather no-party, democratic state, with candidates for the national parliament required to surrender any previous party affiliations before running for parliament. This same political structure remained in position for twenty years, and the projected lifting of the ban on party politics, which was proposed by the Constituent Assembly of 1994,[29] took until 2006 to materialize. Within the cabinet, Museveni was, however, always careful to honour his pledge of broad-based government by allocating a good proportion of posts to easterners and northerners, the groups who did not form part of his core constituency of support.[30]

In the initial recovery period, from 1987 to 1994, Museveni was highly suspicious of the market economy, and followed a heterodox and truculent approach with the international financial institutions, seeking to fix the exchange rate as rigidly as possible (using the Latin American excuse of wishing to contain inflation), showing an extremely lukewarm attitude towards the PAPSCA (Poverty Alleviation Programme for the Social Costs of Adjustment) which the donors had designed to compensate Uganda's retrenched 'new poor'[31] and even at one point,

[29] Lifting the ban on party politics was to be Phase 4 of the process of constitutional development proposed by the Constituent Assembly (Ondoga 1998, page 174). The American Ambassador intervened in this process in 1994 by demanding 'a return to multi-party politics within five years', not the first or the last time that conditionality of this type has backfired (compare the Bolivian case in Chapter 10 below, note 25).

[30] 'This is underscored by the fact that between 1986 and 1988 up to four northern politicians served under the NRM as full cabinet ministers, with an additional eleven serving as deputy ministers or ministers of state' (Ondoga 1998, page 153).

[31] 'The problem of rural poverty is a three-fold one. The first problem is infrastructure. Once one has adopted a free-market economy, whereby private entrepreneurs will be the main actors, it follows logically that the next priority is roads, to allow people to move up and down the country in pursuit of their economic activities and, in the process, develop the country. If there are no adequate roads, then it is difficult to produce goods for sale. *Unfortunately*, in our case, the appropriate ministries did not follow up this issue quickly. Instead, they focused their energies and resources on research, on setting

in 1994, imposing taxes on coffee exports, the one action most likely to enrage the World Bank. However, the Bank had evolved (see Chapter 7 below). At this crucial fork in the road, it decided not to punish Museveni for his defiance of Washington Consensus policies but rather to trust him, with a series of policy-based loans (ESAFs and PRGFs),[32] which provided the basis for the huge fall in poverty of the next ten years. The two key measures which delivered this were the liberalization of coffee and cotton exports—in effect a pro-poor tax reform—and the prioritizing of pro-poor expenditures including primary health and education, rural infrastructure, and above all smallholder agriculture, which served as a prototype for many Poverty Reduction Strategy Papers (PRSPs) in Uganda and other countries. The Bank's trust in Museveni was rewarded. That trust did not materialize as a result of personal charisma, as it did in the case of President Meles' similarly heterodox approach to structural adjustment conditionality in Ethiopia;[33] rather, it was brokered. It was brokered particularly by, first, the DFID consultant responsible for defining the pro-poor list of expenditures, and second, Emanuel Tumusime-Mutabile, then Permanent Secretary to the Treasury, now Governor of the Bank of Uganda, who became a supreme expert in wrapping those fiscal priorities in the kind of pro-poor language which the donors wanted to hear.

These accomplishments marked the switch from a short-term to a long-term poverty strategy in Uganda. Over the following fifteen years there have been a number of confirming achievements, including the achievement of universal primary education in 2002, and elaborations of the original pro-poor vision, including the establishment of a new agricultural strategy in 2002/3, a new concordat with NGOs in 2004,[34] measures to increase the participation of the poor (the Uganda Participatory Poverty Action Programme—UPPAP), and, and most recently, a re-orientation of the basic development strategy towards large-scale industry and agriculture. None of these alter the basic political alignment of the Museveni regime, which is oriented in the first instance towards broad-based growth, in the second place towards the opportunistic use of poverty-reducing instruments towards this end, such as the drive towards universal primary education, and in the third place towards the long-run goal of personal and national self-sufficiency, one dimension of which is a decreased reliance on overseas aid. This last, of course, has implications for one of our suggested foundations of long-term poverty reduction, which is the laying of a tax base. These implications are explored in Chapter 5 below.

up various poverty relief programmes, such as PAPSCA (Poverty Alleviation Programme for the Social Costs of Adjustment), *and generally scattering money in inappropriate directions*' (Museveni 1997, page 182); emphasis added. The other two items in Museveni's three-fold list of basic obstacles to development, apart from lack of infrastructure, are lack of incentives to produce and the culture of reliance on government (ibid). Museveni has travelled a distance from his Marxist roots!

[32] ESAF = Enhanced Structural Adjustment Facility, PRGF = Poverty Reduction and Growth Facility, both of these conditional low-interest programme loans provided for budget support by the World Bank and IMF and administered by the Fund.

[33] For the Ethiopian episode, see Stiglitz (2003), pages 30–3.

[34] This will be analysed in Chapter 6 below.

The politics of *Ghana* in the 1990s and 2000s were in many ways very different from those of Uganda, even though the initial conditions, underlying economic structure, and poverty outcome were all similar. Like Uganda, Ghana was a peasant export economy, based on the export of cocoa to world markets from the first decade of the twentieth century onward, and the wide diffusion within Ghana of smallholder exports contributed from the first, as in Uganda, to an early rise in African living standards and relatively low levels of inequality. In terms of the penetration of the peasant export economy (African sales per capita), and measures of well-being, Ghana's progress ran ahead of Uganda's, and in Chapter 13 below we date the onset of the sharp fall in Ghanaian infant mortality to the 1920s, ten years before Uganda and more than twenty years before the settler economies of Kenya, Zimbabwe, and South Africa. Ghana was also a leader, from the 1920s onward, in African education, and in 1958 the first African country to achieve independence. President Kwame Nkrumah, notorious among economic liberals for his phrase 'seek ye first the political kingdom', pursued from the moment of independence a policy of import-substituting industrialization, roundly criticized for its excesses and its anti-agriculture bias by Nkrumah's adviser Sir Arthur Lewis (Killick 1978; Tignor 2005), and after the 1960s Ghana entered a period of economic and political repression not as dramatic or savage as Uganda's during the same years, but almost as effective in bringing a once proud peasant export economy to its knees (Toye 1995, Vol. 2, Chapter 14).

Revival came in 1983 in the shape of a structural adjustment programme designed by Joseph Abbey, Kwesi Botchwey, and others around the newly-established National Defence Council (NDC; subsequently Provisional National Defence Council or PNDC) under the President Flight-Lieutenant Jerry Rawlings: like Museveni's a reformist process achieved through military intervention but using a determinedly light military touch. The key elements in the reform process were also similar: tax reform and liberalization of customs duties, exchange rate de-control, and privatization of the Cocoa Marketing Board (achieving, however, a smaller impact on the share of the cocoa price achieved by the producer than in the case of the Uganda Coffee Marketing Board: Chapter 13 below).

These were the early years of structural adjustment, and the rhetoric of poverty alleviation was, at first, used neither by the PNDC nor by the Bank. This takes nothing away from the fact that many of the reforms *were* pro-poor: the rural areas were the ones which the PNDC, in the 1990s, knew that it would need to win once the promised democratization of politics arrived. In addition, much of the (P)NDC's liberalization was accompanied by populist pro-consumer rhetoric, which Lindsay Whitfield describes as 'Nkrumahist' (Whitfield 2009c, Chapter 4) and sometimes by fairly Neanderthal pro-consumer actions, such as the burning down of the Makola No. 1 market in Accra in 1981.

Onto this process of liberalization, as the tide within the World Bank began to turn in a pro-poor direction, was grafted in 1988 PAMSCAD (Programme to Mitigate the Social Costs of Adjustment), a programme which, like PAPSCA and the Bolivian Emergency Social Fund, provided food-for-work typically in the health and education sectors to compensate 'new poor' people made redundant by adjustment. Ghana was thus well positioned, from the 1990s onward, to convert the materials already to hand into a long-term pro-poor programme.

One of the big differences between Ghana and Uganda lies in the early abandonment of single-party, quasi-authoritarian politics in favour of genuine multi-party democracy of a kind which in 1992 was rare in Africa. The 1992 elections were won by the NDC, the more rural-allied of the two emergent main parties. Under the economic recovery programme, over and above continuing gains from liberalization in cocoa areas, the three northern regions were finally connected to the national electricity grid and a rural electrification programme was extended to most district capitals (Asaga 2008, page 105). But the pattern of beneficiaries from this golden decade for poverty reduction in Ghana, for a party rooted in the cocoa areas and the rural north, is somewhat surprising. Of the decline in overall headcount poverty in Ghana from fifty-one to twenty-nine per cent over the course of the 1980s and 90s, it appears, a very large share went to the *urban* poor. This concentration of gains amongst the urban electorates of Accra and Kumasi also contrasts with the Ugandan situation. Francis Teal (2006, see also Teal and Awoonor-Williams 2010) calculates that 'growth was not pro-poor among [self-employed] farmers', who only begin to show gains from the sixty-fourth percentile upwards, but that it was amongst workers (*including* farm workers) and self-employed people, all of whom gained over the decade from the richest to the poorest. Because farm workers gained in common with other workers, this cannot be called a return to the bad old days of urban bias, but it perhaps points to the predominance of unintended (spin-off) effects over intended ones. And, in spite of all the gains emerging from the budget surveys, many urban people nonetheless felt a continuing pinch from adjustment, and transferred their vote to the more urban-oriented National Patriotic Party (NPP) in 2000 and 2004.

The NPP has a less populist approach than the NDC; Whitfield (2008) describes this as inspired by the 'Busia-Danquah' (i.e. liberal-intellectual) tradition, by contrast with the NDC's more populist (Nkrumahist) roots. The NPP also has a much more urban (especially Accra-urban) power base than the NDC, and from this point onward an intended policy of targeting on urban interests, including the urban poor, begins to take root, implemented through job creation and, in intention, through transformation of the economy into non-traditional exports. But this transformation, awaited ever since Nkrumah fifty years ago, has yet to materialize, and the coming on stream this year of offshore oil from Ghana will scarcely accelerate it.

The conclusion which we derive from our case studies, therefore, is that the pessimistic conclusion derived by Haggard et al. concerning the political impotence of pro-poor policies is no longer *universally* valid, although it still holds good in a number of places. The choices taken at the 'forks in the road' (Figure 3.1 above) exercise not only the narrowly economic function of influencing resource allocations, but also, through its choice of policy instruments, the political function of *signalling*, or sending messages about the way government is operating and the interests it serves, and at these vital junctures the sending of pro-poor signals has in several cases, notably in Argentina (after 2002), Ghana, Indonesia (after 2000), and Uganda, proved politically advantageous to the cause of pro-poor growth. In opposite cases, such as Indonesia in late 1997 or Bolivia in February 2003, the government's choice, abetted by the aid donors, of distributionally regressive measures in the depths of crisis, confirmed pre-existing distrust of government, prompting political violence and resistance to reforms, delaying adjustment and stopping poverty from falling, indeed causing it to rise over the duration of the crisis from 1998 to 2003. Fear of conflict, breadth of vision among the political elite, and in the case of poorer countries intermediation by aid donors have all played a role in determining the acceptance or rejection of pro-poor signals by elites.

3.3 POLITICAL INSTABILITY AND PRO-POOR ORIENTATION

However, this is only the beginning of the story, because a pro-poor alliance once formed may not hold; and even if it holds, it may not deliver gains for the poor if the strategy around which it coalesces is misconceived.

Whether it does depends on a range of factors. Three which we wish to consider in detail, the next building blocks in our story, are *political stability*, *economic strategy* (both its policy and its institutional dimension), and *international economic relationships*. We consider these in sequence.

As we have already observed, political instability and conflict act as both a stimulus and an obstacle to development. The fear and sometimes the recent memory of instability, as we saw in all the cases just considered, can act as a powerful incentive to stitch together pro-poor alliances which would otherwise not have formed; at the same time, current instability can destroy pro-poor momentum. In Chapter 4, we shall consider this two-way relationship in detail. As a prelude to this, let us imagine that a coalition has formed which contains some pro-poor elements, as in the cases of the previous section; but it is fragile, and is at risk of breaking down if it cannot deliver material gains to all the parties in the coalition. In this environment, what can the state do to preserve political stability? To this end let us examine the simple game presented in Figure 3.2. This model speaks to the question, examined by many political theorists over the last three hundred years, of whether it is possible, to stop society from falling apart, and it builds on the model presented by Cervellati et al. (2008). Like them, we visualize a game between an 'elite', which as in many developing countries has a monopoly of land and physical capital assets, and a 'people', who only have human capital assets (skills and qualifications) and no command over land or equipment. Each of these two groups, elite and people, earns income from either of two sources, private wages, and the social wage (or government budget). The value of the social wage, in terms of the pay-off to both elite and people, is determined by two characteristics, its real value or purchasing power and its allocation between sectors. The logic of bringing allocation between sectors into the story is that, as we have described above, the elite can send the people a signal, by means of its allocation of money to particular budget headings, of the interests it identifies with and the equity with which it plans to arbitrate between them. If the signal is successful, it generates trust, in the sense of a reduced fear of exploitation, and a consequent motivation to hold off from aggressive behaviour by both sides in later periods. More broadly, any of three factors—an increase in the social wage, an 'improved' intersectoral allocation of the social wage, or changes in process which increase the fairness with which, from the people's point of view, society is organized—increase the likelihood that the outcome of the game will be a collaborative one, rather than the 'warre of all against all, in which the parties reduce their strength by mutual opposition to nothing' visualized by Thomas Hobbes in 1651[35] and still visible across many of the poorest parts of the developing world today.

Our story runs as follows. The social wage, W_s, is the product of the real level of social benefits (w_s) provided by government to the people, and their intersectoral composition (c), which we can interpret as a measure of the ability of different parts of the people to cause social disruption:

$$W_s = w_s \cdot c \tag{3.1a}$$

The elite (denoted by the subscript E) determines the distribution of the social wage and private wage between itself ($W_{s(E)}, W_{p(E)}$) and the people, denoted by the subscript P($W_{s(P)}$, $W_{p(P)}$), and in addition has at all points in time the choice between 'provocative' and 'non-provocative' behaviours: the elite can increase or decrease the share of military personnel within government (to the point, in some cases, of a military take-over), they can increase or decrease the share of military expenditure in total expenditure, and when faced by provocative behaviours by the 'people' (such as strikes, roadblocks, suicide bombs, etc.) they have the choice to escalate or not escalate the level of aggression.[36] The people have the choice between rebelling against the elite or accepting its authority. The initial pay-offs are as in Figure 3.2a. If aggressive behaviour by one party is met by non-aggressive (or by unsuccessfully aggressive) behaviour by the other, the 'sucker's pay-off' to losing the conflict is zero, and there is an asset transfer A to the winning side. If there is aggression on both sides, a share α of the assets of both sides is lost in the consequent conflict.

If on the other hand conflict is avoided and a social contract $[(W_p + W_s)_E, (W_p + W_s)]^*$ is agreed, a 'trust dividend' T accumulates to both players in the subsequent period. Trust, on this formulation, derives partly from peace itself, and partly from the acceptance of a signal of 'fair' public resource allocation (c).

$$T_p = f[c(-1], Z \tag{3.1b}$$

where Z is a state variable taking the value 1 in case of conflict and 0 in case of no conflict.

Let us first represent $W_{p(E)} = W_{s(E)} = 2$, Let $W_{p(P)} = W_{s(P)} = 1$, $A = 1$, $\alpha = 0.5$, $T = 0$, as in Figure 3.2b. This is, in essence, a one-sided prisoner's dilemma—one-sided in the sense that the elite group is assumed to have, through the political structure, a larger share of income flows (1.5) than the people (1), partly as a

[35] The full quotation runs:

> [Under a state of nature] every man will and may lawfully rely on his own strength and art, for caution against all other men... For being distracted in opinions concerning the best use and application of their strength, they [i.e. all men] do not help, but hinder one another, and reduce their strength by mutual opposition to nothing... also, when there is no common enemy, they make warre upon each other, for their particular interests (Hobbes, 1651/1965, Part 2 Chapter 17, pages 128–9).

[36] The enlightening analysis of conflict by Nafziger and Auvinen (2000) refers to the extent of provocation within government behaviour as 'military centrality'.

		Player 1 ('elite') behaviours	
Player 2 ('people') values of private and social wage		Non-provocative	Provocative
	Not rebel	$[(W_p + W_s)_e + T_e, (W_p + W_s)_p + T_p]^*$	$[(W_p + W_s)_E + A, 0]$
	Rebel	$0, (W_p + W_s)_p + A$	$\alpha (W_p + W_s)_E, \alpha (W_p + W_s)_p$

Figure 3.2(a) A conflict game in its simplest form.

		Player 1 ('elite') behaviours	
Player 2 ('people') responses		Non-provocative	Provocative
	Not rebel	3,2	4,0
	Rebel	0,3	1.5,1

(b) Possible structure of pay-offs under an 'imposed social contract'.

		Player 1 ('elite') behaviours	
Player 2 ('people') responses		Not provocative	Provocative
	Not rebel	5,5	4,0
	Rebel	0,3	1.5,1

(c) Pay-offs (value of S) under a 'negotiated social contract'.

consequence of its monopoly of land assets; there is no trust on either side. As in the standard prisoner's dilemma, the individual protagonists fear being exploited even more than they fear the state of conflict itself, and so the dominant strategy equilibrium is that they defend themselves against that fear of exploitation (i.e. each arm pre-emptively), so as to give an equilibrium in the bottom right-hand corner. No 'social contract', or binding agreement enabling the elite and people to resolve conflicts of interest by peaceful means after the model suggested by Jean-Jacques Rousseau (1762/1968) materializes, even though the one proposed, at the top left-hand corner, yields more to both parties than the state of conflict. A social wage, equal in value to the private wage, is being paid, but this also is not enough to prevent conflict. Political instability prevails.

We have above described a number of cases in which this kind of conflict equilibrium has prevailed, to the detriment of growth and to the frustration of poverty reduction initiatives: for example, Uganda in the 1980s, Russia in Chechnya between 1993–2000, Indonesia in 1997–2000, Argentina and Bolivia between 2000–3. The same analysis, we have argued elsewhere, applies to Ethiopia and Mozambique in the 1980s and indeed to some political instabilities in industrial countries, including the former Yugoslavia for much of the 1990s and Northern

Ireland in the early 1970s.[37] In all of these cases, in order to maintain the credibility of its threat in face of rebellion by at least a substantial fragment of the population, the government chose the *provocative* option. The result was stalemate (a bottom right-hand corner equilibrium), persistence of riot-type conflict, and in some of these cases an escalation into full-scale conflict also.

The interesting question, of course, is how a shift from war to peace can be engineered. With this model, this can occur if, for example, the payoffs shift to the level portrayed in Figure 3.2c.

In general, if the payoff to both elite and people rises to the 'tipping point' where $[(W_p + W_s)^*_E + T_{e},] > [W_p + W_s)_E + A_s]$ *and* $[(W_p + W_s)_P + T_p]^* > [(W_p + W_s)_P + A_{p},]$ then we move from an exploitative equilibrium (bottom right-hand corner) to a trust equilibrium (top-left hand corner) where conflict is replaced by political stability.

How can this mutually beneficial trust equilibrium be made to occur? From the analysis above we have observed three possibilities:

1. The elite can send a *wage signal*, consisting of a higher average social wage w_s. By raising w_s, this takes the 'people' group closer to the point where the incentive to rebel is dominated by the incentive to not rebel.
2. The elite can send a *distributional signal* (c in our notation) consisting of an altered allocation of expenditures between different expenditure functions, such as human capital (education and health),[38] housing, transport, social protection, and so on. Each reallocation of this type transfers resource from one interest group to another, and conveys a message from the elite to the people, concerning how it intends to deal between competing interests in future. The logic of including a variable of this type is that a shift in the balance of social expenditure towards the social groups which feel the greatest sense of injustice, as well as simply changes in the overall level of expenditure, may be able to defuse latent tensions within the population and reduce the likelihood of riot-type conflict. In Chapter 5 we observe two major ways in which this has been done, in support of social expenditures (Bolivia, Argentina, Ghana) and in support of agricultural expenditures (Uganda, Indonesia), respectively. Each of these signals, of course, can be transmitted through cuts or progressive shifts in taxes, instead of or as well as through increases in expenditure; and indeed it can be transmitted through non-fiscal means such as land reform (Bolivia in the 1950s, South Africa in the 1990s).
3. The elite can propose an *institutional change* which amends the process by which resources are allocated. If effective this increases $W_{s(P)}$, the people's perception of the social wage. In South-East Asia, as we have observed above, political violence during the crisis period, 1997 through 2000, was far greater in Indonesia, where it was associated with attempts by the

[37] For further discussion of the Northern Ireland case see Hudson, Lenton, and Mosley (2011).

[38] Investment in the human capital of the poor can be seen as increasing overall productivity and social cohesiveness (social capital) between the 'elite' and the 'people', and it has served a major distributional signal within donors' recent aid initiatives, as illustrated by Table 2.3 above. John Stuart Mill would have agreed with them. In 1848 he wrote that 'with these [universal education and an effective population policy] there could be no poverty, even under the present social institutions' (Mill 1848/1994, page 16).

> government to stigmatize one particular ethnic group, than in Thailand and South Korea, where government emphasized equitable sharing of the burden of adjustment. During recent crisis-adjustment processes, some governments, notably Latin American ones, have tried to embed equity into the process of governance through constitutional reform. Following the violent confrontations in Argentina in early 2002 and in Bolivia in February and October 2003, discussion forums were established in each country (the *Mesa de Dialogo* in Argentina and the *Asemblea Constituyente* in Bolivia) the purpose of which was to establish discussion processes which might lay the basis for the countries' constitutions to operate in future in a way which made the social contract more voluntary and less coercive. An important guiding principle underlying these conciliation processes was the withdrawal of the military from the level of influence over government which lit the fuse for both of the 2003 outbreaks of violence in Bolivia—a reduction in 'military centrality'.[39] These forums in due course generated new vehicles for the disbursement of the social wage, such as the *Programa Jefas y Jefes* in Argentina and the *Renta Dignidad* in Bolivia, and new, often highly heterodox, policy instruments such as, in each country, measures to finance pro-poor expenditure out of export taxation (Grugel and Riggirozzi 2009b). The suggestion here is that the forums generated trust, not only through these new policy initiatives, but because their mere existence, at least for a time and for a significant number of people, made the idea of justice more credible in those environments.[40]

In this way, the elite has the option open to it of transmitting any or all of these three signals to buy off the scepticism of the people; and if their reception is favourable they diminish the amount of distrust felt by the people towards the elite, a process which if sustained will confer additional legitimacy on the elite, that is, provide the elite with a trust dividend T_e which increases the 'elite pay-off' in the top left-hand cell of the table. How much these manoeuvres achieve will depend on the political leverage of the beneficiary groups; thus, in proportion as the perceived benefit goes to regions and interest groups which are highly politicized and have considerable power to disrupt the state, that increase will generate a higher pay-off. The three signals may be conveyed either separately or

[39] *Military centrality*, in this analysis, therefore connotes not just the share of the military in public expenditure and in government, but the willingness of the elite group to settle differences by discussion rather than by violence. As A.K. Sen comments, 'the fact that, after the murderous attacks in Mumbai in November 2008 by terrorists from a Muslim background (and almost certainly of Pakistani ancestry) the much-feared reaction against Muslims did not emerge was to a great extent due to the public discussion that followed the attacks, to which both Muslims and non-Muslims contributed richly' (Sen 2009, page 353).

[40] The trust of the 'people' group in response to offers of a higher social wage may relate to who is making those offers as well as on how the process is conducted. Offers of immunization, or agricultural extension, or financial services, or schooling made by the NGO sector may have a different effect, in particular a different leverage on local levels of political unrest, from offers made by the government sector, because of differences in effectiveness between the two sectors and because of differences in what is expected in return. If the offer of community services is not made in return for political influence, as is the case in the NGO sector, it may be more effective. Thus we hypothesize that a high density of NGOs may be associated with a relatively high degree of effectiveness of the social wage.

in parallel. A case of their being deployed in parallel is Northern Ireland over the course of the 1990s, where wage signals, in the form of a continuous increase in the real social wage and the share of the budget devoted to health and education, reinforced the efforts being made to incorporate the paramilitary and political representatives of the Protestant and Catholic communities into negotiations, eventually leading to the Good Friday Agreement of 1998 (Hudson, Lenton, and Mosley 2011).

Our hypothesis, then, is that within the social wage relationship:

$$W_s = w_s \cdot c \tag{3.1a}$$

increases in the real social wage (w_s) can be engineered by means of reallocations of expenditure towards more politically militant groups, and distributional improvements as seen from the point of view of the 'people' (c) can be engineered by intersectoral transfers which increase the leverage of militant groups, and by changes in governmental process which increase perceived justice among the people, potent signals towards which may be a reduction in the Gini coefficient of inequality (σ), or reductions in military centrality (M). Thus, seen for now purely from the point of view of the 'people', the condition for moving towards a trust equilibrium becomes:

$$(w_P + w_s \cdot c)_p + T_P[c(\sigma, M)]^* > [W_P + (w(s) \cdot c)_{P'}] + A_P \tag{3.2a}$$

If conflict is to be healed, everything depends on the distributional signal within the social wage (c), converting into sufficient trust among the 'people' group (T) for the equilibrium of the game to move from a conflict equilibrium to a trust equilibrium.

Of course, this is only one blade of the scissors. Before a trust equilibrium can be reached, the pay-off to the elite needs to rise to the point where:

$$[(W_P + w_s \cdot c) * E \ + T_e,] > [W_P + (w(s) \cdot c))_E + A_s] \tag{3.2b}$$

This can occur through a variety of processes, as discussed above: because the elite, perhaps as the consequence of an external shock, finds that it needs to broaden its base of support if it is to achieve a sustainable power-base, as in Argentina, Bolivia, Ethiopia, and Ghana during the 2000s; because the elite discovers that a broader-based development pattern is in its own self-interest, as in the analysis of Gradstein (2006); or finally, in poor countries, as the result of intervention by an external aid donor leading to a broadening in the base of public expenditure, as occurred with some success in the cases of Uganda, Rwanda, Mozambique, and Ethiopia during the 2000s, and is currently being attempted, in the midst of conflict, in the unpromising environments of Afghanistan and the Democratic Republic of the Congo.

If both blades of the scissors (3.2a) and (3.2b) can be made to close, there emerges a further dividend—the 'time heals' effect much analysed by Collier (2007) and in our case rendered by (1b):

$$T_P = f[c(-1)], Z \tag{3.1b}$$

In this way, peace itself engenders trust, which helps to entrench political stability. But of course the mechanism can go into reverse: if the blades of the scissors do not close, the result will be an aggravation of political instability, and an intensification of the vicious circle of political instability, weakness of the state and of social capital, decapitalization, and poverty. A particularly important feature of our analysis is the link between social ties, political structures, and material deprivation. Poverty may persist, or be alleviated, depending on whether mechanisms for creative communication and conflict management exist between elites and those who have the power to undermine the state, as in the Argentina and Bolivia (post-2006) cases mentioned above, or whether the contrary case of a vicious circle applies, as in Indonesia in 1998 and, more particularly, in Bolivia in 2002–3, and we refer to the latter case as a *political poverty trap* (Chapters 10 and 11 below.)

3.4 MACRO- AND MICRO-POLICIES AS SIGNALS

On the view presented above, political stability can be encouraged by the sending of various kinds of policy signal, which lead towards a long-term equilibrium. We focused on three particular signals: increases in the level of the social wage, reorientations of the social wage towards more politicized groups, and amendments in governmental process, to which reductions in income inequality and military centrality may be the key. Those same signals, crucial for the consolidation of political stability, in turn, on the evidence of our case studies, feed back into successful poverty reduction processes. We now discuss the ways in which these changes, on the evidence of our case studies, can be achieved, focusing on four types of signal: heterodox macro-economic policy, public expenditure policy, tax policy, and institutional reform.

1. *Heterodox macro-economic policy.* Especially in Latin America, where the economic gains from structural adjustment were modest and where memories persist (Chapter 2) of the possibilities of an activist alternative to neoliberal economic policies, governments have experimented with increasing the social wage through a return to protectionism, especially, as we saw in the Argentina case, through export taxes, price controls, and capital controls. Neodevelopmentalism, as it is known, is, however, a very different protectionism from that which gave development economics a bad name in the 1950s and 1960s: rather, some elements of the 'Washington Consensus' remain in position, in particular the need to avoid inflationary budget deficits and maintain competitiveness (although, as we shall see, there is huge debate, both in North and South, about how this latter objective should be achieved) and the radical measures described above are implemented. What is particularly relevant to our argument is that neodevelopmentalism (unlike old-style protectionism) almost always contains measures explicitly designed to benefit the poor. Often these consist of pro-poor expenditure programmes financed from the aforementioned export taxes, such as the *Programa Jefas y Jefes* in Argentina, the *Renta Dignidad* in Bolivia (and the conditional cash transfer programmes now found across a majority of countries in Latin America), but other heterodox forms of increasing the social wage are encountered, such as asset transfers, as in Bolivia. The

general approach of using controls, particularly export taxes and minimum wages, as a means of reasserting the power of a weakened state is also to be encountered in our Russian case study. And in Africa pro-poor export taxes are also now to be encountered, including not only Ghana (as we discuss in detail in Chapter 5), but also Zambia and Mauritius. Also in this spirit, capital controls were imposed by Malaysia in 1997 to stabilize the flow of funds out of the country, in spite of a strong preference expressed by the IMF that controls should not be imposed.[41] Of course, all these measures are outside even the new 'augmented Washington Consensus' (see Table 7.3 below): politics here has defeated at least orthodox economics, and the real issue, to be discussed in Chapters 5 and 8 below, is whether poverty reduction is the winner.

2. *Reallocations of expenditure.* It is one of our major themes that the risks of conflict can be eased and poverty reduced by altering the allocation of expenditure between sectors as well as by simply raising expenditure, and the second of these is often (as we shall see in Chapter 5) politically the easier as well as financially the less costly option. From the point of view of maximizing poverty impact, the crux is to focus the social wage on productive sectors which are labour-intensive, since the poorest people are typically those who have only labour income and no capital of any sort. In low-income Asia and Africa, where most people are in rural areas, one crucial way of achieving this is via the green revolution, which raises the yield of food crops by labour-intensive methods and thereby raises both the consumption of poor people and the demand for their labour at the same time, and this, as we have seen, was the principal route by which the dramatic reductions in poverty in Indonesia in the 1970s and 80s were achieved. In the 1990s and early 2000s, this process began to spread to Africa (see Chapter 13 for the impact of these). In higher-income countries, the route of reducing poverty through augmented social expenditure is both politically and administratively more feasible, and in the last decade conditional cash transfers, many of them financed by 'neodevelopmental' export taxes, have revolutionized social protection in Latin America and have been responsible for much of the fall in poverty and inequality levels in that continent.[42] The relative merits of different types of pro-poor expenditure strategies are examined in Chapter 5.
3. *Tax policy.* If it is possible to signal an intention to achieve greater fairness by changing public expenditure, it is also possible to do so through the tax system, both by moving the burden of taxation on to rich people and sectors, and by closing tax loopholes, as we observed above in the case of foreign-owned capitalist enterprises in Bolivia. In Africa, the burden of export taxation has historically had an entirely different structure, being imposed until the 1980s, mainly levied on low-income smallholders rather than on

[41] See Duasa and Mosley (2006) for an analysis of the effectiveness of these controls, and Jomo and Fine (2006) for further discussion of heterodox policies in Asia. The IMF was particularly unsympathetic to limitations on the export of capital, preferring tax-based measures limiting capital inflows on the model pioneered by Chile in the early 1990s (Eichengreen 1999).

[42] In fifteen out of twenty countries in Latin America, inequality has fallen since 2000 (see World Bank, 2006a).

multinational corporations, and the politics of pro-poor tax reform have therefore had to have an entirely different thrust, liberalizing rather than reimposing export taxes. The processes by which these reforms have been achieved are discussed in the later part of Chapter 5.

4. *Institutional development.* Institutions, it is now universally acknowledged, are crucial to development, but of those identified as most crucial by the Bretton Woods institutions, (rule of law; bureaucratic efficiency; democratic accountability; freedom from corruption; and political stability), the only one which we have so far fitted into our analysis is the last. We argue in Chapter 6 that institutions which facilitate access to key markets (notably labour and capital markets) by the poor are also crucial, and that sending pro-poor signals to such institutions is another key pathway through which long-term poverty can be reduced.

3.5 INTERNATIONAL INTERESTS AND PRO-POOR POLICIES

In the previous chapter we saw that the first wave of pro-poor strategies, under MacNamara in the 1970s, was born of a fear that the security not just of some countries, but of the whole world, might be threatened by growing poverty and inequality. The wave receded in the 1980s, under the stress of global recession, but by the time it returned in the guise of the International Development Targets (later Millennium Development Goals), several of the ideas and strategies associated with it, including investment in the green revolution and the urban informal sector, were already driving poverty reduction strategies forward in Asia and Latin America.

During the 2000s, aid and to some extent other forms of international capital flow underwent a metamorphosis: instead of being governed by 'ultimatum conditionality' they were now the subject of what we describe as 'new conditionality' in which recipient countries were ostensibly the prime movers and in which not only their governments but also their NGO sectors were formally involved. In the poorer LDCs, which still depend on aid flows, the effectiveness of this new aid modality is obviously a key building block, determining poverty reduction possibilities beyond all the factors previously discussed, and we analyse this in Chapter 7.

3.6 THE WAY AHEAD

We have thus examined a number of the building blocks which underlie the political rationale to adopt different elements in pro-poor action: coalition formation, political stability, fiscal policies, institutional development, and international interests. These are represented as a causal chain in Figure 3.3. It will be abundantly clear by this point, however, that there is no one right way to achieve a pro-poor growth pattern; rather there are many ways of doing it, each of them appropriate to different power-structures, institutional capacities, and ways of interpreting the data.

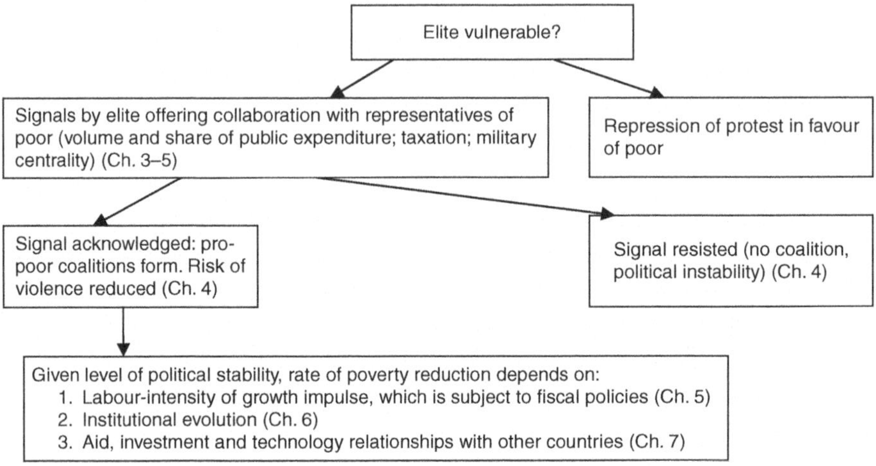

Figure 3.3 Pathways of poverty impact: the amplified decision tree.

We now have some evidence to suggest that the OECD's iron law of political exclusion of the poorest no longer appears to fit the data, and we have surmised that the five relationships mentioned are important 'building blocks' in explaining poverty dynamics in particular countries. We have presented some evidence on how these building blocks 'functioned' in individual case-study countries, but we have said little about how well or badly these ideas generalize across countries. This will be the main concern of the remaining chapters.

These chapters will examine the following propositions:

- *Building block 1: scope for making pro-poor alliances.* We have argued above that fear of conflict, breadth of vision among the political elite, and in the case of poorer countries, intermediation by aid donors have all played a role in determining the acceptance or rejection of pro-poor signals by elites, and thus the making of an initial bargain which has put countries on the road towards pro-poor growth.
- *Building block 2: political stability.* Our first analytical contribution is definitional: we argue, in Chapter 4, that 'riot-type conflict', or conflict short of civil war, which is seldom measured by the literature, is key to understanding the forms of political instability that determine investment and poverty reduction, whether or not this leads to full-blown civil war. We then test the propositions developed above, that the social wage, its composition, and the process or 'rules of engagement' defining the negotiating process between the elite and the socially excluded are crucial to determining the level and incidence of riot-type conflict (and thence overall political instability).
- *Building block 3: fiscal and related influences on pro-poor growth.* In Chapter 5, we examine various ways in which the choice of fiscal policy instruments can impact on poverty. First, we examine the influence of prioritizing particular expenditures, such as welfare, agriculture, and health and education spending, on poverty levels, and then we perform a similar exercise in relation to tax structures. Finally, we illustrate how under the influence of

'neodevelopmentalist' political pressures', as discussed above, fiscal reforms may be combined with other policy instruments such as price controls, minimum wages, and export taxation, and speculate on the implications of these heterodox policies for poverty strategies.

- *Building block 4: pro-poor institutions.* In Chapter 6, we examine the relationship between existing governance measures and economic performance, and find that several of them do not relate reliably to growth, much less to poverty. Building on the proposition that capacity to manage risk and equity of market access are crucial in order to understand the impact of governance institutions on the poor, we construct an index of pro-poor institutions (PPI) containing this measure, and relate the PPI measure to poverty reduction performance.
- *Building block 5: external influences on poverty dynamics.* Chapter 7 picks up the story of international institutions' involvement with poverty reduction, begun in Chapter 2. For the poorer developing countries, we ask whether the mutation of conditionality into an apparently more equal relationship based on trust between borrower and lender has increased the poverty-leverage of aid flows. More broadly, we return to the theme of whether a combination of global crises and the demise of the Washington Consensus have brought about a return of state influence in developing countries, and the implications of this for poverty dynamics.

Each of the sequential building blocks in our argument, then, contains hypotheses or a set of propositions on the causes of poverty emerging from this chapter and our case studies. By testing these propositions we hope to understand better the processes by which poverty is determined and may be remedied.

4

Political violence, state instability, and poverty

4.1 INTRODUCTION

Political violence, or simply the threat of it, is on the analysis so far clearly an important element in determining government policy and well-being. As we saw in the previous chapter, a significant element in the dynamics of poverty is the ability of representatives of poor groups to send a credible threat to the elite and the state's response to that threat; but where this response has been miscalculated, the costs have been considerable, as we saw in the last chapter in the case of President Suharto's refusal to conciliate protesters in Indonesia in 1997 and the Bolivian government's blind determination to push through the proposed tax increases of February 2003. The same analysis applies to the wars which from 1994 through 1996, and then again in 1999, were waged in two of Russia's poorest republics, Dagestan and Chechnya.[1] In all of these cases, the ability to achieve a peaceful solution to conflicts of interest is clearly crucial in determining the poverty outcome.

A considerable literature has emerged in recent years, which seeks to explain war and peace in economic terms. A central part of this literature treats rebellion against the state as the object of a cost-benefit analysis. If the costs of rebellion against the state are low (for example because an individual is poor and ill-educated) and its benefits are high (for example because a state possesses large natural resources, which can be seized at relatively low cost because security is weak) the benefit-cost ratio of rebellion is high and the likelihood of conflict is greatest; hence wars are more likely to start in low-income countries with weak states and abundant oil and other resources than any others (Collier, 2007; Collier and Hoeffler 1998, 2004; Nafziger, Stewart, and Vayrynen 2000). Hence the reason why all of the four countries in the world which are both large (population more than 50 million) and ultra-poor (less than $300 income per capita)—Nigeria, Sudan, arguably Ethiopia and the Democratic Republic of the Congo[2]—are locked in a poverty trap which is also a conflict trap, or at any rate a political instability

[1] In Chechnya, Dagestan, and Ingushetia in 2004, the average gross regional product was $601, similar to that of India and under one-quarter of average Russian income of $2,467. Source: Chapter 12 below, Table 12.1.

[2] Ethiopia is slightly different from the others because it does not suffer from a natural resource curse.

trap. However, there is controversy about whether *only* these cost-benefit, or 'greed', factors account for conflict, or whether political factors such as military centrality, intergroup animosities, democracy, and quality of governance should also be factored into the story. There is also controversy concerning the specification of a number of the independent variables, in particular the distribution of income and wealth.[3] In the context of Africa, there has been an eloquent attempt to rebut the ethnic fragmentation part of the 'grievance' story, which argues that there is no correlation between ethnic fragmentation and growth (e.g. Sala-i-Martin 1997), and indeed that ethno-linguistic and racial 'fragmentation' should not been seen, as argued by Easterly and Levine (1997) as a fundamental source of conflict and under-performance in Africa, but rather as a positive force in controlling conflict and in development generally (Elbadawi and Sambanis 2000).

Our contribution in this chapter is to try and understand political violence and how it can be controlled, building on the simple gaming analysis of the previous chapter and measuring the conflict variable in a broader way than that employed by most of the literature. The literature on the economics of conflict is almost entirely concerned with civil war, but most of the violence which causes collapses in investment and in business confidence, including that examined in the previous chapter, consists not of civil war but of what we may call 'riot-type behaviour' (strikes, demonstrations, marches, roadblocks), much more localized and of shorter-term duration than full-scale civil war, and for that reason falling below the radar of the conflict literature's databases. In addition, the conflict literature is mainly concerned with violence itself, rather than with policies for the pre-emption of conflict. Indeed, although we know that less poverty means less conflict, we know relatively little about, and urgently need to discover, which policies stand a good chance of buying off conflict and political instability in which environments. Our idea is that if we understood more about the causes of riot-type conflicts and the policy factors which cause them to expand or contract, many of which, as we shall see, are economic crisis-related, we would better understand the causes of full-scale war, and would possess an early-warning indicator which if well-managed might prevent its outbreak.

The focus in this chapter, then, is on this broader definition of conflict, aiming to identify the processes by which social tensions often remain at the level of riot-type conflict, but sometimes escalate into full-scale civil war; the processes which minimize that risk; and the knock-on effects of these tensions on poverty. The next section discusses how this broader concept of conflict should be specified, and how it has evolved over time in our case-study countries. Section 4.3 returns to the model of 'riot-type conflict' sketched out in the previous chapter, tests it by two alternative methods (panel data, plus case-study examination of Bolivia and

[3] There is debate, first of all, about whether vertical income distribution is significant at all: Collier and Hoeffler 2004 (Table 4 and conclusion, page 580) argue that it is an insignificant influence on conflict once 'greed' factors are controlled for. Second, there is disagreement about whether the inequality which matters is vertical, or income-related, differential or the so-called 'horizontal' inequalities between races, regions and ethnicities, and finally it is disputed whether the true flashpoint for conflict is inequality itself or government's attitude towards it—whether it is seen as seeking to limit, whether it is seen to be or conniving at, the injustices which inequality causes (Cramer 2003).

Indonesia, two of our case-study countries), and in particular examines the circumstances under which riot-type conflict may broaden into war. Section 4 concludes and presents some implications for short-term anti-poverty policy; other implications, however, fall into the category of long-term actions, and are considered in Chapters 5 and 6.

4.2 THE CONCEPT OF 'RIOT-TYPE' VIOLENCE

Various attempts have been made to measure the intensity of conflict, and we begin from the measure frequently used in regression analyses, ucdp_loc, developed by the Norwegian PRIO database. This uses a four-part classification, distinguishing between countries experiencing 'war', 'intermediate conflict', 'minor conflict', and 'no conflict'. This is the only database which distinguishes between conflicts by intensity of conflict. If we define conflict short of a war as riot-type conflict, closely associated with frequency of coups and revolutions, it is a good deal commoner than civil war, as illustrated by Figure 4.1, and therefore possibly a more significant cause of economic damage in the developing world than the latter.

At this point we need to draw attention to problems with the data. Certainly for the case of riot-type conflict (conflict short of war) and arguably for other cases also, the existing quantitative data on conflict do not describe the reality on the ground well. One illustration of this is that Zimbabwe and Bolivia are both classified by the standard datasets on war and civil conflict (the PRIO and Quality of Government (QoG) datasets) as being conflict-free even though, as our case

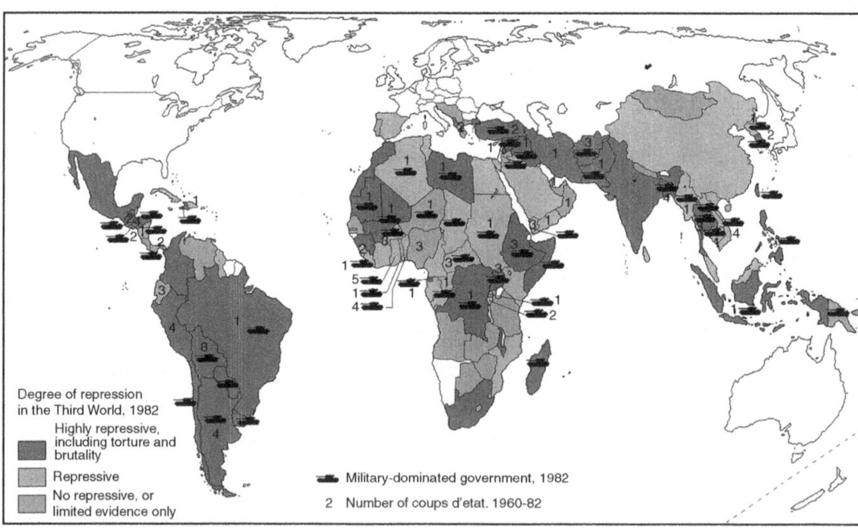

Figure 4.1 Location of riot-type conflict and high military centrality in developing countries.

Source: Adapted from Open University, *Third World Atlas*, map on page 64 'Arms and the military'. © The Open University.

studies (Chapters 10 and 13) describe, each of them has been responsible for several hundred deaths in riot-type conflict since 1999. For this reason, we have doctored the data in Table 4.1 for those two countries.[4] And for Indonesia and Bolivia, we have constructed or adapted our own datasets. In the next two tables, therefore, although the qualitative discussion relates to all our case studies, the quantitative analysis of riot-type conflict is for Bolivia and Indonesia only.

There are six cases of reasonably severe conflict in crisis periods (costing ten or more civilian lives and associated with demonstrations against the government's economic policies) amongst the countries in Table 4.1: Uganda (1981–9), Russia (1994–6 and 1999), Indonesia (1997–8), Argentina (2001–2), Bolivia (2000–5), and Zimbabwe (1999 to the present).[5] Of these cases, we set Uganda aside, even though conflict occurred during a period of global crisis, because the violence was associated not so much with the crisis itself as with a guerrilla war designed to replace a failing regime. In the other five countries, government retrenchment during an economic downturn (IMF-supported in all cases except Zimbabwe) was met with unexpected resistance—expanding into outright civil war in Russia only, which protracted the crisis, drove out foreign investment, and increased poverty. These are the processes which we wish to analyse.

The stages in the analysis are indicated by Figure 4.2. Beginning from the idea that riot-type conflict is often, but not inevitably, the fuse which gives rise to actual civil war, we examine in detail the root causes of riot-type conflict and the policy reasons why that type of conflict expands or contracts, then the crossover from riot-type conflict to civil war.

Let us therefore begin with riot-type conflict, the right-hand branch of this model. As mentioned above, there are few systematic analyses of political instability of this sort. From the few studies which have been done, for example the studies by the OECD (Haggard, Lafay, and Morrisson, 1996; Paldam 1993; Morrisson, Lafay, and Dessus 1993)[6] it is, however, clear that riot-type violence

[4] For these countries, see our dataset for Indonesia, Zimbabwe, and Bolivia, at www.poverty.group.shef.ac.uk.

[5] Because of deficiencies in the dataset, Bolivia and Zimbabwe are not treated by PRIO as suffering even from minor conflict in the periods named; however, the conflict certainly happened and is chronicled in detail in our Chapters 10 and 13.

[6] The two constituent studies use somewhat different methodologies. The study by Paldam (1993) compares nine Latin American balance-of-payments crises between 1980 and 1991 and examines their consequences in terms of strikes and demonstrations, finding that protests on average reach a peak about a year after the onset of adjustment, and they are more lively under democratic than under authoritarian regimes. The study by Morrisson, Lafay, and Dessus (1993), confronted by more severe data problems, constructed a pooled database over the period 1980–90 for 23 African countries. Both industrial strikes and demonstrations are found to be correlated with measures of the intensity of adjustment (this time with a six-month lag—Haggard, Lafay, and Morrisson 1996, page 89). The authors of this study also note that the policy-mix is relevant, for example cuts in recurrent government expenditure are correlated with protest, but cuts in public expenditure are not (Haggard, Lafay, and Morrisson 1996, page 89). Where (more often than not, especially in authoritarian regimes) these protests are met with politically repressive measures (arrests without trial, etc.), these repressive measures are typically short term, and as they are loosened, typically economic policy is loosened as well, with tax cuts, increases in subsidies, and expansion of the money supply to accommodate these (Haggard, Lafay, and Morrisson 1996, page 91).

Table 4.1 Case-study countries: incidence of conflict and political instability, 1960 to present.

	Russia	Latin America cases		Asia cases		Africa cases			
		Argentina	Bolivia	Indonesia	Malaysia	Ghana	Uganda	Kenya	Zimbabwe
War	1995–6 1999–2001 2004	1982 only	None	None	None	None	1981–9 1991 2004–5		None
Intermediate conflict	2002–3	None	None	1981–9 1992 1997–8 2003–4	None	None	1990 1993–2003	2008	None
Minor conflict	1990–1	None	None	1990–1	1981	1981 1983	None	1982	None
No conflict	1993–6	1980–1 1983–2008	1980–2008	1993–6	1980 1982–2007	1980–2 1984–2008	None	1980–1 1983–2007	1980–2008
'Riot-type conflict' (our classification, Bolivia and Indonesia only)			1980–5 1999–2006	1997–2002					

Sources: rows 1–4, series University of Gothenburg dataset on governance (www.qog.pol.gu.se) row 5, our own data series on riot-type conflict for Indonesia and Bolivia (at www.poverty.group.sheffield.ac.uk).
Notes: (1) No available data for Russia 1980–91.

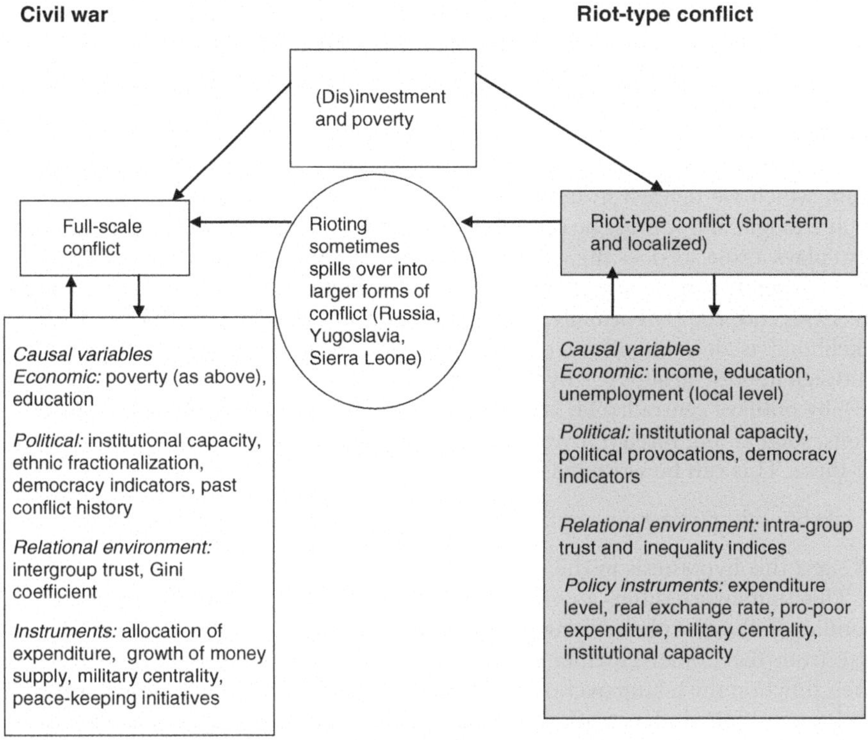

Figure 4.2 Interactions between conflict and causal variables.

is, by comparison with civil war, more short term,[7] more localized,[8] and reactive to an identifiable trigger or provocation rather than planned.[9]

In modelling riot-type conflict, we may take as a point of departure the well-known Collier and Hoeffler model (1998, 2004) of 'rational conflict' in which individuals take a decision on whether or not to rebel against the government, based on their perception of whether the costs exceed the benefits. The benefits consist of the greater power and higher standards of living which will be derived

[7] As the OECD report notes, Haggard et al. (1995, page 80) low-level conflicts 'over time become increasingly difficult to sustain because of the growing costs to participants'.

[8] Whereas with civil war it is the behaviour of *national-level* institutions for management and resolution of social tensions which is relevant to determining the outbreak and persistence of conflict, with riot-type violence it is the capacity and behaviour of those tension-managing institutions (police, courts, ombudsmen/civil rights officials, channels of communication with local government) at *local* level which are relevant. Hence, whereas civil wars often cover an entire country, episodes of rioting are typically confined to a few, mainly urban, locations, in many cases within one city only. Within Bolivia, as discussed in Chapter 10 below, this was typically the city of Cochabamba, or even more often the satellite city of El Alto above La Paz.

[9] This may, as in the case of the proposed income tax increases in February 2003, be a component of a reform programme, either internally instituted or planned with the support of the IMF or other external agency, but it is often something totally separate, as with the arrests of May 2005 in Addis Ababa, Ethiopia.

from subverting the government, which are greater the lower the individual's initial income and education and are higher the larger the tax base which can be taken over, weighted by the probability of success of revolt. The costs consist of the costs of coordinating the revolt and of income foregone if the revolt is unsuccessful.

Our own approach derives from the conditions for a 'trust/no conflict' equilibrium which we defined in Chapter 3 above. These are: the social wage must be high enough, and it must be equitably distributed.[10] The level of the private wage also plays a role, as does the willingness of the elite to negotiate and conciliate (as in the Argentinian *Mesa de Dialogo*) rather than fight (as in Indonesia and Bolivia in 1998 and 2003). Formally, our hypothesis for riot-type conflict is that its likelihood is determined by the level of social wage (W_s), by its distribution between interest-groups (c), by the distribution of income between interest groups (σ), by military centrality M, and by the possibility of external financial interventions, such as aid, foreign investment and IMF policy conditionality, affecting all of these. This can be written as:

$$\text{Likelihood of riot-type conflict} \longleftarrow W_s, c, M, \sigma, \text{external interventions} \qquad (4.1)$$

We test this hypothesis in the next section.

This framework differs in various ways from the Collier-Hoeffler approach to conflict. In the first place, we have eliminated the terms in tax ratio and population size from the Collier-Hoeffler model: riot-type actions typically do not have as their function the taking over of the apparatus of the state, but are localized events with more limited objectives, responding often to localized triggers, as we saw in the previous chapter. Second, we have included process indicators, including measures of the aggressiveness (military centrality) of the elite and the politicization of the opposition, in our explanation of violence.

Third, we have included new policy and institutional variables in the model, including the role of external financial agencies, which, as argued in the previous chapter, may through their influence on the social wage prevent riot-type conflict from escalating. We specify this mix W_s in three different forms:

1. If the incidence of expenditure is *relatively equal*, anger and resentment stemming from inequity are diminished, and the likelihood of conflict is reduced.[11]
2. If the incidence of expenditure is *relatively pro-poor*, there is a large number of beneficiaries, and possibly also an increased sense of fairness and

[10] In Chapter 3 we rendered the condition for the achievement of a trust equilibrium as:

$$(w_p + w_s \cdot c)_p + T_p[c(\sigma, M)]^* > [W_p + (w(s) \cdot c)_{p'}] + A_p \qquad (3.2a)$$

where w_p is the private wage, w_s is the social wage, c is the distribution of the social wage, A_p are the assets available to the private sector, and income distribution σ and military centrality M are likely to play a role in framing of the social contract.

[11] In our Bolivia case study (Chapter 10, see notes 16 and 17) the conflicts of 2003 arose not only because taxes were increased on the low-paid, but because the impositions took place in an environment in which inequality had been increased both by privatization and by tax exemptions granted to a number of the millionaires made rich by those privatizations.

communal rather than individual orientation among most people, conflict may be reduced on both counts.

3. If expenditure is orientated towards *urban groups*, which certainly in El Alto, Bolivia, were the most militant, that may reduce the likelihood of riot-type violence.

By analogy with the (private) efficiency wage principle of labour economics, which states that businesses can maximize their utility by increasing wages and thereby the stability and productivity of the labour force, we call the general approach of seeking political stability through variations in the social wage a *social efficiency wage* approach; adjustments in the social wage influence the stability and productivity of the state.

The transition from riot-type conflict to full-scale war

The other (left-hand) branch of the model of Figure 4.2 is the transition from riot-type conflict to full-scale war. Amongst our case-study countries, this transition was made only by Uganda, between 1981 and 1983 (persisting through to the end of the decade), by Russia, between 1994 and 1996 (intermitted in that year, reignited in 1999, and ending in 2000), and briefly by Indonesia (in East Timor in 2003–4, ending in the latter year). In all of these cases we observe a 'trial of strength'—an attempt by rebels to take advantage of state weakness, which the government was willing to escalate to the level of war rather than concede. In Uganda and Indonesia, victory went to the rebels, and in Russia, eventually to government after the war was scaled down between 1996 and 1999. In Bolivia, Zimbabwe, and Kenya, riot-type conflict continues but has not turned into war. It is clearly of importance to try and understand the difference between the minority of cases when conflict escalates into full-scale war and the majority when it does not. From the cases cited above it is not possible to infer a huge amount. It is thus worth examining other cases where an economic crisis-related dispute extended beyond rioting into full-scale war, such as Sierra Leone (with the transition to full-scale conflict taking place in the early 1980s, and the conflict lasting from the mid-1980s to the mid-1990s), Sri Lanka (with the transition to full-scale conflict again in the early 1980s, and the conflict lasting from the mid-1980s to the present), Yugoslavia (which drifted from riot-type conflict into war in the early 1990s) and Cote d'Ivoire (beginning in the late 1990s and again persisting to the present). In each of these hugely diverse cases, the following generalizations can be attempted:

1. Transition to war was more likely in cases where state weakness deteriorated (Sierra Leone, Cote d'Ivoire, former Yugoslavia), although there are contrary cases (Russia).
2. Transition to war was more likely in cases where there was a sudden downward revision of the standard of living, as in Russia in 1991–4, or in Yugoslavia in 1990, in which year the central bank cut the money supply by forty per cent; it is clear with hindsight that the break-up of the federation was hastened and embittered by this excessively rapid stabilization.
3. Transition to war was more likely if there was a broadening either of the range of localities covered by riot-type conflict for example from an urban to

a rural base, or a shift in modalities, for example from attacks purely on the government to attacks on civilians.

4. Transition to war was more likely if there was a military take-over.
5. Transition to war was more likely if there a severe deterioration of the income distribution during the period of riot-type conflict, especially a deterioration associated with an escalation of ethnic and religious discrimination.
6. *In principle*, transition to war can be halted by external mediation, which eventually occurred in Sierra Leone and the constituent republics of Yugoslavia. But this was after war had broken out. External mediation is almost always reactive rather than preventive.

Thus our 'transition to war' relationship is:

$$\text{Conflict 2} \longleftarrow (\Delta M, Y, G, MC, \text{Conflict 1}) \qquad (4.2)$$

where:
Conflict 2 = full-scale conflict ('war' or 'intermediate conflict' according to the classification of the PRIO index)
ΔM = change in the money supply – a proxy for speed of deflation
Y = income
G = Gini coefficient of inequality
MC = Military centrality—the share of military expenditure in total expenditure, blended with the willingness of the elite group to settle differences by discussion rather than by violence (see page 84 above).
Conflict 1 = riot-type conflict, as specified in (4.1) above

Several of these inflammatory factors already figure in the riot equation, but three: speed of deflation, possibilities for mediation, and locational spread, are new. Several variables treated by the literature as key causes of war, for example IMF loans,[12] do *not* figure as important causes of conflict in this specification. This is because we see their effect as essentially short term and location specific, and therefore to be included in the first stage of the model only.

In the following section, we report the results of tests carried out on the two branches of our conflict model. Results for the riot-type model only are in Table 4.3, drawing on an extended comparison between two of our case-study countries, Bolivia and Indonesia, and the transition to long-term conflict is modelled in Table 4.4. It will be remembered that the data on conflict short of war are fragile.

4.3 TESTS OF MODELS

For the reasons given in the previous section, we model conflict and its link with poverty in two parts, first of all considering factors determining the risks of riot-

[12] This is treated as a factor significantly associated with conflict, for example by Nafziger and Auvinen (2000), see note 10 above.

type conflict, and then broadening the discussion to include the likelihood that this will escalate into overall civil war.

Riot-type conflict: Bolivia and Indonesia

The comparative background to the outbreak of severe riot-type violence in Bolivia and Indonesia in the wake of the East Asian crisis is set out in Table 4.2. In essence, the economic structure, income level, degree of economic openness, underlying socio-political tensions, and many of the policy instruments deployed in the two economies were extremely similar, which makes interesting the question of why the outcome of the two crises was so different, with Indonesia escaping from crisis and from violence by 2001, but Bolivia remaining trapped in violence and political crisis from 1999 through to the present. Our major objective is to tease out what caused the differences in political violence to be so different between the two economies, in the hope that this may help contribute to the broader explanation of why some countries become trapped in a violence-poverty vicious circle whilst others escape.

However, in spite of these similarities in initial conditions and policies, the evolution of the two countries' political economies was, as Figure 4.3 shows, very different. In Indonesia the impact of the global crisis, which began at the end of 1997, was short and sharp: after two years of recession and big increases in poverty, output per capita was once again growing around its trend level of four per cent per annum by the millennium, and although riot-type violence persisted for a longer time, it was essentially over by 2001, three years after the crisis began. By contrast Bolivia experienced a later onset of global crisis, at the end of 1999, but unlike Indonesia has not been able to drag itself to date out of either recession or political violence. Only in 2004 did it begin to register positive per capita growth of real GNP, and this was at only about two per cent, in spite of the oil and gas boom. And political violence, which climaxed in 2003, has persisted through the following years, albeit on a diminishing trend, rather than dying out. Our major purpose is to understand why such similar initial conditions and stimuli produced such a differing response.

We estimate the reduced form for riot-type conflict as a variant of (4.1):

$$\mathrm{Prob(C)} = \mathrm{constant} + a_1\sigma + a_2\mathrm{M} + a_4\mathrm{c} + a_5\mathrm{RER} + \mathrm{controls} \qquad (4.1')$$

where M (military centrality), c (intersectoral allocation of public expenditure), and σ (Gini coefficient of income inequality) are defined as in (4.1′) above, both by ordinary least squares and as a simultaneous two-way relationship. The results are given in Table 4.3.

We find that an increase in poverty and inequality positively contribute to political violence, although only the inequality is statistically significant at conventional levels. Higher military centrality (an increase in the military to total expenditure ratio) also is conducive to political violence. Finally, the coefficients on trust in the government (in Bolivia), and our measure of the social efficiency wage (pro-poor spending) are negative and significant, suggesting that these factors reduce political violence.

Table 4.2 Bolivia and Indonesia: descriptives

	Bolivia	Indonesia
Initial conditions:		
Demographics and geography	Population *c.*10 m, landlocked	Population > 150 m, archipelago of 7,000 islands
Per capita income	Lower-middle income (*c.*$1000)	Lower-middle income (*c.*$1000)
Economic structure	Oil and gas–based economy	Oil and gas-based economy
Political structure	Formally democratic since 1985	Formally democratic since 1970s
Social tensions	Between Aymara/Quechua majority and Spanish-speaking, light-skinned minority	Between ethnic Indonesians and ethnic Chinese
	Separatist tendencies: rich light-skinned Europeans in oil/gas and rich farming regions in east of country seeking to escape from La Paz government in poor west of country (referendum, May/2008, confirmed majority desire to do this among easterners)	Separatist tendencies: very poor East Timorese seeking to break away from Indonesian Republic (now independent, as of 2005?)
Flash-point to be examined:	Riots, February and October 2003 (*c.*100 deaths)	Riots, 1998–2001 (over 2000 deaths nationwide)
Institutions and policy:	Strong microfinance institutions (mainly NGO based)	Strong microfinance institutions, (mainly state-based until early 2000s) Unlike Bolivia, strong micro-saving as well as micro-lending institutions (BRI alone had > 30 million savers in 2007)
Financial sector	No programme of rural-based investment comparable to that in Indonesia, but strong investment in health and education under donor impetus	Heavy investment in agriculture-associated sectors (rural infrastructure, agricultural inputs, research, credit and extension, agro-industry) since 1970s
Public expenditure	1. Blatant tax evasions by 'fat cats' beneficiaries of oil/gas/utility privatizations	Absence of compromise and shared sacrifice; reluctance by President Suharto to relinquish power in 1998; lack of voice mechanisms; scapegoating of ethnic Chinese community
Crisis management	2. Dismissal of *Defensora del Pueblo* (ombudsman) September 2003	Historically (since 1970s) poverty falling rapidly; short crisis 1998–9, during which poverty doubled; since then, violence has dwindled and the momentum of poverty resumed
Dynamics of crisis and of poverty	3. President Sanchez de Losada, by 2003, exhausted and unable to be decisive; the decision-taking vacuum was occupied by a trigger-happy Defence Minister (Carlos Sanchez Berzain) 4. During crisis, media silenced. Catholic Church revealed true scale of violence and deaths in covert broadcasts Historically (1985 to end 1990s) poverty falling very slowly, more quickly since 2006; GDP/capita negative 1999–2003, recovering since then; persisting violence 2000 to date; poverty level over those years static to slightly increasing	

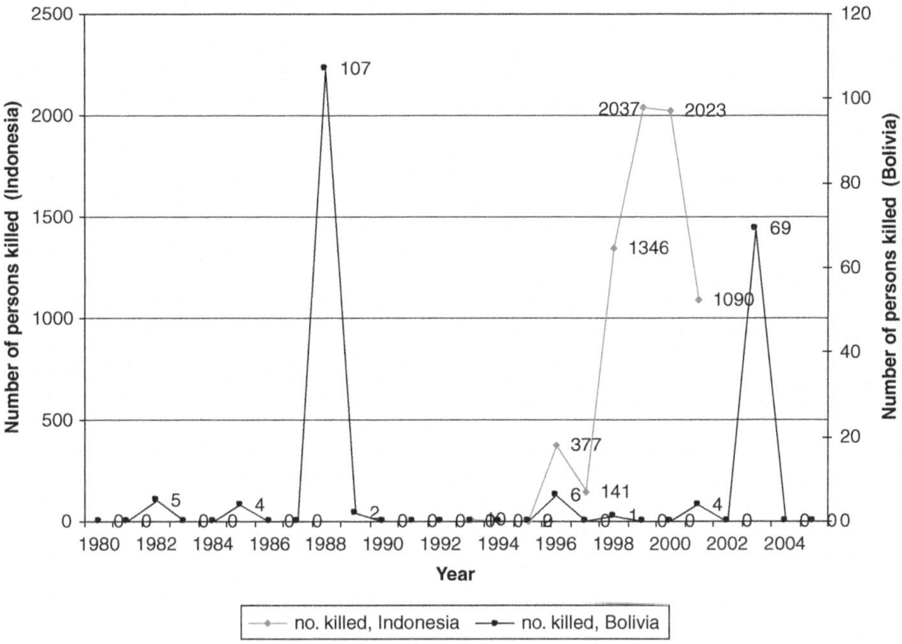

Figure 4.3 (a) Bolivia and Indonesia: time series of political violence, 1980–2007: numbers killed.

The transition from riot-type violence to war

For overall conflict risk, we first estimate the model of transition from riot-type conflict to war (4), using now our full data set of 61 countries, encompassing the Bolivia and Indonesia cases. The estimations are set out in Table 4.4. We experiment with two indicators of the dependent variable, overall vulnerability to conflict—the PRIO index and the ICRG government stability index—and with three formulations of the social efficiency wage: expenditure for the benefit of urban groups, educational expenditure and pro-poor expenditure. The first equation of Table 4.4 indicates a significant (at the ten per cent level) impact of riot-type conflict on full-scale violence, and equations 2 through 4 suggest that, amongst the indicators of the social wage that we have examined, pro-poor expenditure is the best predictor of the social efficiency wage. We therefore, in the final column of the table, incorporate this indicator of the social efficiency wage in a composite conflict model in which conflict, investment, and poverty (measured as infant mortality) are simultaneously determined.[13] The social

[13] Table 4.4 presents only the results in which political violence is the dependent variable. For a full statement of impacts on investment and poverty, see Chapter 5, Table 5.4 below.

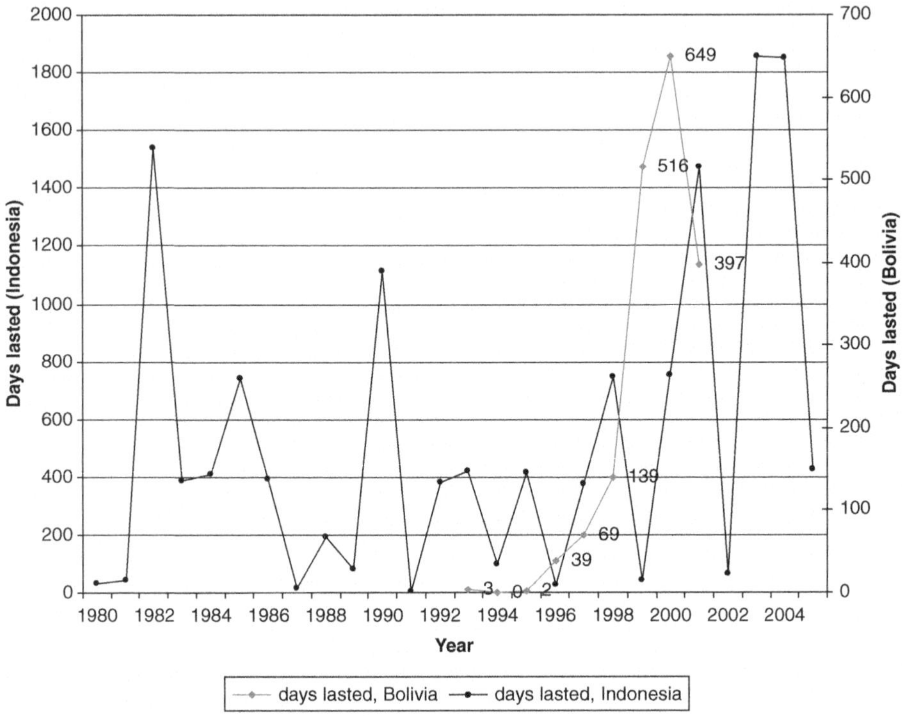

(b) Bolivia and Indonesia: duration of riot-type conflict.

efficiency wage and Gini coefficient measure of inequality emerge as significant predictors of political (in)stability.

4.4 CONCLUSIONS AND POLICY IMPLICATIONS

From this discussion we observe that civil violence is, indeed, a key determinant of poverty. However, on the evidence presented here we believe that the analysis of such violence needs to start further back in the chain of causation than by looking at the full-scale civil war typically examined by the literature. What we call 'riot-type violence', typically confined to shorter time periods and more localized regions than full-scale civil war, may provide an 'amber light' or early-warning indicator of civil war, which if responded to appropriately may be able to prevent the full-scale version from occurring.

However, this requires a different modelling procedure from that applied to civil war, because the causes of riot-type conflict are different. It is shorter term, more localized, more reactive rather than initiatory in nature, and much more than civil war it is a reflection of short-term political variables, in particular the credibility of government and the politicization of the opposition.

Table 4.3 Empirical results: riot-type conflict.

Dependent variable: numbers killed in riot-type conflict, 1990:1 through 2006:IV. Estimation method: OLS

Sample regression coefficients on independent variables	Pooled data, Bolivia and Indonesia	Bolivia only
Constant	825.5**	528.5**
	(5.59)	(7.37)
Headcount poverty	0.16	−3.05**
	(0.10)	(2.67)
Gini coefficient of inequality	−9.18**	
	(2.57)	
Pro-poor expenditure	−32.5**	−8.02*
	(5.22)	(2.03)
Military expenditure	−0.25	26.89**
	(0.05)	(4.76)
Foreign investment	−5.65	
	(0.74)	
P	0.0000	0.0000
'R^2'	0.42	0.32
Observations	100	50

Sources: Deaths in riot-type conflict: Bolivia—own estimations; Indonesia[a], Tadjoeddin (2002).

[a] These are daily data covering the period from January 1979 to June 2006. They are available on an Excel file from p.mosley@sheffield.ac.uk or from chiripanhura@yahoo.co.uk, and can also be downloaded from http://www.poverty.group.shef.ac.uk. We collected data on the following variables: strikes and other industrial disturbances, roadblocks, street demonstrations, and coups d'état. These events are analysed by duration, region, and industrial sector and collected from the following newspapers: *Presencia, El Diario, Hoy, El Mundo, Ultima Hora, La Razon, Los Tiempos.*

Pro-poor expenditure: IMF, *Government Expenditure Statistics Yearbook.*

Military centrality: weighted average of share of military expenditure in budget (from IMF, *Government Expenditure Statistics Yearbook*) and military regime dummy (from Quality of Government database, www.qog.pol.gu.se).

Gini coefficient of inequality, headcount poverty and foreign investment: from World Bank, *World Development Indicators.*

We therefore visualize the transition from peace to war as occurring through two discrete steps—from peace to riot-type conflict, and from riot-type conflict to war. We simulate the first step through the use of a game-theory model in which the likelihood of conflict can be influenced by policy instruments including the level and distribution of public expenditure. In the empirical estimations of the reduced form of this model, indicators of the politicization of the opposition, of the public's mistrust of government, and of local-level, as well as national-level, indicators of unemployment and inequality, emerge as significantly related to the likelihood of violence of this type.

In our examination of the second step, from riot-type to full-scale conflict, we observe that a number of causal factors condition the transition from riot-type conflict to war, in particular the level of macro-economic stability, the quality of governance, and the 'social wage' (the level and composition of public expenditure). We visualize the government as being able to send signals through the social wage which are capable of either inflaming or damping down conflict, and observe that the pro-poor expenditure measure of the social wage is positively correlated with political stability.

Table 4.4 Empirical results: transition from riot-type to full-scale conflict.

Dependent variable	(1) Transition from riot-type conflict to full-scale conflict	(2) ICRG Political instability indicator			
Estimation method	Single-equation probit	3SLS (political violence equation only)			
Independent variables					
Constant	−2.73	−0.74*	4.01	−0.87**	−0.87
	(1.53)	(2.00)	(1.51)	(2.94)	(1.51)
Indicator of riot-type	1.43*				
conflict (conflict 1)		(1.82)			
Social efficiency wage indicator 1: urban social spending		0.056*			
		(1.95)			
Social efficiency wage indicator 2: social expenditure (2)			0.13**		
			(3.38)		
Social efficiency wage indicator 3: 'pro-poor expenditure index'	−0.008			−0.15**	−0.14**
	(0.15)			(4.79)	(4.56)
Military centrality	0.065*				
	(2.19)				
(log) Foreign investment (percentage of GDP)			0.03*		0.029
			(2.43)		(1.49)
(log) exports			0.11		
			(1.71)		
Conflict 1	1.43				
	(1.82)				
ICRG quality of government indicator	−2.43				
	(1.58)				
Gini coefficient of inequality	0.02	−0.024*	−0.16		−0.031**
	(0.61)	(4.00)	(0.87)		(4.08)
Rule of law indicator				0.38	
				(1.57)	
Corruption index (Transparency International)		0.29*		0.18	0.17
		(3.46)		(1.83)	(1.83)
Inflation rate		−0.009	−0.008	−0.004	−.008
		(1.68)	(0.75)	(0.67)	(1.33)
Number of observations	261	145	145	145	61
Diagnostic tests					
'R^2'	0.24	0.45	0.32	0.45	0.11
P	0.0338	0.0000	0.0000	0.0000	0.0000

Variables and sources

Military centrality = share of military in total expenditure, from IMF *Government Expenditure Statistics Yearbook.* Weighted by dummy variable taking the value 1 if government is under military control, 0 otherwise.

Conflict 1 = dummy transition variable from no conflict (PRIO indicator value 0) to riot-type conflict (PRIO indicator value 1), data from PRIO indicator.

Conflict 2 = dummy transition variable from riot-type conflict (PRIO indicator 1) to full-scale conflict (PRIO indicator value 2 or 3), takes the value 1 in periods when there is a transition from riot-type to full-scale conflict and 0 at other times.

Social efficiency wage indicator (1): 'urban social spending', defined as (housing expenditure/GDP) plus (social protection/GDP) plus (education/GDP).

Social efficiency wage indicator (2) defined as (educational expenditure/GDP) *less* (military expenditure/GDP).

Social efficiency wage indicator (3) = 'pro-poor expenditure': (educational expenditure/GDP) *plus* (health expenditure/GDP) *plus* (agricultural expenditure/GDP) *less* (military expenditure/GDP), from IMF *Government Expenditure Statistics Yearbook.*

icrg_qog = ICRG quality of government index.

All data for sixty-one countries from 1980–2007, mostly from World Bank *World Development Indicators* dataset with additions as specified, available from http://poverty.group.shef.ac.uk.

Three fairly firm implications appear to emerge from these results, and one highly tentative one. First, in order to understand war it would appear essential to understand riot-type violence also. If the root causes of violence reside in local-level rather than national-level variables, for example the levels of unemployment and inequality in El Alto, Bolivia, rather than nationally, then it is in local-level rather than national-level policy action and media presentation that a possible resolution to short-term political violence of this sort resides.

Second, economic variables on their own are unable to explain transitions from peace to either riot-type violence or war, and political variables such as military centrality and lack of trust in government are also needed. Measures of politicization and trust, not just objective measures of economic deprivation or affluence, are relevant to the explanation of violence of this type. So also are measures of government proactivity, and the manner in which it and the opposition are represented in the media: what matters is not only how great inequality (for example) is, but what if anything government is perceived as trying to do to mitigate it.

Third, slow and gradual transitions towards viability, and consequently larger IMF support packages, may be more rational than quick transitions to equilibrium if the long-term losses associated with violence caused by over-severe 'quick fixes' are factored in.

Fourth, and highly tentative, there may be a time trend at work due to democratization. Perhaps governments who for a long time got away with ignoring the wishes of the underprivileged can no longer get away with it, and possibly policy may be adapting to this, with pro-poor results.

5

Pro-poor fiscal strategies

5.1 INTRODUCTION

The politics of reducing poverty has both a short-term and a longer-term dimension. In the short term, if the elite makes coalitions with pro-poor elements, and manages the instruments of macro-adjustment in a manner which minimizes the likelihood of conflict, that will reduce deprivation and vulnerability in the near term and in particular the poverty of the 'new poor' who have lost jobs and livelihoods as a consequence of a global slump. However, the time-horizon over which macro-economic downturns last is typically quite short—in most of the cases examined in Chapters 3 and 4, it was between one and five years, although in some cases such as Russia and Bolivia the recession lasted for a longer period. The alliances and policies required to achieve exit from recession may be sustained over the long term, or they may not. But countries which have taken their populations right out of poverty, whether we look at Japan in the late nineteenth and early twentieth century, or Chile, Indonesia, and much of East Asia in the second half of the twentieth century, have needed much more than short-term alliances and policy instruments to do this. They have also needed the kind of policies which will sustain the development process over the planning horizon of a generation and more, and they have needed institutional structures to back that up. In the next two chapters we explore what those policies and institutions might be.

First, let us examine the data on long-run poverty reduction between 1990 and the present. As we can see from comparison of Table 5.1 and Figure 5.1, the countries which have been effective at reducing poverty over the long term are rather different from those which have achieved this over the short period of the 'East Asian' crisis. Within our twenty-year time perspective, the most successful countries at reducing poverty are, within our sample, Uganda and Indonesia, and in a global perspective, almost exclusively in South-East Asia and parts of South Asia, with Chile as an important outlier in Latin America, and Uganda and Ghana in Africa. The recent anti-poverty successes achieved by Argentina, and *a fortiori* Russia appear much more minor in long-term perspective; in fact, all the impressive growth achieved over the period from 2000 to date in Russia has not prevented poverty from showing a net rise over the entire period since 1990. By contrast Bolivia, which had a very 'bad crisis', can be credited with considerable achievements in the 1990s which, although heavily damped by the sustained crisis of the early 2000s, still leave the country with a lower poverty level than it had in 1990.

Table 5.1 Case-study countries: long-term poverty dynamics (1990–2005) in relation to growth performance.

Country	Period	(1) Growth rate of real GDP (% pa)	(2) Poverty reduction (% pa)	(3) = [log(2)/log(1)] 'Growth elasticity of poverty'
Global average	1990–2006	3.2	−2.0	−2.4
Case-study countries: Asia				
Indonesia	1993–2002	5.4	−2.5	−0.4
Malaysia	1988–2005	5.8	−2.4	−0.3
Russian	1988–2009	1.0	0.2	0.2
Federation	1992–2009	0.8	−3.0	−0.5
Latin America				
Argentina	1990–2005	2.9	−0.3	−0.2
Bolivia	1990–2006	2.2	−0.2	−0.1
Africa				
Uganda	1989–2006	5.5	−4.2	−0.8
Ghana	1992–2005	4.0	−3.8	−0.3
Kenya	1991–9	3.2	1.0	0.3
Zimbabwe	1988–2005	−0.5	1.2	2.5

Sources: Indonesia, Uganda, Ghana: Besley and Cord (2007), Table 1.2.
For Russia, see Table 12.4 below; for Bolivia: Table 10.2 below; other estimates are from *World Bank World Development Indicators*. Global poverty elasticity estimate of -2.4 is from World Bank, *World Development Report 2006*, Figure 4.3, page 85.
Notes: (2) a + sign in this column denotes an increase in headcount poverty; a − sign denotes a reduction.

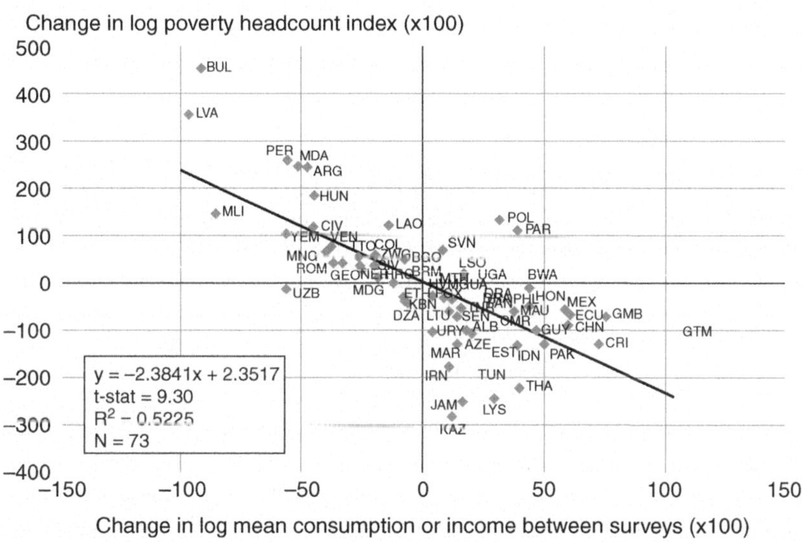

Figure 5.1(a) Long-term poverty and growth scatters: World Bank vs. our own observations. World Bank (various periods between 1990 and 2005).

Source: International Bank for Reconstruction and Development/The World Bank: *World Development Report 2006.*

Source: author's calculations.

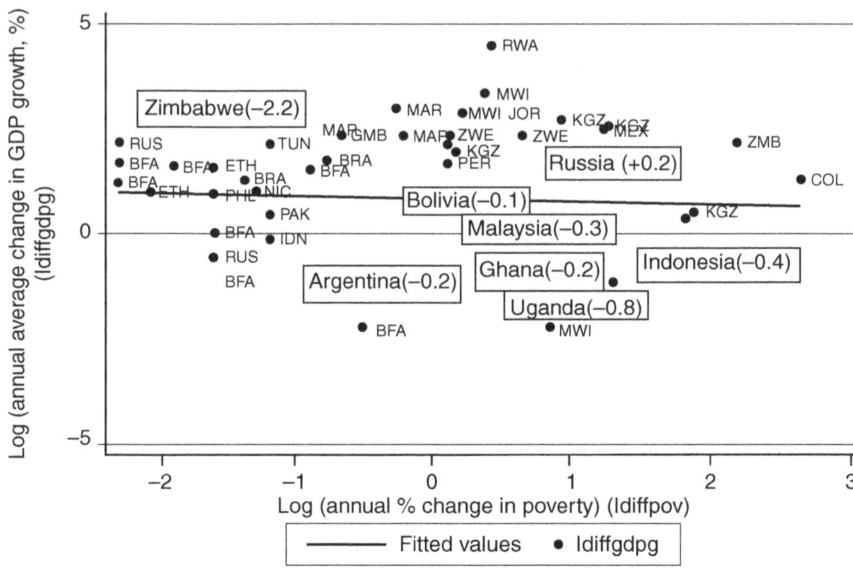

(b) Long-term poverty and growth scatters: our calculations (20-year period 1987–2007, or nearest equivalent).

Regression: log (annual per cent change in poverty) = 6.15** (3.11) – 0.04 (0.53) log (annual growth in GDP), $r^2 = 0.03$, n = 90. OLS estimation.

Source: project database (accessible at www.poverty.group.shef.ac.uk), using World Bank, *World Development Indicators*.

Note: figures in frames are estimated 'poverty elasticities' (ratios of annual log change in poverty to log change in income) for the countries in our sample.

We now examine the long-term poverty dynamics of our case-study countries. Their initial historical conditions are important: all of them except Russia were once colonies, and the manner in which they were colonized is significant for subsequent poverty reduction potential. Argentina, Bolivia, Zimbabwe, and Kenya began at a disadvantage, since large areas of these countries were settled by nationals of the colonial power for the purpose of either commercial agriculture or the extraction of minerals—they became, and remained after decolonization, *settler economies* in which the export economy was driven by a capital-intensive production process only capable of generating limited numbers of income opportunities even during periods of growth. By contrast Indonesia, Malaysia, Ghana, and Uganda did not allow settlement of land by nationals of the colonial power: land settlement was done by the indigenous people, who developed them as *peasant export economies*, producing an export staple: rubber and palm-oil in Malaysia; coffee, spices, and rice in Indonesia; coffee and cotton in Uganda; cocoa in Ghana—principally by labour-intensive, smallholder production methods. The poverty reduction potential of the peasant export model was inherently greater than that of the settler model, because it was more labour-intensive and thereby generated a more equal income distribution. Some countries in both groups managed a measure of industrialization from the inter-war period onwards, but this took on the characteristics of the parent economy. Argentina's was capital-intensive, and by the 1990s associated with growing unemployment and inequality, whereas Malaysia's and Indonesia's were labour intensive, and had by between the 1960s and the 1990s brought down headcount poverty from over half the population to less than ten per cent.

What are the long-term forces which determine poverty? Let us look once again at the countries which we examined in Chapter 3, with an emphasis on the 'long-term poverty reduction stars'—Indonesia, Malaysia, and Uganda, the only countries in our sample to have halved poverty in twenty-five years. What political factors enabled them to do this? Our argument over the next two chapters is that the things which really matter are the stepping stones summarized in Chapter 3: the ability to sustain *alliances with the poor*; political *stability*, which then begets stability in developmental orientation, as analysed in the previous chapter; the achievement of pro-poor *expenditure patterns*, and the ability to support these with an adequate *tax base*; the performance of *institutions* in the public, private, and NGO sectors; and the specific impact of *international institutions* on all of these.

5.2 CORRELATES OF LONG-TERM POVERTY REDUCTION

In developing countries the distribution of assets is likely to be particularly clustered among *elites*, asset-holding groups who also have power to control the allocation of resources. As we argued in Chapter 3, it is unusual for elites to be able to govern on their own: they need the support of others. How likely is it that these groups will include low-income people, or that the benefits of growth will spin off on to them? We now discuss in more detail the five facilitating influences in Chapter 3, which may help to answer this question.

The scope for forging alliances with the poor

As emphasized at the beginning,[1] poor people are neither well represented within conventional political structures, nor are they typically a cohesive group disposed to work together for a common cause. And yet they can achieve a pro-poor reallocation of resources if the state needs them, in particular if there are splits within the elite. These splits may take the form of a pro-poor coup, as in Uganda in 1986, discussed below.[2] But a much commoner model is that of Indonesia in 2000, Argentina in 2003, and Bolivia in 2006, in all of which, as we saw in Chapter 3, the approach of confronting an opposition in which pro-poor groups were strong was eventually replaced, under crisis conditions, by the approach of conciliating them.

[1] See quotation from Haggard et al. (1995) Chapter 1 above, page 10.

[2] This process and its distributional consequences are examined in detail later in this chapter and in Chapter 13 below.

Actions in support of the poor do not need to originate in an explicit agreement or alliance. They may, rather, originate from the elite's fear of what the poor may do if not appeased. In Indonesia and Malaysia in the 1960s, under the stress of large-scale political disturbances, riots triggered by periodic unpredictable increases in the price of rice and threats of a possible communist takeover, the governments of those countries took the decision to invest directly in packages of green revolution inputs—irrigation, credit, extension and fertilizer—for the benefit of small farmers, the consequence of which was a broad-based increase in food productivity through the following two decades, which took the level of poverty in Indonesia 'from nearly eighty per cent in 1960 to barely an eighth of that level thirty years later' (Timmer, in Besley and Cord 2007, page 43; see further, Chapter 11 below). These investments in green revolution technology were not worked out in collaboration with any low-income group, they were motivated by fear of insurrection much more than by affection or even understanding for the poor, and yet they were hugely to their benefit. The same could be said, with reservations, of the injections of subsidy into outlying areas of the Russian Federation during the late 1990s and early 2000s (Chapter 12, Figure 12.7), which were generally far above the average in regions which had experienced civil unrest around the time of the breakup of the Soviet Union—famously Chechnya, but also Yakutia, Khakassia, Komi, Dagestan, and Ingushetia. Like the countries of South-East Asia they illustrate the proposition that pro-poor actions do not always result from an explicit alliance with poor people and may take the form of an implicit attempt to insure against possible rebellion by them.

Thus, the triggers for pro-poor action may be various, but to sustain themselves they require complementary actions. The most important of these is a sustained depreciation of the real exchange rate, because if adjustment is attempted through devaluation there are many low-income gainers, typically people working in export-based industries, whereas in the case of other instruments of macro-adjustment there are few or none that are not distortive. Undervaluation of the real exchange rate, indeed, is one of the most potent tools for stimulating economic growth and generating long-term poverty reduction (Rodrik 2006). The other crucial complementary actions are fiscal—an adequate and stable programme of expenditure in support of poor people, and a tax regime which enables this expenditure to be financed, and it is on the scope for pro-poor fiscal action that the argument of this chapter is focused.

Political stability

On the evidence of our country sample, stability in policy, if not in government itself, is extremely important in long-term poverty reduction. In three of the four countries within our sample which managed to halve poverty in twenty-five years[3]—Indonesia,

[3] Almost. Uganda reduced headcount poverty from fifty-six per cent to thirty-one per cent between 1990 and 2006 (see Chapter 13 below). Indonesia reduced poverty from sixty per cent to eighteen per cent between 1965 and 1990 (World Bank 1990, Chapter 1, page 1), and Malaysia reduced poverty from thirty-five per cent to under ten per cent over the same period. Long-term poverty dynamics for the other countries in our sample are specified in Table 5.2.

Malaysia, Uganda, and Ghana—the ruling party was the same over that quarter of a century, and in Indonesia and Uganda the President was the same over that period. These elements of stability were valuable in enabling government to sustain consistent long-term expenditure plans, such as the rural development programmes which sustained the pro-poor momentum of the Asian green revolutions, and also programmes of long-term investment in education and infrastructure.

The sustainability of labour-intensive, pro-poor expenditure patterns

As we saw in Chapter 3, the countries afflicted by the East Asian crisis developed very different approaches to making their escape from it and protecting against the fragility it had exposed. In some cases, especially in Latin America, as discussed for the cases of Argentina, Brazil, Venezuela, and Uruguay in Grugel and Riggirozzi (2009a), but also Russia, the exit strategy from crisis was to entail a long-term expansion of governmental scope, labelled in Russia *derzhavnichestvo*, defensive reassertion of state power. In all of these countries, the state found itself more vulnerable to capital market volatility than it could ever have foreseen, to the point, in Russia in the mid-1990s, of reaching the borders of state collapse, with rebellions against federal authority in sixteen of the eighty-nine regions, and large-scale capital flight[4] which necessitated large-scale loans from the IMF and World Bank through the 1990s. Exit from crisis, in these cases, was planned not as a short-term reactive process, but as a long-term strategy to reassert and expand the influence of the state and reduce its dependence on the outside world in general and towards the Washington institutions in particular. Various instruments were deployed in support of this long-term project: in Russia, a recentralization of the governmental process, in Argentina, Bolivia and a number of Latin American countries, an appeal to old-style 'developmentalism' (i.e. protectionism in support of import-substituting industrialization) and in many middle-income countries, a not very covert abandonment of the ideals of the 'Washington Consensus', with export taxation and price controls, as well as capital controls, all making a return as elements of the arsenal of anti-crisis defences (see Chapters 9 and 12 below). But protectionism was by no means the only game in town, and the rapid fall in poverty in Uganda in the 1990s is mainly caused by the liberalization of export agriculture, as illustrated in Chapter 13 below.

In the context of expenditure policies, what was key to the pro-poor outcome was not only the size but the intersectoral allocation of public expenditure. As we argued in Chapter 3, labour-intensity is one key element in this, because the poor depend on low-wage employment. In addition, the allocation of public expenditure may be important both in directly determining the poverty outcome, and also in sending a signal concerning the equity with which the government intends to arbitrate between different interests. This may, as our case studies illustrate,[5]

[4] 'Russia, although one of the poorest industrialized countries, exported more than $150 billion of capital since it launched its reform in 1992 (until 2000) and has attracted less foreign investment per capita than its more advanced neighbours' (Stone 2002) page 164.

[5] See especially the studies of Argentina (Chapter 9), Bolivia (Chapter 10), and Indonesia (Chapter 11).

Table 5.2 Case-study countries: possible political determinants of long-term poverty orientation.

	Well-being indicators		Possible political causes							
	(1) Poverty headcount, evolution 1990–2009	(2) Gini coeffiecient of inequality, 1990–2009	(3) Scope for forging alliances with the poor	(4) Evolution of PPE ratio 1990–2007 (%)	(5) Evolution of tax ratio and tax politics 1990–2007	(6) Governance indicators: Democratic transitions	Polity index	Fairness initiatives	(7) Pro-poor institutions (PPI) index	(8) External influences
						1 Democratic transitions	2 Political stability: Polity index average 1990–2008 (start value and end value in parentheses)	3 Fairness measures/ initiatives		Average share of aid in GDP 1980–2008 (%; starting value and end value in parentheses)
Indonesia	Fell from 18% (1987) to 12% (2006) (but with increase to 24% in 1997–8)	Rose from 33% (1987) to 39% (2005)	Background—successful history of pro-poor, pro-smallholder growth 1970–mid-1990s Short-term response to crisis 1997–2001, retrenchment and accelerated exchange rate depreciation, accompanied by scapegoating of Chinese ethnic minority. Long-term response—	Big increases in 70s and 80s; in period specified, rose from 1.3 to 2.9	Fell from 16.9% to 12.3%	1999–2001, transition from dictatorship to democracy	−2 (−7, +8)	Numerous decentratlization and democratization initiatives post-1999; see Chapter 11	Increased from 0.6 (1996) to 2.3 (2005)	1.09 (1.26, 0.033)

			democratization, partnerships with a range of ethnic groups, and decentralization via Kecamatan Development Programme.							
Malaysia	Fell from 15% (1989) to < 10% (2006)	Stable: 47% (1987), 49% (1997)	Short-term response: controls on capital outflows (in the context of low inequality, further brought down by labour market discrimination in favour of bumiputras). Long-term response: alliances with small-scale private business.	n/a	n/a	Same ruling party 1970s to present	+5 (+4, +8)	See Chapter 11	Increased from 1.2 (96) to 2.1 (05)	0.38 (0.56, 0.25)
Uganda	Fell from 54% (1990) to 31% (2006)	Stable: 44% (1988), 46% (2002)	Short-term (1986–94) rural smallholder interests came to dominate the government after victory in a guerrilla war 1981–6, which	Rose from 7% to 15.3%	Rose from 5% to 12%	End of guerrilla war 1985; same president 1986–2009; shift from single-party to multi-party system, 2006	−4 (−7, −2)	Constitutional Commission appointeed 1992	Increased from 0.1 (96) to 0.2 (05)	12.1 (9.1, 14.8)

Continued

Table 5.2 Continued

	Well-being indicators		**Possible political causes**							
	(1) Poverty headcount, evolution 1990–2009	(2) Gini coeffiecient of inequality, 1990–2009	(3) Scope for forging alliances with the poor	(4) Evolution of PPE ratio 1990–2007 (%)	(5) Evolution of tax ratio and tax politics 1990–2007	(6) Governance indicators: Democratic transitions	Polity index	Fairness initiatives	(7) Pro-poor institutions (PPI) index	(8) External influences
			overturned a northern elite in favour of a central/south-western rural alliance. Broad-based support pursued through 'geographical equity', with cabinet posts also to east and north. Limited reliance on market mechanisms. Longer-term (1994–): prioritization of pro-poor expenditures (1994), liberalization of coffee and cotton (mid to late 1990s), increasing involvement of NGOs and private sector, including in new agricultural policy (early 2000s).							

Argentina	'Extreme poor' (indigentes) rose from *c*.10%–15% in 1990 to 27% in 2002, then declined to 12.2% by 2009	Rose from 44% (1986) to 52% (2004)	Short-term (2001–3): exchange rate liberalization, and establishment of a broad-based discussion forum (Mesa de Dialogo), from which emerged alliances with unemployed people and NGOs. Medium-term (2003 onward): broadening of state expenditure, some of it financed by heterodox methods (e.g. export taxes), offering support to low-income consumers e.g. through price controls.	Rose from 8 to 15%	Rose from 9 to 14.3%	Constitutional democracy since 1980s; unstable 2001–03 (four presidents in three years)	+7 (+7, +8)	Establishment of Mesa de Dialogo (see this chapter and Chapter 9)	Increased from 2.4 (96) to 2.3 (05)	0.07 (0.03, 0.06)
Bolivia	Rose slightly from 60% (1990s average) to 65% (2001), then fell to 62% by 2009;	Rose from 51% (1986) to 58% (2002)	Before 2003, no alliances between elite and Aymara-Quechua majority Short-term (2003–5): referendum on oil/gas	Gradual increase in share of health and education, and reduction of military expenditure, after mid-	Rose from 8% to 17%	Constitutional democracy from 1985; elections at four-year intervals 1985–99, but unstable thereafter	+7 (+8, +6)	Asemblea Constitucional, established in 2006, seeks to reform legislative and judicial process so as to achieve equity	Increased from 1.1 (96) to 1.2 (05)	8.8 (5.2, 9.2)

Continued

Table 5.2 Continued

	Well-being indicators		Possible political causes							
	(1) Poverty headcount, evolution 1990–2009	(2) Gini coeffiecient of inequality, 1990–2009	(3) Scope for forging alliances with the poor	(4) Evolution of PPE ratio 1990–2007 (%)	(5) Evolution of tax ratio and tax politics 1990–2007	(6) Governance indicators: Democratic transitions	Polity index	Fairness initiatives	(7) Pro-poor institutions (PPI) index	(8) External influences
	extreme poor fell more sharply, from 45% to 31%		renationalization, constitutional assembly aimed at establishing equity within judicial system, anti-corruption measures. Longer-term (2006–9):quasi-renationalization of hydrocarbons industry; constitutional assembly.	1990s. PPE index rises from 5% (1990) to 12.4% (2007).		(six presidents in six years 1999–2005) Severe riot-type violence (> 100 civilian deaths) 1999–2005.		between ethnicities and regions		
Russia	Rose from 10% (1987) to 29% (2000) then fell to 16% (2009)	Rose from 26% (1991) to 42% (2009)	Short-term 1991–9: privatization and decentralization with foreign aid support. War in Chechnya terminated, 1996–9. Long-term after 1999, recentralization of	Rose from 10.9% to 11.2%	n/a	Presidential and Duma elections at four-year intervals since 1992. Political instability in Caucasus and other dissident regions particularly	+3 (0, +6)	Soviet Union dissolved and Russian federal constitution and parliament inaugurated, 1992. Powers of provincial governments subordinated to those of central	Declined from 1.2 (96) to 1.1 (05)	0.39 (0.04, 0.22) Maximum 1.03 (1994)

			power; renewal of war in Chechnya; increased state subsidies to fragile or rebellious regions.			severe 1992–95 and 1998–99 (war in Chechnya in those periods; Duma stormed 1993).		administration, 1999.		
Ghana	Fell from 51% (1988) to 27% (2005)	Rose from 35% (1988) to 44% (1999) Cocoa privatization and exchange rate depreciation (logically should benefit all in sector, in practice farm workers only); compensation for retrenched urban workers under PAMSCAD; Longer term—some reorientation to urban interests under NPP after 2000.	Short-term 1983–1992: PNDC government, with strong orientation towards cocoa regions and low-income consumers.	Increased from 5% to 6.6%	Rose from 11.4% to 23%	Regular presidential and parliamentary elections since 1992.	1.4 (−7, +8)		Increased from 1.0 (96) to 1.3 (05)	9.1 (4.3, 7.7)

Continued

Table 5.2 Continued

	Well-being indicators		Possible political causes							
	(1) Poverty headcount, evolution 1990–2009	(2) Gini coeffiecient of inequality, 1990–2009	(3) Scope for forging alliances with the poor	(4) Evolution of PPE ratio 1990–2007 (%)	(5) Evolution of tax ratio and tax politics 1990–2007	(6) Governance indicators: Democratic transitions	Polity index	Fairness initiatives	(7) Pro-poor institutions (PPI) index	(8) External influences
Kenya	Rose from 42% (1991) to 52% (1997); no data for 2000s	44% (1995), 42% (1997)	Some movement towards a more pro-poor allocation of resources under Rainbow Alliance government (see right).	Rose from 6.6% to 13.2%	Rose from 17% to 18%	Until 1992, oligarchic system, biased towards western tribal groups. Since 2002, moves towards freer elections and against corruption under new 'Rainbow Alliance', but severe political violence after disputed 2008 election.	−1.5 (−7, +8)	Since 2008, power-sharing between principal government and principal opposition party.	Increased from 1.0 (96) to 1.6 (05)	7.1 (5.6, 4.7)
Zimbabwe	Rose from 26% (1991) to *c.*60% (2006)	Fell from 56% (1991) to 50% (1995)	Short-term (see Chapter 3): smallholders in communal areas, especially veterans of guerrilla war of	4.9% (1990), trend after late 1990s not clear	Increased from 24% (1990) to 26% (1997)	Constitutional democracy with regular elections. Severe political violence at	−3.5 (−6, +1)	Since 2009, power-sharing between President Mugabe and Prime Minister Tsangvirai.	Declined from 1.8 (96) to 1.6 (05)	2.5 (2.4, 0.6). Maximum 12.2% in 1992.

1970s, buttressed by price controls, exchange controls, and land seizures. Longer-term: restriction of benefits to ZANU-PF members in communal areas, but some attempt to palliate general suffering through NGO-financed relief efforts.	elections of 2002 and 2006.

Sources: cols 1 and 2 Inequality data from *World Bank World Development Indicators*. Poverty rates calculated at national poverty lines from national budget surveys:

Argentina—Encuesta Permanente de Hogares (EPH). Note that INDEC, the National Institute of Statistics, changed its methodology in 2003 to reflect changes in socio-economic conditions, from permanent household surveys conducted twice a year to a mixture of continuous and quarterly surveys.

Bolivia—*Instituto Nacional de Estadistica, Encuesta Integrada de Hogares*. For summary see Table 10.2 below.

Russia—from 1992, Russia Living Standards Measurement Survey (RLMS). For summary see Table 12.4 below.

Uganda—*Uganda Bureau of Statistics, Uganda National Household Budget Survey*, 1992, 1996, 2000, 2003, and 2006. For summary of sources also see Appendix to Chapter 13 below.

Ghana—for summary of sources see Appendix to Chapter 13 below.

Col. 3 Scope for forming pro-poor coalitions, from discussion of Section 2 above.

Col. 4 Pro-poor expenditure, originally from *IMF Government Finance Statistics Yearbook*, computed in Table 5.3 below.

Col. 5 Tax ratios, originally from *IMF Government Finance Statistics Yearbook*, computed in Table 5.4 below.

Col. 6 Governance data from University of Gothenburg QoG (Quality of Government) database.

Col. 8 PPI index from Chapter 6 below, Table 5.3 (col. 9). Aid ratios from World Bank World Development Data.

impact on the government's legitimacy and thereby the level of political stability: both the initiation of riot-type conflict and its escalation into war can be influenced, we there argued, by expenditure mixes which signal the government's determination to play fair between the privileged and the underprivileged. Our idea of the 'social efficiency wage' attempts to define this signal: variations in the social wage influence political stability and thus poverty. The relationship between the social wage and political stability depends on the salience of different interest groups in relation to the fragility of government: as the salience of low-income groups within government increases, so the importance of *pro-poor expenditure* (PPE) rises as a determinant of the social efficiency wage. In general, increases in PPE increase equity and thus stability. The change over time in sectoral shares and specifically in PPE are set out in Table 5.2. The constituent elements of PPE are primary health and education, rural infrastructure, agricultural research and extension, and some other social expenditures, and in the section below we explore the politics of some of these components.

Tax policy

Over the short term, an increase in taxation revenue reduces disposable income and well-being. However, over the medium and long term, as we have just argued, poverty-reducing expenditure strategies (such as the green revolution and the universalization of primary health and education) require expansion of the expenditure base; and without an expansion of the revenue base that cannot be achieved without increasing dependence on aid flows and borrowing, which will compromise its quality.[6] Therefore, a long-term poverty reduction strategy requires expansion of the tax base. However, this is not an easy strategy to implement, because tax increases and extensions of the tax net are politically unpopular, and for this reason may be reversed in weak states (Moore 1999). Thus, the possibility exists that developing countries can be caught in a fiscal poverty trap, where poverty stays high because public expenditure does not increase, and expenditure cannot increase because the taxes needed to finance it are politically infeasible. (This is exactly what happened in Bolivia, where the tax increases recommended by the IMF and donors to close the fiscal gap were rescinded after riots in La Paz in February 2003.) To understand long-term poverty reduction, therefore, it is important to understand the political economy of why some countries escape from this trap and others do not; this is the task attempted in the section below.

Institutional quality

Finally, we have not yet addressed the institutional dimension. In Argentina, Bolivia, Russia, Kenya, and Zimbabwe in the late 1990s (and arguably for a time

[6] Indeed, a revenue base is needed to supply the core functions of government, including security, and the latter is precisely what is lacking in many of the 'bottom billion' countries, including much of Africa. See Haggard and Kaufman (2008).

even Indonesia) the processes at work to aggravate poverty included a process of long-term institutional decline, embracing, in different proportions as described by Chapters 9 through 13, discrimination in access to justice by disadvantaged groups, inequities in access to land, corruption in the supply of public services including health, education, and small-scale agriculture, and collapse of discipline in the financial sector. In the first three countries, these factors as much as macroeconomic decline were the major causes of political crisis. These institutional failings both leached away support from governing elites and motivated poor people to search for alternative sources of supply. Since the 1980s, as described in Chapter 2, these alternative sources of supply have increasingly been forthcoming in the shape of national and international NGOs, and in some cases also private sector organizations, which now supply some of the key elements in PPE, such as health, education, microfinance, and agricultural services and even, as we saw in Chapter 4, civil protection. In the poorer countries and the weaker states, indeed, the core of the poverty-reduction effort comes from outside the government sector. For these reasons, we shall need in Chapter 6 to go beyond the sphere of government behaviours with which the argument so far has been concerned. In that chapter, we construct an index of institutional quality, elements of which are previewed in the following table, and seek to understand the links between it and long-term poverty.

Table 5.2 provides a roadmap for the next two chapters. It classifies the long-term poverty reduction performance of each of the case-study countries in terms of the five elements in pro-poor politics discussed above. The best entrance gate for interpreting the table is the third column, 'Scope for forging alliances with the poor', and in that column we bring together our findings on this issue from Chapter 3 with a picture of the long-term response which we develop in the current chapter.

From Table 5.2, we can see, first, how diverse are the political routes by which long-term poverty orientation can be brought about:

- Takeover of the state by individuals owing loyalty to low-income social groups and regions (as for example by Museveni, who was by upbringing a cowherd, and Morales who was an agricultural worker).
- Splits in the elite which cause a middle-class elite to search for low-income partners to work with (e.g. the *piqueteros* of Argentina, and manual workers in the Ghana cocoa industry under the NDC), or, conversely, which cause a 'revolutionary' lower-class elite to search for middle-class partners to work with (e.g. Bolivia from 2003 onward).
- Defensive measures to protect a fragile state (such as the large increases in subsidy given to the fragile outlying territories on the southern periphery of Russia).

Second, the contrast from short-term reactive strategy against crisis to long-term proactive strategy is often associated with regime change—as in Indonesia, Argentina, and Bolivia—and sometimes riot-type conflict as well, as in Indonesia. Third, for those regimes which had some commitment to poverty reduction, there is absolutely no presumption that the transition from short-term reactive strategy to long-term proactive strategy was associated with the growth of the state or the demise of the global 'Washington Consensus'. In some places, notably Argentina and (eventually) Bolivia, the state did reclaim part of its patrimony as a component of the government's poverty reduction strategy, but this was not the case in Russia, where the growth of the state had little to do with poverty reduction, or in Africa and South-East Asia, where long-term expansion of the state was scarcely in evidence and where liberalization and incentivization of smallholder export sectors was the key to the long-term fall in poverty. We develop these ideas further in Chapters 7 and 8.

Of course, some kind of political support for pro-poor actions, as explored above, is only a necessary and not a sufficient condition for pro-poor action; that also requires complementary policy actions, as summarized in the other columns of Table 5.2. We now consider these.

5.3 ELEMENTS OF 'PRO-POOR EXPENDITURE STRATEGY'

In Chapters 3 and 4, we showed that a number of policy actions during the 1990–2008 period, pro-poor and otherwise, which economically appeared quite rational to government decision-makers before the event, turned out to be politically infeasible. Often, in addition, the process of reversing them led to conflict which made existing poverty worse. In Chapter 4 we examined a variety of potential escape routes from this problem, one of which we referred to as the *social efficiency wage*—the level of the social wage which, amongst those options which are feasible, makes the greatest contribution to minimizing socio-political instability and thereby to reducing conflict. The rationale of this approach is that variations in the social wage cannot only alter resource allocations and thereby influence well-being directly, but also that they can send a signal conveying to affected parties the message that the government is committed to achieving greater equity and to negotiating with all parties to achieve this, which can increase the trust of the distrusting and thereby deter conflict. The optimum value of the social efficiency wage obviously depends on the sensitivities of different aggrieved parties and their proclivity to trust or not trust the government, and we experimented in Chapter 4 with a range of different concepts of the interest groups most likely to be distrusting. Increases in any of these concepts of the social wage, we found, were associated with a reduction in the likelihood of conflict and socio-political instability. All of this is relevant to the issue of long-term poverty reduction strategies, in particular because the concept of the social efficiency wage which showed most promise in buying off conflict—'pro-poor expenditure', or PPE—has apparently been an important element in strategies for long-term poverty reduction, as illustrated by our discussion above, especially of the cases of Argentina, Bolivia, Uganda, and Ghana (Table 5.2). In the exploratory discussion of Chapter 4, the main elements in PPE are primary health and education, rural water and infrastructure, and agricultural research and extension, with military expenditure having a negative weight. As we confirmed empirically in the previous chapter, there are good reasons for supposing military expenditure to aggravate conflict and therefore poverty. However, the other elements in the story also need serious examination. Is it true that increases in the ratio of agricultural, health, educational and other social expenditures to GNP reduce poverty; and if so is the argument universally applicable, or does it only apply to particular countries or particular types of expenditure? And under what circumstances are increases in these categories of expenditure politically feasible? We now explore these questions, both across our small-country sample and across our broader sample. It so happens that one of the elements in PPE, 'social expenditure', has recently been the subject of a major study (Haggard and Kaufman 2008), and so we begin by reviewing this.

Social expenditures: the Haggard and Kaufman study

Social expenditure, in the broad sense consisting of social security, health, and education, provides both consumption and investment benefits—an investment in the human capital of the poor and a safety net for those who had no human or physical capital. In Asia, Latin America, and Eastern Europe Haggard and Kaufman's recent book on *Development, Democracy, and Welfare States* (2008, page 1) describes public welfare provision of this type as having originated in the early post-Second World War period, although there are a good number of cases, especially in Latin America, of state welfare support to the poor and unemployed before this time.[7] As Haggard and Kaufman show, provision of this resource has historically varied enormously across continents of the developing world, with social provision being comprehensive in Russia and Eastern Europe, narrowly focused on urban areas in Latin America, thin everywhere in Africa (outside of South Africa), and finally in Asia extremely variable, with some cases of very generous and some of very narrow provision. Especially in Latin America, state social expenditure programmes have been complemented since the late 1980s by targeted pro-poor programmes financed by the state, but using the private sector or NGOs as a vehicle, such as the Bolivia Emergency Social Fund, Ghanaian PAMSCAD, and Ugandan PAPSCA discussed above.[8] Within our case studies, we have observed the importance of social spending as an instrument for mitigating conflict in Uganda, where the pursuit, and achievement in 2001, of universal primary education has been a powerful force legitimating the new National Resistance Movement regime; in Argentina, where an expansion of social assistance to unemployed workers has been an important element in cementing the 'Kirchner consensus' (Haggard and Kaufman 2008, page 281);[9] and finally in Russia, where average real pensions and real wages (though not the minimum wage) faltered during the Yeltsin period, but have risen since 2001, with above-

[7] In their book (2008, page 89) Haggard and Kaufman illustrate that in Uruguay and Chile the foundations of the social insurance system go back to the late 1920s. In addition, for the case of the Vargas regime in Brazil, see the essay by Hilton (1975).

[8] These are programmes of quite narrow scope (less than 0.1 per cent of GDP), and in this sense our sample possibly understates the significance of these quick-disbursing public works programmes, especially in Latin America. The first large-scale programme of this sort was Mexico's *Programa de , Educacion Salud y Alimentacion* (PROGRESA), and in both PROGRESA and its successors, *Familias en Accion* in Colombia, Chile's *Subsidio Familiar*, and the *Bolsa Escola* programme in Brazil, spending is of the order of 0.5 per cent to one per cent of GDP (Haggard and Kaufman 2008, pages 216–17).

[9] Haggard and Kaufman claim, however, that this expansion of unemployment assistance 'came at the expense of cutbacks of health in education' (Haggard and Kaufman 2008, page 281).

average increases in social expenditures in regions on the vulnerable southern and eastern peripheries (see Chapters 4 and 12). In many countries, there has been a switch towards these social policies and away from directly productive pro-poor policies such as agriculture and infrastructure since the 1990s.[10] Haggard and Kaufman conduct a regression analysis to explain these expenditure dynamics. In their fifth chapter, they relate overall generosity of pro-poor funding, first of all, to the adequacy of the tax base. Second, they examine the impact of democracy on social spending, an issue on which there is a large and inconclusive literature.[11] In their own regressions, Haggard and Kaufman use the POLITY index of the degree of democracy, with the proviso that the length of time a democracy has been established is relevant also. Third, the sensitivity of welfare payments to trade openness is assessed, and a final group of influences is supplied by 'recession', the state of the business cycle, to test the likelihood that additional unemployment payments and other welfare payments will be made in times of recession. The first three variables emerge as significant in all of Haggard and Kaufman's regressions, albeit with regional variations in significance.[12]

[10] In Indonesia, for example, most of the effort to help the poor, which in the 1970s and 80s went mainly into agricultural support programmes (see pages 118–19 below) 'under the democratic governments in power since 1999 . . . has been through direct fiscal transfers involving loosely targeted distribution of rice, school vouchers, and cards granting access to health facilities' (Timmer 2007, page 32).

[11] This is summarized by Haggard and Kaufman in their Appendix 2. Within this appendix, there is a preponderance of studies which suggest that indicators of democracy have a positive impact on the quality of life, and a slight preponderance of studies which suggest that indicators of democracy have a positive impact on overall social spending over those which suggest no significant impact. However, within the latter group several studies suggest that democracy increases some elements in social spending and not others, and one (Nooruddin and Simmons 2006), which suggests that democracy is associated with higher education shares of the budget in the absence of IMF programmes, but lower health and education shares in the presence of such programmes. The latter finding is interesting in the light of our claim that compositional effects are important in assessing the impact of the political business cycle (Chapter 3 above).

[12] The table gives a picture of the variables which emerge from Haggard and Kaufman's analysis as significant influences on social spending, by continent.

Independent variable	Latin America	Asia	Eastern Europe
Polity (value of Polity IV democracy index)	**(social security only)	*	***(social security, but not health and education)
Revenue(per cent GDP)	***(not education)	***(not social security)	***
Openness to trade (exports and imports as per cent GDP)	***(negative; social security only)	***(social security only)	***(negative; education and total expenditure only)
Recession (decline in GDP as per cent of previous year)	—	***(education and health only)	—

*** Denotes significance at the one per cent level;

** denotes significance at the five per cent level; and

* denotes significance at the ten per cent level for the variables and regions stated. The analysis examines the impact of the variables stated on total social expenditure, health, education, and social security, and (—) in a cell denotes that none of these variables is significant.

Our own concept of pro-poor expenditure is wider than Haggard and Kaufman's social expenditure. It includes, in addition to their expenditure categories, agricultural expenditure for the benefit of low-income groups, and also expenditure on rural infrastructure, and it excludes military expenditure, shown by Chapter 4 to be positively associated with the likelihood of conflict and hence poverty. Table 5.3 displays the different component categories of pro-poor expenditure, side by side with the material on long-term political change presented in Table 5.2. All of the countries which experienced a substantial fall in long-term poverty over our period—Indonesia, Argentina, Ghana, and Uganda—are also countries in which the long-term trend in pro-poor expenditure (PPE) was substantially upwards. As we will discover, however, this increase in PPE was achieved through widely differing financial and political channels, and in addition it was no panacea: Bolivia more than doubled pro-poor expenditure over the course of the 1990s and early 2000s, but this did not reduce poverty, nor, much to the chagrin of the donors who had financed much of it, did it prevent the upsurge in violence of 2000–3.

In the final column of Table 5.3, we have classified the channels of political influence into three groups, corresponding to the channels through which low-income groups exercised such influence. In Group 1, represented in our sample by Uganda, a president from a low-income group takes over the state by coup d'état, and then engineers the instruments of policy, including expenditure policy, in such a way that most of the gains from growth go to rural groups. In Group 2a, a fragile governing elite is subjected to pressure from a variety of interest groups, and the extent to which pro-poor groups are able to exercise long-lasting influence is key to the poverty outcome. In Argentina, Indonesia, Bolivia, and Ghana, the poor groups able to exercise leverage on the state included the 'new poor', those impoverished by adjustment, for each of whom compensatory programmes, designed in the late 1980s and early 1990s, were scaled up: *Trabajar* in Argentina, the Kecamatan Development Programme (KDP) in Indonesia, the *Fondo Social de Emergencia* (now the *Fondo de Inversion Social*) in Bolivia, and the Programme to Mitigate the Social Costs of Adjustment (PAMSCAD) in Ghana, plus aid-financed programmes in support of social expenditures in the last two cases.[13] In all of these cases actions originally conceived as improvisations in support of the new poor were able to embed themselves into a long-term expenditure policy, albeit by very different routes, as described in the case studies above. Finally in Group 2b, the elite is less obviously fragile and there is little evidence of dialogue between the state and pro-poor groups. However, pro-poor action is nonetheless expressed through centralized or localized action in anticipation of, or in response to, political tension. This model describes Russia in the 2000s, where the growth of

[13] Zimbabwe also falls into this category: the independence government of 1980 was one of the first to buttress its appeal to voters by means of expenditure programmes for the benefit of (almost entirely African) low-income farmers growing mainly food crops in areas of communal tenure (Eicher 1995, etc.). These expenditure programmes started to run out of money in the late 1980s and had to be scaled back. After 1997, the Zimbabwean government switched its strategy from direct support for communal-area farmers to support for war veterans seeking to occupy, by invasion, land belonging to commercial farmers. The encouragement of this approach, represented by the government as explicitly pro-poor, continued to be a basis for policy in Zimbabwe until 2009.

Table 5.3 Sample countries: social expenditure and PPE, 2007 in relation to 1990.

	Change in poverty 1990–2007	Social expenditure:				Additional elements in pro-poor expenditure:		'Pro-poor expenditure' (PPE) = (1) + (2) + (3) + (5) *less* (6)		Evolution of pro-poor coalitions (from Table 5.2), defined as follows: Group1 = takeover by elite with strong representation from low-income (typically agricultural) regions, social or ethnic groups. Group 2a = elite is fragmented; in its position of weakness, accepts support from low income groups. Group 2b = elite neither fragmented nor openly influenced by pro-poor groups, but allocates resources to pro-poor groups to pre-empt or alleviate conflict
		(1) Education	(2) Health	(3) Other social	(4) = (1) +(2) +(3) Total social expenditure	(5) Agricultural support expenditure	(6) Military expenditures	Share of GDP 1990	Share of GDP 2007	
Cases of long-term decline in poverty: Argentina	'Extreme poor' (*indigentes*) rose from *c.*10–15% in 1990 to 27% in 2002, then declined to 12.2% in 2002	3.7 (1.1)	4.4 (4.2)	5.0	13.1	3.5	1.9	8.1	14.7	Group 2a: Peronists lost influence from mid-1990s with unemployment and falling living standards, replaced by *Mesa de Dialogo* with strong pro-poor representation, including in particular from 'new poor'.
Indonesia	Fell from 18% (1987) to 12% (2006) but with increase to 24% in 1997–8	1.3 (0.9)	2.1 (0.6)	3.6	7.0	3.0	7.1 (7.8)	1.3	2.9	Elements of Group 2b since 2000: Until mid-1990s poverty falling, not through coalition but through dictatorial imposition of a fast-growth, labour-intensive, pro-smallholder model. Since 2000, more democratic constitution.

Uganda	Fell from 56% (1992) to 35% (2000), then to 31% in 2006	5.2 (1.4)	7 (2.3)	3.0	15.2	2.4	2.3 (3.4)	7.0	15.3	Group 1: Since 1986, takeover by pro-agriculture coalition dominated by centre and southwest of the country.
Ghana	Fell from 51% (1990) to 39% (1999)	5.4 (3.2)	6.2 (1.3)			0.5 (0.3)	0.7 (0.5)	5.0	6.6	Ambiguous, contains elements of both Group 1 and Group 2a.
Bolivia	Rose slightly from 60% (1990s average) to 65% (2005), then fell to 61% by 2009	5.3 (2.3)	6.9 (2.0)	5.8 (14.4)	18.0 (18.7)	0.5 (0.4)	6.1 (14.1)	5.0	12.4	Group 2a (after 2006): Aymara/Quechua majority able to capture urban middle-class vote, and by this means to establish a pro-poor coalition.
Malaysia	Fell from 15% (1989) to < 10% (2006)	6.2 (5.5)	4.2 (1.4)	na	Na	0.9 (1.9)	2.2 (2.5)	5.0	5.9	Group 2b: From 1960s on, acted to pre-empt inter-ethnic resentment and conflict.
Russia	Rose from 10% (1987) to 29% (2000) then fell to 15% (2006)	3.5 (3.0)	5.2 (5.7)	6.3	15.0	0.2 (0.3)	4.0 (15.5)	10.9	11.2	Group 2b: After 1992, varied social expenditures and minimum wage by region so as to buy support in dissident regions.
Kenya	Rose from 42% (1991) to 52% (1997); some suggestions of fall since then	6.4 (6.7)	4.5 (2.3)	2.5	13.4	1.4 (1.6)	1.6 (2.8)	6.6	13.2	Elements of Group 2b.
Zimbabwe	Rose from 35% (1990) to *c.*60% (2006)	4 6 (7.7)	8.4 (3.5)	2.0	15.0	0.9 (3.1)	3.8 (4.6)	4.9	12.1	Group 2b: used compulsory land transfers to reward loyalty of 'veterans' and others willing to show loyalty to ruling party.

Source: IMF, Government Expenditure Statistics, various years. Definition of social expenditure is that used by Haggard and Kaufman (2008). In column (3), 'other social expenditure' consists of social security, housing, and other social expenditures classified as 'miscellaneous social expenditures' in the IMF Government Finance Statistics.

Notes: Figures in cells represent percentages of GDP

government subsidies was higher in regions, many of them poor, which had a record of rebellion against the state (Chapters 4 and 12) and also Malaysia, where the ruling BN coalition, which contained representatives from all ethnic groups, was able to practise a pro-poor expenditure policy simply by exercising discrimination in the allocation of expenditure in favour of the poorest income group, the ethnic Malays. A similar argument applies to Indonesia from the 1960s through to the mid-1990s.

The politics of PPE: 'social' versus 'productive' expenditures?

How do the different parts of PPE expenditure work against poverty?

There is more to pro-poor expenditure, and especially its investment component, than 'social expenditures' as defined by Haggard and Kaufman, and in particular we must examine the role of expenditures on agriculture and in support of it, whose expansion is strongly related with long-term poverty reduction, as illustrated by a number of econometric and historical case studies (Irz et al. 2000; Mosley and Suleiman 2007; Chapter 13 below). The expansion and deepening of smallholder agriculture offers a unique set of opportunities for escaping from the poverty trap—it is the only strategy which at the same time is labour intensive, directly increases the productivity of poor people, offers linkages in the shape of poverty-reducing input and processing industries, and finally in the case of food crop agriculture reduces the cost of food. The implications of this for poverty strategies reach back quite a long way. In the first two decades of the twentieth century, the first railways were laid to connect the cocoa-producing areas of Ghana, the coffee and cotton-producing regions of Uganda, the oil palm smallholdings and estates of Malaysia, and the coffee and spice smallholdings of Indonesia with export markets—to mention only the peasant export economies within our sample. These investments in support of smallholder export cultivation were accompanied by investments in health and education, of which the most visible (for example the universities of Makerere in Uganda and Legon in Ghana, the first for Africans in Africa)[14] were probably not the ones with the most important impact.[15] All of these were early cases of pro-poor expenditure[16] combining direct support for African agricultural production via research, extension, and infrastructure with indirect support for human capital and social expenditures. Some indication of the early impact of these policies is provided by the fact that infant mortality—the best indicator of poverty that we

[14] The South African universities (Cape Town, Stellenbosch, Witwatersrand, and Pretoria) of course also existed at this time, but although *de iure* open to African students until the onset of apartheid in 1948, they did not in practice admit African students. Nelson Mandela, in 1948, was the only African student of his year at Witwatersrand (Gordon Brown, *Courage*, London: Bloomsbury Press 2007, page 149).

[15] Expenditure of African primary schooling was much higher in the peasant export economies of Uganda and Ghana than in the settler economies of Kenya and Zimbabwe, see Table 13.2 below.

[16] For Asian cases of developmental expenditure in colonial peasant export economies, going far beyond the 'nightwatchman state' of care and maintenance administration, see the essay by Booth (2007).

have for these times—began to fall in Ghana in the early 1920s, and in Uganda ten years later, well before this began to happen in the settler economies of Kenya, Zimbabwe, and black South Africa (Bowden and Mosley 2008, Chapter 13 below, Table 13.2). The expenditure politics that made this support expenditure possible was underpinned by a negative decision of the colonial authorities—the decision *not* to allow settlement of land by Europeans. As implemented in Ghana, Uganda, and other peasant export economies, this decision allowed the emergence of a well-above-subsistence labour force, the beginnings of an African middle class and a relatively equitable income distribution. The opposite decision in, for example, South Africa, Zimbabwe, Kenya, Zambia, and the Democratic Republic of the Congo, created a highly unequal income distribution, and an inequitable state, the consequences of which for the well-being of the poor in those countries are still being felt.

The many achievements of developing-country agriculture in the inter-war period, however, pale in comparison to what was achieved during Asia's green revolution between the mid-1960s and the 1990s, which coincides almost exactly with the period of sharpest decline in long-term poverty ever recorded. Indonesia, for example, 'took less than a generation in the 1970s and 1980s to reduce the incidence of poverty from almost sixty per cent of the population to less than twenty per cent' (World Bank 1990, page 1), and a majority of this poverty reduction was smallholder-agriculture derived (Timmer 2007, page 41). The origin of the green revolution consisted in the discovery that the principles of genetics could be used to produce, by selective cross-breeding, high-yielding varieties of many food crops. In industrial countries such modern seed varieties of cereal crops had been widely diffused since the 1920s, but the breakthrough in spreading them to the developing world is credited to the biologist Norman Borlaug in 1954.[17] Working from the Rockefeller Foundation's Mexican laboratories, Borlaug was able to breed 'dwarfing' high-yielding varieties of wheat with relatively short stalks and, as a consequence, heavy ears of grain which were eventually shown to outyield traditional varieties by a factor of three or four to one, not only in Mexico but in other regions of the temperate sub-tropics such as northern India and northern China.[18] Further south where rice rather than wheat is the dominant crop, the scientists of the International Rice Research Institute (IRRI) were able to breed varieties of rice capable of multiplying yields by a similar magnitude.[19] During the middle 1960s, a period of political turbulence and rising rice prices all over Asia, the elites of India, Indonesia, and other Asian countries took the decision, in the first instance to commit budgetary and overseas aid resources to the import and dissemination of high-yielding varieties of wheat and

[17] Borlaug (1914–2009), awarded the Nobel Peace prize in 1970, has contributed enormously to the dissemination of modern seed varieties not only through his scientific work for the Rockefeller Foundation in India, but also through his popularizing work on the borders of plant genetics, environmental science, and agricultural policy (for example Borlaug 2000). More recently he helped to found, and was on the board of, the Sasakawa Foundation, an international NGO with a mission to spread green revolution technologies in Africa.

[18] For an excellent survey both of the genetics of the green revolution and of its diffusion within Asia, especially South Asia, see the book by Lipton and Longhurst (1989), especially Chapters 2 and 3.

[19] For the rice revolution in Asia see Lipton and Longhurst (1989), and specifically on Indonesia, Collier and Sayogyo (1972), and Timmer (1975, 2004b, 2007).

rice[20] and then to incur the huge resource cost of establishing support systems for them. For smallholder producers, these support systems are the crux. In the near-subsistence village economies of developing countries until the 1960s, low-income producers were caught in a low-yield trap by multiple barriers which prevented them increasing their productivity: climatic uncertainty, fragmentary plots with insecure tenure, aversion to risk and investment, limited infrastructure, and financial exclusion. In no way, in 1960s South or South-East Asia, could smallholders with their own resources buy new seeds, fertilizers, irrigation, infrastructure, or finance for all these: the market was not there, because the private sector found it unprofitable to supply it. The task of replacing the missing markets thus fell on to governments, in the cases where effective states existed; in their absence, as for example in Bangladesh and much of Africa, the role has fallen to NGOs. In Indonesia, which we can take as an illustrative example, irrigation and infrastructure development was carried out from the late 1960s onward by central and local government,[21] fertilizers were supplied in a package with extension advice by the government agency BIMAS (Bimbingan Massal or 'Mass Guidance',[22] smallholder credit—including savings, most unusually for the microfinance of the time—were supplied on a national level by village units of BRI (Bank Rakyat Indonesia or, approximately, Indonesian Peasants' Bank), the state-owned bank which was closest to agriculture, and on a regional level by rural development banks established by provincial administrations,[23] At the same time, the previous policy of controlling the price of rice in the interests of urban consumers was replaced by BULOG (Bureau of Logistics), an agency established to protect a floor price high enough to stimulate production and at the same time keep appropriate price relationships between national and international rice markets (Timmer 1975). All of these inputs were heavily subsidized by the state until the 1980s, but with structural adjustment many of the subsidies have been removed, and since the 1990s the village units of a now-privatized BRI have been cross-subsidizing the parent bank; and the institutional structures now in position

[20] In the summer of 1966, 18,000 tons of hybrid wheat seed were imported into India, in large part to avert the threat of civil disturbance caused by devaluation and rising food prices. According to C. Subramaniam, the Agriculture Minister at the time, 'the stakes were so high it was just like gambling... In retrospect, it was historical compulsion, compulsion of circumstances, which enabled me to force through in one month critical decisions which might otherwise have taken years.' Quoted in Lele and Goldsmith (1989, page 326). For the taking of similar gambles with rice in Indonesia, see Timmer (1975).

[21] Kilometres of road in Indonesia scarcely changed between 1939 and 1970, increasing only by ten per cent, from 75,000 to 84,000 kilometres, during that entire period, but increased by fifty per cent to 122,000 kilometres between 1970 and 1977, at the start of the green revolution period, and more than doubled, to 344,000 kilometres, by 1993 (Timmer 2007, Table 2.4).

[22] BIMAS was developed from the DEMAS (Mass Demonstration) programme, a student extension service started in 1963 by the Faculty of Agriculture at Bogor as a response to the national food shortage. The students first tried to gain the confidence of farmers and then attempted to teach them to use selected seeds and fertilizers, at the same time making sure that input supplies to the targeted farmers were timely (Djurfeldt and Jirstrom 2005, page 61). For discussions of BIMAS see the essay by Patten, Rosengard, and Johnston (2001).

[23] The most notable institutional models for these were the BKKs in central Java and the KURKs of east Java. For detail of these see Hulme and Mosley (1996), Vol. 2, Chapter 10, and Patten, Rosengard, and Johnston (2001).

have, as we saw in Chapter 3, supported the resilience of smallholders in periods of global crisis such as 1999–2003 (Patten, Rosengard, and Johnston 2001). As a consequence of these initiatives, average yields across the whole of South and East Asia had risen from around one metric ton per hectare at the end of the 1950s to over three metric tons per hectare by the end of the 1990s.

The politics of this dramatic new policy experiment were therefore a mixture of fear of food shortage, fear of conflict, partnerships with parties in a position to promote peasant agriculture, and overseas aid support. In the authoritarian regime of President's Suharto's Indonesia, the two biggest surges of fiscal support for rural infrastructure were a direct response to periods of state fragility—the Malari riots of 1974, when the president and his advisers lost control over the rice price, and the 'moment of living dangerously', as Suharto called it, in 1966, when they nearly lost control of the state. The latter was accompanied by a brutal suppression of the Indonesian communist party. Fiscal support for green revolution expenditures was strongly underpinned by aid donors, with the World Bank, one staff member of which described Indonesia in 1991 as 'our best aid recipient, bar none'[24] in the lead. Even in the 1980s, when the government was more secure, the pro-poor bias of policy continued: Suharto, like his Malaysian counterparts, realized that rural spending could be a way of extending Golkar's party organization (the bureaucratic party machine by which Suharto legitimized his hold on power) to the grass-roots level, securing widespread support for his regime.[25] Producing growth that delivered for the poor also deflected the criticism that it delivered even greater patronage resources to Suharto's political clients. Democracy during this period made little headway: in terms of our earlier categorization, this is a 'Group 2b', top-down, poverty reduction process. The collapse of the Suharto regime in 1998 'left no political institutions in place for efficient public governance' (Timmer 2007, page 30). Since the democratic coup in 2000, Indonesia's growth has been lower than in the previous thirty years, less pro-poor, and less agriculturally orientated.

Does democracy therefore operate against pro-agricultural spending, therefore, by contrast with the connection between social spending and democracy, which Haggard et al. have shown to be positive? Not necessarily. Michael Lipton's analysis of *Why Poor People Stay Poor*, in the 1970s (Lipton 1977), did indeed suggest that in developing-country democracies, of which India is a classic case, public spending and pricing policies might be afflicted by a pro-urban and by implication anti-poor bias, which as we have observed does not apply in dictatorships such as Suharto's Indonesia. The desire to offset this bias, by means of aid-supported integrated rural development programmes and the like, was an important focus for the 'MacNamara wave' of rural poverty programmes in the 1970s

[24] Discussions between author and World Bank Country Policy Division, Washington, DC, 5 August 1991. For a more detailed hymn of praise to the relationship between the government of Indonesia and the donors in the 1980s, see the several essays on that country in Perkins and Roemer (1991), especially essay 6, 'Structural adjustment and economic reform in Indonesia', essay 8 'Food price stabilization: rationale, design and implementation', and essay 13, 'Reform of rural credit in Indonesia'.

[25] MacIntyre (1993) adds that agricultural spending provided a rare point of contact between nationalist agendas pressing for rapid growth with a *pribumi* (ethnic Indonesian) emphasis and an orthodox economic focus on comparative advantage.

(see Chapter 2 above), and such programmes have been continued with local resources in democracies such as India, Sri Lanka, and Bangladesh after the donors' enthusiasm to support them waned during the structural adjustment period from the 1980s onward. In these countries, the urban bias and large-farm emphasis of public policy have now been greatly reduced since the 1970s (Besley, Burgess, and Esteve-Volart 2007; Djurfeldt and Jirstrom 2005; Johnson, Hazell, and Gulati 2005)[26] as policymakers discover the benefits of policies such as Sri Lanka's Million Houses Programme and India's Integrated Rural Development Programme, which capture the votes of the many rather than the few. Instrumental in this process, not only as political actors but as institution builders, have been not only agencies of government but also NGOs—most of all in Bangladesh where most of microfinance and most of primary health care are in their hands.[27]

When we switch the discussion to Latin America and in particular to Africa, the issue becomes more fascinating still. In Bolivia, the failure to achieve any significant green revolution or indeed agricultural growth of any description was an Achilles heel throughout the structural adjustment period (Morales 1991).[28] Indeed, it remains one even after all Evo Morales' attempts to improve the degree of democracy; in 2009, food crop yields on the *altiplano* were still around 1.5 tons per hectare, half the Latin American average and far lower than Asian yields. What is the cause of Bolivia's failure to reduce rural poverty, *in spite of* big increases in pro-poor expenditure? Our main explanation is that this is because it has only increased the health and education spending of PPE, and not the pro-agriculture component. But conflict (Chapter 4) also contributed to the disappointments of the Bolivian experience; and so did institutional decline, to be further discussed in the next chapter.

Africa, of course, and especially its food crop sector, is agriculturally in a much weaker state than Asia and Latin America, unable in many countries to raise yields above one ton per hectare, a third of the Asian level, and still, as a consequence, burdened by massively high levels of food imports. The green revolution, even now, has scarcely arrived in most parts of the continent, and much of Africa's persisting poverty is due to this. The trend was broken, as is now widely forgotten, by Zimbabwe, the first African country to develop its own hybrid maize seed variety, SR 52. During the first five years of independence in the early 1980s, Zimbabwe brought the whole of the African communal areas under hybrid seed, backed these up by programmes of complementary input supply reminiscent of the Asian green revolutions,[29] doubled maize production, and for a time greatly reduced the poverty of what has historically been one of the world's most unequal societies (as discussed in Chapter 13 below). But, from 1986 onward, Zimbabwean cereal yields ceased to climb beyond 1.5 tons per hectare, less than half the Asian

[26] Johnson, Hazell, and Gulati specifically analyse the contribution of rural infrastructure in India and other South Asian countries to poverty reduction.

[27] On BRAC in Bangladesh, see, for example, Chowdhury and Bhuiya (2004), and specifically on its programmes for the ultra-poor, Halder and Mosley (2004).

[28] No relation. Juan Antonio Morales, when he wrote this paper, was a professor at the Universidad Catolica de Bolivia and thereafter, until very recently, the Governor of the Central Bank of Bolivia.

[29] For the Zimbabwean green revolution see Rohrbach (1988) and Eicher (1995).

level, and soon they had gone into long-term decline, averaging 0.53 tons per hectare between 2005 and 2009 according to the FAO *Production Yearbook*. This pattern of now-you-see-it-now-you-don't green revolutions was then replicated in a number of other African countries, including Kenya, Zambia, Malawi, and briefly, during the years of transition out of apartheid, the communal areas of South Africa (Djurfeldt et al. 2005; Mosley 2002). The reason was that each of them ran out of money—for credit, fertilizers, extension, irrigation water, and sometimes the hybrid seeds themselves—in a manner that the Asian green revolutions had not done. This of course calls into question African governments' fiscal priorities, and behind those their politics.

The global recession of the 1980s fell hardest on African countries, and reduced nearly all of them to the point where they became heavily dependent on overseas aid inflows—on average, during this decade, fifteen per cent of GNP, and all capital expenditure, was aid-financed, and the donors, in the new global environment of structural adjustment, were determined not to let the aid of the 1980s go to waste as so much of it had done in previous decades (Mosley, Hudson, and Horrell 1987). In this environment budgetary priorities were not determined by African elites, but rather were bargained between them and aid donors, in a way that in Asia and Latin America—save in the poorest countries of those continents, such as Nepal, Bangladesh, and Bolivia—scarcely occurred, since the donors had no leverage.[30] These bargaining processes have been analysed by us (Mosley, Harrigan, and Toye 1995) and more recently by Whitfield (2009a). In terms of poverty reduction, our verdict on most African governments' conditionality negotiations with donor agencies through the 1980s would be that they 'won the battle but lost the war'—that is, they won the battle to only comply with the conditions they wanted to comply with, but because that battle was not part of any overall economic development strategy,[31] the victory was a purely pyrrhic one, except for some rent-seekers, and their economies continued to sink.

[30] For one of the most contemptuous illustrations of this, see the Russian case study, Chapter 12 below.

[31] There are some interesting exceptions to this rule, for example Botswana and Mauritius, but they are numerically minor, and by this time were in the process of escaping from low-income status. A more interesting exception still is Malawi, which initiated its own green revolution package in support of smallholder maize productivity, known as 'Starter Pack'—but in spite of its clear pro-poor thrust received little support from aid donors; see Harrigan (2003). Malawi despite World Bank opposition had fought through the 1980s to retain a fertilizer subsidy and a smallholder rural credit administration that were both intended to overcome capital-market constraints in favour of low-income farmers. But it had no spokesperson, let alone a high-level one such as Tumusime-Mutabile in Uganda or Meles in Ethiopia, to show that these initiatives could be framed as part of a poverty strategy. Rather, the battle was fought purely on grounds of fiscal feasibility. Thus, when the even more pro-poor Starter Pack initiative was mooted in 1998, the Malawian government had no basis of pro-poor credibility with which to build in relation to most donors. The Starter Pack provided 'enough free seed and fertilizer along with extension advice for all smallholders to cultivate 0.1 ha of staple grains . . . and legumes' (Harrigan 2003, page 856). But the World Bank did not support the programme, nor did any other donor subscribe to it except, briefly, DFID, and the programme had to be drastically scaled down from the year 2000 onwards. This was the year when a high-water mark of nearly 2 tons/hectare maize yields was reached, and hybrid seed planting was abandoned. Smallholder yields then progressively fell and had halved by 2003; but the Starter Pack initiative, in spite of its feeble support by donors, has been successful and has lifted Malawian maize yields up to a long-run average of 1.86 metric tons per hectare (2005–9 average from FAO *Production Yearbook*), double the African average.

In the 1990s, this situation began to change. African leaders emerged who did have a long-term economic development strategy, and who, even if this did not contain a ready-made pro-poor component, could readily be persuaded to craft one for the sake of the essential long-term relationship with the international financial institutions. A classic case is Uganda, whose developmental state contained no pro-poor rhetoric until some was inserted in 1994 by his Permanent Secretary for Finance (page 64 above). By contrast with other African 'governance states' the development of agriculture and its infrastructure was given parity of esteem in spending allocations with 'social' expenditures (Table 5.3) and it is from agriculture that most of the remarkable reduction in Ugandan poverty in the 1990s was derived (Appleton 2000; Lawson, McKay, and Okidi 2006). Ethiopia, a larger and even poorer country, followed in 1991 the same route of converting a guerrilla insurrection originating in a deprived part of the country (Tigre) into a state deriving its intellectual motive force from the challenge of confronting that poverty. Its chosen approach, 'agricultural-development led industrialization' or ADLI, retained more elements of the Asian state-led green revolutions than Uganda, for example local rural infrastructure created by mass campaigns, credit provided jointly with extension services in instalments collected by local government agents, and even state ownership of the land. Prime Minister Meles Zenawi was even more willing to lead from the front in the dialogue with the aid donors than President Museveni, and it would not be wrong to describe his relationship with the World Bank of the time, on the evidence of the memoir published by the Bank chief economist's memoir, as an intellectual love affair.[32] Both of these African governments, however, unlike any previous ones, shared a long-term vision of agricultural modernization as the basis for a developmental state, an awareness of the place of pro-poor expenditure within it,[33] and finally an awareness that that vision required a planned long-term expansion of the revenue base to pre-empt a 'stop-go green revolution'. Thus in both countries, there was a shift of public resources into agriculture—especially smallholder maize production, and associated support services such as extension as a means of reducing poverty and broadening the regime's popular appeal. As shown in Table 5.3, this raised the PPE ratio dramatically over the course of the 1990s; it also gradually raised smallholder yields to around 2 tons/ha by the end of the 1990s, or double the

Thus, here a pro-poor initative succeeded not because of support from aid donors, but in the teeth of their apathy and sometimes opposition.

[32] Joseph Stiglitz, the chief economist in question, describes this relationship as follows:

> A doctor by training, Meles had formally studied economics because he knew that to bring his country out of poverty would require nothing less than economic transformation, and he demonstrated a knowledge of economics—and indeed a creativity—that would have put him at the head of any of my university classes. He showed a deeper understanding of economic principles— and certainly a greater knowledge of the circumstances in his country—than any of the international economic bureaucrats that I had to deal with in the succeeding three years (Stiglitz 2003, page 22).

[33] Like Uganda, Ethiopia put emphasis on mass primary education as well as agriculture. However, in terms of poverty reduction performance, Ethiopia has not been able to emulate Uganda's success; the data are disputed, but on some estimates the reduction in Ethiopian poverty during the 1990s from its base level of fifty-one per cent in 1992 is only marginal, possibly as little as one per cent, according to World Bank (2005b).

African average.[34] The engagement of both leaders with democratic institutions was circumscribed. Ethiopia's ruling party allowed itself, unlike Uganda's National Resistance Movement, to compete in multi-party elections, and formed an inter-ethnic coalition, the Ethiopian People's Revolutionary Defence Force or EPRDF,[35] to enable it to do this more effectively. But like many another African incumbent party, it rigged an election, in May 2005, to pre-empt an expected negative verdict at the polls, and treated protesters with violence.[36] These are Group 1 cases, in terms of Table 5.3 above, in which an elite from a low-income region takes over the state, using its lowly origins to bolster its populist appeal but not properly daring to entrust itself to the electorate.

Ghana, the other big poverty reduction success of Africa, is a very different case. First of all, it is a democratic showpiece, and since its return to democracy in 1992 has managed four general elections, and two changes of ruling party, with great panache. Second, it has also historically, much more than Uganda, been a showpiece for urban bias, especially in the shape of the policies of the first president of independent Ghana, Kwame Nkrumah. The PNDC (NDC) governments of the 1990s continued in a 'Nkrumahist' tradition, not a million miles from *desarollismo*, but with weaker unions[37] and a much more accommodating attitude towards liberalization. We have described Ghana's poverty reduction strategy above as a 'Group 2a' poverty reduction process, somewhat analogous to the Group 2a processes currently at work in Argentina and Bolivia, in which the poor are one of many groups whom a vulnerable elite has felt it necessary to try and appease. In Ghana, the poor are three groups: subsistence farmers from the three northern regions, who historically have always voted for the NDC; employees of cocoa farmers in the cocoa-producing regions of the centre, a National Patriotic Party (NPP) heartland; and urban workers, who are better represented at least in Accra by the NPP, but whose floating voters the NDC has sought to prise away. To compete for the votes of the poor, therefore, the parties need to bid both for cocoa regions and for the cities. By comparison with Uganda, therefore, Ghana's poverty alleviation strategy is more oriented towards the cities[38] and, in terms of expenditure more focused on

[34] In both Uganda and Ethiopia, average maize yields rose gradually from around 1 ton/hectare at the beginning of the 1990s to a sustained average of 1.46 tons/hectare (Uganda) and 2.19 tons/hectare (Ethiopia) between 2005 and 2009 (data from FAO *Production Yearbooks*). The average yield in Sub-Saharan Africa remains around 1 ton/hectare, and in many places there is a downward trend due to expansion of cultivation into marginal areas and to the effects of global warming, which has affected Africa more seriously than other parts of the developing world (see Stern 2006, Figure 3.8).

[35] Descended from the Tigre People's Liberation Front (TPLF), the guerrilla group which had taken over Ethiopia in 1991.

[36] There were at least thirty deaths in demonstrations in Addis Ababa in May 2005, and several hundred people many from the NGO sector. One senior staff member of the charity ActionAid, and several other NGO members, were arrested on charges of 'genocide'. Most those charged were released in an amnesty in September 2008.

[37] The 'Nkrumahist bargain' consisted of modernity and welfare provided by the state in return for increased state authority and decentralization of power (Mustapha and Whitfield 2009, page 53).

[38] As will be recalled (Teal 2006), it was especially manual workers, not farmers who shared in the fall in poverty between 1990 and 1999.

Figure 5.2 'Pro-poor' export price liberalization: Uganda and Ghana 1980–2003.
Source: chapters by Akiyama et al. and Baffes in Akiyama et al. (2001), updated and amended.

the social rather than the pro-agricultural components of PPE.[39] The implicit export tax on cocoa used as the main source of public revenue since the 1930s has been brought down as a share of the price received by the farmer through the reforms of the 1990s, but not nearly as fast as the implicit tax on exports of Ugandan coffee or cotton (Figure 5.2); indeed, as shown by the figure, 'urban bias' still survives in the shape of a tax of just under fifty per cent on Ghanaian cocoa exports. We discuss export taxation further in the next section and in Chapter 13.

Just as the NDC sought to extend from a base in the cocoa-producing regions towards the cities, so the more city-based NPP,[40] when it took over in 2000, sought to spread its appeal towards the rural areas also. So instead of consensus being imposed by a dominant ruling party, as in Uganda, in Ghana it has resulted much more from a European-style determination by both parties to seek out the middle ground. As in Argentina and Bolivia, improvements in governance procedure, especially in the organization of elections, have been used as a consensus-building instrument.

Summarizing across our case studies, what we describe in this chapter as 'pro-poor expenditure' is an aggregation of different strands in expenditure politics. The promotion of social expenditures, as per Haggard and Kaufman's classification, is one of these strands, which prioritizes direct support for poor people either as consumers or as members of the workforce, that is, recipients of

[39] Within agriculture, the long-standing dynamism of the cash-crop sector did not translate to the food crop sector at all (Mosley and Suleiman 2007; Tripp and Marfo 1997).

[40] Lindsay Whitfield describes the NPP as being in 'the Busia/Danquah tradition', that is, intellectual and rationalistic, by contrast with the more populist approach of the NDC (Mustapha and Whitfield 2009).

human capital. The promotion of agricultural development is a second approach, which operates especially by stimulating labour markets for low-income people and also, in 'green revolution' cases such as Indonesia, by lowering the price of food. A third approach, already explored in Chapter 4, involves reducing the level of military centrality and specifically a reduction in the share of military expenditure in total expenditure. As illustrated by the cases of Indonesia and Uganda, the pro-agriculture strand appears to be able to bring about particularly dramatic reductions in poverty in low-income, agriculture-dominated countries. The two most dramatic poverty reduction processes in our sample were in Indonesia between 1970 and 1990 and in Uganda between 1990 and the mid-2000s. The first of these was a Group 3 regime, which imposed poverty reduction from above, and the second was a Group 1 regime, where an elite from a low-income region took over the state. This long-term poverty is contemporaneous with and appears to be driven by a long-term improvement in agricultural productivity, to which an expansion of rural infrastructure was very important. Bolivia makes an interesting comparative case; it, too, like most of the countries in this sample, experienced a large increase in the share of social expenditure in the later 1980s and 1990s, and yet poverty did not fall. Our intuition is that one reason for this was Bolivia's failure to deal with problems of agricultural modernization (Morales 1991): cereal yields even by the 2000s had scarcely risen above 2000 kg/hectare, a level more typical of an African than a Latin American country.[41]

Previous literature, as discussed above, suggests at least a latent conflict between the targeting of social expenditure (which is apt to be biased towards, if not uniquely focused on, urban groups) and the targeting of pro-agricultural expenditure (which almost by definition goes to rural groups). Argentina, Bolivia, Ghana, and classically Russia had in the first half of the twentieth century experienced much aggravation of poverty from urban bias. However, reconciliation between the welfare-focused and the agriculture-focused approaches to pro-poor expenditure is quite achievable, as we can see from our case studies. One such reconciliation, much observed in Uganda, Ghana, and indeed many other countries in Africa, consists of financing as much pro-agricultural expenditure as possible out of the domestic development budget and leaving increases in social expenditure to donors whose priorities are heavily towards technical assistance, health, and education. But it is not only donors who have been buying out urban bias—a shift towards broad-based development has also occurred in Argentina which is not donor-aided.

As indicated above, different pro-poor strategies highlighting different components of PPE (pro-poor expenditure) may have a bearing on social impact. In Table 5.4, we develop the simultaneous model of Chapter 4 by examining the influence, within that model, of three different PPE concepts:

1. 'ppe2': social expenditure (health plus education), referred to in the graphs above as *ppehe.*
2. 'ppe3': social expenditure, plus 'pro-agricultural expenditure' (agricultural support less military expenditure).

[41] Average maize yields 2005–9 were 2.52 tons/ha across the country as a whole (source FAO *Production Yearbooks*). Cereal yields on the *altiplano* were a great deal less than this.

Table 5.4 Developing-country panel—estimates of complete system, 1980–2006 (all countries in sample).

Regression coefficients on independent variables	(1) Infant mortality (as indicator of poverty)			(2) Allocation of expenditure: PPE index 4	(3) Violence indicator	(4) Investment (% of GDP)	(5) Aid (% of GDP)
Dependent variable					(political stability index)		
Constant	55.9* (2.39)	7.48 (0.68)	28.6 (0.69)	2.88 (1.34)	2.24** (6.34)	24.1** (26.36)	3.29** (4.69)
PPE index 2 (health plus education)	−4.53** (2.55)						
PPE index 3 (health plus education plus agriculture plus infrastructure)		−0.00047** (3.54)					
PPE index 4 (health plus education plus agriculture plus infrastructure less military expenditure)			−0.0005** (3.93)				
Budget deficit (% of GNP)				−1.04 (0.29)			
Gini coefficient of inequality	0.47 (1.36)	0.25 (1.06)			−0.056** (6.72)		
Total population							−0.004** (4.31)
Political stability index						0.93 (0.82)	
Aid/GNP(%)				1.67** (3.08)			
Inflation					−0.005 (1.90)		
Total investment(%GDP)			0.49 (0.36)				
GDP growth (% p.a)						−0.24 (1.65)	
GDP/capita ($) at 2000 prices							−0.0008** (3.95)
Instruments for specified dependent variable in other equations				Corruption index	Inflation	GDP growth	GDP/capita
Number of observations	369	319	450	362	261	327	327
R^2	0.19	0.24	0.28	0.28	0.37	0.07	0.10
P	0.0161	0.2901	0.0212	0.0161	0.0000	0.2417	0.0000

Source: panel of 61 developing countries for period 1980–2005, mainly from World Bank World Development Indicators. Dataset available at http:www.poverty.group.shef.ac.uk.

Three-stage least squares regression. Figures in cells are regression coefficients (Student's statistics in brackets). **Denotes significance of a coefficient at the 1% level and * denotes significance at the 5% level.

3. 'ppe4': social and pro-agricultural expenditure (ppe3), less military expenditure.

Our explanatory story is therefore that the long-term dynamics of poverty are determined by the variables discussed above and summarized in Table 5.2—the long-term change in PPE, institutional influences, and income inequality, controlling for standard influences on growth such as physical and human capital:

$$\text{Poverty} \leftarrow (\text{PPE, institutional quality index, conflict, Gini, controls}) \quad (5.1)$$

where PPE takes the various forms defined above. Since several of the causal influences on the right-hand side (notably PPE and conflict) are 'endogenous', that is, determined within the model, we estimate this relationship within a simultaneous-equations framework in which all of these causal influences are estimated as functions of so-called instrumental variables, in other words independent influences which influence them but have no part in causing them.

In explaining PPE, which is 'social' plus productive pro-poor expenditure, we can usefully begin from Haggard and Kaufman's analysis, which as we have seen focuses on available revenue, trade openness, and the state of the macro-economic cycle. To these causes we add, on the evidence of our case studies, first of all, *conflict*, as demonstrated especially by our Russian case study in Chapter 12, the level of social expenditure was often driven by the desire to pre-empt a renewal of conflict, and not by compassionate motives; and second, *pressure from aid donors* to push up health and education expenditures.

Thus our explanation of pro-poor expenditure reads:

$$\text{PPE} \leftarrow (\text{revenue, openness, cyclical factors, conflict vulnerability, pressure from aid donors}) \quad (5.2)$$

Conflict vulnerability is of course itself endogenous, as per the argument of the previous chapter, and so we model it as in Chapter 4:

$$\text{'Conflict 2'} \leftarrow (\text{speed of monetary deflation, per capita income, inequality, military centrality, 'Conflict 1' (whose determinants are provocations by government, social capacity to manage conflict))} \quad (5.3)$$

Investment (equation (4) in Table 5.4) is determined by the level of income and political stability.

Finally, aid flows (equation (5) in Table 5.4), a major influence on PPE in poorer countries, are endogenous to, in particular, indicators of recipient need, such as per capita income, and country size.

Estimates of the complete system consisting of these five equations are presented in Table 5.4. As will be observed, the proportion of the variance in poverty that is explained by the causal factors discussed rises from nineteen per cent, to twenty-four per cent, to twenty-nine per cent, as we move from the least comprehensive definition of PPE (basic social expenditures, i.e. health plus education) to the most comprehensive, (i.e. social expenditures plus pro-agricultural expenditures minus military expenditures). Thus, on those occasions where it has been politically possible to operate a multi-track anti-poverty strategy, the implication is that this has increased the effectiveness of pro-poor efforts.

It is also worth examining some of the other relationships in the model to get a broader picture of influences on poverty. As emphasized by much of the Haggard/

Kaufman work and also by our PPE equation (column (2) of the table) no form of promotional anti-poverty policy can function unless supported by an adequate revenue base, and the next section examines tax-based anti-poverty strategies. Especially the investment element of expenditure is also dependent on political stability (Chapter 4 above; see also Alesina and Perotti 1996) and political stability, as discussed in several of our country case studies and also evident in column (3) of the table, has a strong negative relationship with income inequality. Thus both fiscal adequacy and political stability are complementary with pro-poor impact.

We must recall, finally, that the politics of pro-poor expenditure are not just a question of fiscal allocations and their determinants—institutional influences are also important, and neither the fiscal measures in this chapter, nor the measures to manage conflict considered in Chapter 4, could have been put into place without appropriate institutions. The influence of institutions is considered in more detail in Chapter 6.

5.4 TAXATION AND PRO-POOR STRATEGY

Nothing is certain, we are told, except death and taxes; but, in the developing world, the latter part is not true. The predictability of tax systems in the developing world is very low, and from this stems much of its poverty, since none of the poverty-reducing expenditure programmes we have discussed can be sustained without expansion of the revenue base,[42] and failure to attend to this has, as we saw, driven many planned green revolutions and welfare expansions into the sand. This is an area in which the contrast between short-term and long-term rationality is absolute. Every act of (increased) taxation reduces someone's disposable income, and thereby reduces political support for the government, which in a weak state is a big worry.[43] Other things being equal, therefore, increased

[42] In the poorer countries there is the possibility of filling the gap through aid inflows, but as Haggard and Kaufman emphasize, this has efficiency costs, from which the only possible escape route is to rationalize the tax system:

> Governments not dependent on taxes—either because of income from natural resources, from state-owned enterprises, or from aid—will be less responsive to their citizenry and more corrupt than those that rely on taxation . . . A dominant model [of the process by which taxes are justified] is majoritarian and focuses on redistribution: the poor, or alliances of the poor and the middle classes, use majority rule to impose redistribution on the wealthy or blackmail them with the threat of social order or even revolution. However, it may well be that social policy is less redistributive than it appears, and that stable welfare bargains work precisely when the incidence of benefits aligns most closely with the incidence of taxes . . . when people get what they are paying for. For the poor to be represented in the social-policy system, they must also be brought into the fiscal system, so that politicians will be made accountable to their interests (Haggard and Kaufman 2008, page 356).

[43] On this, see Arthur Lewis's comments:

> Most governments find it easiest to tax those who oppose them and to exempt those on whose support they rely, and this fact plays as large a part in determining the distribution of the tax burden as considerations of equity, of incentives, or of savings. Yet the fact remains that in most of these economies it is impossible for the government to play the roles it needs to play in economic

taxation will always reduce well-being and make the state more fragile in the short term[44] even though in the long term the revenues from that taxation are essential to protect it against remaining fragile. If the country is very poor, and aid is available, that may make the problem worse, because raising money through aid always appears, in a fragile state, a more politically rational option in the short term than raising it through taxation. We call this predicament the 'Lewis–Moore Paradox' after Mick Moore who drew attention to its generality in the late 1990s (Moore 1999) and Sir Arthur Lewis, quoted above. But the problem of development being constrained by poor tax performance does not just arise in low-income countries. Within our period it has also arisen, for example, in Argentina and Russia, both of which in the 1990s experienced severe macro-economic instability partly as a consequence of inability to collect the taxes which were due.[45]

As our case studies illustrate, the problem can be solved. In particular, as will be illustrated by Table 5.5 below, a large increase in tax-to-income ratios was achieved between 1990 and the mid-2000s in Uganda, Ghana, Argentina, and Bolivia, combined with a large fall in poverty in the first three of these cases. In what follows, our main preoccupation will be with how the low-tax trap was sprung, and its implications for the poverty outcome. We examine only the four countries mentioned: two low-income African countries and two middle-income Latin American countries.

One historical cause of the low-tax trap is that most poor developing countries have retained from colonial times a tax structure heavily dependent on overseas trade flows.[46] From a developmental point of view, this had three faults: it handicapped the competitiveness of the export sector; it embedded instability into the public finances, because international trade flows are volatile (Greenaway

> development unless it taxes *all* classes more heavily than at present. The major political problem in most of these countries is to persuade the people that this is so, and to gain their consent to the necessary measures. [In particular] the main problem is whether it is politically feasible to levy adequate taxation upon the peasants . . . The greatest political question which a country such as India now has to face is whether it can force [through taxation] a doubling or trebling of domestic saving without involving its people in hatred and violence on a large scale (Lewis 1955, pages 401, 402, 382).

[44] As we showed in Chapter 3, countries which increased tax rates sharply during the 1998–2003 global crisis were more politically vulnerable to riots and demonstrations (and were less effective at reducing short-term poverty).

[45] For a study of tax compliance in Argentina (compared with the much happier experience of Chile) see Bergman (2003).

[46] For the beginning of our period, the 1988 *World Development Report* provides the following data on tax structures:

Country groups	High income	Middle income	Low income
Percentage of income derived from taxes on			
Personal income	35	32	25
Social security and other direct taxation	34	17	4
Domestic sales of goods and services	29	30	32
International trade	2	19	38

Source: World Bank, *World Development Report 1988.*

Table 5.5 Poverty, tax ratios, and tax structure, 1988–2007.

	Poverty trend:	Tax/GDP ratio (%)	Sources of tax revenue:			
			Taxes on international trade and transactions:	Taxes on income, profits and capital gains:	Taxes on goods and services	Other
Argentina	'Extreme poor' (*indigentes*) rose from *c*.10–15% in 1990 to 27% in 2002, then declined to 12.2% in 2002	1988: 9.3 2005:14.2	1988: 13.2 2004: 12.5	1988: 4.6 2004: 22.5	1988: 34.3 2004: 17.2	1988: 44.6 2004: 17.2
Bolivia	Rose slightly from 60% (1990s average) to 65% (2005)	1988: 8.4 2005: 16.8	1988: 18.6 2005: 6.1	1988: 4.5 2005: 12.7	1988: 57.4 2005: 65.3	1988: 19.5 2005: 15.8
Indonesia	Fell from 18% (1987) to 12% (2006) but with increase to 24% in 1997–8	1988: 16.9 2005: 12.3	1988: 6.2 2004: 4.5	1988: 62.6 2004: 42.0	1988: 27.5 2004: 47.7	1988: 3.4 2004: 5.8
Malaysia	Fell from 15% (1989) to < 10% (2006)	1988: 19.6 2005: 18.5	1988: 24.5	1988: 44.8	1988: 25.9	1988: 4.8
Russia	Rose from 10% (1987) to 29% (2000) then fell to 15% (2006)	2006:16.5	1988: 2005: 28.1	1988: 2005: 37.6	1988: 2005: 30.1	1988: 2005: 4.2
Ghana	Fell from 51% (1990) to 39% (1999)	1988: 11.4 2005: 22.3	1987:47.5 2004: 38.4	1987: 24.0 2004: 29.9	1987: 28.2 2004: 29.0	1988:0.3 2004: 2.7
Uganda	Fell from 56% (1992) to 35% (2000), then to 31% in 2006	1986: 5.0 2005: 12.5	1986: 75.3 2003: 30.6	1986: 5.4 2003: 23.5	1988: 19.1 2003: 32.6	1988: 0.2 2003: 13.3
Kenya	Rose from 42% (1991) to 52% (1997); some suggestions of fall since then	1988: 17.6 2007:	1988: 19.8 2003: 3.3	1988: 31.1 2003: 39.3	1988: 47.7 2003: 56.8	1988: 1.4 2003: 0.6
Zimbabwe	Rose from 35% (1990) to *c*.60% (2006)	1988: 24.0 2001: 26.3	1988: 16.9 2005:	1988: 53.6 2005:	1988: 28.1 2005:	1988: 2005:

Source: IMF, Government Finance Statistics Yearbook, various years, except for column 1, poverty trends, which is transcribed from Table 5.2.

and Milner 1991) with obvious political implications for the stability of livelihoods; and last, because a high proportion of poor people were dependent on incomes from that same export sector, it was severely regressive and a barrier to poverty reduction. This constraint applies with particular severity to the group of former African colonies, including Uganda and Ghana, which during the Second World War had introduced taxation on primary exports, in the form of an 'export stabilization fund' at rates up to ninety per cent of the price received by the farmer, and then kept it there for forty years mainly for reasons of fiscal dependence (Chapter 13 below); however, the problem of trade-tax dependence applies with almost equal stringency to Bolivia also.

During the period of increased engagement with the international financial institutions which followed the global crisis of the 1980s, the case for reform of these tax structures was energetically put to client countries by the Washington financial institutions. The main elements in the process which the IMF and the Bank attempted to achieve long-term reform in the tax structures of developing countries, over and above the short-run crisis-adjustment measures discussed in Chapter 3, were typically four (Jenkins 1991; Lledo, Schneider, and Moore 2004; Mosley, Harrigan, and Toye 1995):

- First and foremost, *trade tax reforms* which brought price-structures as close as possible to the prices which reflected true resource scarcities low and as far as possible uniform import duties, removal of quantitative restrictions on trade, and perhaps most crucial of all for the Fund of the time, the elimination of taxes on exports, the goose which laid the golden eggs.
- Second, to achieve the urgent objective of diversifying the tax structure, the development of tax base alternatives to overseas trade. The most obvious option was domestic sales, and the idea of rationalizing existing indirect taxes into one uniform *value added tax* (VAT) quickly became one of the Fund's staple exports.
- Third, to go further with diversification and at the same time raise revenue quickly in a targeted manner, the idea of *user charges* on public services, for example, health, education, roads, and agricultural extension services, was also promoted.
- Fourth, to reverse the brain drain, *punitive rates of direct taxation* were discouraged.

Finally, in the new atmosphere of heightened sensitivity to government rent-seeking, it sought to depoliticize revenue authorities by giving them *administrative autonomy*. The purpose of all of these recommendations was allocative, not distributional: this was the golden age of 'trickle-down', and the objective was above all to restore a growth impulse.

The implementation of this varied menu of reforms over the following twenty years has been described by us and others (Mosley, Harrigan, and Toye 1995; Whitfield 2009). For our four case-study countries, the tax reforms executed (and in some cases reversed) during the structural adjustment period are listed in Table 5.6. Tax reforms are notoriously demanding of high-level technical expertise, which gave many recipient countries an excuse to delay their implementation and fast-track the things that they saw as being more urgent and/or easier to accomplish;[47] at the same time, the atmosphere of policy negotiations in the developing world was evolving by the end of the 1980s, in what turned out to be a long-term way, towards the poverty objective and towards greater give and take in the bargaining process. The consequence of both of these things was that during the 1980s and much of the 1990s, the revenue objective prevailed within the fiscal decisions of crisis-hit governments, often requiring temporary *increases* in import duties which the IFIs wished to be scaled back and the structural reform objective came a bad second. Nonetheless, structural reforms did eventually occur[48] and in what follows we consider their outcome within our African and Latin American sample countries.

African cases: Uganda and Ghana

In Uganda, Ghana, and indeed all the African countries developed on a basis of African smallholder exports,[49] the colonial authorities originated in the 1930s and 1940s, as described in Chapter 13, the practice of diverting a portion of the price of export crops from farmers into the country's treasury to finance development—a practice which was continued after independence in the 1960s. The proportion thus retained varied according to the state of the markets but in some boom years rose to over ninety per cent[50] of the export price (see Figure 5.2 above). It was never described by governments of the time as a tax, rather as a 'development levy' or equivalent phrase,[51] but so effectively did it function as one that, at the end of the 1980s, three-quarters of the Uganda government's total public revenue was accounted for by export duties on coffee alone. All exports other than coffee were wiped out by this export taxation,[52] which at the same time, being almost uniquely targeted on labour-intensive rural producers, was highly regressive.

In 1991, Uganda grasped the nettle of eliminating the export tax (Figure 5.2 above)[53] and creating in its place a structure of import duties, initially at high rates which were then gradually lowered over the latter part of the 1990s (Table 5.6) , at the same time rationalizing the existing set of indirect taxes into a value added tax and initiating a programme of privatization under which, to date, more than a hundred public enterprises have been sold off. A new tax collection service was

47 Morrissey (1995) gives an excellent description of how the tax reform process in Tanzania in the 1980s and early 90s was moulded by this process.

48 Often in response to shocks, as after the 1985 hyperinflation in Bolivia.

49 Peasant export economies as described by Myint (1976); this economic structure also developed in Malaysia, Indonesia, and other countries of South and South-East Asia.

50 Full-time series for this 'tax' are set out in Chapter 13, but for the period of reform in the 1980s and 1990s, see Figure 5.2 above.

51 Governments still using this system of taxation in the 1980s included, in addition to Uganda and Ghana, Cameroon, Benin, Togo, Nigeria, Cote d'Ivoire, Congo, and Congo DRC; see Mosley and Chiripanhura (2009).

52 'For example, tea production fell from a peak of 20,000 tons in the early 1970s to around 2,000 tons by the early 1980s, and cotton production fell from 87,000 tons to 2,000 tons' (Collier and Reinikka 2001, page 31).

53 In the process, the Coffee Marketing Board ceased to be a monopoly, and responsibilities not only for tax collection, but also for the financing, quality control, and transport of the crop were taken away from it (Collier and Reinikka 2001, page 35).

Table 5.6 Sample countries: policy changes affecting the tax system, 1980 to the present.

	Argentina	Bolivia	Uganda	Ghana
1980s	VAT in position since 1975.	1986—following macro-economic crisis, top rates of income tax reduced for individuals from 40% to 10%, and for corporations from 30% to 2%. 1985: VAT introduced at 10%.	Until end of decade: almost complete reliance on export taxes as source of revenue (> 75% of public revenue from coffee exports alone in 1986).	1985: establishment of autonomous revenue authority. VAT introduced 1988. 1988: top rates of income tax reduced from 65% to 55% for individuals, and from 60% to 45% for corporations.
1990s	1990: following macro-economic crisis, reforms reducing import duties and top rates of income tax. 1992–3: drive to increase compliance rates, involving simplification, penal statutes to combat evasion, and closing of loopholes. Establishment of independent revenue authority (1995).		1991: establishment of autonomous revenue authority. 1991/2: removal of export taxes and replacement by import duties. VAT introduced 1991. 1994: temporary coffee export tax. 1995–9: gradual lowering of highest rate of import duty from 60% to 15%.	
2000 to the present	2002: imposition of export tax to fund emergency unemployment relief.	February 2003: abortive attempt to extend range of income taxes, ended by rioting in La Paz. July 2004: referendum confirms majority support for an *Impuesto Directo en los Hidrocarburos* (IDH), a tax on oil and gas exports. 2006: IDH introduced as part of a new regulatory regime for the hydrocarbons sector.		

introduced, the Uganda Revenue Authority, in which staff were paid well above civil service pay scales (Reinikka and Collier 2001). In the process, the structure of taxation has been shifted from one almost exclusively targeted on smallholder rural producers, the majority of whom were poor at the beginning of the 1990s, to one much more oriented towards urban consumers, a good number of whom are well off. Thus, not only the 'Moore-Lewis trap' has been sprung, but sprung in a pro-poor manner: Chen, Matovu, and Reinikka (2001) show that the tax changes of the 1990s led to an increase in the progressivity of the tax system.[54] The fact that much of the Museveni government's power-base was not only rural but specifically concentrated amongst the coffee producers of the 'Luwero triangle' whose loyalty had been crucial to the NRM's success (pages 62–3 above) was clearly favourable to this reorientation of the tax base. Sequencing was important: subsequent extensions of the tax base, including user charges and the temporary export surcharge introduced in 1994, were introduced *after* the all-important removal of the export tax.

The case of Ghana is similar in terms of the centrality of export tax reform: as in Uganda the government monopoly in selling the main export crop, the Cocoa Marketing Board, has been terminated, and an independent revenue authority has been created. However, Ghana differs from Uganda in terms of the scale of marketing liberalization, the creativity of the search for alternative tax bases and the underlying politics. Ghana in the late 1980s derived only about forty-five per cent of its public revenue, rather than Uganda's seventy-five per cent, from export taxes (Table 5.5 below), and its Cocoa Board, by contrast with its Ugandan counterpart, retains responsibility for quality control and supply of inputs including fertilizer. The process of liberalization, again by contrast with Uganda, has involved not the total removal of the export tax but rather its gradual easing to a level of about fifty per cent of the export price, by comparison with twenty per cent at the beginning of the 1980s (Figure 5.2). Notwithstanding this, there has been a distinct reduction, since the end of the 1980s, of Ghana's dependence on primary exports for its revenue and a reduction in particular of the fiscal pressure on the cocoa producer, which suited the political imperatives bearing on the PNDC (later NDC) governments of Ghana in the 1990s well, namely above all to capture and retain support in rural areas.[55] Much more than in Uganda, the diversification of tax revenue has been not just into the building up of VAT revenue but also into collections of direct tax from individuals as well as compa-

[54] See Chen, Matovu, and Reinikka (2001). Liberalization of taxes on smallholder exports has in other African countries with a similar productive structure (in particular Cameroon, Benin, Togo, Madagascar, and Cote d'Ivoire) had a much lesser impact on poverty. We investigate this difference in poverty impacts in Mosley and Chiripanhura (2009) and give, provisionally, three reasons for it: better infrastructure, enabling the benefits of crop price liberalization to be transmitted to small-scale producers; better chemistry with the aid donors, enabling a more stable and productive flow of aid money; and, deriving from this, a more pro-poor expenditure pattern, which as illustrated in Chapter 13 built upon a pro-poor asset structure inherited from colonial times.

[55] 'The NDC... was aware that it was not especially popular in the cities where structural adjustment had produced the greatest pain, but it also knew that the elections would be won and lost in the countryside' (Nugent 2001, page 410).

nies.[56] There has even been a broadening of taxation into previously untapped bases such as the informal sector (Joshi and Ayee 2008).

Latin American cases: Argentina and Bolivia

Argentina and Bolivia are two of several Latin American countries caught up for decades in a vicious circle of macro-economic disequilibrium, inequality of personal income, low compliance with tax obligations, and weakened fiscal capacity (FitzGerald 1978; Lledo, Schneider, and Moore 2004). In Bolivia in 1985, and in Argentina in 1991, attempts were made by new leaderships to break out of the spiral, taking advantage of macro-crises to impose reforms of a liberalizing nature, involving widespread privatizations, liberalization of foreign trade, and large cuts in corporate tax rates to incentivize inward investment.[57] The wholesale nature of the privatizations caused large-scale job losses whose political consequences can now be seen in context. For example, three-quarters of the work force of the Bolivian tin and silver mines became redundant on privatization in the latter part of the 1980s (Mosley 2001), many of whom, desperate and angry, migrated to the satellite-city of El Alto above La Paz, to become the spearhead of the 2003 revolution. Argentina, hugely different from Bolivia in its ethnic composition, productive structure, and income level, nonetheless exhibited a comparable pattern of political response among the crucial lower middle class: contained resentment during the first wave of privatizations in the early to middle 1990s; vocal protest when unemployment and poverty deteriorated further under the stress of contagion from the 'East Asian crisis'; and finally explosion in 2001 when the crisis turned to panic, sucking into the crisis not only the lower but the middle-middle class who woke up to find their savings deposits frozen. In both countries, the sequence was first stunned loyalty, then exit,[58] then voice, and finally uprising.

In tracing the fiscal strand within this process Marcelo Bergman (2003) makes an illuminating comparison between the Argentinian case and that of Chile, the most successful country in Latin America at poverty reduction,[59] which was also fiscally stronger, with a tax compliance rate twice that of Argentina.[60] Bergman argues that 'compliance is rarely the result of altruistic behaviour; rather, [it] is the result of policies that rely on deterrence, that is the ability of tax administration

[56] In 2003, tax collections from the personal sector in Uganda were 19 billion shillings out of total direct tax revenue of 276 billion shillings, or 6.8 per cent. In Ghana they were 1535 million cedis out of total direct tax revenue of 3401 billion, or forty-five per cent (source as per Table 5.5).

[57] For example, in Bolivia the maximum rate of corporation tax was cut from thirty per cent to two per cent (see Table 5.6 above). Under-taxation of income and capital has been a long-recognized Achilles heel of Latin American tax systems. 'There are some countries which have been conspicuously unsuccessful in imposing taxes on the wealthy classes—chiefly, I think, the countries of Latin America' (Kaldor 1963, 414).

[58] In three senses: withholding of taxes due (to be discussed further below), capital flight, and in some cases emigration.

[59] Poverty in Chile fell from forty per cent in 1990 to eighteen per cent in 2003 (Neilson et al. 2008, page 251).

[60] In Argentina, as noted by Bergman, there is an additional problem caused by the federal structure: the provinces are perennially in deficit, and thus erode possibilities for non-inflationary expansion of expenditure at the centre.

and other state organizations to detect effectively and punish citizens who disobey the tax laws' (Bergman 2003, page 594) and locates the relative effectiveness of Chilean deterrence in the stronger legal systems, and greater administrative autonomy, prevailing in that country.[61] We can add, taking note of the experience of Bolivia, Argentina and other countries in our sample, that *relative* tax burdens and the relative intensity of their enforcement are important also. The World Bank nostrum of 'export-led growth and reform', so progressive in its application to peasant-export Africa, aggravated in much of Latin America, and Bolivia most especially, the level of existing inequalities by reducing rates of corporation tax to nominal levels and then not even enforcing those minimal levels.[62] (The comparison with Russia, where the tax base became similarly oligarchic as the export economy shifted from a manufacturing towards a natural resource base in the early 2000s, is highly relevant (Easter (2008) and Chapter 12 below.) Tax compliance rates were low, not just because deterrence of evasion was weak, but because the tax structure was inequitable, and because the pattern of enforcement, moderate on middle-incomes and weak on the rich, diluted any moral leverage that might have existed in relation to middle-income payers. There is an analogy here with the 'social efficiency wage' approach of Chapter 4. Just as a less equitable pattern of expenditure may act as a signal which motivates conflict over resources and militant political action, so also may, as per the Bolivian and Argentinian case in the early 2000s, a less equitable pattern of taxation. In Bolivia, as discussed in Chapter 3, a final straw was supplied by the proposed extension of the tax net, in February 2003, from upper to lower middle-class groups amidst an environment of rising unemployment: in a clinching illustration of the breakdown of governance, it was the police, themselves amongst the groups threatened with inclusion in the direct tax net, who rioted against this proposal, and who were then fired upon by the army.

In Argentina, the 'voice and uprising' phase was sooner to start and fitted slightly differently into the country's politics. By the mid-1990s, whilst Bolivia was still stable, the Argentinian fiscal deficit and unemployment were beginning to escalate (Mussa 2004). In the middle 1990s, Argentina experienced one of its and Latin America's worst episodes of 'anti-poor growth', with per capita income in the lowest income decile shrinking from 43 to 28 constant 1999 pesos per month (Grugel and Riggirozzi 2009, Table 5.2) between 1994 and 1996 even while GDP

[61] Chile acquired a greater 'tax autonomy' since tax administrators were solidly backed by the finance ministry and ultimately by the president, who even allowed his own brother to be investigated for alleged tax evasion. The relative administrative autonomy of the SII (*Servicio de Impuestos Internos*, Chile) contrasts with DGI's (*Direccion General Impositiva*, Argentina) complete subordination to the political elite and (then to) recurring financial crises. 'Tax initiatives were first (in the 1970s) channelled through the military... and later to political appointments following the restoration of democracy... Solid tax compliance programmes were never developed because quick revenues were prioritised' (Bergman 2003, page 608).

[62] In 2003 fiscal receipts from the oil and gas sector were less than half what they were before privatization: Rolando Morales, *La Prensa*, 12 February 2003, page 6. 'The Confederacion de Empresarios Privados de Bolivia', Morales adds, 'indicated that the fall in the country's fiscal revenues [between end-2001 and end-2002, which had caused a shortfall in revenues and required the IMF to be called in] was 7.3 per cent, and that the principal reason for that was a fall of 25.4 per cent over the same period in tax revenues due from the hydrocarbons (oil and gas) sector.'

growth was proceeding at an average five per cent per annum; partly because of the fiscal weaknesses described, and partly because of the government's chosen macro-policy of privatization combined with pegging the peso, one-to-one, to the US dollar. The protests of the *piqueteros* (unemployed workers) described above and in more detail in Chapter 9, began in the later year (Wolff 2007, page 6). This was an amber light to which the government adapted only slowly[63] through until the first half of 2002, at which point they were included in the conciliation round tables (*Mesas de Dialogo*) established by the Duhalde government, and subsequently in the government itself. Thereafter, the issue of confrontation versus cooperation has divided the *piqueteros*, who in return for co-optation into a share of power have lost their radical cutting edge.

If tax administration had been instrumental in the political destabilization of Argentina and Bolivia in the early 2000s, so also by the middle of the decade it had made a considerable contribution to their stabilization. In late 2002, the Duhalde government negotiated a special twenty per cent export tax on earnings from agricultural commodities and hydrocarbons, which became the central source for financial social emergency programmes (Riggirozzi 2009) and in particular to finance food-for-work payments to the unemployed under the *Programa Jefas y Jefes*. Although strongly opposed to the principles of the 'Washington Consensus' (page 46 above)[64] for whom export taxation is one of the worst forms of resource misallocation that can be imagined, politically this was an imaginatively pro-poor recreation of the relationship between taxpayers and civil society. Tax policy was being used at the same time to finance social inclusion, to signal a reversal of the privatization on which the increase of poverty was blamed, and at the same time to quickly close the fiscal deficit. Perhaps no other social contract could have achieved all these objectives. But it is a moot point whether the approach of 'pro-poor export taxes' is politically sustainable. The political forces which may derail it come not from the IMF, but rather from inside—from the agro-exporters who successfully demonstrated against President Fernandez de Kirchner's extension of export taxes in 2008, and from the blunting of the political leverage of the *piqueteros* now that they have come in from the cold.[65]

[63] They did adapt a little. The De La Rua government in 1999 allowed the *piquetero* organizations to present their own local development projects and administer social subsidies themselves (Wolff 2007, page 7).

[64] Of course the export tax was not at all welcome to the IMF; but Argentina was not dependent on aid, which increased its room for manoeuvre, and was in the process of rapidly paying back its IMF loans, achieving this in 2005.

[65] Wolff argues that (both in Argentina and in Ecuador) movements of marginalized sectors 'have become crucial political actors challenging the existing polities while they, for their part, have proven highly successful in "taming" them without really giving in to their demands' (Wolff 2007, page 2). Relevant to this long-term pessimistic view of the sustainability of progressive tax reform is the following view from a generation back:

> O' Connor (1973) argues that in the later stages of monopoly capitalism the large corporations that dominate the US economy demand ever-increasing public expenditure on physical expenditure while at the same time refusing to contribute the necessary profit taxes to pay for them. In consequence, the state is forced to raise taxes from workers (e.g. consumption taxes) but these are inadequate to cover its increased financial requirements: this is the 'fiscal crisis of the [Latin American] state" (FitzGerald 1978, pages 125–6).

In Bolivia, the revolt against social exclusion of the 2000s is much more a matter of a revolt also against ethnic discrimination, culminating in 2006 not only in much greater legislative representation for, but the first president ever to be elected from, the Aymara ethnic group. Although starting with the same political weapon—the *piquete* or roadblock—it was therefore a much broader exercise. Whereas the Duhalde and Kirchner governments became an effective pro-poor force through the incorporation of a low-income pressure group into a labour-based party, the Morales government became one by broadening the appeal of a party representing an oppressed ethnic majority, the MAS (*Movimiento al Socialismo)* to the point that it ceased to frighten middle-class professionals. As in Argentina, it was a commitment of the government from the mid-2000s onward to reverse the trend of neoliberalism, but what was implemented in Bolivia was a much more pragmatic *neodesarollismo* than that implemented in Argentina, with less invocation of the spirit of Prebisch and Peron and much more focus on the atavistic theme of giving the country greater control over its own natural resources—in particular but not only the almost seventy per cent of exports which derive from oil, gas and minerals.[66] As in Argentina, so in Bolivia also, this new policy was mediated through reforms in export taxation, which was the route through which the expected renationalization of the hydrocarbons industry was eventually negotiated. In May 2006, the government announced its intention to renew the leases of the private oil and gas companies, but to increase the share of taxation on their exports, through the Impuesto Directo de Hidrocarburos (IDH), at a rate which varies from company to company but at the maximum is now eighty-two per cent (Domingo 2009, page 172); a far cry from the two per cent corporation tax rates of the 1980s.[67] As a consequence, state revenue from the sale of hydrocarbons has increased nearly four-fold between 2006 and 2007 and, as in Argentina, an element of this tax has been explicitly allocated to social functions, specifically the *Renta Dignidad*, a state pension paid to all Bolivian citizens over the age of 60 (Domingo 2009, page 175). In addition, the issue of land reform was addressed in November 2006: not, however, by attacking individual property rights, but by making underused property more liable to confiscation. As will be discussed in more detail in the next chapter, there were also constitutional reforms, designed again to give the indigenous population a greater stake in the machinery of government. Thus, the collective identity underlying the programme of Morales' MAS, encompassing land reform and reform of state structures, went far beyond the concrete objectives advanced by the *piqueteros*, which from the start were 'largely restricted to micro-political claims: material support for unemployed households and projects promoted by the *piqueteros*, liberty to protest, and rejection of oppressive measures by the state' (Wolff 2007, page 21).

[66] Forty-nine per cent of Bolivian exports in 2006 were of hydrocarbons, and nineteen per cent of minerals (Gray-Molina 2007).

[67] Notice that Argentina and Bolivia, together with Russia, the three middle-income countries in our sample, increased their use of export taxes in the 2000s (Argentina started doing so in 2002 and Russia had always done so), whereas the low-income countries, Uganda and Ghana, reduced or eliminated their use of them. There is an obvious connection with the influence of aid donors—Argentina and Russia not only had insignificant aid flows by the 2000s but had eliminated their use of IMF credit by 2005, thus freeing them from any leverage the Fund might have been able to exert. We discuss the link between funding sources and leverage further in Chapter 7.

Consequences and lessons

Thus, in all these countries we can observe progress towards an exit from the 'Moore-Lewis tax trap', as illustrated in Table 5.5. Not only this, but the progress is of a pro-poor sort: directly in the sense that the tax changes themselves appear to be on balance progressive over the period 1990–2006 (although our methods are rough, and in Bolivia and Argentina, poverty has only begun to fall since the middle 2000s) and indirectly in the sense that they have made feasible the kind of long-term expenditure changes for which expansion of the tax base is a pre-condition. The trade tax/indirect taxes ratio, which we can take as a primitive measure of progressivity since most trade taxes are based on goods produced by the poor (and very often on agricultural labour), whereas indirect taxes are based on the expenditure of everyone, diminishes over the survey period in all the sample countries.[68] One element in this evolution is common across all four cases: a shift out of taxes on foreign trade towards taxes on income and, especially, expenditure. But others are almost opposite: whereas, in Africa, progressivity was achieved by getting rid of export taxes, in Latin America it was sought by putting them on.

From this comparison we can also appreciate the importance of timing and sequencing, as shrewdly managed in the African cases by launching the tax increases of the 1990s into a boom largely made possible by the liberalization of export taxes, as it was wrecked in the Bolivian case by attempting a regressive income tax increase in the middle of a severe slump. As Lewis argued in the 1950s, there is a political limit to what increases in rates or bases are feasible, but the limit is flexible, and can be finessed in various ways, one of which is simply waiting for the right moment. In a recession, in the context of a highly unequal society with severe corruption of the existing tax system and a rigid and inflexible leadership, the room for tax manoeuvre is extremely small, as the Bolivian case illustrates. In a boom, where there is greater equity in income and tax incidence, where the government shows imagination in linking tax payments to the expenditure mix (as in Argentina especially), much more is possible. Institutions also matter fundamentally, as we argue further below; not only in the sense emphasized by Bergman, of institutions which pose a credible threat to non-repayers, but in the sense of institutions which offer credible signals of equity within expenditure patterns and tax structures. A final supportive impulse to effective tax performance is macro-stability. In an atmosphere of chronic crisis, or where as in Bolivia tax changes were attempted and then cancelled, tax policymaking became improvisatory, and as a consequence inconsistent and unstable. As Bergman remarks, in Argentina, by comparison with Chile, 'cyclical economic crises

[68] In Africa, as we have seen, the share of trade taxes was dramatically reduced by the elimination or reform of export taxes (from seventy-five per cent to thirty per cent in Uganda, and from forty-seven per cent to thirty-eight per cent in Ghana). In Bolivia and Argentina, the share of trade taxes also fell. This reflected a general Latin American trend: 'Taxes on foreign trade, which in 1980 represented thirty per cent of all taxes in the average country in the region . . . were partly replaced by domestic taxes, to the point where trade taxes now generate only seventeen per cent of revenue collected' (Lledo, Schneider, and Moore 2004, page 24). We emphasize that the measure of progressivity we have used is a rough and approximate one, and no rigour is claimed for it.

hampered the development of a stable tax policy' (Bergman 2003, page 608). Instability in the macro-economy undermined possibilities for escaping from the tax trap, and macro-stability, which paradoxically was not aggravated by the political business cycle (Chapter 3 above) made the trap easier to spring.

Taxation and governance

If institutions matter fundamentally, how do they matter? 'Taxation' Deborah Brautigam argues:

> Is an underrated tool in the effort to build more capable and responsive states... Democracies are built not only on periodic elections but also on a social contract based on bargaining over the collection and spending of public revenue. [Indeed we can argue] that taxation may play the *central* role in building and sustaining the power of states.
>
> (Brautigam 2008a; also Brautigam, Fjeldstad, and Moore 2008, pages 1–2, italics in original)

What form of 'social contract' between taxation and governance have we observed in our case-study countries, and how does the nature of the contract made bear on the observed poverty outcome? Classically, the social contract has taken the form, fiscally speaking, of 'taxation in exchange for representation': the slogan on which the demand of the American colonists for independence was based (representation, that is, across the web of organizations which determine how society's resources are allocated). We are particularly interested, of course, in the resources which are allocated to lower income groups.

As we have seen, taxation in developing countries has had difficulty in escaping from the straitjacket of taxes on foreign trade, a problem which possibly reached its outer limit in one of our case-study countries, Uganda, where as late as 1986, three-quarters of *all* public revenue was derived from taxes on the export of one commodity, coffee, which were never even publicly described as taxes but rather as compulsory contributions to a 'price stabilization fund'. In systems of this kind taxes have little connection with governance, since those who collect them are accountable to nobody and especially not the representatives of those from whom they are collected; and this lack of connexion indeed bears heavy responsibility for the emergence in another of our case studies, Ghana, of what has been described as a 'vampire state'[69] (the government sucks everything out and gives nothing back): or the opposite of a consensually-agreed contract. Across all of the case studies, indeed, including the special case of Russia, most taxation and especially the part of it derived from trade has been coercive rather than consensually agreed.

Brautigam et al. note various potential ways forward from this predicament. One consists of administrative checks and balances to keep vampires at bay, and in particular the establishment of independent revenue authorities which can buffer the revenue collection function against corruption by special-interest groups. Another consists of what Moore (2008, Chapter 2) calls 'revenue

[69] This term originates with Frimpong-Ansah (1991).

bargaining': a process by which, through the transformation of taxation from coercion into a bargaining process between citizens and the state, the state's institutions are strengthened. Bargaining extends from explicit exchanges of taxation for improved representation, on the one hand, to 'indirect strategic interaction and mutual behaviour adjustment', of which the following examples are given: '(a) the presence of revenue issues on the public policy agenda; (b) collective action by groups of taxpayers around taxation issues, whether through electoral or other channels of representation; and (c) the willingness of government to interact with and respond to taxpayers' expressed or anticipated preferences in making public policy' (Moore 2008, pages 37–8). We wish to explore the circumstances under which this social contract can be made pro-poor, in which taxation is bargained not just in exchange for improvements in the capacity of the state, but explicitly for institutions which enhance the state's delivery of reduced poverty. At the implicit end of the spectrum, several of the changes in revenue structure observed in Table 5.5 achieved an exchange of pro-poor tax reform for a greater involvement of citizens in governance. Changes in the export tax regime, as we have seen, are often at the centre of this process. In Ghana and Uganda, export duties coercively imposed on low-income cocoa and coffee farmers and their employees were gradually diversified into broader-based taxation which was more progressive, more open,[70] and where at least a limited increase in accountability to taxpayers could be achieved through the creation of autonomous revenue authorities, paid at well above civil service rates and under the control of a management board with both government and non-government representation[71] (Fjeldstad and Moore 2009). In Argentina and Bolivia, the same objective—greater progressivity and a stronger tax bargain—was achieved through the opposite process, namely the *imposition* of ad hoc export taxes linked to targeted social expenditures (Argentina 2002) and pensions (Bolivia 2006). This was a more explicitly poverty-oriented social contract, in the sense that tax changes linked to the improvement of social well-being, not as in the African cases by 'indirect strategic interaction' but by public and explicit earmarking of tax revenues. Politically, this was also a highly unorthodox 'social bargain', since export taxes are anathema to the Washington consensus; but they have the political advantage of being quick-acting, easily targetable, and if rightly

[70] We mean, specifically, open in the sense of openly advertised as being a tax. Other elements of openness come into play in this discussion, but their import is less clear. Moore writes that 'in East Africa, the recent shift from authoritarian or one-party states to more pluralistic polities has given locally-based politicians more leverage centrally and is the major reason for the decline of coercive local taxation'; but as far as export levies are concerned this decline has in fact proceeded more quickly in one-party Uganda than in highly democratic Ghana (see Figure 5.2 above).

[71] There is by no means a unanimous verdict on autonomous revenue authorities (ARAs). Lledo et al. claim that they 'have a particularly bad record in Africa' (Lledo, Schneider, and Moore 2004, page 7). Their record is examined by Fjeldstad and Moore (2009). Africa-wide, Fjeldstad and Moore generally take a less sanguine view than we do about the ability of tax structure changes to increase the revenue ratio, but nonetheless conclude that 'our impression is that the creation of ARAs has increased the *potential* of African governments to enhance central government revenues by acting as a conduit for the introduction of a range of sensible reforms in tax administration'. Bergman (2003) shows that the greater autonomy of Chile in relation to Argentina was a factor in causing compliance rates in Chile to be higher than in Argentina.

managed, a basis for a progressive bargaining process between producers and the state.[72]

Tax bargaining can improve governance, then, specifically in the sense of contributing to a pro-poor outcome. In achieving this, we need to emphasize that the timing of the two-way bargain matters. Both the Argentinian and, even more, the Bolivian export-tax bargains were more easily achievable as a consequence of being launched into an oil and gas export boom, so that it could be illustrated that it was the gaining sectors which were being taxed to finance those who were suffering.

In addition, the nature of the 'improvements in governance' which can be expected from tax reform is worth considering. As we have seen, compliance with tax measures is strongly associated with trust and approval of institutional performance (Bergman 2003, page 616). But which institutions? We argue that it is not only the quality of tax institutions which matters, but broader measures of fairness. The failures of tax compliance in Bolivia, leading eventually to conflict in 2003, did not arise just because of faults in the tax authority but, as described earlier, because of injustices and inequities in the overall structure of governance, in particular access to justice, finance, and public service administration (see also Chapter 10 below). The same can be said of Argentina at the turn of the millennium, and for that matter Ghana in the 1980s: it was an overall long-term change in public trust in the mechanism of governance as a whole which made a tax-for-governance bargain easier to achieve. In Chapter 6 we shall argue that the range of institutional indicators required to bring about equity in this sense is incompletely captured by the 'standard' (World Bank) governance sectors, and will suggest additional indicators based especially on the principle of access to markets by low-income groups.

5.5 ASSET TRANSFERS AND OTHER PRO-POOR OPTIONS—A POSTSCRIPT

The main options for long-term poverty reduction which we have been examined in this chapter have been fiscal: transfers of public revenue or expenditure in favour of the poor, rather than transfers of capital. It was not always thus. The dog which, in recent times, has failed to bark in the night is transfers of *assets* from the rich to the poor. Historically, land reforms have been a major instrument for transferring assets, for example in Russia and Mexico before the First World War, in much of Latin America including Bolivia during the 1940s and 1950s, and in Taiwan, South Korea, and other South-East Asian countries including Indonesia

[72] This argument is illustrated by Brautigam's study of Mauritius, which also argues that 'in some instances, pacts shaped by these bargains can serve as a way to make foreign assistance into an earned resource, avoiding the deleterious effects of state dependence' (Brautigam 2008b, page 136). This point is further taken up in Chapter 7.

and Malaysia during the 1950s and 60s. All of these initiatives were sponsored by the national state. During the 'MacNamara era', as discussed in Chapter 2, an attempt was made to put the force of the World Bank and bilateral donors behind programmes of asset transfer and land reform, following the logic that lack of assets was the main cause of poverty and provision of such assets therefore the main potential ladder out of it. Additional support for this logic was provided by the controversial 'inverse farm size rule', which suggested that small farms had higher productivity than large farms[73] (Singh 1990, etc.). Countries whose rural development strategy embraced a donor-supported or Bank-supported land reform process in the 1970s included Brazil, Peru, India, Sri Lanka, Nepal, Bangladesh, and Kenya, in all cases as an element in integrated programmes of rural development—building on the insight of the Asian green revolutions that poverty reduction requires action to remove market failure across a range of input markets, but broadening the sphere of intervention into health and education, which was a major focus of *Redistribution with Growth*. In some experimental cases, the vision of policymakers extended into the transfer into the hands of the poor of assets other than land, for example water rights in Bangladesh. There exists some evidence, for example from Mexico, Peru, and India, suggesting that the land transfers of this time increased the income levels of the poor.[74]

In the 1980s global recession, much of this enthusiasm for pro-poor asset transfers dwindled. Donors' new preoccupation with market liberalization, structural adjustment, and 'getting the prices right' allowed little space for measures which overrode rather than liberated the market, and the only land reform programmes which therefore continued were those, as in India and Sri Lanka, which relied on national governments for their impetus. Once poverty focus returned in the 1990s, there is very little mention, for example in the Poverty Reduction Strategy Papers published by donors and recipients, of what for much of the previous century had been one of the main instruments for achieving social justice in the developing world. This is ironic, because over the last ten years *assessments* of poverty dynamics have been turning ever more towards measuring poverty dynamics through changes in asset values rather than income-based measures of poverty,[75] even while anti-poverty *actions* exhibit the opposite tendency.

The three exceptions to this general rule within our sample, where asset transfers remained a significant element in long-term pro-poor strategies within our period, are Bolivia, Zimbabwe, and Russia. This is no coincidence, as these are the three countries where the disparity in land tenure between *latifundios* and *minifundios*, between those with no land and those with abundant land, was most in evidence. Albeit that in Russia after 1923, the large landholdings were collectivized into state hands, many of them have now reconcentrated themselves back into the hands of oligarchies (Chapter 12 below) and inequality of income in Russia is once again severe.

[73] For a comprehensive empirical review of the debate and the literature on the 'inverse farm size rule' see Singh (1990), Chapter 4, Tables 4.1 to 4.3.

[74] See Mosley (1982b) on Peru; Besley and Burgess (2000) on India; Deininger (2002) fn. 4, page 991.

[75] For example, this kind of asset-based approach underlies most of the essays in Carter and Barrett (2006) and in Addison, Hulme, and Kanbur (2009); see also the first chapter of Valente (2008).

In *Bolivia*, following fifty years of weak attempts to follow up on the comprehensive reforms of 1952, an unsuccessful attempt at a 'neoliberal' land reform was made under the Ley INRA of 1996. This aimed at 'a balance in rural property ownership structures between a market logic and a formal recognition of communal and indigenous landholdings' (Domingo 2009, page 159) but has tended to serve mostly the interests of large landholdings in the eastern regions: in other words to have a pauperizing rather than a progressive impact. Following the Morales landslide of December 2005, the issue of land reform was addressed in November 2006; not, however, by attacking individual property rights, but by making underused property more liable to confiscation (Domingo 2009, page 173). The hope was to reverse the re-concentration of rural property in the hands of large landholders in the eastern part of the country, who have repeatedly demanded by referendum the right to secede from the poor western regions of Bolivia (Chapter 10 below). Land titling has been speeded up under the Morales administration: nearly 500,000 hectares or formerly communal land have been distributed as private plots to poor farmers since the beginning of 2006 (Weissbrot and Sandoval 2007), but policy has fallen short of any encroachment on the *latifundios* in the lowlands, or even restrictions on their maximum size.

Zimbabwe is one of the few countries, possibly the only one in Africa, which always held out against structural adjustment since its beginnings, allowing itself to go only once and reluctantly to the IMF for finance, in 1991, and breaking off the relationship with the Fund shortly thereafter. As discussed above it was one of the first 'green revolution countries' in Africa, but the momentum of agricultural development, first interrupted by financial constraints in 1986, could not be easily reignited even with the help of the Fund's standbys, and unemployment and poverty rates were in long-term deterioration after the mid-1990s. This is the political context of the decision of President Mugabe to sanction compulsory land reform, in the form of invasions of the large commercial farms, after 1999; it was one of the few ways of creating new livelihoods which held out the hope of regaining popularity within his Shona-speaking heartland which was also financially feasible. A pro-poor tag could also be plausibly attached to a process by which large farms were occupied by 'war veterans', who were originally designated to be the main beneficiaries from invasions. However, by 2002 it was already clear that many of the beneficiaries from invasions were not poor people, new or old, but senior civil servants and government ministers.

In *Russia* the context is different from the cases of Bolivia and Zimbabwe, indeed from most cases in the developing world, because the asset which needs to be reallocated is not underused large landholdings in private ownership, but underused collective farms in public ownership. (Indeed this is the third phase of asset transfer in Russia: there has already been a transition from a feudal to a capitalist land system in the second half of the nineteenth century, and a second which collectivized the private farms created by the first reform.) The reform effort during the 1990s and 2000s,[76] has concentrated on large collective farms in

[76] Land reform was done in two steps, which often occurred simultaneously. The first step was to transfer land (sometimes by sale, but often it was given away free) from collective state ownership to collective ownership of the peasants living and working in collective farms. In the second stage,

European Russia (especially the more fertile south) and on these 'overall output based on large collective enterprises is stagnant' (Childress 2002), and employment is falling, slightly, so that although about fourteen per cent of the land is now in private ownership the overall tendency is towards a decline in the real personal incomes of agricultural workers on these farms, even through the boom years of the 2000s (see Chapter 12 below). Signs of change are indeed appearing, such as the astounding fact that half of food production is now coming from household plots within the collective structure (Childress 2002, page 981, quoting Serova and Khramova 2001). But many of these household plots are attached to second country homes (*dachas*) owned by middle class people, not by the poor, and there is extremely little evidence that the very poor (a majority of whom are in any case in urban areas: World Bank 2004, page xvi) are able to capture many of the benefits of land reform. Indeed (Childress continues) 'Private traders and processors have been extremely slow to fill the gaps in output distribution . . . left by the withdrawal of state orders. The severity of rural poverty and underdevelopment in the social sphere is perhaps the most unexpected result [of reform]' (Childress 2002, page 980). The World Bank's comprehensive report on Russian poverty (World Bank 2004) does not even mention land transfers as an influence, positive or negative, on poverty outcomes.

These are the only significant cases of asset transfers in our sample, and in all cases the impact on the poor is at best small. But of course the sample is not a representative one: are we leaving any crucial cases out? The twenty-first century case where most hopes have been pinned on land reform is South Africa—in 1990, one of the most unequal structures of land ownership and governance in the world, possibly the most unequal of all (Deininger and Squire 1996). The government's Land Transfer Programme has indeed been at the centre of policy debate in South Africa. As in Bolivia and in all modern-day Bank-supported land transfer programmes, this is land reform based not on coercion but on a free exchange between willing buyers and willing sellers (Deininger 2002). As of 2008, less than five per cent of the previously white-owned large farms had been transferred into black smallholder ownership, well below the government's hopes of transferring thirty per cent of agricultural land by 1999 (Lahiff 2007). And, on balance, the effect on black smallholder food security of such reform as there has been has been negative[77] (Valente 2008, Chapters 4–5; Valente 2009). Although the 'inverse farm size rule' has been found to hold in principle for South Africa[78] it obstinately fails to translate into a pay-off for the modality of transfer which has been used in the country so far, either in Valente's study or others using different farm samples and indicators of land reform effectiveness (e.g. Bradstock 2005). The reason for this counter-intuitive finding is not completely clear, but especially Valente's qualitative findings suggest that management failings created by the authorities'

individuals received certificates of entitlement to land in collective ownership (see Swinnen and Heinegg (2002), page 1023).

77 Valente uses econometric methods on national sample survey data to assess the overall relationship, accompanied by combined quantitative-qualitative methodology in two provinces in the north and east of the country.

78 'The inverse farm size-efficiency relationship . . . is present in South African agriculture, despite a history of policies favouring relatively large mechanized farms' (van Zyl 1996, page 304).

requirement for farms to be operated under farm models that do not match the beneficiaries' skills may lie at the heart of the problem. Many smallholders neither had any farm management skills on acquiring assets under the programme, nor apparently picked any up on the job as settlers, with the consequence that the contribution which they were able to make to marketed output and even to their own food security was severely limited. In addition, many large farms were simply not subdivided at the point of reform by the incoming settlers but simply occupied as large units by cooperatives, thereby making any benefits from reform harder to realize. The apparent failure of this enormous initiative is one contributory factor underlying the 'anti-poor growth trajectory' of South Africa in the 1990s and possibly in the 2000s also: the paradox is that amidst all of rapid growth, a liberation of the labour market and a massive profusion of pro-poor initiatives in South Africa, unemployment and poverty in South Africa have gone on increasing[79] and the apparent inability of the poor to capitalize on the one asset which it might have seemed easiest for them to acquire cannot have helped.

We have only examined four cases in a highly informal way. These are only cases of the most 'traditional' type of asset transfer, namely land reform, and it may be that more experimental types of transfer, involving water and other natural resource assets, would work more effectively as instruments of poverty reduction. It might also be appropriate to think of the currently highly fashionable expenditure shifts towards human capital (health and education), already analysed in Sections 2 and 3 above, as asset transfers rather than as consumption transfers. For these reasons it would be very premature to suggest from these examples that asset transfers cannot any longer fulfil their historical role of leading the process of poverty reduction; but there are a number of cautionary words for optimists here.

5.6 SUMMARY AND CONCLUSION

We have examined a number of policy alternatives for reducing poverty over the long term. The success of these inevitably connects with the institutional capacities examined in the next chapter.

Politically, the iron law of political impotence of the poor has been overcome by a combination of three routes. The first route, observed in Uganda (and also, outside our sample, in Ethiopia) is where a guerrilla army led by a low-income interest group takes over the elite and commits it to a pro-poor programme. The second route, observable in Ghana, Argentina, and Zimbabwe, is where a weak, divided, or besieged elite opts to provide benefits to a low-income group or groups in exchange for their political support. The third route, observable in Russia and

[79] Between 1995 and 2003 GDP growth ran at an average of four per cent per annum: the unemployment rate rose from seventeen per cent to twenty-eight per cent on the narrow definition (and from twenty-nine per cent to forty-two per cent on a broad definition) and the poverty headcount, between 1995 and 2000, rose from thirty-two per cent to forty-nine per cent. These data are all taken from the *Journal of African Economies* special issue on the South African economy under democracy: see Du Plessis and Smit (2007, page 670) for the growth data, Kingdon and Knight (2007, pages 814–15), and finally for the poverty data, see Aguero, Carter, and May (2007, page 207) who, however, note that there has been 'perhaps some improvement [unquantified PM] since 2000' (*ibid.*).

Indonesia, is where the elite adopts pro-poor policies to pre-empt a threat of insurrection.

Expenditure policies are a powerful instrument of pro-poor action, as they can relatively quickly be targeted on, and switched between, the interest groups whom the government wishes to propitiate. More generally, they can, as illustrated in the last chapter, be used to send a signal to targeted groups as to which interests they identify with and how they expect to arbitrate between them. We examine here the politics of different elements in *pro-poor expenditure*, which is a mixture of social expenditures (health, education, and social protection) and pro-agricultural expenditures (direct support for agriculture, plus infrastructure), with military expenditures having a negative weight. Our empirical analysis suggests that the combination of all of these elements is the ideal way to reduce poverty, but this ideal approach may not be politically feasible. The two most dramatic cases of long-term poverty reduction examined in our sample, Indonesia and Uganda, are both cases where pro-agricultural expenditure (particularly green-revolution food crops in the first case and particularly cash crops in the second) was prioritized over a long time period and was a primary reason for the fall in poverty. The alternative policy of pushing up social expenditures, as the experience of Bolivia and several countries in Latin America illustrates, may not be so effective, even though it is the favoured strategy of the aid donors. One particular reason for this is that it fails to overcome the problem of urban bias, or otherwise put the problem of exclusion of the rural poorest.

Pro-poor expenditure policies cannot realize their potential without an adequate expansion of tax capacity, which as we saw poses its own political problems: weak governments may have a chronic fear of grappling with the necessary reforms to expand tax capacity. But the tax trap can be sprung, as we illustrate from two pairs of comparisons, one between the two African peasant export economies and one between the two Latin American economies in our sample. In all four, limitations in fiscal capacity were the consequence of a post-colonial dependence on natural-resource based taxes, out of which there was diversification during the 1980s and early 90s in dialogue with the international financial institutions, also a move towards autonomous revenue authorities, and these developments of themselves increased the productivity and progressivity of the revenue base. In our Latin American country cases, but not in Africa, the evolution of the tax system has gone one step further, into a reaction against the entire Washington Consensus, born from the bitter experience of the 'East Asian crisis' years, within which the tax element notably consisted of export taxes earmarked against social expenditures. Both of these policy steps have been favourable towards an evolution from purely coercive forms of taxation towards 'revenue bargaining' in which the state bargains with representative elements of the tax base with the purpose of bolstering its own legitimacy: in the Latin American cases, the attachment of improvised export taxes to expenditures in favour of the elderly and the unemployed gave this bargaining a pro-poor twist.

In the 1970s especially, the option of promoting long-term poverty reduction through asset transfers was enthusiastically promoted by aid donors; in the 1980s this policy instrument fell somewhat into disuse. It was revived in a few places in the 1990s, but even where the political difficulties were overcome the poverty reduction impact has not been proven.

Thus, long-term poverty reduction requires a pro-poor political impulse, and a pro-poor political impulse requires a supportive expenditure pattern, and a supportive expenditure pattern requires, at a minimum, enough fiscal firepower to finance it. But these are only the basics of central government. In practice the requirements of pro-poor action are often found not in policy but in the operation of institutions, many of which are not run by government at all. We now consider these institutions.

6

Institutions, state capacity, and poverty

6.1 INTRODUCTION

Throughout our discussion, institutional strength and weakness have determined the ability of anti-poverty efforts to sustain themselves. A desire to build up the institutional capacity of developing countries, especially in relation to the development of land and education resources, underlaid the 'first poverty wave' of the 1970s, as described in Chapter 2, and when many of the initial structural adjustment reforms of the 1980s ran into the sand, it was again to the idea of institutional reform, especially in the fields of bureaucratic transparency and judicial process, that the reformers returned (World Bank 1997). When recovery from the global shock of the end of the 1990s was difficult to achieve and threatened to catch the victims in a poverty trap, institutional failings, and in particular the erosion of services which provided a buffer against poverty, were frequently the cause, as we saw in Bolivia and parts of Russia in Chapter 3; and institutional failings persisting over a longer period have prevented many African countries and others in the 'bottom billion' from getting launched on the road to long-term growth of any sort, let alone pro-poor growth. In particular, where countries were structurally too feeble to protect themselves against insurrection, economic crisis, and the localized rioting associated with it could easily, as we saw in Chapter 4, persist into chronic conflict, or escalate into all-out war,[1] both of which destroyed all possibility of sustained investment.

In Chapter 5, we went further, and identified governance quality and institutional capacity as factors which influence the long-term trend of poverty, supplementary to the expenditure, tax, and other policy measures examined in that chapter and often interlinked with them in the sense that without adequate institutions policy could exercise little leverage over the economy. We now need to define these capacities, which in the literature often have rather elastic meanings, and illustrate how they connect with individual well-being. *Governance quality*, in this chapter, refers to the ability of institutions of government and civil society to fairly select representatives (democracy), govern (government effectiveness and regulatory quality), exercise civil and criminal judgments which command people's respect (rule of law), maintain themselves in face of

[1] Bolivia (1999 to the present) is the best illustration of persistent riot-type conflict from Chapter 5, and Sierra Leone (1987–2000), Cote d'Ivoire (1997 to the present), and Zimbabwe (1999 to the present) are three examples of 'adjustment operations gone bad' in which the fragility and lack of legitimacy of the state converted short-term crises, in all of which the IMF was involved, into long-term chaos.

threats of disruption (political stability), and finally respect people's rights to express themselves freely in public and in the press (voice and accountability); the headings in brackets are the categories used by the World Bank in its Governance Indicators.[2] *Institutional capacity* refers to the effectiveness of government and civil society in allocating resources at the local level, and our particular concern is whether this is done in a pro-poor manner, which even the massive range of governance indicators currently on the market does not attempt to measure. In this chapter we seek to define the political processes which determine governance quality and institutional capacity and how they relate to poverty dynamics. Even more than in previous chapters, it needs to be emphasized that in discussing politics, we are not just talking about government. One of the main characteristics of the structural adjustment process was a transfer of many government functions, including the poverty-reducing ones examined in the last chapter (agricultural support, primary health and education, local infrastructure, and social protection) out of government to NGOs and the private sector, and therefore the idea of 'institutional quality' needs to encompass these institutions as well. As far as it is feasible, we shall seek to document the impact of these public-to-private-and-third-sector shifts, but readers will be aware that the voluntary sector in development, now a $20 billion per annum industry,[3] is a territory characterized by the presence of massive hope and idealism and, still, very few data.

Both governance and institutional capacity are of course highly disputed concepts, which have proved very hard to assess and measure objectively. A good point of departure is provided by the political economy of Arthur Lewis, who more than most governance specialists of the post-war period came into contact with developing-country policymakers, notably in his two-year secondment to the first president of an independent Ghana, Kwame Nkrumah, in the late 1950s.[4] In his *Theory of Economic Growth*, Lewis defined the effectiveness of governance in terms of law and order,[5] democratic rights,[6] and protection of the public services from corruption, which he placed at the heart of his analysis.[7] He assessed the effectiveness of economic institutions in terms of the security with which individuals are able to retain the rewards from work, from asset ownership and trading in markets (Lewis 1955, pages 57–84). This tradition of work operated from first principles, and contained few numbers. When the World Bank in the

[2] The World Bank's governance indicators are described by Kaufmann, Kraay, and Mastruzzi (2006) and are displayed at http://www. worldbank.org/wbi/governance/pubs/govmatters4sra.html. A large range of governance indicators now exists, and these are helpfully summarized in the *Quality of Government Codebook* published by the University of Gothenburg Quality of Government Institute (http://www.qog. pol.gu.se).

[3] $12 billion in 1999 at 1990 prices.

[4] This encounter is discussed in Tignor (2006), Chapter 5.

[5] 'The primary function of a government is to maintain law and order' (Lewis 1955, page 377).

[6] 'The case for democracy' Lewis emphasizes,' is not that it prevents tension, but that open discussion creates a healthier society than is achieved by suppression' (Lewis 1965, page 44).

[7] Amongst nine ways in which the state can harm the process of economic development, Lewis lists 'plundering the citizens', 'promoting the exploitation of one class by another', and 'excessive control' (Lewis 1955, page 408). At one point he asserts that 'most governments are, and always have been, corrupt and inefficient. The art of creating a public service free from corruption has been learnt only slowly, and only in a few countries' (Lewis 1955, page 83).

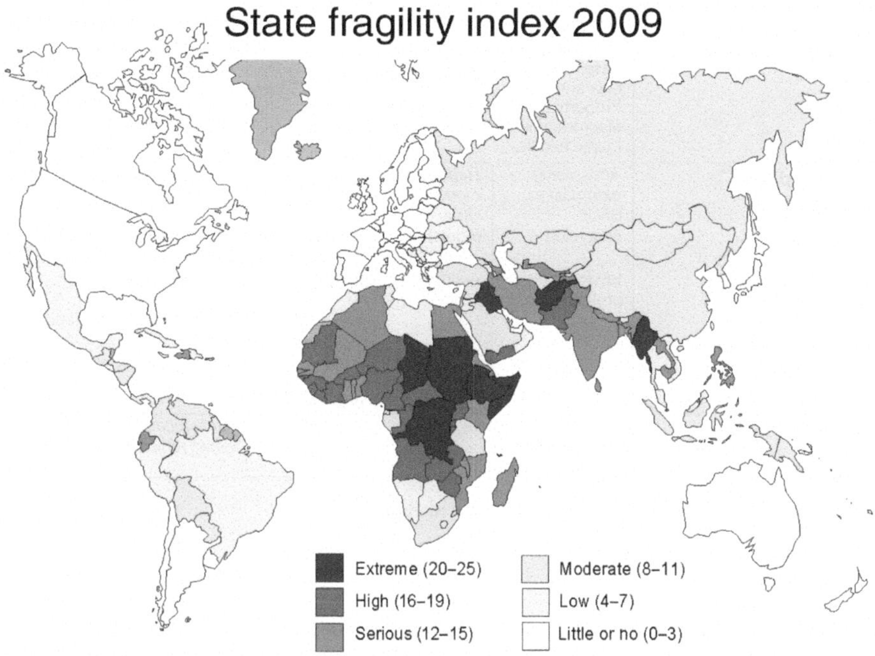

Figure 6.1 Indices of state fragility by country (Polity IV index).
Source: Center for Systemic Peace.

1990s, disappointed with the results which structural adjustment was achieving especially in the poorer countries, decided also to focus on governance as a key to development (Chapter 2 above; World Bank 1997) it attempted to go beyond Lewis by specifying measurable indicators of governance quality, as discussed above (Kaufman, Kraay, and Mastruzzi 2006). These (not far removed from Lewis' specification) are political stability, rule of law, bureaucratic quality, democratic accountability, and limitations on corruption. A composite of these indicators yields the Polity IV map (Figure 6.1), in which weaknesses in governance, embodied in the concept of *state fragility*, are entirely concentrated in low-income Asia and Africa.

It is worth examining how these indicators emerge from the Bank's analysis. The Bank, in its *1997 World Development Report* review of governance, began with an admirable schema (Figure 6.2) which defined the functions of the state as 'addressing market failure' and 'improving equity'. Within each category, it then specified three possible levels of intervention: the 'minimal function' of providing pure public goods without which the state would fall apart, the 'intermediate functions' of protecting the vulnerable and making markets work properly, and the 'activist functions' of promoting redistribution and better-functioning markets.

The list of indicator variables on which the Bank collects governance data (Kaufman, Kraay, and Mastruzzi 2006) is extremely comprehensive, comprising 'several hundred individual variables measuring perceptions of governance,

	Addressing market failure			Improving equity
Minimal functions	**Providing pure public goods:** Defence Law and order Property rights Macro-economic management Public health			**Protecting the poor:** Anti-poverty programmes Disaster relief
Intermediate functions	*Addressing externalities:* Basic education Environmental protection	*Regulating monopoly:* Utility regulation Antitrust policy	*Overcoming imperfect information:* Insurance (health, life, pensions) Financial regulation Consumer protection	*Providing social insurance:* Redistributive pensions Family allowances Unemployment insurance
Activist functions	*Coordinating private activity:* Fostering markets Cluster initiatives			*Redistribution:* Asset redistribution

Figure 6.2 Functions of the state (after World Bank 1997).

drawn from thirty-one separate data sources constructed by twenty-five different organizations' (Teorell et al. 2008, page 61). However, the list is principally concerned with the left-hand half of Figure 6.2, 'Addressing market failure', rather than the right-hand half, 'Improving equity'. Indeed, within the heading of 'Addressing market failure', the concern is, as in Lewis, with indicators of central-government effectiveness: political stability, rule of law, bureaucratic quality, democratic accountability, and restrictions on the level of corruption, rather than with imperfections, and measures to correct them, in individual markets, or with the issue, vital to us, of how these imperfections impinge on different social groups. Much of this chapter is concerned with attempting to fill this gap.

On the question of whether or how these governance indicators affect economic performance, we present evidence from two samples. The first (Table 6.1) is from our 'full' sample of more than one hundred countries, with GDP growth as the dependent variable. The relationship is estimated with and without lags for both low-income countries and all countries.

Only government stability is always significant, and law and order is significant most of the time (i.e. in the full sample and the low-income sample, with and without lags). Three of the World Bank's 'famous five' governance indicators (bureaucratic quality, democratic accountability, and corruption) however, are *never* significant. When we apply a Granger-causality analysis to the same data (Hudson and Mosley 2008, Table 5.1), we find indeed that the only variables which can be seen as causing growth are, once again, law and order and internal and external conflict—the ones which also show up as significant in the regression tests—and that, apart from bureaucratic quality, an improvement in any of the other governance indicators leads to an *increase* in corruption, which, however, by the previous analysis, does not significantly affect growth performance for better or for worse.

Table 6.1 Growth equations

Variable	Full sample	Full sample	Full sample	Low income	High income
Log	.061	.0378	.0398	.191	.1167
population	**0.46**	**0.28**	**0.29**	**1.02**	**0.90**
Log	–.2272	*–.2647*	–.2659*	–.2217	–.1068
area	**–2.04**	**–2.34**	**–2.32**	**–1.24**	**–0.84**
Landborder	9.3e–05	9.7e–05	9.7e–05	1.2e–04	-6.3e–05
	1.79	**1.84**	**1.81**	**1.66**	**–1.06**
Coast	–.1104	–.0745	–.0777	–.2891	.1833
	–0.28	**–0.19**	**–0.19**	**–0.56**	**0.41**
Colony	–.8448	–1.046*	–1.049*	–.8823	1.554*
	–1.92	**–2.35**	**–2.33**	**–1.48**	**2.06**
Religion	–.1324	–.1685	–.1689	–.2132	.1169
	–1.15	**–1.47**	**–1.47**	**–1.60**	**0.55**
Trend	–.0306	–.0238	–.0232	–.0075	–.0537*
	–1.33	**–1.06**	**–1.03**	**–0.24**	**–1.97**
Government	.3443**	.3072**	.3062**	.2271**	.4697**
stability	**6.03**	**5.49**	**5.47**	**3.06**	**6.16**
Law and order	.4403**	.4067**	.4004**	.6467**	–.1964
	3.79	**3.53**	**3.48**	**4.66**	**–0.96**
Bureaucratic	–.0888	–.1929	–.2108	–.2055	–.2741
quality	**–0.57**	**–1.19**	**–1.32**	**–1.09**	**–0.83**
Corruption	–.2119	–.1817	–.1764	–.2762	.1226
	–1.70	**–1.46**	**–1.43**	**–1.70**	**0.75**
Democratic	.1205	.0888	.0899	.0069	.2009
accountability	**1.21**	**0.90**	**0.91**	**0.06**	**1.19**
Earthquake	–1.778*	–1.804*	–1.804*	–5.262**	–.7818
	–2.15	**–2.24**	**–2.24**	**–2.77**	**–1.11**
SSA	–2.191**	–2.2**	–2.203**	–1.131**	
	–3.72	**–3.69**	**–3.65**	**–1.52**	
N. Africa	–.7242	–.7086	–.6973	–.4148	
	–0.74	**–0.71**	**–0.69**	**–0.37**	
S. America	–1.114*	–1.301**	–1.304**	–.5803	–1.68*
	–2.27	**–2.62**	**–2.59**	**–0.87**	**–2.27**
Asia	.9834	1.009	1.022	2.067**	–.0299
	1.87	**1.89**	**1.90**	**2.74**	**–0.05**
Middle E.	–1.31*	–1.291*	–1.301*	–1.162	–1.475
	–2.23	**–2.17**	**–2.16**	**–1.27**	**–1.92**
Island	.3858	.3137	.3097	.5402	–.6834
	0.80	**0.64**	**0.62**	**0.66**	**–1.49**
Base year	–8.4e–05**	–6.9e–05**	–6.5e–05**	2.8e–04**	–1.1e–04**
GDPPC	**–2.79**	**–2.17**	**–2.07**	**2.48**	**–3.37**
Weighted	.5067**	.4458**	.4447**	.6605**	.2959**
growth	**6.20**	**5.54**	**5.53**	**5.00**	**3.60**
Lagged	7.016**	6.852**	6.928**	8.461**	59.21**
aid	**4.48**	**4.40**	**4.43**	**4.85**	**2.17**
GDPPC error		.0609			
Lag 1 year		**0.43**			
GDPPC error		–.2595*	–.2258**	–.2221*	–.562**
Lag 2 year		**–2.16**	**–2.64**	**–2.20**	**–2.93**
Constant	–.3904	.4068	.4204	–1.609	.5212
	–0.40	**0.42**	**0.43**	**–1.16**	**0.34**
Observations	2332	2325	2325	1614	711
chi^2	288.1	277.7	275.2	242.5	139.2

Notes: ordinary least squares regressions. Emboldened text represents t-statistics, **/* denotes significance at the 1%/5% levels of significance. Poorer (richer) countries are defined as those with per capita income less (more) than $10,000 in the base year.

Source: World Bank, *World Development Indicators*; University of Gothenburg, *Quality of Government Indicators* (www. qog.pol.gu.se).

Do these results also hold up across our case-study sample? Our main concern is of course with poverty impact, and so in this sample we examine the effect of governance variables on poverty as well as growth. In several cases, such as rule of law and measurement of corruption, alternative governance indicators to those calculated by the Bank have emerged, and Table 6.2 sets these out.

The data now tell a more confused story, but still one that is consistent with the idea of rule of law as the key governance indicator at the macro-level. In the countries where poverty is declining over the long term between 1990 and 2005—Ghana, Argentina, Uganda, and in a mild way Indonesia—there is, with the exception of Ghana, an improvement over the same period in the rule of law measure and in the DPI 'checks and balances' measure of bureaucratic capacity. (Corruption, according to both datasets, is getting worse in all of these places except Indonesia and Ghana.) In one of the countries which in poverty terms is a puzzle, namely Bolivia, where social PPE and the long-term tax ratio are both on an upward trend, and yet poverty until 2006 was going up rather than down, the decline in rule of law (as expressed in the riot-type violence of Chapter 4) helps to explain this. Political instability and a decline in rule of law are found also in Kenya and Zimbabwe, where poverty is increasing.

In addition to this evidence on the contribution of *governance* to pro-poor growth, we also need to understand the contribution of *institutions*. In many cases institutional performance is tightly interwoven with policy effectiveness, as we can illustrate in relation to some of the pro-poor policy initiatives described in the previous chapter:

- *The green revolution* (Figure 5.4 and pages 117–22 above), a major correlate of poverty reduction in Indonesia and Uganda, required localized markets and distribution channels for inputs such as fertilizer and irrigation equipment, and institutional support (in Indonesia mostly from the public sector, in Uganda much more from the private) was required to make these inputs available at planting time. Often small-scale finance was required as well, and financial institutions needed to be in a position both to supply the loans and to make sure they were repaid on time.
- *Access to primary health and education* (Table 5.3 and pages 111–16 above) requires finance for school fees. Often, as we can document from South Africa, Uganda, and Zimbabwe (Mosley and Rock 2004), microfinance loans have been diverted from their intended function of supporting small business in order to pay these fees. Micro-insurance has also been used extensively in South Asia, more sporadically elsewhere, to support primary health care expenditures.
- *Access to labour markets* (Chapter 2 and pages 99–108) required public, NGO, or private sector support for road-building and other infrastructure. It also required the confidence and trust required to establish labour markets on a regional rather than a village basis.
- *Social protection programmes* (Table 5.3 and pages 111–16 above) required private and 'social' entrepreneurs to establish them, increasingly through private or joint public/private finance initiatives rather than through the 'Indonesian model' of extending the range of public provision.

Table 6.2 Case study countries—measures of state weakness in relation to measures of economic performance, 1990–2007.

	Economic performance			Tax capacity	Governance measures (1990–2007 unless otherwise specified)								2007 value of overall governance quality index (1990 = 100)
	GNP per capita		Poverty measures		Political stability	Freedom of expression	Bureaucratic quality			Rule of law measures		Corruption	
	Average for crisis period (dates as specified)	Average for post-crisis period (dates as specified)			World Bank measure of political stability	Freedom House Polity 2 measure of democracy	DPI checks and balances measure	ICRG quality of government measure	World Bank? Government effectiveness measure	World Bank rule of law measure	Freedom House rule of law measure	Transparency International measure (Ti_corrupt)	
Middle-income countries Indonesia	−3.6 (1997–9)	3.5 (2000–6)	Fell from 18% (1987) to 12% (2006) but with increase to 24% in 1997–8	Fell from 16.9% to 12.3%	Declined from −0.66 to −1.41	Increased from 4.7 to 7.7	Increased from average near 1 to average near 2	..	Declined from 0.08 to −0.39	..	Declined from −0.41 to −1.03	Increased from 2 to 2.2	149
Malaysia	−2.5 (1997–8)	3.3 (1999–2006)	Fell from 15% (1989) to <10% (2006)	Rose from 5% to 5.9%	Declined from 0.76 to 0.48	Increased from 5.58 to 5.75	Static around 4.00	Static around 0.55	Fell from 0.75 to 0.71	..	Declined from 0.8 to 0.39	Declined from 5.3 to 5.1	82
Bolivia	0.5 (1999–2005)	1.5 (2005–7)	Rose slightly from 60% (1990s average) to 65% (2005)	Rose from 8% to 17%	Declined from 0.38 to −1.15	Declined from 8.5 to 7.8	Decreased from 6 to 5	Increased from 0.16 to 0.44	..	Declined from −0.71 to −0.78	Increased from 4 to 13	Declined from 2.8 to 2.5	122

Continued

Table 6.2 Continued

	Economic performance			Tax capacity	Governance measures (1990–2007 unless otherwise specified)								2007 value of overall governance quality index (1990 = 100)
	GNP per capita		Poverty measures		Political stability	Freedom of expression	Bureaucratic quality			Rule of law measures		Corruption	
Argentina	−5.9 (1999–2002)	7.8 (2000–6)	Rose from 38% (Oct 1990) to 57% (Oct 2002) then fell to 34% (end 2005) 'Extreme poor' (*indigentes*) rose from *c*.10–15% in 1990 to 27% in 2002, then declined to 12.2% in 2002	Rose from 8% to 15%	Rose from −2.35 to 0.82	Fell from 9.08 to 7.8	Declined from 5 to 2	Declined from 0.55 to 0.46	..	Declined from 0.23 to −0.56	Increased from 5 to 10		174
Russian Federation	0.9 (1998–9)	7.1 (2000–6)	Rose from 10% (1987) to 29% (2000) then fell to 15% (2006)	Rose from 10.9% to 11.2%	Improved from −1.16 to −1.07	Declined from 6.9 to 5.5	Declined from 5 to 4	Increased from 0.3 to 0.58	..	Declined from −0.89 to −0.84	..	..	89
Low-income countries													
Uganda			Fell from 56% (1992) to 31% (2006)	Rose from 10% to 13%	Improved from −1.34 to −1.31	Increased from 2 to 3.58	Static at a value of 1 throughout	Increased from 0.22 to 0.5	..	Increased from −0.93 to −0.73	Increased from −0.93 to −0.62	Declined from 2.6 to 2.5	125
Ghana			Fell 51% (1990) to 39% (1999); possible further fall since then	Rose from 11.4% to 23%	Declined from −0.70 to −0.29	Increased from 2 to 8.6	Increased from 1 to 3	..	Declined from 0.05 to 0.03	Declined from −0.16 to −0.23	Declined from 0.17 to 0.11	Increased from 3.3 to 3.5	188

Kenya	−1.0 (1999–2002)	2.2 (2003–6)	Rose from 42% (1991) to 52% (1997)	Rose from 17% to 18%	Declined from −0.65 to −1.15	Increased from 1.58 to 7.83	Increased from 1 to 3	Declined from 0.58 to 0.46	Declined from −0.64 to −0.72	Declined from −0.82 to −0.94	Declined from −0.83 to −1.03	Declined from 2.5 to 2.1	203
Zimbabwe		−6.4 (2000–5)	Increased from 35% (1990) to 60% est. (2005)	Increased from 24% (1990) to 26% (1997)	Declined from −0.37 to −1.57	Declined from 2.66 to 1.16	Decreased from 4 to 2	Decreased from 0.44 to 0.19	Declined from −0.03 to −1.1	Declined from −0.28 to −1.46	Declined from −0.28 to −0.79	Declined from 4.2 to 2.6	42

Sources: (1) and (2) GDP and (3) Poverty trend: from Table 5.2 above. Democratic Accountability: Freedom House Polity 2 measure (from ICRG) This is defined on a six point scale. It is a measure of how responsive government is to its people, on the basis that the less responsive it is, the more likely it is that the government will fall, peacefully in a democratic society, but possibly violently in a non-democratic one. The points in this component are awarded on the basis of the type of governance enjoyed by the country in question and takes into account: (1) whether the government alternates and that there are fair elections, (2) evidence of restrictions on the activity of non-government political parties, (3) evidence of checks and balances between the executive, legislature, and judiciary, (4) evidence of an independent judiciary, and (5) evidence of the protection of personal liberties. *Source*: ICRG.

(2) Tax capacity: from Table 5.5.

(3) Law and order: from Polity IV index (wwwsystemicpeace.org/polity/polity4.htm).

(4) Corruption (ICRG index): this is defined on a six-point scale. High values indicate a lack of corruption. It is an assessment of corruption within the political system. It is focused on actual or potential corruption in the form of excessive patronage, nepotism, job reservations, 'favour-for-favours', secret party funding, and suspiciously close ties between politics and business. It is thus much more closely related to corruption associated with the military than a more general level of corruption would be. Source: ICRG.

(5) Legitimacy (from Englebert 2001a). A country is legitimate if its boundaries are consistent with its pre-1900 political frontiers (the countries defined as 'initially legitimate' by this criterion are Botswana, Burundi, Cape Verde, Ethiopia, Lesotho, Mauritius, Rwanda, Sao Tome, Seychelles, and Swaziland), or, if not, it subsequently recovered its previous 'sovereignty, identity and effective existence' and if the post-colonial state did not do 'severe violence' to pre-existing political institutions.

Notes: 'No change' denotes change 2000–5 statistically insignificant.

In all of these illustrations, access to the resources required to reduce poverty required the support of specific institutions. We now list these institutions and the manner in which we propose to incorporate them into a pro-poor institutions index.

First, institutions which *limit the cost of doing business* and develop trust, or social capital, between transactors. Obvious potential examples of these are regulatory bodies and business associations, but the list of groups capable of generating productivity-raising social capital is very much for debate. Putnam's well-known comparison of northern and southern Italy (1993) argued that differences between the two halves of the country not only in political democracy and press freedom (which of course are contained within the list of governance indicators in Table 6.2), but also in overall scope for establishing social networks, helped to explain the differences in economic development between north and south, and Putnam took a broad view of the kind of networks which were relevant, famously including sports clubs and church choirs in the list as well as business associations. More recently, a body of work on developing countries, including Woolcock (1998) and Narayan and Pritchett (1999) has empirically examined the relationships between social networks, trust, and the cost of doing business. Empirical attempts to estimate the level of social capital in particular communities, never mind the level of social capital amongst the poor, have often run into conceptual difficulties, as some forms of social linkage do harm rather than good, and researchers have sometimes retreated into the approach of measuring, by means of attitude surveys or experiments, *trust*—the output which social networks are expected to deliver, rather than the networks themselves (e.g. Barr 2003; Glaeser et al. 2000). Empirically, because trust data are sparse and localized, we do not use this approach here, but rather use the 'state-business relations index' developed by Leftwich, Sen, and te Velde (2008), which assesses, for African countries only, precisely the form of social capital which we wish to measure—namely the 'bridging and linking social capital',[8] which connects, and seeks to minimize, the transaction costs between businesses and governments.[9] This is a better measure of the costs of doing business than any other of which we are aware, and we will use it in our survey, using qualitative methods especially to examine the social linkages between *low-income* borrowers and government.

Second, institutions which provide *access to capital markets by the poor.* In developing-country environments where capital markets are localized and a majority of people are excluded from access to financial services, the scope for putting poor people within reach of the social and agricultural expenditures

[8] In the terminology of Narayan and Woolcock (2000) *bonding* social capital consists of horizontal social linkages within communities, *bridging* social capital consists of social linkages between communities, and *linking* social capital consists of linkages between units within a hierarchy, for example between agencies of government and the governed, or between regulators and the regulated.

[9] The method of compiling the state-business relations index is described in the first chapter of Leftwich, Sen, and te Velde (2008). The components of the index are an organized public sector vis-à-vis the public sector, the adequacy of communications between the two groups, and absence of harmful collusive behaviour (Leftwich et al. 2008, page 11). Especially the last of these indicators also assesses the ability of the minnows to avoid being swallowed up by the pike; and therefore it provides an indication of pro-poor institutional tendencies, although this clearly needs to be supported by qualitative evidence also.

described in Chapter 5 is inevitably limited, and the productivity of the poor is as a consequence low. Microfinance institutions—a blanket term covering loans, savings facilities, insurance, and other types of financial support for low-income people without collateral—have developed, over the last twenty years, a potential means of filling this institutional gap, which has been of huge importance in some low-income countries, notably, within our sample, Indonesia, and to a limited extent Bolivia, Uganda, and Kenya. However, the spread of such institutions has been very uneven, and their impact on poverty is disputed.[10] Moreover, provider institutions are only part of the institutional story: also important are regulatory bodies (whose contamination during the Bolivian crisis is examined in Chapter 10) and institutions which offer a non-financial buffer against shocks, for example famine early-warning systems operated by meteorological agencies, which enable poor people to anticipate shocks by planting drought-resistant crops. The MIX-market index, which we shall use, provides a measure of the penetration of microfinance institutions and is the best available quantitative measure of access to capital by low-income people, but the regulatory and non-financial dimensions of access to capital will need to be assessed qualitatively.

Third, institutions which *provide access to labour markets by the poor.* As we have emphasized, the poorest are those who have nothing to sell but their labour. Institutions which reduce the risks associated with establishing and sustaining labour markets (beyond the trust and microfinance mentioned above) therefore have an important poverty-reducing potential. Often, the supply of low-income labour to the market is constrained by barriers associated with gender relations,[11] ethnic and regional rivalries and conflicts[12] and dominance-dependence relationships,[13] as well as purely economic obstacles such as poor infrastructure, and it is often these relational factors, as well as purely technical factors such as

[10] See Mosley and Hulme (1998) and Morduch and Haley (2000).

[11] Alison Evans provided the following illustration of this problem in Uganda:

> On the demand side of the market [for agricultural labour] employers, who were generally but not exclusively male, stated that it was easier to deal with male workers because there were fewer misunderstandings between men. Many referred to the rumours and innuendo that would start in the village if a woman, and particularly a married woman, worked for another man for payment. The few male employers that did hire female labourers generally hired women that were either widowed, separated, or divorced. On the supply side, men and women both stated that doing manual work for another was no better than begging, and was a reflection of a poor and 'disorganized' home... For a married woman, working for a male employer was considered particularly damaging, not only to her own reputation, but also the reputation of her husband. The concern was expressed in the following terms: 'when a wife goes for casual labour and is paid by another man, she is dissatisfied with her home and is seeking a new husband' (Evans 1992, pages 114–15).

[12] Yoweri Museveni, Uganda's President from 1986 to date, defends his takeover of power and his imposition of a new constitution on the grounds that 'the interests and needs of the people were... not made a focal point because opportunistic politicians had so fragmented society that common interests were lost sight of' (Museveni 1997, page 36), and his argument is that it is not just political systems but national markets that were broken up by pre-1985 sectarianism.

[13] With reference to the persistence of chronic poverty, Geof Wood (2003) referred to the relationships which poor people form with their more powerful patrons as a 'Faustian bargain': in return for support and protection from those patrons, they cut themselves off from access to resources—in particular contact with the market—which they need in order to escape from chronic poverty.

infrastructure and labour market information, which determine who is able to climb the ladders out of poverty and whose deprivation remains chronic. Although, up to a point, it is possible to measure the physical obstacles to labour market development by means of the infrastructure indicators used in Chapter 5, we are doubtful that this can be done for the relational obstacles, and we discuss these in a mainly anecdotal way.

Finally, *institutions of conflict management.* Our study of Bolivia, Argentina, and Ghana, in particular, in Chapters 3 and 4 argued that institutions for the management and pre-emption of conflict—negotiating fora, advocacy, and arbitration bodies—might play a part in determining whether riot-type conflict occurs and whether or not it escalates into war. This idea can be used to extend our argument that signals of the state's capacity to manage conflicts of interest, rather than fall victim to them, will be good for poverty reduction, for some of these signals are conveyed through institutions rather than through policy. The existence of such institutions may influence not only the risk of conflict directly, but also rule of law, trust, and transaction costs in labour and capital markets. However, the adequacy of institutions of conflict management is not easy to measure. There does exist a measure of *state legitimacy* for Africa developed by Pierre Englebert (2000a), which in some ways is the inverse of vulnerability to conflict, but this of course is not the same as a measure of institutions of conflict management, and the measure can also be challenged.[14] Thus, although we shall bring the Englebert measure into our story, we suspect that the essence of these institutions can only be assessed qualitatively.

In the next section, we review the evidence from our case studies on these four measures of institutional capacity, and present both quantitative and qualitative indicators, which are then amalgamated into a 'pro-poor institutions index'. In section 3, we examine the linkage between these indicators of institutional capacity and the evolution of poverty. Section 4 extends the theme initiated in Chapter 3, that there may be a trade-off between political openness and economic performance, to institutional capacity in this sense; and section 5 concludes.

6.2 INSTITUTIONAL CAPACITY AND POVERTY: INDICATORS AND MECHANISMS OF CAUSATION

In explaining long-term poverty, therefore, we need to take into account not only the standard governance indicators, but also several institutional variables which most probably influence poverty and for which we currently have no measure. In search of one, we return to our country case studies. These are divided into three groups—the ones whose governance, on the indicators of Table 6.2, *improved* since the millennium; those whose governance *deteriorated* since the millennium; and, on its own, the ambiguous case of Russia.

[14] With reference to the persistence of chronic poverty, Geof Wood (2003) referred to the relationships which poor people form with their more powerful patrons as a 'Faustian bargain': in return for support and protection from those patrons, they cut themselves off from access to resources—in particular contact with the market—which they need in order to escape from chronic poverty.

Case studies—improvers

Indonesia, as discussed in the previous chapter, kept within the government's grasp, throughout the period 1967–2000, many of the institutions required by the green revolution and by small business development. The emphasis of its pro-poor policy (see Figure 5.3 above) was much more on smallholder agricultural growth than on social expenditures, and during the green revolution years between the mid-1960s and the mid-1980s, credit, road and irrigation infrastructure, agricultural extension, and improved varieties were all supplied by government agencies. Indonesia is a paradoxical case of pro-poor development, because throughout the Suharto period its public sector was corrupt, its private sector (see Chapter 11 below) oligopolistic, and its NGOs and cooperatives, so vital to the poverty reduction effort of other parts of Asia, extremely weak. One of the explanations of this success, as described in Chapter 3, was its macro-policy, which warded off the threat of Dutch disease by aggressive pre-emptive devaluations of the exchange rate, But another explanation was institutional: local administrators were converted, from the 1960s onward, into development agents, providing seeds, extension support, irrigation labour and finance in an integrated package, with ample support not only from oil revenues but also from a sequence of *kecamatan* (rural locality)[15] development programmes financed by the World Bank and other donors. This in itself was nothing unusual, and indeed was replicated all over Asia in the 1960s. What was unique to Indonesia was the way it was used to generate incentives to both save[16] and repay loans within a state-managed system. We may take the case of rural credit: in most regions, this was provided not only by the national rural bank (Bank Rakyat Indonesia) but also by regional development banks established by the local administrations of, for example, Central Java (the *Badan Kredit Kecamatan* or BKKs) and East Java (the KURKs). Banks, in Indonesia as in many Asian countries, were subject to usury laws forbidding them from exploiting borrowers by charging in excess of a fixed 'fair' interest rate (in the mid-1990s, twelve per cent), a trap they escaped from by styling themselves not as banks but as 'bodies' (*badan*) which, not falling within the ambit of the regulatory authorities, could charge whatever rate they chose. Lending to poor and uncollateralized clients within the villages, the regional *badan* were clearly exposed to a high risk of default. This risk they confronted by using local officials within each village as debt-collectors, a job which they had to combine with their responsibilities as extension agents, data-recording clerks, and much else. But the size of the bonuses paid to them as debt-collectors—more precisely the large fraction of their salaries which was withheld if loans fell

[15] The *kecamatan* is a sub-district incorporating a small number of villages.

[16] The practice of providing micro-savings facilities as well as loans was pioneered by Indonesian institutions in the 1980s. BRI (Bank Rakyat Indonesia) alone in 2006 provided savings facilities to some 30 million clients—almost as many as the number of microfinance clients in the entire remainder of the developing world. These saving facilities, which were not available to small businesses in other countries affected by the 1997–9 crisis (see Chapter 3 above, and, for a contrasting example, our discussion of the Bolivian case below) acted as a buffer which helped extract Indonesia from the 1997–8 crisis. Indeed, BRI deposits continued to grow through the recession (Patten, Rosengard, and Johnston, 2001).

overdue[17]—was an effective incentive-mechanism, and in few parts of Indonesia do default rates exceed five per cent (Hulme and Mosley 1996, Chapter 10; Patten and Rosengard 1991). This entire institutional structure was then, so far as possible, embedded within the Golkar party machine, the opportunity to extend which, as described in the previous chapter, was eagerly seized upon by the Suharto government in its quest to enforce the rule of law more effectively —a quest which held together through the entire green revolution period and then, as we have described, spectacularly came apart in 1997, illustrating the failings of the administration's conflict management institutions (Rodrik 1999, Chapter 3 above). Since the advent of democracy in 2000, attempts have been made to put institutional process on a different track. One feature of this has been a flowering, at last, of poverty-related NGOs, who comment favourably (Chapter 11 below) on their new-found ability to access government, contribute to debate and discuss poverty policy. The government, in conjunction with the World Bank, restyled and scaled up the Kecamatan Development Programme as PNPM (*Program Nasional Pemberdayaan Masyakarat* or National Programme for Self-help Community Empowerment). This has all the hallmarks of a PRSP, although not formally styled as such; local people decide on priorities for projects and go on to control and monitor implementation. 'Assessments show that, despite some inevitable problems, the projects have been well-targeted, much cheaper than similar government-run projects. Village surveys show high levels of satisfaction and projects from earlier rounds have proved sustainable' (Chapter 11, page 305). It is the case, however, that in spite of the maintenance of good policy and improvements in pro-poor governance and institutions, national poverty rates remain stuck at their pre-recession level of around twelve per cent, rather than continuing to decline. Our case study (Chapter 11) suggests some institutional reasons for this. Although the flagship pro-poor policy in Indonesia only amounts to about 0.3 per cent of Indonesian GNP ($1.5 billion out of projected GNP of $496 billion in 2008) one key element of institutional performance, labour-intensive employment in the formal sector, has stopped growing, because foreign direct investment, even before the crash of 2008, has itself stopped growing; and underlying this, we speculate, the very effectiveness of restraints on corruption may have undermined investment and risk-taking.[18] As governance in the conventional sense improved in the 2000s, therefore, so did anti-poverty performance tail off. The top-down governmental style which informed its own anti-poverty policy from the 1960s through the 1990s—in terms of the last chapter, a 'Group 2b model'—has been removed from office by popular demand, and successor administrations are still searching for an alternative which can deliver equivalent economic performance.

Ghana inherited from the colonial period not only, as we saw in the previous chapter, the liability of a cocoa tax system which handicapped the country's export

[17] In the extreme case, which is the KURKs of east Java, some local officials act as commission agents, that is, they are paid only commission and no salary, and receive no payment unless arrears are kept down below a specified level (Hulme and Mosley 1996, Vol. 2, Chapter 11).

[18] Attempts to tighten up on corruption may have removed civil servants' incentives to promote projects (based on kickbacks) or may have increased anxiety over making any decisions in an environment of tough but somewhat capricious enforcement' (Chapter 11, page 306).

base, but also the asset, described in Chapter 13, of a relatively educated labour force and a relatively equal income distribution created through the wide diffusion of income opportunities deriving from the cocoa export sector. An attempt was made in the 1950s by the country's first president, Kwame Nkrumah, to convert this export base into a process of import-substituting industrialization described in the previous chapter as 'not a million miles away from *neodesarollismo*' (Latin American-style protectionism),[19] and it was the failure of this attempt and its successors to deliver either a more diversified economy or any sort of political stability which led Ghana into the state of economic collapse described in Chapter 3. The exit strategy followed by Ghanaian governments over the following twenty years, while still coloured by Nkrumah's statism, nonetheless represents quite an astute grafting on to it of the more positive elements in the colonial institutional legacy.

We have described the political party constructed in the 1980s by President Rawlings to lead the country out of chaos, the Provisional National Defence Committee or PNDC, as 'originally, a coalition of leaders of the four elements of Rawlings's support in the 1979–81 period—the lower ranks of the forces, a variety of left-wing student organizations, some of the unionized workers in Accra and some sections of military intelligence' (Toye, in Mosley, Harrigan, and Toye 1995, Vol. 2, page 156). However, the business of converting this coalition into a grouping that could both win democratic elections in Ghana and achieve a working relationship with the IMF and World Bank was to entail a number of transformations. Economically, the most important of these was the cutting loose of the exchange rate and the increased market exposure (by no means total privatization),[20] of the Cocoa Board, which markedly increased the share of the export price going to the farmer, although not by nearly as much as in Uganda. Politically, the PNDC shed the student and much of the military element within its power-base, and in 1992 reconstituted itself without its first initial as the National Democratic Congress (NDC), competing within a multi-party system with, as its principal rival, the National Patriotic Party (NPP), which won from it the elections of 2000 and 2004. The NDC has attempted to broaden its constituency from the urban consumers who were Rawlings's focus in the 1980s, and by virtue of this has achieved considerable electoral success in the poor rural regions of the north.[21] It has never achieved as much success as the NPP in the central cocoa belt, although this success can be interpreted either in economic or in ethnic terms, as loyalty to the Asante ethnic group at the heart of the NPP's power-base. Thus, in terms of the three groups which make up the core of the Ghanaian poor—employees in the cocoa sector, northern subsistence farmers, and 'new

[19] 'The "Nkrumahist bargain" was modernity and welfare provided by the state in return for increased state authority and centralisation of power, which ultimately led to state domination of most of the economic and political space' Whitfield (2009c): 51. Much of this could be said of Chavez's Venezuela, or the Kirchners' Argentina, or indeed Peron's, as we discuss below.

[20] Recall Figure 5.2: the share of the export price taken by Ghanaian cocoa producers increased from around thirty per cent to around fifty per cent only, compared in Uganda which is more like twenty-five per cent to eighty per cent.

[21] For example, in the five presidential elections since 1992 the NDC have always carried (albeit by a margin which decreases over time) the constituencies of the three northern regions (Northern, Upper West and Upper East) by far the poorest in Ghana (Fridy 2007, page 287).

poor' urban workers—the NPP dominates in the first; the NDC in the second and the third, where many of the floating votes lie, is hotly contested between the two main parties.[22] But the acceptance of an economic programme sufficiently liberal-reformist to keep the IMF happy, in the expectation of a long-term relationship with it, is common ground between the two parties, albeit with more reluctance and symbolic populist gestures on the part of the NDC.[23] This represents a contrast with the exit strategies of Russia and Argentina described elsewhere in this volume, which involved not a retreat, however reluctant, but an expansion of the role of the state, and as a greatly desired by-product, a long-term exit also from involvement with the IMF.

The 'liberal consensus' of Ghanaian politics is reflected in the pattern of state-business and state-NGO relations over the two decades. The first-ever Ghana Investment Promotion Centre was established under an NDC government, in 1994, but the NPP, suffering from fewer populist restraints, positioned itself much closer to the import-export lobby, creating an Exporters' Forum in 2001 and an independent Ministry of Private Sector Development in 2004. The Leftwich/Sen/te Velde index of state-business relations rises from zero in 1991 to 0.75 after 2005.

The liberalization of policy in Ghana has benefited not only private businesses but also NGOs, whose proliferation has been encouraged by both major parties (Whitfield, in Mustapha and Whitfield, 2009, page 61). As everywhere, these NGOs are a mixed bag, many of which are not concerned with poverty reduction or resource reallocation of any sort.[24] With the strong encouragement of the aid donors, however, Ghanaian NGOs have been prominent in supporting and broadening the health, education, and welfare thrust of the public expenditure programme, and in giving a sharp upward push to rural infrastructural investment as discussed in the previous chapter, thereby broadening access to rural labour markets.[25] They have also been involved in building up micro-enterprise finance, albeit from a low base. Within microfinance, there has been an emphasis on establishing not the large-scale microlending 'chains' that are observable all

[22] It will be recalled that Ghanaian poverty has fallen much more among workers and the self-employed than amongst farmers (Teal 2006, as discussed in Chapter 5 above), and this may reflect the 'traditional' approach of LDC politics that urban groups are more politically salient than rural ones (see Chapters 1 and 2 above).

[23] Lindsay Whitfield has described the inspiration behind the NDC as being 'Nkrumahist' and populist in character, whereas the inspiration behind the NPP is from a 'Danquah-Busia' or liberal-intellectual tradition (in Mustapha and Whitfield 2009, Chapter 4). J.B. Danquah was a lawyer (and university academic) who played a major part in designing Ghana's independence constitution; Kofi Busia was President between 1967–9, who attempted to arrest Ghana's slide into economic decline by putting the economy on a more liberal course.

[24] The same claim can be made with statistical support in the case of Uganda; see Barr, Fafchamps, and Owens (2005) and pages 166–7 below.

[25] Much more within NPP and aid donor policymaking clusters than amongst NDC supporters, there is a desire to create employment, via a removal of restraints on urban labour markets (e.g. employment protection legislation), which it is hoped may engineer a shift from the more rigid large-business end of the market, where unions have more influence, to the more flexible small-business end. It is also hoped that this 'active labour-market approach', as it is known in industrialized countries, will further reduce urban poverty levels (interview, Professor N. Nuamah, University of Ghana, 18 December 2008).

over Indonesia, Bolivia, and even Uganda, but rather on establishing village savings and loan associations on a decentralized basis. This emphasis on savings may be considered pro-poor, as the poorest are likely to be deterred by risk-aversion from incurring indebtness, but not from saving (Hulme and Mosley 1996, Chapters 4 and 5).

Ghana's achievement in creating, over this period, a low-conflict political environment within conventional multi-party political parameters has been much commended and discussed (Fridy 2007; Gyimah-Boadi 2001; Whitfield in Mustapha and Whitfield 2009, Chapter 4). It is possible to observe in Ghana's politics a gradual progression from the nadir of 4 June 1979, when three past presidents adjudged to have failed the country were summarily executed by a military government, and this progression is institutional as well as political in its cause, as Whitfield relates:

> In an effort to establish dialogue between the NDC government and opposition Parties, the Electoral Commission initiated the formation of the Inter-Party Advisory Committee (IPAC) in March 1994. During the following two years, IPAC provided a forum where disagreements, suspicions and fears were regularly addressed. Ninsin (1998) argues that the deliberations of IPAC were a [successful] exercise in building trust among the political elites, because all parties were incorporated and their leaders were involved in making decisions about the electoral system . . . Before the 1996 elections took place, the political elite had thus forged the institutional bases required for a more stable democratic politics through negotiation . . . Subsequent elections [in 2000 and 2004] charted significant improvements in the electoral process which increased the perception of elections as free and fair among leaders as well as the electorate. Changes in the electoral procedure include the use of vote identity cards, transparent ballot boxes, opening the voter register for public inspection, and new rules of monitoring voting, counting votes, and reporting results . . . Since 1992, official aid agencies have supported the electoral process with significant financial contributions to facilitate these reforms and support the functioning of the Electoral Commission.
>
> (Whitfield 2009c, pages 55–6)

This experience contrasts sharply with that in Ghana's neighbour, Cote d'Ivoire, also a cocoa-based economy which moved from a one-party to a multi-party constitution at almost exactly the same time, in the early 1990s. Whereas Ghana's vulnerability to conflict diminished over the period under examination, Cote d'Ivoire's increased, with a civil war having resulted from a disputed election in December 2010 following a long period of riot-type conflict, and it is reasonable to see this as having much to do with her having more fragile institutions of conflict management.[26]

Interesting in this context is the link between institutional capacity and stability both political (represented, e.g. in the political instability index of Table 6.2, one of the few polity indexes that we were able to correlate with economic development) and economic. Both in the comparison between Ghana and Cote d'Ivoire, we can

[26] Other contributory causes of the crossover between Ghana and Cote d'Ivoire are short-term economic rather than long-term political, recall Chapter 3—Ghana moved to a flexible exchange rate, as discussed, over the course of the 1980s, whereas Cote d'Ivoire continued to adhere to a fixed exchange regime which made her exports less.

argue that an investment in institutional capacity—both institutions of conflict management, as here, and our thesis can be put as 'institutional capacity prevents the political business cycle from turning into political instability': an idea to be developed in section 4 below.

Uganda, in terms of Table 6.2, is an improver on the democratic accountability, bureaucratic quality, and also the crucial law and order dimension of governance. In terms of our classification in the previous chapter, it is a 'Group 1 case', in other words the pro-poor element in its politics derives directly from the elite's, and indeed the President's, domination of the political process. The checks and balances on the use of arbitrary power which undoubtedly exist are in many ways self-imposed rather than constitutionally embedded, and although Uganda is by any standards a star performer in pro-poor growth, some of the most vulnerable and chronically poor are still excluded from this process (Hickey 2005, page 1001), in part as a consequence of chronic border conflicts which the government has not been able to bring under control.

At the outset of the Museveni regime in 1986, the government implemented two changes of enormous relevance to social capital between state, business, and the third sector. First, it invited back to Uganda the Asian businesses which Idi Amin had expelled in 1973 to occupy their previous niches in sugar, retail distribution, and textile manufacturing; at the same time, the Ugandan Manufacturers' Association, moribund since the 1960s, was re-established (Leftwich, Sen, and te Velde 2008, page 50), and protection for both foreign and domestic investors was established by means of an investment code. Second, it attempted at the same time to build a creative partnership with the NGOs who, during the Amin and Obote years, had been quiescent and often subject to harassment. On their own, these actions enormously reduced the cost of doing business: the Leftwich/Sen/te Velde index of state-business relations, which will be formally introduced in section 4, rises from zero in 1991 to 0.62 after 2005. More than in Ghana, the 'business' to which the state seeks to relate is agricultural, and the keystone of the government's poverty strategy, the Plan for the Modernization of Agriculture, has no Ghanaian counterpart. Within this plan, however, there is a continual pendulum-swing between smallholder-first approaches, in which subsistence farmers are replaced by commercial ones, and export-based approaches in which multinational-owned estates and non-traditional exports such as horticulture, fruits, and spices take a larger role. At the time of writing (early 2009) the second tendency is in the ascendant, partly because the government senses a back-to-growth mood amongst the donors and partly because its very success in reducing poverty in the middle 2000s has given it the feeling that, that problem having been solved, growth is the new frontier (interview, DFID Kampala, December 2008).

Ugandan NGOs have grown on an enormous scale since the beginning of the 1990s, and by contrast with the situation in many developing countries, we have a fairly clear picture of their scope. A pioneering study of the Ugandan NGO sector was carried out by Fafchamps, Barr, and Owens in the middle 2000s, which reports that 'there is some evidence that Ugandan NGOs target poor, albeit less isolated, communities' (Barr, Fafchamps, and Owens 2005, page 657). However, much more than in Indonesia and many African countries they have provided a creative impulse in support of the crucial institutional function of access to capital markets. The government has not attempted to force a green revolution through state agencies, as was done by Indonesia and other Asian countries,[27] and the financing lead especially in the case of social expenditures such as health and education is with NGO micro-credit organizations such as FINCA, the Uganda Microfinance Union and FOCCAS. FINCA has branched out from credit into health micro-insurance, and a survey by the author suggests that this innovation, amongst a sample of sixty clients in Kampala, has been able to reduce the variability of income and expenditure and increase rates of investment among clients (Mosley 2004d). In the case of lending to small farmers, much technical support is provided by government NGOs, such as the Sasakawa Foundation, but the technical lead is provided by a commercial bank (Centenary Rural Development Bank), which has embarked on a number of small-farmer schemes, one of which has produced a minor green revolution in maize in Mbale district,[28] and has also experimented with a number of unorthodox schemes for vulnerable clients, including emergency loans and drought insurance.

Whereas the economic basis for recent poverty reduction has, as in Ghana, been a liberalization of peasant exports and both countries are classed, governance-wise, as 'improvers', the subsequent political evolution of the two countries could scarcely have been more different. Whereas the post-1990s governments of Ghana have injected new life into a corroded multi-party democratic model, the Museveni regime, having considered doing the same,[29] persisted until 2006 with the one-party model which it imposed at the time of its 1986 coup, and continues to operate within an atmosphere if not the outright forms of a lifetime presidency. Nor is there any sign, in Uganda, of either of the tendencies which have animated both the old and the new Ghanaian political parties—the 'Nkrumahist' populist and the 'Danquah-Busia' liberal (pages 163–4 above); there exists in Uganda neither the urban power-base for the former nor the liberal-intellectual tradition which built the latter, and the country is governed by an agrotechnocracy[30] oscillating, as described above, between a large and a small-farm emphasis. Parliament, an important albeit constrained influence on policy and institutions in Ghana, has in Uganda 'as in other parts of Africa . . . been effectively sidelined in the poverty reduction process' (Hickey 2005, page 1000).

Argentina experienced a worse crisis around the turn of the millennium than any other 'East Asian-type' country (with the exception of Russia, in which the two

[27] Also Ethiopia: see pages 122–3 above.

[28] This scheme was developed in conjunction with the Kapchorwa Farmers' Association, three of whose members were below the Ugandan poverty line in 1999; according to a small sample of 35 in Kapchorwa district, maize yields among Association members (including the three below the poverty line) trebled between 1999 and 2003 to an average of about 4 tons/ha, equivalent to the average national cereal yield in Indonesia or China. Data from Chiripanhura et al. (2008).

[29] The new constitution established in 1994 provides for a constitutional commission (which reported in 1993), and for a 'Constituent Assembly' (the same concept as that currently being implemented in Bolivia) to debate the Constitution. The alignment of political forces on this issue is regionally based, with northern and eastern groups wishing a return to an unconstrained multiparty system and western and central groups (i.e. the coalition which executed the 1986 coup) wishing to preserve the existing system (Ondoga 1998, pages 174, 182).

[30] For an acute attempt to locate the intellectual origins of the Museveni government's policies in the concepts of 1950s social science (including political modernization theory and disguised unemployment) see Hickey (2005).

shocks of structural adjustment and the East Asian crisis were rolled into one). The severity of this economic shock caused not only, as described in Chapters 3 and 5, short-term political instability but also a reorientation of policy: away from the market and inspired by 1950s-style protectionist industrialization, but respecting the principle of fiscal stringency and welcoming partnerships with non-governmental actors, and hence known as *neodesarollismo* (new developmentalism). As we described in the previous chapter, this change of strategy required the elite in self-protection to seek out support from a range of new interest-groups, acknowledging that their ties with their traditional ally, organized labour, had been weakened by liberalization and needed supplementing. And new allies, of course, required new institutional linkages: the re-orientation of state-business relations, embodied in the creation by the Duhalde government in 2002 of a *Grupo Productivo* (Producers' Group) of representatives from industrial sectors (Riggirozzi 2009, page 135), was therefore only a part of a wholesale re-making of linking social capital which also took in, within the labour movement, 'new poor' professionals who had lost their jobs in the crisis rather than unionized workers, and within civil society more broadly, NGOs and consumer groups. Thus, the centre of gravity of the alliances of the Kirchner government, which took over in May 2003, evolved from the promotion of international capital[31] and economic linkages to a bias towards domestic capital, and from an exclusive commitment to organized, protected labour to a commitment to those struggling in the informal sector.

The government indeed has exercised considerable imagination in co-opting precisely these groups, and specifically those threatening 'riot-type conflict', by whatever means were available. One of the key institutions created in the depths of crisis in 2002, and developed to meet the needs of the last three groups, was Jefas y Jefes (*Programa Jefas y Jefes de Hogares Desempleados*, or Programme for Heads of Unemployed Households). This was a workfare scheme which offered 150 pesos (US $50) monthly to families in exchange for participation in projects such as community service, construction, school maintenance, rebuilding health facilities, road works, communal kitchens, house building, and small-scale production (Grugel and Riggirozzi 2009, page 14), without any significant microfinance element of the type found in Bolivia. This programme broke the link between unemployment, welfare, and trade unions, and indeed was orientated explicitly at those outside the trade unions, especially those (*piqueteros*) who had protested on the streets in 2001 and 2002.[32] The programme was financed, ironically, partly by a loan from the World Bank and partly by income from the new export taxes which the Bank, so long as it had influence in Argentina, was fighting to eliminate.[33] Another emergency programme with an explicit poverty focus was the health plan

[31] Controls were imposed by the Duhalde and Kirchner administrations on the prices of the basic services they provided by privatized utilities, which were popularly held responsible for much of the suffering of the late 1990s and early 2000s (Riggirozzi 2009, page 136).

[32] It has been estimated that eight per cent of the population in receipt of *Jefas y Jefes* funds are *piqueteros* (organized unemployed protesters) and many more are linked formally or informally through family and neighbourhood networks. One leader of the *piqueteros*, Luis d'Elia, of the Fundacion Tierra y Vivienda, even accepted a ministerial post in government, at the Department of Planning (Grugel and Riggirozzi 2009a, page 17).

[33] As discussed in Chapter 3, Duhalde's government imposed a twenty per cent tax on export earnings from agricultural commodities and hypdrocarbons, which became the central source for

Remediar, supported by the IDB, which organized the distribution of basic medicines to the poorest. Overall, these policies were central in re-establishing the credibility of the state, and represent one of the most politically potent examples of the 'new Latin American welfare programmes' examined in the previous chapter. The approach of confining all new social benefits to targeted groups, rather than going back to universal benefits of the kind which Peron and his followers had practised, was one hallmark of *neodesarollismo*, and made it easier to achieve a second key objective of Kirchner's, namely fiscal restraint as a defence against old-style inflation. Meanwhile poverty and unemployment, as illustrated by Table 6.3, have diminished sharply, although not among all groups, for example unemployment rates remain worryingly high amongst young people (Grugel and Riggirozzi 2009, Table 5) and the proportion of people who are economically vulnerable through lack of job rights and social insurance, as the opposition to Kirchner has not been slow to point out, is high and certainly not decreasing.[34]

The initiating element in the process of conflict management which launched many of these new-redistributive institutions was the *Mesa de Dialogo*. Launched with the help of the Catholic Church and the United Nations Development Programme (UNDP), the *Mesa*:

> was designed to serve as an alternative to Argentina's traditionally corporatist structure of social relations. Organized in thematic round tables, it encouraged inputs into governance discussions by a broad range of society-based actors including labour, business, NGOs, *piqueteros*, social movements, political parties, and religious groups. One of its most significant initiatives was to push for the adoption of urgent policies of social inclusion.
>
> (Riggirozzi 2009, page 137)

Some of the *mesas*, or round tables, were explicitly concerned with the establishment of social justice and with the improvement of public administration rather than simply the improvement of economic well-being; in this way, the intergroup reconciliation and the poverty reduction agendas were institutionally linked, and the improvement of administrative process was made a vehicle for the achievement of social stability.

Case studies—decliners

Bolivia

Bolivia, the poorest country in Latin America, figures in governance terms (Table 6.2) as a 'mixed case', declining in terms of government stability but improving in terms of corruption and in terms of law and order. Nonetheless, we shall treat it here as a 'decliner'. This is because outcomes have been so negative—recession

financing social emergency programmes. Argentina's loans to the Bank and Fund were paid off in 2005 (Grugel and Riggirozzi 2009, page 26).

[34] 'Current government figures point to a phenomenal 47.5 per cent of workers without social insurance, a figure which has not changed since 2002' (Grugel and Riggirozzi 2009, page 21).

Table 6.3 Institutional indicators and long-term poverty reduction.

	(1) Poverty trend	(2) Governance indicators	(3) Institutional quality, quantitative indicators:			(4) Institutional quality, qualitative indicators		Pro-poor institutions (PPI) index = (3a) + (3b) + (3c), adjusted for qualitative indicators	
			SBR index	Access to capital	Tax/GDP ratio	Investment/GDP	Institutions for conflict management		
Middle-income cases:			(a) Trust and state/ market relations (SBR index)	(b) Access to capital: microfinance borrowers as % of population	(c) Fiscal support for PPE: Tax/GDP ratio	(a) Access to labour markets: trend in public investment/GDP ratio, plus data on targeted employment schemes	(b) Institutions for conflict management	2007 value of index (1990 = 100)	Change 1990–2007
Indonesia	Fell from 18% (1987) to 12% (2006) but with increase to 24% in 1997–8	Improvement in democracy indicator; no change in other indicators	NA	First microfinance loans in 1970s. Grew from 8.6m clients (5.2%) in 1997 to 34m (15.4%) in 2007	Fell from 15.9% (1990–2) to 12.1% (2002–4)	Investment/GDP: declined from 28.3% (1990) to 20.9% (2005)	Sharply deteriorated 1997–2000, improved 2000–6, see text	107	+7
Malaysia	Fell from 15% (1989) to < 10% (2006)	Slight improvement in democracy indicator, slight deteriorations in rule of law and corruption	NA	NA	Rose from 5% to 5.9%	Investment/GDP: declined from 33% (1990) to 20.4% (2007)		90	−10
Bolivia	Rose slightly from 60% (1990s average) to 65% (2005)	No change in democracy indicator; law and order and corruption indicators both improve	NA	First microfinance loans in late 1980s; grew from 171,000 borrowers (2.2%) in 1997 to 630,000 borrowers (6.8%) in 2007	Rose from 8% to 17%	Investment/GDP: declined from 14.5% (1990) to 12.6% (2007). *Fondo Social de Emergencia* established for public works job creation 1989, still running as *Fondo de Inversion Social*	Deteriorated 1999–2003, see text; *Asemblea Constitucional* (designed 2004–7, implemented 2008)	139	+39
Argentina	Rose from 38% (Oct 1990) to 57% (Oct	Improvement in freedom of expression indicator,	NA	No records until 2000; by 2007, 38,000 active borrowers (0.09% of population)	Rose from 8% to 15%	Investment/GDP: increased from 13.9% (1990) to 21.4% (2005). *Jefas y Jefes* programme	Deteriorated 1999–2001, see text. Broadened	159	+59

	2002) then fell to 34% (end 2005) 'Extreme poor' (*indigentes*) rose from *c.*10%–15% in 1990 to 27% in 2002, then declined to 12.2% in 2002	bureaucratic quality and rule of law both deteriorate				(2002 onward): workfare, targeted at heads of unemployed households	forum (*Mesa de Dialogo*) for negotiations involving state, NGOs and judicial system established, 2002		
Russia	Rose from 10% (1987) to 29% (2000) then fell to 15% (2006)	Improvement in bureaucratic quality; decline in freedom of expression and rule of law	NA	No records until 2000; by 2007 122,000 (0.08% of population)	Rose from 10.9% to 11.2%	Declined from 30.1% (1990) to 20.1% (2005)		91	−9
Low-income cases:									
Ghana	Fell 51% (1990) to 39% (1999); possible further fall since then	Democracy, tax and bureaucratic quality indicator improves; law and order and corruption indicators both stay constant	0.25 (1992–2001), 0.625 (2002–5)	First microfinance loans in 1990s, 700 clients (0.003%) in 1997, rising to 322,000 (1.4%) in 2007	11.3% (1990–2) rising to 19.9% (2002–4)	Investment/GDP: rose from 14.3% (1990) to 27.8% (2004)	1996–2004: numerous reforms to increase transparency of electoral system, see text	175	+75
Uganda	Fell from 56% (1992) to 31% (2006)	Press freedom and corruption deteriorate; Democratic accountability and law and order indicators improve	0 until 1990; 0.375 (1994–2002), 0.875 (2004)	Some microfinance loans through Centenary Bank and NGOs in 1980s, 11,000 clients (0.05%) in 1997, rising to 357,000 (1.2%) in 2007	< 10% (1990–2) rising to 12% (2002–4)	Rose from 12.7% (1990) to 22.1% (2004)	Constitutional conference 1993 defined path to new constitution; many steps in this, including establishment of multi-party rule, not fully implemented, see text	148	+48

Continued

Table 6.3 Continued

	(1) Poverty trend	(2) Governance indicators	(3) Institutional quality, quantitative indicators:			(4) Institutional quality, qualitative indicators		Pro-poor institutions (PPI) index = (3a) + (3b) + (3c), adjusted for qualitative indicators
			SBR index	Access to capital	Tax/GDP ratio	Investment/GDP	Institutions for conflict management	
Zimbabwe	Increased from 35% (1990) to 60% est. (2005)	Democracy and corruption indicators both deteriorate	0.175 rising to 0.469 (1992–2000), 0.55 rising to 0.631 (2001–5)	Some state (through Agricultural Finance Corporation) and NGO finance since early 1980s. 14,000 borrowers (0.1%) in 1997, rising to 43,000 (0.3%) in 2007	21.1% (1990–2) falling to *c.*14% (2002–4)	Declined from 18.6% (1990) to 9% (2002)	Power-sharing government since 2009	71 −29
Kenya	Rose from 42% (1991) to 52% (1997)	Corruption, bureaucratic quality and rule of law all decline	0.25 (pre-1992) rising to 0.875 (2005)	Some state (through Kenya Industrial Estates) and NGO finance since mid-1980s, 3,800 borrowers (0.01%) in 1997, rising to 692,000 (1.9%) in 2007	Rose from 17% to 18%	Declined from 20.6% (1991) to 16.3% (2004)	Power-sharing government since 2008	−4

Cases of *significant long-term improvement* are shaded.

Sources: column (1) poverty headcount at national poverty line, from World Bank *World Development Indicators* CD-ROM.

Column (2) governance indicators, trends summarized from Table 6.2, columns 5–13.

Column (3a) SBR (state-business relations) indicator is from Leftwich, Sen and te Velde (2008), Chapter 1.

Column (3b) microfinance access from Microfinance Information Exchange (www.themix.org), *MFI League Tables*, various issues. Note that data for Indonesia have been amended to include information on one very large microfinance organization (Bank Rakyat Indonesia) on which MIX does not supply data.

Column (3c) from IMF Government Finance Statistics; these tax measures transcribed from Table 6.2.

Column (4a) investment/GDP rate from *World Development Indicators;* qualitative data on special employment schemes from country case studies, Chapters 9 and 10 below.

Column (4b) institutions of conflict management—from country case studies, Chapters 9–13 below.

persisting into the mid-2000s, persisting riot-type conflict, and a mildly increasing trend, until 2006, in the poverty headcount.

As discussed in detail in Chapter 10, Bolivia has a long history of political instability going back to its independence in 1825 (deMesa, Gisbert, and Mesa 2003), with democratically-elected governments frequently being unseated by coups, which then had a tendency to generate retaliation. One attempt to achieve a long-term solution was executed in the early 1950s by means of extensive nationalization and land reform, and a second, by means of 'structural adjustment' following the trauma of 1985, a year in which the government lost control of the macro-economy, resulting in a hyperinflation which at its peak reached 25,000 per cent. The stabilization programme implemented at that point brought back to the presidency Victor Paz Estenssoro, the architect of the 'near-revolution' of the 1950s, and it was accompanied by a far-reaching liberalization programme, involving the closure of a large part of the country's mining and banking industry. Under the stimulus of these supply-side reforms, the economy between 1986 and 1999 grew at around 3.5 per cent, far above its historical trend; and at the same time, the political system stabilized as well. Again well against the Bolivian trend, there were no unconstitutional changes in government between those years, and the level of political violence declined to a nominal level (Chapter 4 above). These attractive developments led the Managing Director of the IMF to declare in 1996 that the vicious circle of political and economic instability had been broken in Bolivia, and that an 'Andean jaguar' had emerged, by analogy with the East Asian tigers, which would take Latin America by storm (Camdessus 1996). This prediction, of course, turned out to be premature; governance and institutions have a great deal to do with this. One element of this is a sudden deterioration in the climate of state-business relations after 1999. The numerous pro-poor actions taken during the period of privatization, from the Emergency Social Fund to the blossoming of microfinance to the rapid growth of health and education expenditures (Chapters 3 to 5) could not, especially for the Aymara/Quechua ethnic majority, conceal the fact that they had not made poverty go down, nor the fact that systematic discrimination against that majority continued. Most were aware that Gonzalo Sanchez de Losada, the President from 1989 to 1997 and the architect of many of the privatizations, was also a mining millionaire and therefore a beneficiary from them: the jaguar, in the view of many of them, had clearly not changed his spots. But corruption, and in particular the deteriorating non-payment of tax on the newly privatized oil, gas, and mineral industries, became much worse after the crash of 1999, and appeared worse still in the context that many people were losing their jobs, and in February 2003 were faced with an extension of the income tax net, while many richer people continued to be tax-exempt.[35] Control was lost over expenditure as well as taxation (notably as a consequence of a huge overspend on pensions), and there was a fiscal deficit of 8.5 per cent of GDP by 2003. (In this respect, the global crisis as experienced

[35] Rolando Morales, *La Prensa*, 12 February 2003, page 6. 'The Confederacion de Empresarios Privados de Bolivia', Morales adds, 'indicated that the fall in the country's fiscal revenues [between end-2001 and end-2002, which had caused a shortfall in revenues and required the IMF to be called in] was 7.3 per cent, and that the principal reason for that was a fall of 25.45 per cent over the same period in tax revenues due from the hydrocarbons (oil and gas) sector'.

in Bolivia contrasts strongly with that experienced in Indonesia, Malaysia, and other South-East Asian countries, where the fiscal deficit did not rise above two per cent.) What had been seen by many as a relatively benign oligarchy now came to be seen even by the urban middle class, as the recession deepened, as an increasingly anachronistic and even malignant one.

Another dimension of institutional deterioration was the collapse of loan discipline in the microfinance industry, which occurred partly because the regulatory authority lost its grip. During the boom in 1997 and 1998 three new finance houses (Fassil, CrediAgil, and Acceso) were authorized by the *Superintendencia de Bancos* to enter the market for micro-loans, and took the opportunity to move upmarket, offering loans for the purchase of consumer durables by the aspiring lower middle class. None of these institutions was adequately capitalized or in possession of sufficient appraisal skills to be able to operate a viable microfinance organization, and all three collapsed during the global crisis. Worse, the portfolios of many other previously reputable and disciplined microfinance organizations, including the market leader BancoSol, became contaminated at this time, and the situation was exacerbated by the decision of the populist new President, Hugo Banzer, to grant loan amnesties over the heads of the *Superintendencia*. The immediate consequence was that average six-month arrears rates, across the twenty microfinance institutions, increased from around three per cent to around twelve per cent between 1999 and 2002. The longer-term consequence was that most of these institutions, finding their cash flow squeezed, cut their lending; and the main sufferers from this were the eight per cent of clients who operated small businesses, many of these around or below the poverty line, and their employees, most of whom were below it. Thus, it was not only access to the capital market, but also to the labour market, which was impaired as small-business sector investment fell through the early 2000s. An attempt to measure the loss in employment resulting from this institutional failure is made by Marconi and Mosley (2006). Some recovery from this predicament was achieved during the middle 2000s, but during the latest recession, in 2009, the cycle appears to be repeating itself. This time round some of the institutions, such as CRECER, which held firm to their poorest clients in 2000–3, appear to be abandoning them if they fall into arrears, and moving upmarket.[36] Evo Morales' government has not implemented his threat, which frightened many microfinance operators during the rise of his radical opposition,[37] to undermine institutional discipline by waiving loan arrears; on the other hand, he has failed to grasp the nettle of deficiency of rural savings capacity, which has been a chronic lack in Bolivia since the 1980s (Marconi 2010). Deficiency of smallholder agricultural productivity has been an Achilles heel in Bolivia for several decades, as the previous chapter showed, and at present there is little sign that the country's new politics is leading to any alleviation of the institutional failures which are responsible for this weakness.

[36] Personal communication, Irina Aliaga, 20 April 2009.

[37] Interviews, CRECER, ProMujer, FINRURAL, and other microfinance organizations, September 2005.

The third and most serious symptom of *desinstitucionalisacion* ('disinstitutionalization' or 'institutional decay')[38] as it is known in Bolivia, was a collapse in the rule of law, with many prosecutions being corruptly abandoned; and the decay of many 'checks and balances' in the civil service, significant amongst which was the sacking by the President, at the height of public anger amongst the Aymara/Quechua population in October 2003, of the *Defensora del Pueblo* (approximately: parliamentary ombudsman) Ana Maria de Campero. As described earlier, this institutional decline hit a population which was already one of the world's most unequal, not only in terms of the income Gini coefficient but also in terms of inter-ethnic inequalities. It was the light-skinned who were being exempted from liability to pay tax and the need to pay back their loans, and it was the dark-skinned Aymaras and Quechuas who not only were not being exempted, but were losing their jobs at an accelerating rate by 2003 (Mosley 2007).

At the same time, and as a consequence of this, there was finally an increase in political consciousness, focused on the satellite city of El Alto above La Paz. The proportion of people voting for one of the two Quechua-Aymara parties, the MIP and the MAS, rose from two per cent to twenty-five per cent at the 2002 election; these parties then committed themselves to extra-parliamentary action through strikes and roadblocks, as well as through the ballot box. As in Argentina, both radical consciousness and the search for *neodesarollista* solutions prospered in an environment of rapidly-rising employment, and not only the MAS but orthodox middle-class opinion became sympathetic to protectionist policies which might generate employment in petrochemicals and other potential linkages to the hydrocarbons industry. Within El Alto some went further, and demanded a tariff barrier around the city, even that it become an independent republic.[39] The government's violent response to this challenge, leading to the eventual flight and humiliation of President Sanchez de Losada, has been described in previous chapters; on the day that the violence came to an end, 17 October 2003, one member of parliament declared, 'This was the day that neo-liberalism finally came to an end in this country'. In the short term, investment, which since 1998 had been on a falling trend in response to political instability, began to flee the country at an increasing rate. It is to be remembered, however, that not all of the economy, and especially not the central bank, fell victim to disinstitutionalization. Inflation remained low and under control, capital controls were avoided and the exchange rate continued to float freely. The autonomy still prevailing in certain parts of Bolivia's governance did much to counter Bolivia's slide into the poverty trap, although it did not prevent it.

We have here an unusual sequence of events, in which the persistence of the poverty trap and the resource shortages associated with it were brought about by institutional decline, rather than causing it—disinstitutionalization was a leading rather than a lagging element in the sequence of causation, the force which polarized politics and pushed investment and output down. In Chapter 10, this process is modelled as a 'political-institutional poverty trap'—a causal sequence from institutional quality to political behaviour to political stability to investment

[38] The phrase appears to have been invented by the Bolivian political commentator, and former MP, Cayetano Llobet (see Llobet 2005).

[39] Special issue of *El Diario* for 23 December 2003, page 2.

and poverty, which in the presence of better agencies of conflict management or better aid donors might have been avoided but in the real world locked the world within a 'political poverty trap' from 1999 until, at least, the elections of December 2005.

In this election, Evo Morales, the Aymara leader of the MAS, was elected president, with fifty-four per cent of the vote. In seeking a route out of the trap, he has made much of his determination to set a personal example in rooting out corruption, and has partly reversed the privatization of the oil and gas industry, hoping by this means to reduce the overt symptoms of inequality. In seeking to create a system which is more transparently fair between different interests, an *Asemblea Constitucional* (constitutional assembly, or standing committee for constitutional reform), he has also sought to take a preventive approach to conflict management, by renegotiating those parts of the constitution which lie at the root of current inequalities, especially those relating to inequities of access to public services between Aymaras and Quechuas. The new agreement, ratified in April 2009 after blocking manoeuvres by the upper house of parliament were finally defeated by a five-day presidential hunger strike,[40] recognizes explicit collective group rights for indigenous communities, in most respects provides for a more decentralized fiscal structure in favour of regions and communities, but with the exception that control over land is brought back, in the spirit of the 1951 reforms, into the hands of central government.[41] As with Argentina's *Mesa de Dialogo*, the emphasis of the *Asemblea* was on procedural reform as an instrument for reducing social tension, but whereas the *Mesa* was more concerned to redistribute income, the *Asemblea* was more concerned to redistribute capital and the rights to it. The ubiquitous Bolivian rhetoric about the 'natural wealth of the earth', which is to be returned to those who occupy it, finds little echo in the much more urbanized environment of Argentina.

Russia—a U-shaped pattern, with fallbacks

Russia is both the most dramatic, and the most ambiguous, of our case studies. It experienced a more severe macro-economic crisis during the years of adjustment than any other, with eight years of continuous decline in GDP, and twelve years of continuous decline in mortality rates, starting in 1992, and during this period moved from being one of two global superpowers to the edge of state collapse, with several core governance functions including the collection of tax, the payment of wages, and even the enforcement of law and order not being upheld across many parts of the country. As in Indonesia and Bolivia, there have been threats of secession, with Chechnya simply the most dramatic and widely-publicized case of the articulation of this threat: of the eighty-nine constituent political entities, or 'federal subjects',[42] of which the Russian Federation has consisted since the break-up of the Soviet Union, more than a dozen, mostly on

[40] Reported in *Independent*, 16 April 2009.

[41] There is a short summary of the provisions of the *Asemblea* in Gray-Molina (2008).

[42] These comprise fifty-five *oblasti* (regions) and *kraya* (federal territories), twenty autonomous republics, and ten other autonomous districts.

the southern and eastern edges of the federation (see Figure 12.1 below) have rebelled against federal authority[43] in ways which vary from refusing to comply with requirements to execute elections, to defying federal laws, to refusing to deliver tax revenues or statistics (Giuliano 2006). This 'fragility at the edges' provided, during the 1990s, a window of opportunity for external actors, such as the IMF, to seek to intervene in determining the direction of Russia's macro-economic and public expenditure policies, a process further examined in Chapter 7.

That governance and poverty both got worse between 1992 and 1999 is clear; what is totally unclear is even what has happened to governance quality since that time, let alone what is the sequence of causation between it and well-being indicators. According to the formal indicators of the World Bank, what occurred after 1999 is that political stability (one of the two 'super-core' measures of governance, according to the regression analysis of Table 6.2) improved sharply, whereas the other, rule of law, remained static, with deteriorations in both corruption and in bureaucratic quality. However, the rule of law and order measurement is suspect—dissent has indeed been more efficiently kept out of the public eye than in the 1990s (Lyall, 2006), but this does not necessarily show that it has been effectively suppressed: Hoff and Stiglitz state that 'in Russia and many other post-communist countries . . . little progress towards either forming a strong constituency for the rule of law, or establishing the rule of law, has been made since the privatization of most state enterprises' (Hoff and Stiglitz 2008, page 1474). What has essentially happened in the political sphere is that since the reforms of 2000 the federal government has been able to exercise far more effective administrative compliance, mainly by fiscal means, than prevailed before the millennium. In the economic sphere and at aggregate level, there has been growth, at any rate until the middle of 2008, reduction in headcount poverty, and since 2004 in mortality also. But there has been enormous dispersion around these mean tendencies, and at local level, the standard of living of some entire oblasts has regressed over the 2000s, with considerable evidence that institutional decay preceded and was responsible for the deterioration of poverty levels.

In Mussurov and Mosley (2008) we make a comparison between two 'new poor regions', with initial (1995) poverty rates of about thirty per cent and quite high gross regional product: Pskov (in the north-west), where poverty has declined dramatically with the growth of the 2000s, and Ulyanovsk (on the Volga), where in spite of growth in real gross regional product, poverty levels have increased since 1995. Both regions, are structurally, rather than just cyclically, poor: they have had, since the late nineteenth century and amplified by the Five-Year Plan periods, good infrastructure and a heavy concentration of economic activity within machine-building, all of it in the 1980s state-owned, and both as a consequence suffered heavily under perestroika in the 1990s. Their evolution since 2000 has been very different. Ulyanovsk, loyal to the man after whom it is named,[44] maintained during the 1990s elements of a command economy (two

[43] During the late 1980s and early 90s, Boris Yeltsin encouraged the autonomous republics to do this as part of his campaign against President Gorbachev (Service 2003).

[44] Lenin's true name was Vladimir Ulyanov; 'Lenin' was a pseudonym assumed years after he became a political activist (Service 1997, page 70).

World Bank commentators describe it at that stage as being 'at the bottom of the list for reform' (de Melo and Ofer 1999, page 13), many of which it still maintains, including ceilings on profits and trade markups and restrictions on food exports to other regions, whereas Pskov's local administration is very heavily orientated towards the private sector. In Ulyanovsk, unlike Pskov, there are very low levels of inward foreign investment (de Melo and Ofer 1999). Indicators of social capital are also inferior in Ulyanovsk; unlike Pskov, it has very low access to non-government media. Only local, primarily government-owned, newspapers are read, there are no privately-owned radio and television stations, and the local democracy indicator is much higher in Pskov than in Ulyanovsk. Although we must be cautious about inferring causation from these data, the superficial impression is that Ulyanovsk is caught in a low-level poverty trap, not too dissimilar from the Bolivian one, with the authorities' response (repression of both the media and the private economy) deterring foreign investment, inhibiting diversification of the local economy, and disincentivizing the formation of both human and social capital, including those skills required to put any momentum behind progressive reform at the local level. All of these resource constraints prevent the labour market from growing quickly and responding to the needs of the new globalized economy, and this, we speculate, was a major cause of persistence in the differing dynamics of local poverty levels.

Zimbabwe

Zimbabwe represents a classic case of economic failure caused by collapse of macro-economic discipline: it holds the all-time record for the highest rate of inflation in the world, which ran into the trillions before stabilization was achieved in 2009, and until that point the macro-economy was in freefall, with substantially negative growth of GDP throughout the 2000s. Here we examine the specific role of governance indicators.

These indicators are indeed negative in their tendency, but not unanimously so. Zimbabwe shows deterioration since 2000 on three governance indicators: accountability, corruption, and bureaucratic quality. It has also experienced deterioration in tax effort in recent years, which has been a contributory factor to loss of control over the public sector deficit and thence to macro-economic chaos. Finally, there has been a deterioration in civil order and a rise in political violence since the late 1990s, a factor which, as Table 6.2 shows, is interactive with a worsening in most indicators of governance; and, both because civil order has deteriorated and because the government has lost budgetary room for manoeuvre, there has been an increase in 'military centrality' (a component of which is the share of military expenditures in GDP), which to date at least has tended to exacerbate rather than ease the level of political and economic instability, and a decline in the share of developmental expenditures such as agriculture, health, and education.[45]

[45] Since the stabilization of autumn 2009 there has been power-sharing in Zimbabwe between President Mugabe and Prime Minister Tsangvirai; the finance ministry and most economic ministries are directed by the latter, but home affairs and control over the military rests with the former.

Any attempt at analysis must be speculative, not least because of an acute shortage of reliable and up-to-date data. Nonetheless, a strong first impression is that initial conditions are extremely important, and that the role of capacity and institutional factors in Zimbabwe's crisis is accommodating and not initiating. Zimbabwe inherited at independence an unequal and dualistic society, with a Gini coefficient of around sixty per cent in 1980, deriving from the allocation of most of the good land, jobs and educational opportunities to Europeans during the colonial period. The ZANU-PF party, on taking over the government at independence, rejected the free-market model already being flirted with by (*inter alia*) Guyana, Ghana, and Cote d'Ivoire, and aimed to rectify the underlying inequity by investing heavily in a structure of state support services, aimed especially at African 'communal' farmers (marketing, credit, extension, etc.), and making heavy use of controlled exchange rates, input subsidies, and other policies proscribed by the Washington institutions. This approach initially achieved remarkable results (for example communal-area grain production doubled between 1980 and 1986, and by the latter year was one hundred per cent under high-yielding seed varieties), but after that year for reasons of fiscal debility could not be sustained. Agricultural Finance Corporation credits for small farmers, for example, began to dwindle from 1986 onward. Between 1987 and 1996 the government on two occasions sought to fill the fiscal gap by going to the IMF, but was able to satisfy the expectations neither of low-income farmers (agricultural production peaked in the early 1990s, and yields began to fall after 1993) nor of donors, who could see that reform was only being implemented in a half-hearted way. At the end of the 1990s the Mugabe regime took the decision to placate low-income farmers by authorizing land invasions in support of war veterans, to reject the advice of and eventually to physically eject representatives of international aid agencies, and finally to deport white commercial farmers, compounding this with the expenditure of large sums on military support for the Kabila regime in the Democratic Republic of Congo. It was these policies, and the associated collapse in investment and of macro-economic discipline, which caused the economic collapse between 2000 and 2008, and not flaws in governance. Some elements of governance eventually bent under the stress of macro-economic collapse (notably corruption, with the revelation that many commercial farms after invasion had been re-occupied by ministers and by high-ranking civil servants, rather than by war veterans). However, in some respects, institutional quality has held up even in face of the most extreme pressures. One illustration of this is tax collection, which held up quite well until late 2005, and another has been the performance of the judiciary, an element in the 'rule of law' variable, which since the millennium has often been good and at times heroic. The Zimbabwe courts have on numerous occasions, and with great courage, refused to ratify decisions under heavy pressure from the ZANU-PF ruling party, one recent illustration being in September 2008, when an MP from the opposition Movement for Democratic Change (MDC), Lovemore Moyo, was elected speaker of parliament in face of furious opposition from ZANU-PF. Since April 2009 the MDC's leader, Morgan Tsangvirai, has served as prime minister, and other ministries including finance have been taken over by the MDC, within a power-sharing agreement in which President Mugabe retains control of home affairs including the army and police. At the time of writing it is too early to say what the economic effects of this arrangement will be; the international financial agencies also are currently following a policy of wait and see and not yet backing the new regime.

6.3 RELATIONSHIPS BETWEEN INSTITUTIONAL INDICATORS AND POVERTY REDUCTION

Our general story has been that six factors can help to explain the long-term process of poverty reduction—the four policy issues (scope for forging alliances with the poor, expenditure mix, regime stability, and tax structure) examined in the previous chapter, and the governance and institutional factors examined here.

In Table 6.3, we display the trends in each of these indicators of governance and institutional capacity, in order to understand their impact on poverty. In several cases, an examination of these indicators clearly adds value to an explanation couched in purely governance terms. In Indonesia, where nearly all of the governance indicators until 1997 were adverse, the building up, almost entirely through state initiatives, of a rural network of infrastructure, microfinance, and hybrid seed supply in the 1970s and 80s opened up access to labour markets by low-income people, which was the foundation of the massive reductions in poverty of those years. In Uganda, where the trend of the press freedom and corruption indicators of governance is strongly negative, improvements in state–business relations and in tax administration enabled investment to be expanded and public expenditure to be put on a pro-poor trend in the 1990s. And in Ghana and Argentina, which have a relatively favourable trend of governance indicators, what makes them favourable is in part what is happening in the field of institutions. For example, in Argentina's period of extreme instability in 2002, when several presidents had come and gone and the level of public trust in government was well captured by the phrase *que se vayan todos*, that trust was mended by the act of bringing the various affected parties, including the socially excluded, around a table (the *Mesa de Dialogo*) which in turn facilitated an improvement in state-business relations and thereby investment and growth. In Ghana, the link is more long term and more elusive, as there was not, as in Argentina, one identifiable group both poor and militant whose inclusion within the political process turned the key to pro-poor growth, and trust in political institutions, having been catastrophically damaged by public executions of past presidents in 1979, was very slow to return. But in Ghana also, an investment in institutions of conflict reduction paid off—improvements in the transparency (literally) of the electoral process[46] have helped to create legitimacy for the political system, and trust in the country's political stability has encouraged private investment. In all these cases, access to pro-poor institutions is clearly key.

[46] Transparent ballot boxes were introduced in the 2000 presidential elections; see Whitfield 2009a, Chapter 4.

However, there are some country cases which do not conform to this pattern at all. The most striking example within our sample is Bolivia, which both in conventional governance terms and in terms of our pro-poor institutions index is a 'good performer' and yet scarcely made a dent, until 2006, in the high level of poverty persisting since the crash and structural adjustment of 2005. Here, as we have discussed, a great deal of the problem resides in dimensions of institutional decay which our quantitative indicators do not expose. For example, Bolivia is a good performer in terms of our indicator of the real volume of microfinance loans as a share of population, which grows almost continuously from 1990 to 2007 (Table 6.3), and yet because the average quality of those loans, in terms of repayment and in terms of targeting, deteriorated, especially between 1999 and 2005, it was not possible for them to make a contribution to maintaining the momentum of smallholder investment, which fell during those years. The anger felt by the entire Aymara/Quechua community at the refusal of President Sanchez de Losada to negotiate with its leader, Evo Morales, 'as a drug dealer' in January 2003 (Chapter 5 above) is not measured in our institutions of conflict management index, but it still had a negative influence on the feasibility of conflict management, and thus on the conflict and political instability which exploded the following October. That explosion was an interaction between the street-by-street political organization of neighbourhood groups (*juntas vecinales*) and the continuingly ham-fisted management of the crisis by the elite, as related in Chapter 10; but that also does not find its way into our measure of conflict management, which only includes *institutions* of conflict management and does not contain individual measures of local-level organization.

In many cases, indeed, a long-term poverty trend has its origin not in national politics but in a local issue which then extends itself on to a national stage. This was illustrated in Chapter 4, which illustrated that economic disruption often has its origins in local conflicts, which then, depending on how they are managed, may or may not spread on to a national scale, as it did in El Alto in 2003 and Central Java in 1998. In Russia, the fear of this possibility drove the recently-appointed President Putin, in early 1999, into the decision to restart attacks on Chechnya to prevent the spread of rebellions against federal authority through the whole of the Caucasus and beyond. But even after the success of this gamble, it has been possible within Russia's federal system for islands of bad governance, including the governor of an autonomous republic possessing thirty-six cars of which four are white Rolls-Royces (Chapter 12), to survive into the twenty-first century as islands of increasing poverty within a general environment of falling poverty levels.

Often, sequencing is important, and institutional change is the prime mover. As we saw in Chapter 3, tax increases at a time of recession can be politically ruinous and lead to reversal and instability, especially when (as in Bolivia) they are regressive and occur in a context when the rich are not being pressured to pay their own taxes. As we saw in the previous chapter, tax increases timed so as to come after a bonus, such as those imposed in Ghana and Uganda in the mid-1990s immediately after marketing reforms which put a higher share of the producer price into the hands of farmers, not only have a better chance of sticking, but also provided a basis for expenditure which in turn underpinned growth. Expansion of infrastructure and rural loan and savings outlets may be an essential precondition for the expansion of labour markets, the process which in Indonesia in the 1970s and 1980s (more modestly in Uganda in the following decade) was the true driver of poverty reduction. And effective institutions of conflict management may be able to pre-empt social tensions and thereby make market access easier. A small example of this can be provided from Bolivia in 2003; in September of that year, a general strike was called across the entire city of El Alto, in protest against government policy (Chapters 3 and 4 above), precluding microfinance clients from going to loan offices to repay their instalments. In many cases this created tension within the household, as most microfinance clients are female and the male partners of many of them were on the street barricades defending the strike. The damage to loan repayment thus caused was defused by improvisation (Aliaga and Mosley 2007): loan staff of CRECER and ProMujer[47] extended their clients' loan terms, accepted payment of loan instalments in kind rather than in cash, and where feasible (for example if they lived in the same street as the client) collected loan instalments on clients' doorsteps, rather than forcing them to run the barricades. In this way, conflict was managed by circumvention. The exercise of institutional ingenuity enabled access to the bottom of the credit market to be maintained in the midst of severe riot-type conflict.

Finally, we need to draw attention to linkages between the right-hand and the left-hand part of Table 6.3, between pro-poor institutions and indicators of governance quality. We illustrate this particularly in relation to one of the two governance indicators which exhibited a significant relationship with economic growth, namely political stability. How did institutional indicators impact on this?

We examine this question by superimposing our pro-poor institution indicator(s) on the time series for our case-study countries depicted in Chapter 3 (Figure 6.3). As we there observe, in those cases where pro-poor institutions improved over the period 1990–2007 (Argentina, Ghana, Kenya, Uganda, and Bolivia), this was associated, except in one case, with a reduction in overall political instability and where pro-poor institutions got worse, political instability deteriorated.

The implication of this is that the *development of effective pro-poor institutions may be able to act as a buffer against bad governance, and by itself contribute to political stability which is a component of that governance.* We have encountered a number of examples of this: the development of a countrywide network of rural saving institutions in Indonesia, which provided protection for low-income households against the 1997 slump which the maladministration of President Suharto had aggravated; the opening up of extension and microfinance services to the private and NGO sectors in Uganda has enabled remote rural households to access services in areas which previously were not provided by government; and

[47] As argued above, there was widespread contamination of microfinance portfolios in Bolivia during the early 2000s, with large increases in default rates. Only four institutions escaped this process, keeping default rates at less than two per cent. The NGOs Crecer and ProMujer, which aim at a lower target group than the Bolivian average, are two of these four. Both Crecer and ProMujer supply credit in groups jointly with education to female clients only, and we argue (Marconi and Mosley 2006) that the social capital thus created, as well as the flexibility described above, may have kept clients loyal and protected their repayment rates and cash-flow.

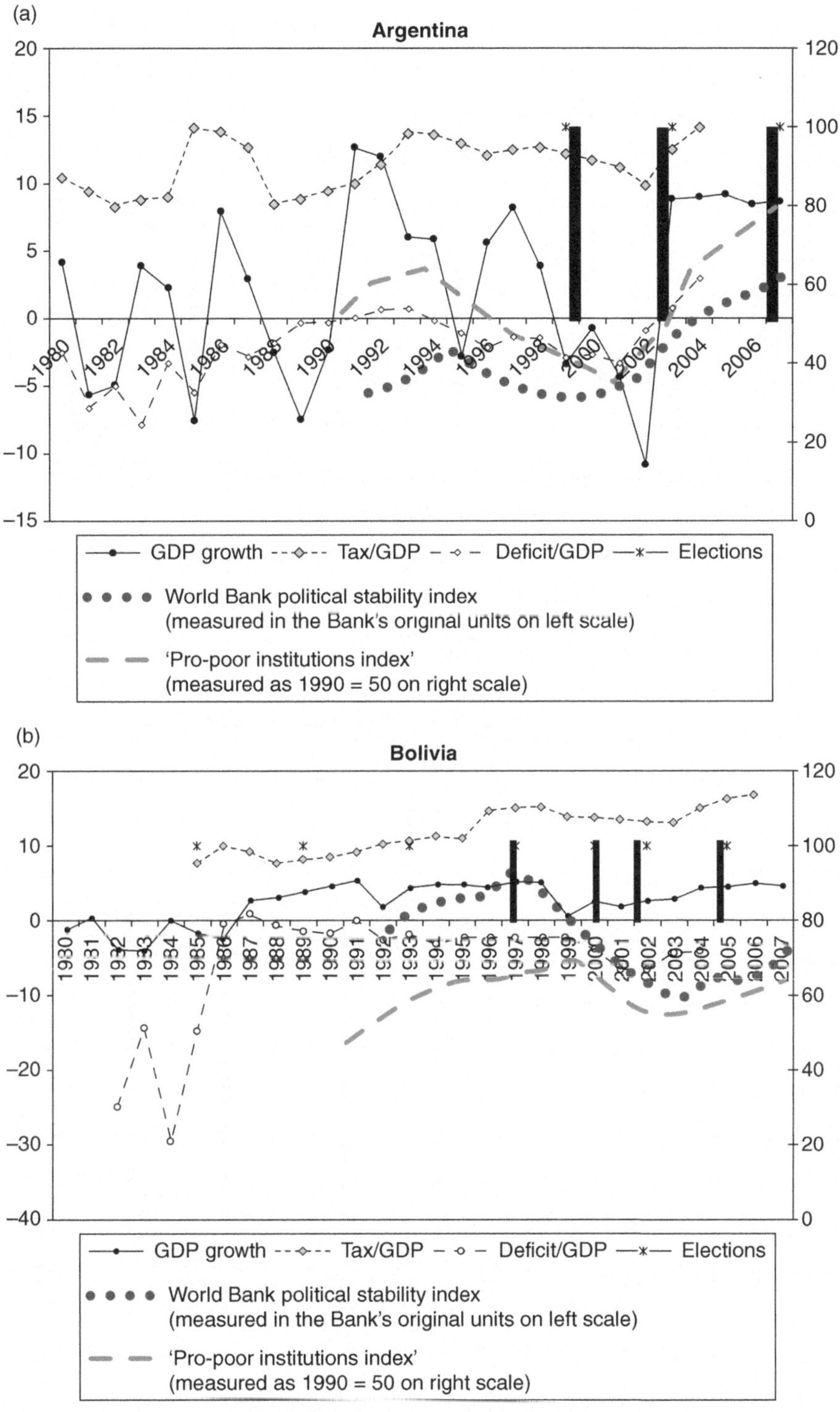

Figure 6.3 'Pro-poor institutional performance', political instability, and the business cycle.

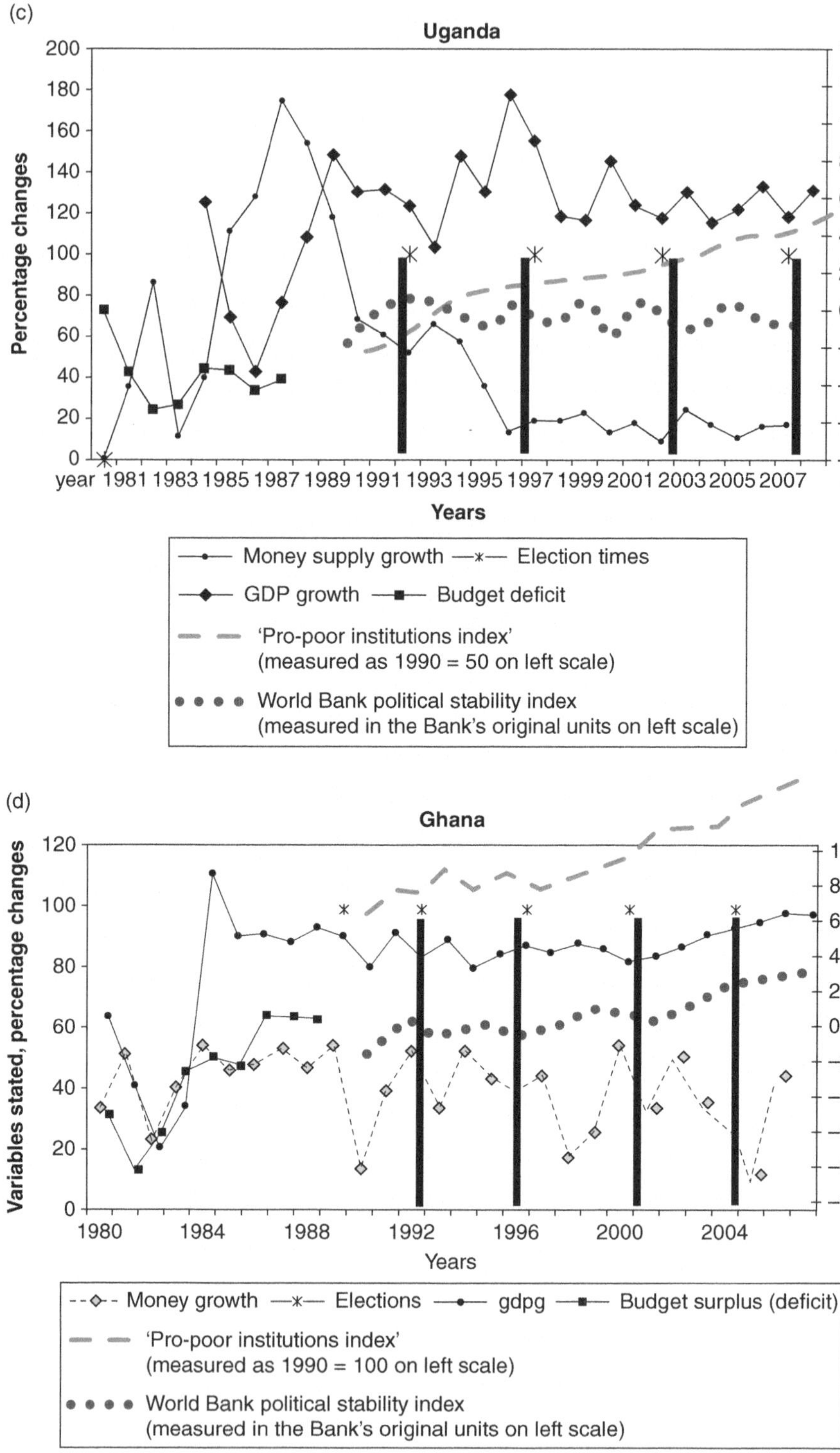

Figure 6.3 Continued

(e)

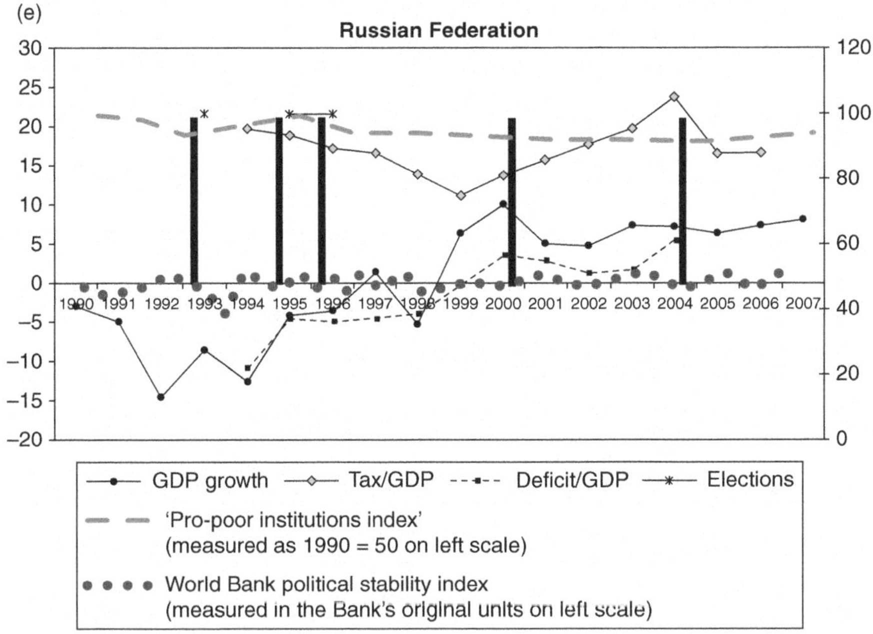

(f)

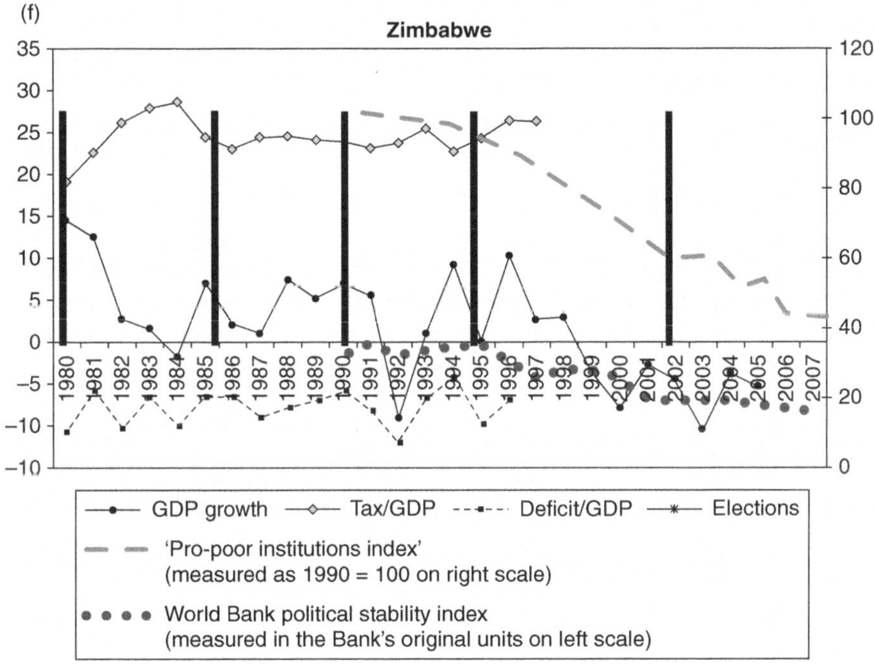

Figure 6.3 Continued

two very different institutions of conflict management (the *Mesa de Dialogo* in Argentina, and the Electoral Commission's Inter-Party Advisory Committee in Ghana) can be credited with having increased the level of public trust and minimized the risks of conflict by broadening the level of participation and transparency in decision-making. Needless to say, this proposition is not an iron law, and we have encountered several exceptions to it, notably the case of Bolivia, where the polity has been chronically unstable since 2000 in spite of several progressive institutional developments. This case draws our attention to the measurement problems of our proposed index previously discussed,[48] and also to the local dimension of institutional capacity. As we saw, local institutional improvisations can often achieve a great deal, even in situations such as El Alto where the national governance environment is grim.[49]

This conclusion links interestingly to the idea of the 'political business cycle', which states that government macro-policy, in developing as much as industrialized countries, is likely to be relaxed in election years. In this context we can now ask, how do institutional influences enter this picture? Block (2002), who has found the election cycle to be alive and well all over Africa in response to the resurgence of democracy in the 1990s, warned that there might be a price to pay for this, in the shape of reduced fiscal and institutional discipline. Our own initial impression is the reverse of this.

We can begin by looking at Table 6.4. This table begins, in the first column, by estimating as a regression, across a sample including all of our case-study countries, the relationship between institutional and political stability which we have just discussed. We find that relationship, once again, to be positive, and when we add in election years as an additional influence they are non-significant—in other words, the pre-election stimulus, which in most of the countries and periods we surveyed does occur (Chapter 3) apparently does not feed through into increased political instability.

But what of *economic* instability? In the last four columns of Table 6.4 we bring this variable into the picture. We do this by estimating as simultaneous relationships the entire chain of causation from institutions to economic stability to political stability to poverty, because both political and economic stability are endogenous, that is, determined by causes within the system we have been discussing, and likely to give biased estimates if presented as individualized relationships. Thus, reading from right to left in Table 6.4, the dependent variables are respectively aid flows, the World Bank political stability index, a simple measure of economic stability (deviations of GDP from trend), and finally the infant mortality indicator of poverty. Within this system (column 2), political stability, which (column 4) is influenced upward by the institutional quality index, increases poverty, and economic instability decreases it. However, the election-

[48] In Bolivia microfinance quality declined between 1999–2003 even while microfinance quantity was increasing, and several qualitative institutional indicators (capacity of mediating services between judicial system and civil society; government capacity for conflict management) deteriorated at this time. See pages 171–5 above.

[49] See the discussion of El Alto in Chapter 10 below.

Table 6.4 Institutional quality, political instability, and the political business cycle.

Independent variables	Estimation method				
	OLS	Simultaneous (three-stage least squares) estimation			
	Dependent variables				
	(1) World Bank political stability index	(2) Infant mortality	(3) Instability of GDP	(4) World Bank political stability index	(5) Aid/GDP
Constant	−2.97** (6.04)	22.8** (5.88)	0.032 (1.06)	−1.87** (4.78)	11.99** (19.92)
World Bank political stability index		−23.11** (5.96)			
'Pro-poor institutions index'	0.008** (2.49)			0.0087** (2.65)	
Openness index	0.019** (3.88)				
Investment		−0.73 (1.83)			
Aid/GDP		−3.57** (12.15)			
Per capita GDP	0.0002** (5.65)			0.0001** (4.43)	−0.001** (9.36)
Instability of GDP		131.15 (1.87)			
Election-year stimulus	0.30 (1.33)		0.0002 (0.23)		
Population					−0.057** (8.52)
Instruments		Investment	Openness	GDP per capita	Population
'R^2'	0.3586	0.0775	0.0359	0.19	0.52
P	0.0000	0.0000	0.2910	0.0000	0.0000
Number of observations	75	75	75	75	75

Sources: data cover the period 1990–2008 for the following countries: Argentina, Bolivia, Cote d'Ivoire, Ghana, Ethiopia, Indonesia, Kenya, Malaysia, Nigeria, Russia, Uganda, Tanzania, Zambia, Zimbabwe (potentially 252 observations). All variables are from World Bank, World Bank Indicators CD-ROM, except:

- Our 'pro-poor institutions'(PPI), indicator assembled from measures for state-business relations, microfinance density, tax ratios, and labour market access (infrastructure), all of these described in detail in Table 6.3. The indicator measured is 'PPI3rev', in other words the state–business relations indicator is excluded, and an allowance is made for capacity to manage conflict.
- World Bank political instability index from Kaufmann et al. (2006) and are displayed at http://www.worldbank.org/wbi/governance/pubs/govmatters4sra.html. Alternative stability indicators are summarized in the *Quality of Government Codebook* published by the University of Gothenburg Quality of Government Institute (http://www.qog.pol.gu.se).
- 'Instability of GDP' is deviation of GDP from its time trend as estimated by an OLS regression.
- 'Election-year stimulus' takes the value (percentage increase in money supply) in an election year, zero in a non-election year.

All data are available on the programme website www.poverty.group.shef.ac.uk.

cycle variable[50] (column 3) has no impact whatever on instability of GDP; the impact of institutional quality on GDP instability is insignificant and on political stability is significantly positive. These results are robust across a range of specifications.[51]

All that the table illustrates, of course, is the absence of a predicted linkage, but there is a good deal of evidence from our case studies to explain how the political business cycle mechanism has, in several cases, been uncoupled from its ability to cause harm. In the presence of an institutional mechanism enabling savings to grow during the 1998–2000 recession, many rural Indonesians were able to protect themselves against recession; pro-poor institutions counteracted both the political and economic business cycle. In Bolivia, by contrast, between 2000–5, the decay of pro-poor institutions which had previously thrived amplified (Figure 6.4) both the political and the economic business cycle. In Ghana, it was widely foreseen that the Electoral Commission's efforts to encourage greater participation in the political process from 1992 onward would encourage incumbent parties to inflate the money supply and the budget deficit, and they did not disappoint expectations (Figure 6.4). However, because those efforts were accompanied by institution building in making the electoral process more transparent, temporary and predictable increases in short-term economic instability not only did not cause longer-term political instability but actually contributed, by building up public trust, to the process by which that condition of instability, chronic and severe at the beginning of the 1980s, could be brought under control.[52] Broadly similar observations apply to the situation of Argentina in 2001, which also was taken out of a state of chronic political instability by the creation of institutions which increased public trust—in this case focused on rights to justice and on policies to reduce social exclusion. The greater the availability of institutions to protect private trust and public assets, we surmise, the less we need to worry about a political business-cycle mechanism.

6.4 CONCLUSIONS

Obviously, state capacity matters for poverty reduction: development without an effective state is impossible, and without pro-poor institutions and adequate governance, little can be expected from the pro-poor policies described in the previous chapter. The intellectual climate of the 1990s and 2000s, indeed, has responded to a disappointing structural adjustment experience especially in the

[50] This is measured as (election-year dummy) times (increase in the money supply) in an election year, zero in a non-election year.

[51] We have attempted to do this by varying the estimation method for political stability (as in equation 1), the range of right-hand side control variables, and also using a fiscal rather than a monetary variable as the measure of the election-year boost to the economy. Results of these estimations are available from the author on request.

[52] Recent research has found that not only this institutional impact, but also the intersectoral composition of the pre-election boost, is important in determining whether the political business cycle imposes an economic cost (Drazen and Eslava 2010; Mosley and Chiripanhura 2010).

poorest countries by diagnosing deficiencies of governance as what principally needs to be set right to achieve the Millennium Goals.

However, within the empirical literature, at least, there is a great deal of ambiguity about what instruments of governance effectively support a fragile state, and how those interact with policy. For clarity we distinguish here between 'governance indicators proper' and indicators of institutional capacity. We find that several of the 'governance indicators proper' do not correlate well with growth or, therefore, poverty reduction performance: indeed, of the World Bank's indicators, *only* political stability and rule of law correlate at all well with growth outcomes. On the opposite hand, we do not have adequate indicators of pro-poor institutional capacity to match the importance which the literature rightly attaches to them, even though the importance of tax capacity has often been stressed. From the discussion of previous chapters, we argue that the essence of pro-poor institutions lies in their ability to enable poor people to access key labour and capital markets and to protect them from conflict. Our proposed surrogates for institutional development in this sense are access to microfinance, the investment ratio (as a proxy for access to labour markets) and the state-business relations indicator developed by Leftwich, Sen, and te Velde (2008). We combine these with a measure of tax capacity to construct a 'pro-poor institutions index'. This index can then be adjusted in a number of alternative ways to incorporate elements of institutional capacity, in particular capacity to manage conflict, which can only be assessed qualitatively.

We discuss in detail the politics underlying state-business relations, access to labour and finance markets, and capacity to manage conflict in our case-study countries. In some places these politics have been associated with liberalization, for example the spread of NGOs into niches previously occupied by the state, as has occurred in the 'aid countries' (all the African countries plus Bolivia) in the 1990s; in Uganda, liberalization in the form of the removal of previous ethnic discrimination against Asian businesses has been very important. These tendencies have also been visible in Indonesia in recent years; but this is a country where most pro-poor institutional development, especially in support of agriculture, has historically been executed by the central and regional state, and this is an initiative which has recently been observed and adapted by a number of African governments. In Latin America since 2000, the impulse of institutional development has also been heavily state-inspired, albeit with considerable regional variation.

Often a redesign of pro-poor institutions, as we demonstrate, underlies improvement in the conventional indices of governance, and in particular political stability. Broadening of access to markets from which the poor are excluded is both pro-poor and pro-stability, and it appears, on our empirical analysis, to submerge the worry expressed by previous commentators, that greater political openness might undermine institutional development.

Poverty dynamics are the outcome of both domestic and global politics, and our discussion so far has emphasized the former. We now reverse this bias. The next chapter discusses international political influences bearing on the poverty reduction process.

7

The global politics of poverty reduction

7.1 INTRODUCTION

In this chapter we explore the international politics that have shaped the current international poverty agenda, and seek to understand how these pressures, as embodied in the bargaining relationships between international financial institutions[1] and developing countries, have impacted on the political processes and poverty outcomes observed through the course of the book.

With increasing force after the crisis of the 1980s, as discussed in Chapter 2, the chief thrust of the main international financial institutions was directed towards *liberalization*, the freeing of the market as an instrument for the promotion of economic efficiency and individual well-being. Liberalization became a global project, embracing industrialized countries, developing countries under the name of *structural adjustment*, and eventually, after 1990, the command economies of eastern Europe and the former Soviet Union also. The end of the cold war changed the geopolitical context surrounding international financial institutions out of recognition, and Russia, one of our case-study countries, changed from being a pivot of resistance to capitalism into a country itself involved in economic and political adjustment to capitalist forces—indeed for a time also struggling for survival as a state. In many of the countries of the low-income developing world, as in Russia, it soon became clear that the unleashing of competitive forces could not necessarily be seen as a force which would make either the state or the market work more effectively. In much of Africa, and elsewhere where the state was weak, the results of adjustment were negative not only in the sense that personal incomes (and therefore poverty) deteriorated over the course of the 1980s and much of the 1990s (Mosley, Sabasat, and Weeks 1995), but also in the sense that states further weakened by the stresses of adjustment, as we saw in Chapter 4, became vulnerable to conflict, and thus to a further twist in the poverty spiral.

The adaptations of international institutions to these planned developments were multiple. In the first place, as described in Chapter 2, the goals changed, and

[1] Our main concern in this chapter is with the International Monetary Fund (IMF), the World Bank, multilateral financial institutions such as the EU development funds, and the bilateral aid donors. Aid (capital flows at zero or concessional interest rates) comes from all these institutions, and is mainly confined to low-income countries with incomes of about $1000 or less. Non-concessional capital flows from all these institutions, and from the private sector, are concentrated to the tune of about seventy per cent on middle-income countries with incomes of more than $1000. See World Bank, *Global Development Finance*, various issues.

a new poverty agenda was born: in this chapter we examine the broad geopolitics that shaped it. We argue that poverty became particularly important to centre-left governments, concerned to maintain public support for a broad internationalist commitment to liberal economic policy by showing that this agenda could work for the poor as well as the rich. We go on to show that this politics has had an impact on poverty policy, in that a new agenda of participatory poverty planning has been bolted onto an only thinly altered, and indeed now reviving, economic consensus on producing growth.

In the second place, of course, the ability of international financial institutions to influence development processes changed also, and this fed through into poverty outcomes. As we have illustrated in the case of the World Bank (Mosley 1986; Mosley, Harrigan, and Toye 1995) influence emerges from *bargaining relationships*, in which both the supplier and the receiver of the finance pursue their own political interests. Below, we pursue the question of what has happened to these bargaining relationships in the new post-cold war, post-new poverty agenda world, and how they have impacted on poverty levels. The findings are somewhat paradoxical. On the one hand, the bargaining leverage of the donors, already weak in the 1980s, in the 1990s and 2000s became weaker still as pressure on the donors to spend the budget intensified, and in the 2000s the aid part of the budget itself was expanded under the impetus of the Millennium Development Goals. On the other hand, however, not only did poverty fall across the range of environments examined in previous chapters, but, in poorer countries, it fell for reasons which, we demonstrate, are directly connected with the degree of influence of the aid donors; we speculate that, in some of these countries, this was because the ultimatum game once played by the donors had been replaced by a *trust game*, one component of which was the preservation of core elements of the Washington consensus, in relation to both policy and institutions, while letting others slip. In middle-income countries, we argue, the bargaining relationships were very different: especially after the 'east Asian crisis', an explicit reaction against the 'Washington Consensus' became apparent (Grugel, Riggirozzi, and Thirkell-White 2008), and Russia, Argentina, and Malaysia, so far from preserving the core of the Washington consensus, expanded their use of policy instruments quite anathematic to that consensus, including export taxes, price controls, and capital controls. The 'policy convergence' of the structural adjustment period has been at least partly reversed, and in this and the final chapter we explore some of the implications of this for poverty levels and the direction of policy.

7.2 THE EMERGENCE OF THE POVERTY AGENDA WITHIN INTERNATIONAL FINANCIAL INSTITUTIONS

At a general level, policy within the Bretton Woods institutions tends to be a broad reflection of domestic approaches to political economy in the West. Electoral incentives encourage political parties to present a package of policies with some ideological consistency, which shapes perspectives on foreign economic policy. More importantly, career progression and appointment processes ensure a uniformity of intellectual and ideological outlook amongst key figures in government. So, to take the most obvious example, the early structural adjustment agenda was plainly influenced by the rise of New Right political parties in the UK and USA. The economic crisis of the late 1970s produced a mutually reinforcing intellectual and political reaction in which neoliberal ideas were deployed to justify a political move to the right, and newly empowered political forces helped to reinforce the influence of the new intellectual agenda.[2] Policy towards the Bretton Woods institutions reflects a subset of broader political influence. Treasury ministries dominate but their views are also sometimes influenced by specifically development-oriented lobbying and by direct national commercial interests. The overall result is a broad reflection of domestic economic priorities and intellectual outlook but coloured by a stronger emphasis on economic orthodoxy and internationalism, tempered by an interest in poverty rather than inequality.[3] These perspectives are then fed through the institutional structures of the Bretton Woods institutions themselves. We go on to explore the mandates and institutional cultures of the two institutions. We argue that both promote a preference for universalist, economic justifications for policy, further reinforcing the enhanced importance of technical debate relative to much domestic policymaking, but that this effect is stronger within the IMF than it is in the more pluralist World Bank. Within the Bank the 'intellectual consensus' that shapes policy shows notable signs of broadening beyond orthodox economics.

Domestic politics in the West

In the process of establishing the Bretton Woods institutions, the desire of John Maynard Keynes was to create institutions that were staffed by economic technocrats, insulated from the irrationalities and vagaries of politics and incentivised to better performance through the principle of separation of powers.[4] Executive Directors are civil servants, rather than politicians. They are usually drawn from finance ministries or central banks and are full-time employees of the Bretton Woods institutions. However, Keynes's victory was only partial. Symbolically, he lost the battle to have the institutions based in financial New York, rather than political Washington. More practically, the institutions' ministerial-level Boards of Governors exercise ultimate oversight over policy. In practice, the Board of Governors is too unwieldy to have more than a very broad guidance but Executive Directors are appointed by governments, remain accountable to them and

[2] For the origins of the 'neoliberal project' see Toye (1993) and Gore (2000).

[3] This section builts on earlier work by Thirkell-White, which explores the domestic politics of policy toward the International Financial Institutions (Thirkell-White 2005a, b).

[4] In particular, and relevantly for the present time, Keynes aimed to create interactions between the Bretton Woods institutions which would insulate them against problems of excessive risk-taking. In May 1945 he wrote to Edward Bernstein at the US Treasury that: 'Different qualities are required [sc. of Fund Executive Directors and Bank Executive Directors], and the range of activities of the two would be widely divergent. I should like to see the Board of the Fund composed of cautious bankers, and the Board of the Bank of imaginative expansionists' Keynes (1945/1980), vol. 26, page 194, Keynes to Bernstein, 29 May 1945.

probably expect their long-term careers to be based in the domestic civil service, even if they are full-time employees of the Bretton Woods institutions (Gardner 1980; Strange 1973; Thirkell-White 2005a).

What this means in terms of day-to-day policymaking varies considerably between Executive Directors (EDs). At one extreme, the US ED tends to be geographically and politically close to the United States Treasury, who provide him or her with a small staff. Policy is fed through Treasury (with occasional input from other branches of government) and is also more peripherally influenced by legislative directives passed by Congress that require USEDs to use their 'voice and vote' in particular ways (Thirkell-White 2005b). At the other extreme, African Executive Directors often represent up to twenty countries, rely on the Fund to provide them with research staff and receive little advice from domestic capitals except, perhaps, on particular lending programmes (Evans and Finnemore 2002).

The politics of US influence over the Fund is particularly well-researched. Although institutional arrangements across countries are variable, the US situation can provide at least a broad proxy for patterns in other significant member countries. In political terms, policy towards the Bretton Woods institutions is a minority concern. The US Executive Directors are appointed by the Department of the Treasury. Much of the time, Treasury's international affairs department simply pursues policy in line with officials' technical opinions and the current Presidential Administration's broader foreign economic policy objectives. From time to time, though, USTR (the United States Trade Representative) will push particular trade issues via the USED and there is also strong evidence that US strategic interests have sometimes affected lending agreements (Thacker 1999, 2006). Especially on trade issues, the influence of Congress is also on the rise. USAID, by contrast, has no influence over IMF policy and plays a relatively small role in policy towards the Bank.[5]

Amongst other members of the Fund and Bank group, institutional arrangements are often less complex. Nonetheless, the same broad constellation of interests tends to dominate. What emerges is a curious hybrid of influence that differs significantly from the electorate as a whole. In domestic systems of government, economic ministries have primary responsibility for monetary and fiscal policy, but fiscal policy, at least, is determined in interaction with a far broader range of bureaucratic (and indirectly electoral) interests. When it comes to policy towards the IFIs, Treasury views are far less diluted and are subject only to a relatively narrow range of interest group pressures. It is not just 'Western' interests that dominate in the IFIs, then, but a particular subset of Western interests, in the following rough order of importance: finance ministry, internationally-oriented business, and development NGOs.

Politics within the Bretton Woods institutions

As already indicated, Keynes's attempts to design institutions that would be relatively free of political interference were only partially successful. Both

[5] Ben Thirkell-White, interviews, Washington, DC, October 2000.

institutions' constitutions require them to be politically neutral and staff tend to see themselves as technocrats, engaged in the pursuit of 'good policy' (Woods 1998, 2006). They clearly seek academic approval for their policy choices and academic criticism probably has a greater impact than disapproval from small segments of the institutions' political guardians.[6] Equally, claims to technocratic authority (and therefore political neutrality) are particularly important in the governance of international institutions. The relationship between sovereign states and international institutions is rather different to that between democratic governments and their populations. It is more difficult, on the global plane, to appeal to the notion of a community of fate in which participants can expect to win some battles and lose others over time (Steffek 2003). Wherever possible, it is better to argue that policy choices are the outcome of a process of neutral, technical optimization, rather than messy political compromise. There is therefore a natural affinity with utilitarian economic arguments (Thirkell-White 2005a, b).

Through both these sets of motivations, trends within the economics profession came to shape institutional policy at least as much as political influence, though which is the driving force varies over time and across issues. For example, the Bank's growing interest in the state and institutions partly pre-dates donors' adoption of governance conditionality in the early 1990s and the Bretton Woods institutions' technical emphasis, derived from the new institutional economics, continues to shape ideas of governance in ways that differ significantly from the emphasis on democracy and human rights that often drives donor agendas (Lancaster 1993; Thirkell-White 2003). In this case, the original impetus was technical and analytical but it was given a great deal of extra momentum and a slight twist in meaning by a changing political climate. Alternatively, in Congressional testimony, Timothy Geithner, now the US Treasury Secretary, has described the ways in which the US government seeks to push its political agendas in the IMF by finding ways to dress them up in technical form and build an intellectual consensus, so that they can eventually be raised within the Executive Board as 'technical issues' (Geithner 1998). Here political goals are sometimes realized, but in ways that are shaped and constrained by the availability of credible technical arguments. Overall, economic and political influence interact with one another in complex ways but it is certainly fair to say that the academic ethos of the Bretton Woods institutions makes them much more concerned to provide economic justifications for their policy choices than would be the case in most domestic policy institutions, reinforcing the pre-existing bias towards technical economic world views created by the structures of accountability reviewed above.[7]

Technical economic prestige is particularly important within the IMF, which is generally a more tightly-managed institution with a macro-economic focus (Barnett and Finnemore 2004; Woods 2006). The Bank is much larger, relatively

[6] Witness, for example, the highly pointed public exchanges between Kenneth Rogoff and Joseph Stiglitz on international financial governance in 2002.

[7] The obvious exception is independent central banks; but recent evidence suggests that even these may not be as independent of political sentiment as they would sometimes like to claim. See Hay (2008) *Good Inflation, Bad Inflation: The Housing Boom, Economic Growth and the Disaggregation of Inflationary Pressures in Britain and Ireland.* Mimeo, July 2008, available at http://subprimeworkshop.blogspot.com (accessed 20 March 2009).

diverse, and has both a more micro focus and a broader development mandate. It has been more open to change driven by its often quite entrepreneurial presidents who are less subordinate to the Bank's Executive Board than the Fund's managing director is to its IMF equivalent (Blackmon 2008). Initially concerned with financing large infrastructure projects, it moved in the 1970s, as we saw in Chapter 2, into both the aid and the poverty business under the impetus of the MacNamara initiative. In the 1980s, the IMF and World Bank came together with the instrument of structural adjustment lending as a response to the global economic crisis of that time; this collaboration, however, was never easy and, over time, the tensions between the two different mandates have also begun to grow (Mosley, Harrigan, and Toye 1995; Polak 1994). Within the IMF, there is a strong preference for measures that can be interpreted as having a strong impact on macroeconomic balance. The Bank's broader 'development' mandate makes poverty reduction a more comfortable policy territory, within which, however, opinions differ quite broadly across the staff.[8]

The geopolitics of the new poverty agenda

The broad political impetus behind the new poverty agenda can be seen as a projection of 'Third Way' political ideas onto the international realm. During the 1990s a reaction to the new right politics of the 1980s began to set in across much of the developed world, though we will focus on the US Clinton Administration and New Labour in the UK. The new centre-left governments were anxious to distance themselves from both their free-market predecessors and the socialist agenda of the 'old left'. The Third Way concept was supposed to provide an escape from the old dichotomies of capitalism versus socialism, state versus market, and growth versus redistribution.

The aim was to promote: 'a dynamic knowledge-based economy that harnesses the market to serve the public interest; a strong civil society; a modern government of partnership and decentralization; and a foreign policy based on international co-operation' (Blair 1998, cited in Dixon and Williams 2001). These governments broadly shared the enthusiasm for a liberal international economy (by now re-labelled as 'globalization'). However, their appeal to left-wing supporters was built on the promise that democratic regulation, more participatory government, and greater space for civil society would ensure that the benefits were widely spread. For those on the left who were sceptical about globalization, including many with ties to the NGO sector, the promise was that economic internationalism could be combined with a more social and political internationalism that would ensure the international promotion of human rights and democracy. Public action would maximize social inclusion by providing social safety nets and effective lifelong education so that those temporarily disadvantaged by more rapid economic change would not suffer permanent social or economic exclusion.

[8] In particular, staff of the International Finance Corporation (IFC), the Bank's arm lending to the private sector, have been impatient with the requirement to comply with the new poverty mandate. In interviews with the author in June 2007, they described the Bank President's insistence that poverty impact must be assessed on all projects including IFC projects as 'just another internal tax imposed on us'.

A more competitive open international economy would produce more periods of short-term unemployment but, with short-term safety nets in place and a commitment to re-skilling and re-training, no one should be permanently disadvantaged. Globalization could be made to 'work for the poor', as an influential DfID white paper put it, and a focus on 'joined-up-government' encouraged the making of at least broad analogies between perspectives on domestic economic policy and development policy.[9]

The overlaps between this broad ideological agenda and what was to become the Poverty Reduction Strategy Paper (PRSP) process, in which the centrepiece of a poor country's development effort was an anti-poverty strategy driven by the recipient country in consultation with civil society and specifically with poor people within that country, should be readily apparent. Growth created through orthodox liberal economic policies remains the point of departure; there is a growing acknowledgement, however, that public action is necessary to eliminate a range of market failures that can prevent such policies from translating into pro-poor growth. An emphasis on democratic processes and civil society engagement, both in the national and in the global sphere, can help to guarantee these positive outcomes.

Precursors for this agenda in aid policy

During the heyday of structural adjustment, the IMF (in particular) argued that concern for its clients' sovereignty precluded it from becoming involved in many domestic policy matters (notably the sectors on which expenditure cuts should fall, which are the centrepiece of the analysis of Chapter 5). The Fund's job was to set out clearly the magnitude of adjustment that was required of countries and to ensure that the policies they came up with were compatible with those limits, but it was not for the Fund to enquire into the distributional consequences of a particular policy mix. Questions about trade-offs between, for example, military spending and primary health care were none of the Fund's business (Nowzad 1982; Polak 1991). This view began to change in the early 1990s in conjunction with a broader change in North-South relationships.

The most obvious manifestation of this change was the rise of governance (or more bluntly 'political') conditionality on the part of bilateral donors. Democracy and human rights promotion were catapulted onto donors' agendas across much of the developed world in a remarkably short period of time in the early 1990s, as described in Chapter 2. The motivations for the change were a combination of liberal self-confidence in the wake of Soviet collapse and the need to find new, publicly palatable, justifications for foreign spending to counteract expectations of a large 'peace dividend'. An expanding agenda was also made possible by developing countries' reduced options for playing one donor off against another once socialist donors had vanished and the West had begun to put more effort into aid coordination (Crawford 2001; Lancaster 1993).

[9] For policy papers written in broadly these terms from both sides of the Atlantic, see Bowman Cutter et al. (2000), DfID (2000), and more broadly, for some relevant critical perspectives on the extension of this kind of thinking to development policy, see Craig and Porter (2006) and Jayasuriya (2006).

Table 7.1 The 'augmented Washington consensus' (after Rodrik 2006).

Original Washington Consensus	Augmented Washington Consensus
	The previous ten items, plus:
Fiscal discipline	Corporate governance
Reorientation of public expenditures	Anti-corruption
Tax reform	Flexible labour markets
Financial liberalization	WTO agreements
Unified and competitive exchange rates	Financial codes and standards
Trade liberalization	'Prudent' capital-account opening
Openness to DFI	Non-intermediate exchange rate regimes
Privatization	Independent central banks/inflation targeting
Deregulation	Social safety nets
Secure property rights	Targeted poverty reduction

Source: Rodrik (2006), Table 1.

Within the Bretton Woods institutions, there was also a growing interest in governance that sprang from more technical roots. Disappointing results from structural adjustment in Africa, including growing academic evidence and NGO lobbying on poverty outcomes, was increasingly focusing attention on issues of governance (World Bank 1989). Attempts were made to re-assemble the Washington consensus (Rodrik 2006) by bolting on to the original (1980s) core principles, which were principally related to freedom of markets, a set of new 1990s principles which as illustrated by Rodrik (Table 7.1) were mainly concerned with institutions.

The rise of the new institutional economics helped to push this agenda forwards by providing intellectual justifications for a link between predictable, transparent institutions, investor confidence, and growth (Dhonte 1997). Under the Clinton administration the pre-existing interest in democracy was re-enforced and closely related to the concept of globalization under the rubric of 'enlargement policy'. In his Presidential campaign of 1992, Clinton argued that the Bush (senior) administration had failed to capitalize on the potential for a peace dividend and that, in a post-Cold War environment, the focus should be on re-invigorating US prosperity through the promotion of American competitiveness at home and the spread of democracy and free markets abroad (Dumbrell 1997). New Labour's attempts to soften enthusiasm for globalization by associating them with an 'ethical foreign policy' functioned in a similar way (Dixon and Williams 2001).

What changed with the rise of centre-left governments, particularly in the UK, was that maintaining a connection to traditional left-wing electoral support placed them under more immediate pressure to show that globalization could deliver for the poor as well as the rich. The governance agenda therefore began to take on a more poverty-oriented character.

The rise of the debt agenda and HIPC 1

NGO and academic pressure was pushing issues of poverty up the Bretton Woods agenda throughout the 1990s but it only reached its current prominent position in the course of the second round of Highly Indebted Poor Countries (HIPC) negotiations in the late 1990s. HIPC reflected the reality that much low-income country debt could not be repaid. However, it was still highly controversial within the Bretton Woods institutions, amongst some bilateral donors, and with many members of the US Congress, who were wedded to the conviction that cancelling international debt was a dangerous precedent, possibly undermining the BWIs' creditworthiness (Callaghy 2004). For right-wingers, IMF lending (especially lending into the arrears of developing countries unable to service their debts) was creating moral hazard, encouraging reckless private sector lending, and, more importantly, preventing markets from disciplining countries with poor policy. Although no one really thought Congress would actually withhold funding for further global debt relief, the debate dragged on for much of the second half of the 1990s and achieved a very high media profile. In the end, Congress approved funding for debt cancellation but with a long list of conditions attached, which reflected a (sometimes incompatible) mixture of the left and right-wing agendas. The legislation both required the IMF to promote market-oriented reform, trade and financial sector liberalization, and privatization (on the one hand), and to 'discourage practices which may lead to ethnic or social strife', tailor its policies better to country circumstances, and recognize the destabilizing effects of 'inappropriate stabilization policies'.[10]

An important outcome of this debate was that the US administration commissioned a group of conservative economists under the leadership of Alan Meltzer to write a report on Bretton Woods reform (International Financial Institution Advisory Commission 2000), recommending that the IMF revert to its core curriculum and abstain from expansionist ventures onto other agencies' turf, such as the proposed IMF Poverty Reduction and Growth Facility. This report was to strongly influence the policy of the Bush Administration for the next ten years. It recommended a more radical separation of the Bank and IMF's tasks, removing the IMF completely from lending to low-income countries so that its role could be made more purely macro-economic and technical and its conditionality more focused. Many of its recommendations were rapidly buried, even by the Bush administration, but its findings and popularity point to the mixed messages that were being sent to the Bretton Woods institutions (and particularly the IMF) even in the midst of the apparent new mandate to put poverty first.[11]

The PRSP concept and its contradictions

The deal that was eventually struck in 2000 conceded the issue of debt cancellation on the condition that the proceeds would go to poverty reduction. In this way, technical issues of moral hazard and optimal resource allocation could be trumped by an ethical commitment to poverty reduction (Busby 2007). The

[10] For a fuller account, see Thirkell-White (2005a, b). For some indication of Treasury responses in the short-term, see US Treasury (2000a, b).

[11] On some of the aftermath to the Meltzer report in Washington see Thirkell-White (2005b) and Callaghy (2004). For a critique of its recommendations for taking the IMF out of the business of low-income lending, see Bird and Mosley (2004) in Vines and Gilbert (2004).

politics that produced this result, though, were highly complex and distinctly fragile. Indeed, shortly after HIPC 2 was announced, Camdessus argued that: 'It shows us above all, how fragile our collective commitments are, and how small the chances that they will be fulfilled without a universal mobilization of public opinion, as has been the case with Jubilee 2000' (cited in Callaghy 2004). Congressional debates over IMF reform demonstrate clearly that any pro-poor shift in political opinion during the 1990s was shallow and contested, rather than radical and complete.

A key element in the new compromise was the invention of Poverty Reduction Strategy Papers (PRSPs) as the instrument through which the required pro-poor reforms were to be channelled. As David Hulme has noted, two very different sources generated the ideas that underpin the PRSP design. The first was Uganda's home-grown Poverty Eradication Action Plan, approved in summer 1997. This plan arose out of dissatisfaction in Uganda about World Bank proposals for the country to reduce poverty simply through the prioritization of primary health and education expenditures. Ugandan ministers and technocrats felt these proposals did not do justice to other elements in the country's national poverty strategy, in particular the agriculture, tax, and finance elements (see Chapters 5 and 6 above) and were supported by bilateral donors and international NGOs, especially Oxfam. This led to Uganda supplementing the Bank's poverty assessment with a participatory poverty assessment (PPA) and drafting a plan directly aimed at national poverty eradication—the PEAP. As Hulme relates, this:

> raised the profile of poverty and broadened the range of policies the country would use to tackle it. It also served political purposes: demonstrating to donors that HIPC money would reach the poor and that Uganda's 'non-party' democracy promoted civil society participation in policymaking. World Bank officials based in Kampala observed the PEAP process and reported this back to Washington, DC.
>
> (Hulme 2010, pages 4 and 14)

The second source of ideas was the Comprehensive Development Framework (CDF) drafted by the World Bank President, James Wolfensohn in early 2000, which sought to re-orient the process of the World Bank in response to continuing criticism of its top-down style, of which conditionality was a component. The CDF would be long-term and holistic, would be based on a Bank–country partnership led by the recipient country, would involve civil society consultation and use the latest 'participatory' techniques. It would also be results oriented. From these two different sources, a set of five core principles were used to build PRSPs.[12] That year, it was agreed that PRSPs would be the mechanism by

[12] These were:

1. Country-driven: involving broad-based participation by civil society and the private sector in all operational steps.
2. Results-oriented: focusing on outcomes that would benefit the poor.
3. Comprehensive: recognizing the multidimensional nature of poverty.
4. Partnership-oriented: involving coordinated participation of development partners (bilateral, multilateral, and non-governmental).
5. Based on a long-term perspective for poverty reduction.

Source: World Bank website (http://go.worldbank.org/ZLBKFM2V90).

which HIPC resources would be handled, and in 2002, it was decided that all development assistance disbursed by the Bank and Fund would require a PRSP also. As virtually all OECD donors require recipients to be compliant with the Bretton Woods institutions, this meant that a PRSP became essential to access any foreign aid.

In principle, the PRSP, later Poverty Reduction Strategy or PRS,[13] process provided the Bank and the donors with a mechanism for replacing top-down, short-term conditionality based on compulsory liberalization with a mutual and long-term planning process in which the recipient country truly owned the process of policy reform. In practice, little mutualization of the development policy process occurred. With the exception of Uganda, which embarrassed the Bank by claiming that its own PEAP concept had been globalized by the Bank without its permission,[14] most countries' PRSPs continued to be drafted in Washington, sometimes by Bank staff and sometimes by consultants (Stewart and Wang 2006). One reason for this was that the capacity of developing countries to prepare long-term plans had been depleted, not least by the fact that the Bretton Woods institutions had for twenty years been encouraging the closure of national planning units and promoting a focus on short-term, macro-economic management. Nor had the locus of authority been altered: although presented as being 'country executed' and 'nationally owned', PRSPs could not come into effect until an IMF/Bank joint staff appraisal had been conducted and the executive boards of both organizations had approved the strategy. This was not the end of conditionality, or even of *ex ante* conditionality; rather it was a shift to what we call 'new conditionality' (Mosley, Hudson, and Verschoor 2004), in which the recipient country is encouraged to be the first mover in the bargaining process, ample scope exists for flexibility and the formation of trust-relationships between donor and recipient, and participation by alternative providers of development inputs, notably NGOs and the private sector, is welcomed. Conditionality is now, however, attached to the overall governance and policy framework, as discussed in Chapters 5 and 6, rather than to specific policy actions.

7.3 BARGAINING, 'NEW CONDITIONALITY' AND POLICY OUTCOMES

The international financial institutions thus entered the new millennium in an environment several elements of which, transparent throughout the age of structural adjustment, had now become murky and confused. Even within the Fund,

[13] The change from PRSP to PRS was made in 2002. It was highly appropriate, as the framing of poverty strategies was, to quote the last of the five principles (footnote 12) based on a 'long-term perspective for poverty reduction' and could by no means be encapsulated in a single paper.

[14] 'A widely told joke at the [Uganda] Ministry of Finance runs: "The World Bank saw what we were doing and wrote down a description of the PEAP process. They sent that back to DC where people changed the initials from PEAP to PRSP. Two years later other Bank staff visited us to teach us about the Bank's amazing new process—the PRSP."' Interview of Margaret Kakande by David Hulme, reported in Hulme 2010, pages 4 and 29.

which still was willing to own up, with a great deal of heart-searching, to practising conditionality,[15] there was confusion about which elements in conditionality were truly essential and which expendable; and the Bank, as we have seen, was not even willing to admit that it still imposed conditions. Formally, following a period in the 1990s of trying to make conditions more poverty related (for example by requesting improvements in the level of social expenditures and the quality of governance in addition to standard free-market conditions),[16] conditionality had been abandoned by both the Bank[17] and the bilateral donors[18] as being incapable of enforcement. However, the Bank and Fund continued to have and to exercise the right of veto over recipient countries' PRSs; and beyond this, since middle-income countries were not subject to PRSs, to search for ways of exercising leverage over the use of aid money even though that leverage could no longer, formally, be styled as such, and was now often expressed through euphemisms such as 'dealing with poor performance', 'engaging with weak recipients', or simply 'making 'budget support aid more effective'.[19] Indeed, conditionality had not gone away; but its parameters had changed, as described above. We now wish to understand the consequences of this change in the rules of the game. The argument will be that, within these changed parameters, the bargaining process, the mix of policy instruments and the poverty outcome are all influenced by the *trust-relationships* which form (or fail to form, or break up) between negotiators for the donor and the recipient. These trust-relationships, where they did form, then provided recipient countries with expanded room for manoeuvre in relation to the 'openness agenda' desired by the Washington institutions. We now pursue this argument in relation to our country case-study countries.

IFIs and the evolution of 'conditionality as bargaining process'

Over twenty years ago we argued (Mosley 1987) that conditionality of whatever sort could most appropriately be seen as a *bargaining process* between conflicting objectives: in this particular case, the conflicting objectives of the

[15] The IMF has stated that beyond a core of 'essential issues' comprising a commitment to macroeconomic stability there should be a' policy space' in which members' choices would not affect the Fund's willingness to support them. The Fund has recommended that conditionality should be 'streamlined', and adopted new staff guidelines on conditionality in 2002 along these lines (IMF 2001, 2004). However, 'Killick (2006) finds little systematic evidence to show that borrower governments are being given more policy space, and an internal IMF review found that there is no evidence of a reduction in the number of structural conditions following the introduction of the streamlining initiative' (Whitfield 2009a, page 86).

[16] For this transitional period, see Mosley, Harrigan, and Toye (1995), introduction and Chapter 1.

[17] 'The dynamics between aid donors and recipients explain *why conditionality fails*. Recipients do not see the conditions as binding, and most donors are reluctant to stop giving aid when conditions are not met' (World Bank 2000, page 193, italics added).

[18] See United Kingdom, Department for International Development *et al.* (2005) which argues that ultimatum conditionality is unworkable.

[19] Engagement with poor performance' was the phrase used in DFID workshops attended by the author at IDS, University of Sussex, on 4 July 2000, and 'Budget support as more effective aid?' is the title of the influential World Bank book by Koeberle, Stavreski, and Walliser (2006). The theme of conditionality is revisited, under that name, by the Bank in most chapters of the book by Koeberle et al. (2005).

donor[20] of development finance and the recipient. At that point—the deep global recession of the 1980s, to which the World Bank sought to respond by means of conditional programme finance—we represented the donor and recipient as having a mutual interest in the disbursement of resources budgeted for development, and a conflict of interest over the intensity of conditionality attached to those resources. In its simplest form, this conflict can be represented in the form of a game, such as that portrayed in Figure 7.1a. The game begins with the donor asking the recipient to carry out reforms of policy (such as tax increases, as in the case of Bolivia 2003) or of governance (such as reductions in corruption, as in all of our African country cases) in return for the provision of a loan or grant. In all cases, and this has only changed marginally since the emergence of the PRS process in the 2000s, any deal will be split into 'tranches', or instalments, and disbursement of the later tranches depends on whether the earlier ones have been complied with. Whether or not a deal is done, and money flows from donor to recipient, depends partly on the donor's and the recipient's perceptions of each other's trustworthiness, and partly on the political pressures bearing on the donor to spend the budget. Two alternative cases can be imagined, and drawing on our earlier analysis we shall label these cases 'Zimbabwe 1995' and 'Russia 1998'. In both of these cases, there is certainly distrust on the donor's side about whether the conditions will be complied with (which indeed is reasonable, as if the recipient had wanted to comply with them *ex ante*, s/he would have done so without the pressure of conditionality), and there may also be suspicion by the recipient of the donor's motivations. Where the cases differ is in the political pressures bearing on the donor. In case (a), the top part of the table, we have an orthodox prisoner's dilemma, in which the pressures bearing on each side are equivalent: both sides would prefer to do a deal than not to do a deal (so that the pay-offs are higher in the top left-hand corner, where the donor trusts the recipient to comply with the conditions and the money flows, than in the bottom right-hand corner, where the donor does not trust the recipient and negotiations break down); but each side fears the consequences of doing a deal and having their trust exploited by the other more than the consequences of failing to do a deal. This, indeed, was the situation between Zimbabwe and the IMF in the mid-1990s: Zimbabwe, like many other countries, had breached policy conditions repeatedly on previous standbys in 1991 and 1993, but the Fund and the Bank's need of Zimbabwe was not great either in a geopolitical or in a financial sense, Zimbabwe not having accumulated the kinds of debts on which default was likely to threaten the global financial system (Chapter 13 below). Thus, the dominant strategy equilibrium, for the two parties in the relationship, was '*recipient*, do not comply with conditions; *donor*, do not disburse' and this outcome—increasing and overt delinquency by Zimbabwe on the Fund's conditions, then suspension of disbursement by the Fund in 1996, leading eventually to cancellation of the relationship—duly occurred. There has been no lending by the Bank–Fund group to Zimbabwe since 1999 (nor has it been requested; since 2000 the Mugabe government has pre-emptively broken off aid relationships with many multilateral and bilateral donors, leaving the NGOs as the only providers of support to the country). The word 'overt' is key to our subsequent

[20] Throughout the remainder of this chapter we shall stick to the terminology *donor* for the provider of development finance, even though in a number of country cases (e.g. Russia, Argentina, Malaysia among our case studies) the relationship is in fact a commercial one.

(a) The conventional, symmetric prisoner's dilemma: equilibrium at bottom right

		Player 1 ('donor') behaviours	
Player 2 ('recipient') responses		Trusting (e.g. 'disburse next installment of loan')	Untrusting (e.g. 'not disburse next installment of loan')
	Trustworthy (e.g. 'comply with conditions')	1,1	2,–2
	Untrustworthy (e.g. 'not comply with conditions')	–2,2	0,0

(b) The one-sided prisoner's dilemma: equilibrium at bottom left

		Player 1 ('donor') behaviours	
Player 2 ('recipient') responses		Trusting (e.g. disburse)	Not disburse
	Trustworthy (e.g. 'comply with conditions')	2,2	0,–1
	Untrustworthy (e.g. 'not comply with conditions')	1,3	0,0

Pay-offs are given in the order (player 1, player 2).

Figure 7.1 Conditional budget support operations by the World Bank and IMF: two conflict-of-interest models.

argument. It signals that Zimbabwe did not attempt to defend, still less to apologize for, its slippage on conditionality, and, not being willing to seek accommodation with the donors by negotiating an agreement on fundamentals, lost the trust that might have preserved the inflow of funds.

Russia in the 1990s (discussed in more detail in Chapter 12 below), represents a variant on this case, in which once again there is mutual distrust between donor and recipient, but this time the donor fears the consequences of failing to disburse even more than the consequences of being 'exploited' by the recipient. In common with other large developing countries such as India, Mexico, Brazil, and indeed Argentina (Chapter 9), all of whom held international debts of more than $100 billion, some of the causes of this fear were financial: any failure by the Bank/Fund group to maintain disbursements of structural adjustment loans ran the risk of causing a default across the recipient country's entire financial system, prompting the Bretton Woods institutions to lend defensively in spite of repeated and transparent failure to comply with conditionality, in order to head off this threat. But in Russia, of course, there was the additional threat of nuclear weapons in unstable ownership, the consequence of which was that neither the Bank nor the Fund, in 1998, hesitated to support Russia with massive loans during the financial crisis of that year even in face of massive evidence that previous loan conditionalities had been abused.[21] This we call the

[21] As the testimony of the IMF's resident representative makes clear, this threat was quite sufficient to spook the Fund into setting aside whichever parts of its fiscal conditionality the Russian government might choose to discard:

> They say that Indonesia is too big to fail, but Russia is something totally different. Think of the nuclear weapons! I never made the programs [sc. the policy conditions attached to loans, PM] easier because of this, but it is just realism that we have to integrate them into the modern world

creditor's dilemma: implementation by the creditor of the threat to withhold funding hurts the creditor and the interests surrounding him much more than non-implementation, and therefore is not a credible threat.

One way of looking at the 'Russian case', and indeed at all cases where there is an opposition of interests between donor and recipient, but the donor needs the recipient much more than the other way about, is to model conditional programme lending as a *one-sided* prisoner's dilemma (Figure 7.1b). The key features of this variant of the model are (1) the donor derives utility from a continued lending relationship—hence his pay-off from continuing to lend rather than breaking off lending in the bottom left-hand cell is one rather than minus two as in Figure 7.1a; (2) the dilemma is asymmetric, because although the recipient gains from being able to exploit the donor (in the sense of achieving both finance and non-compliance with conditions) it is not clear what a donor would gain from refusing to lend to a recipient who complies with conditions. Accordingly, the top right-hand cell in Figure 7.1b has been amended so that the donor derives no utility from exploitative behaviour of this sort. With these altered parameters, the dominant strategy equilibrium of the game moves to the bottom *left*-hand corner of the table, in which lending continues even though conditions are not complied with. Empirically, this is a commonly observed outcome with both the World Bank and the IMF; however, it is also an inefficient outcome, because the recipient is not managing policy instruments in a way that at least the donor considers to be vital for the long-term recovery of the economy, and because failure is being openly indulged, with a consequent loss of donor credibility. The calls cited earlier for abandoning conditionality, possibly in favor of 'selectivity'—the giving of aid only to recipients whose policy and institutions are already acceptable—derive from a logic of this type.

These models of how the conditionality game may play out in different environments are neither complete nor exclusive; they simply illustrate two frequently encountered possibilities. In particular, they telescope what is often a lengthy and varying process of negotiation and follow-up into one instant. In *Aid and Power* (Mosley, Harrigan, and Toye 1995) we examined the processes by which donors and recipients play the conditionality game so as to maximize the advantage which they can derive from it. Donors seek to combat the creditor's dilemma by *facilitation*, or offering technical assistance money to remove technical obstacles to reform (the case of tax policy obstacles was considered in Chapter 5), by *stiffening* or employing measures to reinforce the position of those in government who are committed to reform, and by *bribery*, the making of promises of funding if and only if key conditions are met. For their part, the recipients can simply fail to implement, and see whether they are punished; they can conceal their preferences, that is, offer up as a big concession something that they would have done anyway; or they can seek out alternative sources of funding. In the 1980s and 1990s, oil-exporting countries, especially in the Middle East, were often able to provide development aid in defiance of the wishes of the

> economy, or we will have a nightmare. It would only take five or six crazy people in Russia, and just imagine what might happen.

(Interview with Horiguchi, head of IMF mission in Russia, November 1999, reported by Stone (2002), page 138). For an elaboration of this argument and details of Russian breaches of conditionality see further Chapter 12 below.

Bretton Woods donors, and in the 2000s, as we shall see further in the final chapter, this mantle is increasingly passing on to the shoulders of the Chinese.

In general, our findings for the 1980s and early 90s were that the less the donor needs the recipient (either as an outlet for funds or as a political ally) and the more the recipient needs the donor (because of the gravity of its debt or foreign exchange position or because it does not believe it can borrow from other sources), the less room for manoeuvre the recipient has, and the more likely s/he is to change her policies as a consequence of conditionality being imposed. Countries with a well-developed awareness of their strategic interests and considerable geo-political weight, such as Russia in our example, would be much better positioned to win a Game B in which, over a considerable period, conditions are flouted and budget support lending disbursed, than Zimbabwe, in our example, or any of the low-income countries of Africa. Even at that time, we noted, there were severe dangers in equating 'strength' in the conventional economic sense (e.g. fast growth and low deficits) with bargaining strength: in Russia, as in Argentina and Brazil in the late 1990s crisis, financial *weakness* in the sense of large and unpayable debts, which would aggravate the weakness of the global economy if not financed, was consistent with and indeed contributed to the strength of the recipient's bargaining position.[22] More recently, in the changed aid and bargaining environment of the 2000s Whitfield (2009c) has extended our picture of the bargaining process in the context of African countries. In addition to the factors mentioned above, she emphasizes the influence of the political history and traditions of individual countries in determining bargaining strength. Specifically, she develops the notion of *negotiating capital* as an extension of our idea of relative bargaining strength. She describes the majority of African countries in her sample,[23] including Ghana as well as Mozambique, Mali, Tanzania, and Zambia, as having very weak negotiating capital, but notes that in Botswana, and to a lesser extent Ethiopia, negotiating capital was strong and that this enabled the governments of these countries to persist with their desired development programme and where they thought necessary to resist the pressures of the Washington institutions. Ethiopia is clearly an interesting case in the sense that, like Zimbabwe in Figure 7.1a, it had insignificant assets in the sense of physical and financial capital to negotiate with—indeed, it is one of the poorest countries in the world—and so it had to fall back on other resources, including clarity of vision and negotiating skills.[24]

[22] John Maynard Keynes put the matter this way: 'If I owe you £1000, you have a problem; if I owe you £10 million, I have a problem' (see Skidelsky 2000).

[23] Whitfield's case studies relate to Ghana, Mali, Mozambique, Tanzania, Rwanda, Ethiopia, and Botswana.

[24] Where do these negotiating skills come from? Whitfield (2009c, page 20) notes that:

> What marks our successful cases out is the confidence to translate a country's conditions into negotiating capital and deploying it effectively in aid negotiations. Confidence can come from different sources, such as the ideology of the government, the background of the ruling political party and political leaders, and the degree of popular legitimacy and support that a government enjoys. Finally, institutions for managing aid matter. Those countries that have been most successful in negotiating aid have kept donors at arm's length while formulating their own policy positions and have largely kept them out of their domestic administrative systems.

Which if either of these conflict-of-interest models best fits the experience of developing countries during our period of 'new conditionality',[25] and what are the poverty implications? The rest of this chapter is concerned with this question. We shall approach it once again by reviewing our country cases. A summary of the overall argument is presented in Table 7.2 below.

Middle-income country cases

Malaysia avoided going to the IMF throughout the 1990s and 2000s, assisted by some unorthodox tools of policy explicitly disapproved of by the IMF, including capital controls, as described in Chapter 11.

Russia, as described in Chapter 12, negotiated three enormous adjustment loans from the Bank and Fund between 1992 and 1998. Compliance with conditionality on these loans[26] and especially the conditions related to the level and targeting of social expenditure was minimal; indeed in an otherwise laudatory report (World Bank 2004) the Bank reveals Russia to have the least well-targeted social expenditure within a group of former Soviet and east European economies. In essence, during the 1990s the Russian government was taking advantage of the considerable bargaining power granted to it by virtue of its fragility and its possession of nuclear weapons. It was deeply hurt and embarrassed to need this finance, and as part of its drive to recover state capacity as rapidly as possible paid back its loans to the Bank and Fund early, in 2005. With the same objective, it has made abundant use of interventions in the market (capital controls, minimum wages, export taxation, and price controls) of which the Washington authorities profoundly disapprove but which they now have even less power to influence than in the 1990s.

Argentina is a more complicated middle-income case than Russia or Malaysia because, unlike those countries, it has a history of quite intimate involvement with the Fund and Bank going back as far as the early 1980s, and in his account of the economic collapse which was to occur at the millennium the Fund's former chief economist, Michael Mussa (Mussa 2004) goes to great lengths to emphasize that the crisis was by no means entirely the Argentinian government's fault, and that responsibility for the crisis is shared.[27] This shared responsibility between the Washington institutions and the Argentinian government has been carried through into the post-crisis relationship, and following the collapse of the hugely

[25] Harrison (2004, Chapters 4 and 5) describes the environment of donor-recipient relations during the 2000s as 'post-conditionality'. We hold to our existing description here: conditionality, as we argue above, has not been supplanted, but it has mutated.

[26] 'The policy performance of the Russian government under the Fund-supported programme since early 1996 had been—to put it politely—less than entirely satisfactory, especially in controlling the fiscal deficit' (Mussa 2004, page 350).

[27] 'Argentina is different from most other cases where the Bank has provided exceptionally large financial support. Virtually continuously throughout the 1990s, Argentina operated under the auspices of and close scrutiny of a Fund-supported programme. In contrast, in other cases where the Fund provided exceptionally large financial support (Mexico in 1995; Indonesia, Korea and Thailand in the Asian crisis; Brazil in the crisis of late 1998 and early 1999) a Fund-supported programme was started only after the crisis was already under way' (Mussa 2004, page 318).

Table 7.2 Case-study countries: evolution of bargaining parameters and policy outcomes.

	(1) Per cap. income ($, 2007)	(2) Relationships with WB and IMF 1990-2007: (a) IMF Loan/aid transactions, 1990–2007	(b) WB policy quality ('CPIA') score	(c) Aid/GDP %	(3) Bargaining parameters: (a) Debt stock ($bn, 2005)	(b) Fiscal deficit (%) Mean 1990-2007 (st. dev. in brackets)	(4) Applicable bargaining model (see Figure 7.1 and text pp 201–6).	(5) Evolution of policy variables: (a) Pub. exp./GNP	(b) Labour and capital markets	(c) External sector: Protection on imports	Exchange rates	Export taxation	External capital controls	Overall policy openness scores
Middle-income cases:														
Malaysia	5,490	None?	NA	*Low and falling:* 1.11% (1990) 0.25% (2004)	51	0.75 (2.42)	None: no IMF/WB flows	**18.1,** static (20.2 1990 to 19.1 2007)		0.087	Flexible through-out. Black market premium never more than 2%.	None.	No controls 1979–1996; IMF score 12 (1997–2003)	Sachs-Warner: open since 1963
Argentina	5,150		NA	*Low and falling:* 0.12% (1990), 0.05% (2007)	114	−0.75 (1.62)	Mainly Model (recipient domination) 1991–2005, then exit.	**17.1,** static (16.4 1990 to 17.2 2007)	Price controls imposed 2003 on all essential foodstuffs	0.294	Flexible since 2001	Imposed 2002	Controls on 1979–93, off 1994–96, score 6 (1997) rising to 9 (2003)	Sachs-Warner: open since 1991
Russia	5,780		NA	*Generally low, peaked in* 1999: 0.04% (1990) 1.03% (1999) 0.22% (2004)	229	−0.17 (5.62)	Model 2 (recipient domination) 1991–2005? Then exit.	**24.6,** static (22.1 1992 to 22.6 2007)	Price and wage controls , also minimum wages, in force since 1992.	Na	Partly flexible since 1992 (but currency still not convertible)	Imposed both by central and state governments 1992–	No data until 1992, controls on 1993-96, score 10 (1997), rising to 13 (2000), falling again to 10 (2003)	Not listed (Sachs-Warner)

Table 7.2 Continued.

	(1) Per cap. income ($, 2007)	(2) Relationships with WB and IMF 1990-2007: (a) IMF Loan/aid transactions, 1990–2007	(b) WB policy quality ('CPIA') score	(c) Aid/ GDP %	(3) Bargaining parameters: (a) Debt stock ($bn, 2005)	(b) Fiscal deficit (%) Mean 1990-2007 (st. dev. in brackets)	(4) Applicable bargaining model (see Figure 7.1 and text pp 201–6).	(5) Evolution of policy variables: (a) Pub. exp./ GNP	(b) Labour and capital markets	(c) External sector: Protection on imports	Exchange rates	Export taxation	External capital controls	Overall policy openness scores
Mixed (partly middle, partly low-income cases)														
Indonesia	1,420		WB compliance: 90% 1991, 1995 CPIA: grade 4 1999, grade 2 2003	*Low and falling:* 1.5% (1990) 0.03% (2007)	138	−0.52 (1.59)	Model C (trust between WB and elite) until 1998, then uneasy balance between Models B and C	**18.9,** static (23.4 1990 to 18.9 2004)	Persisting controls on interest rates to 2000	0.137	Flexible since 1970 (at which point dual exchange rate system ended)	None	No data	Sachs-Warner: open since 1970
Bolivia	1,100	ESAFs I–IV 1988–94, PRSP 2000, IMF standby 2003	WB compliance: 85% 1991, 70% 1999 CPIA: grade 1 1999, grade 2 2003	*High and static:* 11.8% (1990), 9.1% (2004)	6	−3.12 (1.76)	Model C (trust between WB and governing elite) until 2002, Model A (breakdown) in 2003, then uneasy balance between Models B and C	**18.2,** static (17.9 1990 to 15.2 2007)		0.129	Flexible: low black-market premia	Imposed on petroleum sector 2006	Controls off 1979-81, on 1982–6, off 1987–96, score 2 (1997) rising to 4 (2003)	Sachs-Warner: open since 1985

Low-income cases													
Uganda	300	SAF, then ESAF 1988–91, ESAFs 1996–2000	WB compliance: 76% 1994	*High and rising*: 15.8% (1990) 17.3% (2005)	4		Model B (slippage) gradually evolving into model C (trust)	33.2, falling slightly (38.9 1990 to 33.7 2007)	0.103	Flexible since 1988	Enforced at rates up to 90% 1980–92, partially removed 1992–3, finally removed 1995	Controls on 1979–1996, score 8 (1997), falling to 2 (1998-2003)	Sachs-Warner: open since 1988
		PRGF 2003	CPIA grade 1 1999 and 2003										
Ghana	520	WB structural adjustment credits 1984, 1989	WB compliance: 70% 1985, 75% 1990, 64% 1994	*High and rising*: 9.7% (1990) 15.4% (2005)	7	−2.72 (3.14)	Model B (slippage) gradually evolving into Model C (trust)	25.6, rising (20.9 1990 to 25.9 2007)	0.330	Flexible: black market premia below 10% after 1990	Enforced at rates up to 85% 1980–92, gradually reduced 1992–9, but export duties still > 40% of export price	Controls on 1979–96, score 10 (1997–2003)	Sachs-Warner: open since 1985
		IMF standby 1985–7	CPIA: grade 1 1999, grade 2 2003										
		ESAFs I–III 1989–92, 1996–8, PRGF 2001, 2004											
Kenya	**580**	SAF, then ESAF I–III 1988–91	WB compliance: 60% 1985, 22% 1989, 42% 1994, 30% 1998 CPIA: grade 3 1999 and 2003	*Traditionally high, fell sharply in 1990s*: 14.4% (1990) 3.9% (2004)	**6**	**−3.35 (0.90)**	Model B (slippage) 1990–5, Model A (almost complete breakdown of lending relationship) 1995–2002	**19.5**, rising (13.1 1990 to 21.8 2007)	0.275	Partly flexible since 1993; but black-market premium above 20% in several years		Controls on 1979–96, score 6 (1998–2003)	Sachs-Warner: closed 1967–1993; limited reform thereafter

Continued

Table 7.2 Continued.

(1) Per cap. income ($, 2007)		(2) Relationships with WB and IMF 1990-2007: (a) IMF Loan/aid transactions, 1990–2007	(b) WB policy quality ('CPIA') score	(c) Aid/ GDP %	(3) Bargaining parameters: (a) Debt stock ($bn, 2005)	(b) Fiscal deficit (%) Mean 1990-2007 (st. dev. in brackets)	(4) Applicable bargaining model (see Figure 7.1 and text pp 201–6).	(5) Evolution of policy variables: (a) Pub. exp./ GNP	(b) Labour and capital markets	(c) External sector: Protection on imports	Exchange rates	Export taxation	External capital controls	Overall policy openness scores
		ESAFs IV–V 1992, 94, 97 (interruptions 93, 96, 98), PRGFs 2001, 2003					Resumption of Models B with elements of C 2002 to present							
Zimbabwe	340	ESAFs I–II 1993–5, interrupted April 1995, no resumption to date	WB compliance: 50% 1992, 14% 1994	3.9% (1990) 4% (2004)	4	−7.75 (2.59)	Model B (slippage) 1991–7, Model A (complete breakdown), 1997–2009, now emerging signals of willingness to re-establish aid relationship	14.4, static (16.7 1990 to 16.0 2004)		0.229	Not flexible: exchange controls in position since independence in 1980. 'Black market premium averaged above 90% in the 1970s and 80s' (Sachs and Warner 1995, page 95)		Controls on 1981–96, score 10 (1997) rising to 13 (2003)	Sachs-Warner: never open
			CPIA: grade 4 1999, grade 5 2003											

Sources: Column 1, World Bank, *World Development Report* 2008, appendix Table 1.
Column (2a): loans and credits are headed 'IMF' for International Monetary Fund operations and 'WB' for World Bank operations, except for Structural Adjustment Facilities (after 1989, Enhanced Structural Adjustment Facilities), denoted here as 'SAF' and 'ESAF' respectively. All data from IMF, *Annual Reports* and World Bank, *Annual Reports*.
Column (2b) 1991–9 Compliance with World Bank conditionality ('WB compliance'): author's estimates from Mosley, Harrigan, and Toye (1995), Table 5.3. 1999 onward: Country Performance Institutional Assessment (CPIA) scores from Eifert and Gelb, Chapter 12 in Koeberle et al. (2003). CPIA scores available for low-income countries only.
Column (2c): aid/GNP ratio, from World Bank, *World Development Indicators* CD-ROM.
Column (5): *Public expenditure*; from IMF, *Government Expenditure Statistics Yearbook*, annual. *Labour and capital markets, exchange rates, export taxation, import protection*; from country case studies, Chapters 9–13 below. External capital controls; from IMF, *Annual Report on Exchange Arrangements and Exchange Restrictions, various issues.* Until 1997 information is provided only on a one-zero or on-off basis; thereafter information on different capital controls is disaggregated and the intensity of capital controls is measurable on a scale from 0 to 13.

unpopular emergency measures implemented to contain the crisis in late 2001 (the 'Corralito', or freezing of savings) the former Bank economist, Mario Blejer, became in 2002 governor of the BCRA, the Argentinian central bank. Thus, the international financial institutions were able to regroup: an IMF standby was agreed, and the Bank co-financed the social payments to the *Programa Jefes y Jefas* (Chapters 5 and 6 above) for heads of unemployed households and a number of other sectoral loans. Within the new lending relationship, the Kirchner governments from 2003 on, as the holders of $114 billion of debt, enjoyed considerable room for reverse leverage and policy manoeuvre, and as described in Chapter 9 they have exploited this through policies which, as in Russia, reverse much of the momentum of neoliberalism, including, in particular, export taxes and increases in the level of import duty and price controls on foodstuffs and other essential goods. However, much though the Kirchner government has taken advantage of the 'policy space' which the Washington institutions have allowed it, the Argentinian government has adhered to the fundamentals, or as the IMF calls them the 'essential issues';[28] the exchange rate has been kept flexible, the budget deficit has been kept under control and inflation has remained moderate.[29]

Thus, in all of these three cases, the IMF, World Bank, and other providers of finance had scant leverage over recipient-country policy, the financial institutions made little attempt to impose ultimata, and there were very substantial departures from even the augmented Washington consensus model in terms of interferences with the price mechanism. At the macro-economic level, however, discipline was broadly maintained, and inflation and budget deficits were kept low.

Intermediate (middle-to-low income) country cases

The three cases considered so far derived most of their capital flows from the market, and in none of them were overseas aid flows a significant factor. By contrast, the remaining six countries in our sample, being poorer (average per capita income at the millennium less than $2000), received substantial aid flows from international donors, and in all of these countries except Indonesia investment rates were heavily dependent on aid flows. Did this greater aid dependence, now of course often mediated through Poverty Reduction Strategies rather than through old-style conditionality, bring about a greater adherence to the Washington consensus? As the remaining case studies illustrate, the basic answer to this question is yes; but, as we shall argue, the conditionality relationship in several cases was transmuted into trust-relationships which allowed the recipients considerable room for manoeuvre.

[28] The phrases 'policy space' and 'essential issues' reflect the terminology in which the IMF itself expressed its willingness to allow flexibility to its clients in the determination of economic policies, providing that a core of macro-economic fundamentals was adhered to (see footnote 16 above).

[29] During the period since 1990, Argentina's budget deficit peaked at three per cent in the crisis year 2001. Its inflation rate peaked at twenty-five per cent immediately after the removal of the one-to-one peg between the peso and the dollar, and since then has been in single or low double figures (having been well over one hundred per cent throughout the 1980S).

In Indonesia, the shift towards an aid relationship which was based neither on ultimatum nor on donor surrender began not at the millennium, but immediately after the chaos of 1967. The story is told in this way by the recently-appointed World Bank President of the time, Robert MacNamara:

> The reason I went to Indonesia was—it shows how little I knew about development—because I went into the office one Saturday morning. I got out the atlas... I turned it open to the page that has all the countries of the world listed with their populations... and I wrote down for the larger population countries in the world the amount of Bank lending. I got down to Egypt and Indonesia, and there was none. And so—that was Saturday—on Monday I asked why. In Indonesia the reason was—which I didn't realize—they had under Sukarno at the end of his regime, '67 or somewhere around that, they had a 600,000 per cent inflation over a ten-year period—600,000 per cent! Well, that's past. Sukarno's gone, Suharto's in there now. So I went out there. They didn't know what to do with me. They gave a luncheon for me one day around a table like this. They didn't know what to do with an ex-defence minister, so they sat me here and right on my right was the Chief of Naval Operations... So during the lunch—I had tried to find something to talk to him about—I said, 'Sir, would you mind if I asked you a personal question? He said, 'No, of course not.' I said, 'Well, would you mind telling me what your compensation is?' 'Oh no', he said, I'd be happy to. It's a rice ration for myself, my wife and each of our children, plus $16 per month.' I thought, that guy can't possibly live on rice plus $16. Anyhow, I go in to see Suharto, and said, 'We haven't loaned you anything because the society was totally mismanaged in terms of economics, but I understand you wish to change. Are you interested in the World Bank operating here?' 'Yes.' 'Would you wish us to establish an office?' 'Yes.' 'Who are your key people?' 'You know who they are; they're the Berkeley Mafia.' They were, as I remember, five ministers from Berkeley (who) had taken their PhDs in the mid-50s under Professor Malcolm Davison, whom I had studied under twenty years earlier in undergraduate school. Some very good guys. So I met them. And out of all that I concluded that here was a society that (a) needed help, (b) wanted it, (c) had some what appeared to me to be able economists who would lead it, and (d) who appeared to have the full support of the president. So I was determined... to set this thing up in a way that would work. And my only point is that some things worked well by a somewhat arbitrary process.
>
> Interviewer: The message you're telling us is that you need a president who intervenes pretty strongly and radically sometimes.
> MacNamara: I think so.[30]

This is the essence of what we shall later want to describe as 'core conditionality', founded on mutual trust and intellectual camaraderie between members of the donor and recipient elites, with huge flexibility required and granted in face of severe breaches of conditionality, caused notably by large-scale corruption in the state oil monopoly, Pertamina.

Thirty years later, mobilization of students and workers was a key factor in the downfall of the Suharto regime, within which the relationship between donors and recipients had been exceptionally close.[31] Once the transition to democracy

[30] Robert MacNamara, interview with John Lewis, Richard Webb, and Devesh Kapur, interview 3 October 1991. World Bank/IFC Archives, Oral History Program.

[31] In 1991, when I was carrying out a review of macro-economic policies for the World Bank, a senior Bank staff member described Indonesia as being 'the Bank's best client in the developing world-bar none' (interview, World Bank Country Policy Department, July 1991).

occurred, though, civil society's role returned to one that is quite analogous to the PRSP vision; and the traditional Indonesian virtues of budgetary austerity and flexible, indeed aggressively competitive, exchange-rate policies were restored.[32] A series of newly-incumbent Indonesian governments introduced institutional and democratic reforms designed to demonstrate their distance from the authoritarianism and corruption of the Suharto era (Robison and Hadiz 2004). These measures included the production of a voluntary draft PRSP, which eventually turned into the National Poverty Reduction Strategy (SPNK). The Bank has also sponsored a pioneering and successful experiment in infrastructure provision (called KDP, *Kecamatan Development Project*) by providing block grants at the *kecamatan* level that are distributed and monitored through local participatory processes.

Both these processes have created new spaces for the Indonesian poor to engage in dialogue over poverty-related policies. However, civil society movements have not been able to translate this policy role into having a significant impact on the Indonesian political process (Tornquist 2006). Civil society groups representing the poor have not managed to form or strongly influence political parties and, in keeping with experiences elsewhere, the poverty strategy process has been entirely divorced from mainstream budgetary processes and has consequently made little impact on the legislature. Poverty policy, in the form of the KDP programme, has returned to the Indonesian agenda (after a hiatus during the 1990s) but spending in KDP amounts to only 0.34 per cent of Indonesian GDP. Meanwhile the government has done little to alter patterns of growth that are increasingly capital-intensive, making Indonesia's post-crisis growth less pro-poor than it was during the authoritarian and corrupt Suharto era.[33] Civil society involvement, in the tight confines of PRSP-style processes, has not been enough to counter the growing influence of a pre-Suharto era business elite that is increasingly able to capture the policy process (Robison and Hadiz 2004).

In Bolivia, a considerable measure of trust had developed between donors and the governments of the period 1985–97 under the impetus of a successful stabilization in 1985–6, widespread privatization, and a shift of expenditure towards health and education[34] assisted by innovative donor-financed schemes to compensate the new poor such as the Emergency Social Fund (Chapter 5 above); the Managing Director of the IMF admiringly referred to Bolivia in 1996 as an emergent 'Andean jaguar', by analogy with the east Asian tigers.[35] However, under the stress of the global recession the climate soon darkened, and Bolivia's PRSP was produced at the turn of the millennium by UDAPE *(Unidad de Analisis*

[32] The budget deficit in Indonesia has never exceeded three per cent of GDP within the period since the early 1980S, and the inflation rate (consumer prices index) has been in single figures throughout, with the exception of the crisis year 1998.

[33] Figures on KDP volumes and judgements on Indonesian growth are both taken from World Bank (2006).

[34] Health and education spending increased from 12–16 per cent of GDP during 1995–9 (Dijkstra 2005, page 447). For the process of stabilization, macro-economic reform and privatization between 1985 and 1997, a good source is Chapter 5 of Sachs (2005), who pays tribute (page 12) to the 'remarkable leadership of the late President Victor Paz Estenssoro and his top economic aide and later president, Gonzalo Sanchez de Losada'.

[35] In a speech in La Paz in June 1996 (Lazarte Rojas 2005, page 18) (for further discussion see Chapter 10 below).

de Politica Economica), a unit in the Treasury Ministry, in the midst of a period of global recession and associated political instability, described in Chapter 10 below, which saw five presidents sworn in during the period from 2000 to 2005. The third of these was Gonzalo Sanchez de Losada, a mining millionaire and both an architect and a beneficiary of the privatizations of the 1980s, whose re-election in 2002 the donors welcomed in the hope of re-establishing a progressive, liberalizing trust equilibrium in place of instability. The alliance came catastrophically unstuck, not least because the donors believed that the group who in principle should have been at the heart of the PRSP consultation process (the Quechua/Aymara poor of the *altiplano*) could be bought off by increases in targeted health and education expenditures rather than directly involved in that process.[36] Neither President Sanchez de Losada,[37] nor the donors, saw the hurricane coming, and in particular the latter failed to warn the government of the political dangers associated with raising income tax in February 2003, when unemployment had doubled in the previous two years (see Chapters 5 and 10). Although only the American Ambassador, and not representatives of the other donors, had attempted to warn the electorate off voting for Evo Morales,[38] the winner of the election which followed the resulting political violence, the cause of liberalizing policy reform in Bolivia was greatly damaged by the donors' and specifically the PRSP's, lack of vision. And yet, having won the election resoundingly, his party the *Movimiento al Socialismo* only moved towards socialism, and away from the Washington Consensus, in the most hesitant of ways (see Table 7.2). Rather than nationalize the gas companies, it taxed their royalties; rather than nationalize, or forgive the overdues of, the microfinance organizations, it reinforced their drive towards viability and their movement up-market; and government interference in the foreign exchange market and with external capital movements continued to be as minimal as in the days of control of government by a centre-right elite. Export taxes did return (in extension for a progressive extension of the old age pension: Chapter 5 above), but not Argentinian-style price controls; and such land reform as has so far been attempted, no doubt as a sop to secessionist tendencies in the east of the country, has been highly 'market-based' (ibid.). Although not at all 'the end of the embrace'[39] with neoliberalism, this was at least a more equitable and principled accommodation with it than had been achieved by previous Bolivian elites.

[36] 'The dialogue process had a limited agenda. It was concerned with social policies, but it did not include topics about which people felt strongly, such as access to land, employment, control of natural resources such as gas, macro-economic policies, regional trade agreements, and structural reforms. A further limitation was the absence of Parliament and the political parties from the dialogue process' (Dijkstra 2005, page 448).

[37] The Sanchez de Lozada government failed to produce PRS monitoring reports in 2002–3, possibly because there were few incentives to do so once Bolivia had received HIPC debt relief.

[38] On 26 June 2002 the US Ambassador, Manuel Rocha, stated: 'I would like to warn the Bolivian electorate that if it chooses candidates who are trying to make Bolivia once again an exporter of cocaine, that result would prejudice future aid flows from the United States' (in the column *Usted Elige* (It's Your Choice) in *La Prensa* for 27 June 2002, as reported by Lazarte Rojas (2005, page 373).

[39] The phrase is that of Grugel and Riggirozzi (2009).

Low-income country cases

Following a period of political turbulence lasting from 1970 to 1986, the *Ugandan* relationship with the World Bank group restarted less than happily in the late 1980s with a series of reconstruction credits disbursed through gritted teeth by a World Bank aware of President Museveni's distaste for market mechanisms, and in particular for exchange rate flexibility. As described above and in Chapter 5, the turning point came in the early 1990s, when he was first persuaded to do away with export taxation on coffee and cotton, but more fundamentally when his Permanent Secretary for Finance[40] in 1994 *initiated*, with external technical assistance, the system of prioritization of pro-poor expenditure which was eventually, three years later, to become the spearhead of the government's Poverty Eradication Action Programme. For the donors this had a valuable demonstration effect, as at that time it was rare for an African government to take the lead in the design of poverty strategies. Where the Ministry of Finance had led, the donors, the NGOs, and even the President himself, who, as illustrated in Chapter 5, was by no means convinced of the merits of either liberalization or poverty alleviation initiatives, had the good sense and the pragmatism to follow. The Finance Ministry's poverty initiative (in common with other bona fides such as rapid progress with universal primary education, a rising PPE ratio, reduced military expenditure, and eventually, by 1996, clear evidence that poverty was coming down rapidly) sent a signal to the donors that the government was not only committed to the poverty reduction objective, but willing to take a leadership role in achieving it. This exercise of leadership by MFPED built trust or, in Whitfield's terminology, *negotiating capital*, between the recipient government and representatives of the international financial institutions, which overrode the donors' worries both about breaches of formal conditionality and about corruption (Booth 2003; Mosley and Suleiman 2007). Through this growth of trust, the threat of investment and growth being damaged by donor withdrawal (Model A), distinctly present in 1990, had receded entirely by the millennium. By this point, in effect, the conditionality game had broken down: not in the sense that either side in the game had walked away (Model B) or surrendered (Model A), but rather in the quite new sense that a compromise had been reached, in which the donors overlooked minor breaches of conditionality in exchange for agreement over the core principle of a coherent poverty reduction strategy. This was of course what also happened in Bolivia and Indonesia; but there the agreement to forgive slippage was tacit, whereas in Uganda it gradually evolved into an overt agreement to provide long-term finance centred around core conditionalities only, which became the prototype of the Poverty Reduction Strategy Paper model. Indeed, Uganda has now reached the point where performance criteria are jointly negotiated between donor and recipient rather than simply being specified by the donor (Adam and Gunning 2002). The return to Uganda on this new model of donor-recipient relations was two-fold: on the one hand, it delivered steady and sustained aid flows, but it also delivered legitimacy for a

[40] Formally the Permanent Secretary of MFPED, the Ministry of Finance, Planning and Economic Development.

rural-based resistance movement that still needed to show it was different from the tradition of 'centralized policy-making and state terror, which had greatly diminished expectations of the state as a guarantor of public goods or human welfare' (Brock, McGee, and Ssewakiryanga 2002). Uganda's very success in establishing poverty reduction frameworks may now be leading to an altered emphasis at the centre of government. In 2008 the government announced that it wished to move from working within a short-term PRS framework to a longer-term (four to five years) development planning framework, focused on wealth creation and in particular on the development of large farms; the following year it was announced that the Poverty Action Fund was to be wound down after 2009 and increasingly, in advance of the elections projected for February 2011, the vision was of a government which, having outgrown the need for poverty strategies, picks winners on the East Asian model (Hickey 2010).

In Ghana, as in Uganda, the government created room for manoeuvre for itself with the Washington institutions through an amiable bargaining style and the offer of bona fides, or signals of a willingness to focus on a core curriculum of macro-stability, export promotion, and poverty reduction, which was also the central preoccupation of the Washington authorities. These signals were rather different from those offered in the Ugandan case, since Ghana, although also a peasant export economy recovering from a long period of economic chaos with episodes of military government, had a quite different elite and quite different political traditions from Uganda. Whereas Uganda's elite, post-1986, had emerged as the victors of a guerrilla war and was dominated by central and south-western rural interests, Ghana's, post-1979, had emerged from the enlightened military coup of Flight-Lieutenant Jerry Rawlings, leading to a much more *dirigiste* and urban-dominated elite than that of Uganda's National Resistance Movement, with an affection for controls on prices and markets that Whitfield has described as 'Nkrumahist', after Ghana's first president, who had attempted in the 1960s to develop a programme of import-substituting industrialization financed by export crop surpluses.[41] The reforming elite of the Provisional National Defence Council (later National Democratic Committee, NDC) allowed the external marketing functions of the Cocoa Board to be privatized but kept internal marketing under its own control; allowed a measure (albeit a reduced measure) of export taxation on cocoa to continue through to the present;[42] retained subsidies on fertilizer; and perpetrated other interferences in the market which in other less-trusting environments were punished by withdrawal of aid flows.[43]

Because of these deviations from orthodoxy, Ghana's slippage rate on conditionality during the 1980s and 90s was a good deal higher than Uganda's (Table 7.2). Yet, very like Uganda, it learned to develop one rhetoric for internal and another for external consumption, and on external account it built up social capital with the international financial institutions by 'sticking to basics' and

[41] This 'Nkrumahist' tradition is discussed by Killick (1978) and, much more cursorily, in Chapter 13 below.

[42] Even now the cocoa farmer only receives about 55–60 per cent of the export price, by comparison with more than eighty per cent in Uganda (Figure 5.2 above).

[43] For the treatment by the donors of fertilizer subsidies in Malawi, see Mosley and Suleiman (2007), also footnote 46 below.

achieving the exchange rate and marketing reforms which at least would keep the basis export staples, gold and cocoa, competitive. Because progress was being made on these core conditions and because enlightened people in the donor community, notably Peter Heller, the lead IMF negotiator, were willing to acknowledge this, Ghana's large-scale slippage on other conditions, even the fact of its inflation rates often going well into double figures, was never punished *à la* Zimbabwe (Figure 7.1, Model A), but initially was condoned (Model B) and eventually led to trust between the lead negotiators in the donor and recipient communities and an expansion of aid flows: a model which we have already observed operating in Uganda and elsewhere and which below we shall describe as a *trust equilibrium*. Additional factors tending to create social capital between donor and recipient were, as in Uganda, creativity in working out measures to protect the 'new poor', that is, the PAMSCAD programme to mitigate the social costs of adjustment, which achieved relatively little in terms of poverty reduction but had immense symbolic value as a signal of determination to develop the pro-poor agenda.[44] Thus, the net result was that, in Zimbabwe, Kenya, and also Malawi, slippage on conditions was punished because of lack of trust between donors and recipients, whereas in Ghana and Uganda, an equivalent amount of slippage went unpunished. By contrast, therefore, with the World Bank's view that aid donors were not selective enough in their conditionality, our own research suggests that they were selective on grounds which had little to do with objective compliance with conditions.[45]

In other parts of Africa this taking of heterodox initiatives goes further, under the influence of more creative (East Asian-inspired) forms of protectionism. In Mauritius, for example, one of the very early examples of a trust equilibrium in Africa, the government was able in the early 1980s, in the midst of a World Bank structural adjustment programme, to impose protection at 128 per cent on imports of clothing and semiconductors which were competitive with its own nascent manufacturing industries, and yet to avoid penalties for its slippage.[46]

[44] See Mosley, Harrigan, and Toye 1995, vol. 2, page 195.

[45] 'Foreign aid has contributed to policy reform; but it could do so more effectively if donors were more selective in their recipients and instruments' (Devarajan, Dollar, and Holmgren 2001, page 35).

[46] See Gulhati (1987) and Gulhati and Nallari (1990, especially Chapters 2–3). Mauritius in the 1980s, just like Ghana, Uganda, and Indonesia in this volume, walked out of a poverty trap, in this case the trap of sugar monoculture, with falling prices and escalating population, in which the country was embedded in the 1960s (Meade, 1967). It received two structural adjustment loans from the World Bank in the early 1980s, which were disbursed without argument even though the country was practising a neo-developmentalist policy at right angles to the structural adjustment policies which the Bank was at the time seeking to impose—very high rates of protection on competitive imports, quotas on imports of textiles, garments, and consumer durables, progressive taxes on sugar exports (on the politics of which, see Brautigam's essay in Brautigam, Fjeldstad, and Moore (2008)), and credit subsidies to exporters. It was and is also a highly democratic multi-party political system where no single party was able to command a majority, and where policies were therefore the result of compromises brokered between different interest groups. This early exemplar of indulging slippage on conditionality in cases where macro-economic fundamentals are right, with highly beneficial results both for growth and for poverty (for example, unemployment fell from twenty-two per cent in 1983 to four per cent in 1987 (Gulhati and Nallari 1990, page 59)) has been far too little studied. Although details are limited, the evidence suggests that the factors causing trust to emerge and slippage to be condoned were precisely the same as those which later applied in Uganda, namely a coherent and proactive micro-economic strategy, coupled with austerity, increased flexibility on exchange rates, and

Later, in Ethiopia, which as we have seen was able to achieve a great deal more bargaining autonomy, or negotiating capital for itself than Ghana or Uganda, the Prime Minister was explicitly to claim that effective development policy in Africa needed to detach itself from the Washington Consensus:

> The neo-liberal market reforms that have been the hallmark of Western and World Bank intervention in Africa for more than two decades have 'failed to generate the kind of growth they sought'. They were correct in identifying the predatory nature of African states as 'the central problem'. They were also right in addressing huge macro-economic imbalances... But they had been 'unable to transform the rent-seeking nature of the state', merely weakening the state and reducing its influence instead. I believe in a strong developmental state. Developmental states do not intervene in the market in a wanton fashion. They intervene in the market to address pervasive market failures... It is a combination of market instruments and non-market instruments to optimize the outcome. That has been the model of, let's say, South Korea and Taiwan.[47]

In its prescription, this is classic Third Way politics, translated on to an African stage: the central momentum of development must come from free markets, but to make that development is pro-poor, barriers to market access by the poor must be removed, which will require the exercise of 'non-market instruments'.[48] However, within our sample only Ghana amongst low-income countries, and Malaysia, Argentina, Russia, and Bolivia, among middle-income countries, represent any serious attempt to implement this philosophy; and of these, only Malaysia comes anywhere near the model of South Korea and Taiwan.

In this book we have represented the other two African countries in the sample, Kenya and Zimbabwe, somewhat as 'black sheep', who by contrast with Uganda and Ghana fell out of favour with the donors and experienced rising poverty levels in the 1990s and 2000s. However, the process of their estrangement from the donors is a little strange and deserves further investigation, since in the 1980s and the first half of the 1990s the levels of slippage by Kenya and Zimbabwe on Bretton

agreement on macro-economic fundamentals. (At that time, poverty was not the issue that it later became.) However, the degree of departure of policy from the Washington Consensus model is greater than in any of our sample countries, with the possible exception of Russia.

[47] Prime Minister Meles Zenawi of Ethiopia, interviewed by *Financial Times*, 7 February 2007, quoted in Whitfield (2009a, page 367). In Stiglitz (2003), Chapter 3, see also Chapter 5 above, there is a highly enthusiastic account of the personal chemistry which caused social capital to form in the 1990s between the government of Ethiopia and the World Bank.

[48] Although not mentioned by Prime Minister Meles, this is almost exactly what Arthur Lewis was asking for sixty years previously when he wrote:

> The economics that is relevant to the problems of (low-income countries) is not the economics of marginal utility, but the economics of laws, institutions, tenures, nationality, race, religion, ideology and kindred determinants of economic equity and of the rate of economic progress.
>
> If wages were equal to marginal productivity there would be no problem because labour in these places would be so cheap. But outside the factory and the classroom, wages bear no relation to marginal productivity. Although labour is superabundant it is also very dear. Prices are therefore a false guide to the real economic situation, and *policy must be in defiance of prices if the economic situation is to be met.*
>
> Rhodes House Oxford: Mss. Afr.s. 350, pages 10–11. Emphasis added.

Woods system conditionality, although substantial, were no worse than those of Ghana, Uganda, or most other African countries (Harrison 2004, page 119; Chapter 13 below) and their levels of private-sector development were far superior; indeed for a time in the early 1990s Zimbabwe made a breakthrough into the manufacturing of clothing for export.[49] Both Kenya and Zimbabwe also had NGO communities able and willing to mend many of the gaps in state structures of education, health, agricultural extension, and low-income financial provision. What, therefore, went wrong?

Our explanation for this divergence is simple and personalized: Kenya and Zimbabwe 'lacked a Tumusime-Mutabile'. Emanuel Tumusime-Mutabile, now the Governor of the Bank of Uganda, was at the time the Permanent Secretary to the Uganda Ministry of Finance, the technocrat who created the set of bona fides required to convince the donors that the Uganda government was committed to a core of long-term poverty reduction measures and had the capacity to carry them through.[50] Ghana has also had such technocrats able to tell the donors what they wanted to hear and stop the President, if necessary, from interfering: initially the trinity of P.V. Obeng, Joe Abbey, and Kwesi Botchwey, who for a long time was the minister of finance. Kenya and Zimbabwe, during the crucial parting of the ways in the second half of the 1990s, had nobody with the necessary combination of leverage, organizational ability and eloquence to convince donors that corruption and slippage on conditions were inescapable small things[51] and the government's commitment to poverty reduction via a PRS process the big thing; and nobody capable of restraining Presidents Mugabe and Moi as they began, rather than mastering the Ghanaian and Ugandan facility of speaking with two voices and leaving aid negotiations to the technocrats, to go increasingly off-message.[52]

Thus, a long period of case B dynamics in most African countries lasting from the early 1980s to the middle 1990s, in which most recipients took budget support loans from the Bank and Fund and then failed to comply with the conditions, was followed by polarization, in which Kenya and Zimbabwe were placed alongside Cote d'Ivoire, Burundi, Cameroon, Malawi, and other problematic cases in category A, where aid flows were cut down to essential support for the health and education sectors, whilst Uganda and Ghana progressed, alongside other 'governance states' such as Tanzania, Mozambique, and Rwanda, into a high-trust category which we have not yet formally labelled, with high and stable aid flows awarded on the basis of initially a string of Enhanced Structural Adjustment Facilities and, eventually after the millennium, a PRSP. Then Kenya got a reprieve. The election of December 2002 was won by Mwai Kibaki, a former Finance Minister who had left the previous government to set up his own party and had during the 1990s been imprisoned and roughly treated by the Moi government.

[49] In the early 1990s, indeed, Zimbabwe had contracts for the supply of nightwear, underwear, and shirts with the quality UK retailer Marks and Spencer.

[50] For an account of the macro-economic origins of this process in 1992, see Dijkstra and Van Donge (2001, page 843).

[51] It is true that some of the corruption in Kenya in the mid-1990s was on a grand scale, such as the Goldenberg financial scandal, in which more than $500 million was embezzled. But corruption in Uganda was by no means insignificant; it was simply viewed by the donors through a different lens.

[52] The Malawi government also lacked this capacity for wrapping their desired policies in the packaging which the donors required, and lost aid as a consequence: see Chapter 5 above, especially discussion surrounding note 31.

For a time the donors crowded back into Kenya, and the IMF awarded Poverty Reduction and Growth Facility credits in 2001 and 2003, but allegations of continuing corruption proved much harder to keep at arm's length from the donors than was possible in Uganda, and Kenya has found it hard to retrieve the levels of aid stability, investment, and growth achieved in Uganda and Ghana (Table 7.2). Meanwhile, the Mugabe regime in Zimbabwe decided that it could do without the donors, and embarked on an economic policy which took it a long way towards a command economy, with sanctioned invasions of commercial farms by 'war veterans' and a tightening of controls on exchange rates, consumer prices, and marketing of the country's principal food crop, maize. However, the coming of a command economy in Zimbabwe by a long way postdates the rift with the donors, which occurred in March 1995.

In Table 7.2, we examine the pattern of external involvement with our sample countries in relation to various dimensions of policy. First, we look at the pattern of financial flows, and first ask: what determined the size and stability of such flows into developing countries, and thence the impact of such flows on investment and poverty? Very directly in the Ghana and Uganda examples quoted here, and in a more shadowy and fragile manner in Bolivia, Argentina, and (latterly) Kenya, we can see something replacing some of the conflict games played out in Figure 7.1, and that something is *trust*, or *social capital*, within the community whose core is comprised by negotiators for the donor and recipient governments and arguably extends for some distance into civil society.[53] Social capital in general has been found capable of explaining inter-country variations in growth, even when conventional causal influences such as policy, physical capital, and human capital are held constant (Knack and Keefer 1997; Whiteley 2000). What we are suggesting here is simply that the social capital that exists between just two entities—negotiators for the donor and recipient authorities—is a factor of production that is particularly important for explaining the productivity of resources invested in aid negotiations, or indeed conditionality negotiations of any sort, including negotiations between the Fund and middle-income countries. The creation of social capital, we argue, involves the replacement of expectations of untrustworthiness held concerning the protagonists in the aid-bargaining game of Figure 7.1. If the pay-offs attached to trusting and to trustworthy behaviour are both increased, the basis for a conflict equilibrium within those games collapses, and distrust—either in the form of deadlock and cancellation of lending, case A, or surrender by the donor, case B—is replaced by trust, as in the 'all-in matrix' of Figure 7.2. We now have a 'trust equilibrium', the evolution of which has been described in a number of our case studies.

The next question, of course, is how the distrust equilibrium transforms into a trust equilibrium. Above we have stated our explanatory hypothesis: trust between donors and recipients is principally created through the provision by the recipient of a *credible signal of trustworthiness*, such as that provided to the World Bank by

[53] The definitions of social capital and trust are complex, but in essence social capital consists of those networks of social relationships which increase income, and one of the ways in which they do this is by creating trust between transactors, which reduces the cost of doing business and thereby raises the rate of investment (including, in the present case, investment by aid donors in recipient economies) and growth. Social capital is thus an input into the creation of trust.

		Player 1 ('donor') behaviours	
Player 2 ('recipient') responses		Trusting (e.g. disburse)	Not disburse
	Trustworthy (e.g. 'comply with conditions')	3,3	2,–2
	Untrustworthy (e.g. 'not comply with conditions')	–2,2	0,0

Figure 7.2 The all-in matrix: trust made rational.

Emanuel Tumusime-Mutabile in 1994, in which cuts in primary health and education, rural water, and infrastructure, and agricultural research and extension were omitted from the Uganda government's retrenchment programme in order to advance the cause of poverty reduction. Such signals, we argue, influence the donor's perception of his long-term pay-off, and can often deflect attention from cases of slippage on non-fundamentals. We refer to these signals as bona fides: a substitute for collateral, which provides a subjective feeling of trustworthiness rationalizing and providing subjective protection for a lender's decision to continue to lend. A further illustration of a bona fide is provided by Tanzania between 2000 and 2005, where various surrogate signals of recipient commitment to pro-poor reform, including the setting up of rigorous poverty monitoring procedures, were offered in place of evidence of actual poverty reduction (interviews with DFID staff, Cape Town, May 2005). Another example is Ethiopia in 1997–8, where the World Bank was willing to continue to lend even though the IMF's fiscal conditions had been breached, because the President of Ethiopia on his own initiative had set out a recovery plan that the Bank saw as coherent (see Chapter 5 above and Stiglitz 2003, Chapter 2). It is to be emphasized that the question of what makes a bona fide into trust is still rather unclear and in need of research: a number of cases exist where African governments have offered what seem *prima facie* to be perfectly good poverty reduction plans for funding as bona fides only for them to be rejected by sponsors, and it is clear that interpersonal chemistry between individual donors and recipients is often important, over and above the objective content of the bona fides. Three factors which additionally appear to increase the likelihood of bona fides being accepted are measures to improve the channels of communication between donor and recipient (for example increased frequency of meetings, or the setting up of a donor office in the recipient country, rather than relying on visiting missions); the exercise of flexibility and pragmatism, rather than rigid performance criteria, by donors; and the availability to the donor of Plan Bs which can protect his position if the Plan A of increased trust in the donor comes unstuck—an illustration of this kind of insurance is the option of increased support for NGOs in the health, education or agriculture sector if government services are not able to deliver. With greater *risk efficacy* or protection against risk, donors can take afford to take higher risks[54] and all of the bona fides we mention are measures which incentivize donors to do this, or protect them against their trust being misplaced.

[54] The proposition is tested and empirically confirmed by Lenton and Mosley (2011).

Whether measured in the form of density of social networks or as their consequence, trust, social capital is not easy to operationalize.[55] We endeavour to measure it in terms of *donor willingness to sustain the budget support relationship*,[56] against a sample of 14 developing countries over the period 1986–2007:[57] there are thus 300 observations. In both formulations, trust shows a significant association with PPE, a negative association with military expenditure, and a positive association with a dummy variable signifying willingness to initiate pro-poor initiatives—all of these interpreted as bona fides. It shows a positive association with various process variables, including frequency of contact between donor and recipient. (Corruption, notably, is not significant.) Trust, thus measured, is then a positive influence on budget support aid and a negative influence on the instability of aid.[58] Once trust is built up, therefore, it has consequences that go

[55] The definition and measurement of trust has been the focus for a large literature spanning philosophy and the whole of the social sciences. An excellent discussion of processes which induce trusting behaviour is provided by Gambetta (1988). For experimental procedures for the measurement of trust see Glaeser et al. (2000) and Barr (2003).

[56] This can be measured either as frequency of interruption of the budget-support lending relationship from whatever cause (see Mecagni 1999), or as donors' willingness to forgive breaches of conditionality (the response-coefficient of lending to implementation of conditionality).

[57] The countries are: Argentina, Bolivia, Cote d'Ivoire, Ethiopia, Ghana, Indonesia, Kenya, Malaysia, Nigeria, Russia, Tanzania, Uganda, Zambia, and Zimbabwe.

[58] The equations which illustrate these propositions are:

(1) Trust (measured as donor's willingness to forgive slippage) = −764** −27.08* compliance with:
(2.56) (2.34)

conditionality +14.9** ln (PPE) −4.7* ln (military expenditure) −1.11 corruption
(3.65) (2.08) (0.15)

+9.88* recipient-initiator dummy +8.56**residence dummy +0.45** time fixed effects
(2.33) (6.54) (2.97)

+1.22** country fixed effects, number of observations = 350, pseudo R-squared = 0.3508
(6.85)

(2) Budget support aid = 85.5** −0.97** (distrust measure) +1.71** compliance with conditionality
(4.65) (9.93) (6.64)

−0.30** ln (PPE) + 0.58** ln (military expenditure) −1.21** (corruption) +0.42** (openness dummy)
(4.99) (6.94) (9.77) (4.14)

−0.045** time fixed effects + 0.043 country fixed effects, number of observations = 215
(4.99) (2.03)

pseudo R-squared = 0.4923

Sample: 14 countries (as listed in Table 6.4), 3SLS analysis applied to period 1986–2004.

** denotes significance of a coefficient at the one per cent level and * denotes significance at the five per cent level. Full data set and details of estimations and test statistics are available at www.poverty.group.sheffield.ac.uk.

beyond the restoration of aid flows. It alters behaviour. If donors are more trusting, aid flows are more stable and they thus come to be treated as permanent rather than transitory income. This expectation influences investment rates, with consequent benefits for the recipient economy. And if donors become less trusting, then instability in aid flows prejudices the stability and also the *level* of domestic development spending, which then has an important bearing on poverty levels (Mosley and Suleiman 2006; Bulir and Hamann 2003, 2005). And in the 1990s, the pattern of aid flows becomes bifurcated, between those aid recipients who did and those who did not enjoy these trust-relationships. In Table 7.2, the sequence of bargaining relationships through which our different case-study countries passed is recorded, reflecting the discussion above. Did the new modalities of aid, and in particular the emergence of trust relationships between donors and recipients, encourage those recipients, especially under the stress of crisis, to reverse the momentum of liberalization and expand the scope of state activity? The answer is complex, because liberalization and openness are not unitary things: it is quite possible to have, for example, open capital markets and at the same time controlled labour markets, or markets in which internal capital flows are free but which impose restrictions on external capital movements (Sachs and Warner 1995; but see the critique by Edwards 1998). In addition, as we recall from our discussion of the Washington Consensus and confusion in Table 7.1, 'good policy' in its modern interpretation embraces the governance as well as the policy dimension. However, we postpone discussion of governance to the next section of the chapter, and in Table 7.2 are recorded six of the dimensions of openness of policy considered by Rodrik in Table 7.1: freedom of internal capital and labour markets, tariffs and quotas on external trade, flexibility of exchange rates, external capital controls, export taxes, and finally the overall size of government. The individual openness scores of case-study countries on each of these criteria are then assessed in relation to the overall openness measure used by Sachs and Warner (1995).

We find that the revolt against liberalization appears to be stronger in the case of middle-income than of low-income countries. First, the growth of state expenditures is stronger in middle-income than low-income countries (Figure 7.3). Second, the incidence of heterodox policies (the 'dark squares' of Table 7.2) is higher in middle-income than in low-income countries. One dimension of this is that the massive unemployment of the late 1990s especially in 'East Asian crisis' countries was ascribed by many of their inhabitants to preceding strategies of liberalization and privatization, with the consequence that the political changes of that period led to *neodesarollista* policies designed to restore the influence of the state in the face of globalizing pressures, and endow it once again with the ability to create employment and livelihoods (Grugel, Riggirozzi, and Thirkell-White 2008). As the analysis of Chapter 3 showed, these pressures were strongest in Latin America, and not only in our case studies of Bolivia and Argentina, but also in Venezuela, Uruguay, and Ecuador, which broke with the Washington Consensus not so much in their expansion of the state but rather in their determined use of non-price-based policy instruments (Grugel and Riggirozzi 2009). There were also, as we observe in Chapter 12, powerful pressures in Russia, also a middle-income country, to re-entrench what in the mid-1990s what had been a fragile state, and *derzhavnichestvo*, the reassertion of state power, becomes the primary

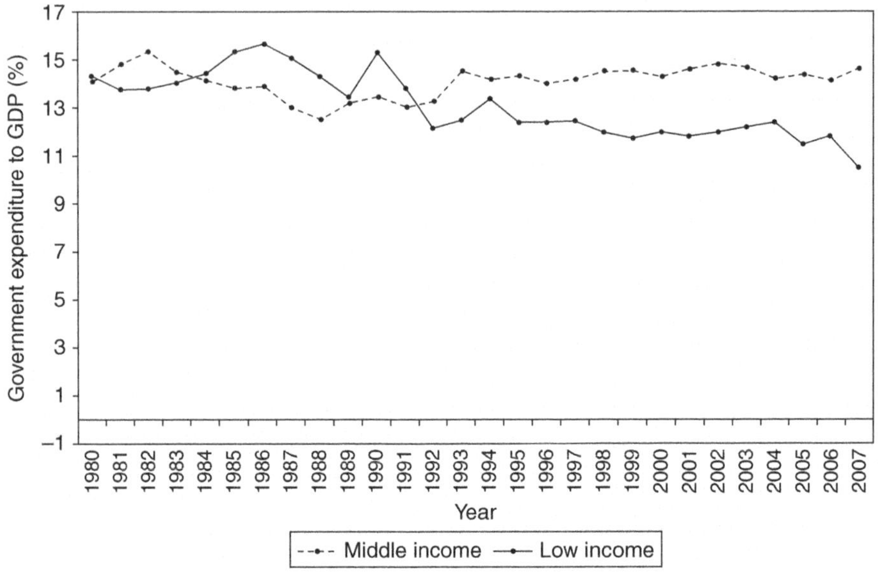

Figure 7.3 Low and middle-income countries: share of government in national income.
Source: World Bank World Development Indicators, reproduced and abstracted at http://poverty.group.shef.ac.uk.

imperative underlying policy in the 2000s. Reflecting these pressures, we see the imposition in the 1990s and early 2000s of controls on prices and wages in Russia and Argentina; export taxation in these countries plus Bolivia; and controls on external capital movements in all of these countries plus Indonesia and Malaysia. To be sure, the definition of what could be included in the Washington consensus had broadened and softened over time, as illustrated in Table 7.1, but no definition of the Washington principles known to the author includes export taxes within the definition of policies which could encourage growth or make economies work more efficiently. Indeed, export taxes had been the number one target for the early structural adjustment reformers seeking to reverse economic decline in poor developing countries and especially Africa (World Bank 1989). But however much Washington might see such interventions as the root of the problem, crisis exit strategies in middle-income countries were increasingly to see them as part of the solution.

Low-income countries, by virtue of and in proportion to their fiscal weakness and aid-dependence, lack the freedom of policy manoeuvre which is available to richer countries; and deviations from neoliberal orthodoxy, as shown in Table 7.3, are indeed less pervasive in the low-income countries within our sample. Some low-income countries, notably Uganda within our sample, conform fairly accurately still to the neoliberal model.[59] However, such deviations from orthodoxy exist, and they are related to the way in which international aid policies have evolved. Quantitatively and in terms of the first policy indicator in the table (the

[59] But even in Uganda the convergence on a neoliberal model was not complete (Dijkstra and van Donge 2001, page 842).

Table 7.3 The 'return of the state' and departures from the Washington consensus.

	Major increases in government share of expenditure	Major breaches in the 'Washington Consensus'	Nature of deviation from Washington Consensus	Shares of production			
				1990		2006	
				Ag	Ind	Ag	Ind
High-income countries (per capita income > $1500)		Russia	Export taxes, capital controls, price controls, minimum wage legislation	7	38	6	38
		Argentina	Export taxes, price controls, minimum wage legislation	13	44	9	35
		Malaysia	Export taxes, price controls, capital controls	13	43	8	52
		Bolivia	Export taxes	24	27	14	26
Low-income countries (per capita income < $1500)	Kenya	Ghana*	Export taxes (albeit reduced) on cocoa, fertilizer subsidies, capital controls	49	16	38	21
		Kenya*	Protection on imports, capital controls	31	20	31	17
		Zimbabwe	Exchange controls, maize movement controls, price and wage controls	11	43	22	27

Source: Table 7.1 and World Bank, *World Development Reports*, 1990 and 2006. In first column, a 'major increase' in the share of government is an increase of more than twenty-five per cent in that share. In final columns, data for Russia and for Malaysia are for 1995.

share of public expenditure to GNP), aid, across the board, has been associated with an enlargement in the size of the state in terms of expenditure (Remmer 2004), rather than the privatization and increased room for market forces which structural adjustment was expected to deliver. However, and perversely, increased levels of aid are also associated with lower levels of taxation, discussed in Chapter 6 as a fundamental determinant of state capacity.[60] This problem is further discussed in the next section.

Qualitatively, there is some evidence that the emergence of trust relationships between aid donors and recipients provided recipient countries with room for manoeuvre which they used, more or less adroitly, both to increase their political leverage and in some cases to increase their competitiveness by non-orthodox

[60] Note that Remmer's data cover the period 1970–99. In the period immediately after the East Asian crisis there occurred a great deal of state expansion attempting to protect against a recurrence of that crisis, some of which was aid-financed (Chapter 3 above), which is not covered by Remmer's data. In the global crisis of 2008/9 the whole process happened again (Chapter 8 below).

means.[61] But, just as every unhappy family is unhappy in its own way, every country which deviated from the neo-liberal orthodoxy also deviates in its own way in response to local political pressures and creativities, rather than adhering to a template. As we recall from our previous discussion, Ghana retained a measure of export taxation on cocoa, provided state subsidies on fertilizer, and imposed substantial controls on the export of capital from the country; Bolivia imposed taxation after 2006 on hydrocarbon exports; and Kenya retained quite a high level of protection on imports, as well as imposing some (not nearly as extensive as in middle-income countries) controls on capital exports. Outside the sample, Malawi experimented with fertilizer subsidies, and Ethiopia represents a case where the reasoning underlying the case for protection in terms of compensating for market failures was set out in much more explicitly developmentalist terms, and where the recipient in 1993 explicitly announced its intention to proceed with a programme of 'agricultural development-led industrialization' (Whitfield 2009, Chapter 5; see quotation keyed by footnote 47 above). The governance states of Africa may, as Graham Harrison claims, represent 'the Bank's best efforts to embed neoliberalism in Africa' (Harrison 2004, page 4), but even in the poorest states neoliberalism is not exactly what has been embedded. The one policy territory where the neoliberal model did take hold in the 1980s and retained its hold through all the turbulence of succeeding decades was the establishment of flexibility in the exchange rate,[62] and this applies as much in the middle-income cases such as Russia and Argentina as in the low-income, aid-dependent cases. In the aid-dependent cases, which had never experienced Latin American or eastern European levels of monetary and inflation instability, it is notable that we in addition see a shift to greater monetary autonomy for the central bank and in general a greater role for monetary, rather than fiscal, instruments in the setting of macro-policy (Adam and O'Connell 2006). This has served as an additional vehicle for liberalization and stabilization, as it has stiffened central banks against the passive accommodation of large state-enterprise deficits which was a feature of the 1970s and 1980s (Adam and O'Connell 2006, especially Chapters 6–7).

It is to be emphasized, however, that we do not yet, as a consequence of all these rebellions against orthodoxy, see a spread during the 1990s and 2000s of export-based industrialization on the model established by Indonesia, Malaysia, other East Asian countries, and indeed Mauritius. The fall in poverty achieved in the 1990s and 2000s, unlike that of the 1960s and 1970s, is not to be explained in terms of a transformation in the productive structure away from primary production and towards industrialization. As Table 7.3 indicates, within our sample such a transformation only occurred in Malaysia and, in a small way, in Ghana. In spite

[61] The qualifier 'in some cases' is crucial. Protectionism can be used either to protect the economically weak, which embeds inefficiency and corruption, or to build up the weak so that they become strong, as in the Far Eastern model, and as in the example of Mauritius above. In the context of Africa and most low-income countries, the Bank tended to assume that the latter strategy would always be followed.

[62] In Africa, 'Nominal exchange rates are now market-determined, via regular auctions or an interbank market, and black market premia now mainly reflect controls on capital account transactions, and are very low except in countries experiencing acute macro-economic instability' (Adam and O'Connell 2006, page 8).

of the differences of all the efforts made by poor countries in this period to distance themselves from the neoliberal model as a guide to policy, their productive structures remain heavily dependent on the export of primary staples. Until the economic collapse of the late 1990s, the low-income country which had gone furthest down the export-based industrialization path is probably, and ironically, Zimbabwe.

These variations in protectionist experience are catalogued in Table 7.3. In all of the low-income cases, we would argue, the offer of bona fides, in the shape of macro-economic stringency, the offer of a proactive poverty reduction strategy and in some cases assurances of an attack on corruption, were used to construct an umbrella of trust which then in several cases sheltered the recipient from the evidence that many elements in the Washington Consensus had been abandoned. In a majority of these cases, as we shall now examine, the resulting large and steady financial flows yielded a poverty reduction dividend.

A distinction between low and middle-income countries persists when we examine the impacts of aid on poverty. As we have observed (Chapter 5 above) the allocation of expenditure between sectors, in the shape of the pro-poor expenditure (PPE) index, is a significant determinant of headcount poverty and infant mortality, and we found it to be one of the main channels through which poverty has fallen over the medium term. It is therefore crucial if we are to understand the poverty leverage of aid to understand whether aid flows can influence the level of pro-poor expenditure. The finding of our panel-data regression analysis (Figure 7.3) is that there is a significant and positive influence of aid on growth in low-income countries, represented as the hollow circles in the diagram: for every one per cent increase in aid, the PPE ratio increases by 0.36 per cent.[63] Thus, one of the mechanisms by which aid reduces poverty may be represented as follows: as part of the processes by which aid recipients have been encouraged to take ownership of their poverty strategies, several of those aid recipients have offered a package which, in different proportions and according to their varying political priorities (Chapter 5), combines increases in primary health and education spending, increases in agriculture spending, cuts in military expenditure (which between them raise PPE) and progressive changes in the tax base. The fact that in low-income countries aid is typically a very high proportion of public expenditure (Table 7.1) is a strong incentive to them to do so. A high-PPE package, within a PRSP proposal, acts as a bona fide intended to signal the priorities of the recipient and unblock the desired aid flow; and, with quite a high probability but depending on the chemistry which forms between donor and recipient, obstacles to aid disbursement deriving from the persistence of controls on prices and trade can be overcome. Usually this signal works, as in Uganda, Ghana, Ethiopia, and other African countries which have negotiated high aid flows based on a strong commitment to poverty reduction; but occasionally it fails, as in the Malawian case described above.

We can now begin to pull the threads of the discussion together. In middle-income countries donors had no bargaining leverage, and the usual outcome was some degree of slippage on conditionality, or, otherwise put, considerable

[63] Note that the relationship between aid and PPE in middle-income countries, represented by the solid black circles in Figure 7.3, is across middle-income countries as a whole non-significant.

departures from the pattern of policy which the donors favoured and where invited into the policy dialogue (as in Argentina in 1991) had sought to impose—the outcome was therefore typically Model B, slippage condoned by the donors, involving of course large and increasing deviations from the free-market Washington Consensus model, especially during the East Asian crisis, as discussed in Chapter 3. In 'mixed' and low-income countries, donors had more leverage, but the cases where they both used that leverage and the recipients were weak enough to have to surrender to it (Model A) were few and far between: Kenya and Zimbabwe in the middle 1990s are the main cases considered here, although the over-heavy conditionality applied to Indonesia during the East Asian crisis (Chapter 3 above) and the case of agricultural input subsidies in Malawi are also relevant. Where Model A occurred, lending and investment fell, and these are also the cases of long-term increasing poverty within our sample. What was much more common in poorer countries was once again surrender by the donor (case B), mutating in some cases into trust based on 'agreement about core anti-poverty strategy principles' (case C), and we have analysed above the circumstances which caused this case to occur. These low-income cases often contain some elements of a movement towards the Washington consensus, for example in the case of exchange-rate policies, agricultural pricing policies, and monetary policy, but in other markets we can see conscious movement away under the stimulus of a 'developmental' approach to economic policy—as in Bolivia in the case of export taxes, and Ghana in the case of both labour markets and export taxation. In most of our case C case studies—Uganda, Ghana, Indonesia except during the period of turbulence during the 'East Asian crisis', and possibly Kenya in the middle 2000s—we can observe falling poverty, clearly associated with aid flows focused around a PRSP-type concordat on the mix of public expenditure. Since aid flows are both a higher share of income and, on the evidence of Table 7.3 and Chapter 5, have higher poverty leverage in low than in middle-income countries, we would argue that external financial relationships in all probability were better able to influence poverty levels in the poorer than in middle-income countries. But there are exceptions to this general principle and several cases of dramatic poverty reduction within middle-income countries, for example the maintenance of World Bank loan programmes in Argentina after the 2001/2003 crisis was significant in financing pro-poor public expenditure programmes and in particular the *Programa Jefas y Jefes* (Chapters 6 and 9).

7.4 INTERNATIONAL FINANCIAL INSTITUTIONS, GOVERNANCE, AND POVERTY OUTCOMES

This picture of international financial relationships is, of course, incomplete, as it focuses on *policy instruments*, the battleground of the 1980s and 1990s, and not on *governance*, the battleground of the late 1990s and 2000s. This matters both because governance issues are an integral part of bargaining between donors and recipients, and also because they may take us towards a less sanguine picture of the aid–poverty relationship than that so far presented.

In the late 1990s, in poor countries and in Africa in particular, there was as discussed above much concern that aid and structural adjustment policies were not working and that the failure of the one was related to the failure of the other. The diagnosis, for example of the World Bank's 1997 *World Development Report* (World Bank 1997) was that it was unreasonable to expect a national economy to respond to price-based stimuli such as more flexible exchange rates if the basic capacities of government—its ability to keep order, protect private property and maintain public services—were not working. These capacities, collectively known as *governance*, then became a major focus for a re-launch of the efforts of aid donors, linked in of course with the formal enunciation of the Millennium Development Goals and as discussed above with the broadening of the Washington Consensus. The analysis of Graham Harrison (2004), for example, identifies in Africa a category of 'governance states', defined as countries (the examples he gives are Mozambique, Tanzania, and Uganda) which have so far internalized the imperatives of good governance that they have ceased to perceive any conflict of interest between themselves and the Washington institutions, and rather see themselves as partners in the common enterprise of, not only poverty reduction, which commands a good measure of consensus and is commended precisely for that reason, but also the spread of free-market institutions, which does not.[64] Whether better governance has helped to make policies converge towards the Washington Consensus is of course an issue highly relevant to the effectiveness-of-aid and development finance debates which we have been examining. As a point of departure we shall examine a paper by Brautigam and Knack (2004) which suggests a pessimistic answer to this question, an answer which threatens to bruise the optimism of findings such as Figure 7.4. Under the stimulus of this paper we shall return to the governance data presented in our Chapter 6. The general story will be that the use of a wider range of governance indicators than the Bank's standard set exposes much more policy divergence, and leads to less gloomy conclusions about aid effectiveness, than emerges from the use of standard governance indicators.

Brautigam and Knack examine aid effectiveness, not in the sense in which we have analysed it so far—in terms of the impact of aid on growth or poverty—but rather in terms of its impact on institutions. The institutions they select as measures of state capacity are tax ratios and the International Country Risk Guide (ICRG) index, 'a commercial service providing information on political risks to overseas investors'; providing subjective in-country estimates of the levels of bureaucratic quality, rule of law, and corruption[65] (Brautigam and Knack 2004, page 266). They find that high levels of aid tend to sap rather than encourage state

[64] For example: 'The World Bank has openly and keenly worked to promote the expansion of international capitalism within its operations . . . since the mid-1990s the Bank has become increasingly supportive of the WTO's free trade agenda.'

[65] More precisely, the indicators in the ICRG quality of governance index are specified as follows: *Corruption in government (0–6)*: lower scores indicate that 'high government officials are likely to demand special payments', 'illegal payments are generally expected throughout lower levels of government' in the form of 'bribes connected with import and export licences, exchange controls, tax assessment, police protection, or loans'.
Quality of bureaucracy (0–6): high scores indicate 'autonomy from political pressure', 'strength and expertise to govern without drastic changes in policy or interruptions in government services' when governments change' and 'established mechanisms for recruiting and training'.

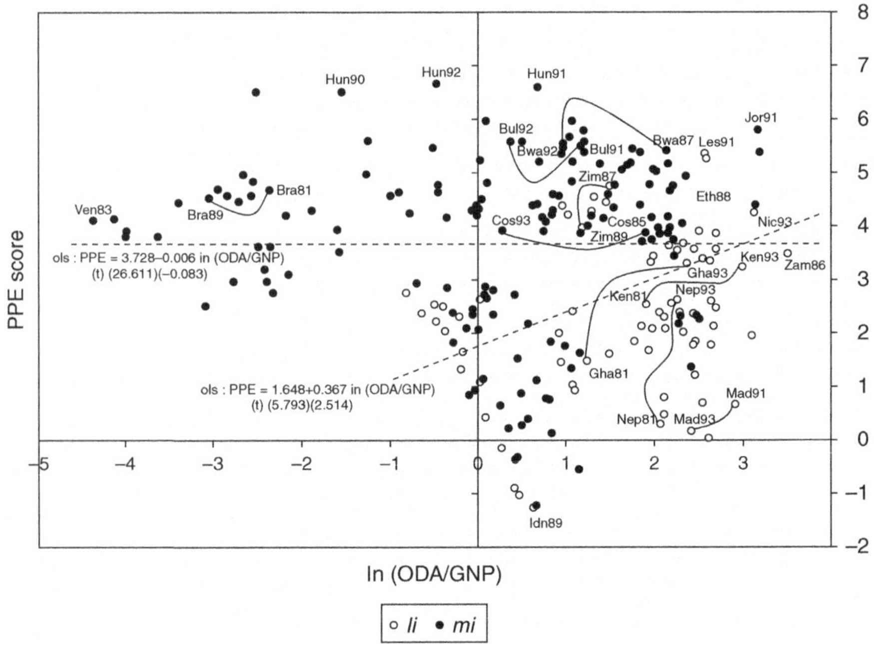

Figure 7.4 Middle- and low-income countries: aid in relation to PPE score.

Sources: PPE score from IMF, Government Expenditure Statistics Yearbook: ODA/GNP ratio from World Bank World Development Indicators. Data are for sixty low and middle-income countries during the period 1990–9, obtainable from www. poverty.group.shef.ac.uk. Mosley, P., Hudson, J., and Verschoor, A. (2004) Aid, poverty reduction and the 'new conditionality', *The Economic Journal,* **114**, F217–F243, Figure 1. Blackwell Publishing, published on behalf of The Royal Economic Society.

capacity, in the specific sense that in regressions of 32 African countries covering the period 1982–95[66] high aid is associated with lower tax effort and lower values of the ICRG index, a subjective indicator of governance quality which incorporates corruption, bureaucratic quality, and rule of law. Other statistical studies of aid and governance, including Boone (1999), Knack (2001), van der Walle (2005), and Moss, Petterson, and van de Walle (2006), who refer to the existence of an 'aid-institutions paradox' and even the possibility of an 'aid curse',[67] and most recently

Rule of law (0–6): this variable 'reflects the degree to which the citizens of a country are willing to accept the established institutions to make and implement laws and adjudicate disputes. Higher scores indicate 'sound political institutions, a strong court system, and provisions for an orderly succession of power'. Lower scores indicate 'a tradition of depending on physical force or illegal means to settle claims'. At changes in government, new leaders 'may be less likely to accept the obligations of the previous regime' in low-scoring countries.

[66] The estimated regressions control for the levels of economic decline and political violence, and also use instrumental variable methods to deal with endogeneity; yet 'when we correct for the potential endogeneity of aid, we see an even stronger relationship between aid levels and declines in the quality of governance and in the tax share of GNP' (Brautigam and Knack 2004, page 266).

[67] This phrase is used by Moss, Petterson, and van de Walle (2006), clearly drawing on the analogy with the 'natural resource curse' literature.

Unsworth (2009)[68] have drawn similar conclusions: that aid crowds out governance. Brautigam and Knack's recommendation is not to reduce aid, but rather to deliver it more selectively 'with few if any strings to proven, developmental governments in recognition of the fact that funding is fungible and that an overabundance of uncoordinated donors can crush local ownership and boost transactions costs' (Brautigam and Knack 2004, page 277) and with planned exit strategies, after the model of the Marshall Plan (Brautigam and Knack 2004, page 278).

In Chapter 6 above we examined a great deal of material on institutions, especially within our case-study countries, and we now wish to bring this material into relationship with the Brautigam–Knack crowding-out thesis to see whether its conclusions about the long-term effectiveness of aid are likely to be well-founded. For this study we are principally interested, of course, in the long-term *poverty* effectiveness of aid.

The institutional material surveyed in Chapter 6 examined two kinds of state capacity indicators—in the first place measures of what we called 'standard governance indicators' including rule of law, bureaucratic quality, and corruption (the three variables in the ICRG index), and in the second place measures of what we called 'institutional quality with a pro-poor bias' including measures of state-business relations, access to labour and capital markets, and institutions of conflict management. (Tax capacity also figured in this list of institutional quality measures, even though it is also a policy variable.) Our reason for expanding the list of institutional indicators in this way was because we did not believe that the standard governance indicators adequately captured the ability of institutions to reduce poverty. The values of these institutional indicators, ancient and modern, are recorded in Table 7.4 below in relation to the poverty trend and some of the possible explanations of it presented in previous chapters.

In the next two diagrams, we examine the hypothesis that aid discourages good governance. First, in Figure 7.5 we examine the link between aid and tax revenue with our data. As in the investigations by Brautigam and Knack, and also by Remmer (2004) the relationship is negative, although in our case it is insignificant.[69] The diagram draws attention to some of the outliers from the overall trend, and our discussion in Chapter 5 above has examined in detail some of the factors which have enabled outliers within our sample—Ghana, Uganda, Bolivia—to buck the trend and achieve increases in tax revenue, including the creation of independent revenue authorities, linkage of tax to social benefits, inventiveness in the extension of tax bases, and simply clever timing.

[68] Unsworth's paper, entitled 'What's politics got to do with it?' argues that there is a need for 'rethinking the essentially flawed assumptions underpinning the Paris Declaration and the Accra Agenda for Action: that better behaviour and more/more predictable finance from donors can be traded for action by 'partners' to improve governance and development performance' (2009, page 892).

[69] The estimated relationship is:

$$\text{taxgdp} = \underset{(16.22)}{16.28^{**}} - \underset{(0.80)}{0.07}\,\text{aid} - \underset{(0.55)}{0.40}\,\text{wbgi\_pse} - \underset{(0.37)}{0.003}\,\text{population} - \underset{(0.20)}{0.011}\,\text{per capita GDP},\quad \text{r-squared} = 0.017$$

where wbgi_pse is the World Bank's political stability indicator. In this multiple regression, the controls (the right-hand-side variables other than aid) have been selected so as to be, as far as possible, the same as those used in the Brautigam–Knack regression.

Table 7.4 Impact of aid on governance.

	Poverty trend	Policy model	Aid trend (%)	Conventional governance indicators (Brautigam–Knack)		Unconventional governance indicators (from Ch 6)		2007 value of PPI index (1990 = 100)
				Tax	ICRG	State-business relations index	Access to small business capital: microfinance borrowers as % of population	
Middle-income cases:								
Malaysia	Fell from 15% (1989) to < 10% (2006)	None: no IMF/WB flows	Low and falling: 1.11% (1990) to 0.25% (2004)		Static at 0.55	NA	NA	90
Argentina	Rose from 38% (October 1990) to 57% (October 2002) then fell to 34% (end 2005) 'Extreme poor' (*indigentes*) rose from *c.*10%–15% in 1990 to 27% in 2002, then declined to 12.2% in 2007	Mainly Model B (recipient domination) 1991–2005, then exit	Low and falling: 0.12% (1990) to 0.05% (2007)	Rose from 9% to 14.3%	Declined, 0.55 to 0.44	NA	No records until 2000. By 2007, 38000 active borrowers (0.09% of population)	159
Russia	Rose from 10% (1987) to 29% (2000) then fell to 15% (2006)		Generally low, but peaked in late 90s crisis: 0.04% (1990), 1.03% (1999) 0.22% (2004)		Declined, 0.58 to 0.37	NA	No records until 2000. By 2007 122000 (0.08% of population)	91
Mixed (partly middle, partly low-income cases)								
Indonesia	Fell from 18% (1987) to 12% (2006) but with increase to 24% in 1997–8	Model C (trust between WB and elite) until 1998, then uneasy balance between Models B and C	Low and falling: fell from, 1.5% (1990) to 0.03% (2007)	Fell from 16.9% (1990) to 12.3% (2005)	Increased, 0.12 to 0.33	NA	First microfinance loans in 1970s. Grew from 8.6 mn clients (5.2%) in 1997 to 34 mn (15.4%) in 2007	107

Bolivia	Rose slightly from 60% (1990s average) to 65% (2005)	Model C (trust between WB and governing elite) until 2002, Model A (breakdown) in 2003 then uneasy balance between Models B and C	High and static: 11.8% (1990), 9.1% (2004)	Rose from 8% to 17%	Increased,.16 to.44	NA	First microfinance loans in late 1980s; grew from 171,000 borrowers (2.2%) in 1997 to 630,000 borrowers (6.8%) in 2007	139
Low-income cases:								
Uganda	Fell from 56% (1992) to 31% (2006)	Model B (slippage) gradually evolving into Model C (trust)	High and rising: 15.8% (1990) 17.3% (2005)	Rose from 5% in (1986) to 10% (1990) and 13% (2006)	Increased, 0.22 to.50	0 until 1990; 0.375 (1994–2002), 0.875 (2004)	Some microfinance loans through Centenary Bank and NGOs in 1980s. 11,000 clients (0.05%) in 1997, rising to 357,000 (1.2%) in 2007	148
Ghana	Fell 51% (1990) to 39% (1999); possible further fall since then	Model B (slippage) gradually evolving into Model C (trust)	High and rising: 9.7% (1990) 15.4% (2005)	Rose from 11.4% to 23%	Declined, 0.61 to 0.41	0.25 (1992–2001), 0.625 (2002–5)	First microfinance loans in 1990s. 700 clients (0.003%) in 1997, rising to 322,000 (1.4%) in 2007	175
Kenya	Rose from 42% (1991) to 52% (1997)	Model B (slippage) 1990–5, Model A (almost complete breakdown of lending relationship) 1995–2002; resumption of Models 2 with elements of 3, 2002 to present	Traditionally high, fell sharply in 1990s: 14.4% (1990) 3.9% (2004)	Rose from 17% to 18%	Declined, 0.58 to 0.46	0.25 (pre-1992) rising to 0.875 (2005)	Some state (through Kenya Industrial Estates) and NGO finance since mid 1980s; 3,800 borrowers (0.01%) in 1997, rising to 692,000 (1.9%) in 2007	96
Zimbabwe	Increased from 35% (1990) to 60% est. (2005)	Model B (slippage) 1991–7, Model A (complete breakdown), 1997–2009, now emerging signals of willingness to re-establish aid relationship	Moderate and static:3.9% (1990) 4% (2004)		Declined, 0.44 to 0.19	0.175 rising to 0.469 (1992–2000), 0.55 rising to 0.631 (2001–5)	Some state (through Agricultural Finance Corporation) and NGO finance since early 1980s 14,000 borrowers (0.1%) in 1997, rising to 43,000 (0.3%) in 2007	71

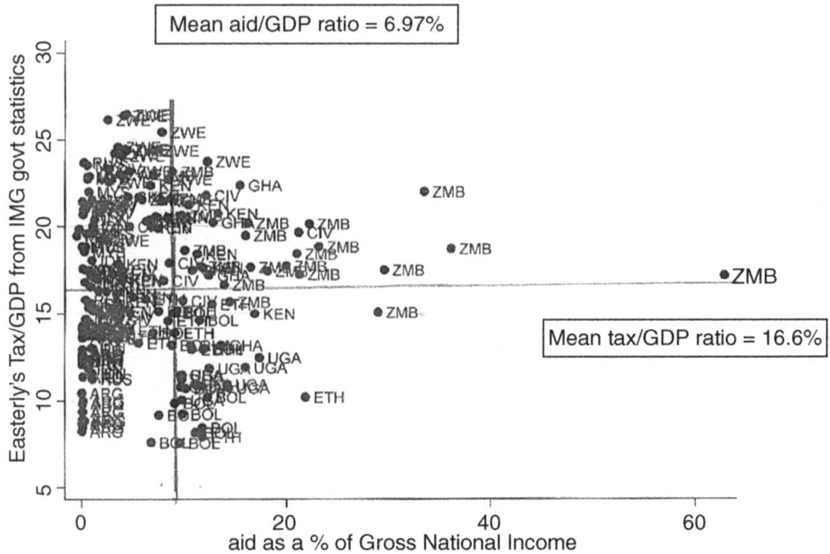

Figure 7.5 Fourteen-country sample: aid and tax ratios, 1990–2007.

Next, we examine the other indicator of governance quality considered by Brautigam and Knack, the ICRG index. Here, we find that the impact of aid is highly sensitive to the governance indicator employed. Whereas on the ICRG measure aid crowds out governance quality, as shown by Brautigam and Knack (first column of Table 7.5) and confirmed by our own estimations in the second column, the ICRG measure is not the only possible measure of governance and, as we have argued in Chapter 6, its constituent elements (corruption, rule of law, and bureaucratic quality) omit several dimensions of the ability of institutions to combat poverty, including the capacity of institutions to tackle market failures affecting poor people, the capacity of institutions to manage local and national conflict, and as an index of both of these the capacity and creativity of the NGO sector. In Chapter 6 we sought to tackle this problem by means of our 'pro-poor institutions' (PPI) measure, and in the third column of Table 7.5, we find that if this measure is brought into the story, which we do by 'interacting', that is, multiplying, our PPI measure by the conventional ICRG measure, the crowding-out effect of aid on institutional quality disappears. Indeed, if we examine the impact of aid on the PPI measure of institutional quality alone (Figure 7.6), the overall impact is significantly *positive*[70] although, as can be observed from the diagram, there is plenty of dispersion around the regression line reflecting

[70] The two-variable relationship represented in the scatter in Figure 7.6 is:

ppirev=107.07** + 1.55** aid, r-squared = 0.1465, observations = 57
(19.25) (3.07)

The captions on the individual observations illustrate and remind us of some of the country cases (the countries in the top right-hand quadrant of Figure 7.6) where the link from aid and other flows to

Table 7.5 Regressions of aid on alternative governance measures.

Regression coefficients on independent variables:	**Estimation method**					
	OLS			**3SLS**		
	Dependent variables					
	(1) ICRG-QOG (Brautigam–Knack)	(2) ICRG-QOG	(3) ICRG-QOG)*PPI	(4) Trust	(5) Aid	(6) Poverty
Constant	9.83**	0.49**	58.8	0.0889	1.38	69.70**
	(3.37)	(19.42)	(0.82)	(0.77)	(0.29)	(4.28)
Governance measures: initial value of (ICRG-QOG) index	−0.78**					
	(4.27)					
PPI index				0.0018**		
				(2.69)		
Aid	−0.061	−0.0019	0.31			−1.40
	(1. 60)	(0.84)	(0.82)			(2.07)
PPE ratio						−0.76
						(1.15)
Trust					42.2**	
					(3.87)	
WB political stability index		0.038*	7.39**	−0.061**		
		(2.10)	(2.76)	(2.95)		
Political violence	−2.36					
	(1.78)					
Openness index				−0.002**		
				(3.17)		
Population		−0.0001	−0.025	−0.0038	0.109	
		(0.57)	(0.64)	(1.41)	(1.24)	

Continued

Table 7.5 *Continued*

Regression coefficients on independent variables:	**Estimation method**					
	OLS			**3SLS**		
	Dependent variables					
	(1) ICRG-QOG (Brautigam–Knack)	(2) ICRG-QOG	(3) ICRG-QOG)*PPI	(4) Trust	(5) Aid	(6) Poverty
Population change/initial population	1.52 (1.58)					
GDP per capita		0.0029 (1.05)	0.400 (0.34)			
Democracy indicator (Freedom House Polity 2 measure)						−1.80* (2.23)
R-squared	0.60	0.0432	0.1464	0.5595	0.1842	0.0869
Number of observations	32	137	95	31	31	31
P	NA	0.0432	0.0061	0.0000	0.0000	0.0006

Notes: Data are for 1980–95 (column 1) and 1990–2007 (all other columns). Figures in parentheses are student's t-statistics; ** denotes significance at the one per cent level and * denotes significance at the five per cent level.

Variable definitions: all from World Bank World Development Indicators, augmented and summarized at www.poverty.group@sheffield.ac.uk; but note: aid = ratio of aid to GDP; trust = slippage on conditionality* (value of World Bank and IMF loans/GDP).

Sources: Column (1): Brautigam and Knack (2004), Table 3, column (1). Other columns: own regressions using World Bank, World Development Indicators and other sources; entire database at www.poverty. group@sheffield.ac.uk PPI index is from Chapter 6 above, Table 6.6.

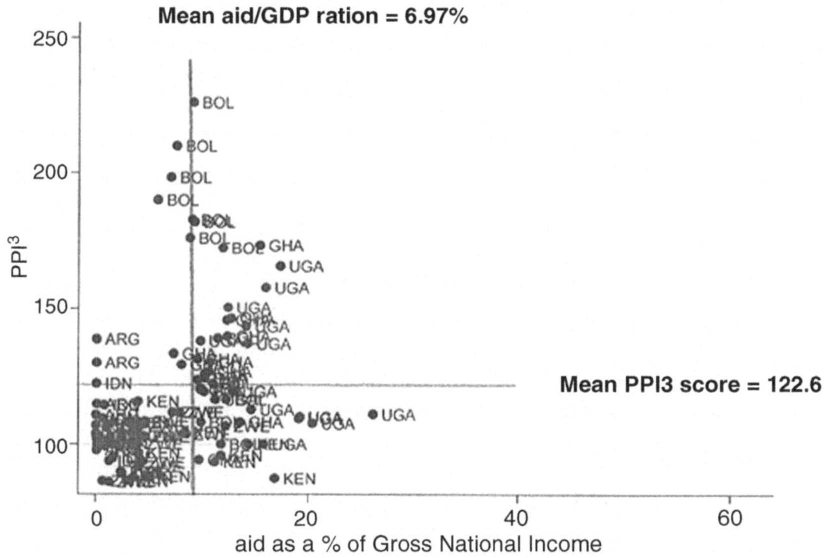

Figure 7.6 Fourteen-country sample: aid and PPI ratios, 1990–2007.

country-specific responses. If, as one of the authorities quoted by the Brautigam–Knack study suggests, 'aid dependence is a state of mind, where aid recipients lose their capacity to think for themselves and thereby relinquish control',[71] much depends on the forces which in individual countries induce that state of mind. We offer two hypotheses here. First, to understand the overall relationship between aid and institutions it is useful not only to look at the relationship going from aid to institutions but also at the relationship going from institutions to aid, and in this context to treat institutional quality as a bona fide which recipients can use to build trust relationships with donors, in augmentation of the approach sketched out earlier in the chapter. Second, the linkage going from aid to institutional quality clearly has a great deal to do with the motivation and behaviour of the NGO sector, both because the NGO sector is a large part of the activities which, especially in the poorest and weakest states, determine the capacity to reduce poverty, and because it is a sector which donors have quite deliberately cast in the role of complement or even substitute for government in order to improve the delivery of poverty-reducing services.

In the right-hand half of Table 7.5 we examine the first of these ideas: the PPI index is presented in the guise of a bona fide, an assurance which develops trust and motivates donors to make long-term commitments of aid, like the policy variables which we examined in the previous section, as well as an institutional

institutional quality appears to have been most positive: Ghana all the time, and Uganda, Bolivia, and Argentina much of the time.

[71] Rehman Sobhan, quoted in SIDA, *Aid Dependence and Donor Policy: the case of Tanzania with lessons from Bangladesh's Experience* cited in Brautigam and Knack (2004), footnote 12.

capacity which is influenced by aid flows. In other words, the relationship between aid and institutional capacity is two-way, and must therefore be simultaneously modelled. This is done by three-stage least squares methods in the final three columns of Table 7.4. We observe, first, from the trust equation (column 4) that increased values of the PPI index serve as an effective bona fide to incentivize trust, which then (column 5) performs, like good policy, the function of boosting and stabilizing aid volumes, which then (column 6) enables poverty to fall faster in regimes which have achieved trust relationships within the donor–recipient community. From this approach we learn, second, that the relationship between aid and institutions is not linear but simultaneous, multiple, and interactive—indeed, as we have observed from our case studies, it often operates not through one flow crowding out one entity called 'institutional capacity' but rather through multiple and often uncoordinated flows exercising impacts on many institutions which are sometimes destructive but sometimes creative and supportive.

Generalizing about which is which, of course, is not easy. One of the keys, as we have emphasized, is the triangular dynamics between the donors, the recipient government, and the NGO sector. But sadly, it is still the case after thirty years of exponential growth in expenditure, and research, on NGOs that little is known about this relationship which is more than impressionistic: the data continue to be very bad. In our case studies we have illustrated something of the dynamism of the relationship between government and microfinance NGOs in Bolivia, and NGOs as a whole in Uganda—these are clearly not cases of crowding out. There are other legendary cases where large government-to-government and government-to-NGO aid flows have helped to generate a synergy which has generated a great deal of pro-poor creativity, notably Bangladesh. More negatively, there exists one quantitative study outside our sample by Bano (2008) which indicates, in Pakistan, a strong correlation between aid and absence of members, which in turn '*indicates the possibility* (our emphasis) of a causal relationship where aid leads to [an increase in the] material aspirations among leaders of NGOs, which in turn result in lower performance and an ability to mobilize members'[72] (Bano 2008, page 2297). However, these are only straws in the wind, and there is nothing like the weight of evidence which might be able to indicate which of these two tendencies might be expected to predominate in which environments. This indicates an important priority for future research.

7.5 CONCLUSIONS

In defining the international context within which anti-poverty action takes place, we have focused on the international financial institutions, led by the IMF and

[72] Membership, used as an index of social capital, is taken as the dependent variable here, and not any measure of the output, productivity, or poverty-reducing potential or achievement of NGOs (Bano 2008, page 2297). For an impressionistic but very vivid account providing support for the view that incremental aid resources crowd out NGO service quality in Africa, see the book by Theroux (2003), especially Chapters 8 and 15.

World Bank. Over the last thirty years, the dominant trend in global economic policy, the rise and fall of neo-liberal policies, has been faithfully reflected in the conduct and policy prescriptions of those institutions, and one element within the 'fall' phase of the last fifteen years, has been the emergence of a 'third way' politics which sought to transcend left-right political divisions in favour of an equitable partnership between states and markets. These 'third way' ideas have indeed been reflected in the thinking and recommendations of the international financial institutions, and the global commitment to halve poverty, as embodied in the Millennium Development Goals, is one result. But, as Ravi Kanbur has put it, 'the end of history lasted such a short time' (Kanbur 2001, page 1083); even if there is global consensus around the idea that reducing poverty is a good idea, consensus has not emerged around the detail of how to do it. In this chapter, we have examined the different ways in which the operations of the international financial institutions impacted on the policies and institutions of developing countries, notably our case study countries, and the consequences of this for poverty and well-being.

We have sought to understand the linkage between international institutions and developing-country governments in terms of a *bargaining process* which may, under certain circumstances, collapse and be replaced by a core of mutual interest and trust. In the 1980s, donors had not thought through the process by which they expected to overcome political opposition of interest-groups opposed to liberalization; but a pattern quickly emerged in which that opposition was surrendered to if the recipient had sufficient countervailing power—either because of its geopolitical leverage or because its loan portfolio was large—and confronted only if the recipient was weak in both senses. The latter cases were rare; and yet a lot of liberalization happened, because it had advantages for governments, in particular in terms of revenue. Gradually they learned the advantages of thinning down the conditions to bare macro-economic essentials, forgiving non-essentials, and letting the recipient make the first move, an approach which enabled, in a number of cases, a critical mass of trust to be created within the broad donor-recipient community. With the addition of poverty rhetoric, this evolved by the millennium into what came to be known as the 'PRS approach'; and yet minus the rhetoric, that approach had already evolved pragmatically by the 1980s in several countries where the necessary local trust relationships existed between the key actors. Indonesia, within our sample, was one of these countries; but also, in Africa, was Mauritius, and it is to be stressed that a formal aid relationship was not required, as we have illustrated throughout this book, for the advantages of a pro-poor strategy to become manifest. Under the umbrella of these trust equilibria, numerous dilutions and violations of the Washington consensus occurred, as noted above, especially but not only in the middle-income countries. Especially where steady increases in pro-poor expenditure were achieved, a process which aid flows did materially assist in low-income countries, poverty tended to fall more than elsewhere.

Although there is something close to consensus that aid increases income and reduces poverty in the short term, it is far from clear that aid improves institutional quality, and many of the recent attempts to 'broaden the Washington Consensus' relate to measures to improve the capacity of state institutions. All this concern emerges from a wide literature which shows negative correlations between aid measures and some measure of institutional capacity. The implication of this literature is that the optimistic conclusions so far drawn about aid impact are at risk, as they may be undermined by creeping institutional decay.[73]

This literature, we argue, is speculative and over-simple. Rather than proving some iron law by which aid crowds out institutional capacity, what it does is establish one-way correlations between aid and a highly restrictive measure of institutional quality, some elements in which (e.g. corruption) have no demonstrable connection with growth or poverty. We therefore re-estimate the institutional impact of aid by means of a two-step procedure which examines the simultaneous relationship between aid and institutional capacity, treating institutional capacity as a bona fide, or a signal which like credible policy commitments can build trust. Once this is done, and once institutional capacity is redefined to assess the ability of institutions to overcome market failures, we no longer find that aid crowds out institutional capacity. The shadow appears to have been removed from the finding that aid reduces global poverty. But the data reveal wide variations in the effectiveness of aid across countries, which appear to be connected with the performance of the NGO sector. With the data in their existing state, no more can be said.

In conclusion, it is worth seeing the events described in this chapter in a thirty-year perspective. The global crisis from which those events emerged, in 1979–81, was a crisis for the Bank and Fund no less than it was a crisis for developing countries. They found themselves faced both with widespread default and with a demand for a financial product—medium-term programme finance—which the market was not at the time supplying. The new financial product which was developed to meet the need was structural adjustment lending (in its various forms, leading eventually to budget support lending and the Poverty Reduction and Growth Facility), for which liberalization was the *quid pro quo.* Almost all the developments examined in this chapter stem either from liberalization or from reactions against it. At one stage, the 'aid compromises' made to overcome these problems appeared to the international financial institutions quite alarmingly successful, to the point that in 2006 and 2007 the Fund's services were scarcely required: most loans had been paid back, and few new ones needed to be made. Some IMF staff were made redundant (Ariel Buira, personal communication). But by the time of writing, the boot had shifted to the other foot. To the surprise of many, it emerged that global crises were, in defiance of the international financial architecture, still capable of occurring. We shall examine the poverty implications of this renewed outbreak of crisis in our final chapter.

[73] This is suggested by the paper by Rajan and Subramaniam (2008) which reports that the overall impact of aid on growth is insignificant, and particularly weak where the period over which aid impacts materialize is allowed to be long-term (Rajan and Subramaniam allow for a time horizon of up to forty years).

8

Summary and conclusions

> Perhaps in these spheres the right thing always has to be done for the wrong reasons.
>
> Arthur Koestler, *Arrival and Departure*

8.1 RECAPITULATION OF MAIN ARGUMENTS

The rapid reduction of poverty over the last decade and a half has been one of the great achievements of recent history. Global poverty, as measured by the World Bank yardstick of an income of $1.25 a day, has already halved, from 41.7 per cent in 1990 to 22 per cent in 2008, and is expected to fall further to 15.1 per cent in 2015 (Hulme 2010, Chapter 7, page 12). This has in all probability never occurred before.

In this book we have tried to understand the political reasons why this achievement has happened, to set these reasons in historical perspective, to explore the disturbing cases where the trend is still adverse, and to draw lessons which will enable continued progress to be made. It has emerged that much of this progress has been unwilled, in the sense of not being directly aimed at by those who took the relevant policy actions; rather it was a by-product of actions aimed in the first instance at political survival. Thus, the iron law of political exclusion of the poor has been well and truly overcome. But not by altruism—the presidents of the most successful countries at reducing poverty, Museveni and Suharto, were by no means philanthropists—rather by the channelling of elite self-interest.

What kinds of policies and institutions have enabled developing countries first to cope with shocks in a pro-poor manner, and then to achieve pro-poor growth which builds on the 'pro-poor tendencies' mentioned above? Six of the most useful insights which we believe emerge from our research are the following:

1. *'Riot-type conflict' is a useful early-warning indicator of larger political instability, and social efficiency wage policies—expenditure policies which have the ability to buy off riot-type conflict—have an important role in offsetting such conflict and preventing it from turning into larger-scale instability.* In Chapter 4 we devise, measure, and test the concept of riot-type conflict. Riot-type conflict is violence which is not sufficiently devastating or widespread to be classed as civil war, and in all of Indonesia, Argentina, Bolivia, Russia, and Zimbabwe within our sample, it increased dramatically under the stress of economic recessions including the 'East

Asian crisis'. Whether it quickly abated or became persistent was an important determinant of poverty dynamics within these case-study countries, and we illustrate this within the context of a four-equation model, which illustrates the links from political variables to policy to riot-type conflict to, in some cases, a wider escalation of that conflict. In the case of the last link in this chain, there is a statistically significant relationship between probability of escalation and the manner in which conflict is managed, indeed, within the sample it is possible to observe, in Indonesia in 1998 and in Bolivia in 2003, how poor conflict management led to a significant escalation of hostilities, and an increase in poverty. We thus interpret riot-type conflict as an 'amber light' providing early warning of danger, and provide evidence for a number of strategies which empirically appear to be able to reduce the likelihood of such dangers.

One of these strategies is increases in what we call the *social efficiency wage,* which is the level of the social wage that minimizes political instability, by analogy with the efficiency wage of labour economics, which is the level of the private wage that, acting through the stability and productivity of the labour force, maximizes long-term private profit (Hudson, Lenton, and Mosley 2009; Stiglitz 1976). In any environment the definition of the social efficiency wage will depend on the identity of the social groups which are most politicized and best positioned to organize riot-type conflict, for example in Bolivia this group is the urban inhabitants of the satellite city of El Alto above La Paz, but in Russia it is the mainly rural autonomous republics of the Caucasus (Chechnya, Ingushetia, Dagestan, Kabardino-Balkaria, North Ossetia, and surrounding regions). We work with three definitions of the social efficiency wage: mainly rural, mainly urban, and mixed. Each of these is strongly correlated with pro-poor expenditure, and each of them, in our regressions (Tables 4.4 and 5.4 above) significantly reduces the probability of conflict. Increases in military centrality (weighted average of share of military expenditure and role of military expenditure in government) increase the probability of conflict. We thus speculate that increases in the social efficiency wage have the ability to embed, and create legitimacy for, regimes whose legitimacy is fragile, as in the cases of Uganda, Ghana, and post-2003 Argentina.

How does the social efficiency wage mechanism work? We argue that it sends a signal concerning not only the interests with which the government is aligned, but concerning its determination to arbitrate fairly between those interests. A government which sends, through the social efficiency wage, signals of an intention to reduce inequities and to allocate taxes and subsidies fairly is, in this sense, more likely to be able to achieve political stability than one which does not. These signals are likely to be complementary with institutions which secure greater transparency in the allocation of government resources (e.g. ombudsmen, autonomous tax authorities, constitutional commissions such as those set up in Bolivia and Argentina in the mid-2000s). They are also complementary with improvements in the transparency of the electoral process, as the experience of Ghana after 1992 illustrates. It is in this qualitative sense that we can say that 'improvements in democracy' will improve political stability. They have done, and what predatory elites can get away with without triggering conflict has definitely reduced over time, but the way in which their room for manoeuvre has been reduced is often not by formal measures such as multiplying the number of political parties, so much as by informal signals, within which the social efficiency wage mechanism plays a part.

2. *'Pro-poor expenditure' is not only an important element in the social efficiency wage—thereby reducing political instability, but has the ability to reduce poverty through other channels.* A relatively quick reduction in poverty levels can be achieved by targeting public expenditure on economic sectors which have a relatively high 'poverty elasticity', or tendency to reduce poverty per unit of expenditure—either because they are labour intensive, or because they provide goods and services which feature heavily in the consumption of poor people, or because they provide linkages to sectors whose growth will reduce poverty—as when an increase in construction activity induces growth in production of furniture which is made in the informal sector. On all of these criteria, growth in expenditure in primary health, primary education, and rural infrastructure is likely to be pro-poor, and only a little more debatably, so is growth in expenditure on agriculture, on social protection, and reduction in military spending. To test this intuition and refine our definition of *pro-poor expenditure* (PPE), we examine the linkage between pro-poor expenditure and poverty, by simultaneous-equation methods, against short-term, large-sample data from the East Asian crisis period (Mosley and Chiripanhura 2009, Chapter 3); against medium-term data for 1990–2007 (ibid., Chapter 5), and finally against historical data for Uganda, Ghana, Kenya, and Zimbabwe for 1914–2007 (ibid., Chapter 13). From all of these tests, pro-poor expenditure emerges as a significant correlate of poverty, the best fit being to the case in which agriculture, social expenditure, and military spending, as well as health and education, are all included.[1] As mentioned above, we speculate that it 'works' not only by signalling the government's intention to promote a fair and equitable allocation of resources (thereby reducing the likelihood of conflict), as per the social efficiency wage theory but also simply by augmenting the demand for activities in respect of which poor people are heavily represented in production or consumption.

The political perspective we have taken adds another dimension, as political weight is not necessarily concentrated in pro-poor expenditure sectors. However, our case studies (Mosley and Chiripanhura 2009, Chapters 5 and 9–13) illustrate two different kinds of political pressure in favour of increased levels of PPE:

(a) *Where the elite is rural based* (e.g. Uganda, Ethiopia, Zimbabwe): in this case, the elite will naturally wish to augment the agriculture and rural infrastructure element in PPE, sometimes as far as launching a green revolution campaign, which will assist poor rural *producers*.
(b) *Where the elite is urban based* (e.g. Argentina, Russia): in this case, the elite will naturally wish to augment the social subsidies, housing and health and education elements in PPE, which will be of assistance to urban *consumers*.

The diversity of elements in PPE affords considerable scope for building pro-poor coalitions which appeal to a diversity of interest groups, as our case studies illustrate.

[1] There are, however, data problems: more abundant data are available for health and education than for agriculture and social sectors.

3. *The same applies, at least potentially, to pro-poor taxation. Specifically, the role of export taxation in supporting a pro-poor politics is complex, but rightly designed it is highly creative.* Taxation and tax structures are crucial for poverty reduction; but in a long-term context only, since in the short term higher taxes reduce income. Over the longer term, increases in taxation are vital to finance the expansion of public expenditure on which development is based. These require a strategy for escaping from the 'tax trap' identified by Moore (1999) which shows that poor countries with weak states have difficulty in increasing or diversifying their tax base (because higher taxes further reduce support and trust for, by hypothesis, an already fragile government) and consequently in building a stable base for expenditures, a problem often exacerbated by large aid flows. In Chapter 5, we examined the political routes which our sample countries have chosen in order to spring this trap. These have required, first of all, a sense of timing: the disastrous attempted Bolivian tax increase of 2003, in which taxes on the lower middle class were increased during a recession when many of the upper class were visibly not paying tax, is a case in point. Second, administrative reforms, including the placing of tax collection responsibilities with an autonomous revenue authority, are often useful in raising the tax/GDP ratio. Third, a shift from a tax base consisting almost entirely of agricultural/natural resource production and exports to a more diversified tax base making use of taxes on sales (e.g. VAT), income, and capital can often be configured so as to not only raise revenue but reduce poverty. A case in point is the liberalizing reforms of the early 1990s in Uganda and Ghana, which sharply reduced taxation on mostly smallholder exports of, respectively, coffee and cocoa, and played a considerable part in the large reductions in poverty of those years. However, earmarked *increases* in export taxation can also have both a progressive and a democratizing effect (as noted also by Brautigam (2008) in Mauritius), by contractually steering income from richer people in a booming sector towards expenditure for the benefit of poorer people. Examples of this are the taxes on Argentinian oil and primary produce exports of 2002, which were earmarked for co-financing, with the World Bank, of the *Programa Jefas y Jefes* for unemployed heads of households, and the increased taxes on exports of Bolivian oil and gas in 2006, which financed increases in the level and coverage of the government state pension.

4. *Institutional quality is a key element in assisting and embedding the emergence of a pro-poor politics, but although the importance of institutions in development is now widely recognized, the definition of pro-poor institutions is not well advanced. We suggest and specify a concept of 'pro-poor institutions' which we believe advances the debate and shows promise in explaining some puzzles in the politics of poverty—notably the link between aid and institutions.* Institutions are important for development: that much is well understood, but the question of which institutions help to achieve which development goals in which environments is not well understood. In Chapter 6 above, we began by examining the statistical relationship between the standard 'World Bank indicators' of governance (rule of law, democratic accountability, political stability, bureaucratic quality, and corruption) on *growth* (not yet poverty) and find that, of these standard governance indicators, only rule of law and political stability are robustly correlated with, and help to Granger-cause, GDP growth. We then argue that even these governance

indicators do not properly gauge the ability of institutions to reduce poverty, a capacity which we relate to the ability of institutions to deliver poverty-reducing inputs, which include access to labour and capital markets but also capacity to reduce conflict, as in (1) above. We compose an exploratory 'pro-poor institutions (PPI) index' which is intended to meet this need (Table 6.3), and contains five components: the state-business relations index created by Leftwich, Sen, and te Velde (2008); a measure of access by the poor to capital markets; a measure of access by the poor to labour markets; a measure of capacity to manage conflict reflecting the arguments described in (1) above; and reflecting the arguments described in (3) above, the ratio of taxation to income. This PPI index shows promise in explaining the poverty dynamics of our case-study countries; it also shows promise in resolving one of the paradoxes of the aid literature, which is that although aid increases short-term growth, it appears to undermine long-term institutional quality (Brautigam and Knack 2004). We find that, when our PPI index rather than standard World Bank indicators of tax effort and the ICRG governance index are used, aid flows do not undermine but rather they support long-term institutional quality (Table 7.4).

5. *Bargaining relationships between international financial institutions have in some cases—notably but not exclusively aid recipients—transmuted into trust-relationships: we analyse the dynamics of these and argue that they are important for determining the level, stability, and poverty impact of aid flows.* Especially in poor countries, aid flows are clearly an important determinant of poverty reduction potential. Over sixty years since the origins of the Bretton Woods system, one of the main instruments used to increase the effectiveness of these flows is policy conditionality, which has served as a kind of collateral substitute, seeking to increase the effectiveness of loans and grants made by international financial institutions (IFIs). Conditionality, however, has been widely evaded, and during the last ten years, at least, there has been an attempt to replace conditionality with a form of contract which is longer term and better 'owned' by recipients—the Poverty Reduction Strategy (PRS) framework. In Chapter 7, we identify *trust* between members of the donor and recipient communities as a key element determining the success of PRS-type and other conditionality-based operations, which if a critical mass forms may be able to break down conflict-based bargaining relationships between the donor and the recipient. We test, and in relation to our large sample confirm, the hypothesis that the key determinants of trust are willingness by the recipient to offer gestures which credibly define a pathway towards core donor objectives (which we refer to as bona fides), the existence of networks allowing for frequent communication between donor and recipient, and the availability of expedients which protect the donor against having his trust abused and increase his risk efficacy—including the existence of alternative aid vehicles such as NGOs—in addition to a host of elusive and often personalized factors which define the chemistry between donor and recipient communities. In environments where trust between donor and recipient communities is high, such as Indonesia, Uganda, and Ghana, aid flows are larger and more stable, and poverty reduction impact proportionately higher, than in low-trust environments such as Kenya, Zimbabwe, and Bolivia.

6. *We document how, initially under the stress of the global recession of 1997–2003, and especially in middle-income countries, policy patterns and the bases of*

support for the state have shifted away from the Washington Consensus model. As is common in times of recession, the terms of developing countries' engagement with the international economy were blamed by many citizens of those countries for the 'East Asian' crisis: specifically, policies of privatization and, more broadly, a high degree of exposure to international trade and investment, augmented by structural adjustment policies, were seen by the elites who took over in the early 2000s, especially in the Southern Cone of Latin America, as responsible for the severity of job losses during the crisis and as weakening both the economy and the state. In our research (Grugel and Riggirozzi 2009a) we seek to explain the politics of how, in some countries of Latin America (notably Bolivia, Argentina, Ecuador, Venezuela, and Uruguay) the state sought to retrieve its position by means of policies of *neodesarrollismo* (new developmentalism) which combined some of the features of 1950s protectionism (price and wage controls, export taxes, high and selective tariffs) with other characteristics of the late 1990s and early 2000s accommodation to globalization (flexible exchange rates, low budget deficits, highly targeted social subsidies, and indeed sovereign debt default, as studied by two of our colleagues in the World Economy and Finance Programme (Dhillon and Garcia-Fronti 2009). Especially in Argentina, Ecuador, and Bolivia, this revolt against neoliberalism has involved the incorporation into government of militant 'new poor' groups, and at least in the first two countries has had substantial poverty-reducing results since 2000 (Grugel and Riggirozzi 2009b, Chapters 4 and 5). In Grugel, Riggirozzi, and Thirkell-White (2008) we extended the examination of crisis-affected countries' search for autonomy into Asia, and our Chapter 7 showed how in some African countries, notably Ghana and Ethiopia, the establishment of trust relationships with donors provided an incubator in which all manner of policies alien to the Washington Consensus were able to grow. However, these African and Asian variants lacked the rhetoric, the intellectual coherence, and the populist appeal of *neodesarollismo*.

Between them, we believe, these ideas provide a useful set of analytical tools for the understanding of the politics of poverty reduction. Higher levels of the 'social efficiency wage', a reorientation towards locally relevant versions of pro-poor expenditure, and a reorientation towards locally relevant institutions, can in our judgement reduce poverty where that is politically feasible, and we have indicated in our case studies some of the circumstances in which it has been politically feasible. Additionally, in poor countries, the achievement of trust relationships which break down the latent conflict between donor and recipient-based interest groups, where that can be achieved, yields a dividend in terms of poverty reduction, although that may be achieved at a price in terms of deviations from the Washington Consensus.

8.2 THE 2008–9 GLOBAL CRISIS AND A LOOK FORWARDS

In 2008 and 2009, the world economy was hit by a fresh crisis, originating in widespread default on US mortgage debt but rapidly spreading to all parts of the globe and in particular to the developing world. Like the earlier East Asian crisis

(Stiglitz 1998), this one has been blamed on inadequate regulation of the banking system, allowing, in particular, too large a role to government-owned banks in developing countries (Andrianova, Demetriades, and Shortland 2008). Now that the banking system has become heavily contaminated, state participation in the banking system has been further increased in 2008 and 2009, in both developing and industrialized countries, to protect against runs on weak banks, but the recession has been severe, and in 2009 the world economy experienced negative growth, for the first time since the 1940s. In 2011, the threat of global recession re-emerged, this time not because of runs on weak banks, but because of runs on weak industrialized countries—in particular Greece and Italy.

Since the roots of the crisis, in the US mortgage market in the spring and summer of 2008, were associated with complex financial instruments such as derivatives and collateralized debt obligations which are concentrated in industrialized countries, many initial prognoses such as the IMF's *The Implications of the Global Financial Crisis for Developing Countries* (IMF 2009) took the view that the damage to the developing world might be relatively small (IMF 2009, page 8). However, some developing countries are clearly already suffering. The most vulnerable (IMF 2009, Chapter 6) are in three groups, all with very open economies: eastern European countries exposed to severe capital flight (e.g. Latvia, Hungary, and Ukraine), low-income countries which had just begun to gain a foothold in global capital markets from which they have now been expelled (e.g. Kenya, within our sample, and Nigeria), and very low-income, often conflict-hit countries which have very high ratios of aid to GNP (e.g. Rwanda, Afghanistan, and the Democratic Republic of the Congo).

At the global level, there has been coordinated action, and indeed action which lacks the deflationary bias of the international financial institutions' response during the 1980s crisis. The IMF's capital has been doubled, at the G20 meeting in April 2009, to $200bn, and the largest economies, notably the US, the UK, and China, have deliberately increased real public spending with the intention of insuring the world economy against the consequences of a collapse in bank lending. However, on other policy issues there is less unanimity. The former UK chancellor and prime minister, Gordon Brown, mindful of the consequences of lack of coordination during the 1930s recession, warned (at the same G20 meeting) that 'protectionism protects nobody', but it is clear that, at the level of individual vulnerable economies, such protection is both economically and politically a short-term necessity. One area in which this is particularly relevant is capital controls. As we saw in Chapter 3, Malaysia managed during the 'East Asian' crisis to escape many of the political consequences of the crisis by imposing capital controls in response to it, and a leading NGO, Action Aid, has warned that it sees premature liberalization of the capital account as a major reason why the consequences of the recession on LDCs have been aggravated during the last year (Action Aid 2009, pages 8 and 15). Of course, that liberalization has not been indulged in across the world; rather, as we have argued (Chapter 7 above) most middle-income countries have retained such controls, and they have only been removed by those low-income countries who need to offer them as a bona fide to the donors. As in previous recessions, the difference between those countries who have freedom of policy manoeuvre and those who have not is being cruelly exposed.

Thanks to the developments discussed in this book, the latter group of countries is now smaller than it was. Of the countries in our case-study sample, Russia, Indonesia, Argentina, Ghana, and Uganda, at least, are certainly better positioned to withstand the current global recession than the previous one; and more broadly, even Collier's 'bottom billion' of extremely deprived and vulnerable countries has now shrunk to two hard cores: an African group, not even now the majority of African countries but prominently including all the large problem countries of Africa—Ethiopia, Nigeria, Sudan, and Congo DRC, together with the group labelled by David Hulme as 'sub-siberian Asia'—Turkmenistan, Kyrgyzstan, Afghanistan, Pakistan, Nepal, Burma, Cambodia, and the Tibet and Xinjiang provinces of China. Every single country in this group is conflict-ridden. It is reasonable to hope that the approach we have adopted in this book, of applying the test of political feasibility at the same time as the test of economic optimality and seeing development policy through the same lens as policies for the prevention of conflict, may be helpful in further reducing poverty within these two clusters.

Part 2

Case studies

9

Argentina

Jean Grugel and Pia Riggirozzi

The main purpose of this chapter is to explore the emergence of poverty as a political issue in Argentina, examine institutional responses to it and gauge their success, and offer some thoughts as to the longer term sustainability of key aspects of the new pro-poor policies and pro-poor growth that emerged out of the ashes of the 2001 economic collapse. That we should consider Argentina a suitable case for a comparative study of the politics of poverty would have been incomprehensible even twenty years ago. Argentina was one of the most prosperous countries outside the small core of intensive capitalist economies, due to its exceptionally strong export-led agrarian growth in the early years of the twentieth century, relatively small population, and steady state-sponsored expansion of industrialization, public education and the provision of public goods. In addition, state elites did not recognize poverty either as a political issue or socio-economic problem. It was increasingly difficult for elites to refuse to 'see' poverty, however, by the 1980s, as the effects of recurrent and deep economic woes began to bite. By the beginning of the new millennium, governing elites were forced to abandon the myth of Argentina as the Europe of Latin America as cyclical economic crises deepened and the government defaulted on its international debt commitments. Negative growth followed, along with a spectacular explosion of poverty and rising levels of conflict and violence.

Since 2002, a set of institutional responses, which we have elsewhere designated a post-neoliberal strategy for growth (Grugel and Riggirozzi 2007, 2009a; Grugel, Riggirozzi, and Thirkell-White 2008), has been put in place to try and mend the economy whilst also attending to the some aspects of poverty. Post-neoliberalism combines elements of statist governance, job creation, a strategy of inflation control through price fixing, cash transfers, and export promotion growth. They reflect to some extent a return to a pre-neoliberal concern with social peace through industrialization and the expansion of unemployment and welfare rather than a wholly new or focused pro-poor approach. But, crucially, this return to the paradigms of the past is taking place in a very different environment from the one in which Argentina's original welfare system emerged. Post-neoliberal concerns with poverty are due more to the decision of governing elites to seek to engineer a new phase of economic growth and co-opt the organized working class, than a direct concern with the very worst manifestations of poverty or the fate of the very poor or indigent. Equally, such policies should be understood as evidence of elite concerns about the stability of market-led, democratic governance in the wake of widespread and bitter social protest about rising poverty, social exclusion, and government failures.

The new pro-poor agenda is, in other words, linked with the mobilizational capacity of the working class and the newly unemployed and, in particular, the threat of anti-government mobilization from below on a scale that might lead to regime disintegration. These capacities were magnified in the period after 1999 as a result of a combination of inappropriate economic policies, some of which were sponsored and supported by international financial institutions, and an institutional matrix that ignored the process of rapid pauperization that was taking place. It was the mobilization of the 'newly' poor, we contend, that lay behind the social uprisings at the turn of the millennium and that contributed to the development of a new attempt at more socially-inclusive economic growth.

9.1 POVERTY AND INEQUALITY IN HISTORICAL PERSPECTIVE IN ARGENTINA

The political economy of development, growth, and poverty in Argentina cannot be fully separated from the trends that have characterized development across Latin America in general. Latin American societies are fundamentally unequal; that is, *grosso modo*, the misery which many of its inhabitants experience stems not from a shortage of national resources but from their exceptionally asymmetrical distribution and highly unequal access to capital, services, and basic goods (Birdsall and Lodoño 1998). Szekely and Birdsall attribute the high levels of poverty across Latin America in general primarily to high levels of historical inequality and the failure of governments to address persistent inequality in income and assets through the twentieth century (see also Chapter 10 below). Latin America is, as Centeno and Hoffman put it, a 'lop-sided continent'. In Argentina, however, this general trend has played out in very a particular way. Argentina experienced a process of state building, industrialization, and welfare creation that allowed it to minimize levels of extreme poverty (though not inequality) whilst co-opting the organizations of the urban working class with the consequence that poverty was not a political issue—and the very poor were largely without political voice—for most of the twentieth century. This history sets it somewhat apart from the rest of the region.

The origins of extreme inequality across Latin America lie in the liberal export-oriented period of growth and nation building which opened in the 1880s. In Argentina, liberalism led to the emergence of agrarian capitalism based on the production of wheat and beef for overseas markets. Export agriculture based around the port of Buenos Aires consolidated the dominance of the city over the rest of the country and the large farmers of central Argentina over smaller rural interests in the north and south of the country. So successful was the Argentine export economy in this period that Argentina was amongst the highest per capita income countries by 1913 (Maddison 2000). The success of agro-exports allowed Argentina to pull away from the rest of the region, attracted European migration on a massive scale, and cemented the social and political resources, as well as the economic capital, of the landed upper classes. Economic growth during this time was not accompanied by a strengthening of the state. Growth did not mean the emergence of a powerful set of institutions at the centre. The central state in Argentina did not 'learn to tax' as Kaldor (1963) put it. Instead, the country's federal structure meant that dominant local economic elites were able to remain in control of political, economic, and social assets. Over time, institutional weaknesses and elite privilege contributed not only to the periodically explosive class tensions that erupted but also to the country's difficulties in responding to the steady erosion of its export markets through the twentieth century.

Argentina was badly affected by the First World War and the global recession of the 1920s. The result, as in the rest of Latin America, was the (temporary) collapse of the oligarchy-dominated model of liberal economics and export agriculture in the 1930s. But the recession of the 1930s did not undo the federal pact in Argentina or fatally undermine the resources of landed elites. It did mean, however, that a new process of industrial growth was grafted onto the old agro-export strategy. This dualism was not the result of a conscious strategy of two-pronged growth so much as a contingent compromise that emerged in Argentina, as in the larger Latin American countries generally, around this time. The crisis of the 1930s was thus initially resolved by economic growth and the expansion of the internal market. It was encased by the 1940s in narratives of nationalism and class politics as the newly dominant Peronist coalition tried to use the state to further industrial expansion. In the absence of elite agreement—and indeed in the teeth of elite opposition—Peronism ended up strengthening the office of the presidency rather than the autonomous capacity of the state and implementing industrialization and statist policies by diktat rather than consensus.

Nationalism provided the frame for appealing to an emerging working class, along with elements of the expanding public sector middle class, as it appeared to offer access to social and economic rights and resources and prompted feelings of solidarity, belonging and identity—particularly important in Argentina given its history as a settler country with a large immigrant population. New social groups challenged dominant liberal ideologies, resulting in the rise of popular nationalism (Collier and Collier 1991; see Di Tella 1965). Rural and urban workers and those adversely affected by the export-led growth provided a growing constituency that opposed the 'liberal project' and economic internationalism. These groups provided support for the new nationalist/interventionist economic policies that, by the mid-1940s, were taking shape as an alternative to liberalism with the advent of Peronism. After Juan D. Peron won the elections in 1946, the government initiated an industrialization plan (Lewis 2005). Key to its success was that industrialization did not replace the needs for the export economy; quite the reverse, in fact, as the agricultural sector, which boomed again after 1945, provided some of the capital for industrial growth (although eventually foreign loans were also needed, marking the onset of a capital-dependence that has marked Argentine growth since the 1950s).

Labour-intensive industrialization and job creation were the keys to the rising living standards that Argentina experienced in the boom years between the 1940s and the 1970s. Prosperity was the result not just of economic growth (in fact growth overall was slower in Argentina than the Latin American average). It was tied to the establishment of welfare institutions that accompanied industrialization. Peronism created a welfare regime managed via labour unions, cooperatives, recreational groups, and other social network associations based on social insurance and the public provision of education and health care (Barrientos 2006; James 1988). By the 1950s, social insurance schemes covered around seventy per cent of the labour force (Mesa Lago 1978): more than any other country in the region.

Welfare politics cemented support for Peronism and laid the foundations for the popular mystique that Peronism continued to enjoy even after the death of its founder. At the same time, the creation of a dominant and stable political coalition based around the unions ensured the survival of redistributive institutions after the overthrow of Peron in a conservative military coup in 1955. In short, the introduction of protectionism and state control of industrial development provided the material means for the introduction of a form of citizenship based on social entitlements rather than independent liberal voice. Nationalism and populism came together to offer a very distinctive anti-poverty approach, based on nurturing the organizations of working class solidarity, the trade unions, and the political voice of the urban working class. Social policies were constructed around patterns of broad access in the areas of social spending—education and health—and enjoyed relatively stable budgets. The system of implementation via the unions, meanwhile, obviated the need to deliver through the state. But, precisely because welfare reinforced the links between governments and trade unions, social protection was mainly directed at the labour force (rather than the poor) and it tended to neglect the rural population and the poorest groups in society. This segmented provision of social and economic rights has contributed, over the long term, to the creation of lasting difficulties in terms of universalizing access to, and the public provision of, social welfare and justice; the very poor were left without protection. Nevertheless, the welfare system did mean that, overall, levels of poverty were much lower in Argentina than in the Latin American region as a whole, with only around eight per cent of the total population living below the national poverty line before 1970.

The political economy of Peronism ushered in a degree of contingent class compromise in Argentina, as agro-business and financial groups found they had little choice but to accept the new politics based in reality on the veto power of interest groups, rather than liberal or social democracy. Industrialization under the import substitution model remained heavily dependent on the surpluses provided by agricultural exports, which meant in turn not only external vulnerability but, more particularly, the retention of elite privilege and a continuous process of negotiation between power holders as the state tried to deliver for landowners and exporters (in practice if not rhetorically) as well as the urban working class (Teubal 2001, page 36). The weaknesses of the formal political system and the shifting balance between interest groups and social classes which actually determined the direction of policy contributed to the political instability and economic uncertainty that characterized the country until the 1990s.

It is important to recognize that rising living standards for the working class and the creation of a welfare regime were not accompanied by stable democracy or even non-democratic political stability. Quite the reverse, in fact, happened.

Peron's pro-working class populism was followed by a conservative revolution in 1955 that tried to re-impose a liberal economic order and to disarm the populist state. Despite the apparent eclipse of Peronism, however, the mobilized and organized working class resisted the overthrow of the trade union controlled welfare institutions (Teubal 2001). Distributional conflicts and social and political instability dominated the period after 1955, creating uncertainties as to the direction of political and economic governance. This led to erratic 'stop-go cycles' by the late 1960s, where economic expansion was followed by contraction and political stalemate that culminated in the military dictatorship between 1976 and 1983 (Basualdo 1987; O'Donnell 1973, 1982). The coup in March 1976 was fiercely anti-Peronist, leading to intense persecution of union leaders and party militants. The ruling Junta launched a 'Process of National Reorganization' that in political terms meant social demobilization through terror. Congress was closed, censorship imposed, trade unions banned, and state and municipal governments brought under military control.

9.2 THE NEO-LIBERAL TURN AND THE GATHERING CRISIS

Against this backdrop, the recurrent problems in financing the expansive social services created under Peronism came to the fore. The cyclical downturns and bouts of inflation that were a standard part of the import-substitution period across Latin America, coupled with the extreme boom-bust growth pattern that was a particular feature of the Argentine economy, contributed to stagnating investment in infrastructure, in health services and education in particular, and to a deterioration in living standards. It was in the context of deepening repression in the 1970s that the import substituting model slowed fatally under the weight of energy price hikes, the complexity of protectionist tariffs, the loss of industrial competitiveness, the difficulties of internal capitalization, and a general loss of faith in nationalist approaches to development (for different perspectives see Biglaiser and Brown 2005; O'Donnell 1979). Import substitution—and with it the promises of state investments in employment and public investment in education, health, and infrastructure—finally ground to a halt in the 1980s debt crisis as credit shortages forced Argentina to default on its debt. There followed a period of intense economic instability, and with it, the emergence of poverty on an unprecedented scale. The percentage of the population living in poverty tripled between 1980 and 1990, by which time it constituted twenty-nine per cent of the total population. This was the backdrop to Peronism's embrace of orthodox economics in the 1990s, to the horror of its traditional working class voters, and the wholesale adoption of Washington Consensus policies.

The failure of import substitution projects, together with severe repression of the unions and the Left under the dictatorship (1976–83) opened a space in Argentina for the introduction of new ideas of political and economic liberalization, assisted by the weaknesses of the first democratically elected government of Raul Alfonsín (1983–89) and its inability to construct a coalition around heterodox approaches to stabilization. In the resulting hyper-inflationary chaos, the benefits of adopting IFI-sponsored solutions to crisis seemed clear. In fact, such was Argentina's willingness to embrace the consensus that Morley, Machado, and Pettinato (1999) argue that, of all of Latin America, it was Argentina that conformed most closely with an ideal-type, neo-liberal state.

For much of the 1980s the standard prescriptions for development across the developing world (Chapter 2 above) focused on shrinking the state, or reducing the scope (and cost) of its activities. Instead, a minimal 'regulation' state was to provide the basis for effective market-led governance (Cerny 1995). The primary goal of the neo-liberal orthodoxy was thus to reform the relationship between the state and the market. The role of the state was reduced to the provision of the rule of law and core public goods; and, crucially, the state was seen as operating best in terms of policy decisions when it was insulated from 'politics' and popular pressures. A leaner, more focused state, it was thought, would emerge, and to compensate for the elimination of 'wasteful' welfare schemes and tighter fiscal discipline, a range of safety net pro-poor public services, different in concept and mode of delivery and aimed at different social groups from the more traditional welfarist policies of earlier years, would be introduced.

The introduction of neo-liberalism in Argentina was only possible after 1989 as a result of societal exhaustion caused by brutal dictatorship followed by hyper-inflation and a generalized sense of 'urgency' that the government of Carlos Menem, apparently committed to the new liberalism, manipulated to his advantage (Palermo and Novaro 1996, page 124). The state was able, almost for the first time, to impose pay settlements from above through weakening trade union power (Acuña and Smith 1994) and strengthening executive authority. Following the decision to bring the presidential succession forward in 1989, the state reform and economic emergency laws granted power to the executive to modify critical aspects of economic and socio-political relations simply by presidential decree. As a result, Menem suspended state subsidies for industrial promotion, allowed foreign investors to compete in Argentina on equal terms with national capitalism and downsized the public administration simply by presidential decree (see Bambaci, Saront, and Tommasi 2002). In contrast to his predecessor who issued ten decrees, Menem enforced a total of 308, ranging from deregulation to privatization and tax collection (Ferreira Rubio and Goretti 1996). He also neutralized the opposition of domestic firms, especially from those dependent on state protection such as textiles, electronics, and auto-parts and cut away at the collective bargaining capacity of the trade unions by negotiating strategically with individual union leaders who won concessions in return for support. At the same time, the government managed to build an alliance with the newer business groups that were able to benefit from the liberalization of trade and the privatization of state-owned assets, companies that were largely less dependent on the domestic market and employed fewer manual and semi-skilled workers (Acuña, Galiani, and Tommasi 2006, pages 21–3; Murillo 1997).

More than anything else, it was the Convertibility Plan that sealed Argentina's new liberal economy. Introduced in 1991, the Plan pegged the Argentine peso to the dollar and thus created the conditions for currency stability, reducing annual inflation from 200 per cent in 1989 to less than five per cent by 1994 (Pastor and Wise 2004, page 8). At the same time, the introduction of the Plan convinced the IFIs of Argentina's commitment to reform and they recommenced their activities in the country. The global financial enthusiasm for emerging markets in the early 1990s, meanwhile, led to a huge influx of foreign investment, mainly in the newly privatized sectors of the economy, climbing from US$3.2 billion in 1991 to US$11 billion in 1992, and to US$10.7 billion in 1993 (Rock 2002, page 65).

What were the effects of these dramatic changes to the political economy of Argentina on growth, welfare, and poverty? Macro-economic stability, together with the return of credit, led to an immediate increase in consumption and to a period of economic growth. Between 1991 and 1995 growth was in excess of four per cent per year—as high as the 'golden period' of economic expansion in the 1940s. But, as in Latin America as a whole, Washington Consensus results were negative in terms of social equity (Huber and Solt 2004) and de-industrialization, privatization, financial liberalization, and welfare reform had particularly nefarious consequences. Argentina had prospered in the period 1940–70 due to a combination of growth, public expenditure, and near-universal welfare. By contrast, growth in the early 1990s was accompanied by the shrinking of the state. The federal government gradually divested itself of responsibility for social service provision and social services such as education and health were passed onto state government as a way of reducing public expenditure. The first consequence of this was widespread job losses in the public sector. The federal government was thus able to shed more than 200,000 jobs between 1990 and 1992, of which only around forty per cent of workers were re-hired by state governments (Rock 2002).

Meanwhile, the privatization of public utilities and pensions, and the reform of social security, intensified the social exclusion experienced by the growing number of workers excluded from formal sector employment (Birdsall, de la Torre, and Menezes 2008). Whilst the residual power of the unions meant that the government had to retain a fully funded tier managed by trade unions (Cortés and Marshall 1999), this concession did nothing to prevent the impoverishment of non-unionized workers, whose living standards plummeted under the impact of labour market and public sector reform. So, if the traditional working class did badly, the very poorest groups in society fared worse—and, most significantly this group expanded rapidly in number. Children and young people paid a particularly heavy price as attendance at schools began to decline and the numbers of children working in risky and exploitative industries increased. According to a UNICEF report on Argentina in 2002:

> Fifty three per cent of children and young people under 18, more than 6 million live in poor households... 46.7 per cent of the almost 14 million of poor people in the country are minors who belong to families that do not have sufficient income to obtain basic goods such as housing, warm clothes, health, and education.
>
> (UNICEF 2002)

The very poor and the new poor were left behind even during the years of economic growth (World Bank 2003). But they reached breaking point after 1999. In this context, urban poverty and extreme poverty, both rose abruptly as the boom of the early to mid-1990s ended and recession set in. In 1998, just over twenty-five per cent of the population of Gran Buenos Aires, home to over ten million people, was officially living in poverty. By 2000, this had risen to over twenty-nine per cent and by 2001 to thirty-four per cent, before rising to a staggering fifty-two per cent in 2002.

For the poor, many of whom had only a decade earlier been part of the formal sector and employed in unionized industries, the dramatic decline in the quality of life was difficult to cope with. In the urban conurbation of Gran Buenos Aires, the percentage of the population without health care coverage reached an unprecedented forty per cent of poor neighbourhoods, and even included almost twenty per cent of middle class areas. This newly dispossessed group was to some extent cross-class—the poor now seemed to include not only ex-workers but also middle-class groups and public sector workers who had failed to find employment in the new market economy (Arrossi 1996; Feijoo 2001). The 'new poor' as they were quickly termed, were a politicized, vocal, and numerically significant social stratum, mainly composed of suddenly impoverished members of the lower middle class and upper working class who retained traditions of social organization and habits of mobilization (Feijoo 2001). Their sense of bewilderment and despair at the suddenness of their social collapse is hard to measure. Whilst most studies point to the emergence of new forms of political organization through roadblocks and spontaneous protest, there were also severe social costs to the new poverty. Some studies indicate a sudden rise in public and private violence as people struggled to cope with changed social and economic circumstances. Save the Children reported an upswing in societal and family violence and a study of schoolchildren within the Province of Buenos Aires revealed that thirty-three per cent of children felt abandoned or neglected, twenty-three per cent felt that they suffered emotional abuse, eighteen per cent felt physically mistreated at home, and two per cent reported sexual abuse. Rising levels of domestic violence were mirrored by increased police brutality in poor neighbourhoods and heavy-handed policing (Amnesty International 2002), and a willingness on the part of political authorities to sanction the kind of violent repression of popular organizations during the protests of 2001–2.

In short, Argentina experienced an unprecedented process of social decline, impoverishment, and collapse after 1995. The immediate causes were a combination of the effects of social policy reform, changes to the labour market, declining jobs and wages, and a slowdown of the economy in response to international crisis. Argentina's historically experienced high levels of income inequality that had been ignored or mediated through industrialization and welfare expansion between 1940 and 1970 had been intensified in the 1990s, whilst the process of economic growth was difficult to sustain and took places in sectors that did not take up the slack created by de-industrialization. By the end of the decade, the long-term trend of inequality, coupled with the negative growth as the economy entered recession, and the steady impoverishment of already vulnerable social groups marked the beginning of a critical confluence of factors that led ultimately to the crisis of 2001. Allied to this was a popular exhaustion with the discourses of market-led democracy (Grugel and Riggirozzi 2009b). Mass protest was virtually inevitable.

9.3 THE CATALYST FOR CHANGE: THE CRISIS OF 2001–2002 AND CRISIS RESPONSES[1]

The economic collapse of 2001 was, in strictly economic terms, a result of the rigidity of the Convertibility Plan, combined with the fallout from a fiscal policy that had been over-expansionary in the boom years of the early 1990s and had left the government few reserves on which to fall back in hard times. This exposure became critical after 1995, when the tequila crisis affected investor confidence in emerging markets and left the Argentine government with no instruments through which to mediate the onset of crisis and the problem of capital flight. The growing deficit was financed with increasing indebtedness. Argentina's recovery after 1995 was slow and, as a result, the economy was unable to withstand the effects of the Asian crisis of 1997, the Russian crisis of August 1998, and currency devaluation in Brazil, Argentina's main trade partner.

In 1999, a new centre-left government took office, led by Fernando De la Rúa of the *Alianza por el Trabajo, la Justicia y la Educación* (Alliance for Work, Justice and Education). The *Alianza* promised reform but, once in office, was too weak to resist external and domestic pressures to maintain the fixed exchange rate and the neo-liberal agenda. In an effort to demonstrate his commitment to financial stability, De la Rúa brought back Domingo Cavallo, the architect of Convertibility, as Minister of Finance in March 2001. Cavallo announced a 'Zero Deficit Plan', cutting pensions and public sector wages by as much as thirteen per cent, and reduced federal transfers to the provinces still further. Social protest followed. *Piquetero* (movements of the unemployed) uprisings, which had first emerged in Salta after the 1993 privatization of the national oil company, spread quickly across the country and street protests erupted to oppose the planned cuts, propose renationalization, and demand non-payment of the external debt. In November 2001, meanwhile, the IMF withdrew its support for the government which, in a desperate reaction to stop capital flight, imposed restrictions on bank withdrawals and money transfers, a policy that became known as the Corralito. In response, the middle classes joined the unemployed and public sector employees in seizing public spaces to demonstrate against the government. As Feijoo (2001) pointed out:

> In 2001, the new poor realized that their social collapse was unstoppable. They were going to carry on falling. It was at that point that new political actors appeared, representing the new poor . . . not the historical leaders of the working class because, when the labour market collapsed, the unions, as the political representatives of the working class, went with it.

One of the most visible groups within the new poor in the 1990s was the *piqueteros*, organizations of ex-workers with social and cultural ties to the trade union movement:

> *Piqueteros* are poor. But they don't belong to the historical world of marginality and structural poverty . . . Rather *piqueteros* are the consequence of the disarticulation of

[1] See Grugel and Riggirozzi (2007) and Riggirozzi (2009), which act as the inspiration for this section, for further details.

> the country's formal wage-earning working class. That explains why they are persistent and organized. They have historical links with organized socio-economic actors such as trade unions.
>
> (Interview conducted by Pia Riggirozzi, January 2006)

As a result, cooperation between *piqueteros* and trade unions was not uncommon, especially because the unions were themselves galvanized into action and joined the protests, leading to massive street demonstrations, the formation of vocal neighbourhood assemblies, and the emergence of a plethora of new sites of social struggle within disused factories and the neighbourhood. Protests spread rapidly across the country, with thousands of barter clubs based on non-official 'currencies' coming into existence, and some abandoned factories even went into production as cooperatives. In the end, then, it was popular protest by groups such as these against the withdrawal of the state, in the context of economic meltdown, that brought the Washington Consensus period to a close in Argentina in the early years of the twenty-first century. As GDP fell precipitously by over twenty per cent between 1999 and 2002, poverty, especially urban poverty mushroomed, reaching a staggering fifty-seven per cent in October 2002.

De la Rúa responded with a declaration of a state of siege and unleashed a wave of repression which led to over twenty deaths. The slogan of the demonstrations, *Que se vayan todos* ('Out with all of them'), was a measure of the enormous distance that had opened up between governing elites and society. Cavallo resigned, followed quickly by De la Rúa. In mid-December the country defaulted on its financial obligations and within two months the value of the peso had dropped by more than a third (it was to fall still further in the coming year). In the face of such extreme economic and social chaos, the political order collapsed: presidents came and went in quick succession, until a temporary parliament-led government under Peronist Eduardo Duhalde, previously leader of Congress, assumed some degree of institutional command in January 2002. The challenges facing the interim government were huge. In addition to the difficulties of managing the default and promoting growth, the government faced the very real possibility of social rebellion. Poverty continued to rise on a monthly basis and the number of people living in extreme poverty reached twenty-seven per cent in 2002, more than double the figure of just twelve months earlier.

In the face of this kind of social activism, Duhalde sought above all to restore traditional forms of governance and stability. Governmental concerns focused overwhelmingly on guaranteeing the survival of political order. As such, it seemed imperative to take control of the new sources of production, rein in the proliferation of alternative currencies and reintegrate the new social actors, even ones opposed to the system, such as *piqueteros*, into the formal channels of state-society networks. With this in mind, it is hardly surprising that the government rejected orthodox stabilization programmes which would have focused on regaining investor and IMF confidence, but would have risked alienating the government still further. Instead, Duhalde turned to old ideas and the residual legitimacy of the national development project that had been overturned in the 1980s and 1990s. This policy response, which may well have been instinctive and reflected the residual legitimacy of ideas associated with a golden period of growth and prosperity, marked a critical break with neo-liberalism.

Policies were thereafter informed by heterodox critiques of neo-liberalism and contingent responses to crisis, articulated inside Argentina by a broad range of independent economists (some of them belonging to the 'Fenix Group' from the Universidad de Buenos Aires) as well as by opposition groups including the *piqueteros* and unionists who were brought into dialogue as a way of building bridges with civil society. Whatever differences there may have been over the detail of policy, for all these actors industrial reactivation, and the generation of employment, was key to recovery. Duhalde also promised the introduction of some new pro-poor policies through state-sponsored, safety-net welfare policies and a renegotiation of the external debt. One of his first—and most symbolic—measures was to abandon convertibility and to convert bank deposits and debts into pesos. Effectively, this meant devaluation, and it was the most dramatic evidence of government commitment to domestic industry in more than fifteen years. It generated an important 'bounce back effect' in terms of exports and, in turn, stimulated the productivity of competitive tradable goods. This was accompanied by the introduction of a policy of price controls to encourage consumption and prevent inflation. These measures were followed by a twenty per cent tax on export earnings from agricultural commodities and hydrocarbons, the income from which was to serve, in part, as the basis for emergency social programmes. The Corralito was lifted in early December 2002. Following hard negotiations, a seventy per cent reduction in the debt to private creditors was agreed, and in January 2003 an arrangement was reached with the IMF for a US$3 billion loan. The administration was also able to resume payments to the World Bank and the International Development Bank, which, in turn, allowed new loans to come on stream in early 2003.

The devaluation of the Argentine peso was aided by changing dynamics within the international political economy. A dynamic upswing in the global economy led to favourable exchange terms in commodity markets, benefiting Argentina along with other developing countries. China's entry in the WTO in 2001 also opened markets. But while the international context created opportunities, the way development strategies unfolded depended on the domestic politics. In Argentina, the emergence of a strong domestic political alliance between the government and the so-called *Grupo Productivo* (Producers' Group), formed by representatives from industrial sectors, was decisive. The *Grupo Productivo* had developed as a lobby group in the 1990s in relation to the privatization policy and adopted a stronger line after the recession in 1998, arguing for policies to promote national businesses. It went on to become highly influential in shaping a new national economic strategy around the needs of domestic industry. The *Grupo* strongly supported devaluation and the reactivation of national industry by lowering the costs of production and fostering export and trade. As such, this alliance brought into the centre of the political and economic arena industries that provided substitutes for foreign imports and financial resources to back up government policies.

In order to stem the rising tide of political contention, meanwhile, the government launched a consensus-building initiative, the Mesa de Diálogo, in January 2002, with the support of the Catholic Church and the UNDP. Organized in thematic round tables, the Mesa encouraged inputs from a broad range of actors across society, including labour, business, NGOs, *piqueteros*, social movements, political parties, and religious groups. One of its most significant initiatives was to push for the adoption of state policies to foster social inclusion. According to Marcela Masnatta of the UNDP, a founder member: 'The most important achievement . . . was that we were able to agree . . . on a programme of Citizen Income, which was discussed as a universal right, a form of social inclusion. The recommendation from the Mesa was that the state should guarantee a minimum income to all citizens.' The Mesa went on to recommend three specific areas for urgent action: food supplies, medicines, and the creation of income subsidies for the poorest. These recommendations fed into the creation of the *Programa Jefas y Jefes de Hogares Desempleados* (Programme for Male and Female Unemployed Households), set up in January 2002 initially with funds from export tax revenue, supplemented after January 2003 with World Bank loans. Significantly, the Jefas y Jefes programme broke the traditional link between welfare, employment, and the trade unions. It was a workfare scheme which offered 150 pesos a month (US$50) to families in exchange for participation in projects such as community service, construction, school maintenance, rebuilding health facilities, road works, communal kitchens, housebuilding, and even more small-scale production. It reflected the fact that the casualization of labour in the 1990s had already created a vast pool of low paid workers; to this was added the vast numbers of those suddenly without jobs or income. In this context, working-class concerns were no longer limited to wages or employment. Jefas y Jefes quickly reached two million people. As an immediate response to extreme crisis, it was remarkably effective, although over time it became part of traditionally cliental networks of welfare distribution, operating to favour Peronist supporters and creating a degree of control over the unemployed. Other, more minor, policies followed, including Remediar, supported by the IDB, which organized the distribution of basic medicines to the poorest social groups. Overall, these policies were central in re-establishing the credibility of the state and in bringing about the first signs of economic recovery in early 2003.

9.4 CONSOLIDATING THE POST-NEOLIBERAL PARADIGM

In May 2003 the interim administration gave way to the elected government of Nestor Kirchner, Peronist ex-governor of the province of Santa Cruz. Kirchner, who campaigned on a clearly anti-neoliberal programme, was one of two Peronist candidates; the other was ex-president Carlos Menem, who retained a significant level of support within the party machine. First-round results indicated a split Peronist vote, with twenty-four per cent for Menem and twenty-two per cent for Kirchner, the rest of the votes being scattered among other candidates. Given that no one had received the necessary forty-five per cent support to win the elections outright, a run-off was scheduled between Menem and Kirchner. But Menem pulled out before the second round could take place, leaving Kirchner to become president by default and in an apparently weak position. Despite these inauspicious beginnings, in less than three months Kirchner enjoyed an eighty per cent support rating, almost certainly explained by his image as a socially conscious, socially responsible politician and his forthright commitment to job creation and domestic industry.

Committed from the outset to continuing the policies initiated by Duhalde, Kirchner retained Roberto Lavagna, regarded as the chief architect of the economic recovery in 2002–3, as Minister of the Economy until 2005. Initially in conjunction with Lavagna, Kirchner focused government policy on rebuilding Argentina's industrial base, public works, and public services; and, in a clear reversal of Menemismo, the state began to take on a role in stimulating economic growth. The government also sought to re-negotiate the terms under which some foreign companies operated the public services privatized in the 1990s. The exchange rate proved a particularly critical tool of government policy, and taxes on the export sector were increased in order to raise revenue. A judicious devaluation of the peso in January 2002, meanwhile, allowed the export boom to continue. Meanwhile, in order to ensure social support, Kirchner effectively deployed a combination of pro-poor rhetoric and nationalism that, like Peronism in the 1940s, proved useful for resolving distributive conflicts (Itzigsohn and vom Hau 2006, page 204), allowed the government to present itself as a decisive break with the neo-liberal era, and mobilized electoral support and public opinion. Even the pro-poor social investments inherited from the past were turned into political capital for the government.

Paradoxically, though, and in marked contrast to the earlier period of nationalist development, contemporary nationalism was presented under Kirchner as fully compatible with markets and global integration. The circle was squared in two ways. In the first place, the favourable international climate for Argentine exports meant that the outside world was seen as supportive of internal economic development. Second, the growth of the domestic market, based on the production of goods produced inside Argentina, was job-creating. Furthermore, export expansion and domestic industrial expansion meant that Kirchner was able to reduce dependency on external funding. So, in contrast to the 1990s when the government of Carlos Menem was portrayed as having effectively given national control of interest rates and the currency in order to satisfy foreign investors, Kirchner was able to satisfy a range of national aspirations through commitment to flexible exchange rates and a more expansive monetary policy. Thanks in part to the slack in the economy and the room for domestic expansion, combined with the hugely favourable international environment, growth took off and reached nine per cent a year between 2003 and 2007.

As Argentina became less dependent on fresh money from the IFIs, the government's bargaining capacity vis-à-vis the IFIs increased. Economic recovery and the competitiveness of national industry gave the state more control over the economy, allowing for higher levels of state investment, an expansion of public works and the introduction of forms of tighter regulation over public service companies and banks; policies that not only contradicted IMF rules but also made clear that Argentina was no longer willing to tolerate foreign creditors dictating national economic norms. At the same time, these policies reduced the leverage of the IMF as 'lender of last resort'. Kirchner's strategy became known as *desendeudamiento* (de-borrowing) meaning the renegotiation of existing debt with international institutions and private creditors on as favourable terms as possible, without asking for any further loan and cancelling payments with national reserves. In the end, the US$9.8 billion debt was settled in December 2005, creating the image inside Argentina that a new, more autonomous period of development was opening up (Riggirozzi 2007, page 137; also Cooper and Momani 2005). Kirchner's decision to seek independence from IMF pressure by paying the debt owes as much to questions of political management as economic policy. Nurturing an image of a sovereign state in Argentina was important in a country where the electorate had been so injured by external-induced reform programmes. At the same time, it genuinely allowed the government much greater room for manoeuvre, economically, politically, and even diplomatically. As a result of his success, Kirchner was able to hand the office of the presidency over to his wife, Cristina Fernandez, elected on a programme of continuity, in October 2007.

Overall, the recovery from the crisis opened a new cycle of political economy in Argentina. Revenue acquired after 2003 as a result of export-led economic growth has allowed the government to increase welfare spending on unemployment insurance and pension benefits in the public sector, raise transport subsidies, fix the costs of and increase state participation in various public services, and invest in public works. But, while the style of government is nationalist, both Kirchner, who died in late 2010, and Fernandez were and are committed to conservative fiscal policies. As a result, social policies under the new *desarrollismo* have clear limits (Grugel and Riggirozzi 2007). Growth and falling levels of poverty allowed the government to carry out some politically sensitive reforms—mainly in the areas of tax, welfare, and institutional and human rights reforms. Steps have been taken towards a re-regulation of the labour market and some reform has been introduced to the two-pillar retirement system, fostering the return of workers to the public system, and extending the numbers of non-contributory pensions. Collective bargaining has been re-introduced in the hope of encouraging steady, but controlled, wage increases, and the tripartite council for defining the level of minimum wages has been reintroduced, allowing the minimum wage to reach three times its 2003 level by 2008. But the costs of these policies have been passed on to industry for the most part and the state has avoided big increases in its social security budget (Cortes 2009). As a result, the pro-poor dividend engineered by the new post-neoliberalism has mainly benefited the waged, formal sector workers, taking them out of poverty but leaving workers in precarious and informal jobs with low pay without the benefits of social protection. At the same time, the targeted anti-poverty programmes have not been extended (though they have not been closed) and they remain clearly insufficient for tackling income poverty. Cash transfers remained unchanged in spite of inflation, meanwhile, with the result that inflation has eaten away at their worth. By 2007, the value of the cash benefits was down to fifteen per cent of the minimum wage (Cortes 2009).

9.5 CONCLUSION

The extreme crisis of governance that opened in 2001 and 2002 is over. Between them, the Kirchner/Fernandez governments have been able to manage the two principal governance challenges, namely social desperation on a scale that threatened to bring down the political system and the need for a new macroeconomic matrix. As a result, a partial but still unstable new political economy has emerged; but the cost has been an extraordinary accumulation of executive power that sometimes risks falling into (semi-democratic) authoritarianism. And, with the euphoria of recovery over, it is time to ask about the long-term sustainability of post-neoliberalism and its success in pro-poor terms.

There is little doubt of the success of the post-crisis governments in reasserting the command and capacity of the state in the new political economy. Effective and well-targeted policies combined with nationalism to manage the crisis in a way that was broadly sensitive to the aspirations of the poor. But *effective* policies after crisis do not necessarily equal *sustainability* over the long term. The first depends upon the rapid introduction of politically legitimate crisis-resolving strategies; the second on the institutionalization of a coherent and consensual programme over the longer term. There are few signs that post-neoliberalism is either fully consensual or legitimate domestically. There are criticisms concerning the process of decision-making and the concentration of power in executive hands, for example, and growing opposition, especially from agro-export elites who have paid the costs of the Kirchner/Fernandez strategy of expanding welfare while maintaining fiscally conservative policies. These groups are more central than ever to the economy because of record commodity prices worldwide and a favourable exchange rate; yet they remain outside the governing coalition and it is doubtful whether they could ever be brought in, given their traditional hostility to Peronism. Decades of cultural and social hostility between Peronism and the landed elite explain the hostility to the Kirchner/Fernandez decision to raise export taxes, as much as opposition to the tax itself. This crisis exploded in 2008, shortly after Cristina Fernandez took office in a fierce protest against government policy of increasing the tax burden further, leading, once again, to shortages, roadblocks, and protests, this time by the wealthy rather than the poor.

As well as disagreements over tax, there is no real consensus about how to continue to finance social spending, or indeed what the contours of the new social policy should be. The government seems to take a view that social spending can be paid for through increasing tax on exports, certainly an approach that means that its core electorate wins benefits without paying costs. But, as the protests of 2008 indicate, this opens up a range of social tensions that are not always easily managed by the government. Yet there is no doubt that export tax is less contentious than the option of increasing taxation on income and wealth, proposals that have traditionally been discarded in Latin America because of elite opposition.

With regard to poverty, meanwhile, the first point to note, perhaps, is that, from a purely governance perspective, the poverty issue seems to have been 'managed' successfully. Recent growth has undoubtedly been job-creating and, therefore, pro-poor. Many of the new poor have, at least temporarily, been bought off by jobs and the prospect of some wage increases. Cortes (2009) suggests:

> The poverty question is losing ground on the policy agenda as state social intervention is shifting—although not always explicitly—away from 'poverty' toward 'labor issues'. In this respect, Argentina's emerging model of social policy is based on a dichotomy between the introduction of measures that enhance rights for formal sector workers while neglecting the rest of the labor force, thereby intensifying the formal/informal labor divide.

It is not hard to see that not nearly enough has been achieved to reduce overall levels of poverty and indigence. The clock has not been turned back. Rather

Argentina seems to have accommodated itself to accepting that poverty is now here to stay: the debate turns on how much and whom it affects. Certainly Kirchner's post-neoliberal responses have not done enough for the extremely poor, who largely remain outside the formal labour market. What of the 'new poor' who played such an important political role in the crisis? The recovery has cut away at the bonds of working class–middle class solidarity that emerged in 2001 and the middle classes have, on the whole, recovered relatively quickly. The category of 'new poor' is losing, if it has not already lost, its coherence as a distinct social category. The most badly affected of the working class, especially those who were already part of the long-term unemployed before 2001 or were dependent on casual and informal work, remain firmly in the grip of poverty and social exclusion. These groups still remain in or near destitution. The government's own figures indicate that 33.8 per cent of the population remains below the poverty line, including 12.2 per cent who are indigent, that is, unable to meet their own basic needs of food, health, and housing. A further 9.1 per cent of the population lives only just above the poverty line (with annual incomes between 745 and 931 Argentine pesos or approximately US$243 and US$304). Additionally, post-neoliberalism recovery policies do not address directly the pockets of embedded unemployment amongst young people, both middle and working class, who paid an inordinately heavy price in the crisis of 2001–2, many of whom are still without decent jobs. There is also an issue generally around the quality of jobs generated in the recovery after 2003, which are often temporary and without the welfare benefits that were once regarded as standard in Argentina. Current government figures point to a phenomenal 47.5 per cent of workers without social insurance, a figure that has not changed since 2002.

So, while it is the case that the number of people living in poverty has fallen, the drop is far more modest than might have been expected in view of the rate of economic growth. Not surprisingly, the centre-left opposition to Kirchner has focused its critique of the government on its failure to generate long-term responses and in particular quality jobs. In their study of early post-neoliberalism, Gerchunoff and Aguirre are clear that export-led, bounce-back growth of the period 2003–7 will not, on its own, solve the poverty problem in Argentina:

> Are we witnessing a new positive connection between material progress and social progress in a new trickle down fashion? It depends on how we define things. If by trickle down we understand that economic growth will increase sources of employment . . . the answer is yes. If more ambitiously we understand that this will reduce the gap between rich and poor and that will bring a solution to those who lack job qualifications and lag behind in the job market, the answer is no.

Not much has changed for us to disagree with that view. Moreover, the decline in international prices for Argentine exports after 2008 is only likely to make the problem more acute. It is clear that new forms of imaginative and well-funded welfare and education schemes are required to repair the social damage created by the combined effects of a decade of neo-liberalism and economic meltdown. But it is equally the case that the government's commitment to fiscal conservatism, combined with its need to keep the agro-exporters at least moderately happy, makes this extremely difficult, if not impossible.

10

Bolivia

Paul Mosley[1]

10.1 INTRODUCTION: POLITICAL VIOLENCE AND VARIETIES OF STABILIZATION EXPERIENCE

On 12 and 13 October 2003, over sixty people[2] were killed in a confrontation between civilian protesters and the armed forces in the city of El Alto, Bolivia. The incident marked the climax of a series of disturbances which at the time of writing still continue, and which mark Bolivia as one of the gravest sufferers, in human terms, from the wave of capital-account crises which have buffeted the developing world since their onset in East Asia in 1997, and which have now spread to peripheral countries of Europe including Latvia, Ireland, Greece, Portugal, and more recently Italy. In this chapter we seek to understand the linkages between the economy, the political system, and the experience of poverty with reference to the case of Bolivia, where the recent crisis has restored an ancestral pattern of instability following an apparently successful escape from this vicious circle during the 1990s. Our concern is both to explain the particularities of why recovery has proved so elusive in Bolivia, and also in more general terms to illustrate what the lessons may be for institutions and governments which may have responsibility for dealing with crises of this type in the future.

Our analytical approach is to visualize developing countries as being vulnerable to being caught in a 'poverty trap'—an interactive process between poverty and its causes, which if a crisis is wrongly handled may enmesh them in a long-term process of decline. 'Poverty trap' models have recently re-emerged in the development literature as explanations of the persistence of poverty in individuals and countries, but they typically do not contain political variables. What is attempted here is in general terms to explain the persistence of crisis in terms of the working of political institutions as well as economic factors, and in specific terms to ask whether and how more pro-poor patterns of policy might in specific cases such as Bolivia's be an effective instrument for escaping from such a crisis. The original

[1] Especial thanks to the following: Irina Aliaga, Ramiro Alvarez, Jean Grugel, Fernando Landa, Julio Loayza, Reynaldo Marconi, Juan Antonio Morales, Walter Nunez, Rodney Pereira, Pia Riggirozzi, Fernando Romero, Esteban Vesperoni, and seminar participants in Essex and UDAPE (La Paz). All translations from Spanish are mine unless otherwise stated.

[2] Some accounts record more than eighty deaths in this incident alone, for example Suarez (2003).

'poverty trap' or vicious circle of poverty' literature, starting with Nurkse (1953), uses a causal mechanism in which, in its simplest form, low income causes low investment, which perpetuates low income (as illustrated in the left-hand part of Figure 10.1). More recent versions of the vicious circle, including Carter and May (1999), World Bank (2000), and Barrett and Carter (2006), have added additional mechanisms to this vicious circle, of an essentially economic nature.[3] Our own argument develops this approach by suggesting that what Bolivia has been caught in, since it became enmeshed in the global crisis, is a *political poverty trap*. As in a conventional poverty trap model, poverty remained high on account of low and unstable investment rates; but what kept investment rates low was in part a collapse of trust in the political process to achieve democratic decision making, an erosion of the institutional structure, and riot-type conflict, all of which were aggravated by economic crisis. Policy choices (at both the macro and the micro level) provide a potential escape from this trap, and it will be a major objective to investigate the extent to which events in Bolivia were the consequence of a failure to take advantage of these opportunities.

The 'political poverty trap' approach specified in (b) forms the core of our general explanatory story. In the Bolivian case, two additional country-specific factors—relationships with aid donors, and the geographical concentration of poverty and political militancy—play an important part both in setting the initial conditions and in determining the course of the drama. These initial conditions are examined in section 2. In section 3, we test the poverty trap model pictured in Figure 10.2 against the available data for Bolivia. Section 4 takes a comparative perspective and

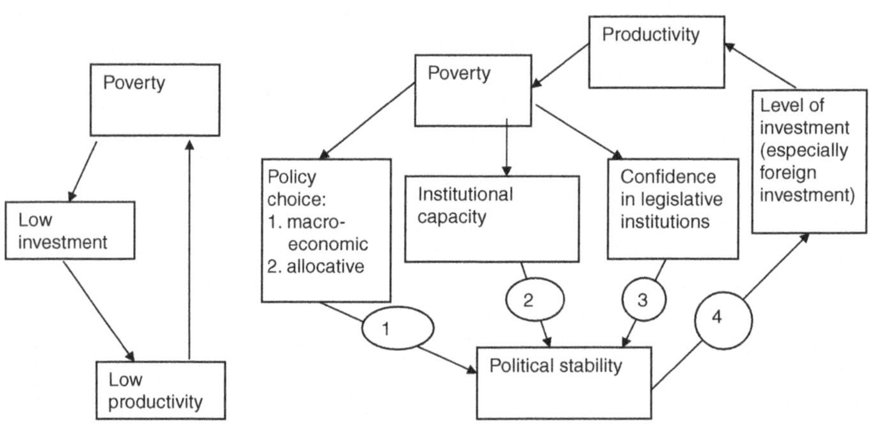

Figure 10.1 Varieties of poverty trap.
(a) Basic economic (as per Nurkse 1953) **(b)** Politico-economic.

[3] These include linkages from poverty to health, participation in labour markets, risk management capacity, and absence of group insurance mechanisms. For a discussion of recent poverty trap models see Barrett and Carter (2006) or Mosley, Petterson, and van de Walle (2006).

asks whether the variables in the poverty trap model help to explain why Bolivia experienced a particularly severe political and economic crisis between 2000 and 2005 in comparison to other countries afflicted by the 'East Asian' crisis, and in particular whether other countries avoided the crisis by taking up options which were available to but neglected by Bolivia. Section 5 concludes.

10.2 THE 2000–2006 CRISIS IN ITS LONG-TERM SETTING

Bolivia's democratic state, established in 1825, has a notorious record of political instability, fragility, and reversion to a totalitarian model. During the hundred and sixty years from independence to the hyperinflation of 1985 there were around 150 changes of government (deMesa, Gisbert, and Mesa 2003), and a number of episodes of military dictatorship. Between 1952 and 1985 a whole succession of governments sought to break the constraints to the country's persistently poor economic development performance by means of structuralist measures, including the thoroughgoing land reform of Victor Paz Estenssoro in 1952, nationalization of the mines in the same year and of the country's natural gas reserves in 1965, and persistent and widespread controls on the exchange rate and other 'key prices'. At the onset of the global structural adjustment process, in the early 1980s, the government initially resisted pressures for expenditure cuts and price de-control, and the failure of these attempts led eventually to one of the great hyperinflations of modern times, reaching its peak at an annual rate of 24,000 per cent in August 1985.

As might have been expected, the scale of deflation and liberalization required to achieve economic stabilization was exceptionally painful, and in particular involved massive production and employment cuts in the country's former main export staples—the tin and silver mines.[4] But gradually, by these means, both the polity and the economy came back towards normality: inflation was brought under control, growth in the real economy was positive from 1987 until the onset of the global crisis in 2000, and most of the elected governments of this period, contrary to Bolivian precedent, ran their full four-year term. Of these administrations, the most radical in its liberalizing measures was that of Gonzalo Sanchez de Losada, a mining millionaire,[5] between 1993 and 1997, which initiated (under the so-called 'Law 21060') the privatization of the main public utilities (oil and gas, telephones, electricity, and water) and drastically reduced controls on trade and capital movements. It was during this period that the Managing Director of the IMF expressed his hope that Bolivia would sustain its economic

[4] Chavez (1992, page 6) estimates the number of tin miners put out of work at 23,000 out of a workforce of 30,000 or seventy per cent, and Morales (1991) at eighty per cent. Only about 2,000 tin miners are now at work.

[5] It is relevant to the subsequent argument that Sanchez de Losada had been a major gainer in the privatization process in Bolivian mining. He had bought the assets of the few mines which remained profitable after the 1985 hyperinflation, and had amalgamated them into a profitable private corporation known as CORPOSUR.

growth, and convert itself into an 'Andean jaguar', by analogy with the East Asian 'tiger economies'.[6]

But this recovery had risks embedded within it. The shift from a growth pattern based on mineral exports to an oil and gas-based economy posed major problems for employment creation and poverty reduction, since mining is labour intensive, whereas the oil and natural gas sector is capital-intensive (Table 10.1). And within both food and cash-crop agriculture, which is also labour-intensive, structural adjustment stimulated little growth,[7] making the problem worse. Also, the geographical distribution of gains went to the rich east rather than the poor *altiplano* in the west, where most indigenous Aymara and Quechua people lived. As a consequence, inequality, and specifically inter-ethnic and inter-regional inequality, grew through the period of stability from 1986 to 2000, and in a way that was openly increased by the government's acts of privatization. Poverty has been measured in Bolivia over a much less lengthy period than inequality; but of the available measures of poverty, headcount poverty and poverty measured by access to health and education services appear to have diminished over the period prior to 1999, so that growth over this period can be characterized as (rather weakly) pro-poor (Landa and Jimenez 2005).

The governments of this period, aware of these long-term threats, made gestures in the direction of self-protection, including decentralization (van Cott 2002), extravagant growth in public sector employment, the pioneering Fondo de Inversion Social (Social Investment Fund), which channeled aid funds into the development of social infrastructure for low income groups, and support for a number of innovative ventures in microfinance (Mosley 2001; Marconi and Mosley 2006), in which Bolivia has a reasonable claim to be a global market leader. All of these initiatives were joint ventures with the aid donors, on whom Bolivia is much more dependent than any other Latin American country,[8] and who encouraged the government to feel that it could be proud of what it was achieving. They turned out, however, not to be enough.

10.3 THE CRISIS OF 1999–2005, AND ALTERNATIVE EXPLANATIONS OF ITS 'PERSISTENCE'

The 'East Asian crisis', having arrived in Latin America via Brazil at the beginning of 1999, hit Bolivia later still, in the second half of the year. Once it arrived, however, its effects were severe: indeed, there was a return to the chronic

[6] In a speech in La Paz in June 1996: Lazarte Rojas 2005, page 18.

[7] The one very important exception to this generalization is the coca industry, which grew fast during the period of structural adjustment and is very labour-intensive. De Franco and Godoy (1990) calculated by means of a computable general equilibrium model that a ten per cent increase in cocaine production raises Bolivian GDP by two per cent and lowers Bolivian unemployment by six per cent (Painter 1994, page 56).

[8] Bolivia has a ratio of aid to GNP of nearly nine per cent (Table 5.2 above); no other Latin American country has a ratio of more than one per cent, and the average for the continent as a whole is 0.2 per cent.

Table 10.1 Bolivia 1986–2004: growth of output and employment.

	Whole economy		Agriculture		Mining		Petroleum and gas	
	Average growth of output	Average growth of employment (private sector only)	Average growth of output	Average growth of employment*	Average growth of output	Average growth of employment	Average growth of output	Average growth of employment
1995–8	4.7	−1.7	2.1	nd	0.0	−1.1	5.6	−0.6
1999–2004	2.1	1.0	2.9	2.7	−1.6	0.1	9.5	−0.3
2004–9	4.6		2.9		18.8		2.6	

Annual average growth rates

Source: Instituto Nacional de Estadistica, Anuario Estadistico 2005, Tables 4.02.01.01 and 3.04.05.01, updated for surrounding years.

* Fruits, vegetables, grains, dairy, and meat products

economic and political instability which had characterized the years prior to 1985. The next four years were all years of falling per capita GDP, five new presidents came and went in the following five years, and lethal political violence occurred in every year except 2000, with a climax in 2003 (Table 10.2).

The first episodes of severe civil violence occurred in 2000, when four people were killed in protests against price increases imposed by the recently-privatized water authority in Cochabamba.[9] In February 2003, a further thirty were killed in rioting in La Paz, most of them policemen who had refused to implement an order to disperse low-paid workers protesting against a proposed extension of the income tax net, whereupon the army was sent in.[10] The climactic confrontation between the security forces and civil society took place in October 2003. It followed the announcement of a general strike in El Alto and La Paz by the COB (*Central Obrera Boliviana*—Bolivian Confederation of Trade Unions) in protest against a government plan to export Bolivian natural gas in an unprocessed state through Chile. The army, under government orders, broke a blockade of the Senkata petroleum depot, on the south side of El Alto, by force on 13 October, and this action escalated into a more general insurrection across the whole of El Alto in which, on 13 and 14 October, at least fifty-nine people were killed.[11] On 14 October, the vice-president, Carlos Mesa, detached himself from the government in the light of the killings, and when, on 17 October, President Sanchez de Losada fled the country to escape what had become a lynch mob, Mesa was sworn in as interim president. His 21-month administration ended also with a general strike initiated in El Alto, in June 2005.[12] The election of the country's first Aymara-Indian president, Evo Morales, has not ended the climate of instability: in sectarian rioting between groups of miners in Oruro in October 2006, a further fourteen persons were killed, and two more died in demonstrations in Cochabamba in January 2007.[13]

Why did these incidents of political violence occur, and what is their broader importance for understanding the politics of poverty reduction? At the level of proximate causes, one account given in the wake of the February 2003 violence by the Governor of the Central Bank, Juan Antonio Morales, stressed the long-term

[9] These episodes are described in detail in *Pulso*, issues 37 through 39, 7–27 April 2000.

[10] The proposed income tax increases were part of the conditionality imposed by an IMF mission, which had proposed to provide a $3.9 PRGF (Poverty Reduction and Growth Facility) credit in return for credible reductions in Bolivia's fiscal deficit of 8.5 per cent of GDP. Before the proposal could be implemented, it was leaked to the press and, when a riot was started by students in the Plaza Murillo, the La Paz square where the presidential palace stands, the police, who were amongst the low-paid workers at risk of being brought into the income tax net under the new proposals, did not defend the palace, and stood aside. Miguel Lora, *Pulso*, 7–13 February 2003, page 11.

[11] For a very simplified geography of El Alto, see Figure 10.3 below. A detailed overview of the events of 'Black October' is given in the special issue of *La Prensa* for 23 December 2003. Some eyewitness accounts also exist in book form, for example Garcia, Prada, and Tapia (2004).

[12] The worst dispute was between members of mining cooperatives and of a privatized mining company working on different levels of a tin mine in Huanuni, near Oruro, in which twelve miners were killed and more than 60 injured. The analysis of this incident in 'Vuelve la Inestabilidad a Bolivia', *Pulso* 368 (6–12 October 2006), pages 5 and 12–13, concluded that Bolivia has returned to 'pure ungovernability' and 'is [once again] gently advancing towards the abyss'.

[13] See *Bolivia Rising* (http://boliviarising.Blogspot.com/2007/01/democracy-is-people-antonio-peredo.htmlJanuary 2007.

Table 10.2 Bolivia: evolution of the economy in relation to elections and political violence, 1997–2009.

	1998	2000	2001	2002	2003	2004	2005	2006	2007	2008	2009
Real economy											
Growth	1070	1016	949	883	870	960		1100			
GNP per capita (in current US $)											
Real GDP growth (%): absolute (at m.p.)	5.2	2.4	0.0	2.7	4.1	4.1	4.4	4.8	4.5	6.1	3.3
Per capita		−0.7	−6.6	−7	−1.5	0.4	0.2	2.8			
Investment	23.8	17.5	13.5	15.6	13.6	13.4	14.3	13.7	14.8	16.5	16.5
Investment/GNP (%)											
Foreign investment/GNP (%)	11.9	10.7	8.7	8.3	4.5						
Poverty indicators	5.3	4.8	5.2	5.4	8.0		5.4	5.0	5.1		
Urban unemployment rate (INE) (%)		6.0			13.5						
Headcount poverty (INE) (%)		65.5	64.3	63.3	64.1	63.6	60.6	59.9	60.1	59.2	58.3
Extreme poverty (%)		45.1	38.8	39.5	34.5		38.1	37.6	37.7	32.7	31.8
Gini coefficient of inequality (%)	62.7	64.4	61.5	63.5	62.4	61.4	60.1				
Political changes and incidence of violence											
Changes of government			Vice-President Quiroga succeeds on death of Banzer		June: election won by Sanchez de Losada. October: Sanchez de Losada resigns and flees from country after El Alto riots. His Vice-President, Carlos Mesa, takes over.		June: Carlos Mesa resigns following further riots in El Alto. Provisional govt appointed under Eduardo Rodrigues (chief justice) December general election: won by MAS under Evo Morales			Morales re-elected with 61% of the vote	
Incidence of political violence: Deaths in policy-related violence		11	2	12	89	..	1	14	2	..	..

Sources: Instituto Nacional de Estadistica (www.ine.gov.bo); Banco Santa Cruz/Muller y Asociados, *Estadisticas socio-economicas 2001, 2003, 2005*; Unidad de Analisis de Politica Economica (UDAPE); Klasen et al. 2005; INE, *Anuario Estadistico 2004*, Table 3.06.03.04, page 339; World Bank 2005, Tables 1.1. Estimates of headcount poverty from UDAPE, 'En los dos ultimos años se redujo el porcentaje y el numero de pobres extremos', November 2009. 'Normal' headcount poverty line (at 2002 prices) is Bs 233/month (rural) Bs 321/month (urban), Bs 327/month (La Paz), Bs 272/month (El Alto). 'Extreme poverty line' is Bs 133/month (rural), Bs 170/month(urban), Bs181/month (El Alto). CEDLA unemployment data are reproduced in *Pulso* (La Paz), (195), 2–8 May 2005. 'Deaths in policy-related violence' and 'Days lost through strikes and demonstrations' are our own measure, which is elaborated in Mosley (2006b), Appendix 2.

factor of inequality (especially 'horizontal' inter-ethnic inequality), and the failure of the government's short-term measures to relieve it:

> [The increases in] Bolivia's external debt and the external aid aimed at reducing poverty benefited mainly the middle class. Even if improvements were achieved in the Human Development Index and poverty fell, the distribution of income deteriorated, as it did across the whole of Latin America. The deterioration of income distribution in a poor and supremely politicized country is perhaps among the main causes of the tragedy of [last] February.[14]

However, several countries also suffering from high levels of inequality, including some in Latin America, did not suffer from the same high levels of overt social conflict: so one thing that has to be explained is why this cause led to particularly grave effects in Bolivia. Our story in what follows will be that four Bolivia-specific factors, all contained within the political poverty trap model of Figure 10.1, help to explain this. These are institutional decay, the sudden politicization of the Aymara/Quechua ethnic group, the channelling of their discontent into the strategic location of El Alto, and the wasting by government of various opportunities to head off the conflict which arose as a consequence. Political instability, we argue, then drove away foreign capital, and the loss of investment perpetuated low income, completing the vicious circle. We now discuss these four triggers in sequence.

'Deinstitutionalization'

In various ways, the visible impact of inequality was aggravated by institutional decay, or 'deinstitutionalization' as the phenomenon is generally known in Bolivia. One major aspect of this is corruption, and specifically corruption arising from the process of 'capitalization' (as the form of privatization selected in Bolivia was known) of state assets, especially oil, gas, and minerals. This inflicted an *allocational* problem, due to the fact that factors of production were often not being allocated on the basis of efficiency but on the basis of ability to lean on the government: a *fiscal* problem, one illustration of which is that in 2003, the privatized oil and gas companies were paying less than half the tax revenue they were paying before privatization;[15] and a *distributional* problem, because the gains from corruption accrued mainly to the rich and not to the poor. It was largely the evidence of huge gains to the fat cats from the privatization of the oil and gas sector at a time of austerity (and specifically income tax increases) for the mass of the population which caused the apparently rather extraneous and rarefied issue of petroleum exports via Chile to become a flashpoint in October 2003.[16] A second

[14] Juan Antonio Morales, 'Que le ha pasado a Bolivia?' (What has happened to Bolivia?), *Pulso*, 14–20 March 2003, page 7.

[15] Rolando Morales, *La Prensa*, 12 February 2003, page 6. 'The Confederacion de Empresarios Privados de Bolivia', Morales adds, 'indicated that the fall in the country's fiscal revenues [between end-2001 and end-2002, which had caused a shortfall in revenues and required the IMF to be called in] was 7.3 per cent, and that the principal reason for that was a fall of 25.4 per cent over the same period in tax revenues due from the hydrocarbons (oil and gas) sector.'

[16] In 2003, this was aggravated by two factors. First, many of the gains from growth, and from growth in the oil sector in particular, fell to the advantage of the already rich east and south-east of the

element of deinstitutionalization, intimately related with the decline in investment illustrated by Table 10.2, is based in the financial sector. The heavily microfinance-based[17] recovery of the banking sector gradually became contaminated during the boom of the late 1990s, in particular by the entry into the market of consumer-credit houses seeking to lend unsustainable amounts of debt to low-income groups without proper appraisal or security (Rhyne 2002). When the recession hit, many clients defaulted on their loans (average six-month arrears rates in the microfinance sector rose from two per cent to twelve per cent between 1997 and 2001), and some of the more politically powerful of them leaned on the Banzer administration of 1999–2001, sometimes collectively as a debtors' cartel, to override their creditors and have their debts annulled. Some of the more loyal clients of the government were successful in this, and in this way financial discipline was undermined.[18] Third and perhaps most serious was the erosion of civil rights. An important illustration of this process was the refusal of President Sanchez de Losada, in September 2003, to re-elect Ana Maria Romero de Campero as *Defensora del Pueblo* ('ombudsman' is only a loose translation). The office had been established in 1998, as one of the achievements of the Banzer years. A person who had spent five years upholding the law, and specifically civil rights law, was removed at a time of extreme pressure on those civil rights by the personal edict of the President, against, it turns out the advice of many of his senators and MPs.[19] The incident was a crucial one in triggering the violence of October 2003.[20]

During the recession, indeed, the entire legal process in Bolivia became incapable of protecting civil or private property rights in a just or equitable manner, if they were the property rights of the poor. Within a system where, against sins of corruption and tax evasion plated with gold, the lance of justice could be seen to break without hurt, it was obvious, not only to the socially excluded, that existing institutions were not working. This was to be a major factor in bringing about political change.

country rather than the poor west (this has been felt particularly keenly during the period of rising oil and gas prices since the onset of the Iraq war in 2003). Second, President Gonzalo Sanchez de Losada, as the person who acquired many of the more profitable assets from a collapsing mining industry during the structural adjustment period, was himself an early epitome of the class who had made, and exported, a great deal of money out of Bolivia as a consequence of the privatization process.

[17] The microfinance institution BancoSol, born out of a non-governmental organization initially capitalized by USAID, was for several years in the mid-1990s the most profitable bank in Bolivia.

[18] This generalization is true as a general tendency but it is not remotely true for all financial institutions. Four microfinance institutions in particular (FIE, Caja los Andes, PROMUJER, and CRECER) resisted the trend towards increasing arrears during the recession, in part because their management stood up to government pressure to cancel arrears, in part because they were better designed to withstand shocks (for example by means of the 'internal account' of the last two institutions named, which acted as an insurance mechanism), and in part because of intense institutional loyalty amongst customers of all these institutions (Marconi and Mosley 2006).

[19] Interview, MNR senator, 21 September 2005.

[20] See *La Prensa*, 23 December 2003, and also the interview with Ana Maria Romero de Campero in *Pulso* (218), 10–16 October 2003, in which she describes Bolivia as a 'democradura' (half democracy, half dictatorship).

The metamorphosis of party politics

It is well acknowledged that across the whole of Latin America political parties have for a number of reasons fallen short of orthodox democratic ideals (Foweraker, Landman, and Harvey 2003, Chapter 5). In Bolivia between 1986 and 1999, this was particularly apparent to members of the Aymara/Quechua ethnic majority in the form of political and social exclusion. The three main parties, whose members were all light-skinned people embracing a centre-right, pro-liberalization, pro-international capital, pro-US stance (MIR, ADN/NFR, and MNR) were forced to engage in coalitions in order to govern, 'constantly changing position, like good lovers, each one sometimes on top and sometimes underneath',[21] as delightfully described by the columnist and former MP Cayetano Llobet. The horse-trading involved in making these coalitions compromised not only their ability to make rational decisions of fiscal policy,[22] but even more their ability to represent in any credible way the interests of the socially excluded.

As Table 10.3 illustrates, this merry-go-round has now been completely shattered during the five short years of the Bolivian recession. None of the three parties which shared power throughout the structural adjustment period fought the 2005 election as serious candidates, and the country is now governed by an Aymara-Indian dominated party (the MAS, or *Movimiento al Socialismo,* led by Evo Morales) which until 2002 had only three per cent of the seats in parliament.[23] The US Ambassador clumsily sought to influence the 2002 election by telling the electorate not to vote for the MAS, a tactic which spectacularly backfired.[24] From the 2002 election onwards, all pretence of respecting the parliamentary rules of the game was abandoned by both government and opposition. Quispe, on behalf of the MIP, promised a return to the roadblock tactics of 2000;[25] Morales sought to supplement or replace the parliamentary process with a meeting between the President and a broad front of civil society interests: 'workers, small farmers including coca growers, pensioners, financial services clients';[26] and President Sanchez de Losada himself not only confined his dialogue with Morales (still the leader of the coca growers' union) to the issue of coca eradication,[27] but chose the month of January 2003, just as the chances of a peaceful solution to the crisis were beginning to look problematic, to launch a

[21] Llobet 1999, page 47.

[22] For example, the extravagant pensions reform of 2002.

[23] The first serious attempt by a political party contender to represent the interests of the socially excluded, in the 1990s, was CONDEPA (*Conciencia de Patria,* Conscience of the Nation). CONDEPA, led by a 'white' professional arguing for poverty reduction on grounds of compassion, certainly raised the consciousness of the middle class concerning the gravity of social exclusion in Bolivia, but fell victim to widespread accusations of corruption (Llobet 1999) and was not able to sustain or consolidate its rapid rise.

[24] On 26 June 2003 the US Ambassador, Manuel Rocha, stated: 'I would like to warn the Bolivian electorate that if it chooses candidates who are trying to make Bolivia once again an exporter of cocaine, that result would prejudice future aid flows from the United States' (in the column *Usted Elige,* in *La Prensa* for 27 June 2002, as reported by Lazarte Rojas (2005), page 373.

[25] See *Pulso* (399) (21–27 April 2000).

[26] As reported in *Pulso,* 10–16 January 2003, page 4.

[27] See Victor Orduna, *Pulso* (179) (10–16 January 2003) and Lazarte Rojas (2005), page 451.

pre-emptive strike against the coca growers of the Chapare, in which thirteen people were killed. From this point on, peace had little chance.

Thus, in face of the widening schisms and deprivations aggravated by the global crisis, not only did many of the key institutions which might have healed it come apart at the seams, but the parliamentary process which might also have healed it was partly or wholly bypassed by all of the main contenders.

It was the merit of Evo Morales, at the same time as he was contributing to this process of bypassing parliament, to persuade not only his core Aymara constituency but much of the middle class (at any rate in the western *altiplano*) to back his efforts *within* the parliamentary arena.[28] He began this process in 2003, we argue, by successfully playing a 'trust game' against Sanchez de Losada. He persuaded not only his core constituency, but large parts of the urban middle class, to detach themselves from their traditional loyalties to the elite coalitions, even though this meant backing a man described by all the government-supportive media as a *narcotraficante* (drug-dealer). He also had to cope with the threat of secession from the rich east of the country,[29] which he did partly by appointing a vice-president from Santa Cruz, Alvaro Garcia Linera, whose intellectual credentials, as a professor of mathematics and the author of an Andean socialist philosophy (Linera 2009) nicely balanced the President's trade union background.

Poverty, inequality, and militancy

In relation to Bolivia we may begin by examining what the indicators say and where the conflict was located. The indicators are set out in Table 10.2. Headcount poverty, after probably falling during the boom of the 1990s (Landa 2003; Landa and Jimenez 2005) rises sharply in 2000, is then flat through the recession, and falls steadily after 2006, especially in its severe poverty dimension. Health, education, and other social indicators improve continuously, including during the recession (Klasen 2005). The INE (*Instituto Nacional de Estadistica*) estimate of

[28] We carried out a survey in La Paz and El Alto in September 2005 (Mosley 2006) with the purpose of understanding the links between interpersonal and political trust. This survey interviewed 105 people drawn equally from the ranks of microbusiness operators, manual workers, and professionals. The results suggest that the proportion of professionals intending to vote for Morales was more or less equivalent to the proportion of workers and microbusiness owners intending to vote for him.

	Intentions, September				*Outcome, December**
	Microbusinesses	Workers	Professionals	All	
Quiroga	6.5	5.7	30.6	14.7	29
Doria Medina	6.5	17.1	5.6	9.8	17
Morales	32.3	48.6	36.1	39.2	44
Other		2.9	2.0	2.0	10
Would not say	22.6	25.7	24.5	24.5	

(ii) Voting intentions and outcomes, 2005

[29] For the geographical distribution of poverty, see the poverty map at Figure 10.3. In 2001, the headcount poverty index in El Alto was 66.9 per cent, and in Santa Cruz 19.1 per cent (data from INE, as for Table 10.2).

Table 10.3 Parties in Bolivian Parliament, 1997–2009.

% of vote		1997	2002	2005	2009
'Governing coalition'	ADN-NFR (Banzer)	22.1	(Reyes Villa) 20.9		
	MIR (Paz Zamora)	16.7	16.3		
	MNR (Duran)	18.2	(Sanchez de Losada) 22.4		
	CONDEPA (Alvarado)	17.1			
	PODEMOS (Quiroga)			28.5	
Aymara/Quechua led parties	Movimiento al Socialismo (Morales)	3.2	20.9	53.7	62.8
	Eje/Movimiento Indigena Pachacuti (Barrenechea)	0.8	6.0		
	Seven other parties				37.2

Sources: Van Cott (2003), Table 1, page 753; Lazarte Rojas (2005), appendix; *La Razon* 13 December 2009.

open unemployment, which is only a short series, notably rises sharply in 2003, the year of greatest conflict. Other unemployment series show much greater variations: the CEDLA (*Centro de Analisis del Desarollo Agrario y Laboral*) urban unemployment series doubles between 2000 and 2003 (Table 10.2 above), and there are indications that in the city of El Alto, the level of unemployment trebled over this period (Table 10.2 above; *La Prensa*, special edition 23 December 2004; *Pulso* (195), 8 May 2003). El Alto, between 1985 and 2003, had grown from a small, exposed, dusty shanty-town adjoining the La Paz international airport into the Soweto of Bolivia, a vast melting-pot for Aymara and Quechua people in many cases uprooted from their previous livelihoods in mining or in agriculture,[30] on whom the economy of the entire western half of Bolivia depended.

It is, therefore, *not* possible to say that the onset of renewed social conflict and political instability in Bolivia as a whole, in 2000, is correlated with a sharp rise in the conventional measure of poverty. Further, the escalation of that conflict, in 2003, is not correlated with any visible increase in most of the conventional measures of poverty in Bolivia as a whole. What occurred in 2003, rather, was that an increase in conflict confined to urban and peri-urban areas on the western side, in the *altiplano*, the main territory of the Aymara, was associated with an increase in *unemployment* in those same regions, and in particular with an increase in unemployment in El Alto, the most politicized part of the country. Even within El Alto (Figure 10.2b) the epicentres of conflict were in Senkata, Villa Ingenio, and Alto Lima—the parts of the city with worst access to water, sanitation, and other public services.

As the left-hand part of Figure 10.2 shows, El Alto, and indeed most of the places where political violence has occurred since 2000, is not amongst the localities of highest poverty in Bolivia,[31] although the contrary is often asserted

[30] El Alto indeed 'is unique in Latin America for being an almost wholly indigenous city', Lazar 2004, page 5.

[31] The highest poverty levels in Bolivia are in the *altiplano* south-east of La Paz, between Coroico and Potosi (see Figure 10.2a). According to INE, *Annuario Estadistico 2004,* Table 3.06.03.04, the

in the media.[32] However, it has five characteristics which, we argue, predispose it towards high levels of conflict. First, there are worsening trends both in unemployment, as discussed, but also in other indicators of deprivation, notably water and sewerage. Second, there are very high levels of intra-personal inequality,[33] including intra-ethnic equality; rising much faster than conventional poverty indicators. Third, recent withdrawal of some key services needed to support a livelihood; in particular, microfinance was cut back countrywide by most agencies during the recession from 1999 onward (page 275 above; Marconi and Mosley 2006) and El Alto is the most microfinance-dependent region in Bolivia. Fourth, its strategic location means that to paralyse western Bolivia and La Paz in particular, all that is needed is to blockade El Alto. The country's main airport is in El Alto (which was its original *raison d'être*); the three main roads from La Paz to Peru, Argentina, and the east of the country, and the pipelines by which natural gas is transferred from the production areas to La Paz and out of the country, all pass through there. Fifth and maybe most crucial, El Alto is emphatically the place in Bolivia where poverty is most politicized. The system of *juntas vecinales* (neighbourhood groups), linked by CoJuVe, the Confederation of Neighbourhood Groups,[34] made communication easy, as did access to modern technology:[35] the uprising of October 2003 is one of the first revolutions to have been largely organized by mobile phone.

It was also of great importance to communication that El Alto is made up mainly of recent migrants from all parts of Bolivia, and in particular of former miners and peasants. For the peasant confederation the CSUTCB, for the landless peasants' movement the *Movimiento Sin Tierra*, and for the trade union confederation the COB, El Alto was the main organizational focus, reinforcing and seeking to unify the efforts of the *juntas vecinales*[36] and providing them with an idealistic, albeit not fully articulated, policy framework. This was autarchic and protectionist in nature, mixing atavistic notions of 'returning Bolivia's natural resources to their rightful owners' with ideas reminiscent of early development economics advocating industrialization based on those resources as a strategy for escaping from Bolivia's poverty trap. Some of the rhetoric emerging from El Alto during the period of the blockade is more reminiscent of late nineteenth-century Russia than any place in the twenty-first century:

percentage of persons in poverty in El Alto according to the 2001 census was 66.9 per cent (compare 58.9 per cent for Bolivia as a whole, or 19.1 per cent for Santa Cruz).

[32] See for example *La Prensa*, 23 December 2003, page 22.

[33] For data on inequality in Bolivia and elsewhere see Table 5.2 above.

[34] The CoJuVe was partly financed by Evo Morales' MAS: interview, Katy Lopez, ProMujer El Alto, September 2005.

[35] Interview, Fernando Romero, former minister of finance, 16 September 2005.

[36] The rebellions of 2003 and 2005 not only set workers against business owners, but also neighbourhoods against neighbourhoods, and women against men. (Mostly female) street-traders, receiving microfinance loans and needing to break the blockade to get their inputs and sell their produce, were in many cases the partners of (mostly male) workers required by the COB or the *junta vecinal* to be on the blockade. The *juntas vecinales* operated a licensing system, requiring traders to hold permits (*fichas*) if they were to continue to trade; many traders, during the blockade, were threatened with the withdrawal of these permits and even with the destruction of their kiosks unless they took part in the blockade (interviews, February 2004; see also Aliaga and Mosley 2007).

(a) Bolivia

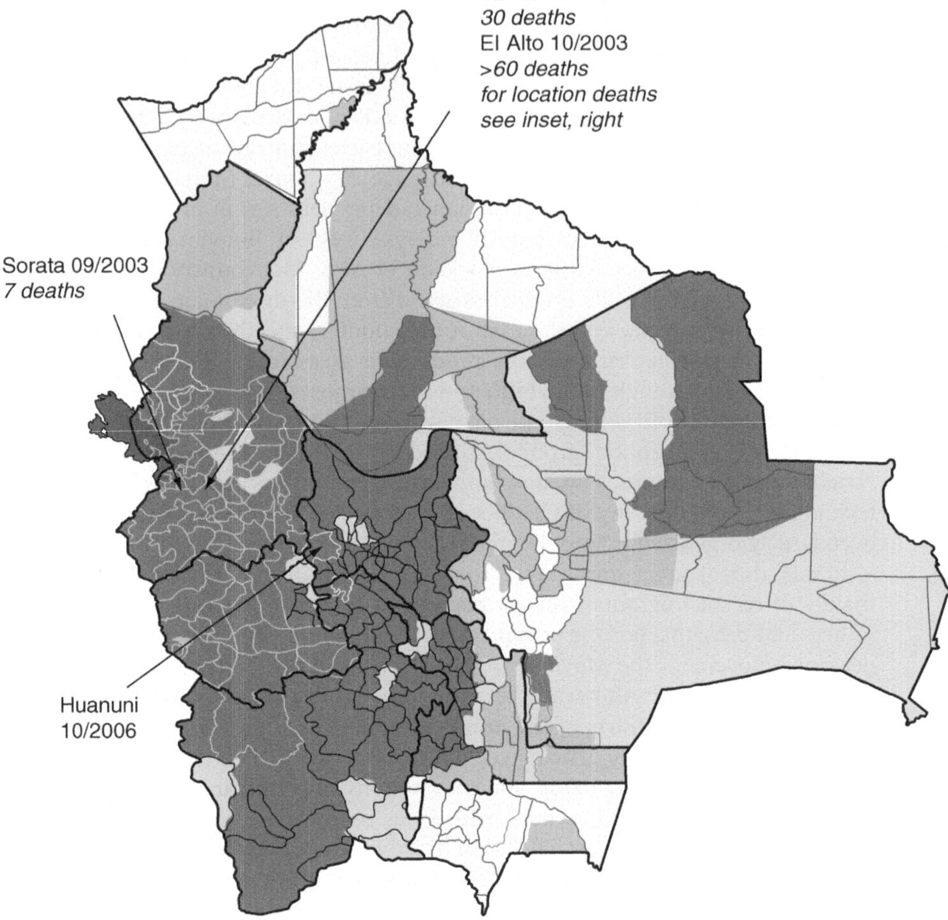

Figure 10.2(a) Political violence in relation to social deprivation: Bolivia (Shading denotes intensity of poverty. Locations circled denote areas of political violence, with dates; indicated numbers of deaths in brackets.)

Source: Instituto Nacional de Estadistica, *Pobreza y desigualdad en municipios de Bolivia*, INE/UDAPE/World Bank 2004, map p. 94, 'Severidad de probreza extrema 2001, medida por consumo'.

> Neighbourhood reunions and workshops took place in which . . . the possibility of making El Alto into a modern industrial city [with a freeport, protected by its own tariff barrier], with employment for all, was debated. The conclusion of most of these discussions was that the only real opportunity of development for the country as a whole, and hence for El Alto, was to recapture for the state the asset represented by oil and natural gas and to add value to it by means of industrialization.[37]

[37] Unsigned article, *Pedagogia de la Sangre: las Lecciones de Octubre* (What we learn from Bloodshed: the lessons of October 2003), *La Prensa* (La Paz), 23 December 2003, page 20. During 2003 several articles were published in the Bolivian press illustrating how Bolivia's oil and natural gas resources could be

(b) El Alto

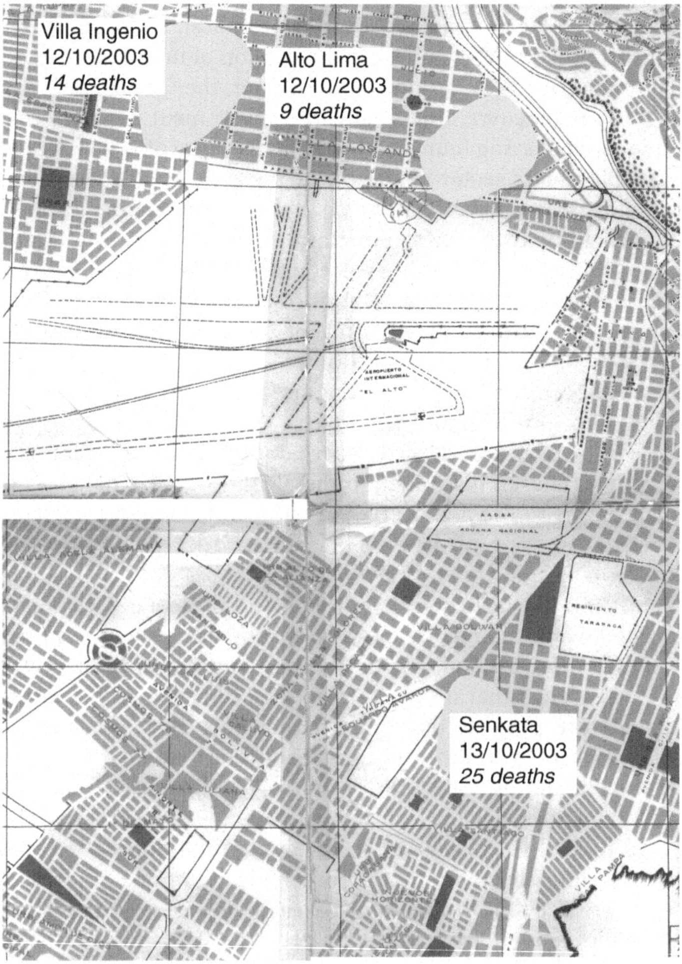

(b) Political violence in relation to social deprivation: El Alto.

Source: *La Prensa* 23/12/2003; Contemporary accounts, in particular Garcia, Prada, and Tapia (2004).

El Alto's high degree of political vision and organization was thus, during this period, blended with its ability to serve as a conduit for most of the grievances of the poorest. This unique role greatly augmented the probability of those grievances turning into violence.

converted in petrochemicals, plastics, and other derivatives far more labour-intensive than existing oil and gas extraction activities. See for example *El Diario*, 5 February 2003, where it is claimed that value added from natural gas exports could be multiplied by a factor of between two and ten depending on whether the processing is 'simple' (electricity generation) or 'compound' (second and third generation petrochemical products). In particular, opportunities existed for selling gas-generated electricity to Brazil and Argentina from power stations located over the eastern and southern borders: an agreement of this kind with Argentina was signed to great acclaim in June 2006.

The choice of adjustment instrument and the role of aid donors

The three factors so far mentioned—the rise of radical, ethnically-based political parties, deinstitutionalization, and the politicization of urban poverty in El Alto—certainly circumscribed the frame determining the government's room for economic-policy manoeuvre. But, finally, the government did not use that room for manoeuvre well. Having found itself at the beginning of 2003 (Table 10.2) with an unsustainable public sector deficit of 8.5 per cent of GDP, it then sought to close that deficit, as we have seen, partly by an inflammatory extension of the income-tax net, and partly by inflammatory proposals to direct oil and gas via a new pipeline through Chile. Neither of these decisions was fiscally necessary: certainly the deficit needed to be cut, but it could have been cut by less politically provocative means, most of all a closing of the tax loopholes from which the natural-resource millionaires were profiting.[38]

It might have been hoped that the donors—or at any rate some or all of the 'gang of four' who deal with all the budgetary support and macro-policy advice given to Bolivia[39]—would warn the Sanchez de Losada government of the danger associated with its chosen instrument of fiscal adjustment. They did not. Indeed, the president of one of them appeared on national television to defend the need for a downward extension of the income tax network on 11 February, the night before first the police and then the whole of La Paz rioted against the injustice (Lazarte Rojas 2005, page 18). The World Bank's representative very uncharacteristically claimed that it did not see fiscal policy and other short-term policy issues as a Bank, much more a Fund, responsibility,[40] and the Corporacion Andina de Fomento (CAF) argued that it saw its role at the time as to achieve implementation of expenditure projects on which money was unspent and development thereby delayed,[41] not tax reform. The degree of coordination between the donors, and between them and the Sanchez de Losada government of whose decentralizing, open-economy policies they greatly approved, was exemplary. This was the problem. The difficulty was not (as so often) that the donors were not singing from the same hymn-sheet, but that they were. Had but one of them warned the emperor that he was about to have his clothes forcibly removed, it is possible that some of the forces tending to close the poverty trap shut might at the last minute have been arrested.[42]

[38] Other potential options included cuts on expenditures benefiting only the professional middle class (notoriously the Sanchez de Losada pension reform included mainly white, middle-class beneficiaries, and was one of the first public sector reforms made by the Morales administration, see below).

[39] The IMF, the World Bank, the Inter-American Development Bank and the Corporacion Andina de Fomento.

[40] Interview, Carlos Mollinedo, World Bank La Paz, 14 September 2005.

[41] Interview, Oscar Bonifaz Paz, CAF, La Paz, 22 September 2005.

[42] The CAF, somewhat locking the stable door after the horse has bolted, is currently disbursing a *Prestamo de Distension Social* (Loan for Reducing Social Tensions). The concept is laudable, and consists essentially of Emergency Social Fund-type expenditure focused on areas of political tension such as those in Figure 10.3.

Modelling of the political poverty trap

The argument is, then, that the four factors analysed—deinstitutionalization, the changing party system, the El Alto factor, and the government's abuse of its room for manoeuvre—converted an external shock into a political poverty trap. We now seek to gain more insight into this process by modelling it. The model to be estimated was presented in the right-hand part of Figure 10.1: the link between political violence and its causes, investment and poverty.

The results of estimating this simultaneous-equation system are presented in Table 10.4. The rationale behind the specification is as follows.

Political violence (relationship (1)). Political violence in Bolivia arose from inequality (both horizontal and vertical) aggravated by institutional decay, the organization of El Alto and poor policy: in other words we see elements of both the 'greed' and 'grievance' explanations of conflict emphasized by Collier and Hoeffler (2004). The rapid rise of unemployment in El Alto in 2002–3, and the blockage of constitutional channels of protest, clearly aggravated the desperation and hopelessness of many inhabitants and, in the language of the 'greed' approach, lowered the costs of protest, especially a protest whose costs, as in the case of this type of violence, fell well short of civil war. At the same time, the level of injustice and distrust of government felt by the Aymara/Quechua population (and increasingly the middle class), and the increasing level of political mobilization of that population, particularly in El Alto, are causes of conflict more associated with 'grievance' type explanations. All of these variables feature in our estimating equation, with trust represented by the monthly index of 'confidence in government policy' collected by the opinion poll agency *Apoyo* and political mobilization represented by the popularity ranking of parties committed to extra-parliamentary action (the MAS and MIP). One merit of our dataset, in principle, is that we have data on actual political violence, in the sense of deaths in conflict associated with stabilization policies (roadblocks, demonstrations, etc.) rather than the 'political instability' indicators typically used in research of this type (e.g. the ICRG and World Bank datasets), which rely on the subjective opinions of key informants reported to public opinion surveys.

Confidence in government (relationship (2)). In our estimation of support for the government (linkage (2)) for Bolivia, we use, from the standard literature on voting functions, 'time since last election', unemployment, and change in personal consumption, and add in our estimator of political violence (quarterly deaths in street riots and demonstrations) into the list of explanatory factors.

Violence, investment, and poverty (relationships (3) and (4)). The final links in this part of the poverty trap are those between political instability and investment. We surmise that political instability will depress both domestic and, especially, foreign investment as in the analysis of Alesina and Perotti (1996), and that this lower investment, completing the 'vicious circle', will lead in subsequent periods to higher poverty.

Our poverty trap model is one of simultaneous causation, in which the causes of political violence are themselves endogenous to indicators of poverty and other causal variables within the model; hence a simultaneous-equation estimation technique, three-stage least squares (3SLS) is employed, in which the right-hand variables which are endogenous are replaced by appropriate exogenous, or

Table 10.4 Regression analysis of 'political poverty trap' model.

Dependent variables / Independent variables	Political violence (linkage 1)		Confidence in government (linkage 2)		Investment rate (linkage 3)		Gini coefficient of inequality (linkage 4)	
Period	Pre- and post-crisis 1996–2006	Crisis 2000–6	Pre- and post-crisis 1996–2006	Crisis 2000–6	Pre- and post-crisis 1996–2007	Crisis 2000–6	Pre- and post-crisis 1996–2008	Crisis 2000–6
Regression coefficients on independent variables:								
Constant	226.3**	–403.5**	71.3**	524.3**	107.0*	11.7**	60.5**	53.3**
	(3.54)	(7.71)	(10.64)	(7.62)	(2.61)	(28.2)	(9.34)	(3.02)
New government dummy			–0.52*					
			(1.86)					
Unemployment (INE data), urban areas only	–53.6*		–5.31**	–86.8**				
	(2.42)		(4.00)	(6.94)				
Unemployment (CEDLA data), urban areas only		0.53						0.92**
		(0.50)						(3.69)
Gini coefficient of inequality	4.62*	6.43**						
	(1.96)	(4.58)						
Confidence in government	–6.19**	–0.11				0.045**		
	(3.65)	(0.41)				(5.35)		
Political militancy indicator	1.42*	0.15*			–0.34**			
	(2.22)	(4.38)			(3.09)			
Political violence indicator				–1.76**	–0.82*	–0.002		
				(4.89)	(2.38)	(0.38)		
Investment rate							–0.28**	–1.83*
							(2.49)	(2.84)
Pro-poor expenditure							–0.33**	–1.92*
							(4.98)	(1.38)
Poverty (headcount index)					–1.95**		0.17*	
					(2.80)		(1.67)	
Number of observations	44	28	44	28	44	28	44	28
R^2	0.91	0.95	0.59	0.86	0.68	0.79	0.55	0.81

Note: Three-stage least squares (3SLS) estimation; data are quarterly for the duration of the recession from first quarter 1999 to final quarter 2005 (hence n = 40). Instrumental variables are in italics.

Definitions and sources

Political violence indicator: Deaths in policy-related conflict (street violence and demonstrations): index constructed from original sources, see Table 10.2 above. *Headcount poverty, Gini coefficient of inequality, INE unemployment rate total investment rate, foreign investment rate*: from Instituto Nacional de Estadistica (INE), Estadisticas socio-economicas 2004. *CEDLA unemployment rate:* from Centro de Estudios para el Desarollo Laboral y Agrario, La Paz. *Trust in government:* Apoyo Opinion y Mercado, *Informe de Opinion,* August 2005 issue plus updates. *Political militancy indicator:* proportion of seats held by parties involved in extra-parliamentary action (MAS and MIP).

Figures in parentheses under coefficients are Student's t-statistics: ** denotes significance of a coefficient at the one per cent and * denotes significance at the five per cent level.

instrumental, variables, which are correlated with the endogenous right-hand side variables. The estimates are presented in Table 10.4, with the instrumental variables in italics.

The results of the regressions confirm as significant all the links hypothesized as making up the 'political vicious circle' model of Figure 10.3. *Political violence* (linkage 1) is associated with, amongst economic ('greed') variables, high levels of the Gini coefficient of *inequality* (reflecting the correctness of the instincts of the Governor of the Central Bank, page 10 above), but, as discussed in the text above, it responds insignificantly to conventional poverty measures: violence has increased, between the late 1990s and early 2000s, whilst poverty has slightly fallen. Amongst the political 'grievance' variables in our model, violence is negatively associated with the Apoyo index of trust in government and positively associated with a rise in the share of militant parties. *Trust in government* (linkage 2) rebounds at the beginning of each electoral period and responds negatively to levels of unemployment (as in industrial countries) but also responds negatively to political violence. Investment (and in particular inward investment from abroad, linkage 3) are responsive to the violence indicator and the political militancy indicator, declining particularly sharply during periods such as 2000 and 2003, when political instability is high and improving when calm is restored, in keeping with the cross-section findings of Alesina and Perotti (1996). Finally, and completing the political vicious circle, the Gini coefficient of inequality (linkage 4) responds negatively in response to declines in foreign investment and to increases in poverty and the social efficiency wage (*ppe*).[43]

The results are robust to changes in specification, for example the experimental changes in estimating sample and control variables reported in the right-hand part of each column of Table 10.4. When we move from data for the pre-and crisis period to the crisis period only, and when we amend the set of instrumental variables used to estimate the parameters of the poverty trap, the estimated impact of the core variables in the model does not significantly alter: the key linkages continue to be those from investment and the composition of public expenditure, to inequality, to political violence, to confidence in government, and back to investment.

10.4 THE MORALES PERIOD (2006 TO THE PRESENT) AND AN INTERNATIONAL PERSPECTIVE

Thus, as in our Argentina case study (Chapter 9) a greater measure of political stability has come about as a result of a previously marginalized low-income

[43] The 'social efficiency wage' (see Chapter 5 above) is the set of public expenditures visualized as influencing political stability, and its definition is therefore sensitive both to the distribution of well-being and to the relative militancy of different social groups in each country. As a proxy for the social efficiency wage we here use 'pro-poor expenditure' (*ppe*), the ratio of expenditure likely to benefit low-income groups (primary health and education, rural water and sanitation, agricultural research and extension) as a proportion of total government expenditure. It is by no means clear how robust this definition of the social efficiency wage, which suggests that pro-poor expenditure will increase political stability, is across countries. However, on the evidence of the right-hand column of Table 10.4, it seems to work reasonably well in Bolivia.

group being incorporated into government, but in this case it has taken over the government rather than being a pressure-group exercising leverage on it. Since taking office at the beginning of 2006, the man who before taking office described capitalism as 'the worst enemy of humanity'[44] has implemented, in a notably moderate manner, a number of anti-neoliberal, pro-poor reforms, notably in the fields of: fiscal policy, devoting the proceeds of export taxes, as in Argentina, to transfers to the poor;[45] financial reform, establishing a new state bank, the *Banco de Desarollo Productivo* (Bank for Development of Productive Sectors) for small-scale agriculture and manufacturing; and constitutional reform, increasing the stake of the Aymara/Quechua majority in both parliament and the civil administration through a constitutional assembly, a governance instrument which is reminiscent of the Argentinian *Mesa de Dialogo* but aims at a quite different target group. Morales' rhetoric of 'capturing the fruits of the soil for the benefit of those who extract them' is attuned, of course, to the poor, dual, natural-resource based economy which Bolivia is, and to the legacy of ethnic discrimination which has occurred in that country (as also, of course, in Peru and Ecuador), rather than to the industrial economy which Argentina is, and in particular it is a very long way away from the rhetoric of *neodesarollismo*, a term not much used in Bolivia,[46] even if many of the constituent policies are similar. And although the new administrations of Bolivia and Argentina have both been seeking to move away from the Washington Consensus and from dependence on North America, the partnerships which they have used to do this, involving, in Bolivia's case, the creation of alliances and aid relationships with left-wing partners such as Venezuela and Cuba, has no parallel in Argentina. For their part, the mainstream aid donors, in spite of receiving some hysterical advice immediately after Morales' accession,[47] have not withdrawn their capital or returned to the kind of fiscal advice whose acceptance helped to destroy Sanchez de Losada; but a test will come when the oil price, which currently is functioning as a brake preventing the fiscal or the poverty situation from getting any worse, starts to fall again.[48]

Our concern is of course with the poverty implications of all this, and on this score the performance of the Morales administration is impressive: it has managed to reduce poverty levels, and in particular severe poverty levels, from the high plateau on which they were trapped throughout the years of neo-liberal growth from 1990 to 2005 (Table 10.2). The irony is that this has been achieved without any progress in relation to either manufacturing or agriculture, two of the Morales administration's principal targets for transformation: the profile of growth

[44] Andrew Mueller, 'The cuddly crusader' [profile of Evo Morales], report in *Independent on Sunday*, 7 May 2006.

[45] This is done in particular through two channels, the *Renta Dignidad*, which is a basic state pension, and the *Bono Juancito Pinto*, which is a conditional cash transfer for the benefit of mothers and children in low income groups.

[46] One member of the Bolivian government's Unit for the Analysis of Economic Policy (UDAPE) described neo-developmentalism to me as 'a word almost unheard of here'. Interview, Fernando Landa Casazola, 14 December 2009.

[47] See for example Michael Radu. 'The end of Bolivia?' 21 December 2005, at www.fpri.org.

[48] At the time of writing (January 2011) the Morales administration has been forced to withdraw a planned cut in petroleum subsidies. This illustrates its continuing weakness in face of the threat of secession from the east of the country, and arguably also its inability to impose fiscal discipline.

remains disturbingly natural resource dependent, and therefore capital intensive, and yet poverty has come down. Exactly how this has happened is not clear, but one possible interpretation is that poverty has been reduced more on the consumption side, by reducing the cost of consumption for low-income people in employment, than on the production side by expanding the number of modern sector jobs or self-employed livelihoods, such as a diversification of the export base might achieve. (Indeed Bolivia, of all countries, is now suffering from Dutch disease, with a buoyant exchange rate making the achievement of export competitiveness additionally problematic.) If our diagnosis is right, the profile of poverty reduction in Bolivia over the last few years therefore compares better with, say, Ghana amongst our country case studies, where the dramatic fall in poverty of recent decades was similarly consumption based (Nsowah-Nuamah, Teal, and Awoonor-Williams 2010) than with, say, Indonesia, Uganda, or even Malaysia (Chapters 11 and 13 below), where the poverty-reduction dynamic derived from the familiar source of rapid growth along a labour-intensive production function.

The Morales administration, finally, has been accused, especially since its landslide electoral victory in December 2009, of *caudillismo*, of exercising control by developing the personality cult of the leader in place of the development of institutions—an accusation which, if true, carries with it the risk that no long-term development of equitable political and economic institutions is happening, even if short-term poverty reduction is.[49] That accusation has also been levelled at the Kirchners in Argentina, as it was half a century ago at their predecessor Juan Domingo Peron, and even if the reasons underlying the accusation are different,[50] the implications are the same, namely that the processes of poverty reduction currently visible in both countries are politically fragile, by comparison with the case of, say, Chile,[51] which has been more effectively burned by its own experience of *caudillismo*. Anyone who makes optimistic long-term predictions that 'the political poverty trap can be sprung' is, in Bolivia, at particular risk of looking foolish, in the light of what happened to the 'fresh starts' of 1952 and 1985. But in Bolivia since 2006 there has been, at least, an attempt to wrestle with fundamental problems of governance and access to distributive justice, as well as the achievement at last of a downturn in the poverty rate: that in itself is non-trivial.

[49] See 'Bolivia prefirió el caudillo' *Pulso*, 13–19 December 2009, front page. *Caudillo* translates approximately as 'boss', with connotations of domination by personality rather than by the exercise of legitimate constitutional authority, by explicit comparison with Latin American leaders such as Peron in Argentina in the 1950s. An article in the edition of *Pulso* quoted above accuses the Bolivian people of having let their hearts govern their heads by awarding power to Morales on the grounds purely of his personal charisma, as many Argentinian voters did with Peron.

[50] Presidents Kirchner and Fernandez concentrated considerable personal wealth in their hands through property investments (see 'Argentina's first couple deliver prosperity for themselves', *The Guardian*, 27 July 2010). By contrast, President Morales, who maintains an engagingly modest lifestyle, has concentrated power in his hands rather than wealth.

[51] For an account of poverty reduction in Chile see the paper by Neilson et al. (2008).

11

Indonesia and Malaysia

Ben Thirkell-White

11.1 INTRODUCTION

The crisis that hit Asia in July 1997 was particularly shocking to the international community because it happened in countries that had previously been regarded as paragons of economic management. Not only had they achieved spectacular growth since the mid-1960s, but that growth had not created significant inequalities and had dramatically reduced poverty levels. The first task for this chapter is to set out some of the politics of this early success.

Despite some broad similarities in patterns of pre-crisis growth, the crisis experience itself was very different in the two countries. Malaysia's crisis was far less severe, partly because of stronger regulation going into the crisis and, possibly because of a distinctly unorthodox approach to crisis resolution involving capital outflow controls. In Indonesia, on the other hand, the crisis rapidly deteriorated into a sharp downward spiral that fits closely with the model of the political poverty trap introduced in Chapters 3 and 4. Economic difficulties led to questions about President Suharto's political will to deal with the crisis. Suharto's intransigence and apparent favouritism towards wealthy, politically connected business groups, including many owned by his family members, created growing political hostility and instability. That reduced market confidence, preventing any recovery in investment, deepening the crisis. Matters were only resolved when the New Order regime collapsed and a sweeping set of institutional and democratic reforms were introduced. The second task of the chapter is to explain these different trajectories with particular attention to the political factors that shaped them.

Finally, Indonesia's post-crisis policies and institutional structures were heavily shaped by interactions with the IMF and World Bank. There were some very positive aspects of that but there are also worrying signs that the poor are not having a very significant impact on post-crisis politics in Indonesia. The chapter will conclude with some indications as to why this is the case.

11.2 THE POLITICAL ECONOMY OF INDONESIA AND MALAYSIA BEFORE THE 1980s

In both countries, patterns of political authority and broad social bargains were established in the 1960s, which were to continue to act as the reference points for debate about economic policy and political structure until the crisis period. The 1960s and 1970s were also a period of impressive poverty reduction in both countries. In this section, we begin by reviewing these patterns and go on to explore the role that pro-poor policy played within them, drawing lessons for longer-term policy strategies in other countries.

Indonesia and Malaysia both appeared as star performers in the World Bank's *East Asian Miracle Report* (World Bank 1993). The *Miracle Report* emphasized the role of sound macro-economic policy and relatively liberal markets, rather than intervention in markets, in promoting growth. It added that this had been supported by strong investment in human capital and sound agricultural policies (particularly, marketing boards that did not dramatically distort prices, and investment in green revolution technologies). Indonesia and Malaysia both broadly fit this model. What the Bank said little about, though, was the politics behind this policy mix, except that it involved strong government with a technically competent bureaucracy. The Bank was also famously ambiguous about the role of industrial policy in each country's performance. In the North East Asian economies, the Bank found it hard to ignore the claim that industrial policies had been a key part of the promotion of export-oriented growth. In South-East Asia, however, there was much more evidence of wasted expenditure and corruption.

We do not need to resolve questions about the economic outcomes of industrial policy here. However, in *political* terms, it is important to recognize that industrial policies of various kinds played a strong role in shaping domestic politics at the national level. By the early 1970s, both countries had authoritarian or semi-authoritarian governments that legitimated themselves largely through their ability to promote broad-based economic growth. For much of the 1970s, the most visible manifestation of this was industrial policy, which was officially designed both to produce growth and to redistribute resources from rich to poor and from 'foreigners' (which included a long-term resident Chinese diaspora) to nationals. As well as reflecting a particular economic vision, nationalist policy was a response to the kinds of issues of national unity that were present in many post-colonial environments. Neither country had been a unitary state, except under colonial rule and both had inherited ethnically and religiously diverse populations and contested political boundaries. In both countries, traditional economic nationalism was coupled with direct attempts to promote *indigenous* capitalists who could play a lead role in the domestic political economy. This played an important role in shoring up state legitimacy by underpinning broader state-building projects with active attempts to produce a national business class.

Although economic nationalism was politically important in both countries, it was tempered with a sense of pragmatism. Nationalist policy co-existed with more orthodox and outward looking economic policies. Both countries began to open up to foreign investment relatively early, though they also sought to direct it to some industries and not others so that it would not interfere with nationalist priorities. Within that broad framework political and economic regimes diverged significantly.

Background

Malaysia

At independence the population of Malaysia was made up of around fifty per cent indigenous Malays, thirty per cent ethnic Chinese, and twenty per cent Indians. Malays had been predominant in government and the civil service during the colonial period but the vast majority of business and capital was in the hands of foreigners or the ethnic Chinese. The combination of Malay political power and Chinese economic power has profoundly shaped Malaysian politics ever since.

Since 1969, every Malaysian election has been won by the Barisan Nasional (BN), an alliance of elite parties from each ethnic group, under the leadership of UMNO (the United Malays National Organization). This inter-ethnic alliance has been difficult to defeat since, given the prevalence of identity politics, the obvious opposition platform is to be 'more ethnic' than the corresponding Barisan party (so the PAS,[1] the Malay opposition, campaigns on an Islamic-nationalist platform, while the Chinese DAP[2] campaigns on a liberal, and implicitly anti-affirmative action, one). Only some kind of inter-ethnic coalition can hope to win power at the national level, but forming alliances with other ethnic groups risks undermining opposition parties' core support base.[3]

The economic manifestation of BN power has been the New Economic Policy, which was introduced following inter-ethnic riots in 1969. It was designed to 'reduce and eventually eradicate poverty, by raising income levels and increasing opportunities for all Malaysians, irrespective of race' and 'accelerate the process of restructuring Malaysian society to correct economic imbalance, so as to reduce and eventually eliminate the identification of race with economic function'. More specifically the government set three targets to be achieved by 1990: a reduction of poverty from fifty per cent to less than twenty per cent; restructuring of employment so that, in all sectors and occupations, it reflected the racial composition of the country; and restructuring of corporate ownership so that at least thirty per cent would be owned by *bumiputeras* (Gomez and Jomo 1999).

[1] Parti Islam SeMalaysia.

[2] Democratic Action Party.

[3] Probably the best account is Jesudason (1996).

The limited chances of electoral victory do not mean that the opposition is wholly irrelevant to Malaysian politics. Particularly in times of political difficulty, the central coalition has altered its policies to incorporate opposition demands or even whole political parties, leading to Jesudason's characterization of Malaysia as a 'syncretic' state (or Case's description of it as a hybrid regime' (Case 2005).

A variety of means were employed to further those goals. In the early period, inter-ethnic equity was pursued through a form of import-substituting industrialization, adapted to ensure that benefits accrued disproportionately to the *bumiputera* population. There were employment quotas for Malays and education quotas to ensure that they were qualified to fill available posts. The government channelled funds into the new industries through '*bumiputera* trust agencies', which held assets on behalf of the *bumiputera* community. The Industrial Coordination Act (ICA) of 1975 also imposed thirty per cent equity quotas for *bumiputera* ownership of most businesses operating in Malaysia. However, this was as much a tool to regulate foreign investment as it was to ensure local ownership. Exemptions to ICA requirements were granted to foreign investors if they were setting up to produce for export, rather than engaging in market-seeking investment to access the Malaysian domestic market. The result was that most foreign direct investment was labour-intensive export production, so as to avoid ICA restrictions (Gomez and Jomo 1999).

Potential opposition from foreign or ethnic Chinese owned business, then, was partly assuaged by ensuring that pro-*bumiputera* nationalism limited potential business opportunities, rather than ruling them out completely. There were also conflicts of interest between the two groups as Chinese business tried to direct nationalist energies into sectors of concern to foreigners and foreigners could benefit from 'pioneer' export status but Chinese business could not (Jesudason 1989). The potential divisiveness of redistribution was also eased by the success with which the overall strategy promoted growth. A strong commitment to macro-economic stability, mobilization of savings for investment in infrastructure and active encouragement of export-oriented industry from the late 1960s onwards created a broadly buoyant economic environment so that all could benefit, even if *bumiputera* would benefit most.

Indonesia

The 1950s and 1960s in Indonesia had witnessed an uneasy political coalition between military nationalist and communist forces under Sukarno. Attempts to hold this coalition together had resulted in unworkable economic nationalist policies and high inflation (Schwarz 1999). Suharto came to power in 1965. The legitimacy of his authoritarian New Order regime was based on the claim that, given the experience of the Sukarno period, a firm hand was needed to hold the country together and deliver economic growth. Much to everyone's surprise, Suharto delivered on the promise of promoting economic growth (Hill 1996), though he also ruled in an extremely authoritarian fashion, outlawing most forms of extra-government political debate or organization (Crouch 1979; Liddle 1992; Schwarz 1999).

New Order economic management was driven by the relationship between three imperatives: orthodox macro-economic policy, economic nationalism, and various forms of political patronage (Robison 1997). The economic crisis Suharto inherited, along with a candid awareness of his own limited grasp of economics, initially led him to place great reliance on a cadre of well-trained orthodox economists based in Bappenas and Bank Indonesia (known as the 'technocrats' or the 'Berkeley mafia').[4] Their early stabilization policy and courting of foreign investors were instrumental in re-starting growth in the late 1960s (Hill 1996; Winters 1996).

Whilst this adjustment was unexpectedly successful in aggregate, foreign investment was heavily (two-thirds) concentrated in oil and gas and the remainder tended to be market seeking in areas that competed directly with indigenous business, creating growing political unrest. Following riots in 1974, and in a context of growing oil earnings in the mid-1970s which eased economic constraints, more emphasis was placed on creating domestic industry and providing opportunities for *pribumi* (native Indonesian, as opposed to ethnic Chinese) entrepreneurs. Measures included emphasis on directed credit for small *pribumi* business, regulations on foreign investment including a fifty-one per cent domestic equity requirement, further reservation of economic sectors to *pribumi*, and measures to promote industrial deepening. These measures were also combined with large experiments in state-owned heavy industry funded out of Pertamina's oil revenues. However, nationalism was also always strongly tinged with patronage—political connections and securing the loyalty of the Indonesian military were more important than ethnicity or business acumen in shaping the disbursement of resources (Robison 1986, 1997; Winters 1996). Pertamina's debts were also a more noted beneficiary of state credit than *pribumi* industry (with the exception of the agriculture sector, which we will discuss shortly).

Overall, then, both countries matured into strong, bureaucratically competent states ruling in an authoritarian (Indonesia) or semi-authoritarian (Malaysia) fashion. The implicit social contract in both places was that limited democratic rights would be tolerated in return for state-guaranteed stability and the state's successful promotion of industrialization and growth. Economic nationalism played an important role both in promoting national development and in managing ethnic tensions. In both cases, it was also partly a mechanism for patronage. However, in Malaysia, the problems of ethnically structured economic opportunities were real and some forms of industrial policy were well implemented and arguably successful. Patronage played a smaller role. In Indonesia, the Chinese population was a much smaller minority and nationalism was more often a cover for patronage. However, in both cases, nationalist policies were restricted to some areas of the economy, while other areas were open to foreign investment and macro-economic policy was sound.

The political environment and poverty reduction

Both countries showed remarkable achievements in poverty reduction during this period. They did so through a combination of investment in rural areas, growth of labour-intensive urban employment, and strong linkages between the two. Investment in agriculture helped to increase rural livelihoods and delay urban migration

[4] For Robert MacNamara's account of the early history of aid relationships between the Bank and the Berkeley mafia, see Chapter 7 above.

while growth took off. Rice cultivators were provided with highly subsidized irrigation schemes, micro-credit and access to fertilizer. Both countries also offered guarantees of rice prices, but at broadly market levels without the distortions that occurred through marketing boards in many parts of Africa. Later, as job opportunities expanded, increased urban wages lured some away from agricultural areas but also increased prices for rural goods, further boosting rural livelihoods (Drabble 2000; Fujimoto 1991; Timmer 2004a, 2007).

Growth in urban employment was particularly important in less-populated peninsular Malaysia, so that by the 1980s, even rice paddy that had benefited from government irrigation schemes was, in some places, going uncultivated due to increased urban migration (Fujimoto 1991).[5] In Indonesia, with a larger, poorer population rural production continues to be significantly more important but rural livelihoods are significantly affected by urban prosperity.

In both countries, significant investment in improving rural productivity and the infrastructure that could link the rural and urban economies were key in promoting pro-poor growth. Alisdair MacIntyre argues that spending on rural infrastructure was the only consistent beneficiary of 'nationalist' investment during the 1970s (other than the debt overhang from Ibn Sutowo's adventures with Pertamina's funds) (MacIntyre 1993). Martin Drabble notes that agriculture accounted for around fifteen per cent of development spending in Malaysia during the early NEP period (Drabble 2000).

Investment in rural areas, in turn, was a function of the political settlements that we outlined in the previous section. In Indonesia, Suharto's rise to power was accompanied by a brutal suppression of the rural-based Indonesian communist party. There was a real threat of communist insurrection in the countryside in the early years. However, that threat alone cannot explain the longer-term commitment to rural spending and low real exchange rates. Over time, Suharto, like his Malaysian counterparts, realized that rural spending could be a way of extending Golkar's party organization to the grass-roots level, securing widespread support for his regime. MacIntyre adds that agricultural spending provided a rare point of contact between nationalist agendas pressing for rapid growth with a *pribumi* emphasis and an orthodox economic focus on comparative advantage (MacIntyre 1993). Producing growth that delivered for the poor was also part of the broader social bargain that sustained regime legitimacy and sustainably delivered patronage resources to Suharto's political clients. Rapid growth for all (assisted from time to time by oil revenues) created a certain tolerance of at least modest levels of patronage politics required to cement together Suharto's governing coalition.

In Malaysia, the link between Malay nationalism and growing agricultural productivity is perhaps more direct. The Malay population were, initially at least, concentrated in rice farming and rural areas have continued to be a key element of BN support. Indeed, one strategy for maintaining BN electoral dominance has been the gerrymandering of the electoral system to provide disproportionate representation of rural (and therefore Malay) communities (Crouch 1996). Both to fulfil NEP promises on poverty reduction and to

[5] Fujimoto adds that design problems and poor maintenance also contributed in some areas.

prevent Malay defections to PAS, the Islamic opposition party, a great deal of money was channelled to rural areas. Development projects were advertised as UMNO projects and party members frequently got preferential access to subsidies and grants.

In the early period of Alliance government, there was a somewhat ambiguous attitude to rice policy. Peasant rice farming was seen as the heart of Malay culture and therefore something that the government should be protecting. At the same time, though, there was a feeling (stronger later under Mahathir's leadership) that rural attitudes were also something that would hold Malays back from competing effectively with the Chinese. Policy was directed at creating national self-sufficiency within the context of those constraints, though Alliance policy inadvertently created rising rural income differentiation through agricultural credit schemes that were easier to access by wealthier farmers. With the arrival of the NEP, rice self-sufficiency received a lower priority and farmer income became more important. The government introduced a guaranteed minimum price for rice and rapidly expanded irrigation schemes, agricultural credit, and subsidies for both inputs and rice production (Fujimoto 1991; Rudner 1983). Overall these policies were successful in raising farmer income in the short term, while over time, poverty reduction increasingly began to take place through migration to urban areas.

11.3 THE POLITICS OF ECONOMIC CRISIS IN INDONESIA AND MALAYSIA

We reviewed some of the literature on the place of distributional questions in crisis resolution in Chapter 3 and introduced the findings of some of our own quantitative research. We argued, following Rodrik, that pre-existing inequalities and ethnic cleavages ('latent social conflict' in Rodrik's terms) can make crisis handling more difficult. These difficulties, though, can be mitigated by successful institutions of conflict management that are able to inspire trust in governments' ability to deal fairly with the distributional conflicts that emerge with financial crisis (Rodrik 1999). Our own research then extended these ideas by pointing to the potential for governments to provide signals to their populations of pro-poor intent, which could help to head off the risk of social unrest. These might include pro-poor expenditure policies or other mechanisms that showed a clear commitment to mitigating the social consequences of crisis. We argued that such signals were more likely to be received and responded to in an environment of broad trust in government. They were more likely to happen where the elite were aware of the need for poor support to secure their political position and where policies could be devised that served a combination of elite and popular interests.

This case study of Indonesia and Malaysia helps us to see how these broad patterns can play themselves out in particular historical contexts. The legacy of the policies reviewed in the previous section should have put both countries in a good position to weather crisis. Indeed, Rodrik's investigation of the political economy of crisis was partly driven by reflections on successful Asian adjustment to earlier shocks in the late 1980s. Both countries came into crisis with relatively low levels of income inequality. In Malaysia income inequality was higher and had historically mapped quite closely onto ethnic inequality, potentially increasing the risk of political instability. However, the Malaysian government also had a strong history of dealing with ethnic inequality. Although Malaysia is only a semi-democracy, it does have strong institutions for dealing with horizontal (inter-ethnic) inequality. In Indonesia, levels of inequality remained low right up to the crisis. However, 'institutions of conflict management' were more problematic.

Although the political settlements we set out above continued to shape broad understandings of the political system in both countries up to the crisis, the late 1980s had triggered incremental but significant changes that form the backdrop to attempts at policy signalling during crisis. During the 1980s and 1990s, activist state attempts to promote distributional goals began to wane in both countries in favour of the promotion of an elite domestic business class, partly created through processes of privatization. To begin with, the further opening to foreign investment that accompanied these changes offset the potential impact on inequality but in the run up to the crisis allegations of elite-government collusion began to grow, in a context of slowly rising inequality.

Attempts at signalling during the crisis took place against this backdrop, which had begun to threaten the social bargain in which authoritarian political practices were accepted in return for strong and equitable growth. In Indonesia, distrust of government had gone further before the crisis and government responses were particularly problematic. The result was a downward spiral of capital outflows, political tension, declining investor confidence, and further reluctance to invest. In Malaysia, the government was in a slightly stronger position. Perspectives on equity had been directed into a discussion of inter-ethnic inequality since independence. Although inequality rose during the 1990s, it was largely driven by *intra*-ethnic inequality, as government policy concentrated more on promoting a symbolic class of Malay millionaires and less on widespread job creation. In some ways the focus on inter-ethnic inequality continued to undermine the potential for opposition to the ruling coalition, but the political structure's inability to deal with *intra* ethnic issues was a potential vulnerability. Fortunately, though, Mahathir's crisis resolution policy hit on a solution (capital controls) that served social goals, offered some protection to his elite support and sent strong signals that the government was actively trying to assist its population.

Our account of the crisis begins with a brief overview of the changes during the 1990s, which had begun to increase social cleavages and make political structures more fragile. We then go on to the crisis itself, and the roles that government policy played in exacerbating (Indonesia) or mitigating (Malaysia) its effects.

Political change in the pre-crisis period

Indonesia

During the 1980s in Indonesia, more difficult economic conditions (partly resulting from the spectacular failure of some of the nationalist ventures) undermined the turn to nationalism. Some power was returned to the technocrats that had been so central in Indonesia's orthodox policies in the early New Order Period. They pressed for the implementation of a programme of orthodox liberalization (Winters 1996).[6] At the same time, though, the liberalization programme was also shaped by increasingly powerful conglomerates that had grown up through the spin-offs from earlier nationalist policies (Robison 1986, 1997). These politically well-connected businesses did not want to see a total withdrawal of government patronage but they were looking for easier access to foreign investment and to some potentially lucrative state monopolies (infrastructure provision, telecommunications, utilities, etc.). Liberalization reflected those interests but there were some less popular moves as well, such as the privatization of the customs service to reign in corruption that had got out of control and was damaging growth (Robison 1997; Winters 1996).

Contrary to orthodox expectations, a somewhat reduced role for the state did not reduce corruption. The late 1980s and early 1990s saw an investment boom, as large numbers of new private banks emerged and the stock market took off. 'Inadequate rules and enforcement capacity allowed companies to go public without adequate disclosure, insider trading was rife and fake share scandals occurred frequently' (Robison 1997).

With the benefit of hindsight, the lesson that emerged was that states are not *only* the 'problem' in creating corruption (through the well-known rent-seeking opportunities associated with directed credit or trade protection); the state's regulatory role is also essential in avoiding rent-based behaviour in private market relationships. The system of political economy that had emerged in Indonesia during the 1990s increasingly functioned on the basis that property rights were guaranteed, primarily, through political connections, rather than through the rule of law (Thirkell-White 2007b).

The growing importance of political patronage led to an increasingly transparent concentration of wealth in the hands of a narrow and highly visible political elite, including many members of the Suharto family. A concentration of corporate wealth was also reflected in a modest increase in income inequality in the immediate pre-crisis period, albeit from very low levels by international standards: the Gini moves from 0.32 to 0.36 between 1990 and 1996 (Timmer 2004a).

Insiders were aware that this concentration of patronage had created conflicts within the regime, as Suharto lost some of his traditional allies in the military.[7] Military funding had traditionally been very significantly 'off budget', with officers funding their operations and their lifestyles through various kinds of business and some of these opportunities were undermined by changing economic priorities. Suharto responded by trying to find new support, particularly amongst Indonesia's Muslim population. He sponsored the creation of ICMI (Ikatan Cendekiawan Muslim se-Indonesia: association of Muslim intellectuals) and put it under the leadership of his anointed successor Habibie. The ICMI was partly staffed by academically inclined intellectuals but it also provided an organizing centre for

[6] Economic nationalism was a 'failure' in the sense that many high-profile ventures went expensively bankrupt MacIntyre (1993), Winters (1996). However, at least one observer argues that this paved the way for later success; see Rock (1999).

[7] The best accounts of changing politics during this period are Mietzner (1999), Schwarz (1999), Hefner (2000b).

Muslim elites within the state (including the military) and, further afield, cover for a modest awakening of extra-state Muslim political activities, after a long period of repression. The ICMI was also perceived by Muslim outsiders as a sign of Suharto's increasing piety and an indication that he might be more open to political influence—this included radical groups such as KISDI, who had links within the Indonesian military. Suharto was certainly looking for support from 'green' (i.e. Muslim) generals to replace his lost power base. The rise of ICMI was also accompanied by modest political opening on broader fronts (particularly in terms of press freedom), suggesting that Suharto may even have been looking to popular support to boost his position.[8] However, this opening was tentative and, after 1994, seemed to be largely reversed (Schwarz 1999).

Most of what was taking place politically was concentrated in the areas of the economy that were reserved for domestic business. Meanwhile, though, both these businesses and foreign owned factories were continuing to create jobs for most of this period. Poverty continued to decline right up to the brink of the crisis. However, partly because of the all-too-transparent abuses involved in state-business relationships, inequality may have played a larger role in ordinary Indonesians' views of government policy.

In retrospect, there were signs that, even before the crisis, Suharto's political legitimacy was severely strained. The political opening in the early 1990s followed by a reversal in the late 1990s did seem to have produced greater political mobilization and some academic observers were talking about 'the final count-down' (Heryanto 1997). Certainly, the New Order regime has begun to erode the populations' trust that it really was using its authoritarian control to pursue the general interest. Suharto was also increasingly short of support from any quarter, which narrowed his political options and breadth of vision when the crisis struck.

Malaysia

Turning now to Malaysia, similar patterns were at work but in a more moderate form, showing greater continuity with the previous period. As we have seen, 1970s NEP policy was strongly associated with state-owned businesses operating for the domestic market (while export growth was encouraged through Foreign Direct Investment). From the mid-1980s onwards, though, a combination of recession and ideological shifts pushed attempts at Malay betterment away from a fairly broad-based strategy of employment creation through import-substituting industrialization and towards the creation of a symbolic class of millionaire *bumiputera* entrepreneurs, through a peculiarly Malaysian form of privatization. State corporations were sold off, licences were issued to firms to compete in sectors which had been public monopolies and infrastructure projects were contracted out, all to 'entrepreneurs' that were close to the government. The result was the creation of a

[8] This is significant because, traditionally the New Order had tried to demobilize the population, partly to avoid a repeat of the traumatic and bloody repression of the Indonesian Communist Party in the early 1960s. It even had an official political policy of 'floating mass', which essentially involved preventing any kind of political engagement with the population at large, except during New Order 'elections', which were largely occasions for demonstrations of mass loyalty.

range of large conglomerates owned by newly consolidated politico-business class, including some ethnic Chinese businessmen with strong ties to the Malaysian political elite. At the same time, recovery was fuelled by the influx of East Asian investment into the region following the Plaza Accord (Gomez 1999; Gomez and Jomo 1999).

Nonetheless, the switch from a broad-based strategy of growth with heavy state influence to a more market-based one with a smaller group of direct beneficiaries produced significant conflict within UMNO over the implications (particularly in terms of personal access to patronage, but also in terms of the kind of political economy that was being produced) (Shamsul 1987). This shift helped to stimulate the rise in inequality noted in the introduction to this section and that rise in inequality has been largely across ethnic groups (rather than between them, which was the pre-NEP pattern). That rising inequality was creating some tensions in Malaysian politics that also had the potential to trigger unrest in the context of crisis.

The crisis

Indonesia

The general course of the economic crisis in Indonesia can be followed by looking at the evolution of the exchange rate over time (Figure 11.1). Indonesia first came under pressure in August 1997, following the devaluation of the Thai baht. The government, and most external commentators, initially saw Indonesia's problems in terms of economic contagion. An orthodox response of an exchange rate float combined with a sharp rise in interest rates was widely praised but didn't produce the expected results. The government then invited in the IMF, hoping that the IMF's arrival would, of itself, create a return in confidence.

Suharto was expecting a fairly simple IMF programme, largely endorsing the government's existing moves. 'We are not asking for money, as we already have

Figure 11.1 US$: rupiah exchange rate 1997–8.

policies . . . we just need the IMF to look at these programmes as it has experience' (quoted in *FT* 20 October 1998).

In practice, though, the IMF programme was a good deal more extensive, requiring a range of structural reform measures and the closure of sixteen banks, including two that were owned by Suharto's close relatives. The bank closures were an economic disaster, creating a run on the entire Indonesian banking system. Critics of the IMF approach argue that there was insufficient deposit insurance in place and insufficient clarity over the extent of future closures (Radelet and Sachs 1998). On the other hand, Suharto also undermined the potential confidence-enhancing effects of the closures by immediately re-opening the banks belonging to his relatives and re-instating fifteen previously postponed infrastructure contracts, with dubious economic benefit but clear advantages for well-connected business (Lane et al. 1999; Robison and Rosser 2000). The rupiah declined further and then went into freefall in early December, in response to rumours about Suharto's declining health.

The conflict between IMF preferences for a large-scale re-engineering of the Indonesian political economy and the political imperatives of patronage came to a head in the second IMF programme. The Fund insisted on a truly radical set of reforms, which cut to the heart of Suharto's patronage network (believing that confidence could be restored by an impressive commitment to reform). The evidence suggests that Suharto signed the programme with little intent of actually doing anything to comply with it (Riesenhuber 2001; Thirkell-White 2005a).

Whether or not the strategy *could* have worked, continues to be a matter of some debate.[9] However, for our purposes, what matters is that from Suharto's perspective, the suggestions the technocrats proposed were more politically problematic than old-style adjustment (which is roughly what his previous experience had led him to expect) *and* turned out to be a spectacular failure. By December he was clearly playing for his own political survival. Ultimately his attempts failed but they tell us a good deal about the political unrest and violence that took place in Indonesia following the crisis. A wide range of violence took place in Indonesia over the crisis period,[10] but, for the sake of simplicity, we concentrate on violence that seems to have been a fairly direct response to short-term government policy in response to crisis, rather than a continuation of pre-existing communal violence in the outer islands. We see a small amount of localized rioting in January and February 1998, followed by a lull in early March, and then escalating tensions through late spring, culminating in the dramatic riots of 12 May in Jakarta, which led to the downfall of Suharto's regime.

Chinese Indonesians were particular targets of violence, which points strongly to at least some economic motivation. Rises in the rice price in January and February were an important contributory factor to the early rioting. Similarly, the

[9] For the view that structural reforms were largely irrelevant and represented the price Indonesia would be required to pay for IMF assistance, see McLeod (1998). For the more fundamental criticism that radical governance reform in a crisis was like screaming 'fire in the theatre', see Radelet and Sachs (1998). McLeod has slightly changed his mind subsequently, believing that he had underestimated the institutional fragility of the Indonesian regime.

[10] For the best review of violence during this period, see Sidel (2006).

violence in May gathered pace after dramatic rises in the price of fuel and other commodities, instigated as an acceleration of previous IMF commitments in the run-up to a new round of negotiations.

However, these economic events were also surrounded by a very complex set of political developments which cannot be isolated from them. As we saw, during the late 1990s, there were increasing splits within the Indonesian elite organized around the distribution of patronage, but overlapping with religious affiliations. Within government, Habibie's rise to power built on alliances with political Islam, mediated through his control of ICMI. Suharto largely supported this, seeking both popular support and support from Muslim military officers, given the growing tensions with more traditional, technocratic, Christian groups springing from first family financial interests.

When the crisis struck, elite political manoeuvres were closely tied up with mass mobilization. In particular, Suharto's need to maintain patronage networks and his attempts to court support with Indonesian radical Islam, both pushed him towards a particular response to the crisis (Hefner 2004). By early 1998, it was clear that Suharto had rejected the IMF approach to crisis. Instead, he was looking at ways of dealing with economic collapse that were more obviously compatible with his economic survival. The strategy he seems to have adopted was one of heightening popular tensions by portraying economic problems as driven by the Indonesian Chinese community. Rice price rises were portrayed as the result of hoarding and speculation by the (almost universally Chinese) distributors. They were met by calls for price restraint and complaints about economic manipulation, rather than a strong focus on elements of the 'social efficiency wage'. At the same time, leading Chinese businessmen were called to a meeting requesting their 'contribution' to alleviating the crisis and the Wanandi brothers (prominent Chinese businessmen with links to the 'technocratic' end of the political establishment) were arrested on spurious charges of a bomb plot.

This strategy had three advantages. It diverted popular animosity from the regime and towards a convenient scapegoat. It provided a potential negotiating tool with the IMF, by showing how tense the social situation was in Indonesia and how urgent the need for an alternative strategy (at this point, Suharto was flirting with the idea of a currency board as a means of halting the decline of the rupiah). Finally, it also secured his support with the radical wing of Indonesian political Islam at a popular level and with the kind of political and military figures he had been courting since the early 1990s, such as General Prabowo.[11]

The political significance of the crisis was operating at two levels, then. Suharto was trying to find a way to maintain his elite support in the face of immediate economic pressure and significant threats to systems of political patronage. At a popular level, the crisis posed a serious threat to the political bargain that

[11] The complexities of shifting alliances in the late New Order period are labyrinthine. For details, see amongst others Schwarz (1999), Hefner (2000b), and Sidel (2006).

secured regime legitimacy: authoritarianism and corruption were only tolerated if they created political stability and economic growth.

Suharto clearly felt that the solution was to try and direct popular unrest against his own political rivals and rely on elite support to tide him through. An obvious conclusion to draw might be that the plan backfired because he had under-estimated the potential for popular revolt. That may be partly true, but it is also important to understand the extent to which elite opposition groups were also involved in trying to direct popular protest.

Protests involved both popular rioting and more carefully organized student protest. Student activists were involved in trying to spread their demands for *reformasi* to a wider audience and opposition politicians (Amien Rais, Megawati Sukarnoputri, Eric Salim) and would be power holders in a post-New Order political system (particularly reformist general Wiranto) were trying to forge links with the students to build their power bases and enhance their reformist credentials. At the same time darker forces in the Indonesian military clustered round General Prabowo appear to have been actively instigating riots in the hope that riots would force a crackdown, propelling them into positions of political influence in a more militarily oriented government.

In general, Indonesia provides us with a strong example of the ways in which sending the wrong political signals in the midst of crisis, against a back-ground of eroded trust in government, can create politically and economically damaging results. In the 1980s, the combination of a strong recent record on poverty reduction and job creation, and a macro-economic response emphasizing external adjustment through the exchange rate was enough to get Indonesia through a crisis with little unrest. In the late 1990s, though, the nature of reforms required to deal with crisis was more threatening to regime legitimacy and the government was in a more politically vulnerable position. Although the formal 'institutions for conflict management' (in Rodrik's terms) may not have changed significantly, informally the regime was more fragile. Suharto had got himself into a situation in which his elite and popular support were both in question, yet he was under pressure to decide between the two in a very public and transparent fashion. He tried to finesse this problem through political means but these attempts ended in failure.

It is this failure of responsiveness (along with levels of trust in governments' ability to do so that are built up in the pre-crisis period) that is the key to institutional failings in resolving social disputes that can emerge during crisis. One might argue, as Rodrik has, that democracies can do a better job under these circumstances as a government reflecting the interests of the elite can be voted out of office. This certainly can take place but is not guaranteed to happen. A secure authoritarian regime with an enlightened view of its role (or a fear of the poor) might be more responsive than a democratic regime that is a focus for political deadlock (as in Thailand) or in which all political parties apparently represent an unresponsive elite (arguably the case in some of our Latin America cases).

In terms of social conflict itself, the numerical data only tell us part of the story (though an important part). The logic of our claims about the interaction between institutional management, trust, and political signals suggests that what matters is a combination of the material effects of crisis and the signals they send about the kind of government that exists. Problems with equity in political management in Indonesia were particularly damaging because they transparently broke what was already a fragile social bargain. If the only reason for tolerating Suharto's government was that it provided economic security, the failure to do so during crisis was likely to be especially damaging.

The kind of social conflict in Indonesia does raise some questions about our assertion that these dynamics during crisis are associated with 'the poor'. Careful research on the social impact of crisis in Indonesia suggests that the rural poor did not suffer strong, direct, adverse effects prior to 1997. Exchange rate depreciation was generally favourable to rural groups through its positive impact on producer prices, offsetting some of the worst effects—though the return of urban migrants to rural communities did increase pressure on livelihoods (whilst reducing the full impact on urban workers).[12] Nonetheless, the politics of crisis was framed domestically in terms of a rich-poor divide and that went on to have an impact on the post-crisis settlement, as we will see in the final part of this chapter. In other words, a variety of explicit or implicit coalitions involving the poor may emerge from crisis conflicts with a strong distributional aspect.

Finally, having discussed pre-crisis vulnerabilities and political constraints, it is worth asking, whether Suharto's genuine political problems could have been overcome by more imaginative economic policies that finessed the growing polarity between 'the cronies' and 'the people'. External and IMF advice was certainly not helping in this regard. Even if the Fund didn't actually push Suharto into the rapid reduction in fuel subsidies in 1998, it was certainly putting pressure on Suharto to choose publicly between elite and public support (and was encouraged to do so by its leading shareholders). Some have argued that earlier attention to social safety nets or a more direct assault on the problem of corporate debt (workouts, haircuts, etc.) could have headed off these difficulties (McLeod 1998; Radelet and Sachs 1998). The key problems, though, were that the debt issue was itself highly politically divisive domestically and that the pattern of Indonesian growth was one in which poverty was dealt with primarily through job creation rather than welfare transfers. As a result there was little infrastructure in place to assist with a rapid expansion of social safety nets and what was in place was tainted by corruption. By the time of crisis, institutional and political failures seem to have over-determined other options, short of regime change. Eventually, of course, that is what happened and we will review attempts to re-establish political order in the final section of the chapter. Part of what distinguished the Malaysia experience, by contrast, was Mahathir's ability to find policy options that both served elite interests and limited the social consequences of crisis.

Malaysia

In Malaysia, the crisis was far less severe. Malaysian banking regulation was stronger than in the rest of the region and the government had tried to control the investment boom in the mid-1990s by introducing reporting requirements for banks' foreign borrowing (Jomo 2004).

[12] For data, see Strauss et al. (2004).

Nonetheless, the devaluation of other currencies in the region heightened pre-existing concerns about Malaysian competitiveness. The labour market was extremely tight and some observers felt that the government was relying on incoming migrant labour, rather than doing enough to encourage technological upgrading. These concerns were exacerbated by an apparent government unwillingness to take the problem seriously. Prime Minister Mahathir refused to cancel a number of large infrastructure 'megaprojects', raising concerns about government willingness to balance the budget and, more dangerously, focusing foreign investor attention on 'crony capitalism' (since some of the large politically well-connected companies were heavily involved in contracting on the projects) (Thirkell-White 2005a).

Instead, Mahathir tended to blame the crisis on foreign speculators, almost taking pride in the extent to which the stock market would fall every time he made a speech (Khoo 2000). He oversaw attempts to limit speculative attacks by limiting Ringgit denominated loans to foreigners and trying to close down access to the swaps market in Singapore. There were also some high-profile bail-outs of well-connected companies.[13]

At the same time, though, there was a far more orthodox agenda being implemented in Malaysia, associated with Mahathir's second in command, Anwar Ibrahim. There were promises of an 'austerity budget' in October, though the markets were not impressed by what was delivered. Then, in December, the government introduced a 'virtual IMF package'. The market rallied briefly but ongoing turbulence in the region and increasing market concerns that Malaysia was not doing the kind of corporate restructuring that the IMF had demanded elsewhere soon put the economy into reverse (Thirkell-White 2005a).

By June, the government had decided that the orthodox strategy was not working. Mahathir appointed Daim Zainuddin as 'Minister of Special Functions' charged with dismantling the 'virtual IMF policy'. A fiscal stimulus package was announced in July and interest rates were lowered in August.

These moves turned out to be the precursor for introducing capital controls and firing Anwar, who was then imprisoned on charges of sodomy and corruption. At that point Malaysians took to the streets in large numbers, first at Anwar's house and then later at the national mosque. The protests were largely non-violent and eventually emerged into a political party, the 'National Justice Party', which campaigned in the 1999 elections on a platform of human rights, anti-corruption, and strengthened democracy (in coalition with the other opposition parties). The elections produced a very bad result from UMNO but not bad enough to actually deprive the BN of power at the centre (Khoo 2004). The economy rebounded fairly rapidly after the controls were implemented and the Malaysian economy has generally recovered.

Despite higher inequality going in to crisis, and sharp ethnic cleavages, Malaysia came through the crisis far more smoothly. This relative success needs to be put down to either better institutions or more successful policy choices during crisis.

13 For a good overview, see Haggard (2000).

Malaysia perhaps demonstrates just how difficult it is to assess the 'quality' of political institutions. At one level, the Malaysian political system has been quite good at reducing inter-ethnic tensions. It has also emphatically delivered on promoting economic growth and reducing poverty (which was initially a largely Malay condition). At another, it has created a situation in which it is extremely difficult to articulate dissent over *intra*-ethnic inequality. It is the rise in intra-Malay inequality (with the shift from a broad-based economic nationalist NEP to a narrow-based, more free-market 'millionaire' producing one) that was at issue in the crisis. It should be no surprise that the political dissent that emerged was primarily from within the Malay community and addressed at both cronyism and high-handed authoritarian government that did not respond to popular concerns. Anwar was symbolic of both.

If dissent was a response to the perception that only rich Malays were benefiting from government policy, the capital controls were potentially quite politically dangerous, as they could be interpreted as designed to protect Malay crony business—and many reformist Malaysian observers saw them in exactly that way. Fortunately, though, crisis resolution was also quite effective. Mahathir's tendency to blame foreigners for the crisis may also have been a good strategy for maintaining domestic peace (though a problematic one for restoring investor confidence). It served to emphasize the extent to which the government was doing what it could in the face of forces beyond its control.

Equally importantly, recovery was quite swift in the wake of the capital controls. The material consequences of policies do matter, particularly when they take effect quickly. Debate continues about whether recovery was *because* of the controls—no one knows what would have happened in Malaysia if they had not been in place. What is clear is that the impact of the crisis on livelihoods in Malaysia was far less severe than in Indonesia. Malaysians that might have been inclined to protest found their livelihoods recovering quickly and the government could plausibly take credit for that as the result of its policy strategy. Equally, the controls were not *simply* a screen behind which Mahathir could bail out his elite 'cronies'. They were introduced in conjunction with a range of measures to ensure ongoing competitiveness. They were designed to safeguard Malay business but Malay business was also being asked to do something to justify the help it was being given. That helped government attempts to portray the controls as a strategy that favoured everyone in Malaysia, not just its closest business allies.

11.4 RESTORING POLITICAL STABILITY AND IMPLEMENTING PRO-POOR POLICY AFTER CRISIS

We conclude this chapter by moving forward from the crisis to look at the extent to which post-crisis reforms re-established political stability and embedded pro-poor growth. Neither country witnessed the kind of long-term political turmoil that ensued in Bolivia (Chapter 10) and broad political stability was established quite quickly. Nonetheless, the crisis and the way it was dealt with have left problematic residues in both countries.

In the aftermath of the fall of the Suharto regime, Indonesia restored broad political stability more quickly than most observers expected. Suharto's successor, B.J. Habibie, presided over a relatively smooth transition. He seems to have realized that his best hope of political survival lay in presenting himself as a liberal reformer, implementing many of the governance reforms recommended by the IFIs, boosting press and political freedom, and preparing for genuinely free and fair elections. His involvement in a high-profile corruption scandal finished any aspirations he may have had for the presidency but his legacy of democracy reforms established the pattern for a series of elections in which power has changed hands peacefully.

Economic recovery, though, has been more problematic. Indonesian growth recovered very slowly and, though now in the respectable 5–6.5 per cent GDP per annum region, continues to lag behind the performance of the 1980s and 1990s. From our point of view, a particular concern is that post-crisis growth has also been less pro-poor. To quote the World Bank's research 'after a low average annual pro-poor growth rate of 2.7 per cent in 1999–2002, this declined even further to a mere 0.3 per cent in 2002–4' (World Bank 2006a). The return to growth did return overall poverty rates to their pre-crisis levels quite quickly but little progress has been achieved since then. Unemployment remains high at around 9–10 per cent and the Gini coefficient of inequality has risen to 39.4 per cent in 2005 (from around 36 per cent just prior to the crisis and 30–33 per cent for most of Indonesia's growth; Table 5.2).

That should not be taken to imply that democracy has produced no gains for pro-poor policy. Poverty has played a strong role in the rhetoric of all presidential candidates. Most have come to power making strong promises to reduce poverty across the country. Poverty-related NGOs also comment favourably on their newfound ability to access government, contribute to debate, and discuss poverty policy. The government, in conjunction with the World Bank, have introduced a very successful and novel form of locally-controlled aid disbursement, originally called KDP (*Kecamatan* Development Project) and now scaled-up as PNPM (*Program Nasional Pemberdayaan Masyarakat* or National Program for Self-Help Community Empowerment). Block grants are disbursed at *kecamatan* level (sub-districts incorporating a small number of villages). Local people decide on priorities for projects and go on to control and monitor implementation. Assessments show that, despite some inevitable problems, the projects have been well-targeted, and are much cheaper than similar government run projects. Village surveys show high levels of satisfaction and projects from earlier rounds have proved sustainable.

However, although PNPM is *the* flagship pro-poor policy in Indonesia, spending on it only amounts to about 0.3 per cent of Indonesian GDP.[14] Total public expenditure is only now returning to its pre-crisis levels of around six per cent of GDP. Whilst the education component of that has increased to seventeen per cent, spending on public infrastructure, welfare programmes, and job creation for the

[14] Estimated at US$1.5 billion for 2009, in relation to estimated GDP of $496 billion.

poor remain low. Equally importantly, there has been a halt to the growth of labour-intensive employment in the formal sector, driven by lower overall levels of investment and foreign direct investment in particular. This, in turn, is probably related to continually low scores on governance indicators, which, with the exception of 'voice and accountability' are lower across the board than they were in 1996 (World Bank 2007) and perhaps due to rising minimum wages.

There are various possible explanations for this problematic performance. One is that the deinstitutionalization of the Suharto era has created a legacy that will take time to overcome. Certainly, economists have noted that Indonesian ministries have been unable to spend the budgets allocated to them for reasons that are tied up with the attempted transition from systems that worked on the basis of patronage to a more orthodox bureaucratic, managerial model. Attempts to tighten up on corruption may have removed civil servants' incentives to promote projects (based on kickbacks) or may have increased anxiety over making any decisions in an environment of tough but somewhat capricious enforcement.

Another explanation is that the transition to a more orthodox, liberal framework for economic governance in Indonesia undermined previous attempts at industrial policy. As we saw above, some industrial policy in Indonesia was clearly problematic. Nonetheless, active attempts to attract labour intensive manufacture for industry did seem to play a strong role in poverty reduction. It may be that a purely liberal approach to investment will continue to result in too much investment in capital intensive extractive industry (mining or oil production) as it did in the 1960s and 1970s. Alternatively, it may be that investment in labour intensive production would materialize if problems of governance could be resolved and if the government can maintain a check on rising minimum wages.

Whether the problem is corruption or a lack of government power and will to actively shape investment, there are strong signs that the political system is not helping to put poverty reduction at the heart of Indonesian policy in the democratic era. To quote Ole Waever's grim assessment: 'Democracy has clearly become the only game in town. However, the elite monopolize, bend and abuse the rules of that game. Most of the supposedly democratic rights and institutions are in place, but they are largely defunct or deficient' (interview, Jakarta, July 2006). The civil society groups that mobilized to push reform agendas in the run up to the fall of Suharto have failed to transform themselves into political parties. Political parties behave more like loose alliances of individuals than tightly disciplined organizations with a clear ideological position.[15] The system of proportional representation and fragmentation of the party system helps to reinforce this lack of clarity as presidents tend to co-opt politicians from a wide range of political parties to form 'rainbow coalition' cabinets (Slater 2004). It is therefore very unclear how a vote for a particular party will translate into positions in the Executive. Party members may also have little incentive to scrutinize and criticize

[15] This view was expressed to me by a very wide range of observers interviewed in Jakarta in July 2006, including NGO activists, UNDP governance reform workers, economists, and members of the political parties themselves.

government policy (since nearly all parties are, to some degree, part of the government) and the electorate is not presented with a clear choice between different policy programmes when it comes to voting. Additionally, particularly during the early period of tenure in the DPR, politicians are as much interested in recouping their 'investment' in acquiring political office as they are in genuine legislative scrutiny.[16] The result has been a fracturing of political power and a weakness of electoral oversight, which encourages either plain populism or bold statements of intent by presidents that are rarely followed through into implementation (Slater 2004).

This situation is exacerbated by elite capture of the party apparatus from above and weak organization from below (perhaps not surprising, given the history of New Order depoliticization). Superior funding and organizational structures have helped to maintain the power of Suharto era political parties. Golkar, the popular vehicle of Suharto's New Order, and Megawati's PD-P (which grew out of one of the New Order's two officially sanctioned 'opposition' political parties) are still capturing the largest share of the vote. The close ties between big business and politics that were central to the Suharto era have reconfigured themselves to operate under the new democratic conditions. The need of politicians and parties for finance and political cooperation, combined with the relative poverty of the Indonesian electorate, encourage political parties whose primary relationship is with elite-level funders, rather than a grass-roots membership. The only partial exception is the Islamist PKS (*Partai Keadilan Sejahtera* or people's justice party), which fights on an anti-corruption platform but seems to have less to say about economic policy. Recent surveys show heartening ongoing support for democracy as the best system of government in Indonesia, but also very low levels of trust in almost all varieties of public official and politician.

Overall, Indonesia demonstrates that democratic reform can be a powerful tool for restoring political stability. However, it can be difficult to make even democracy work for the poor. This may be particularly so in middle-income countries where ongoing poverty reduction may require active attempts to foster more labour intensive production through influence over investment, as well as merely channelling social services to a very poorly served countryside. On the other hand, Indonesian democracy is still very young and an active civil society may yet be able to organize itself into a more effective opposition over time.

In Malaysia, although there were powerful examples of political favouritism, there were also genuine attempts at reform. As we saw, much of the debate during crisis revolved around the extent to which Malaysia's government would bail out well-connected 'crony' business at the expense of the general population. In the immediate post-crisis period, there were reasons for thinking that these fears had been overstated. Corporate governance reforms began under Mahathir's

[16] Again, this is almost universally accepted in Jakarta. A high ranking UNDP employee working on programmes for parliamentarians argued that much of the work he had done in helping parliamentarians debate legislation over the first term of the DPR had been undone by the high turnover of elected members. The new members were not yet close enough to an election to concentrate on anything other than acquiring funds. Similar views were expressed by World Bank staff, NGO activists, and bureaucrats, again during author interviews in Jakarta 2006a.

leadership but really took off after his resignation in 2002. His successor, Ahmad Abdullah Badawi, then stepped up the agenda of anti-corruption programmes and reform, making personal probity the basis of much of his appeal in the 2004 elections.[17] The result was a dramatic return of fortune for UMNO. Although a small number of high-profile bail-outs may have led the market to expect firms connected to the Prime Minister to prosper in the post-crisis period, there is no evidence that they actually did so, in fact rather the reverse (Johnson et al. 2006). Fears that the capital controls would be a means for avoiding post-crisis reforms, then, were misplaced.

Crisis restructuring reduced the ownership share of politically well-connected business and increased the influence of 'government-linked corporations' (or GLCs) which now account for thirty-six per cent of the market capitalization of the KLSE, fifty-four per cent of the composite index, and account for more than fiftly per cent of the top twenty-five stocks. The government put its stake under the charge of a holding company, Khazanah Nasional Bhd, which it hopes to convert into an investment arm along the line of Singapore's Temasek. A flurry of activities designed to improve the efficiency and performance of these companies followed, raising some hopes for a renewed focus on improved corporate governance (Thirkell-White 2007b).

However, these changes co-existed with strong signs of continuity. The ninth Malaysia Plan (announced in 2006) promised support for domestic industry on the basis of efficiency including, for instance, strong signals about a more transparent and competitive approach to government procurement. On the other hand, this image of encouraging domestic competitiveness is undercut by an ongoing emphasis on *bumiputera* preference (so, despite 'transparent and competitive' tendering, there continue to be quotas of projects that must be awarded to *bumiputera* companies). Over time, any intentions Abdullah may have had for genuine reform were worn down by internal party pressure. By 2007, his administration was clouded by a string of allegations of corruption and judicial abuse (Guan 2008). The UMNO chose to respond through increased ethnic chauvinism, rather than reforms or reaching out to non-Malay opposition and was heavily punished for that in the 2008 elections. The results saw the BN's electoral share fall below sixty-six per cent for the first time since independence (Pepinsky 2009). That result has certainly kept alive hopes that increased corruption and elitism can be reined in through growing multi-ethnic electoral competition. However, despite a broad electoral pact holding the opposition parties together, there were strong signs that the non-Malay electorate has little stomach for electing MPs from the PAS, the Islamist Malay opposition party and that Malays are still sceptical of the DAP. The fact that it was primarily non-Malays who defected from the BN again weaken the claim that ethnic politics has been overcome in favour of some form of pro-poor (or at least anti-elite) electoral coalition (Pepinsky 2009).

Overall, in both countries, we see that short-term political reform can play an important role in easing tensions in a crisis situation. However, making that reform pay real dividends for the poor is increasingly difficult in a middle-income country context. It is likely to require long-term political action including

[17] For greater detail, see Case (2005).

attempts to find ongoing policies that create growth in domestic business (to satisfy elites) in ways that also continue to generate employment. In Malaysia, the population continues to struggle to exercise significant control over the danger of business capture of government policy but there is at least some scope to send messages of discontent to the *Barisan Nasional* government through increasingly dramatic electoral decline. In Indonesia, results to date have been quite disappointing. They certainly underline the extent to which electoral democracy is, in itself, no panacea for promoting pro-poor growth. However, it is certainly far too soon to write off Indonesia's democratic experiment. The task is to find ways to deepen Indonesian democracy in ways that create more effective pressure for pro-poor policy.

12

Russia

Paul Mosley and Altay Mussurov[1]

12.1 BACKGROUND

In Russia, more than in any other country within our sample, the battle between state and market was won by the state. This is most transparently true, of course, of the communist period between 1917 and 1992, during which private enterprise was illegal, most land and businesses were compulsorily owned by government, and civil society and democratic institutions scarcely existed. But even before the revolution and after structural adjustment, the role of the Russian government in the economy was greater than in other middle-income countries and the current trend under Putin and Medvedev, after a short liberalizing interlude in the 1990s, is once again towards the reassertion of state power.

The state's victory has also had an external dimension. Like other industrializing countries with geo-political ambitions, nineteenth and early twentieth-century Russia invested much of its public expenditure on military purposes; by 1945, at appalling and unprecedented human cost,[2] this had made Russia the world's second superpower (Kennedy 1989) and within a few years, the only nuclear power to attempt to rival the USA. During the cold war, the Soviet Union was concerned to embed and extend its control over the 'non-aligned' developing countries through all possible means, including diplomatic trade policy and overseas aid flows to some sixty to seventy developing countries.

Our concern in this chapter is with the distributional consequences of this outcome, and especially with the politics of income inequality and poverty during the crises of 1992–8 and their aftermath. As in other chapters we wish to understand the link between political structures, the choice of policies, and the poverty outcome. There now exists a very substantial literature on these issues in Russia, especially at the macro-level, and our own particular contribution is to

[1] Many thanks in particular to Alexei Gradzhinkin, Vladimir Gimpelson, Natalya Zubarevich, Lilia Ovcharova, Alla Chirikova, Nicholas Mosley, and others who assisted the authors with the field research in January 2008; also to Robert Russell, Linda Hanna, and others in the Russian department at Sheffield who attempted to teach me basic Russian. The usual disclaimer applies.

[2] The enormity of the sacrifices which the Second World War inflicted on the Russian population is still being re-estimated, but best current estimates range around 26 million civilian and military dead between 1941 and 1945 (Gatrell, and Harrison 1993, Table 6), or three times the *total* global numbers killed in the First World War.

examine the relationship between policy and individual well-being at the *regional* as well as at the all-Russia level. Russia is a federation of eighty-nine constituent territories or 'federal subjects', and our hope is that by illustrating the diversity of experience between these territories we can illuminate the politics of poverty globally.

In both the economic and the political dimension, the degree of transition towards liberalization has been intermediate, and if present day Russia is certainly not a democracy or a free-market economy, neither is it the autocratic command economy of the Soviet period, or of several post-Soviet transition economies today. Much of the economy has been privatized, but in many cases into the hands of oligarchs with great political power, and huge segments of unviable industry[3] and low-productivity agriculture persist. This has implications for the public finances as well as for competitiveness, since both at federal and at regional level, and in spite of recent centralizing reforms, taxes are still difficult to collect from the powerful. The political system, as emphasized above, began its transition towards the market and towards democracy under quite exceptional conditions, in which the legacy of communism was that there were 'no democratic institutions, parties, or civil society to rekindle' (McFaul, Petrov, and Ryabov 2004, page 14), and many of the particularities of the 'semiauthoritarian state' (Lyall 2006), or if you prefer semi democracy, which Russia now has are owing to these distinctive initial conditions. The new political parties which have emerged in Russia since 1991 hold little power over the state, in part owing to the negative feelings inspired by the (Communist) Party which preceded them. None of the presidents who have run Russia since liberalization, Yeltsin, Putin, and Medvedev, have been members of a political party, and during the Yeltsin period no party, not even those which the government chose to sponsor, was able to command even a plurality of political support (McFaul, Petrov, and Ryabov 2004, page 37, Chapter 5 *passim*). But, as Shevtsova comments (2007, page 893) 'by failing to cope with the deepening crisis and paralysis of power, [Yeltsin] provoked among Russians the longing for power and an "iron hand"'. To achieve this, as in many Latin American governments of the 1970s (O'Donnell 1979), power has now been concentrated in the hands of a leader who relies on the bureaucracy, security forces, and big business for support. It is paradoxical that the degeneration of Yeltsin's leadership strengthened demands, not for independent institutions that could prevent further abuses of power, but for a new and more powerful

[3] Large-scale agriculture also, when transferred into private hands, has experienced only limited improvements in efficiency. One very fertile 4000-hectare collective farm near Voronezh, was privatized in 1996 but still lacks gas and running water:

> The collective had once employed more than six hundred workers; [the manager] was now, in 2007, responsible for 160, a drastic reduction but still a disastrously inefficient use of labour. Left to himself, he would have laid off at least two-thirds of the present workforce—some because they were unskilled, others because they were idle and yet more because they were permanently impaired by alcoholism. But, he gestured emphatically, 'my hands are tied [by local-level political pressure through the works council, and by lack of capital]. This is the best, the richest soil in the world and yet we only get crumbs from it. What else can I do? I have to laugh. Shall I cry? No-one will listen if I cry!'
>
> (Dimbleby 2008, page 150)

authoritarian leadership. As one consequence of this, the presidential party (United Russia) now dominates the popular vote,[4] and it remains the case that inter-party competition of the kind that now characterizes much of the industrialized and developing worlds is not a force for democracy in Russia. Freedom of personal and political expression improved emphatically during the Yeltsin period, but since that time has fallen back. The national television stations are firmly under state control, as are most national newspapers, with distinguished exceptions (such as *Novaya Gazeta*), and direct elections have been abolished for all offices except the presidency. Public anti-government demonstrations are routinely banned, and individuals whose views are considered to be a nuisance to the state (including the chess champion Gary Kasparov, now the leader of one of the seven minor political parties not listed above)[5] not infrequently find themselves subjected to periods of detention or restriction on their movements.

Central to the argument of this book is the relationship between poverty, liberalization both political and economic in individual countries, and the wider world. Russian policy has a long tradition of being inward-looking[6] but under the stresses of structural adjustment, which were more severe in Russia than elsewhere (Figure 12.1 below) the economy became more open to flows of both trade and foreign capital, including loans from the international financial institutions (IFIs), especially the World Bank and International Monetary Fund (IMF). Over and above sector-level loans to the energy, financial, and infrastructure sectors, the Bank and Fund made three enormous loans to Russia during the 1990s designed to bridge the fiscal gap and ease the immense social costs associated with the transition. These loans, which amounted to some $40 billion over the course of the 1990s,[7] were conditional on the standard performance criteria attached to budgetary support from the Bank and Fund, including liberalization of trade and capital movements, privatization of state industries, and measures to secure the payment of overdue taxes. Very few of these policy conditions were in fact complied with. As a wide literature has confirmed (Collier 1997; Mosley, Harrigan, and Toye 1995; Svensson 2000b, 2003) even small and weak countries are able to exercise strong reverse leverage, enabling them to dodge conditionality, on international financial institutions, by virtue of those institutions' need to spend their budget and in particular the pressures on them to rescue their clients from

[4] In the presidential elections of March 2008, United Russia received 64.3 per cent of the vote, the Communists 11.6 per cent, the Liberal Democrats 8.1 per cent, and Just Russia 7.7 per cent; United Russia only controls 341 of the 450 seats in the Duma.

[5] Interview with Gary Kasparov by Fergal Keene, BBC Radio 4, 16 January 2009.

[6] 'I want you to listen to this', said a Russian journalist interviewed by John Steinbeck in 1947. 'And he read something like this. "The Russians of Moscow are highly suspicious of foreigners, who are watched constantly by the secret police. Every move is noticed and sent into central headquarters. A guard is placed on all foreigners. Furthermore, Russians do not receive foreigners in their houses, and they seem to be afraid even to talk to them very much."

There was a good deal more in this vein, and at the end our friend looked up and said "What do you think of it?" And we said, "We don't think you can get it past the censor."

He laughed. "But this was written in 1634. It is from a book called Voyages in Muscovy, Tartary and Persia, by a man called Adam Olearius"' (Steinbeck 1947, page 192).

[7] This was composed of: $4 billion World Bank Structural Adjustment Loans; $6 billion IMF standby 1992, $6.4 billion IMF Systemic Transformation Facility 1993, $17 billion IMF Extended Facility, including supplement from Japanese aid authorities, 1998.

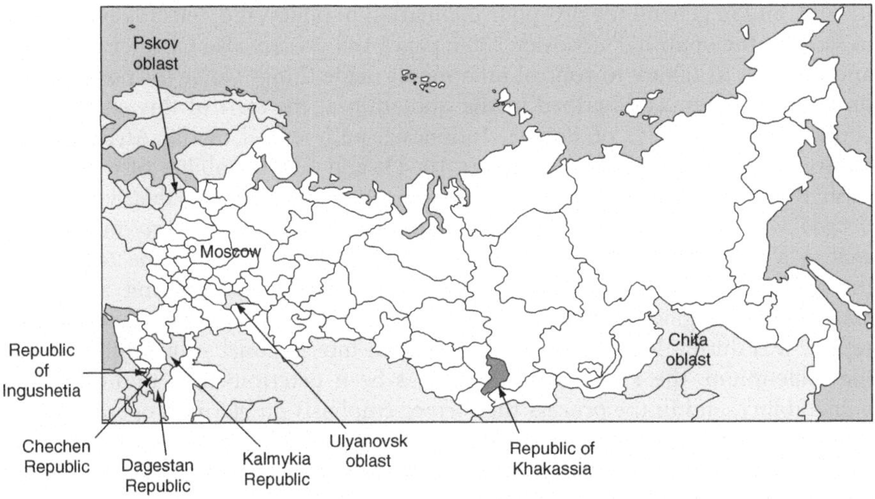

Figure 12.1 Regions of the Russian Federation (case-study regions highlighted).

debt problems—once again resurgent in Russia at the time of writing. And Russia, even in its extremity of the early 1990s, is not a small and weak country. Indeed, the mere presence of its nuclear missiles, as the testimony of the IMF's resident representative makes clear, was quite sufficient to spook the Fund into setting aside whichever parts of its fiscal conditionality the Russian government might choose to discard:

> They say that Indonesia is too big to fail, but Russia is something totally different. Think of the nuclear weapons! I never made the programs [*sc.* the policy conditions attached to loans, PM] easier because of this, but it is just realism that we have to integrate them into the modern world economy, or we will have a nightmare. It would only take five or six crazy people in Russia, and just imagine what might happen.[8]

Thus, to pre-empt the risk of a Communist win at the June 1996 presidential election, very much on the cards in the light of the parliamentary votes of the time,[9] a $10 billion extended facility was agreed in February, subject to four conditions (lifting controls on capital flows, liberalizing foreign trade, revising the tax code to remove tax concessions in favour of oligarchs, and resuming privatization), only the last two of which were ever implemented, and then in a highly distorted manner. Thus, so far from redressing the Russian government's tendencies towards lax fiscal governance, the IFIs indulged them. One consequence of this was distributional: having been urged, in common with most recipient governments of the 1990s, to increase the share of social expenditure

[8] Interview with Horiguchi, head of IMF mission in Russia, November 1999, reported by Stone (2002, page 138).

[9] In the December 1993 elections, the party of the prime minister, Viktor Chernomyrdin, had won fifteen per cent of the vote, the left-leaning party also established by the Kremlin won less than ten per cent and the CPRF (Communist Party of the Russian Federation) and its rural affiliate won almost twenty per cent (McFaul, Petrov, and Ryabov 2004, page 37).

in GNP and in general the pro-poor inclination of policy, the Yeltsin government in fact did the opposite[10] (Mosley 2006, pages 188–91; see also Chapter 5 above), and through its failure to control inflation, it made things worse for poor people on fixed incomes, as described in the quotation at the start of this chapter. By contrast with the case of Bolivia, Indonesia, and several of the African cases reported in this volume (see Chapters 10, 11, and 13), the ability of the IFIs to push Russia onto a more pro-poor policy course even during this 'vulnerable decade' was effectively zero. This was a failure for the Bank's poverty mission, as well as a bargaining failure.[11] A great idealistic crusade against the ravages of the transition, which the Bank at one time visualized as offering a distinct extension of its global influence, perished with barely a whimper. And this, to repeat, was during Russia's period of maximal international vulnerability. Since the millennium, the Putin government has been determined to minimize this vulnerability, and in the process the former emphasis on *glasnost*, openness, has been replaced by a consensus engineered around the concept of *derzhavnichestvo*—literally, preoccupation with power, or in Shevtsova's (2007) more idiomatic translation, 'Russia is a great power or it is nothing.' There is no longer a need to borrow from the IMF or any other donor, and all pretence that Russia's social policies or any other element of its economic policy are open to influence from international bodies has been abandoned.

We now examine the dynamics of *internal* vulnerability and attempts to bolster the Russian state against it. When the Soviet Union was dissolved in 1992, Russia adopted a federal constitution, in which some powers, including taxation and public expenditure, were devolved from the centre to the regions. At this moment of weakness fourteen of the eighty-nine federal subjects took advantage of their bargaining power by employing the miscellany of voice and threatened exit strategies listed in Table 12.1: six (Tatarstan, Tuva, Sakha-Yakutia, Bashkortostan, and North Ossetia, as well as Chechnya) stopped paying taxes to the centre. Tatarstan, as well as Chechnya, declared independent sovereign status. These strategies were accompanied, especially in the regions which were bearing the worst economic stress, by strikes, as in the coal-mining regions of Kemerovo, the Kuzbas, and the Donbas in 1989 and 1991, the first mass strikes experienced in the Soviet Union for over sixty years, and by 'riot-type conflict', as also encountered in time of recession by Indonesia, Bolivia, and Argentina within our sample of countries affected by crisis.[12]

Between them, the manoeuvres illustrated in Table 12.1 took Russia, between 1990 and 1999, to 'the precipice of state failure' (Giuliano 2006, page 276). They mark the opening rounds of a game to which the federal government's response

[10] Over and above the attempted macro-conditionality described above, the World Bank government attempted to persuade the Russian government to target its expenditure on low-income individuals. It was totally unsuccessful in doing this at the level of individuals and income groups; but some redistribution to disaffected low-income *regions* through fiscal transfers did take place, as discussed below.

[11] This was also, to a lesser degree, true in smaller Eastern European countries with less bargaining power (Mosley 2003, page 196).

[12] During the 'East Asian' crisis period East Timor also seceded from Indonesia, and the eastern provinces of Bolivia, at the time of writing, have held a referendum on the possibility of seceding from the La Paz government. See Chapters 10 and 11 above.

Table 12.1 Voice, violence, and secessionist strategies in Russia's republics, 1989–94.

Republic	Tatar-stan	Tuva	Chechnya	Yakutia	Bashkor-tostan	Kalmykia	Karelia	Buryatia	Dagestan/ Ingushetia	N. Ossetia	Komi	Kabardino-Balkaria	Chuvashia	Udmurtia	Mari-El	Mordovia
Descriptives																
Gross regional product 2004, $per capita (Russia = 2,550)	2467	1135	NA	6175	2944	1395	2827	1392	755/448	1281	5035	1071	1698	2460	1505	2141
Headcount poverty rate per cent, 2004	13.5	45.3	NA	20.5	16.1	61.9	17.3	33.9	22.3/61.3	18.2	15.5	24.7	26.1	23.3	40.1	30.6
Constituents of index of secessionism, 1989–94:																
Declared sovereignty	1	1	1	1	1	1	1	1	1	1	1	1	1		1	1
Boycotted RSFSR presidency referendum, 1991	1	1	1							1						
Established presidency	1	1	1	1	1	1	1				1	1	1		1	
Passed language law	1	1		1				1					1			
Titular language sole language		1														
Set own tax policy, or stopped paying taxes	1	1	1	1	1					1						
Refused to sign Yeltsin's	1		1													

Continued

Table 12.1 Continued

Republic	Tatar-stan	Tuva	Chechnya	Yakutia	Bashkor-tostan	Kalmykia	Karelia	Buryatia	Dagestan/ Ingushetia	N. Ossetia	Komi	Kabardino-Balkaria	Chuvashia	Udmurtia	Mari-El	Mordovia
federation Treaty, 1992																
Held sovereignty referendum	1				1											
Adopted constitution	1	1	1	1	1	1	1		1	1	1	1		1		
With right to secede?		1		1												
Republic law supreme?	1	1	1	1	1	1	1									
Boycotted/ invalid referendum on Yeltsin, April 1993	1		1													
Boycotted referendum on RF constitution, December 1993	1		1													
Incidence of 'riot-type conflict'			X						X							
Subsequent governance events																
Armed conflict			Invasion and civil war, 1992–6, renewed, 1999–2000						Invasion, 1992	Caught in invasion of S. Ossetia by Georgia, 2008						

Source: Giuliano (2006), revised and updated. Indicators of riot-type conflict are from Orttung (2000).
Shaded regions feature also in regional case studies, section 5 below.

varied according to the region. Very frequently, even in Chechnya, the initial governmental response to this turbulence was fiscal. As Treisman (1999, see also Treisman and Gimpelson (2000)) brilliantly illustrated during the 1990s, the Russian federal government has routinely used the allocation of subsidies as a lever with which to buy off grievance, and indeed the buying off of grievance (as expressed by declarations of autonomy, failure to vote for Yeltsin, and man-days lost to strikes), was the best available predictor of fiscal allocations to the regions in the 1990s, by contrast with social need, measured by the level of social infrastructure. Indeed the allocation of federal subsidies was actually regressive, in the sense that it went more often to regions with good social infrastructure than to regions where it was bad (Treisman 1999, Tables 5, A1 and A2). Thus, at least across this sample, it was the threat of political disruption which drove fiscal allocations, and not poverty. This appears to fit the 'pessimistic' theory of the politics of poverty sketched in our opening chapter. But where political disruption coincided with poverty, as in Dagestan and Ingushetia, the consequences were progressive at the regional level, although the gains were often appropriated by local elites.

However, there were of course later moves in the game. By 1994 the Yeltsin government had decided to respond to the continuing revolt in Chechnya, with which there had been a tradition of riot-type conflict and worse going back at least to the 1820s,[13] with guns rather than butter, whereas Tatarstan, which had also rebelled in 1991, was conciliated with 'the kind of constructive ambiguity that allows the elites on both sides to claim a constitutional and political triumph—to the benefit of both parties' (Dimbleby 2008, page 294). The war in Chechnya, which by 1996 had claimed at least a hundred thousand lives, half of them civilian, was abandoned in that year and then revived in 1999 by the newly reappointed prime minister, Vladimir Putin, leading to the establishment of a fragile peace the following year. A revolt in Dagestan (where there had also been a revolt in 1991, but by separatists rather by the regional government, hence classified only as 'riot-type conflict' in Table 12.1) was likewise suppressed by federal government forces in 1999. During the Putin period, partly as a response to this violence, there has been both a massive growth of the state, and following the principle of *derzhavnichestvo*, a radical recentralization of power. Since the Beslan siege of 2004 regional governors are appointed by the federal state rather than elected, where often the state rejects the rule of law, that offers many opportunities for corruption (Hoff and Stiglitz 2008; Shevtsova 2007). The political atmosphere in the Caucasus continues to be very tense, and in 2008 international mediation was required when Russia beat back a Georgian incursion into North Ossetia, occupying the neighbouring Georgian territory of South Ossetia for a time. Within this context,

[13] Russia invaded Georgia in 1801, and there have been many cross-border raids since that time. In the winter of 1944 the entire population of Chechnya was deported to Kyrgyzstan and resettled on collective farms there. They were allowed to return during the Khrushchev thaw in 1956. A stereotype of the Caucasian ethnic minority regions as being devious and unresponsive to legitimate economic incentives has persisted certainly since Lermontov's character Maxim Maximich described them in 1840 as having 'no capacity for any kind of education . . . but beware, they like fleecing travellers. Look here, they'll try and get vodka money out of you' (Bela', in Lermontov 1840/1992, page 8) and elements of this exasperation persist in remarks about the Caucasus by President Putin in the 2000s, as discussed below.

the role of social expenditure has been not to increase the share of the poor in *overall* income, but rather to redistribute nominal amounts to regions considered by the centre troublesome enough to need buying off, but not so troublesome as to merit a wholesale military crackdown as in Chechnya. On the southern periphery, Ingushetia, Mari-El, Tatarstan, and now Dagestan, all examined further in section 5 below, are among the former dissident territories whose recent falls in poverty in the Putin period are to be explained in this way.[14] Within the industrial areas of central Russia, Crowley's analysis (1994) of industrial relations in the steelmaking and steelworking industry shows how protest in these and other strategic sectors, which since 1991 have 'scarcely made a sound' (Crowley 1994, page 590), was bought off by appropriately-tailored material incentives in kind (such as housing subsidies) and in cash, together with an awareness of mutual dependence between workers and enterprises.[15] Thus, around a macro-economic trend in which national income was increasing dramatically after 2000, deviations from the nationally static share of social expenditure (Table 12.2) consisted in many cases of an attempt to buy off political tensions at the local level, and the nature of this response helps to determine the local-level poverty outcome. In addition, in one single case there was also significant pro-poor political agitation at the national level. This was the case of the Pensioners' Party, established in 2004 as a response to the erosion of the value of the state pension (Table 12.2).

In the 2005 local elections, it was expected that United Russia would achieve an easy victory, but it was in fact beaten into second place by the Pensioners' Party in a number of seats, including Tomsk and a number of seats in Siberia. However, the discomfiture this caused to the leadership was quickly pre-empted. The leader of the Pensioners' Party had been one of Putin's long-standing allies and had campaigned for him in the 2000 presidential election, and the tensions associated with his establishment of the Pensioners' Party were quickly resolved, both economically, through an increase in real federal pension in 2005, and politically. In 2006 the Pensioners' Party merged with two other minor parties to form Just Russia, which has been welcomed by Putin as the authorized opposition to the presidential party, United Russia.

To set the scene for the discussion of the politics of poverty which follows, it remains to delineate the functioning of the labour market, which determines a large part of poverty, since the poorest have no assets but labour power to convert into a livelihood. Since the massive expansion of the educational system in the

[14] In the Caucasus, this has been done not only through state social expenditures, but also through microfinance NGOs. The Caucacus region was the fastest growing in terms of microfinance disbursements of all areas in the Esatern Europe and Central Asia region (Microfinance Centre for Eastern Europe and the former Soviet Union, Warsaw, monthly report, September 2008).

[15] As a steelworker from Magnitogorsk told an American historian, 'We're completely dependent on them. Food, clothes, apartments, furniture, day care, summer camps, vacations—everything is allocated by them according to their lists, with which they rule over our lives. Everyone has something to lose.' Since the initial period of maximum strike activity in the late 1980s and early 1990s, 'most strike activity, outside of coal mining, has occurred among transportation workers and white collar employees (doctors, teachers, and air-traffic controllers). While there may be alternative explanations for strikes among these particular workers, almost all lie outside the traditional heavy industrial sector, where worker collective action could be expected to occur and where enterprise goods and services have been concentrated' (Crowley 1994, pages 604 and 611).

Table 12.2 Russian Federation: functional allocation of government expenditure, 1990–2008.

	1994	1995	1996	1997	1998	1999	2000	2001	2002	2003	2004	2005	2006	2007	2008	2009
Defence	28.5	*49.6*	*63.9*	*81.4*	*65.1*	115.6	191.7	247.7	295.4	355.7	430	581.8	683.4	834.0	1043.6	1191.2
Agriculture, forestry, fishing, and hunting	14.2	*22.3*	*25.2*	*31.1*	*24.3*	35.5	55.0	67.4	59.8	68.1	78.6	78.7	110.8	146.4	238.3	279.1
Education	27.3	*56.2*			*99.7*	147.6	214.7	277.8	409.4	475.6	593.4	801.8	*1036.4*	1343.0	1658.1	1783.5
Health	19.6	*41.0*	*56.2*	*77.1*	*67.4*	103.7	153.4	181.4	253.7	297.6	370.3	797.1	*962.2*	*1381.5*	1546.3	1653.0
Social protection, of which: pensions	*55.1*	*125.1*	*189.6*	*245.5*	*237.7*	381.7 (279.6)	551.1 (360.6)	808.3 (533.8)	1040.5 (722.6)	879.9 (140.9)	1,407.4 (1,059.4)	1,755.6 (1,254.6)	2,080.4 (1,438.3)	2,477.7 (1,669.7)	3,333.3 (2,282.3)	4,247.7 (2,825.8)
Total expenditure (billion roubles)	280.5	*486.1*	*652.7*	*839.5*	*842.1*	1258.0	1960.1	2419.4	3422.3	3964.9	4,669.7	6,820.6	8,375.2	11,378.6	13,991.8	16,048.3
Pro-poor expenditure ratios: Social protection/total expenditure (per cent)	19.6	25.7	29.0	29.2	28.2	30.3	28.1	33.4	30.4	22.2	30.1	25.7	24.8	21.7	23.8	26.4
Pro-poor expenditure ('PPE': agriculture + health + education + social protection/total expenditure)	41.4	50.3			50.9	53.1	49.7	55.1	51.5	43.4	52.4	50.3	50.0	47.0	48.4	49.6
Defence/total expenditure	10.1	10.2	9.8	9.7	7.7	9.1	9.7	10.2	8.6	8.9	9.2	8.5	8.1	7.3	7.4	7.4
Memorandum items: nominal exchange rate (roubles/$)	2.19	4.55	5.12	5.78	9.7	24.6	28.1	29.1	31.3	30.6	28.8	28.2	27.1	25.6	24.8	31.7
Real exchange rate 2000 = 100	102.9	112.9	137.8	145.6	128.5	90.6	100	120.2	123.6	127.3	137.3	149.2	163.5	172.7	184.4	172.3
Nominal pension/poverty line, per cent	129	101	116	113	115	70	76	90	100	102	106	98	100	102	115	127

All figures in roman type are in billions of roubles (*italic figures in trillions*); other figures are in units stated.

Source: IMF, *Government Finance Statistics Yearbook*. Data are for 'Consolidated central government' after 2002, 'general government', plus local government (column 1 and selected measures in column 2). Data for 1995–2009 period from Russian State Federal State Statistics Service, *Social Conditions and Welfare of the Russian Population, various issues, Health in Russia, various issues, Russian Statistical Yearbook, various issues.*

inter-war period Russia has been a high-wage economy, unable since the ending of the Gulag system to force down the cost of labour by direct conscription[16] and unable to import low-wage labour from neighbouring countries even on the same scale as western Europe and the southern United States. More than this, it is a flexible-real-wage economy (Gimpelson 1999); by contrast with Hungary, Poland, and other transitional countries, which adjusted to falling demand by shedding jobs and creating unemployment, Russia kept employment levels remarkably stable in response to the negative shock of the crisis, as observed in our illustration of reform on collective farms above, and allowed the real wage to take the strain of financial adjustment.[17] Where real incomes increased in this way it was mainly among the higher income groups, from the oligarchs downwards, and when jobs and, much more often, real wages were cut they were typically amongst the poorest income groups, leading to a situation in which Russia moved in four years, 1991–5, from one of the most equal societies in the world in communist times to a more unequal society than the United States (Brainerd 1998)[18] and from the plateau of severe inequality reached in the middle of the 1990s, there has been no significant alleviation up to the time of writing (Table 12.3 below). During the slump of the 1990s, the required wage cuts were achieved not only by cutting nominal wage levels (or failing to adjust them in face of inflation), but also through the Russian particularity of simply failing to pay the wages which were due. Wage arrears, well into the 2000s, have been a major cause of poverty among the lower paid in Russia (Lehman, Wadsworth, and Acquisti 1999), aggravating the tendencies observed by Brainerd; and, as illustrated by Mussurov (2007), political protest was strongest where arrears were most severe, catching some individuals in a political protest-social exclusion trap. The Putin government now claims (Shevtsova 2007) that wages are paid on time.

From this outline we have observed some of the political parameters and behaviours which have influenced well-being levels among different groups in Russia, both short-term during the crises of the nineties and longer-term during the subsequent recovery period. At federal level, there exist in post-transition Russia no coalitions capable of making a dent in the principle that the poorest are generally the politically weakest (the gains of the Pensioners' Party in the

[16] The economics of forced labour are analysed by Miller and Smith (2007). Some Gulags remained open until the 1980s. A photograph of one of the less notorious ones, Perm 36 in the Urals, not closed until 1987, is provided by Dimbleby (2008), spread between pages 340–1.

[17] In other words, the supply curve of Russian labour is steep, and adjustment in the labour market is of prices (i.e. wages) rather than quantities: interview, Vladimir Gimpelson, Moscow, 25 January 2008. Within the stable quantum of employment during the 1990s crisis, there was a shrinkage in federal employment and an increase in employment by regional governments (Treisman and Gimpelson 2001, page 149). For further analysis bringing in also the demand side of the economy, see section 5 below.

[18] Shevtsova (2007, page 897) characterizes the income distribution in the following way:

> The structure of Russian society is hardly a recipe for stability. Between 1 and 2 per cent of the population constitute really rich people; 15–20 per cent are middle class, able to save and to contribute money to their children's education; 60–65 per cent dwell in the 'twilight zone' between the middle class and the poor; 15–20 per cent are fighting for survival; and 5–7 per cent have fallen to the social 'bottom'. Such a 'pyramid' social structure is inherently prone to turmoil.

Table 12.3 Russia: selective poverty indicators based on official estimates, 1980–2009.

Year	(2) Headcount Index	(3) Gini	(4) Real wage (1990 = 100)	(5) Nominal pension/ poverty line	(6) Unemploy-ment rate	(7) Death rate per 1000	(8) Poverty line in roubles per month ($ in brackets)
1980	0.113	0.276				11.0	
1990	0.101		100		0.1	12.0	
1991	0.114	0.260	97				
1992	0.335	0.289	65	119	5.1	13.1	1.9
1993	0.315	0.407	65	138	5.9	13.6	20.6 (20.7)
1994	0.224	0.409	60	129	8.3	14.0	86.6 (39.5)
1995	0.248	0.387	43	101	9.6	14.9	246.1 (57.9)
1996	0.220	0.387	49	116	9.8	14.9	369.4 (72.1)
1997	0.207	0.390	51	113	12		411.2 (71.0)
1998	0.233	0.394	44	115	13.6	14.0	493.3 (50.8)
1999	0.284	0.399	35	70	12.9	15.5	907.8 (36.8)
2000	0.290	0.395	42	76	10.0		1,210 (43.0)
2001	0.275	0.397	50	90	9.0	15.7	1,500 (51.4)
2002	0.246	0.397	59	100	8.7	16.2	1,808 (57.6)
2003	0.203	0.403	65	102	8.0	16.4	2,112 (68.8)
2004	0.176	0.409	72	106	8.1	16.0	2,376 (82.4)
2005	0.177	0.409	81	98	7.3	16.1	3,018 (106.7)
2006	0.152	0.416	92	99	7.0	15.2	3,422 (125.8)
2007	0.133	0.423	107	102	5.9	14.6	3,847 (150.3)
2008	0.140*	0.422	119	115	7.1	14.6	4,593 (184.8)
2009	0.16*	0.422	115	127	8.4	14.2	5,153 (162.3)

Source: Mussurov and Mosley (2007), Table 1, updated from World Bank (2010).

Notes: column 2, headcount index of poverty = share of individuals with incomes below the official poverty line (Federal Statistics Agency measure; note that the method of calculating the poverty line was amended in 1991 and in 2000). In 2009, poverty line was defined as an adult income of 5572 roubles, or £115, per month (4,100 for pensioners; 4,930 for children; 5,153 overall population) as reported in Goskomstat, *Social Conditions and Well-Being of the Population of Russia for 2010*, Table 5.10. For 2008–9, starred data* are based on World Bank 2010, Figures 1.3 (page 5) and Figure 2.4 (page 23). Note that the *Guardian*, 'Millions more Russians shunted into poverty', *Guardian*, 1 September 2009, claims, on the basis of a Goskomstat estimate of 27.5 million people below the poverty line in April 2009, that 'all of the gains in poverty during the period 2000–8 have been utterly wiped out', which would imply a poverty rate of around 0.25 in 2009, rather than the figure in the table (column 3). Gini Index = income inequality measure from Goskomstat (*Socio-Economic Indicators of Russian Federation for 1991–2009*)

Column 4, real wage = inflation-adjusted wage from Goskomstat (*Socio-Economic Indicators of Russian Federation for 1991–2009*) the previous year.

Column 5, pension/poverty line = ratio of nominal monthly pension to the poverty line.

Column 6, unemployment rate on ILO definition.

Column 7, mortality rate on UNICEF definition.

mid-2000s being merely a blip), and international institutions have had no pro-poor leverage whatsoever, but political pressures for a regular readjustment of the minimum wage have enabled some gains for individuals just below the middle of the income distribution. At regional level, the situation is different, first in response to variations in the tightness of local labour markets, and second we have already observed evidence that voice and (threatened) exit, rather than loyalty, behaviours may be capable of delivering fiscal benefits, as long as the threat is not taken too far.

The rest of this chapter consists of an exploration of these regional variations in poverty and anti-poverty action. In section 2, we examine in more detail trends in the macro-economy during the 1990s and 2000s. In section 3, we show how those trends impacted on different measures of poverty, deprivation and well-being. Section 4 establishes a predictive model seeking to explain how those measures of well-being and ill-being, and their relationship to the national growth rate, varied across regions. Section 5 tests this model, and section 6 draws policy conclusions and carries the story forward through the global crisis of 2008/9 and its aftermath.

12.2 CRISIS AND RECOVERY 1990–2010: PATTERNS OF POLICY

Since the Second World War there have been three crises which can reasonably be called global, in the first half of the 1980s, at the end of the 1990s, and at the end of the 2000s. For Russia, the first two crises were rolled into one. Russia went into its process of structural adjustment, or adjustment to market forces, late, had great difficulty in achieving the required adjustments, and then was hit by the second global crisis, in 1998, before it could extract itself from the first. Hence, if Russia is compared on a graph with other adjusting countries (Figure 12.2) it is observed to experience just one very deep, long-lasting trough between 1991 and 1999: structural adjustment and the 'East Asian' crisis are rolled together into one.

With what policy instruments did the federal Russian government respond to this mega-recession? We can make a useful distinction between short-term instruments of response (as analysed in Chapters 3 and 4 above) and longer-term instruments and institutions, as analysed in Chapters 5 and 6.

Examining first the short-term response, the analysis by Treisman and Gimpelson (2001) shows how, in the new and improvisatory political environment of the 1990s, the political business cycle took a quite different shape from that observed in the West. Since, in the Russia of the early 1990s, consumer debt was minute, mortgages virtually unheard of, and taxes imposed on companies rather than individuals, the instruments by which the economy could be manipulated were different from those used in industrialized countries. The highest-leverage instruments with which to give a pre-election boost, in such an economy, were not interest rates and taxes, but rather revenues from newly privatized companies, together with rates of state pensions and, especially, minimum wages.[19]

[19] Treisman and Gimpelson explain very clearly why the minimum wage in Russia has such leverage:

> First, adjustments to the minimum wage occur through a very public political process, and thus constitute a political signal that is far more visible to most voters than change in, say, the average real wage. Secondly, all public sector wages are based on a uniform scale anchored to the minimum wage, and social allowances and family benefits are also calculated with reference to the official minimum wage. Therefore, any increase in the minimum wage is likely to have a broader social impact.
>
> (Treisman and Gimpelson 2001, page 239)

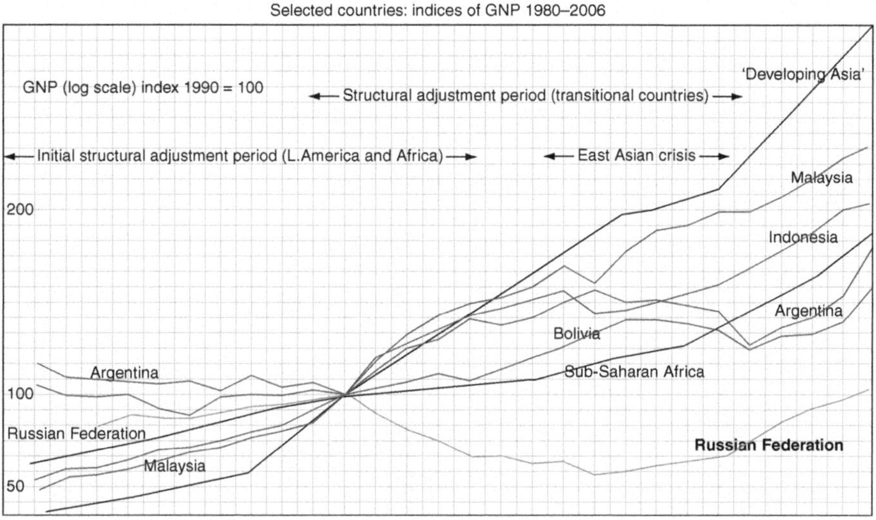

Figure 12.2 Russia and comparator countries: evolution of GNP growth and poverty 1980–2005
(a) GNP growth rates.

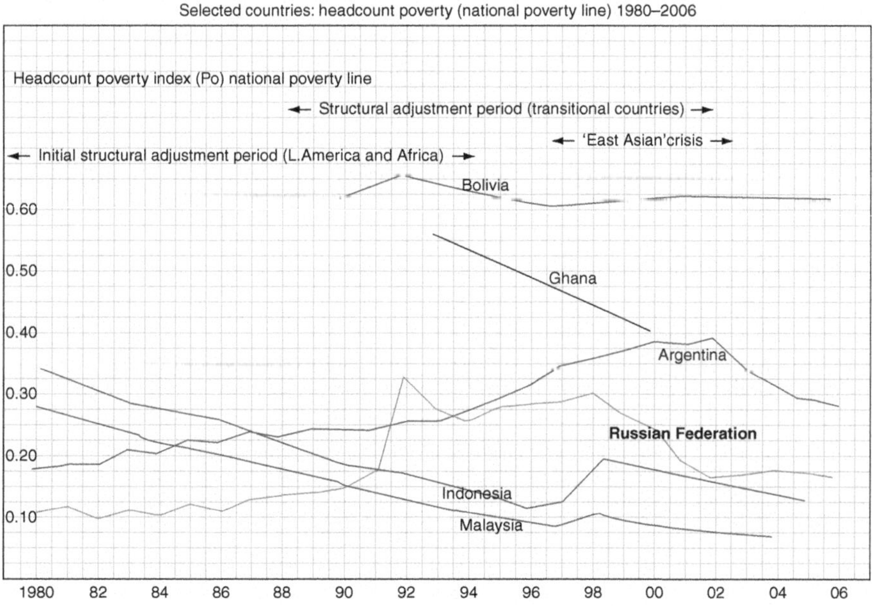

(b) Headcount poverty.

Table 12.4 Russia: short-term and long-term policy responses, 1992–2009.

	Adjustment and 'East Asian crisis' period, 1992–9	Recovery period, 1999–2007	Second global crisis, 2007–9
Short-term adjustment instruments—internal:			
1. Minimum wage/poverty line, per cent 10 (1999)	39 (1993)	27.5 (2007)	78.8 (2009)
2. Subsidies and other recurrent transfers, per cent total expenditure (per cent GNP)	41.2	25.2	
Short-term adjustment instruments—external:			
3. Real exchange rate, per cent change per annum (1)	−2.4 (1994–99)	11.5	1.7
4. Capital controls	Always in force 1993–9 (average score = 11.6)	Always in force (average score = 12.0)	Always in force (average score = 12.0)
Medium-term adjustment instruments and institutional changes:			
5. Nominal State pension/poverty line (2002 = 100) (2)	107.3	96.8	114.6
6. Social protection expenditures, total (per cent GDP)	30.3 (1999)	21.7 (2007)	26.4 (2009)
Structural changes:			
7. Oil, gas and minerals/GNP:			
Share (per cent)	7.9	10.0	9.1
Rate of growth (per cent)	−2.1	1.3	−2.0

8. Manufacturing/GNP Share (per cent)	25.1	17.6	15.0
Rate of growth (per cent)	−4.7	−1.9	−3.4
9. Employment, end of period (million)	64.5	70.8	69.3
(rate of change over period, per cent p.a.)	−1.4	0.6	−0.4
10. Capital-intensity	607 (1992)	692 (2007)	755 (2009)
measure	679 (1999)		
(fixed assets at book value/employment in thousands)			
Rate of growth p.a. (per cent)	0.69	*0.10*	*1.91*
Basic macro-economic descriptives:			
11. GDP level, end of period ($)	2270	5780	6080
12. Growth rate of GDP per cent	−4.3	6.3	1.9
Headcount poverty rate, end of period per cent	0.28	0.14	0.16(3)

Sources: Measures of expenditure (lines 1, 5, and 6) from Russian State Federal State Statistics Service, *Social Conditions and Welfare of the Russian Population, 2003, 2010.* Measure of subsidies and transfers (line 2) from IMF, *Government Expenditure Statistics Yearbook* and Ministry of Finance of the Russian Federation, *The State Budget.* Real exchange rate (line 3) from IMF, *International Financial Statistics.* Capital controls (line 4) from IMF, *Annual Report on Exchange Arrangements and Exchange Restrictions,* various issues. Structural indicators (lines 7–10) from Russian State Federal State Statistics Service, *National Accounts, 2010, Russia in Figures,* various issues. Macro-economic descriptives (lines 11–12) from World Bank, *World Development Indicators* (CD-ROM).

Notes: (1) A positive value denotes a depreciation of the real effective exchange rate.
(2) 2002 only.
(3) For the sources used to derive this estimate, see Table 12.3 above.

Thus, in the months prior to the presidential referendum of April 1993, the 'emergency' parliamentary election of December 1993 (which followed the storming of the Duma) and December 1995, and the presidential election of June 1996, there is a significant increase in the real minimum wage of between 0.16 and 2.18 per cent and, except in the first case, an increase in the real minimum pension also, resulting in an immediate increase in the real average wage and a decline in real wage arrears (except in December 1995) (Treisman and Gimpelson 2001, Table 1). In the 1993 case only, this wage increase led to a decline in the proportion of the population in poverty. In an experimental atmosphere in which what would work could only be guessed at, the Yeltsin administration guessed right and was thus able to 'work the lags in the system' so as to be able to buy the support it needed to hang on to power.

As we see in Table 12.4, these responses gave Russia's adjustment a different character from that of other adjusting countries. The structural shift away from labour-intensive manufacturing into capital-intensive oil and gas exports (rows 7 to 9 of the table), encouraged by a flexible exchange rate (row 3) and by high and sticky wages, as previously discussed, diverted the centre of gravity of the economy on to a capital-intensive production function (row 10 of the table), which made it difficult to reduce poverty rapidly even when, with the onset of the Putin period, renewed growth finally arrived. Moreover, as we shall see, when the third global shock arrived in 2009, these same parameters left Russia vulnerable to a sudden collapse of the economy and a consequent rise in the poverty level.

12.3 POVERTY AND ANTI-POVERTY POLICY: NATIONAL AND REGIONAL PERSPECTIVES

As discussed above, Russia has now returned to sustained economic growth, which at the time of writing has resumed after the 2009 recession. The World Bank, in its recent review, describes this economic recovery as being 'pro-poor' (World Bank 2004, page xii, para. 9). But is this accurate? We may begin by looking in a little more detail at the trend of poverty levels. As shown in Table 12.3, aggregate poverty levels for the Russian Federation as a whole rose dramatically across the country in the early 1990s to a level almost three times that of the previous decade, remained on that higher level throughout the decade as economic growth rates continued negative, and then fell gradually through the growth phase of the early 2000s, only to jump back in the first quarter of 2009 to its 2005 level.[20] The amount by which it jumped back is disputed, and one report has claimed that during the recession of 2009 all of the poverty gains made since 2000 have been wiped out.[21] But even if that claim is discounted and the lowest poverty

[20] In the last three quarters of 2009, poverty fell again. One clear reason for this was the four pension adjustments applied during the year. Specifically during the recession years 2008 and 2009, pensions were increased by a great deal more than the poverty line (see the 2008 and 2009 entries in Table 12.3).

[21] 'Millions more Russians shunted into poverty', the *Guardian*, 1 September 2009, claims, on the basis of a Goskomstat estimate of 27.5 million people below the poverty line in April 2009, that 'all of

estimate, which is the World Bank's, is adopted, a back-of-the-envelope calculation suggests that between 1999 and 2009 per capita GDP grew by a factor of approximately three, from just over $2000 to just over $6000, whereas the poverty rate was at best halved, from twenty-eight per cent to about sixteen per cent. This gives a 'poverty elasticity', or ratio of percentage change in poverty to percentage change in income, of around one-third. This is only a small fraction, possibly as little as one-eighth, of the global cross-section estimate of poverty elasticity presented in the 2006 *World Development Report* (recall Chapter 1, Figure 1.1 above). In other words, on a comparative scale, Russia is not very effective at reducing poverty. We have indicated earlier some of the reasons for this: the structure of production is capital-intensive, and because of high wages employment levels are upwardly inflexible, both of which tend to make it hard to bring poverty down even if growth rates are dramatic.

Of course, it is not wise to measure poverty on the basis of one indicator. Other indicators of well-being, however, also present a rather worrying picture even during the years of growth. Inequality also rises sharply though the early 1990s and then remains on a plateau; mortality rates, very unusually for any country in modern times, increase continually for a decade and only begin to improve in 2004. The state of health services in Russia continues to be alarming, and the World Health Organization rates Russia 127th among its 192 member states in terms of the general health of its population (Russian Federal Statistics Office 2007b). The huge shocks inflicted by the long-lasting recession on the population, imposed on it the need for a range of adaptive behaviours during the crisis and for many years afterwards, as illustrated by a number of surveys (Lokshin and Yemtsov 2001; Stillman and Thomas 2008).

We now wish to disaggregate this picture between regions, which becomes possible with the publication after 1995 of data on the GDP ('gross regional product'), fiscal expenditures and social conditions of all of the eighty-nine 'federal subjects'.[22] The first thing which we notice (Figure 12.3) is that, in essence, the rich regions (two to five times federal per capita GNP) are of two types—in the west, the city states of Moscow and St Petersburg and, in the east, the resource-rich states of northern and central Siberia. By the same token, the poor regions are also of two types—'always poor' or 'chronic poor' regions with a mainly agrarian economy and poor infrastructure on the southern periphery (Dagestan, Bashkortostan AR, Kalmyk AR, Ossetia, and Ingushetia, incorporating Chechnya), the last two of these also recently afflicted by conflict, and 'newly poor' or 'conjunctural poor' regions in the centre along the Volga and in the east along the line of the Trans-Siberian railway (Irkutsk, Chita, Tuva, Krasnoyarsk, Novosibirsk), mainly industrial regions decimated by the decline of the state heavy industry sector after 1991.

the gains in poverty during the period 2000–8 have been utterly wiped out', which would imply a poverty rate of around 0.25 in 2009, rather than the figure in Table 12.3.

[22] These data are published as Federal State Statistics Bureau, *Regiony Rossii*, annual from 2000. The only other study which to our knowledge examines regional GDP trends is Yemtsov (2003). This study, however, examines only the period 1995–2000 and is almost entirely concerned with issues of GDP convergence among regions, and does not discuss issues of living standards or poverty levels.

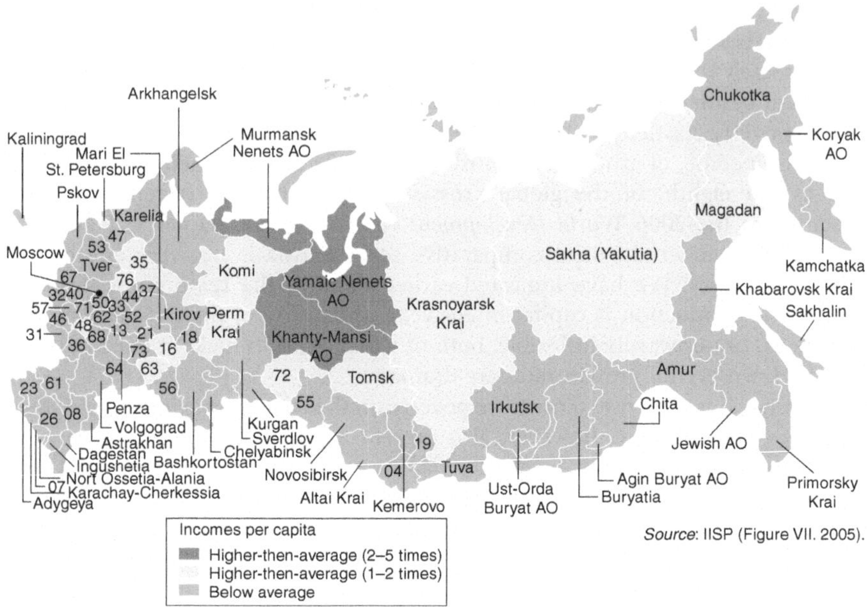

Figure 12.3 Per capita gross regional product by region, 2002.

We now examine the dynamics of poverty across the regions of Russia during the period of perestroika and after. As originally argued by Dollar and Kraay (2002) there is a tendency across the countries of the globe for poverty to fall with increasing rates of economic growth, and we wish to see whether this tendency is also evident across the regions of Russia. As illustrated by Figure 12.4 there was *in general*, across the eighty-nine federal subjects, a tendency for poverty (at any rate between 2000 and 2005) to decline as growth rates increased; however, the best-fit ratio of the percentage change in poverty to the percentage change in regional GNP (the 'poverty elasticity') is across Russian regions only −0.53, which, as mentioned above, is well below the global average. Moreover, in thirty of the eighty-nine federal subjects in the 1996–9 period, and in a smaller number in the 2000s, positive growth rates of GDP in particular regions were accompanied not by reductions in poverty but rather by increases: growth was of a type which did not increase at all and in fact reduced the likelihood of escape from poverty. These regions are catalogued in Table 12.5.

One important reason for the low overall poverty elasticity in Russia, of course is embedded in the characteristics of structural adjustment itself. Adjustment to global market forces involved a shift from non-tradables to tradables, involving, in Russia as in a number of other countries, the substitution of unprofitable state manufacturing activities in both heavy and light engineering industry, mostly labour intensive, by oil, gas, and minerals exports, which currently account for a quarter of GNP and over eighty per cent of exports (Hanson 2007a, Figure 4).

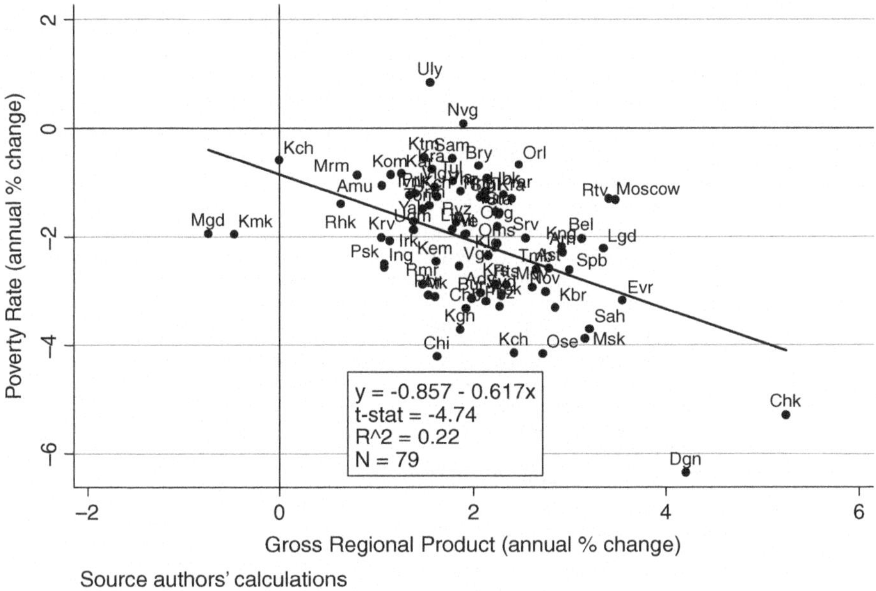

Figure 12.4 Poverty and growth experience, Russia versus global.
(a) Russia: poverty in relation to GRP 1996–2008.

Source: Authors' calculations using data from *Regiony Rossii* (2010 edition).

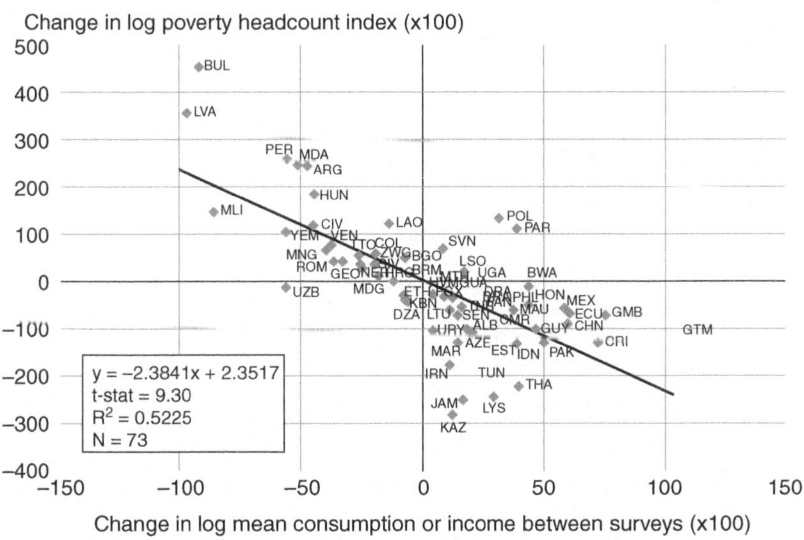

(b) Global cross-section: poverty (log headcount index) vs. change in log mean consumption or income 1990–2005 (between-survey calculations).

Source: *World Bank, World Development Report 2006, Figure 4.3.*

Table 12.5 Patterns of growth and poverty, 1996–9 and 2000–5.

1996–9		2000–5	
Positive growth, fall in poverty *Southern*: North Ossetia/Alania Republic	**Positive growth, increase in poverty** *Central*: Belgorod, Vladimir, Voronezh, Kostroma, Kursk, Moscow (oblast and city), Oryol, Smolensk, Tambov, Yaroslavl *North-western*: Archangelsk, Vologda, Leningrad, Murmansk, Novgorod *Southern*: (Kabardino-Balkans Republic, Krasnodar Krai, Astrakhan, Rostov). *Volga*: Mordovia Republic, Nizhny Novgorod, Penza, Perm, Samara, Saratov *Siberian* (Buryatia Republic, Tuva Republic) *Far Eastern*: Khabarovsk Krai, Sakhalin	**Positive growth, fall in poverty** *Central, North-western federal, Volga, Ural,* and *Siberian*: all territories. *Southern*: all territories except Kalmykia. *Far Eastern*: Yakutia, Primorsky Krai, Khabarovsk, Amur, Sakhalin, Jewish AO, Chukotka AO	**Positive growth, increase in poverty** *Southern*: Kalmykia Republic
Negative growth, decline in poverty *Southern*: Adygeya Republic, Dagestan Republic *Siberian*: Irkutsk	**Negative growth, increase in poverty** *Central*: Bryansk, Ivanovo, Kaluga, Lipetsk, Ryazan, Tver, Tula *North-western*: Karelia Republic, Komi Republic, Kaliningrad, Pskov, St Petersburg *Southern*: Ingushetia Republic, Karachay-Cherkessia Republic, Stavropol Krai, Volgograd *Volga*: Baskortostan, Mari El, Tatarstan, Udmurtia, Chuvashia, Kirov, Orenburg, Ulyanovsk. *Ural:* Kurgan, Sverdlovsk, Tyumen, Chelyabinsk *Siberian*: Altay Republic, Khakassia Republic, Altai Krai, Krasnoyarsk Krai, Kemerovo, Novosibirsk, Omsk, Tomsk, Chita *Far Eastern*: Yakutia Republic, Primorsky Krai, Amur, Kamchatka, Magadan	**Negative growth, decline in poverty** *Far Eastern*: Magadan	**Negative growth, increase in poverty** *Far Eastern*: Kamchatka

Source: Mussurov and Mosley 2008, Appendices 1 and 2.

These, as discussed earlier, are highly capital intensive[23] and for that reason unable to convert any significant part of the growth to which they give rise into livelihoods for poor households with limited skills.

[23] See Table 12.4, row 10. A similar evolution towards a capital-intensive pattern of production—and once again, towards increases in poverty in several regions—was apparent, also with dramatic political consequences, in Bolivia between 1990 and 2005 (Mosley 2007).

Table 12.6 Political tendencies in the regions by poverty experience, 1996–2005.

Poverty experience 1996–2005	Positive trend (10 best cases %)	Negative trend (10 worst cases %)
Political behaviour: Incidence of protest	23.7	18.8
Incidence of voting for principal opposition party (Communists)	11.5	12.4
Policy inputs: Social expenditure (%change in budget share, 1996–2005)	+77.5	+18.4

Source: Authors' calculations based on *Regiony Rossii*, 2007 edition.
Notes: Poverty experience: the 'ten best cases' are those regions with the highest response of poverty to growth over the 1996–2005 period, that is, Ingushetia, Irkutsk, Chita, Pskov, Chelyabinsk, Adygeya, Mari El Republic, Karachay-Cherkassia, Tuva, St Petersburg. The 'ten worst cases' are those regions with the most perverse response of poverty to growth over the 1996–2005 period, that is, Koryak autonomous oblast, Ulyanovsk, Ivanovo, Khakassia Republic, Novgorod, Ryazan, Kostroma, Oryol, Krasnoyarsk Krai, Vladimir.

We can now observe in more detail who were the gainers and the losers from the adjustment process. The gainers were people with skills adapted to the requirements of the 'new economy' and regions intensive in natural resources; the losers (the 'perverse cases' with increasing poverty levels shaded in the top right-hand corners of Table 12.4) were individuals with low levels of skill and regions on the eastern and southern periphery which, as previously described, either never had any labour-intensive tradable activities or lost them with the onset of *perestroika*.

The pattern of winning and losing regions is reflected in the pattern of both political response and policy inputs, as illustrated by Table 12.6. The regions in which poverty rose experienced higher levels of political protest in the sense of willingness to take part in demonstrations, but not, interestingly, in terms of actual protest votes against the United Russia party. And in response, the regions in which poverty was on a falling trend had much higher levels of social expenditure, and other local-specific policy instruments than the regions in which poverty was on a rising trend. In some (Ingushetia, Tuva) falling poverty is clearly due to injections of federal subsidy to head off protest, and in others (Chita) the influence of inflows of (Chinese) migrant labour is observable. Clearly we are dealing with a two-way interaction between poverty levels and policy interventions, which, as we shall see, operated in different ways in different regions, and the nature of which we now wish to investigate in more detail.

The opening up of the regional Pandora's box, therefore, provides an insight both into economic performance and into political behaviour that is not available from the aggregate data. A number of the regions and groups which did not gain from the renewed onset of economic growth after 2000, including, as we saw, pensioners in January 2005, sought to achieve by political action what the newly established market was unable to deliver to them. Did this political action achieve any kind of influence on patterns of public action (expenditure, legislation protective of the poor, and price controls) at the regional level, and thence on the regional pattern of poverty and well-being? The following sections consider these questions.

12.4 APPROACH AND EXPLANATORY STORY

The general argument so far, then, is that in Russia since 2000 economic growth has indeed been important in helping the Putin government re-entrench its grip on power,[24] but that the quality of that growth leaves it still vulnerable, United Russia's enormous majority notwithstanding, especially in face of macro-economic downturns such as that which occurred in 2009. This vulnerability has been exposed once again by mass protests against the alleged rigging of the parliamentary election in December 2011 (*The Guardian*, 2 December 2011, p. 37). Our analysis has grouped the main factors influencing the pro-poor quality of growth into four:

1. *International influences*, which during the time of vulnerability in the nineties helped to close the Russian government's fiscal gap, but even at that time were not able, as we saw, to do much to influence the allocation of resources between poor and non-poor groups. Since the millennium, the ability of international institutions to influence this allocation process has shrunk further.
2. *Structural forces influencing the inter-sectoral pattern of growth and its impact on the labour market*, within which the possibility of transition out of poverty is determined.
3. *Federal-level policy instruments*, such as the minimum wage, the exchange rate, and the level of federal expenditures.
4. *Local-level policy instruments*, such as the level of subsidy going to particular regions and the local taxes and regulatory measures imposed by those regions.

We now seek to model these causal influences. The point of departure is that the low overall poverty elasticity of growth in Russia represents a potential political liability for the government, as it is symptomatic of the emergence of an under-employed underclass lacking the skills to hold down jobs in the new, albeit rapidly-growing, economy, and constituting a political threat especially if this poverty combines with other grievances. In those regions (depicted in Table 12.1) where a perverse poverty elasticity is combined with ethnic or other demands for autonomy, this threat to the federal state was clearly perceived, and as we saw, the state frequently pumped resources into such regions to pre-empt politically destabilizing action. The resources which it injected might come in various forms: subsidies on the prices of 'sensitive' items such as food and heating fuel, increases in pensions, variations in the mix of public expenditures, and variations in the minimum wage. Collectively we refer to these alternative channels for injecting public resources into the economy as the *social efficiency wage*—an increase in the social wage designed to achieve greater economic stability, by analogy with the private efficiency wage of labour economics, in which increases in the private wage achieve increases in the stability and productivity of the labour force.

Our model (Figure 12.5) is a Russianized version of the generic model used to explain the determinants of pro-poor action in Chapter 5. It visualizes a government determined, in whatever way it can, to maximize its chances of retaining its

[24] 'The general sense of rising prosperity has been one of the bases, perhaps the most fundamental of all, of Putin's popularity' (Hanson 2007a, page 872).

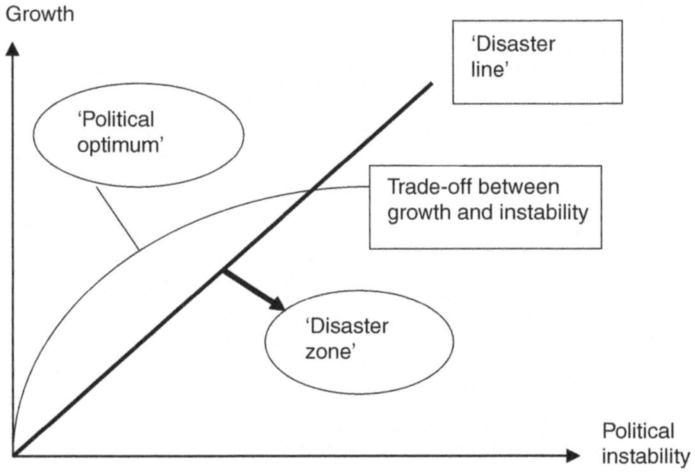

Figure 12.5 Economic performance and political stability—the trade-off and the disaster zone.

hold on power (which is the essence of *derzhavnichestvo*), and using the social efficiency wage as an instrument to enable it to do this. We assume that the government's hold on power will be improved by economic success (e.g. high rates of economic growth) but damaged by political instability. A high level of civil disruption combined with poor economic performance is a calamity for any government, and defines a 'disaster zone' in which the likelihood of holding on to power is very poor. We visualize that any rational government will wish, as an absolute priority, to keep away from this disaster zone, that is, it will choose the point, on the trade-off between these two objectives, which takes it the furthest possible distance away from the abyss at the bottom right-hand corner of the diagram.

The significance of the social efficiency wage instrument, in this context, is that if correctly chosen it will increase the incumbent government's chances of keeping away from the cliff-edge. We reason that up to a certain point, increases in the social wage (e.g. from W_1 to W_2 in the diagram of Figure 12.6), will move the trade-off so as to give it a better change of holding on to power. These upward shifts in the trade-off can be mediated through any of the policy instruments previously described.[25] (During the 1990s, as we have seen, the Russian government won itself additional room for manoeuvre also by the use of loans from the international financial institutions, but has now come to see these as a liability rather than an asset.) Many extraneous factors are also capable of shifting the trade-off either to the government's advantage or to its disadvantage, for example reductions in the oil price and changes in economic structure, such as the shift of

[25] Changes in the expenditure mix, changes in the level of social expenditures, variations in pensions, and variations in subsidies/price controls seem to be the alternative formulations of this instrument most practised in Russia (see page 320–6 above).

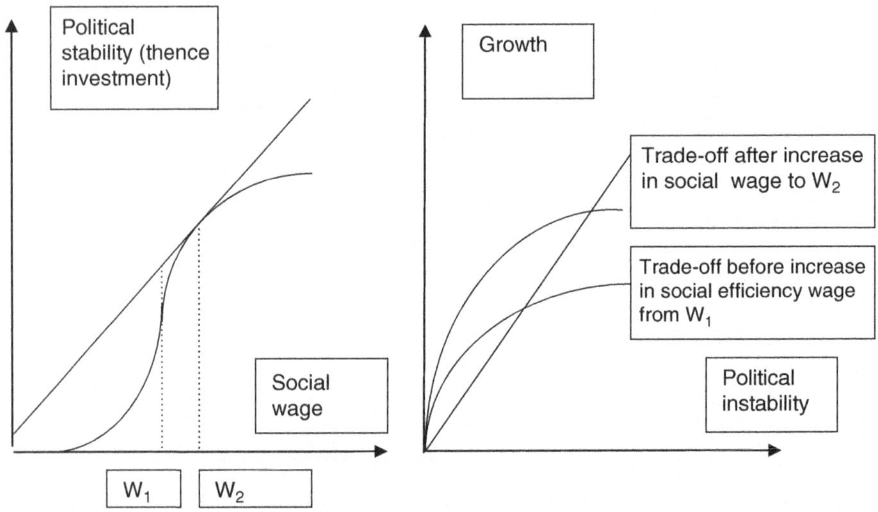

Figure 12.6 The 'social efficiency wage' and the government's survival prospects.

growth towards oil products and services previously discussed, reduce the economy's job-creating ability and thus move the trade-off in the direction of greater vulnerability. How effectively, in such an environment, a government is able to increase its room for manoeuvre depends therefore on both luck and judgement: on luck, in the sense of how much its freedom of manoeuvre is shrunk by forces beyond its control, such as the decline in the oil price, but also on judgement in the sense of how well it is able to gauge the impact of changes in expenditure, through the channels of influence identified earlier, on the sensitivities of local interest groups.

The model which we seek to estimate in the next section (Figure 12.6) is, therefore, a model of circular causation which brings together the core determinants of poverty in Russia. There are three relationships in the model:

1. Resource inputs, the government's revenue position, government reputation and other long-term factors determine the position of the fundamental trade-off between stability and growth portrayed on Figure 12.5, and subject to the factors discussed in (2) and (3) below, the prospects for economic stability.
2. Policy instruments which can be adjusted in the short term such as the allocation of labour between sectors (the 'social efficiency wage' described above) influence the extent to which the trade-off can be moved and thence the extent to which within the current electoral term the government can improve its chances of holding on to power (increase its room for manoeuvre). This relationship will also deteriorate (i.e. move downwards) if there is an escalation in the level of political violence.
3. To the extent that the instruments described in (2) are successful and combine with favourable economic preconditions (e.g. high regional growth rates and a concentration of growth in labour-intensive sectors, as discussed above) poverty falls. The model reduces, under certain parameter values, to a

'vicious circle of poverty' model (as portrayed in the Bolivian case study, Chapter 10 above) in which lack of resources constrain the ability to buy off protest which weakens the state, and one dilemma for weak governments is how to escape from this vicious circle. Russia is not ordinarily thought of as a weak state, but the duration and severity of economic crisis, as we saw, transitorily made it one during the 1990s, and a major priority for the Putin administration, as discussed above has been to shield the federal administration against any risk of being re-enmeshed in the vulnerabilities experienced at that time.

12.5 EMPIRICAL TESTS

Regression analysis of determinants of poverty

In this section we estimate the reduced forms of the three basic linkages in the model: the poverty equation (3), the equation for the social efficiency wage (2), and the equation for economic instability and conflict (1), against data for each of the eighty-nine 'federal subject' territories of Russia, with a view to understanding the determinants of regional variations in poverty levels and in the elasticity of poverty with respect to the renewed growth of the years 2000–7. We operate with a number of alternative specifications of our key variables: the social efficiency wage is alternatively defined as social spending, social spending plus housing, pensions expenditure and the level of the minimum wage; and 'the threat of conflict' is variously defined as indicated willingness to protest against the government as expressed in opinion polls by the Russian national survey agency, VTsIOM opinion polls and as votes for the Communist party (the principal opposition party). Our estimates are displayed in Table 12.7.

Determinants of poverty and deprivation (equation (3))

Our poverty equation (equation (3)) expresses poverty as a function of the propensity to take on low-income labour (the capital intensity) of the regional economy, and of the level of the social efficiency wage. Our estimates (Table 12.7) suggest that both of these factors are significant in determining poverty elasticity: poverty is significantly responsive to social expenditure (only at the ten per cent level in equation (2)), to the level of regional infrastructure, and to the salience of the energy sector.[26] We take this as a proxy for capital-intensity: the oil and gas sectors, which accounted for twenty-seven per cent of output and sixty per cent of the country's exports in 2006, employ fewer people than the Russian railways, and employ only two per cent of the employed workforce (Hanson 2007a, pages 873–4).

[26] Note that the coefficient of the energy sector on poverty is *positive*, in other words, the more energy-intensive a region is, the more, other things being equal, that tends to *increase* poverty.

Table 12.7 Russian Federation: poverty, social expenditure, and conflict: simultaneous analysis. Data for eighty-nine 'federal subject' regions 1995–2006.

Estimation method:	XT fixed-effects regression	Three-stage least squares regression		
Dependent variable:	Poverty headcount	Log (poverty headcount)	Log (social expenditure)	Log (political protest)
Regression coefficients on independent variables:				
Constant	2.09** (2.11)	−4.56** (2.46)	4.20*** (11.66)	4.13 (0.59)
'Social efficiency wage 1'	0.26* (1.67)	2.05** (4.14)		0.19 (0.18)
Log (social expenditure)				
'Social efficiency wage 2'				
Log (social expenditure with housing)				
Road expenditure	0.038 (0.19)			
Energy sector	0.09** (2.02)	0.10 (0.86)		
Log revenue			−0.086** (3.22)	
Log (political protest indicator)			0.10 (1.38)	
Regional democracy index			0.003 (1.16)	
Log unemployment				0.80** (2.17)
Log consumer price index				−0.76 (0.87)
Year dummy 6	0.19*** (2.46)			
Year dummy 7	0.50*** (6.55)			
Year dummy 10	−0.19** (2.41)			
Number of observations	222	38	38	38
R^2 (within group)	0.5287	0.0691	0.2630	0.2494
R^2 (between groups)	0.0782			
R^2 (overall)	0.2574			
p-value	0.0000	0.0000	0.0000	0.0000

Source: *Regiony Rossii*, 2007 edition.

Notes: Figures in parentheses underneath coefficients are Student's t-statistics. *** denotes significance of a coefficient at the 1 per cent level, ** denotes significance at the 5 per cent level and * denotes significance at the 10 per cent level.

Social expenditure and the 'social efficiency wage' (equation (2))

As emphasized by Haggard and Kaufman (2008), underlying political pressures, as well as political institutions such as the degree and forms of democracy, help to explain the level of social spending and the allocation of spending between economic sectors. As indicated by Table 12.2, social expenditure has expanded substantially in real terms since 2000, as one element in the expanded role of the state which is apparent both in Russia and in other post-crisis countries since 2000 (Grugel and Riggirozzi 2009; Hanson 2007a). We see this, specifically in the Russian context, as a variable whose role is not only to redistribute resources equitably but explicitly to pre-empt the possibility of conflict. We embody this idea in our specification of equation (2), relating the level of the social wage to measures of the threat of conflict as well as to the political structure variables (revenue and local democracy) specified by Haggard, revenue and local democracy indicators. We find that all of these indicators are significant influences on the social wage. In particular, local social expenditures have been higher in areas where the local separatist threat is more significant (Ossetia, Dagestan, Tuva Republic, and of course Chechnya). There is also a response, not always significant, of the social wage to the level of headcount poverty.

Political militancy and the threat of violence (equation (1))

We have argued that pro-poor action, and thus the poverty elasticity, is driven by the threat of violence, as well as by underlying fiscal capacities and political characteristics. In the final column of the table, we find that the threat of violence is augmented by the level of unemployment within a region and diminished (insignificantly) by the level of the social wage. Militancy is also significantly associated with local economic conditions and to one of our other political indicators, the vote for the Communist Party leader, Zyuganov. It is also higher, following our earlier argument, in rural areas which suffered very badly in the slump and have not recovered in the subsequent boom.[27]

Qualitative analysis of 'poverty-increasing' and 'poverty-reducing' districts

Thus, poverty is driven by both economic structure and policy, policy is driven by political imperatives of which the greatest is state security, and state security, both at the federal and at the regional level, is influenced by the state of the economy. Although Table 12.7 gives us an initial picture of this pattern of causation and its relation to regional poverty dynamics, it leaves us, of course, well short of understanding the local dynamics which caused some regions to benefit substantially from post-2000 growth, but others to experience an increase in poverty, and to become socially excluded.[28]

As discussed above (page 327) poverty in Russia is of two types, the *chronic poverty* of 'always poor' regions and people which have consistently lacked the skills and resources required for an adequate income, and the *conjunctural poverty* of 'newly poor' regions and people which enjoyed safe and protected livelihoods during the communist period which were then stripped away by the shift to a market economy. During the slump of the 1990s both kinds of poverty became

[27] In the 2006 Russian Living Standards Measurement Survey (interview, Ludmila Khakulina, Levada Centre, Moscow, 22 January 2008) the proportion of 'very poor' was given as:

Moscow 7%	Middle cities 14%
Large cities 10%	Rural 20%

[28] For analysis of social exclusion in Russia, see in particular the papers by Lokshin and Yemtsov (2001), Brainerd (2001), and the World Bank (2004).

worse; during the recovery of the 2000s, as we have seen, some regions became much better off and others worse off, and we wish to compare between the two. We do this (Table 12.8) by making three case-study comparisons between 'successful' and 'failing' regions, one for regions which were *always poor* prior to 1990 on Russia's southern periphery and two for *new poor* regions (one in European Russia and one in Siberia) which had been industrialized for a hundred years but which deteriorated sharply during the *perestroika* period.

The first comparison (columns 2 and 3 of the table) is between two 'new poor regions', with initial (1995) poverty rates of about thirty per cent and quite high gross regional product: Pskov (near to St Petersburg and the Baltic states and well-connected to western and eastern Europe), where poverty has declined dramatically with the growth of the 2000s, and Ulyanovsk (on the Volga), where in spite of growth in real gross regional product, the poverty level has increased since 1995. Both regions, in terms of the terminology introduced on page 327, became 'newly poor' in the 1990s: they have, since the late nineteenth century and amplified by the Five-Year Plan periods, good infrastructure and a heavy concentration of economic activity within machine-building, all of it in the 1980s state-owned, and both as a consequence suffered heavily under *perestroika* in the 1990s. Their evolution since 2000 has been very different. Ulyanovsk, loyal to the man after whom it is named,[29] maintained during the 1990s, under three different governors, elements of a command economy (two World Bank commentators describe it at that stage as being 'at the bottom of the list for reform' (de Melo and Ofer 1999, page 13), many of which it still maintains, including ceilings on profits and trade mark-ups and restrictions on food exports to other regions, whereas Pskov's local administration is very heavily orientated towards the private sector.[30] In Ulyanovsk, unlike Pskov, there are very low levels of inward foreign investment (de Melo and Ofer 1999), and the main domestic industry, aircraft manufacture, has become so inefficient that 'even Aeroflot does not want to buy its low-quality airplanes' (Orttung 2000, page 597). Indicators of social capital are also inferior in Ulyanovsk: unlike Pskov, it has very low access to non-government media. Only local, primarily government-owned, newspapers are read, there are no privately-owned radio and television stations, and the local democracy indicator is much higher in Pskov than in Ulyanovsk. Although we must be cautious about inferring causation from these data, the superficial impression is that Ulyanovsk is caught in a low-level poverty trap, with the authorities' response (repression of both the media and the private economy) deterring foreign investment, inhibiting diversification of the local economy, and disincentivizing the formation of both human and social capital, including those skills required to put any momentum behind progressive reform at the local level. All of these resource constraints prevent the labour market from growing quickly and responding to

[29] Lenin's true name was Vladimir Ulyanov; 'Lenin' was a pseudonym assumed years after he became a political activist (Service 1997, page 70).

[30] Although orientated towards the private sector Pskov is a mixture of new-style entrepreneurship, encouraged by the region's nearness to St Petersburg and the EU Baltic states, and old-style oligopoly and patronage, much of it centred on the oblast-owned alcohol production monopoly, *Pskovalko* (Dininio and Orttung 2005; Orttung 2000, page 442).

Table 12.8 Selected Russian regions 1996–2005: case-study analysis of poverty-increasing and poverty-reducing cases (poverty-reducing cases in **bold**).

	'Newly poor' regions: European Russia		'Newly poor' regions: Siberia		'Always poor' regions: southern periphery	
	Pskov (Northwestern)	Ulyanovsk (Volga)	Chita	Khakassia	Ingushetia (Southern)	Kalmyk Autonomous Republic (Southern)
Initial conditions (1995):						
Poverty headcount (per cent) at poverty line 1,056 roubles/cap/month (Russian Federation = 24.8)	**30.8**	32.0	**29.9**	21.2	**59.5**	42.3
Gross regional product per cap. ($)	**1,230**	1,063	**1,864**	3,018	**314**	818
Unemployment (1998, per cent)	**15.9**	11.1	**19.8**	9.6	**50.9**	31.3
Economic performance 1996–2005:						
per cent annual growth GRP	**1.9**	2.5	**2.0**	0.9	**1.5**	−4.2
per cent change poverty	**−5.6**	7.5	**−9.3**	1.2	**−8.3**	−1.4
Growth elasticity of poverty	**−2.94**	3.00	**−4.43**	1.33	**−5.5**	0.33
Indicators of social efficiency wage and other indicators of economic policy 1996–2005:						
per cent change in social expenditure	**85.9**	9.2	**63.2**	−39	**91.6**	15.8
Price and/or export controls in 2005?	**No**	Yes	Yes	Yes	**Yes**	Yes
Foreign investment level (and rank for investment potential out of 89)	**(63)**	(42)	**(52)**	(73)	**(77)**	

Continued

Table 12.8 Continued

	'Newly poor' regions: European Russia		'Newly poor' regions: Siberia		'Always poor' regions: southern periphery	
	Pskov (Northwestern)	Ulyanovsk (Volga)	Chita	Khakassia	Ingushetia (Southern)	Kalmyk Autonomous Republic (Southern)
Other observations		Persisting restrictions on trade and industry (e.g. ceilings on profits and trade mark-ups, restrictions on food exports to other regions, during 1990s food rationing).				Wastage of much of development budget on white elephant projects, see text
Political indicators: Regional democracy index	**34.0**	25.0	**26.0**	18.0	**17.0**	20.0
Protest index per cent voted		28.9			**17.0**	
Communist	**15.2**	14.1	**12.6**	7.2	**1.0**	10.6
Social capital indicators: Press freedom	**High**	Low	**High**	Low	**Low**	Low
Other observations		Low independence of city leadership from regional government. No access to independent media (see text below)				

Sources: Poverty levels, social expenditures, gross regional product from *Regiony Rossii*, obtainable at www. infostat.ru.

Figure 12.7 Russia: secessionist threats, budgetary allocations, and poverty dynamics.
(a) Causal sequence.

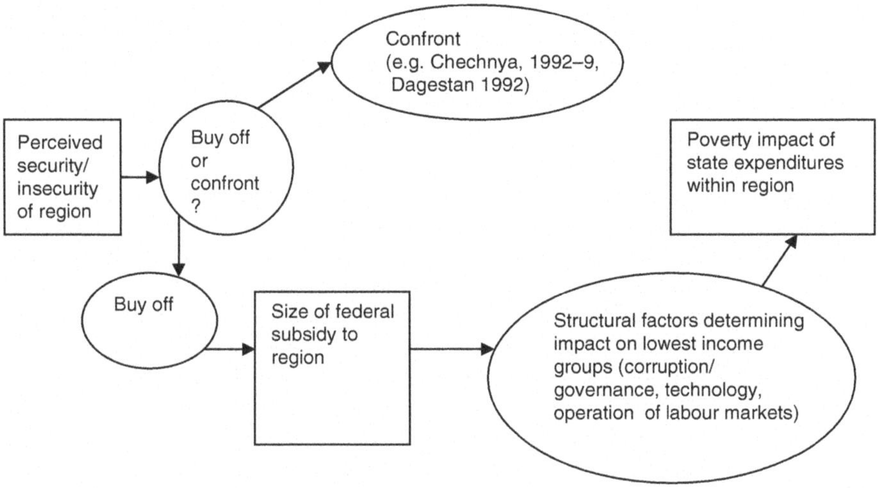

(b) Mapping.

the needs of the new globalized economy, and this, we speculate, was a major cause of persistence in the differing dynamics of local poverty levels.

Next we compare two regions of Siberia. The 'improving' region is Chita, an important base of the military-industrial complex in Siberia on the Trans-Siberian railway quite close to the Chinese border, and the 'declining' region is Khakassia, on the upper Yenisei river in central Siberia. Three relevant points of contrast are the trend of private investment: (1) close to zero in Khakassia but increasing much more rapidly in Chita; (2) the labour market—dynamic and flexible in much of Chita (much of its workforce consists of Chinese immigrants willing to accept jobs at a lower rate than Russians) and rigid and monopsonistic in Khakassia (which is basically a 'company region', almost entirely devoted to the production of aluminium); and (3) political orientation—relatively radical in Chita—the city has had a radical tradition ever since 1825 when it provided a sanctuary for the Decembrists, the participants in the attempted rebellion intercepted and punished that year by Nicholas I. Even now, support for United Russia in this 'city of exiles', as it is widely known, is, by contrast with Khakassia, well below the national average.

Finally we consider two 'always poor' regions with headcount poverty rates of over fifty per cent, an agrarian economic base, and poor infrastructure, both of them in the Muslim-dominated south Caucasus zone (see Figure 12.7). These are Ingushetia, adjacent to Chechnya, which has reduced poverty substantially since the late 1990s, and the Kalmyk Republic, which has experienced an increase in poverty. The major observable policy difference is that Ingushetia has experienced a larger inflow of federal spending, indeed eighty-eight per cent of its budget is provided by the federal government.[31] This is a loyalty bonus which rewards the fact that Ingushetia, unlike Chechnya, did not rebel during the 1990s. Financed by this bonus, social spending has grown rapidly since the 1990s, and there has also been a greater diversification of the fundamentally agrarian economy into petrochemicals and oil and gas derivatives. In essence Ingushetia and its neighbour Dagestan, like many an African country, have in the 2000s been experiencing aid-led growth—the aid in this case being provided by subsidies from the federal administration. None of this has improved the quality of governance, which on one account 'is widely regarded by its people as a kleptocracy kept in power by military force, electoral fraud, and Russian support' (Orttung 2000, page 175) and yet Ingushetia has a lower democracy index than the Kalmyk Republic, whose President, Kirsan Ilyumzhinov, more than rivals Ingushetia in political violence and has poured much of his republic's investible resources into a string of white elephant projects, including four personalized white Rolls-Royces, a virtual casino open to anyone with access to the international computer network, a gold-plated statue of Buddha, and a 'chess complex' designed to put Kalmykia on to the map as the chess tournament capital of Russia.[32] Finally, it must be stressed that one

[31] *The Independent*, 3 September 2008, page 22, the source of this quotation, reports the murder on 1 September of Magomed Yevloyev, the owner of a website critical of the Ingush government. It was in Ingushetia that the Beslan massacre of 2005 occurred, in which over 300 people were shot in a battle between terrorists and security forces, most of them schoolchildren.

[32] 'Overall, [Ilyumzhinov] owns thirty-six cars which are garaged in a variety of cities around the world so that the president can use them when he travels' (Orttung 2000, page 177).

key element in Ingushetia's standing as the most improved performer poverty-wise in Russia is a simple bounce-back from the appalling levels of destitution encountered during the mid-1990s as the consequence of much of the capital stock being destroyed by the civil war.

12.6 CONCLUSION

In this chapter we have sought to understand and analyse the experience of Russia since the crisis of 1998, which at the aggregate level is an experience of slow and gradual reduction of poverty since the millennium following a long-drawn-out and severe recession during the 1990s. Underlying the slowness of the reduction in poverty, we have argued, is a fundamental characteristic of the Russian structural adjustment process—a shift (Table 12.4) away from labour-intensive and previously heavily protected manufacturing towards the more tradable, but more capital-intensive, oil, gas, and minerals sectors, plus associated services, which are only to a very limited extent capable of providing livelihoods for the millions shaken out of the non-traded sector by the process of adjustment. As a consequence, the growth which has taken place has produced only very limited reductions in poverty in many areas, and in some places increases throughout the boom of the 2000s. Where these locations coincide with existing ethnic and other resentments, the Russian state is still vulnerable, we argue, in spite of its resounding success in the 2008 elections.

Although the concept of poverty and the interests of the poor have not been important in Russia as a factor influencing policy at the *federal* level, they have often, and in widely varying ways, influenced political action at the *local* level. The main principle underlying the actions of the Putin government, we have argued, has been *derzhavnichestvo*, the reassertion of the power of the state, and we have interpreted the regional variations in experience which pervaded Russia during the 2000s as variations in the way in which that imperative interacted with the strategies, the economic structures and not least the geographical locations of the eighty-nine regions. As will be recalled from Table 12.1, the regions which gave the government most reason for nervousness by rebelling against federal authority in the 1990s were scattered around the country's periphery, portrayed on Figure 12.7. Faced with the choice of whether to buttress its security by means of guns or butter, the Putin administration increasingly, after the conclusion of the Chechen war in 1999, chose butter, in the shape of increased federal subsidy payments to those regions which had implemented or threatened insurgency in the 1990s (such as Chechnya, Kalmykia, Buryatia, and Tatarstan), or were adjacent and potentially contagious with those regions, such as Ingushetia and Ossetia.[33] But not all of these subsidies, of course, bore fruit in the form of poverty reduction. As explained in the case studies, whether they did so depended on a range of factors, some connected with local governance, some connected with the structure of local

[33] Recall the discussion of this approach by Gimpelson and Treisman (2000); see also discussion at pages 341–3 above.

industries, and some connected with the operation of the labour market. The possible chains of causation are summarized in Figure 12.7.

Thus, much of the serious poverty reduction in Russia of the 2000s, but by no means all, occurred on the fringes of the federation, where the security risks were greatest and where the authorities were determined to pump in, in the form of a 'social efficiency wage', whatever resources were needed to pre-empt a recurrence of conflict and disorder. The deployment of a social efficiency wage strategy was effective in reducing poverty, but not always. Sometimes the strategy failed to work effectively because of corruption and megalomania within the government's nominated partner administration, as in Kalmykia, and sometimes—as in Komi, in the sub-arctic region—because the prevailing production function was simply too capital intensive to generate many livelihoods for low-income people. But where the prevailing production function was labour intensive and the local elite could see the merits of an inclusive expenditure strategy, as in Chita, the reduction in poverty levels was quite significant, and if enough money was thrown at the problem poverty reduction sometimes occurred even in environments such as Ingushetia where the second condition was not satisfied. Thus, many parts of Russia, like many parts of Africa (Mosley, Hudson, and Verschoor 2004) have in recent years been experiencing aid-led growth, with the aid in this case coming from inside the country, rather than from outside, with the same implications of dependence of the peripheral regions, and the same accusations by the donors of wasteful use of aid.

This was not, of course, the only route by which poverty was reduced in Russia in the 2000s, but it was an important one. Other significant factors determining the poverty elasticity of particular regions included governors' capacity commitment, policies towards foreign investment (as in Pskov), the flexibility of the local labour market (as in Chita) and the (in)adequacy of technical training and quality control (as in Ulyanovsk). But by contrast with the situation at federal level, there were many political forces pushing local administrations towards the adoption of pro-poor policies, contrary to a conventional wisdom which insists that, especially in strong and centralized states like that of Russia, the poor are unlikely to have political leverage. By the same token, in some regions where the social efficiency wage is low, there is evidence of the opposite tendency, namely a 'political poverty trap' mechanism in which poverty and institutional weakness react on one another—if the strategy used by the centre to motivate the periphery is unsuccessful, the result, as in Ulyanovsk and Kalmykia, is a 'failed sub-state', and an increase in poverty levels.

These persisting fragilities are now once again being exposed, as in 2008/9, the macro-economy once again turned sour for Russia. As the consequence of the global crisis, the price of oil (which it will be recalled, accounts for forty-four per cent of the federal budget and for nearly sixty per cent of exports) fell from $147 per barrel in July 2008 to $41 in December, which put immediate pressure on the rouble. Russia's credit rating was downgraded in December 2008, unemployment rose quite rapidly before stabilizing (Table 12.3), and the fiscal balance moved from massive surplus to a deficit of six per cent (World Bank 2010, page 33). In 2010, the economy is thought to have returned to growth, and unemployment has now stabilized, but there are some signs of a changed international bargaining environment born of this shock, for example a lack of determination to force a hard bargain with Ukraine on the price of Russian gas piped through that country, and also a reinforcement of protectionism, with a new duty on imported cars announced in December 2008, which was met with widespread public protests (*Guardian*, 22 December 2008). Even for the world's largest country, the attainment of security remains an elusive concept.

13

Four African case studies: Ghana, Uganda, Kenya, and Zimbabwe

Sue Bowden and Paul Mosley[1]

13.1 INTRODUCTION

Although the problem of persistent poverty in developing countries has attracted considerable attention in the literature recently, culminating in the announcement of the Millennium Development Goals, few recent studies of poverty in developing countries have adopted a long-term time perspective. With the exception of recent work by Nunn (2007) and Acemoglu et al. (2001) nearly all of the huge recent research effort on poverty in developing countries has focused on data from the last twenty years, and on policy initiatives related to those data. In part, this is because the measure of deprivation most commonly used for international comparisons, headcount poverty, has been recorded only since the late 1980s or, in some cases, the 1990s. However, if poverty is deeply rooted and transferred from generation to generation, as much recent literature suggests,[2] any explanation of that poverty needs to find a way of analysing its long-term causes. In this chapter, we attempt to do this by means of a dynamic political economy model, focusing on Sub-Saharan Africa.

[1] Our thanks to Blessing Chiripanhura for his most valuable research support, also to Gareth Austin, Anne Booth, Ewout Frankema and participants at the Economic History Society conference at Warwick, 1–3 April 2009.

[2] See Addison, Hulme, and Kanbur (2009), especially the essays therein by Calvo and Dercon, Harriss and Quisumbing. Awareness of long-term persistence of poverty is of long-standing. It was nearly forty years ago, as we recall from Chapter 2, that the World Bank reported that 'more than a decade of rapid growth in underdeveloped countries has been of little or no benefit to perhaps a third of their population' (Chenery and Syrquin 1975, page xiii). Persistence of poverty over long periods has been observed in industrialized countries. Regions reporting little or no improvement in the living standards of poor people during long periods of growth include Russia during the second half of the nineteenth century (Gerschenkron 1959) and of course, Britain during its industrial revolution from 1760 to 1830 (see Crafts 1997; Feinstein 1998; Maddison 2000).

13.2 OUR ARGUMENT

Our starting point is that the poorest people, everywhere, are those who have nothing to sell but their labour; those who hold a claim to any form of productive capital asset (including, for the purposes of this argument, land, skills, and social connections as well as physical capital equipment) will for that reason be above this lowest level (Iliffe 1987). Hence, a production pattern that is pro-poor will be a production pattern that is intensive in low-income labour, and this will typically be associated with a relatively equal income distribution; incrementally, poverty *reduction* will be associated with investment in poor people's capital both human and infrastructural. There are two important reasons for putting the stress on income distribution. First, under an equal income distribution the demand for manufacturers (hence productivity) will be greater than under an unequal income distribution (Alesina and Perotti 1996; Alesina and Rodrik 1994; Murphy, Shleifer, and Vishny 1989).[3] Second, the level of inter-group resentment and civil unrest, which depresses investment and growth, will also be less where income is more equally distributed (Nafziger and Auvinen 2000).

We see income distribution in developing countries in the twentieth century as determined by the nature of the strategies employed to make colonies viable during the colonial period. The 'Scramble for Africa' during the late nineteenth century, and its economic and political rationale, has been the focus of much debate (Offer 1993; Robinson and Gallagher 1961). What is not in question is that any country, once colonized, needed a strategy to minimize the net cost that it imposed on the metropolitan country.

We characterize the two main strategies employed to achieve viability by African colonies, following Hancock (1943) and Myint (1976)[4] as *settler-based* and *peasant-export-based* economic strategies. Settler economies are those in which the chosen strategy was to allow European settlers to appropriate agricultural land. These settlers often found themselves operating in competition with

[3] A number of observers from within high inequality countries such as Zimbabwe during the inter-war depression enviously observed the high levels of demand achieved in societies where inequality was lower. This includes the Governor of Southern Rhodesia, who noted in 1933:

> Of the West Indian colonies perhaps Jamaica affords the most interesting comparison. The population of Jamaica, which is 98% coloured and black, is almost the same in numbers as our native population. The landed cost of imports into Jamaica was something like £4 million, whereas the corresponding figure for this colony was about £1,210,000, which with the addition of local purchases represents a purchasing power of about 30s. per head. Now supposing that only 25 per cent of our native population increased their purchasing power from 30s to 70s per head, the Jamaican level, this would mean an increase in the value of the native trade of at least £500,000 per annum . . . Surely then, on commercial grounds alone, apart from any moral obligation, it should be the policy to encourage the native in the attainment of higher standards.
>
> (National Archives of Zimbabwe: S1216/SC1/100/110, memo to Associated Chambers of Commerce, 10 March 1933)

[4] Hancock (1943) and Myint (1976) Chapter 2. These two categories are not exhaustive; there is also a third model, which we do not consider here, consisting of concessionaire colonies (French Equatorial Africa, much of the Belgian Congo, and much of Angola and Mozambique), where European-owned agriculture consisted of plantations rather than settler farms. We do not consider this third category in our case-study analysis.

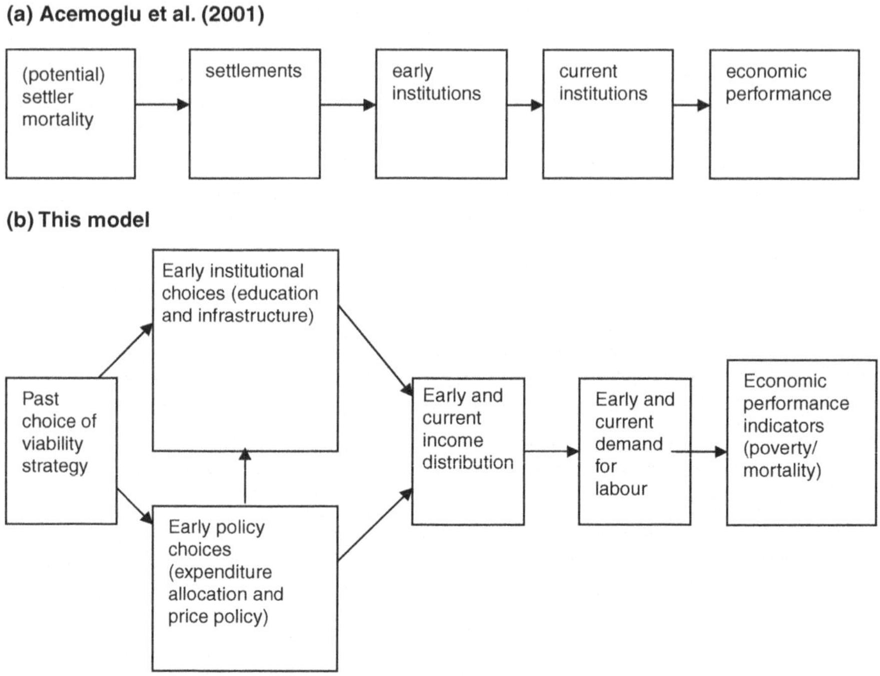

Figure 13.1 Alternative causal sequences determining the level of poverty and deprivation.

indigenous farmers. In peasant-export economies, the chosen strategy was to prohibit Europeans from owning land. As a result, agricultural production and exports were in the hands of indigenous African smallholders.[5] In our view, the choice of strategy determined early institutional decisions related to education and infrastructure and also policy choices related to expenditure allocation and price policy. Between them, these choices affected income distribution and, as a consequence, the demand for labour; income distribution and the demand for labour, in turn, fed through into measures of deprivation. Figure 13.1 illustrates our interpretation of the causal sequence crucial in the determination of poverty dynamics, in relation to that presented by Acemoglu et al.

From these differences in policymaking structures, we argue, there emerged an important difference in resource allocation: low-income Africans had better access to public capital goods, both physical and human, in peasant-export than in settler economies, and a pattern of recurrent expenditure emerged that was more pro-poor. The political rationale for this lay partly with the metropolitan countries, because all of them were under pressure to develop the export base of the colonies as a defence against the erosion of market share which they were already beginning to encounter in world markets. In the peasant-export economies this could only be

[5] Hancock and Myint's ideal types extended across the developing world, and were not confined to Africa. For a discussion of 'settler' economies, see Denoon, *Dependent Development*, and Mosley (1983). Discussion of peasant-export economies is rather more country specific; see, for Uganda Joergensen (1981) and for Ghana Kimble (1963).

achieved, in the short term, by measures to promote the productivity and sales of African smallholders, whereas in the settler economies they could hope that capital provided by European settlers would finance the necessary infrastructural investments to make those exports viable.[6]

At the local level, a voice was given especially in the peasant-export economies to African chiefs and other regional-level authorities, which then from the 1920s onward came increasingly to demand their proper share of resources for roads, education, health, and other inputs required to raise the productivity of the poor.[7] By the end of the 1920s, we argue, this difference in governance patterns had driven a wedge between the productive potential of the African poor and lower-middle income groups in peasant-export economies by contrast with settler economies.

We illustrate in Table 13.1 a division of African economies between the 'settler' and the 'peasant export' type as of the mid-1930s, by which point the key differences in economic structure had fully emerged.[8] As Table 13.1 demonstrates, in the settler economies, and there only, the control of expatriates over land quickly translated itself into control over the apparatus of government, leaving much less scope for investment in the human resources of the African poor.

The detailed research reported in this chapter focuses on four economies, all former British colonies. Ghana and Uganda illustrate the peasant export experience. Kenya and Zimbabwe illustrate the settler approach to colonial development—although it must be acknowledged that Kenya is not a perfect ideal type and contains, especially in the west of the country, some peasant-export characteristics. The availability of comprehensive and reliable data sources determined our choice of these economies as exemplars.

We develop our argument in five steps. Section 3 introduces the new data set created to illustrate and test our hypotheses. In section 4, we compare the performance of settler and peasant-export economies in terms of expenditure allocations, production functions, and patterns of governance. We argue that three components of this policy regime were particularly important: the mix of public recurrent and development expenditures between sectors, the level of investment in the human capital of the poor, and the rate of taxation imposed on the poor, in particular on exports by primary producers. In section 5, we relate

[6] In some settler colonies, notably Kenya within our sample, this expectation did not always materialize (see Brett 1973).

[7] Kimble (1963) and Joergensen (1981) discuss these political pressures and their economic consequences. The terms of trade, and thus the living standards of the poor in particular, declined severely during the 1914–18 period, in particular, to the point where a joint meeting of chiefs of the Gold Coast Colony, in March 1918, took political action, and forbade anyone to sell their cocoa at a price lower than 15s. per head (Ghana National Archives: SNA692, Case33/1918, Memorandum 5 March 1918 to Governor; quoted in Kimble (1963), pages 49–50). In Uganda, also, there were pressures from the chiefs to provide compensation for people's sufferings during the wartime period, against which the small population of white settler producers remaining in Uganda put up some resistance: for these pressures and the colonial government's response to them in the 1920s see Joergensen (1981) pages 161–5.

[8] The criterion for being a 'settler' economy is that five per cent or more or the total land area *was reserved* for Europeans in 1920. During the first years of the twentieth century, when the colonial state did not control the entire country, the criterion is ambiguous, because it was common in some African countries for Europeans to settle land on their own initiative without having any formal title to it.

Table 13.1 African countries: settler and peasant-export economies, *c.*1938.

Settler:	Share of land alienated or reserved for Europeans %	Elective representation of non-Africans on legislative body %	Peasant export:	Share of land alienated or reserved for Europeans %	Elective representation of non-Africans on legislative body %
South Africa	87	92 (note 1)	*Ghana*	*0*	*36 (note 3)*
Zimbabwe (Southern Rhodesia)	*49*	*100 (note 2)*	*Uganda*	*0*	*0 (note 4)*
Zambia (Northern Rhodesia)	3	92	Tanganyika	0	0 (note 5)
Kenya	*7*	*72*	Nigeria	0	0 (direct elections at municipal not federal level; elsewhere, indirect rule through native authorities)
Angola	12	76	Mali	0	N/a
Congo DRC (Belgian Congo)	9	80	Upper Volta (Burkina Faso)	0	N/a
Swaziland	65	N/a	Rwanda	1	0 (no direct elections, chiefs exercising quasi-feudal authority)

The four exemplars on which the discussion of this chapter focuses are in *italics*.
Sources: see Appendix

Notes: 'N/a' = not available

1. In Transkei, four African representatives chosen either by election or by chiefs' nomination. In all other states, representation of Africans vested in Governor-General.
2. Representation of Africans in legislative assembly by appointment through Minister of Native Affairs, not by election.
3. Proportion of elected European members fixed by 1928 constitution. After 1958, no elected European members.
4. No direct elections to Uganda legislative assembly; members nominated by chiefs at county level.
5. No direct elections; indirect rule through native authorities.

these factors to the trend of real wages and mortality in the selected countries. In section 6 we interpret post-independence poverty dynamics in these economies as an interaction between contemporary policy reforms and the institutional heritage of the colonial period. Section 7 subjects our hypotheses to statistical testing and section 8 concludes.

13.3 THE DATA SET

In order to test our argument we derived new data sets. We first discuss the measure of poverty used in this research. Many views exist on how best to select indicators of poverty, deprivation, or well-being. Historically, the first indicators to be used (e.g. Rowntree 1901) defined poverty in terms of the number or proportion of people who fell below a given income standard, defined as the cost of meeting minimum consumption needs—the poverty headcount, or headcount ratio. The poverty-headcount approach has been revived in the shape of the World Bank's 'dollar-a-day' measure, which uses the one standard metric of income below $1 per diem at 1990 purchasing-power parity, in place of national poverty lines, in order to standardize the measure of deprivation across all countries (World Bank 2000). Most analysts, and in particular the global Millennium Development Goals, supplement the poverty-headcount measure with other metrics, including measures of maternal and infant mortality, and education (Bowden, Chiripanhura, and Mosley 2008; Ssewanyana and Younger 2007). The poverty-headcount measure, in every country, exists only for a small number of years, mostly since the middle 1980s, and therefore is not suitable for assessing long-period trends in deprivation. In this section, we present the case for using infant mortality as a measure of deprivation in those cases where data on headcount poverty are not available.

First, we find a close statistical relationship between headcount poverty and infant mortality for countries and periods for which we have data. A regression for these countries over the period 1990–2005, based on the World Bank's World Development Indicators, yielded the relationship:

$$\text{Poverty headcount} = \underset{(11.93)}{19.2^{**}} + \underset{(11.10)}{0.28^{**}}\ \text{infant mortality},$$

$$r^2 = 0.30,\ n = 291$$

Second, the main causes of high infant mortality[9] are related to standards of living, to material deprivation, and specifically to the most extreme form of poverty, which is famine. Even better than the absolute number of people below the conventional poverty line (minimum consumption requirements line), the infant mortality rate captures the idea of *extreme* poverty—the most vulnerable who are so deprived of basic capabilities that they cannot stay alive.

Third, lowered infant mortality is associated not only with current poverty but also with future poverty. This is because, through the standard mechanisms of the demographic transition, persistently lowered mortality rates increase the perceived likelihood of child survival (Livi-Bacci 2001). This in turn diminishes the economic rationale for having a large family, which diminishes the total fertility level (the total number of children born to each parent), which is an important correlate of poverty levels. Finally, infant mortality, unlike headcount poverty, is available for many developing countries since the early twentieth and in some cases the nineteenth century. It has its limitations,[10] but it is available over a much longer historical period, and is well correlated with the 'World Bank standard' (headcount) measure of poverty during years when both indicators are available.

[9] That is, high vulnerability to life-threatening disease, low availability of basic nutrients, lack of access to medical services, lack of access to clean water and other assets which protect health, and high incidence of civil conflict-related deaths.

[10] As per absence of data for the war years, until the mid-twentieth century the records of infant deaths are based on the recollection of interviewees, not observation by doctors, so mortality data will be inaccurate if memory is defective or testimony is wrongly transcribed. Equally, registrations often omitted the births and deaths of children whose lives were very short. See Clairin (1966).

It is, in some senses, a better in-principle measure of human (under) development than the World Bank income measure, because it better captures the health, nutrition, and extreme poverty dimensions of deprivation. Infant mortality, moreover, is a principal component of the Human Development Index. Thus, we adopted one-period variations in the level of *mortality*, in particular infant mortality below the age of one, as our indicator of deprivation in order to evaluate long-period changes in well-being.

Second, we estimated measures of real wages for our sample economies. Using in each case the sources developed and listed in the Appendix, we defined money wages as the average unskilled wage in the formal, enumerated sector and quantified money wages; identified and quantified local consumer price indices; and used these local consumer price indices to deflate money wages. We identified the key characteristics of peasant as against settler economies in terms of the share of land alienated or reserved for Europeans and the elective representation of non-Africans on legislative bodies.

Finally, still using the sources listed in the Appendix, we quantified a variety of policy variables that we argue are likely causes of poverty, including the share of 'pro-poor expenditure' (our own concept, defined in section 4 below), agricultural value added per head, and measures of conflict and political instability.

The new data set is summarized in Table 13.2. As that table demonstrates, there were persistent differences over time between settler and peasant export economies in terms of not only welfare indicators, real wages, and mortality, but also the policy variables, which, on our interpretation, are the proximate causes of well-being, namely agricultural sales, our indicator of productivity in the subsistence and smallholder sector, and pro-poor expenditure by government.

13.4 THE IMPLICATIONS OF COLONIAL STRATEGIES

The contrast between settler and peasant export strategies also fed through to capital expenditure decisions. By 1925, several hundreds of thousands of low-income Ghanaians and Ugandans had a connection to the line of rail within immediate reach, whereas black rural South Africans, Zimbabweans, and (with the exception of one line) Kenyans had no access to rail transport[11] and road connections were pushed into the poorest and most remote parts of the peasant export economies.[12] This differential pattern of provision applied not only to physical capital but also to what a later World Bank report on poverty (World Bank 2000) was to refer to as 'investment in the human capital of the

[11] By 1938, Ghana had 550 miles of railway track running through African smallholder areas and Uganda 350 miles. Kenya had only the 120 miles of the Nairobi-Nanyuki branch line, which ran partly through European and partly through African areas. Zimbabwe had none, as none of its lines of rail ran through African reserves. Railways made a significant difference to the costs and thus the competitiveness of African producers.

[12] Sir Gordon Guggisberg (Governor 1921–9) 'was accused, and cheerfully accepted the accusation, of being a fanatic about the Northern Territories' (the poorest region of Ghana, treated by previous administrations more as a labour reserve than as a terrain for development), (Wraith 1967, page 156).

Table 13.2 Comparative evolution of selected settler and peasant-export economies, 1911–2006.

	Settler economies								Settler economies (average 1+2)				Peasant-export economies								Peasant-export economies (average 3 + 4)			
	(1) Zimbabwe				(2) Kenya								(3) Uganda				(4) Ghana							
	M	W	AS	PPEC	M	W	AS	PPEC	M	W	AS	PPEC	M	W	AS	PPEC	M	W	AS	PPEC	M	W	AS	PPEC
1911–20	225	73	0.10	4.5		100	0.06	3.8		**86**	**0.08**	**4.2**		77	0.39	−3.6	295	84	2.67	−0.4		**81**	**1.53**	**−2.0**
1921–30	246	69	0.12	8.9	400	80	0.08	10.1	**309**	**84**	**0.10**	**9.5**	245	117	0.91	7.9	206	139	3.89	14.2	**227**	**129**	**2.36**	**11.8**
1931–40	267	88	0.09	9.8	287	76	0.07	9.8	**285**	**84**	**0.08**	**9.8**	171	209	1.19	14.4	110	148	2.28	18.9	**136**	**178**	**1.54**	**14.3**
1941–50	264	88	0.22	14.2	182	87	0.24	10.4	**223**	**88**	**0.23**	**12.3**	126	146	1.26	13.8	106	150	3.30	18.7	**115**	**148**	**2.28**	**16.2**
1951–60	178	112	0.44	18.4	145	109	0.72	11.7	**161**	**110**	**1.01**	**15.0**	126	285	5.84	22.7	115	172	6.52	18.7	**120**	**228**	**6.18**	**16.8**
1961–70	161	148	0.73	16.9	120	130	2.14	9.4	**143**	**145**	**1.32**	**13.2**	104	541	6.68		120	267	9.84	29.0	**112**	**404**	**8.41**	**21.1**
1971–80	120	150	2.38	15.4	85	150	6.29	11.2	**102**	**150**	**4.38**	**13.3**	109	372	11.1		105	233	23.8	20.3	**107**	**302**	**17.4**	**16.8**
1981–90	77	180	3.14	20.4	71	164	9.5	14	**74**	**172**	**6.37**	**17.2**	104	217	13.7	5.7	86	275	19.3	15.3	**93**	**246**	**16.5**	**18.4**
1991–2000	68	121	2.37	12.7	68	160	11.8	13.2	**68**	**140**	**12.0**	**13.0**	95	398		8.7	80	385	14.9	15.5	**85**	**391**	**14.9**	**12.1**
2001–6	91	88	0.14	4.8	78		9.2	6.4	**84**		**4.62**	**5.6**	79	458		16.4	65		22.6	13.7	**73**		**15.2**	**15.2**

Sources: see Appendix.
Notes: M = under-1 mortality rate; W = real wage; AS = agricultural sales per capita; PPEC = 'pro-poor expenditure, less coercion' = expenditure on education, health, agriculture, and social protection, less military as police expenditure, as proportions of total expenditure. All data presented are ten-year arithmetic mean values of the variable stated.

poor'. Even by the Second World War, no university or institution of higher education offering access to black students existed in any part of Kenya, Zimbabwe, or South Africa. By contrast, Ghana had Achimota, founded in 1920, and Uganda had Makerere, founded in 1922, which had the power to award University of London external degrees and through the 1930s and 1940s took in students from other African countries without a university including Kenya, Tanganyika, and Zanzibar.[13] At the secondary level, Ghana and Uganda had enrolment levels significantly higher than those in the settler economies did. This not only made a direct contribution to equalizing their income distributions, but also enabled a minority of Ghanaian and Ugandan Africans to unlock the gateway to the higher reaches of the civil service. Even at the primary level of education (which impacts more directly on the poverty reduction process), investment in education was much stronger in the peasant-export than in the settler economies, and integrally related with the growth of peasant exports.

The pattern of recurrent expenditures also had the political function of signalling the alignment of governments with specific interest groups (Hudson et al. 2011). As indicated by Frankema (2011), public expenditure shares across different colonial African states are very diverse, with some remaining minimalist or nightwatchman 'states' (Booth 2007) and others evolving into 'developmental' states with substantial human resource investment; we would add, drawing on our argument above, that the composition of human resource investment between poor beneficiaries (as in Uganda and Ghana) and rich beneficiaries (as in South Africa) matters also. Within our sample, we find that in the peasant export economies, much more than in the settler economies, the government shifted over the course of the 1920s from an expenditure pattern oriented towards security and 'coercive' expenditures towards an expenditure pattern orientated towards pro-poor developmental activities for the benefit of the African majority—and in particular education, health, and smallholder agriculture. Table 13.2 delineates pro-poor expenditure as the share of pro-poor functions (health, education, and agriculture) in GNP, net of 'coercive' (military, police, and prison) expenditure. The latter may be seen as depleting potential pro-poor impact, both because military expenditure is more capital- and import intensive than agricultural and human capital production, and because high levels of military centrality are associated with civil disturbance which is disruptive of development.[14] As Table 13.2 demonstrates, from the 1920s the share of public expenditure attached to these 'poverty-reducing' functions was higher in the peasant-export than in the settler economies. Henceforward, we refer to this share as *pro-poor expenditure*.

[13] Both Achimota and Makerere Colleges, during the inter-war period, awarded their students external degrees of the University of London. The colleges were not granted their own degree-awarding powers until after the Second World War. For the detail of the health and education reforms implemented by Guggisberg in the 1920s see Wraith (1967) Chapters 5–6.

[14] See Nafziger and Auvinen (2000). For the origins of the concept of pro-poor expenditure, see Mosley et al. (2004), which provides evidence in support of the idea that agriculture, education, and social services have a relatively high propensity to impact on the livelihoods of the poor.' The concept of 'coercion' is due to Jorgensen (1981).

The result of these differences in political structure, and consequently in expenditure allocations, was to produce a difference in the production functions of the two groups of economies and, in particular, in the pro-poor impetus attaching to each of these groups (Booth 2007 for illustration of this in South-East Asia; Gardner 2010; and Huillery 2010 for Africa). As first argued by Baldwin (1963), whether or not the law of one price holds, there is certainly no law of one technology, and this has important implications for development. As between different developing countries, different sectors differ enormously in their input requirements per unit of output, and thence in their ability to reduce poverty. Particularly crucial is whether leading (fast-growing) sectors are intensive in resources supplied by the poor. In the first instance this means labour, because the poorest people in the poorest countries have little else they can sell (World Bank 2000). As a broad generalization, growth in which the leading sector is (among non-traded goods) construction and services and above all smallholder agriculture is pro-poor (partly through its demands for low-income labour, but also by achieving a reduction in the price of foods consumed by the poor). By contrast, economies in which the dominant sectors are capital intensive (such as, in most economies, oil and gas production, mineral production, or military expenditure) have much less pro-poor production functions.[15] Peasant-export economies, because their politics did not restrict the development of smallholder agriculture and other pro-poor activities[16] were more effective than settler economies at stimulating activities whose benefits either were directly aimed at, or spilled over on to, poor people. We refer to the latter as *poverty externalities.*[17]

[15] In respect of smallholder and plantation agricultural activities, Baldwin quotes labour utilization coefficients of 6.0 per $1,000 of output for the tea industry of Ceylon (Sri Lanka) for the 1960s, 2.1 in the Cuban sugar growing industry, 3.5 in the rubber industry of West Africa and 2.6 in the rubber industry of Malaya. By contrast, coefficients for mineral and extractive industries are much lower: 0.033 and 0.026 for the oil industry in Venezuela and Saudi Arabia respectively; 0.08 for bauxite production in Guyana; 0.13 for the Zambian copper industry; and 0.31 for iron ore production in India. All these examples are from Baldwin (1963), page 82, note 1. For a long-period discussion of factor proportions in the economic history of Africa, see Austin (2008), which emphasizes the condition of labour scarcity and relative land abundance prevailing across much of Africa in the twentieth century.

[16] At its peak in 1927, Ghanaian cocoa accounted for over forty per cent of world output, and over seventy per cent of all Ghanaian exports consisted of (mainly smallholder) exports of cocoa (Gold Coast, *Blue Book* 1927).

[17] The poverty elasticity or 'marginal propensity to reduce poverty per unit of growth' d log P/d log Y, may be characterized as:

$$\mathrm{d}\log P/\mathrm{d}\log Y = \frac{\partial \log P}{\partial \log(e_i A_i\,[\sigma/Y])} \cdot \frac{\partial \log (e_i A_i\,[\sigma/Y])}{\partial \log Y}$$

where,

P is poverty and
Y is income,

and also:

σ is a measure of vertical inequality of income distribution (e.g. Gini coefficient);
A_i is the leverage (share in output) of any sector i within the economy;
e_i is a measure of the 'poverty externalities' provided by that sector (the propensity to reduce poverty attached to each of the sectors A_i).

13.5 REAL WAGES, QUALITY OF LIFE, AND POVERTY DYNAMICS IN THE TWO SYSTEMS

We have argued that different political power structures produced different allocations of capital assets to the poor in colonial times. We now trace through the implications of these differences in allocation patterns for long-period trends in living standards and poverty rates. Our starting point is the Lewis model of economic development with unlimited supplies of labour.[18] The fundamental premise of the Lewis model is that so long as there is surplus labour in the subsistence sector, the supply curve of labour to the other sectors of the economy is flat, at a level determined by the productivity of the subsistence sector. The consequence is that the real wage and the standard of living will be pegged to those, regardless of productivity, for as long as the labour surplus persists; and thereafter will rise, as in neoclassical development models. Thus, the productivity of the subsistence sector, as well as demand-side factors, is crucial to determining the real wage; and the productivity of the subsistence sector may be influenced by a number of factors, including labour shortage (as identified by Lewis),[19] land shortage (identified by Lewis as being particularly relevant in the case of Ghana and other labour-scarce countries of Africa),[20] a range of policy influences amongst which we have identified the composition of expenditure as being particularly important, and finally extraneous influences such as political stability.

In the context of this discussion, Figure 13.2 presents our estimates of long-term real wage trends in our four sample countries. We find that real wages remained tied close to the subsistence level (with occasional ephemeral surges

It will be clear that the higher is the level of poverty externalities e_i, the higher is the overall poverty elasticity.

[18] See Lewis (1955). The Lewis model was itself inspired by evidence of near-subsistence wage rates throughout the industrial revolution period in Britain (1760–1840). At the time Lewis wrote the main evidence available to him was the three-volume study by J.L. and Barbara Hammond, (*The Village Labourer; The Town Labourer; The Skilled Labourer*) together with the data gathered by Deane and Cole, eventually published as Deane and Cole (1964). Both sources suggested that real wages in Great Britain had a tendency to be stagnant or near-stagnant during the Industrial Revolution period, 1760–1840. Subsequent research on this period used a wider range of sources and indicators of well-being than that available to Lewis. Much of this literature supports his initial intuition that the Industrial Revolution period was characterized by stagnant real wages made possible, as in developing countries, by 'disguised unemployment' within subsistence activities in the service, agricultural and home-working sectors (Crafts 1997; and Feinstein 1998; Horrell and Humphries 1992). The Lewis model has already served as inspiration for a number of long-period empirical studies of real wage rates in the developing countries such as Eisner (1961) for Jamaica; Arrighi (1970) for Zimbabwe; Wilson (1972) for South Africa; Huff and Caggiano (2007) for Burma, Thailand, and Malaya.

[19] And quite explicitly in the case of Ghana, a country which he came to know well in the 1950s as adviser and which in his view was characterized by 'an abundance of land *and an acute shortage of labour*' Lewis (1953) paragraph 28. Emphasis added. For this period of Lewis's career, see Tignor (2005) Chapters 5 and 6.

[20] In a modest way, this occurred in the 1920s as the smallholder production frontier was extended, not only with respect to Ghanaian cocoa, but also with respect to Ugandan cotton. In relation to Ghana, Lewis argued that 'mineral-bearing lands, or lands with just the right suitability for cocoa, are relatively scarce . . . if these scarce lands are owned by peasants, the peasants may of course become rich' (Lewis 1953, page 443). For discussions of labour scarcity and its significance in African development see Hopkins (1973) and Austin (2008).

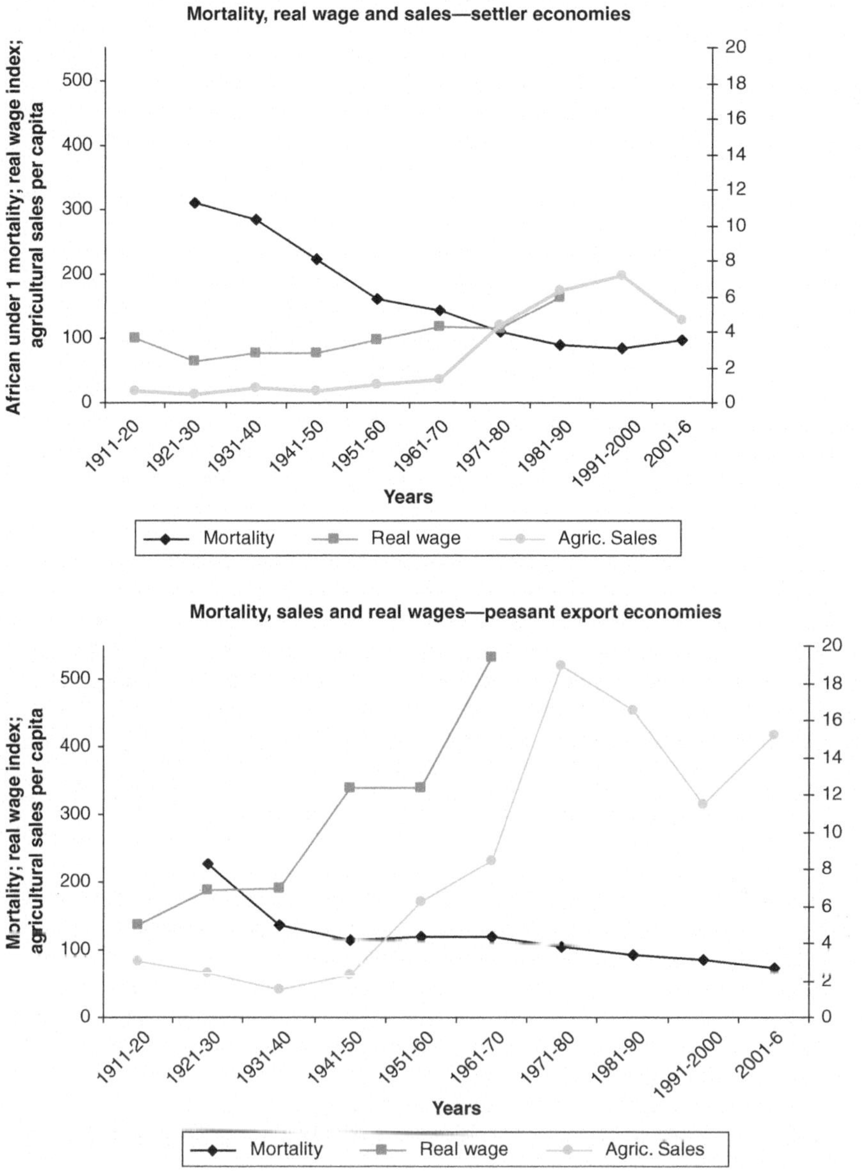

Figure 13.2 The settler–peasant-export dichotomy: mortality, real wages, and smallholder sales.

Sources: See Appendix.

Table 13.3 Settler and peasant-export economies: prices paid to farmers as a share of export realization, 1920–2007.

	Settler economies			Peasant-export economies		
	Zimbabwe (maize)	Kenya (maize)	Average, settler economies	Uganda (coffee)	Ghana (cocoa)	Average, peasant export economies
1911–20	0.91			0.62	0.70	0.66
1921–30	0.87	0.63	0.42	0.69	0.73	0.71
1931–40	0.82	0.57	0.69	0.31	0.47	0.39
1951–60	0.76	0.58	0.64	0.30	0.52	0.41
1961–70	0.69	0.89	0.79	0.18	0.61	0.39
1981–90	0.67	0.79	0.73	0.28	0.36	0.32
1991–2000	0.80	0.81	0.81	0.77	0.55	0.66
2000-present				1.00	0.74	0.87

Note: all data presented are ten-year arithmetic mean values of the variable stated.

Sources: see Appendix.

during boom periods) in the settler economies of Kenya and Zimbabwe for the first half of the twentieth century; they then rose for the next twenty years, but in Zimbabwe, not in Kenya, they returned to this level at the end of the century. We further find that real wages rose above the subsistence level in the peasant-export economies of Uganda and Ghana as early as the 1920s;[21] and, in spite of relapses in the 1940s and 1970s in both countries, they never, during the second half of the twentieth century, fell back to the settler level. In addition, there appears to be a strong link from real wages to infant mortality, our selected indicator of poverty. A sustained fall in the infant death rate began, on the evidence available to us, in Ghana in the early 1920s, in Uganda ten years later, but in the settler economies not until twenty years after that, in the 1950s.

During the 1930s, in spite of a collapse of world cocoa and coffee prices, there was only a small reduction in the supply of Ghanaian and Ugandan primary exports (Table 13.3) and thus in producer incomes.

Thus, for a combination of reasons, a floor was placed, under the labour supply curve by the end of the 1920s, in the peasant-export economies, but not in the settler economies.[22] Figure 13.3 demonstrates this proposition, differentiating between the two types of economies.

In the settler economies of Kenya and Southern Rhodesia, the evolution of policy and thus of African incomes was very different. The governments of each of

[21] This finding of increasing real wages in Ghana and Uganda from the 1920s onwards, and of much lower growth in Kenya, has been dependently confirmed also by Frankema and van Waijenburg (2010), using a different data set.

[22] Radical critiques of the Lewis model have emphasized that in Kenya and Zimbabwe (and also classically in South Africa), the persistence of labour surplus owed a great deal to deliberate policy measures designed to create a surplus, rather than simply to the weakness of African smallholder agriculture (Arrighi 1970). These measures included discrimination in commodity markets (discussed below), hut taxes, and in the early days of settlement outright coercion of labour by government agents. Some of these labour-market interventions, especially conscription of African labour for public works, were also applied in peasant-export economies but on a far lesser scale.

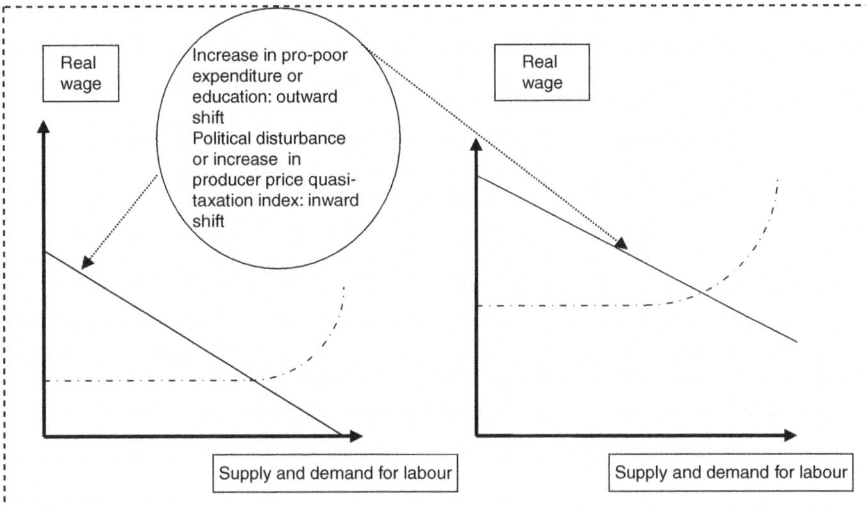

Figure 13.3 Influences on supply and demand for labour in settler and peasant-export economies.

those countries established commodity-control schemes to protect the livelihoods of white farmers against price collapse. Formal discrimination between black and white producers was still illegal under the constitutions of each of those countries at that time, and so informal discrimination was resorted to. Agents of the newly established Government Maize Control Boards bought African maize surpluses within African reserve areas, and then sold the African maize on the export market at the depressed prices of the time, leaving European producers to supply the protected high-priced local market (Mosley 1983, Chapter 2). Under the stress of these pressures, African livelihoods (especially in regions where crop production was least resilient) were pushed down towards the subsistence minimum. As world commodity prices rose during the late 1930s and after the Second World War, buyers' commercial interest in keeping the buying price as low as they could manage merged with the fiscal interest of the colonial administration. Between them, these interests established their own form of commodity control, in the form of boards[23] across all of the peasant-export economies. These marketing boards[24] derived public revenue from paying the (African) smallholder producer less than the export realization, as illustrated in Table 13.3 (Bates 1981, pages 137–45; Appendix; see also Figure 5.2 above).

This taxation of smallholder agriculture, with its huge poverty reduction potential, closed the gap in poverty reduction performance between the

[23] For example, the Ghana Cocoa Marketing Board, the Uganda Coffee Marketing Board, and Cotton Lint and Seed Marketing Boards.

[24] The name 'marketing boards', in this context, was simply a euphemism for taxes on African smallholder exports, and their importance for our present argument is that what they were taxing was in large part the motor by which poverty had previously been brought down in the peasant-export economies.

peasant-export economies and the settler economies.[25] During the period of smallholder commodity marketing boards, from the 1940s through the early 1980s, the ability of peasant export sectors to grow, and therefore to reduce poverty, was heavily compromised by the burden of export taxation.

At the end of the Second World War, the pattern of expenditure was influenced, both in the settler and in the peasant-export colonies, by investments in secondary and higher education, and in industry, in pursuit of economic independence and in rather modest imitation of the import-substituting industrialization attempted at the time in Asia and Latin America.[26] The proceeds of the levies on smallholder export production financed much of this investment. This evolution in expenditure patterns occurred at a similar rate in the settler and the peasant-export colonies, and thus the 'performance gap' between the two groups of colonies in terms of pro-poor expenditure did not widen as it did in the 1920s and 1930s, but rather remained constant between the 1940s and 1960s.

13.6 THE POST-INDEPENDENCE EXPERIENCE

Following the lead of Ghana in 1955, most African countries, both of the settler and peasant-export type, became politically independent during the 1960s and 1970s. In all cases, they received large infusions of concessional aid from both bilateral and the newly established multilateral donors at the point of independence and in most cases for decades afterwards.[27]

At first, through the 1960s and 1970s, the approach was successful in raising investment and growth rates across most of Africa and specifically, through high levels of investment in health and education, in lowering child and adult mortality (Table 13.2). By the end of the 1970s, however, agricultural production per capita was falling across Africa as a whole, and food imports were rising (Bates 1981, page 1). Across Africa as a whole, but specifically in our four case-study economies, there were severe governance problems. These were of two kinds. The first was a chronic fiscal debility which prevented African governments, even through the relatively fat years of the 1970s, from maintaining a sustained investment in the kind of 'green revolution' programmes which had revolutionized smallholder agricultural productivity across Asia (and pushed up the 'supply curve') in the same decade. The second was a wave of political violence and instability.[28]

[25] The governments of settler economies, by contrast with peasant-export economies, had an interest in keeping the price of controlled commodities as high as possible in order to support the European farmers to whom they were beholden. Through most of the post-war period, because power was in the hands of agricultural producers rather than agricultural consumers, they were able to keep the price of board-controlled commodities above the export realization.

[26] For Ghana, these attempts at import-substituting industrialization are particularly well summarized by Killick (1978).

[27] Africa has long been the most aid-dependent continent, as well as the poorest, and in all the cases under examination, the resources provided by aid donors have been crucial in influencing the balance of forces determining the rate of poverty reduction. See, for example, World Bank (1990, 2000).

[28] This was at its most dramatic in Uganda where the savagery and dispossession associated with the rule of Idi Amin caused per capita incomes in Uganda to fall by forty per cent between 1970 and 1987 (Reinikka and Collier 2001).

There were common threads running through each of these cases. First, was the continuing weakness and lack of legitimacy, in most African countries, of the post-colonial governmental apparatus. Second, there was resentment at the size and the injustice of the gap between rich (often white) and poor (almost invariably black). Finally, there was a widening of this gap after independence (especially in the peasant-export economies). This was the result of corrupt utilization of commodity stabilization funds and other surpluses created by government patronage. Consequently, the pro-poor expenditure ratio (Table 13.2) suffered in the 1970s, *both* in the peasant-export and in the settler economies. Africa, having ended the 1970s with its governance apparatus severely damaged, duly suffered more than any other region of the developing world.

By the end of the 1980s a large-scale shift in the portfolio of the World Bank and other aid donors had occurred, away from the long-term project lending provided for in the Bank's 1944 articles of agreement and towards a long-term programme lending 'structural adjustment lending'[29] conditional on the liberalization of the economy. Government control over the economy had come to be seen by the international financial organizations (World Bank 1997) as the root of African economic, and specifically agricultural, weakness, and as the 1980s global recession deepened, these organizations determined to exact liberalization of the economy as the price of their financial support.

If the structural adjustment prescription, as applied to all African economies, was broadly the same, the response was massively different. In particular, in respect of our sample, the two peasant-export economies grew rapidly, and reduced poverty even more rapidly, during the 1990s and early 2000s (Table 13.2). The headcount poverty rate in Ghana fell from fifty-one per cent to thirty-nine per cent during the 1990s and then to twenty-seven per cent by 2005 (Nsowah-Nuamah, Teal, and Awoonor-Williams 2010, page 1). In Uganda, it fell over the same years from fifty-four per cent to thirty-two per cent: a transition rivalling any achieved in any country, even in East Asia, over a similar period. In the settler economies, by contrast, poverty, in a headcount sense, increased on a long-term basis over the same years. Even more importantly for the long term, there was a bifurcation in institutional capacity: tax-to-GDP ratios increased quite sharply in Uganda and Ghana in the 1990s, but fell in the settler economies.

The most crucial reason for this bifurcation in performance was that for the reasons discussed above the peasant-export economies possessed, and the settler economies did not possess, a stock of labour-intensive assets available to be liberalized—in the shape of cotton, coffee, and cocoa smallholdings.[30] Second,

[29] 'Structural adjustment', in this context, meant policies (principally measures which liberalized the markets for crops, foreign exchange, and capital, and thereby facilitated an opening-up of the economy) which changed the structure of incentives, and thereby were able to boost the economy's supply side—by contrast with demand-side measures, which restricted demand and therefore reduced output. By means of these policies, the Bank hoped to be able to give an expansionary impetus to the economy, to contrast with the deflationary bias of the IMF's advice and policies. This boost eventually happened, but in Africa took many years, most of the 1980s and 1990s in fact, to materialize (Mosley, Harrigan, and Toye 1995).

[30] The incomes of about eight-five per cent of Ugandans were affected by what happened to coffee revenues, according to Collier and Reinikka (2001). The diffusion of proceeds from cocoa and coffee favoured three groups in particular: (1) workers (given that peasant production is very labour intensive);

and directly connected with the ebbing of the 1970s tide of political violence and instability described above, patterns of both recurrent and capital expenditure were reformed in a far more pro-poor direction in the peasant export economies than in the settler economies.

Thus was formed, for the first time since the 1920s, a political coalition in Africa in support of pro-poor action—in this case between aid donors, large and small farmers,[31] and trading interests willing to take a bet on benefiting from the liberalization of smallholder commodity production. The incentives to collaboration in support of such coalitions were much greater because the costs of the coalitions coming unstuck, in the form of a renewal of war atrocities from whose effects many Ugandans are still recovering, were obvious to all parties. A similar argument applies in the peasant-export economies of Ethiopia, Rwanda, and Mozambique, each of which came to the end of savage conflicts in the 1990s.[32]

Although the reforms described above relate to the poverty content of *recurrent* expenditure, they also have implications for the pro-poor reorientation of capital expenditure, especially in the case of the universal primary education objective. No pro-poor chemistry at this time occurred in the settler economies, where (with the recent exception of Zambia) the poverty element of the policy dialogue was notoriously tense and uncreative.[33] Within the context of the model of Figure 13.3, both the liberalization of export taxation and the emergence from the governance crisis of the 1970s can be seen as shift parameters that raised the productivity of the small-farm and subsistence sector and thereby moved the supply-of-labour curve (on Figure 13.3) outward, and raised the real wage, much more rapidly in the peasant export than in the upward economies. Government investment in the productivity of the small-farm and subsistence sector (PPE) likewise acts as an upward pressure on the supply function in the subsistence sector. These influences (which we have argued are determined by policy and institutional parameters established many decades ago), in conjunction with the demand function for modern-sector labour, determine the real wage; and the real wage, in conjunction with the production function along which the modern sector operates (the 'poverty externalities' defined above) determines the dynamics of poverty. This is the essence of the causal chain which we shall seek to test in the following section. We now seek to model this pattern of causation.

(2) backward and forward linkages industries; (3) especially in the case of food crops grown on those farms, rural and urban consumers. See Reinikka and Collier (2001), especially Chapters 4 and 5.

[31] In Uganda, the fact that the President had won a guerrilla war and had a rural power-base amongst smallholders in the south-western region was crucial to the pro-poor bias of public expenditure (a similar argument applies to Tigre and Wollo in Ethiopia).

[32] Ghana was a slightly different case, because in the 1980s it was recovering, not from civil war, but from twenty years of systematic mismanagement of its economy.

[33] In the cases of Kenya and Zimbabwe, this is particularly clear. Indeed, by 1999 the aid donors had been expelled from Zimbabwe.

13.7 REAL WAGE AND MORTALITY REGRESSIONS

Specification of the model

Our model uses infant mortality as a measure of poverty (or the reverse of well-being). In the preceding discussion, we examined the political influences bearing on the well-being of the poor and its principal components, labour incomes and agricultural sales. A key contribution of this chapter has been to chart time series of these principal components and to identify a key policy variable influencing them, namely government pro-poor expenditure and investment in the physical and human capital of the poor. We now specify the causal chain which we wish to estimate.

The germ-cell of our model is the supply–demand model of the labour market originally specified by Lewis, where the demand for modern sector labour corresponds to the marginal revenue product of labour, and therefore declines with increases in the amount of labour hired:

$$L_d = \alpha_1(L, w) \tag{13.1}$$

where

L_d = demand for labour,
L = labour force and
w = real wage of unskilled labour within the modern sector

The supply of labour is governed by the conditions under which labour is willing to detach itself from the subsistence economy, being 'unlimited' in those cases where there are many applicants for every job at the going wage. In 1954, Lewis speculated that labour would leave the subsistence economy as long as the wage offered exceeded by a sufficient margin the average productivity of labour in the subsistence (or 'traditional') sector (Lewis 1954, page 409). This formulation has the merit of focusing attention on the productivity of the subsistence sector on small-scale farms and elsewhere as the basic driver of the real wage and thence of poor people's well-being.[34] On this view,

$$L_s = \alpha_2(Y_s/L, w) \tag{13.2}$$

where

Y_s = output from subsistence and small-farm sector, and
L_s = labour supply

Our main innovation has been to argue that both the level and the mix of taxation and public expenditure make a difference to the operation of this model, and thence to the long-term poverty index; so also do political disturbances. We therefore insert four variables: the real level of public expenditure; the extent to which that expenditure focused on low-income Africans; the level of agricultural

[34] 'The prices of tropical commercial crops will always permit only subsistence wages until, for a change, capital and knowledge are put at the disposal of the subsistence producers to increase the productivity of tropical food production for home consumption' (Lewis 1954, page 442).

quasi-taxation; and the level of political disturbances, into the supply function (1): the first two of these influences affect the supply price of labour positively and the last two negatively.

$$L_s = \alpha_2(g, ppe, t, SPI)(L, w) \qquad (13.2')$$

where

g = real level of government expenditure
ppe = share of total expenditure committed to 'pro-poor' functions
t = level of quasi-taxation (export price, less price received by farmers) on agricultural exports
SPI = socio-political instability index

Solving for the equilibrium real wage, reached at the point where (13.1') equals (13.2), we have

$$W^* = f[(\alpha_1/\alpha_2)(g, ppe, t, SPI)(Y_s/L)] \qquad (13.3)$$

That is, the real wage level can be expected to evolve over time at a rate determined by the fundamental factor, identified by Lewis, of the productivity of the subsistence sector, and by variations in the fiscal instruments that bear on the productivity and asset holdings of the poor (g, ppe, and t) and political disturbances (SPI).

Because almost all the livelihood of the poor derives either from wages or from agricultural (crop and livestock) incomes, themselves also subject to political disturbances, it is reasonable to suppose that these three factors have a large part in explaining our chosen indicator of poverty, infant mortality, M:

$$M = f(W^*, Y_s/L, SPI) \qquad (13.4)$$

Finally, political instability is not exogenous but is determined by those forces which determine the incentive to rebel against the government, including in particular the real labour income and educational level of potential rebels and the extent to which government policies provokes or seeks to calm incipient conflict.

$$SPI = f(Y_s/L, ede, MC) \qquad (13.5)$$

where

ede represents investment in education and MC is 'military centrality', or the factors, including the level of military expenditure, determining the level of provocation or otherwise of the civil population by the government

The basic system that we estimate, therefore, consists of an equation determining long-term poverty (13.4), one element of which is real wages which are determined by the real wage equation (13.3), and another element of which political instability is endogenous, through (13.5) to individual well-being (Collier and Hoeffler 1998, 2004; Nafziger, Stewart, and Vayrynen 2000). Table 13.4 details our OLS estimates of the basic estimating equation for mortality (13.4), separately for each of the case-study countries. Several of the variables in the data set, notably mortality, agricultural productivity, and pro-poor expenditure, are subject to a

Table 13.4 Single-equation OLS mortality regressions.

Regression coefficients on independent variables:	Peasant-export economies		Settler economies	
	Ghana	Uganda	Kenya	Zimbabwe
Constant	319.2**	304.0**	151.7	300.9**
	(8.27)	(19.69)	(2.62)	(18.39)
Real agricultural value added per capita (first difference; kg/ha)	−0.14	−0.19	−1.83**	−0.58*
	(0.29)	(1.70)	(2.63)	(1.64)
PPE ratio	−3.23**	−4.67**	−0.65	−2.03
	(4.65)	(4.98)	(0.80)	(1.68)
Share of export price received by farmer	−90.9*	−84.4**	−61.5	−40.6*
	(2.15)	(3.43)	(0.77)	(2.52)
Conflict dummy	−7.79	−0.21	−8.29**	−1.26**
	(0.28)	(0.28)	(3.52)	(2.94)
Time (years since 1914)	−2.11**	−2.65	−0.98**	−2.46**
	(6.99)	(8.65)	(2.90)	(12.68)
R^2	0.78	0.85	0.72	0.96
N	49	65	13	58

Dependent variable: infant (under 1) mortality. Estimation period: 1914–2009.
All relationships estimated as single equations by OLS. For sources, see Appendix.

time-trend, which we control for by including it explicitly in the estimating equation.

All of the independent variables in Table 13.4 have the expected sign. Our interpretation is that legal frameworks which are consistent with wide-scale improvement of smallholder agricultural productivity 'put a floor' under the level of the real wage (Figure 13.3), which in turn reduces the mortality indicator of poverty. In addition, policy influences play a role. First, increases in the PPE ratio (the share of pro-poor expenditures in the total), increases in the share of the export price received by the producer, and decreases in political instability are all significantly associated with reduced levels of mortality. Second, the policy variable, the PPE ratio, has more leverage on mortality in the peasant-export economies, Ghana and Uganda (third row of the table), whereas agricultural productivity (real value added per capita) has more leverage in the settler economies, Kenya and Zimbabwe.

Two of the determinants of mortality in our model, agricultural productivity and political instability, are endogenous. Hence there is a risk that simple OLS regressions such as those presented in Table 13.4 may present biased estimates of the determinants of mortality. To offset this bias, we present in Table 13.5 estimates of the determinants of mortality derived by instrumental variables methods, in which separate equations for the real wage and political instability are estimated simultaneously with the mortality equation. These estimates also differentiate between the different components of expenditure contained within the pro-poor expenditure ratio.

Across the sample as a whole, within the set of expenditures which our prior analysis has identified as 'pro-poor', educational expenditures appear to be much the most significant in terms of bringing down poverty, and in particular more

Table 13.5 Simultaneous-equation regressions: mortality, wages, and political instability index.

	Peasant-export economies (Ghana and Uganda)			Settler economies (Kenya and Zimbabwe)			Whole sample		
Dependent variable:	Infant (under 1) mortality	Real wage index	Conflict dummy	Infant (under 1) mortality	Real wage index	Conflict dummy	Infant (under 1) mortality	Real wage index	Conflict dummy
Regression coefficients on independent variables: Constant	130.2**	193.7**	6.57**	222.4**	68.0**	0.68	−171.4**	135.8**	5.95**
	(5.47)	(3.77)	(13.01)	(5.43)	(5.82)	(0.34)	(7.49)	(3.41)	(13.75)
Agricultural value added per capita (first difference; kg/ha)	−0.35	2.92**		−1.59**			1.46*	3.58**	
	(0.83)	(3.08)		(3.71)			(1.96)	(4.60)	
Real wage (first difference)	−0.30		0.003	−0.49**	2.16**	0.009	−0.27*		0.005*
	(1.44)		(1.12)	(2.70)	(7.04)	(0.71)	(2.13)		(2.46)
Conflict dummy	14.85**			3.94**			9.90**		
	(6.73)			(3.09)			(5.94)		
Share of education in total expenditure	−5.82**			−8.01**			−10.71**		
	(3.60)			(7.69)			(5.31)		
Share of health in total expenditure							−4.27		
							(0.74)		
Share of agriculture in total expenditure							11.1**		
							(6.47)		
Share of military in total expenditure		−11.09			6.01*			−4.91	
		(1.64)			(2.24)			(0.89)	
PPE ratio (net of military expenditure)			−0.21**			0.16			−0.19**
			(4.68)			(1.67)			(6.00)
Producer's share of export price	31.7			86.7**			38.5*		
	(1.61)			(3.27)			(2.26)		
R^2	0.45	0.16	0.70	0.84	0.18	0.01	0.70	0.19	0.21
Hansen-Sargan overidentification statistic	0.14			0.06			0.22		
Number of observations	107			57			137		

Sources: see Appendix.
Estimation method; 3SLS. Estimation is for period 1914–2007 unless otherwise stated.

Notes: figures in parentheses below coefficients are Student's t−statistics. ** against a coefficient denotes significance at the one per cent level and * denotes significance at the five per cent level.

significant than health or agricultural expenditures. In the mortality equation, a one per cent increase in the share of educational expenditures in total expenditure is highly significant across the sample as a whole and associated, when the sample is subdivided, with an eight per cent reduction in the infant mortality rate in the settler economies, or a five per cent reduction in the peasant-export economies. This effect appears to be stable across the time period of our sample, but is stronger during the colonial period, prior to 1960, than during the post-colonial period.[35] The real wage is significantly determined, as Lewis predicted, by agricultural productivity. The likelihood of conflict is determined both by the real wage and, more significantly, by the pro-poor expenditure ratio. This supports our hypothesis that the allocation of expenditure exercises an influence on poverty, not only indirectly through its impact on the likelihood of conflict, but also as a direct influence on indicators of well-being. This method of estimation appears to deal satisfactorily with the problem of endogeneity of the real wage and of conflict. The Sargan test statistics indicate that the system of equations is adequately identified.

13.8 CONCLUSION

We have argued that improvements in smallholder agricultural productivity were the prime mover in enabling poverty, in some poor African countries, to be reduced, and that some of the recent successes in this field represent the realization of assets established many decades ago. At a different rate within different types of colonial and post-colonial structure, these improvements in agricultural productivity have put a floor underneath the subsistence-determined wage of the Lewis model (1954). In so doing, they helped, especially in the peasant-export economies, to even up the income distribution and thus achieve a further development dividend through their contribution to conflict reduction. They have not done this unaided. The composition of public spending, which is determined by the character of the prevailing political regime and its ability to maintain the rule of law, has exercised a measurable influence on the ability of the economy to reduce poverty. Within the set of expenditures whose influence we identified as being pro-poor, by far the most robust of these influences is that working through educational spending.

At this point, our argument intersects with the argument about institutional impact put forward by Acemoglu et al. (2001). There is no doubt that effective institutions, as they argue, are an abiding positive influence on economic development. However, we take a different view of which institutions are important. According to our interpretation, the institutions that have been important in determining long-term trends in well-being in Africa were the allocation of land, the level of capital expenditure on infrastructure, and the allocation of

[35] Within a three-equation system comprising infant mortality, real wages, and conflict identical to that estimated, the coefficient of educational expenditure on infant mortality is strong (a coefficient of 15.4) and significant at the one per cent level across our sample as a whole for the period prior to 1960, whereas it is insignificant for the period after 1960.

recurrent expenditure between 'developmental' and 'non-developmental' functions. The initial decision at the turn of the twentieth century to establish colonies as either settler or peasant-export economies influenced these factors. Prior political decisions, in other words, determined institutional development. The institutional structure, which on our analysis optimized the rate of poverty reduction, was not so much a structure that protected the colonists' property rights against expropriation, but rather a structure that protected African smallholders' property rights. Over time, this structure (much though it was buffeted by export taxation and political instability between the 1940s and the 1970s) contributed to a stock of physical and human capital amongst smallholders within peasant-export economies. As a result, the governments of those countries were able to draw on this stock in a poverty-reducing manner during the 1990s, with the help of a big liberalization dividend as the level of quasi-taxation by marketing boards was finally reduced. By contrast, in the settler economies of Kenya and Zimbabwe the level of inequality was persistently higher and the intersectoral allocation of government expenditure persistently less favourable to lower income groups. The 'historical stock' of poverty-reducing institutions and assets which Uganda and Ghana had been able to accumulate was not available to them in anything like the same degree, and the poverty trend since the middle 1980s, in both countries, has been much less favourable. In other words, our argument is that long-period poverty trends were determined by poverty-reducing institutions, which, in turn, were determined in part by colonial policies.

APPENDIX

Data sources used for creation of data set

The full data arrays are presented in Bowden and Mosley (2010).

1. Sources for identifying land and electoral characteristics of settler and peasant economies

   Share of land alienated or reserved for Europeans percentage and *elective representation* of non-Africans on legislative body: extended and adapted from Mosley (1983), Table 1.1 using in particular data from Hailey (1938).

2. Under-1 mortality (M)

   Before 1950, from Kuczynski (1949), vol. 1 for Ghana and vol. 2 for Kenya and Uganda. For Zimbabwe (Southern Rhodesia), data are from Mosley (1983), Appendix to Chapter 3. After 1960, all data are from World Bank, *World Development Indicators* (CD-ROM), various issues. All data are derived from annual observations. Data for Kenya and Zimbabwe, all years, relate to *African population only.*

3. Sources used to estimate real wages

   Money wages (MW): are given for all countries in shillings per month (£1 = 20 shillings) or, exceptionally after 1970, currency units indicated. The indicator of money wages used is the average African unskilled wage in the formal, enumerated sector; this includes formal-sector agricultural activities such as large farms and plantations, but does not include wages on smallholdings. Men and women workers are both included and wage data disaggregated by gender are presented in Bowden, Chiripanhura, and Mosley (2008) and Bowden and Mosley (2010).

   Zimbabwe: to 1946, *Annual Reports of the Chief Native Commissioner*; thereafter, *Monthly Statistical Digests*, various.

   Kenya: to 1946, *Blue Books*, supplemented by archival sources as listed in Mosley (1983, page 157); thereafter, *Statistical Abstracts* with interpolations from Labour Department archives, also after 1960, International Labour Organization, *Yearbook of Labour Statistics* 2009.

   Uganda: before 1960, wages and employment generally from *Blue Books*, supplemented by data from Powesland (1957) and Jorgensen (1981), especially his Table 2.3, also by Labour Department, *Annual Reports.* After 1960, from World Bank, *World Development Indicators.*

   Ghana: to 1945, wage rates and employment from Gold Coast, *Social and Economic Progress: Annual Reports*, section on 'wages and cost of living'; 1945–60 from Birmingham, Neustadt and Omaboe (1965); after 1960, from World Bank, *World Development Indicators.*

   Consumer price indices: (PI): before 1960

   Zimbabwe: Mosley (1983), Chapter 4 appendix, updated by means of *Index of retail prices of foodstuffs consumed by Zimbabwe Europeans,* in *Annual Yearbooks of Southern Rhodesia,* various.

Kenya: *index of import prices of goods consumed by Kenyan Africans CIF Mombasa*, derived from Kenya Blue Books and reported in Mosley (1983), Chapter 4. Appendix.

Uganda: from *Blue Books*, 1928, 1938, and 1944, sections on prices, wages, and imports; the items of consumption used to compile the deflator prices are cotton piece goods, kerosene oil, bicycles, sugar, soap, maize flour, and bananas (*matooke*). For 1947–77, we use Uganda Government, *Kampala Lower Income Cost of Living Index*, as published in successive issues of the *Statistical Abstract* and *Quarterly Economic and Statistical Bulletin* (typically Table UO6). After 1982, the consumer price index as published in Ministry of Finance and Economic Planning, *Financial Statement and Budget Report*, annual, is used. During the period 1977–82, the *Quarterly Economic and Statistical Bulletin* is also used, but this was a period of considerable political turbulence and the price data published in this period is problematic (see for example Joergensen 1981, pages 298–9 and Table 6.7). The entire period 1971–82 should be regarded as a weak link in the Ugandan part of the table.

Ghana: Gold Coast, *Social and Economic Progress: Annual Reports*, section on 'wages and cost of living' and imports; items of consumption used to compile the deflator prices are as for Uganda, with the addition of wheat flour and minus bananas. From 1939–63, supplemented by wage index for unskilled workers in Accra 1939–63, in Birmingham, Neustadt and Omaboe (1965), Table 6.12.

After 1960, all countries: from World Bank, *World Development Indicators.*

Real wages, for all times and all countries, are money wages, MW, deflated by the consumer price index, PI.

4. Characteristics of poverty

   Price to producer as proportion of export price (ptf)

   Uganda to 1978: *Annual Trade Reports*; after 1978, Figure 3.8, 'Development of Producer Prices in Uganda', in Akiyama (2002).

   Ghana, to 1978: *Annual Trade Reports*; after 1978, Figure 2.6, 'Cocoa producer prices in West Africa' in Varangis and Schreiber (2002).

   Share of export price received by producer

   Uganda to 1978: *Annual Trade Reports*; after 1978, Figure 3.8, 'Development of Producer Prices in Uganda', in Akiyama (2002).

   Ghana, to 1978: *Annual Trade Reports*; after 1978, Figure 2.6, 'Cocoa producer prices in West Africa' in Varangis and Schreiber (2002).

   Agricultural sales (AS) are agricultural sales of African origin per head of African population, derived from *Blue Books* and *Annual Trade Reports* of the countries specified. They are defined as sales within the following countries:

   Zimbabwe: maize, 'small grains' (finger and bulrush millet), groundnuts, cotton, smallholder tobacco, fruits, vegetables.

   Kenya: maize, smallholder coffee, smallholder tea, smallholder pyrethrum, fruits, vegetables, sugar.

   Ghana: maize, cocoa and derivatives, kolanuts, fruits, vegetables, sugar.

Agricultural value added per head (*avad*) is an estimate, calculated at constant 1975 US dollar prices, of agricultural sales (see above) per head of African population. For years after 1960 the estimate is derived from the World Bank World Development Indicators CD-ROM. Prior to 1960, the data were derived from *Blue Books* and *Annual Trade Reports* of the countries specified. We converted per capita sales of these crops, net of an estimate for the value of inputs, to constant 1960 prices by use of country consumer price indices.

Educational expenditure as share of total expenditure (ede): includes all public and private, including mission school, expenditure of education, from *Blue Books*; and after 1970, from IMF *Government Finance Statistics Yearbook.*

5. Pro poor expenditure

Pro-poor expenditure (PPE): combined share of agriculture, health and education in GDP, from *Blue Books*, and after 1970 from IMF *Government Finance Statistics Yearbook.*

Pro-poor expenditure less coercion (PPE-C): combined share of agriculture, health, and education, less share of 'coercion' (military, police, and prison expenditure) in GDP, from *Blue Books*; and after 1970, from IMF *Government Finance Statistics Yearbook.*

Political instability index: measured as the product of the ucdp.loc conflict index in the World Bank/University of Gothenburg Quality of Government series (www.qog.gu.se) and 'military centrality', defined as the share of military expenditure in total expenditure (source: IMF *Government Finance Statistics Yearbook*).

References

Acemoglu, D., Johnson, S., and James A. Robinson (2001) 'The colonial origins of comparative development: an empirical investigation', *American Economic Review,* **91** (December), 1369–1401.

Action Aid (2009) *Where does it hurt? The impact of the financial crisis on developing countries.* London: Action Aid.

Acuña, C. and Smith W.C. (1994) 'The political economy of structural adjustment: the logic and of support and opposition to neoliberal reforms' in W.C. Smith, C.H. Acuña and E. Gamarra (eds) *Latin American Political Economy in the Age of Neoliberal Reform.* New Brunswick, N.J.: Transaction Publishers, 17–66.

Acuña, C., Galiani, S., and Tommasi, M. (2006) 'Understanding the political economy of structural reform: the case of Argentina', Documento de Trabajo, Universidad de San Andres, Departamento de Economía and Departamento de Humanidades, June.

Adam, C. (2008) 'Rules and reactions: policy choices and external volatility', paper presented at Centre for Study of African Economies conference, Oxford, 19–20 March.

Adam, C. and O'Connell, S. (2006) Monetary policy and aid management in Sub-Saharan Africa, unpublished paper, University of Oxford and Swarthmore College.

Adam, C. and Gunning, J. Willem (2002) 'Redesigning the aid contract: donors' use of performance indicators in Uganda', *World Development,* **30,** 2045–56.

Addison, T., Hulme, D., and Kanbur, R. (2009) *Poverty Dynamics: Interdisciplinary Perspectives.* Oxford: Oxford University Press.

Aguero, J., Carter, M., and May, J. (2007) 'Poverty and inequality in the first decade of South Africa's democracy: what can be learnt from panel data from KwaZulu-Natal?' *Journal of African Economies,* **16** (2008), 782–813.

Ahluwalia, M. (1976) 'Inequality, poverty and development', *Journal of Development Economics,* **3**, 307–42.

Akiyama, T. (2002) 'Background, process and results of recent coffee market liberalisation', in T. Akiyama, J. Baffes, D. Larson and P. Varangis (eds) *Lessons from Market Reforms Over the Last Two Decades.* Washington, DC: World Bank.

Alesina, A. and Drazen, A. (1991) 'Why are stabilisations delayed?' *American Economic Review,* **81**, 1170–88.

Alesina, A. and Perotti, R. (1996) 'Income distribution, political instability, and investment', *European Economic Review,* **40**, 1203–28.

Alesina, A. and Rodrik, D. (1994) 'Distributive politics and economic growth', *Quarterly Journal of Economics,* **109** (May), 465–90.

Alesina, A., Roubini, N., and Cohen, G. (1997) *Political Cycles and the Macroeconomy.* Cambridge MA: MIT Press.

Alesina, A., Tabellini, G., and Campante, F. (2008) 'Why is fiscal policy often procyclical?' *Journal of the European Economic Association,* **6** (September), 1006–36.

Aliaga, I. and Mosley, P. (2007) 'Microfinance under crisis conditions: the case of Bolivia', chapter 11 in T. Dichter and M. Harper (eds) *What's Wrong with Microfinance*? Rugby: Practical Action Publishing.

Alkire, S. and S. Seth (2015) 'Multidimensional poverty reduction in India between 1999 and 2006: where and how?' *World Development,* **72,** 93–108.

Amnesty International (2002) *Text of the submission by Amnesty International on its Concerns Regarding the Argentine Government's Application of the United Nations Convention on the Rights of the Child* (available at http://www.amnesty.org/en/library/asset/AMR13/018/2002/en/dom-AMR130182002en.html accessed 12 December 2007).

Andrews, E. and Ringold, D. (1999) *Safety Nets in Transition Economies: Towards a Reform Strategy,* Washington, DC: Social Protection discussion paper 9914.

Andrianova, S., Demetriades, P., and Shortland, A. (2008) 'Government ownership of banks, institutions and financial development', *Journal of Development Economics,* **85**, 218–52.

Appleton, S. (2000) 'Changes in poverty in Uganda 1992–2000', unpublished paper, Oxford: Centre for the Study of African Economies.

Arrighi, G. (1970) 'Labour supplies in historical perspective: a study of the proletarianisation of the African peasantry in Rhodesia', *Journal of Development Studies,* **6**, 198–233.

Arrossi, S. (1996) 'Inequality and health in the metropolitan area of Buenos Aires', *Environment and Urbanization,* **8** (2), 43–70.

Aryeetey, E. and McKay, A. (2007) 'Ghana: the challenge of translating sustained growth into poverty reduction', Chapter 6 in T. Besley and L. Cord (eds) *Delivering on the Promise of Pro-poor Growth.* New York and Oxford: Oxford University Press.

Asaga, M. (2008) Interviewed by Ivor Agyeman-Duah in *An Economic History of Ghana: Reflections on a Half-century of Challenges and Progress.* Edited by Ivor Agyeman-Duah. Banbury. UK: Ayebia Clarke Publishing.

Astorga, P., Berges, A., and Fitzgerald, V. (2005) 'The standard of living in Latin America during the twentieth century', *Economic History Review,* **58**, 765–96.

Austin, G. (2008) 'Resources, techniques and strategies south of the Sahara; revising the factor-endowments perspective on African economic development, 1500–2000', *Economic History Review,* **61**, 587–624.

Ayo, D. (2014) 'Hacia una economía "plural". El capitalismo de camarilla en Bolivia: De cooperativistas y caterings' [Towards a "pluralistic" economy. Crony capitalism in Bolivia: Of co-operatives and catering-company scandals]. *Nueva Cronica* (La Paz), **144** (May 15–31), 6–7.

Ayres, R. (1982) *Banking on the Poor: the World Bank and World Poverty.* Cambridge, Mass: MIT Press.

Bacha, E. and Taylor, L. (1978) 'Brazilian income distribution in the late 1960s: "facts", model results and controversy', *Journal of Development Studies,* **14**, 271–97.

Baldwin, R. (1963) 'Export technology and development from a subsistence level', *Economic Journal,* **73**, 80–92.

Bambaci, J., Saront, T., and Tommasi, M. (2002) 'The political economy of economic reforms in Argentina', *Journal of Policy Reform,* **5** (2), 75–88.

Bano, M. (2008) 'Dangerous correlations: aid's impact on NGOs' performance and ability to mobilise members in Pakistan', *World Development,* **36**, 297–313.

Barder, O. and Birdsall, N. (2006) *Setting Targets to Make International Development Aid More Effective,* presentation at Wilton Park Conference, Sussex, October.

Barnett, M. and Finnemore, M. (2004) *Rules for the World: International Organisations in Global Politics.* Ithaca: Cornell University Press.

Barr, A. (2003) 'Trust and expected trustworthiness: experimental evidence from Zimbabwean villages', *Economic Journal,* **113**, 614–31.

Barr, A. and Fafchamps, M. (2006) 'A client-community assessment of the NGO sector in Uganda', *Journal of Development Studies,* **42**, 611–39.

Barr, A. and Fafchamps, M., and Owens, T. (2005) 'The governance of non-governmental institutions in Uganda', *World Development,* **33**, 657–79.

Barrientos, A. (2006) 'Poverty reduction: the missing piece of pension reform in Latin America', *Social Policy and Administration,* **40** (4), 369–84.

Barrientos, A. (2013) *Social assistance in developing countries.* Cambridge: Cambridge University Press.

Barron, P., Kaiser, K., and Pradhan, M. (2004) 'Local conflict in Indonesia: measuring incidence and identifying patterns', unpublished paper, World Bank; presented at Cornell conference', 75 years of development research, 7–9 May.

Bartilow, H. (1998). *The Debt Dilemma: IMF Negotiations in Jamaica, Grenada and Guyana.* London: Macmillan.

Basualdo, E. (1987) *Deuda externa y Poder Economico en la Argentina.* Buenos Aires: Editorial Nueva America.

Bates, R. (1981) *Markets and States in Tropical Africa.* Boston: Little, Brown.

Bates, R. (1983) *Essays in the Political Economy of Rural Africa.* Cambridge: Cambridge University Press.

Bauer, P.T. (1954) *West African Trade: a Study of Competition, Oligopoly and Monopoly in a Changing Economy.* Cambridge: Cambridge University Press.

Bauer, P.T. (1981) *Equality, the Third World and Economic Delusion.* London: Methuen.

Bebbington, A., Hickey, S., and Mitlin, D. (eds) (2008) *Can NGOs Make a Difference? The Challenge of Development Alternatives.* London: Zed Books.

Bell, C.L.G. (1974) 'The political framework', Chapter 3 in H. Chenery, M. Ahluwalia, C. Bell, J. Duloy, and R. Jolly (eds) *Redistribution With Growth: Policies to Improve Income Distribution in Developing Countries.* New York and Oxford: Oxford University Press.

Bergman, M. (2003) 'Tax reforms and tax compliance: the divergent paths of Chile and Argentina', *Journal of Latin American Studies,* **35**, 593–624.

Bertocchi, G. and Canova, F. (2002) 'Did colonisation matter for growth? An empirical exploration into the historical causes of Africa's underdevelopment', *European Economic Review,* **46**, 1851–71.

Besley, T. and Burgess, R. (2000) 'Land reform, poverty and growth: evidence from India'. *Quarterly Journal of Economics,* **115**, 389–430.

Besley, T. and Cord, L. (2007) *Delivering on the Promise of Pro-poor Growth: Insights and Lessons from Country Experiences.* Basingstoke: Palgrave Macmillan.

Besley, T., Burgess, R., and Esteve-Volart, B. (2007) 'The policy origins of poverty and growth in India' Chapter 3 in T. Besley and L. Cord (eds) *Delivering on the Promise of Pro-poor Growth: Insights and Lessons from Country Experiences.* Basingstoke: Palgrave Macmillan.

Biglaiser, G. and Brown, D.S. (2005) 'The determinants of economic liberalization in Latin America', *Political Research Quarterly,* **58** (4), 565–74.

Bird, G. and Mosley, P. (2004) 'The role of the IMF in developing countries' in D. Vines and C. Gilbert (eds) *The IMF and its Critics.* Cambridge: Cambridge University Press.

Birdsall, N. and de la Torre, A. (2001) *Washington Contentious: Economic Policies for Social Equity in Latin America.* Washington, DC: Carnegie Endowment for International Peace.

Birdsall, N. and Lodoño, J. (1998) 'No tradeoff: efficient growth and more equal human capital accumulation' in N. Birdsall, C. Graham, and R. Sabot (eds) *Beyond Tradeoffs: Efficient Market Reform and Equitable Growth in Latin America.* Washington, DC: IDB/ Brookings Institution Press.

Birdsall, N. and Székely, M. (2003) *Poverty, Equity and Social Policy in Latin America.* Working Paper No. 24. Washington, DC: Center for Global Development.

Birdsall, N., de la Torre, A., and Menezes, R. (2008) 'Fair growth. Economic policies for Latin America's poor and middle-income majority', Center for Global Development, Inter-American Dialogue. Washington, DC: Center for Global Development, Inter-American Dialogue.

Birmingham, W., Neustadt, I., and Omaboe, E.M. (1965) *A Survey of Contemporary Ghana.* London: Allen and Unwin.

Blackmon, P. (2008) 'Rethinking poverty through the eyes of the International Monetary Fund and World Bank', *International Studies Review,* **10** (2), 179–202.

Blair, A. (1998) 'The third way: new politics for a new century'. *Fabian Society Pamphlet 588.* London: Fabian Society.

Block, S. (2002) 'Political business cycles, democratisation and economic reform: the case of Africa', *Journal of Development Economics,* **67**, 205–28.

Block, S., Ferree, K., and Singh, S. (2003) 'Multiparty competition, founding elections and political business cycles in Africa', *Journal of African Economies,* **12**, 444–68.

Bohn, H. (1998) 'The behaviour of US public debt and deficits', *Quarterly Journal of Economics,* **111** (August), 949–63.

Boone, P. (1996) 'Politics and the effectiveness of foreign aid', *European Economic Review,* **40**, 289–329.

Booth, A. (2007) 'Night watchman, extractive, or developmental states? Some evidence from late colonial south-east Asia', *Economic History Review,* **60**, 241–66.

Booth, A. and Mosley, P. (eds) (2003) *The New Poverty Strategies.* London: Palgrave Macmillan.

Booth, D. (2003) *Fighting Poverty in Africa: are PRSPs Making a Difference?* London: ODI.

Booth, D. and F. Golooba-Mutebi (2013) 'Developmental patrimonialism? The case of Rwanda', *African Affairs,* **111**, 379–403.

Borlaug, N. (2000) 'Ending world hunger. The promise of biotechnology and the threat of antiscience zealotry', *Plant Physiology,* **124** (October), 487–90.

Boughton, J. and Mourmouras, A. (2002) 'Is policy ownership an operational concept?' IMF working paper 02/72.

Boughton, J. and Mourmouras, A. (2004) 'Whose programme is it? Policy ownership and conditional lending', Chapter 9 in D. Vines and C. Gilbert (eds) *The IMF and its Critics: Reform of Global Financial Architecture.* Cambridge: Cambridge University Press.

Bourguignon, F. and Morrisson, C. (1992) *Adjustment and Equity in Developing Countries: a New Approach.* Paris: OECD Development Centre Studies.

Bowden, S. and Mosley, P. (2010) 'Politics, public expenditure and the evolution of poverty in Africa 1920–2009', unpublished paper, Universities of Sheffield and York.

Bowden, S., Chiripanhura, B., and Mosley, P. (2008) 'Measuring and explaining poverty in six African countries: a long-period approach', *Journal of International Development,* **20** (December), 1049–80.

Bowman Cutter, W., Spero, J., D'Andrea Tyson, L., et al. (2000) 'New world, new deal: a democratic approach to globalization', *Foreign Affairs,* **79**, 80–98.

Bradstock, A. (2005) 'Changing livelihoods and land reform: evidence from the Northern Cape Province of South Africa', *World Development,* **33** (November), 1979–92.

Brainerd, E. (1998) 'Winners and losers in Russia's economic transition', *American Economic Review,* **85**, 1094–117.

Brainerd, E. (2001) 'Economic reform and mortality in the former Soviet Union: a study of the suicide epidemic in the 1990s', *European Economic Review,* **45**, 1007–19.

Bratton, M. and van der Walle, N. (1997) *Democratic Experiments in Africa: Regime Transitions in Comparative Perspective.* Cambridge: Cambridge University Press.

Brautigam, D. (2008a) *Taxation and Governance in Africa: Take a Second Look.* American Enterprise Institute for Public Policy Research, Development Policy Outlook Papers No1 (www.aei.org).

Brautigam, D. (2008b) 'Contingent capacity: export taxation and state-building in Mauritius', Chapter 6 in D. Brautigam O. Fjeldstad and M. Moore (eds) (2008) *Taxation and State-building in Developing Countries: Capacity and Consent.* Cambridge: Cambridge University Press.

Brautigam, D. and Knack, S. (2004) 'Foreign aid, institutions and governance in Sub-Saharan Africa', *Economic Development and Cultural Change,* **52**, 255–85.

Brautigam, D., Fjeldstad, O., and Moore M. (eds) (2008) *Taxation and State-building in Developing Countries: Capacity and Consent.* Cambridge: Cambridge University Press.

Brett, E.A. (1973) *Colonialism and Underdevelopment in Kenya.* London: Heinemann Educational.

Brock, K., McGee, R., and Ssewakiryanga, R. (2002) 'Poverty knowledge and policy processes: a case study of Ugandan national poverty reduction policy', *IDS Research Reports 53.*

Brunnermeier, M. Crockett, A., Goodhart, C., et al. (2009). *The Fundamental Principles of Financial Regulation (Geneva Report on the World Economy, No.11).* Geneva, CEPR/ ICMB.

Buchanan, J.M. (1980) 'Rent seeking and profit seeking' in J.M. Buchanan, R. Tollison, and G. Tullock (eds) *Toward a Theory of Rent-seeking Society.* College Station, Texas: A and M University Press.

Buira, A. (2004) *Challenges to the World Bank and IMF: Developing Country Perspectives.* London: Anthem Press.

Bulir, A. and Hamann, J. (2003) 'Aid volatility: an empirical assessment', *IMF Staff Papers,* **50**, 64–89.

Bulir, A. and Hamann, J. (2008) 'Volatility of development aid: from the frying pan into the fire? *World Development*, **36**, 2048–67.

Burgess, R. and Pande, R. (2005) 'Do rural banks matter? Evidence from the Indian social banking experiment', *American Economic Review,* **95**, 780–95.

Busby, J.W. (2007) 'Bono made Jesse Helms cry: Jubilee 2000, debt relief and moral action in international politics.' *International Studies Quarterly,* **51** (2), 247–75.

Cain, P. and Hopkins, A.G. (1987) 'Gentlemanly capitalism and British expansion overseas, II: new imperialism, 1850–1945', *Economic History Review,* **40**, 1–26.

Callaghy, T. (2004) *Innovation in the Sovereign Debt Regime: from the Paris Club to Enhanced HIPC and Beyond.* Prepared for the World Bank Operations Evaluation Department, written July 2002, published 2004.

Camdessus, M. (1996) *Speech at Annual Meeting of the Directors of the World Bank and IMF*, Washington, DC.

Carl, E. and M. Wakefield (2001) 'The Saving Gateway and the Child Trust Fund: is welfare 'well fair'?' IFS Commentary 85, London: Institute for Fiscal Studies.

Carter, M. and Barrett, C. (2006) 'The economics of poverty traps and persistent poverty: an asset-based approach', *Journal of Development Studies,* **42** (February) 178–99.

Carter, M. and May, J. (1999) 'Poverty, livelihood and class in South Africa', *World Development,* **27**, 1–20.

Case, W. (2005) 'How's my driving? Abdullah's first year as Malaysian PM'.' *Pacific Review,* **18** (2), 137–57.

Cerny, P. (1995) 'Globalization and the changing logic of collective action', *International Organization,* **49** (4), 595–625.

Cervellati, M., Fortunato, P., and Sunde, U. (2008) 'Hobbes to Rousseau: inequality, institutions and development', *Economic Journal,* **118** (August), 1354–84.

Chang, G.H. and Wen, G.J. (1997) 'Communal dining and the Chinese famine of 1958–61', *Economic Development and Cultural Change,* **45**, 1–34.

Chauvet, L. and Collier, P. (2008) 'Helping hand? Aid to failing states', paper presented at Centre for Study of African Economies conference, 19–20 March.

Chauvet, L., Collier, P., and Duponchel, M. (2009) 'What explains aid project success in post-conflict situations?' paper presented at Centre for Study of African Economies conference, Oxford, 22–24 March.

Chen, D., Matovu, J., and Reinikka, R. (2001) 'The quest for revenue and tax incidence', in R. Reinikka and P. Collier (eds) *Uganda's Recovery: the Role of Firms, Farms and Government.* Washington, DC: World Bank.

Chen, S. and Ravallion, M. (2004) 'How have the world's poorest fared since the early 1980s?' *World Bank Research Observer,* **19**, 141–69.

Chenery, H. (1960) 'Patterns of industrial growth', *American Economic Review*, **50** (September), 624–54.
Chenery, H. and Syrquin, M. (1975) *Patterns of Development 1950–1970*, Washington DC: World Bank.
Chenery, H., Ahluwalia, M., Bell, C., Duloy, J., and Jolly, R. (1974) *Redistribution With Growth: Policies to Improve Income Distribution in Developing Countries*. New York and Oxford: Oxford University Press.
Childress, M. (2002) 'Policy questions for a second decade of rural change in central/eastern Europe and the former Soviet Union', *Journal of International Development*, **14**, 979–87.
Chiripanhura, B., Grugel, J., Mosley, P., and Thirkell-White, B. (2009) 'Why adopt pro-poor policies? Varieties of adjustment strategy during the global crisis (1997–2004)', unpublished paper, University of Sheffield.
Chowdhury, A.M.R. and Bhuiya, A. (2004) 'The wider impacts of BRAC poverty alleviation programme in Bangladesh', *Journal of International Development*, **16**, 369–87.
Clairin, R. (1966) *Estimates of Infant and Child Mortality From Data Available in Africa*. Paper presented at First African Population Conference, University of Ibadan, 3–7 January. Rhodes House, Oxford: 600.12 s.22.
Clark, T., Goss, E., and Kosova, L. (2003) 'Economic well-being and popular support for market reform in Russia', *Economic Development and Cultural Change*, **56**, 753–68.
Clark, W. (1984) *Cataclysm: the North-South Conflict of 1987*. London: Sphere Books.
Collier, P. (1997) 'The failure of conditionality' In C. Gwin and J. Nelson (eds), *Perspectives on Aid and Development*. Washington, DC: Overseas Development Council.
Collier, P. (2007) *The Bottom Billion: Why the Poorest Countries are Failing and What Can Be Done About It*. Oxford: Oxford University Press.
Collier, P. and Hoeffler, A. (1998) 'On economic causes of civil war', *Oxford Economic Papers*, **50**, 563–73.
Collier, P. and Hoeffler, A. (2004) 'Greed versus grievance in civil war', *Oxford Economic Papers*, **56**, 563–95.
Collier, P. and Reinikka, R. (2001) 'Reconstruction and liberalization: an overview' in R. Reinikka and P. Collier (eds) *Uganda's Recovery*. Kampala: Fountain Press.
Collier, R. and Collier, D. (1991) *Shaping the Political Arena: Critical Junctures, the Labor Movement, and the Regime Dynamics in Latin America*. Princeton NJ: Princeton University Press.
Collier, W. and Sayogyo (1972) 'Employment opportunities created by the high-yielding rice varieties in several areas on Java', *Ekonomi dan Keuangan Indonesia* (Economy and Finance in Indonesia), **20** (2), 105–32.
Colton, T. (2002) *Transitional Citizenship: Voting in Post-Soviet Russia*. Cambridge, MA: Harvard University Press.
Cook, M.L. (1998) *The Politics of Labor Law Reform: Comparative Perspectives on the Mexican Case*. Ithaca: New York State School of Industrial and Labor Relations, Cornell University.
Cook, M.L. (2007) *The Politics of Labor Reform in Latin America: Between Flexibility and Rights*. University Park: Pennsylvania State University Press.
Cooper, A. and Momani, B. (2005) 'Negotiating out of Argentina's financial crisis: segmenting the international creditors', *New Political Economy*, **10** (3), 305–20.
Cornia, A., Jolly, R., and Stewart, F. (1987) *Adjustment with a Human Face: Protecting the Vulnerable and Promoting Growth*. Oxford: Oxford University Press.
Cortés, R. and Marshall, A. (1999) 'Estrategia Económica, Instituciones y Negociación Política en la Reforma Social de los 90', *Desarrollo Económico*, **154** (39),
Crafts, N. (1997) 'Some dimensions of the 'quality of life' during the British industrial revolution', *Economic History Review*, **50**, 617–39.
Craig, D. and Porter, D. (2006) *Development Beyond Neoliberalism?: Governance, Poverty Reduction: Governance, Poverty Reduction and Political Economy*. London: Routledge.

Cramer, C. (2003) 'Does inequality cause civil war?' *Journal of International Development*, **15**.
Crawford, G. (2001) *Foreign Aid and Political Reform: a Comparative Analysis of Democracy Assistance and Political Conditionality*. Basingstoke: Palgrave.
Crouch, H. (1979) 'Patrimonalism and military rule in Indonesia', *World Politics*, **31** (4).
Crouch, H. (1996) *Government and Society in Malaysia*. Ithaca: Cornell University Press.
Crowley, S. (1994) 'Barriers to collective action: steelworkers and mutual dependence in the former Soviet Union', *World Politics*, **46**, 589–615.
Daseking, C. and Powell, R. (1999) 'From Toronto terms to the HIPC initiative: a brief history of debt relief for low-income countries.' *IMF Working Paper* WP/99/142.
De Franco, M. and Godoy, R. (1990) *The economic consequences of cocaine production in Bolivia: historical, local and macroeconomic perspectives*. Unpublished paper, Harvard, Mass: Harvard Institute for International Development.
de Janvry, A., Fargeix, A., and Sadoulet, E. (1992) 'The political feasibility of rural poverty reduction', *Journal of Development Economics*, **37**, 351–67.
de Melo, M. and Ofer, G. (1999) *The Russian City in Transition: the First Six Years in Volga Capitals*. World Bank Development Research Group, Policy Research Working Paper.
de Mesa, J., Gisbert, T., and Mesa, C. D. (2003) *Historia de Bolivia*. La Paz: Editorial Gisbert.
De Vries, M.G. (1987). *Balance of Payments Adjustment 1945–1986: the IMF Experience*. Washington, DC: IMF.
Deininger, K. (2002) 'Agrarian reforms in Eastern European countries: lessons from international experience', *Journal of International Development*, **14**, 987–1005.
Deininger, K. and Squire, L. (1996) 'A new data base measuring inequality'. Washington, DC: World Bank.
Denoon, D. (1979) *Dependent Development*, Cambridge: Cambridge University Press.
Department of International Development (DfID) (2000) *Making Globalisation Work for the Poor*. White Paper on Overseas Development. London: Her Majesty's Stationery Office.
Dercon, S. (2008) 'Risk and technology adoption', paper presented at Centre for Study of African Economies conference, Oxford, 19–20 March.
Dervis, K., de Melo, J., and Robinson, S. (1982), *General Equilibrium Models for Development Policy*. Cambridge: Cambridge University Press.
Desai, M. (1991) 'Human development: concepts and measurement', *European Economic Review*, **35** (April), 350–7.
Devarajan, S., Dollar, D., and Holmgren, T. (eds) (2001) *Aid and Reform in Africa*. Washington, DC: World Bank.
Devereux, S. (2005) 'Can minimum wages contribute to poverty reduction in developing countries?' *Journal of International Development*, **17** (Oct), 899–913.
Dhillon, A. and Garcia-Fronti, J. (2009) *Legal and economic aspects of sovereign debt default: the Argentina case*, Full Research Report, RES-165-25-0006. Swindon: ESRC.
Dhonte, P. (1997) 'Conditionality as an instrument of borrower credibility'. *IMF Papers on Policy Analysis and Assessment*. PPAA/97/2.
Di Tella, T. (1965) 'Populism and reform in Latin American' in C. Veliz (ed.) *Obstacles to Change in Latin American*. Oxford: Oxford University Press, 47–74.
Dijkstra, G. (2005) 'The PRSP approach and the illusion of improved aid effectiveness: lessons from Bolivia, Honduras and Nicaragua', *Development Policy Review*, **23**, 443–64.
Dijkstra, G. and van Donge, J.K. (2001) 'What does the 'show case' show? Evidence of and lessons from adjustment in Uganda', *World Development*, **29**, 841–63.
Dimbleby, J. (2008) *Russia*. London: BBC Publications.
Dininio, P. and Orttung, R. (2005) 'Explaining patterns of corruption in the Russian regions', *World Politics*, **57** (July), 500–29.

Dixon, R. and Williams, P. (2001) 'Tough on debt, tough on the causes of debt? New Labour's third way foreign policy'. *British Journal of Politics and International Relations,* **3** (3), 150–72.

Djurfeldt, G. and Jirstrom, M. (2005) 'The puzzle of the policy shift—the early green revolution in India, Indonesia and the Philippines', Chapter 4 in G. Djurfeldt, H. Holmen, M. Jirstrom, and R. Larsson (eds) (2005).

Djurfeldt, G., Holmen H., Jirstrom, M., and Larsson, R. (eds) (2005) *The African Food Crisis: Lessons from the Asian Green Revolution,* Wallingford: CAB International.

Dollar, D. and Kraay, A. (2002) 'Growth is good for the poor', *Journal of Economic Growth,* **7**, 195–225.

Domingo, P. (2009) 'Morales, the MAS and a revolution in the making'. Chapter 6 in J. Grugel (ed.) *Governance after Neoliberalism in Latin America.* Oxford: Macmillan.

Downs, A. (1975) *An Economic Theory of Democracy.* New York: Harper and Row.

Drabble, J. (2000) *An Economic History of Malaysia c.1800–2000: The Transition to Modern Economic Growth.* Basingstoke: Macmillan.

Drazen, A. (2003) *Political Economy in Macroeconomics.* Princeton NJ: Princeton University Press.

Drazen, A. and Eslava, M. (2010) 'Electoral manipulation via voter-friendly spending: theory and evidence', *Journal of Development Economics.*

du Plessis, S. and Smit, B. (2007) 'South Africa's growth revival after 1994', *Journal of African Economies,* **16**, 668–705.

Duasa, J. and Mosley, P. (2006) 'Capital controls re-examined; the case for "smart" controls', *The World Economy,* **38**, 1203–26.

Dumbrell, J. (1997) *American Foreign Policy: Carter to Clinton.* Basingstoke: Macmillan.

Dutt, P. and Mitra, D. (2008) 'Inequality and the instability of polity and policy', *Economic Journal,* **118** (August), 1285–315.

Easter, G. (2008) 'Capacity, consent and tax collection in post-communist states', Chapter 3 in D. Brautigam O. Fjeldstad, and M. Moore (eds) (2008) *Taxation and State-building in Developing Countries: Capacity and Consent.* Cambridge: Cambridge University Press.

Easterly, W. and Levine, R. (1997) 'Africa's growth tragedy: policies and ethnic divisions', *Quarterly Journal of Economics,* **62**, 1203–50.

Edwards, S. (1998) Openness, productivity and growth: what do we really know?', *Economic Journal,* **108**, 383–99.

Eichengreen, B. (1999) *Toward a New International Financial Architecture: a Practical Post-Asia Agenda.* Washington: Institute for International Economics.

Eicher, C. (1995) 'Zimbabwe's maize-based green revolution: preconditions for replication', *World Development,* **23**, 805–18.

Eifert, B. and Gelb, A. (2006) 'Improving the dynamics of aid: toward more predictable budget support', Chapter 12 in S. Koeberle, Z. Stavreski, and J. Walliser (eds) *Budget Support as More Effective Aid? Recent Experiences and Emerging Lessons,* Washington, DC: World Bank.

Eisner, G. (1961) *Jamaica 1830–1930; A Study in Economic Growth.* Manchester: Manchester University Press.

Elbadawi, I. and Sambanis, N. (2000) 'Why are there so many civil wars in Africa? Understanding and preventing violent conflict', *Journal of African Economies,* **9**, 244–69.

Englebert, P. (2000a) 'Solving the mystery of the AFRICA dummy', *World Development,* **28**, 1821–35.

Englebert, P. (2000b) 'Pre-colonial institutions, post-colonial states, and economic development in tropical Africa', *Political Research Quarterly,* **53** (March 2000), 7–36.

Epaulard, A. (2003) *Macroeconomic Performance and Poverty Reduction.* IMF Working Paper WP/03/72, April, Washington, DC: International Monetary Fund.

Evans, A. (1992) *Uganda: Rural Labour Market.* Rome: FAO.

Evans, P. (1995) *Embedded Autonomy: the State and Industrial Transformation*. Princeton: Princeton University Press.

Evans, P. (1997b) 'The eclipse of the state? Reflections on stateness in an era of globalisation', *World Politics*, **50** (1).

Evans, P. (ed.) (1997a) *State-society Synergy: Government and Social Capital in Development*. Berkeley: University of California Press.

Evans, P. and Finnemore, M. (2002) 'Organizational reform and the expansion of the South's voice at the Fund.' *G-24 Discussion Paper Series 15*.

Fan, S. and Pardey, P. (1992) *Agricultural Research in China: its Institutional Development and Impact*. The Hague: ISNAR (International Service for National Agricultural Research).

Fan, S., Hazell, P., and Thorat, S. (2000) 'Government spending, growth and poverty in rural India', *American Journal of Agricultural Economics*, **82** (November), 1038–51.

Feijoo, M. (2001) *Nuevo País, Nueva Pobreza*. Buenos Aires: Fondo de Cultura Económica.

Feinstein, C.H. (1998) 'Pessimism perpetuated: real wages and the standard of living in Britain during and after the industrial revolution', *Journal of Economic History*, **58** (1998), 625–58.

Feinstein, C.H. (2005) *An Economic History of South Africa: Conquest, Discrimination and Development*. Cambridge: Cambridge University Press.

Ferreira Rubio, D. and Goretti, M. (1996) 'Cuando el Presidente Gobierna Solo. Menem y los Decretos de Necesidad y Urgencia hasta la Reforma Constitucional (Julio 1989-Agosto 1994)', *Desarrollo Económico*, **36** (141), 443–74.

Fiess, N., Chiripanhura, B., and Mosley, P. (2008) 'The political economy of political violence: Bolivia and Indonesia 1980–2007', unpublished paper, ESRC World Economy and Finance project, presented at Royal Economic Society, Warwick, 17 March.

Fishlow, A. (1972) 'Brazilian size distribution of income', *American Economic Review Papers and Proceedings*, **62**, 391–402.

Fiszbein, A., R. Kanbur, and R. Yemtsov (2014), 'Social protection and poverty reduction: global patterns and some targets', *World Development*, **61**, 167–177.

FitzGerald, V. (1978) 'The fiscal crisis of the Latin American State', Chapter 6 in J. Toye (ed.) *Taxation and Economic Development*. London: Frank Cass.

FitzGerald, V. (2008) 'The distribution of income and earnings in Latin America during the twentieth century: an initial investigation', *Journal of International Development*, **20**, 1028–1049.

Fjeldstad, O.-H. and Moore, M. (2009) 'Revenue authorities and public authority in Sub-Saharan Africa', *Journal of Modern African Studies*, **47**, 1–18.

Foster, M. and Mijumbi, P. (2001) 'How, when and why does poverty get budget priority: poverty reduction strategy and public expenditure in Uganda'. *ODI Working Paper 163*. London: Overseas Development Institute.

Foweraker, J., Landman, T., and Harvey, N. (2003) *Governing Latin America*. Bristol: Polity Press.

Frankema, E. (2011) 'Colonial taxation and government spending in British Africa, 1880–1940: maximising revenue or minimising effort?' *Explorations in Economic History*, **48**, 136–49.

Frankema, E. and van Waijenburg, M. (2010) 'African real wages in Asian perspective', unpublished paper, University of Utrecht and Northwestern University.

Fridy, K. (2007) 'The elephant, umbrella, and quarrelling cocks: disaggregating partnership in Ghana's Fourth Republic', *African Affairs*, **106**, 281–305.

Frieden, J. and Rogowski, R. (1996) 'The impact of the international economy on national policies: an analytical overview' in H. Milner and R. Keohane (eds) *Internationalisation and Domestic Politics*. Cambridge: Cambridge University Press.

Frimpong-Ansah, J. (1991) *The Vampire State in Africa: the Political Economy of Decline In Ghana*. London: James Currey.
Fujimoto, A. (1991) 'Evolution of rice farming under the new economic policy', *The Developing Economies*, **29**, 431–53.
Gambetta, D. (1988) *Trust: Making and Breaking Co-operative Relations*. Oxford: Basil Blackwell.
Garcia, A., Prada, R., and Tapia, L. (2004). *Memorias de octubre*. La Paz: Muela del Diablo Editores.
Gardner, L. (2010) 'From Gladstone to a new deal in British Colonial Africa, 1919–1938; a new era in colonial governance', unpublished paper, University of Cape Town.
Gardner, R. (1980) *Sterling-dollar Diplomacy in Current Perspective*. New York: Columbia University Press.
Gatrell, P. and Harrison, M. (1993) 'The Russian and Soviet economies in two world wars: a comparative view', *Economic History Review*, **46**, 425–52.
Gebre-Madhin, E. and Haggblade, S. (2004) 'Successes in African agriculture: results of an expert survey', *World Development*, **32**, 745–66.
Geithner, T. (1998) 'Testimony.' before the Subcommittee on Oversight of the Committee on Banking and Financial Services, US House of Representatives, 21 April.
Gerschenkron, A. (1959) *Economic Backwardness in Historical Perspective*. Cambridge, Mass: Harvard University Press.
Ghosh, A., Lane, T., Schultze-Ghattas, M., Bulir, A., Hamann, J., and Mourmouras, A. (2002) *IMF-Supported Programs in Capital Account Crises*. Occasional Paper 210. Washington, DC: International Monetary Fund.
Gimpelson, V. (1999) 'The politics of labour-market adjustment', Chapter 1 in J. Kornai, S. Haggard, and R. Kaufman (eds) (1999) *Reforming the State: Fiscal and Welfare Reform in Post-Socialist Countries*. New York: Cambridge University Press.
Gimpelson, V. and Treisman, D. (2000) 'Fiscal games and public employment: a theory with evidence from Russia', *World Politics*.
Gimpelson, V., Kapeliushnikov, R., and Ratnikova, T. (2008) 'Does fear have big eyes? Fear of unemployment and wages in Russia', unpublished paper, Higher School of Economics, Moscow.
Giuliano, E. (2006) 'Secessionism from the bottom up: democratisation, nationalism, and local accountability in the Russian transition', *World Politics*, **58** (January), 276–310.
Glaeser, E., Laibson, D., Scheinkman, J., and Soutter, C. (2000) 'Measuring trust', *Quarterly Journal of Economics*, **112**, 437–58.
Gomez, E.T. (1999) *Chinese Business in Malaysia: Accumulation, Ascendance, Accommodation*. London: Curzon.
Gomez, E.T. and Jomo, K.S. (1999) *Malaysia's Political Economy: Politics, Patronage and Profits*. Cambridge: Cambridge University Press.
Gonzales, A. (2007) 'How many borrowers and microfinance institutions (MFIs) exist?' Microfinance Information Exchange (MIX), Washington, DC. Available at www.themix.org.
Gonzalez de la Rocha, M. (1988) 'Economic crisis, domestic disorganization and women's work in Guadalajara', *Bulletin of Latin American Research*, **7** (2), 207–23.
Gonzalez de la Rocha, M. (2006) 'Vanishing assets: cumulative disadvantage among the urban poor', *Annals of the American Academy of Political and Social Science*, **606** (July), 116–27.
Gore, C. (2000) 'The rise and fall of the Washington consensus as a paradigm for developing countries', *World Development*, **28**, 789–804.
Gore, C. (2015) 'The Multilateral Development Goals and the post-2015 Development Agenda'. Special issue of *Journal of International Development*, **27**, August.
Gray-Molina, G. (2007) 'El reto postneoliberal de Bolivia' [The post-neoliberal challenge facing Bolivia] *Nueva Sociedad*, no. 209, available at http://www.nuso.org.

Greenaway, D. and Milner, C. (1991) 'Fiscal dependence on trade taxes and trade policy reform', *Journal of Development Studies,* **27**, 95–132.

Gray-Molina, G. (2008) 'A deeper look at Bolivia's 'indigenous constitution', *CRISE: Centre for Research on Inequality, Human Security and Ethnicity.* Queen Elizabeth House, Oxford, **5** (Winter 2008/9).

Grugel, J. (1998) 'State and business in neo-liberal democracies in Latin America', *Global Society,* **12**, 1998.

Grugel, J. and Payne, A. (2001) 'Regionalism, development and the state in the Caribbean basin' in B. Hettne, A. Inotai, and O. Sunkel (eds), *National Perspectives on the New Regionalism in the South.* London: Macmillan.

Grugel, J. and Riggirozzi, P. (2007) 'The return of the state in Argentina', *International Affairs,* **83**, 87–107.

Grugel, J. and Riggirozzi, P. (eds) (2009a) *Governance after Neoliberalism in Latin America.* Basingstoke: Palgrave Macmillan.

Grugel, J. and Riggirozzi, P. (2009b) 'The end of the embrace? Neoliberalism and alternatives to neoliberalism in Latin America', Chapter 1 in J. Grugel and P. Riggirozzi (eds) *Governance after Neoliberalism in Latin America.* Basingstoke: Palgrave Macmillan.

Grugel, J., Riggirozzi, P., and Thirkell-White, B. (2008) 'Beyond the Washington Consensus? Asia and Latin America in search of more autonomous development', *International Affairs,* **84**, 499–517.

Guan, L.H. (2008) 'Malaysia in 2007: Abdullah administration under siege', *Southeast Asian Affairs.*

Guitian, M. (1992) 'The unique nature and responsibilities of the International Monetary Fund', *International Monetary Fund Pamphlet Series 31.*

Gulhati, R. (1987) *Recent Economic Reforms in Africa: a Preliminary Political Economy Perspective,* Washington, DC: EDI Policy Seminar Report Series, no. 8.

Gulhati, R. and Nallari, R. (1990) *Successful Stabilisation and Recovery in Mauritius.* Washington, DC: Economic Development Institute of the World Bank, Case Series, Analytical Case Studies no. 5.

Gupta, S. and Tareq, S. (2008) 'Mobilising revenue', *Finance and Development,* **45** (September), 44–47.

Gurr, T.R. (1970) *Why Men Rebel.* Princeton NJ: Princeton University Press.

Gyimah-Boadi, E. (2001) 'A peaceful turnover in Ghana', *Journal of Democracy,* **12**, 103–17.

Haggard, S. (2000) *The Political Economy of the Asian Financial Crisis.* Washington, DC: Institute for International Economics.

Haggard, S. and Kaufman, R. (eds) (1992) *The Politics of Economic Adjustment.* Princeton N.J.: Princeton University Press.

Haggard, S. and Kaufman, R. (2008) *Revising Social Contracts: the Political Economy of Welfare Reform in Latin America, East Asia and Central Europe.* Princeton NJ: Princeton University Press.

Haggard, S. and Maxfield, S. (1996) 'The political economy of financial liberalisation in the developing world', in H. Milner and R. Keohane (eds) *Internationalisation and Domestic Politics.* Cambridge: Cambridge University Press.

Haggard, S., Lafay, J., and Morrisson, C. (1996) *The Political Feasibility of Adjustment.* Paris: OECD.

Hailey, L. (1938) *An African Survey.* London: Royal Institute of International Affairs.

Haldane, A. Irwin, G. and Saporta, V. (2004) 'Bail out or work out?' Theoretical considerations', *Economic Journal,* **114** (March), 130–49.

Halder, S. and Mosley, P. (2004) 'Working with the ultra-poor: learning from BRAC experiences', *Journal of International Development,* **16** (April), 387–407.

Hancock, W.K. (1943) *Argument of Empire.* Harmondsworth: Penguin.

Hanmer, L. and Naschold, F. (2000), 'Attaining the international development targets: will growth be enough?', *Development Policy Review,* **18**, 11–36.

Hanson, P. (2007a) 'The Russian economic puzzle: going backwards, forwards or sideways?' *International Affairs,* **83**, 869–89.

Hanson, P. (2007b) 'Federalism with a Russian face: regional inequality, administrative capacity and regional budgets in Russia', *Economic Change.*

Harrigan, J. (2003) 'U-turns and full circles: two decades of agricultural reform in Malawi, 1981–2000', *World Development,* **31**, 847–63.

Harrison, G. (2001) 'Post-conditionality politics and administrative reform: reflections on the cases of Uganda and Tanzania', *Development and Change,* **32**, 657–79.

Harrison, G. (2004) *The World Bank and Africa: the Construction of Governance States.* London: Routledge.

Hart, K. (1973) 'Informal income opportunities and the structure of urban employment in Ghana', *Journal of Modern African Studies,* **11**, 61–89.

Hatton, T. and Bailey, R. (2000) 'Seebohm Rowntree and the postwar poverty puzzle', *Economic History Review,* **53** (August), 517–43.

Havrylyshyn, O. and Odling-Smee, J. (2000) 'Political economy of stalled reforms', in *Finance and Development,* **37** (3).

Hay, C. (2008) *Good Inflation, Bad Inflation: The Housing Boom, Economic Growth and the Disaggregation of Inflationary Pressures in Britain and Ireland.* mimeo, July 2008, available at http://subprimeworkshop.blogspot.com (accessed 20 March 2009).

Hefner, R. (2000a) *The Political Economy of the Asian Financial Crisis.* Washington, DC: Institute for International Economics.

Hefner, R. (2000b) *Civil Islam: Muslims and Democratisation in Indonesia.* Princeton: Princeton University Press.

Helleiner G. (1983) 'The IMF and Africa in the 1980s', *Princeton Essays in International Finance,* **152**, July 1983.

Helleiner, E. and Cameron, G. (2006) 'Another world order? The Bush administration and HIPC debt cancellation' *New Political Economy,* **11** (1), 125–40.

Hertog, S. (2010) 'Defying the resource curse: explaining successful state-owned enterprises in rentier states', *World Politics,* **62**, 261–301.

Heryanto, A. (1997) Indonesia: towards the final countdown. *Southeast Asian Studies 1997.* Singapore: Institute for Southeast Asian Studies.

Hess, G. and Orphanides, A. (1995) 'War politics: an economic, rational voter framework', *American Economic Review,* **85**, 828–46.

Hickey, S. (2005) 'The politics of staying poor: exploring the political space for poverty reduction in Uganda', *World Development,* **33**, 995–1009.

Hickey, S. (2010) 'The government of chronic poverty: from exclusion to citizenship?' *Journal of Development Studies,* **46**, 1139–56.

Hickey, S. and Bracking, S. (2005) 'Exploring the politics of chronic poverty: from representation to a politics of justice?' *World Development,* **33**, 851–65.

Hickey, S. (2013) 'Beyond the poverty agenda? Insights from the new politics of development in Uganda', *World Development,* **43**, 194–206.

Hill, H. (1996) *The Indonesian Economy Since 1966: Southeast Asia's Emerging Giant.* Cambridge: Cambridge University Press.

Hills, J. and Stewart, K. (2005) *A More Equal Society? New Labour, Poverty, Inequality and Exclusion.* Bristol: Policy Press.

Hilton, S. (1975) 'Vargas and Brazilian economic development, 1930–1945: a reappraisal of his attitude toward industrialisation and planning', *Journal of Economic History,* **35** (December), 754–78.

Himmelfarb, G. (1984) *The Idea of Poverty: England in the Early Industrial Age.* London: Faber and Faber.

Hobbes, T. (1651/1965) *Leviathan: or, Forme and Power of a Commonwealth.* London: Andrew Crooke, reprinted, Oxford: Oxford University Press World's Classics.

Hoff, K. and Stiglitz, J. (2008) 'Exiting a lawless state', *Economic Journal,* **118** (August), 1474–98.

Hoffman, K. and Centeno, M. (2003) 'The lopsided continent; inequality in Latin America' *Annual review of Sociology,* **29**, 363–90.

Hopkins, A. (1973) *An Economic History of West Africa.* London: Longman.

Horrell, S. and Humphries, J. (1992) 'Old questions, new data and alternative perspectives: families' living standards in the industrial revolution', *Journal of Economic History,* **52** (December), 849–80.

Huber, E. and Solt, F. (2004) 'Successes and failures of Neoliberalism', *Latin American Research Review,* **39** (3), 150–64.

Hudson, J., and Mosley, P. (2008) 'Aid volatility, policy and development', *World Development,* **36**, 2082–103.

Hudson, J. and Mosley, P. (2009) 'Aid and governance', unpublished paper.

Hudson, J., Lenton, P., and Mosley, P. (2011) 'The "social efficiency wage", unpublished paper, University of Sheffield.

Huff, G. and Caggiano, G. (2007) 'Globalisation, immigration and Lewisian elastic labour in pre-World War 2 south-east Asia', *Journal of Economic History,* **67**, 33–69.

Huillery, E. (2010) *The Black Man's Burden: the Cost of Colonisation of French West Africa.* Paris School of Economics, working paper.

Hulme, D. (2008a) 'The making of the Millennium Goals Part 1: human development meets results-based management in a world of complex interdependence', unpublished paper, presented at Glasgow Conference, 25–26 June.

Hulme, D. (2008b) *Global Public Policy and the Millennium Development Goals: a Short History of the World's Biggest Promise.* Manchester: University of Manchester, Brooks World Poverty Institute Working Paper.

Hulme, D. (2010) *Global Poverty: how Global Governance is Failing the Poor.* London: Routledge.

Hulme, D., and Mosley, P. (1996) *Finance Against Poverty,* 2 vols. London: Routledge.

Iliffe, J. (1987) *The African Poor: a History.* Cambridge: Cambridge University Press, African Studies Series 58.

Independent Group on British Aid (IGBA) (1981) *Real Aid: a Strategy for Britain,* Oxford: Oxfam.

Independent Institute for Social Policy (IISP) (2007) *Economicheskoe razvitie regionov* (Economic development of the (Russian) regions). Moscow: IISP.

International Labour Organisation (ILO) (1973) *Employment, Incomes and Equality: Report of a Mission to Kenya.* Geneva: ILO.

International Monetary Fund (IMF) (1998) 'External evaluation of the ESAF: report by a group of independent experts' (available at http://www.imf.org).

Irz, X., Thirtle, C., and Wiggins, S. (2000) 'Agricultural productivity growth and poverty alleviation', *Development Policy Review,* **19**, 449–66.

International Monetary Fund (IMF) (2001) 'Strengthening country ownership of Fund supported programs'. Paper prepared by the Policy Development and Review Department, 5 December (available at http://www.imf.org).

International Monetary Fund (IMF) (2004) *Report on the Evaluation of Poverty Reduction Strategy Papers (PRSPs) and The Poverty Reduction and Growth Facility (PRGF).* Washington, DC: IMF Independent Evaluation Office.

International Monetary Fund (IMF) (2008) 'Reform of quota and voice in the International Monetary Fund—report of the Executive Board to the Board of Governors.' 28 March 2008 (available at http://www.imf.org).

International Monetary Fund (IMF) (2009) *The Implications of the Global Financial Crisis for Low-income Countries.* Washington, DC: IMF (available at http://www.imf.org).

Itzigsohn, J. and Vom Hau, M. (2006) 'Unfinished imagined communities: states, social movements, and nationalism in Latin America', *Theory and Society*, **35** (2), 193–212.

Ivanova, A., Mayer, W., Mourmouras, A., and Anayiotos, G. (2001) 'What determines the success or failure of Fund-supported programmes?' Paper presented at the second annual IMF research conference, 29/30 November.

James, D. (1988) *Resistance and Integration. Peronism and the Argentine Working Class, 1946–1976.* Cambridge: Cambridge University Press.

Jayasuriya, K. (2006) *Statecraft, Welfare and the Politics of Inclusion.* Basingstoke: Palgrave.

Jelmert Jorgensen, J. (1981) *Uganda: a Modern History.* London: Croom Helm.

Jenkins, G. (1991) 'Tax reform; lessons learned', Chapter 11 in Perkins, D.H. and Roemer, M. (eds) *Reforming Economic Systems in Developing Countries.* Cambridge, Mass: Harvard Institute for International Development.

Jesudason, J. (1989) *Ethnicity and the Economy: the State, Chinese Business and Multinationals in Malaysia.* Singapore: Oxford University Press.

Jesudason, J. (1996) 'The syncretic state and the structuring of oppositional politics in Malaysia', in G. Rodan (ed.) *Political Opposition in Industrialising Asia.* London: Routledge.

Jirstrom, M. (2005) 'The state and green revolutions in East Asia' in G. Djurfeldt, H. Holmen, M. Jirstrom, and R. Larsson (2005) *The African Food Crisis: Lessons from the Asian Green Revolution.* Wallingford: CAB International.

Joergensen, J. (1981) *Uganda: A Modern History.* London; Croom Helm.

Johannes F. and R. Klitgaard (2013) 'How much do rights matter?' *World Development*, **51**, 187–206.

Johnson, M., Hazell, P., and Gulati, A. (2003) 'The role of intermediate factor markets in Asia's green revolution: lessons for Africa?' *American Journal of Agricultural Economics*, **85**, 1211–16.

Johnson, S., Kochar, K., Mitton, T. and Tamirisa, N. (2006) *Malaysian Capital Controls: Macroeconomics and Institutions.* Washington, DC: IMF, IMF working paper WP/06/51.

Jomo, K.S. (2004) 'Were Malaysia's Capital Controls Effective? in K.S. Jomo (ed.) *After the Storm: Crisis, Recovery And Sustaining Development in Four Asian Economies.* Singapore: Singapore University Press.

Jomo, K.S. (2006) *The New Development Economics: After the Washington Consensus.* London: Zed Books.

Jomo, K.S. and Fine, B. (2006) *The New Development Economics: After the Washington Consensus.* London: Zed Books.

Joshi, A. and Ayee, J. (2008) 'Associational taxation: a pathway into the informal sector?' chapter 8 in D. Brautigam, O.H. Fjeldstad, and Mick Moore (eds) *Taxation and State-Building in Developing Countries: Capacity and Consent.* Cambridge: Cambridge University Press.

Kaldor, N. (1963) 'Will underdeveloped countries learn to tax?' *Foreign Affairs*, **41** (January), 410–19.

Kalecki, M. (1943) 'Political aspects of full employment', *Political Quarterly*, **14**, 322–31.

Kanbur, R. (2001) 'Economic policy, distribution and poverty: the nature of disagreements', *World Development*, **29**, 1083–94.

Kapur, D. (2002) 'The changing anatomy of governance of the World Bank', in J. Pincus and J. Winters (eds) *Reinventing the World Bank.* Ithaca: Cornell University Press, 54–75.

Kaufman, D., Kraay, A., and Mastruzzi, M. (2006) *Governance Matters V: Aggregate and Individual Governance Indicators for 1996–2005*, Washington, DC: World Bank.

Kennedy, B., Kawachi, I., and Brainerd, E. (1998) 'The role of social capital in the Russian mortality crisis', *World Development*, **26**, 2029–43.

Kennedy, P. (1989) *The Rise of the Great Powers*. London: Fontana Press.

Kessler, G. and Di Virgilio, M. (2008) 'La Nueva Pobreza Urbana: Dinámica Global, Regional y Argentina en las Ultimas Dos Décadas', *Revista de la Cepal*, **95** (August), 31–50.

Keynes, J.M. (1945/1980) *The Collected Writings of John Maynard Keynes, vol. XXVI: Shaping the Post-war World. Bretton Woods and Reparations*. Cambridge: Macmillan and Cambridge University Press for Royal Economic Society.

Khoo, B.T. (2000) 'Economic nationalism and its discontents: Malaysian political economy after July 1997', in R. Robison, M. Beeson, K. Jaysuriya and H.-R. Kim, (eds) *Politics and Markets in the Wake of the East Asian crisis*. London: Routledge.

Khoo, B.T. (2004) *Beyond Mahathir: Malaysian Politics and its Discontents*. London: Zed Books.

Killick, T. (1978) *Development Economics in Action*. London: Heinemann Educational.

Killick, T. (1984a) *The Quest for Economic Stabilisation: the IMF and the Third World*. London: Heinemann Educational.

Killick, T. (1984b) *The IMF and Stabilisation: Developing Country Experiences*. London: Heinemann Educational.

Killick, T. (1995) *IMF Programmes in Developing Countries*. London: Routledge and ODI.

Killick, T. (2006) 'Conditionality and IMF flexibility', in A. Paloni and M. Zanardi (eds) *The IMF, the World Bank and Policy Reform*. London: Routledge.

Killick, T., Marr, A., and Gunatilaka, R. (1998) *Aid and the Political Economy of Policy Change*. London: Routledge and ODI.

Kimble, D. (1963) *A Political History of Ghana: the Rise of Gold Coast Nationalism 1850–1928*. Oxford: Oxford University Press.

Kingdon, G. and Knight, J. (2007) 'Unemployment in South Africa, 1995–2003: causes, problems and policies', *Journal of African Economies*, **16**, 813–49.

Klasen, S. (2005) *Economic Growth and Poverty Reduction: Measurement and Policy Issues*. Paris: OECD Development Centre, Working Paper 246.

Klugman, J. and Braithwaite, J. (1998) 'Poverty in Russia during the transition: an overview' *The World Bank Research Observer*, **13**, 37–58.

Knack, S. (2001) 'Aid dependence and the quality of governance: cross-country empirical tests', *Southern Economic Journal*, **68**, 310–29.

Knack, S. and Keefer, P. (1997) 'Does social capital have an economic payoff?' A cross-country investigation' *Quarterly Journal of Economics*, **112**, 1251–88.

Koeberle, S., Bedoya, H., Silarsky, P., and Verheyen, G. (eds) (2005) *Conditionality Revisited: Concepts, Experiences and Lessons*. Washington, DC: World Bank.

Koeberle, S., Stavreski, Z., and Walliser, J. (2006) *Budget Support as More Effective Aid?* Washington, DC: World Bank.

Kornai, J., Haggard, S., and Kaufmann, R. (1999) *Reforming the State: Fiscal and Welfare Reform in Post-Socialist Countries*. Cambridge: Cambridge University Press.

Kraay, A. (2006) 'When is growth pro-poor? Evidence from a panel of countries', *Journal of Development Economics*, **80**, 198–227.

Krueger, A. (1974) 'The political economy of the rent-seeking society', *American Economic Review*.

Kuczynski, R.R. (1949) *Demographic Survey of the British Colonial Empire*, vol. 1: West Africa, vol. 2: East Africa, etc. London: Royal Institute of International Affairs.

Kuznets, S. (1955) 'Economic growth and income inequality', *American Economic Review*, **45** (March), 1–28.

Lahiff, E. (2007) *Land Reform in South Africa: Progress to Date*. Paper presented at World Bank workshop on 'Land redistribution: towards a common vision, Pretoria, July.

Lal, D. (1983) *The Poverty of 'Development Economics',* London: Institute of Economic Affairs, Hobart Paperback 16.
Lancaster, C. (1993) 'Governance and development: the views from Washington.' *IDS Bulletin* **124** (1).
Landa, F. (2003) *Pobreza y distribucion del ingreso en Bolivia entre 1999 y 2002,* unpublished paper, La Paz: INE/UDAPE.
Landa, F. and Jimenez, W. (2005) *Bolivia; crecimiento 'pro-pobre' entre los años 1989 y 2002,* unpublished paper, La Paz: UDAPE.
Lane, T., Ghosh, A., Hamann, J., et al. (1999) *IMF-supported Programs in Indonesia, Kora and Thailand; a Preliminary Assessment.* Washington, DC: IMF.
Lawson, D., McKay, A., and Okidi, J. (2006) 'Poverty persistence and transitions in Uganda: a combined qualitative and quantitative analysis', *Journal of Development Studies,* **42**, 1225–52.
Lazarte Rojas, J. (2005) *Entre los espectros del pasado y las intercertidumbres del futuro: politica y democracia en Bolivia a principios del siglo XXI* (Between the spectres of the past and future uncertainties: politics and democracy in Bolivia at the beginning of the twenty-first century). La Paz: Plural Editores.
Leandro, J., Schaefer, H., and Frontini, G. (1999) 'Towards a more effective conditionality: an operational framework', *World Development,* **27**, 285–300.
Leftwich, A., Sen, K., and te Velde, D. (eds) (2008) 'The economics and politics of state-business relations in Africa', unpublished report to Department for International Development.
Lehmann, H., Wadsworth, J., and Acquisti, A. (1999) 'Grime and punishment: job insecurity and wage arrears in the Russian Federation', *Journal of Comparative Economics,* **27**, 595–617.
Lele, U. and Goldsmith, A. (1989) 'The development of national agricultural research capacity: India's experience with the Rockefeller Foundation and its significance for Africa', *Economic Development and Cultural Change,* **42**, 305–43.
Lenton, P. and Mosley, P. (2011) 'Incentivising trust', *Journal of Economic Psychology,* forthcoming.
Levitsky, S. (2000) 'The "normalization" of Argentine politics', *Journal of Democracy,* **11** (2), 56–69.
Levitsky, S. (2005) 'Argentina: democratic survival amidst economic failure' in F. Hagopian and S. Mainwaring (eds) *The Third Wave of Democratization in Latin America Advances and Setbacks.* Cambridge: Cambridge University Press, 63–89.
Lewis, S. (2005) 'States and markets in Latin America: the political economy of economic interventionism', *Working Paper 09/05.* London: Department of Economic History, London School of Economics.
Lewis, W.A. (1947) *Colonial development in British territories,* unpublished manuscript, Rhodes House, Oxford: Mss. Brit.Emp.s.350.
Lewis, W.A. (1953) *Report on the Industrialisation of the Gold Coast.* Accra: Government Printer.
Lewis, W.A. (1955) *The Theory of Economic Growth.* London: George Allen and Unwin.
Lewis, W.A. (1965) *Politics in West Africa,* Whidden Lectures 1965. London: George Allen and Unwin.
Lewis, W.A. (1967) *Reflections on Nigeria's Economic Growth.* Paris: OECD Development Centre.
Leys, C. (1975a) *Underdevelopment in Kenya: the Political Economy of Neo-colonialism.* London: Heinemann.
Leys, C. (1975b) 'The politics of redistribution with growth', *IDS Bulletin,* **7** (August), 4–8.
Liddle, R. (1992) 'Indonesia's democratic past and future' *Comparative Politics,* **24**, 443–62.

Lin, J.Y. (1990) 'Collectivisation and China's agricultural crisis in 1959–61', *Journal of Political Economy*, **98**, 1228–52.

Lindert, P. and Williamson, J.G. (1999) 'English workers' living standards during the Industrial Revolution: a new look' in J. Mokyr (ed.) *The British Industrial Revolution; An Economic Perspective*. Boulder: Westview Press.

Lindsay, J.M. (1994) *Congress and the Politics of US Foreign Policy*. Baltimore and London: Johns Hopkins University Press.

Linera, A.G. (2009) *Forma valor y forma comunidad: aproximacion teorica-abstracta a los fundamentos civilizatorios que preceden al Ayllu Universal*. La Paz: Muela del Diablo Editores.

Lingnau, H. and V. Lang (2015) 'Defining and measuring poverty and inequality post-2015', *Journal of International Development*, **27** (April).

Lipton, M. (1977) *Why Poor People Stay Poor*. London: Maurice Temple Smith.

Lipton, M. and Longhurst, R. (1989) *New Seeds and Poor People*. London: Allen and Unwin.

Livi-Bacci, M. (2001) *A concise history of world population*, third edition. Oxford: Blackwell.

Lledo, V., Schneider, A., and Moore, M. (2004) *Governance, Taxes and Tax Reform in Latin America*. Institute for Development Studies, Sussex: IDS Working Paper 221.

Llobet, C. (1999) *Opas seremos?* La Paz: Plural.

Llobet, C. (2005) *SobreMesa*. La Paz: Editorial El Observador.

Lokshin, M. (2008) *Does Poverty Research in Russia Follow the Scientific Method?* World Bank Policy Research Working Paper 4528 (www.worldbank.org).

Lokshin, M. and Yemtsov, R. (2001) *Household Strategies for Coping With Poverty and Social Exclusion in Post-crisis Russia*. World Bank: Poverty Reduction and Economic Management Sector Unit, Policy Research Working Paper 2556.

Lyall, J. (2006) 'Pocket protests: rhetorical coercion and the micropolitics of collective action in semiauthoritarian regimes', *World Politics*, **58** (April), 378–412.

MacGregor, S. (1981) *The Politics of Poverty*. Harlow: Longman.

MacIntyre, A. (1993) 'The politics of finance in Indonesian economic development: command, confusion and competition', in S. Haggard, C. Lee, and S. Maxfield (eds) *The Politics of Finance in Developing Countries*. Ithaca: Cornell University Press.

MacNamara, R. (1973) *Statement at IMF/World Bank Joint Meeting*. Washington, DC: World Bank.

Maddison, A. (2000) *Economic Growth 1500–2000: a Millennium Survey*. New York: Harper Collins.

Marconi, R. (2010) *Microfinanzas y Suma Qamaña; lecciones and desafíos* (Bolivian microfinance and Andean socialism: challenges and lessons learned), unpublished typescript, La Paz, November.

Marconi, R. and Mosley, P. (2006) 'Bolivia during the global crisis 1998–2004: towards a 'macroeconomics of microfinance', *Journal of International Development*, **18**, 237–61.

Marr, A. (2007) *A History of Modern Britain*. London: Pan Macmillan.

Martin, M. (1991) *The Crumbling Facade of African Debt Negotiations: no Winners*. Basingstoke, MacMillan.

Martins, P. (2013) 'Growth, employment and poverty in Africa: tales of lions and cheetahs', unpublished background paper for *World Development Report 2013*, London: Overseas Development Institute.

McFaul, M. (2002) 'The fourth wave of democracy and dictatorship; non-cooperative transitions in the postcommunist world', *World Politics*, **54**, 212–44.

McFaul, M., Petrov, N., and Ryabov, A. (2004) *Between Dictatorship and Democracy: Russian Post-communist Political Reform*. Washington, DC: Carnegie Endowment for International Peace.

McLeod, R. (1998) 'From crisis to cataclysm? The mismanagement of Indonesia's economic ailments.' *The World Economy*, **21** (7), 913–30.

Meade, J. (1961) *Report to the Government of Mauritius: The Economic and Social Structure of Mauritius.* Port Louis: Government of Mauritius.

Meade, J. (1967) 'Population explosion, the standard of living and social conflict', *Economic Journal,* 77 (306).

Mecagni, M. (1999) 'The causes of program interruptions', in H. Bredenkamp and S. Schadler (eds) *Economic Adjustment and Reform in Low-income Countries: Studies by the Staff of the International Monetary Fund.* Washington, DC: IMF.

Mejia Acosta, A. and de Renzio, P. (2008) *Aid, Rents and the Politics of the Budgetary Process.* Institute of Development Studies, Sussex: IDS Working Paper 311.

Mellor, J. (2000) 'Agricultural growth, rural employment and poverty reduction; non-tradables, public expenditure and balanced growth'. Unpublished paper prepared for World Bank Rural Week 2000, March.

Mesa-Lago, C. (2002) 'Models of development, social policy and reform in Latin America', background paper for the UNRISD Project Social Policy in a Development Context, Geneva.

Mesa-Lago, C. and Muller, K. (2002) 'The politics of pension reform in Latin America', *Journal of Latin American Studies,* **34** (3), 687–715.

Microfinance Information Exchange (MIX): for full reference please see Gonzales (2007), and for data see www.themix.org.

Mietzner, M. (1999) 'From Soeharto to Habibie: the Indonesian armed forces and political Islam during the transition', in G. Forrester (ed.) *Post-Soeharto Indonesia. Renewal or chaos?* Singapore: Institute for Southeast Asian Studies.

Migdal, J. (1988) *Strong Societies and Weak States: State-society Relations and State Capabilities in the Third World.* Princeton NJ: Princeton University Press.

Migdal, J., Kohli, A., and Shue, V. (eds) (1994) *State Power and Social Forces: Domination and Transformation.* Cambridge: Cambridge University Press.

Mill, J.S. (1848/1994) *Principles of Political Economy* (with Chapters on Socialism). Oxford: Oxford University Press World's Classics.

Miller, M. and Smith, J. (2007) 'Punishment without crime? Prison as a worker discipline device', unpublished paper, University of Warwick.

Mishkin, F. (1999) 'Symposium: Global Financial Instability' *Journal of Economic Perspectives,* **13**, 3–20.

Momani, B. (2004) 'IMF recruitment practices and the convergence of ideas.' Paper presented at the ISA annual convention, Montreal.

Moore, M. (1999) 'Death without taxes: democracy, state capacity and aid dependence in the Fourth World', in G. White and M. Robinson (eds) *Towards a Democratic Developmental State.* Oxford: Oxford University Press.

Moore, M. (2007) *How Does Taxation Affect the Quality of Governance?* IDS Working Paper 280. Brighton: Institute of Development Studies.

Morales, J.A. (1991) 'Ajustes estructurales en la economia campesina boliviana', *Debate Agrario* (Lima), **9**, 121–62.

Morduch, J. (1999) 'The role of subsidies in microfinance: evidence from the Grameen Bank', *Journal of Development Economics,* **60,** 229–48.

Morduch, J. and Haley, B. (2000) *Analysis of the Effects of Microfinance on Poverty Reduction,* New York University, NYU Wagner Working Paper.

Morley, S., Machado, A.R., and Pettinato, S. (1999) 'Indexes of structural reform in Latin America', *Serie Reformas Económicas* 12 (Santiago de Chile: CEPAL).

Morrissey, O. (1995) 'Political commitment, institutional capacity and tax reform in Tanzania', *World Development,* **23**, 637–51.

Morrisson, C. (1992) *Adjustment and Equity in Morocco.* Paris: OECD.

Morrisson, C., Lafay, J.-D., and Dessus, S. (1993) *La Faisabilité politique de l'ajustement dans les pays africains.* Document technique 88. Paris: OECD Development Centre.

Mosley, P. (1978) 'Images of the 'floating voter'; or, the 'political business cycle' revisited', *Political Studies,* **26** (September), 375–95.
Mosley, P. (1981) 'Aid for the poorest: some early lessons of UK experience', *Journal of Development Studies,* **17** (January), 214–26.
Mosley, P. (1982a) 'Agricultural development and government policy in settler economies: the case of Kenya and Southern Rhodesia, 1900–60', *Economic History Review,* **42,** 751–73.
Mosley, P. (1983) *The Settler Economies.* Cambridge: Cambridge University Press. Reprinted, 2009.
Mosley, P. 'Achievements and contradictions of the Peruvian agrarian reform: a regional perspective', *Journal of Development Studies* 21 (April 1985), 440–448.
Mosley, P. (1987) 'Conditionality as bargaining process: a study of World Bank Structural Adjustment Lending 1980–86', *Princeton Essays in International Finance,* **168,** October 1987.
Mosley, P. (2000) 'Globalisation, economic policy and convergence', *The World Economy,* **23,** 613–34.
Mosley, P. (2001) 'The IMF after the East Asian Crisis: merits and limitations of the "long-term development partner" role', *The World Economy,* **24/25,** 597–629.
Mosley, P. (2002) 'The African Green Revolution as a pro-poor policy instrument', *Journal of International Development,* **14,** 695–725.
Mosley, P. (2003) 'The World Bank and the reconstruction of the "social safety net" in Russia and eastern Europe', Chapter 7 in S. Kosack, G. Ranis, and J. Vreeland (eds)*The IMF and World Bank in Global Perspective.* London: Routledge.
Mosley, P. (2003b) 'Micro-insurance: scope, design and assessment of wider impacts', Institute of Development Studies Bulletin, vol. 34 (Oct 2003).
Mosley, P. (2004a) *Severe Poverty and Growth: a Macro-micro Analysis.* Chronic Poverty Research Centre Working Paper 51. Manchester: Chronic Poverty Research Centre.
Mosley, P. (2004b) 'Pro-poor politics and the new political economy of stabilisation', *New Political Economy,* **9** (June), 271–97.
Mosley, P. (2004c) 'Institutions and politics in a Lewis-type growth model', *Manchester School,* **72** (December), 749–771.
Mosley, P. (2006) 'The World Bank and the reconstruction of the 'social safety net' in Russia and eastern Europe', Chapter 7 in G. Ranis, J. Vreeland, and S. Kosack (eds) *Globalisation and the Nation State: the Impact of the IMF and World Bank.* London: Routledge.
Mosley, P. (2007) 'The political poverty trap: Bolivia 2000–2007', unpublished paper, ESRC World Economy and Finance Project.
Mosley, P. (2009) 'La "trampa politica de la pobreza": Bolivia 1999–2009', *Cuadernos Economicos* (Madrid), **78** (December).
Mosley, P. and Chiripanhura, B. (2009) 'Liberalisation and poverty in Africa since 1990—why is the operation of the 'invisible hand' uneven?', *Journal of International Development,* **21** (August).
Mosley, P. and Chiripanhura, B. (2010) 'The African political business cycle: varieties of experience', paper presented at CSAE annual conference, Oxford.
Mosley, P. and Hulme, D. (1998) 'Microenterprise finance: is there a conflict between growth and poverty alleviation?' *World Development,* **26,** 783–90.
Mosley, P. and Rock, J. (2004) 'Microfinance, labour markets and poverty in Africa: a study of six institutions', *Journal of International Development,* **16** (April), 467–500.
Mosley, P. and Suleiman, A. (2007) 'Aid, agriculture and poverty reduction', *Review of Development Economics,* **11,** 139–59.
Mosley, P., Harrigan, J., and Toye, J. (1995) *Aid and Power,* second edition, 2 vols. London: Routledge.

Mosley, P., Hudson, J., and Horrell, S. (1987) 'Aid, the public sector and the market in less developed countries', *Economic Journal*, **97** (September), 616–42.

Mosley, P., Hudson, J., and Verschoor, A. (2004) 'Aid, poverty reduction and the "new conditionality"', *Economic Journal*, **114** (July), 217–44.

Mosley, P., Subasat, T., and Weeks, J. (1995) 'Assessing adjustment in Africa', *World Development*, **23**, 1459–75.

Moss, T., Petterson, G., and van de Walle, N. (2006) *An Aid-institutions Paradox? A Review Essay on Aid Dependency and State Building in Sub-Saharan Africa.* Washington, DC: Centre for Global Development, Working Paper 74.

Mourmouras, A. (2009) 'The political economy of adjustment in a world of special interest politics', unpublished paper, International Monetary Fund, presented at Sheffield Seminar, 11 March 2009.

Murillo, M.V. (1997) 'Union politics, market-oriented reforms, and the reshaping of Argentine corporatism' in D. Chalmers (ed.) *The New Politics of Inequality in Latin America.* Oxford: Oxford University Press, 72–95.

Murphy, K., Shleifer, A., and Vishny, R. (1989) 'Industrialisation and the big push', *Journal of Political Economy.*

Museveni, Y. (1997) *Sowing the Mustard Seed: the Struggle for Freedom and Democracy in Uganda.* Oxford: Macmillan Education.

Mushtaque, A., Chowdhury, R., and Aminul Alam, M. (1997) 'BRAC's poverty alleviation programme: what it is and what it achieved', Chapter 6 in G. Wood and I. Sharif (eds) *Who Needs Credit? Poverty and Finance in Bangladesh.* Dhaka: The University Press Limited.

Mussa, M. (2004) 'Argentina and the Fund: anatomy of a policy failure', Chapter 12 in D. Vines and C. Gilbert (eds) *The IMF and its Critics: Reform of Global Financial Architecture.* Cambridge: Cambridge University Press.

Mussurov, A. (2007) 'Determinants of wage arrears in Russia'. Paper presented at International Studies Association Conference, Chicago, February.

Mussurov, A. and Mosley, P. (2008) 'The evolution of poverty in Russia 1998–2007', unpublished paper, ESRC World Economy and Finance project, presented at Political Studies Association conference, Swansea, 3 April.

Mustapha, A.R. and Whitfield, L. (eds) (2009) *Elites and Poverty in Africa.* Oxford: Oxford University Press.

Myint, H. (1976) *The Economics of the Developing Countries.* London: Hutchinson University Library.

Nafziger, W. and Auvinen, J. (2002) 'Economic development, inequality, war, and state violence', *World Development*, **30**, 153–63.

Nafziger, W., Stewart, F., and Vayrynen, R. (2000) *War, Hunger and Displacement*, 2 vols. Oxford: Oxford University Press.

Narayan, D. and Pritchett, L. (1999) 'Cents and sociability: household income and social capital in rural Tanzania', *Economic Development and Cultural Change*, **47**, 871–97.

Narayan, D. and Woolcock, M. (2000) 'Definitions of social capital', *World Bank Research Observer.*

Neilson, C., Contreras, D., Cooper, R., and Hermann, J. (2008) 'The dynamics of poverty in Chile', *Journal of Latin American Studies*, **40**, 251–73.

Newman, J., Pradhan, M., and Jorgenson, S. (1990) 'Did workers gain from Bolivia's Emergency Social Fund?' *World Bank Economic Review.*

Ninsin, K. (1998) 'Postscript: elections, democracy and elite consensus', in *Ghana: Transition to Democracy.* Accra: Freedom Publications.

Nooruddin, I. and Simmons, J. (2006) 'The politics of hard choices: IMF programs and government spending'. *International Organisation*, **60** (October), 1001–33.

Nordhaus, W. (1975) 'The political business cycle', *Review of Economic Studies*, 42, 169–90.

Nowzad, B. (1982) 'The IMF and its critics', *Princeton Essays in International Finance.*, Princeton: Princeton University, Department of Economics, 146.

Nsowah-Nuamah, N., Teal, F., and Awoonor-Williams, M. (2010) 'Jobs, skills and incomes in Ghana; how was poverty halved?' Oxford: Centre for the Study of African Economies, Working Paper 2010–11.

Nugent, P. (2001) 'Winners, losers and also rans: money, moral authority and voting patterns in the Ghana 2000 election', *African Affairs,* **100** (July), 405–29.

Nunn, N. (2007) 'Historical legacies: a model linking Africa's past to its current underdevelopment', *Journal of Development Economics,* **83**, 157–75.

Nurkse, R. (1953) *Problems of capital formation in underdeveloped countries.* London: Allen and Unwin.

O'Connor, J. (1973) *The Fiscal Crisis of the State.* New York: St Martin's Press.

O'Donnell, G. (1973) *Modernization and Bureaucratic Authoritarianism.* Buenos Aires: Paidós.

O'Donnell, G. (1979) 'Tensions in the bureaucratic-authoritarian state and the question of democracy' in D. Collier (ed.) *The New Authoritarianism in Latin America.* Princeton: Princeton University Press.

O'Donnell, G. (1982) *1966–1973. El Estado Burocrático Autoritario. Triunfos, Derrotas y Crisis.* Buenos Aires: Editorial Belgrano.

Offer, A. (1993) 'The British empire: a waste of money?' *Economic History Review,* **46** (May), 215–38.

Okidi, J., Ssewanyana, S., Bategeka, L., and Muhumuza, F. (2007) 'Uganda's experience with operationalising pro-poor growth, 1992 to 2003', Chapter 7 in T. Besley and L. Cord (eds) *Delivering on the Promise of Pro-poor Growth.* New York and Oxford: Oxford University Press.

Olson, M. (1965) *The Logic of Collective Action.* Cambridge, Mass: Harvard University Press.

Ondoga ori Amaza (1998) *Museveni's Long March: From Guerrilla to Statesman.* Kampala: Fountain Publishers.

Orttung, R. (ed.) (2000) *The Republics and Regions of the Russian Federation: a Guide to Politics, Policies and Leaders.* New York: East-West Institute.

Painter, J. (1994) *Bolivia and coca: a study in dependency.* Boulder, CO: Lynne Rienner Publishers.

Paldam, M. (1993) 'The socio-political reactions to balance of payments adjustments in LDCs: a study of nine cases from Latin America', unpublished paper, University of Aarhus.

Palermo, V. and Novaro, M. (1996) *Política y Poder en el Gobierno de Menem.* Buenos Aires: Grupo Editorial Norma.

Pastor, M. and Wise, C. (2004) 'Picking up the pieces: comparing the social impacts of financial crisis in Mexico and Argentina'. Paper prepared for presentation at the CIGI-20 Meeting. Flacso, Buenos Aires, Argentina, 20–21 May.

Patroni, P. (2001) 'The decline and fall of corporatism? Labour legislation reform in Mexico and Argentina during the 1990s', *Canadian Journal of Political Science,* **34** (2), 249–74.

Patten, R.H. and Rosengard, J. (1991) *Progress with profits; the Development of Rural Banking in Indonesia.* San Francisco: International Centre for Economic Growth.

Patten, R.H., Rosengard, J., and Johnston, D. (2001) 'Microfinance success amidst macroeconomic failure: the experience of Bank Rakyat Indonesia during the east Asian crisis' *World Development,* **29**, 1057–69.

Pepinsky, T. (2009) 'The 2008 Malaysian elections: an end to ethnic politics? *Journal of East Asian Studies,* **9**, 87–120.

Perkins, D.H. and Roemer, M. (1992) *Reforming Economic Systems in Developing Countries.* Cambridge, Mass; Harvard University Press.

Perkins, J.H. (1997) *Geopolitics and the Green Revolution: Wheat, Genes and the Cold War.* New York: Oxford University Press.

Polak, J. (1991) 'The changing nature of IMF conditionality.' *Princeton Essays in International Finance.* Princeton NJ: Princeton University, Department of Economics.

Polak, J. (1994) *The World Bank and the IMF a Changing Relationship*. Washington, DC; Brookings Institute.

Polity IV Project. Available at www.cidcm.umd.edu/inscr/polity/#data.

Poulton, C., Davies, R., Matshe, I., and Urey, I. (2002) 'A review of Zimbabwe's economic policies 1980–2000', unpublished paper, University of Zimbabwe and Imperial College at Wye.

Powesland, P. (1957) *Economic Policy and Labour: A Study in Uganda's Economic History.* Kampala: East African Institute of Social Research (East African Studies, 10).

Pritchett, L. (2005) 'The political economy of targeted safety nets'. *World Bank Social Protection Discussion Paper No 0501.*

Putnam, R. (1988) 'Diplomacy and domestic policy: the logic of two-level games'. *International Organization,* **42** (3).

Putnam, R. (1993) *Making Democracy Work: Civic Traditions in Modern Italy.* Princeton N.J.: Princeton University Press.

Radelet, S. and Sachs, J. (1998) 'The East Asian financial crisis: diagnosis, remedies, prospects'. Unpublished paper, Harvard Institute for International Development.

Rajan, R., and Subramaniam, A. (2008) 'Aid and growth: what does the cross-country evidence really show?' *Review of Economics and Statistics,* **90**, 643–65.

Ranis, G., Vreeland, J., and Kosack, S. (2006) *Globalisation and the Nation State: the Impact of the IMF and the World Bank.* London and Abingdon: Routledge.

Ravallion, M. and Chen, S. (1997) 'What can new survey data tell us about recent changes in distribution and poverty?' *World Bank Economic Review,* **11**, 357–82.

Reinikka, R. and Collier, P. (2001) *Uganda's Recovery.* Kampala: Fountain Press.

Remmer, K. (1993) 'The political economy of elections in Latin America, 1980–1991', *American Political Science Review,* **87**, 393–407.

Remmer, K. (2004) 'Does foreign aid promote the expansion of government?' *American Journal of Political Science,* **48**, 77–92.

Rhyne, E. (2002) *Mainstreaming Microfinance: How Lending to the Poor Began, Grew and Came of Age in Bolivia.* Bloomfield, CT: Kumarian.

Riesenhuber, E. (2001) *The International Monetary Fund under Constraint: Legitimacy of its Crisis Management.* The Hague: Kluwer Law International.

Riggirozzi, P. (2007) 'Argentina: State Capacity And Leverage In External Negotiations' in J. Robertson (ed.) *Power and Politics after Financial Crises.* Basingstoke: Palgrave-Macmillan, 125–43.

Riggirozzi, P. (2009) *Advancing Governance in the South: What Roles for International Financial Institutions in Developing States*? Basingstoke: Palgrave-Macmillan.

Robison, R. (1986) *Indonesia: the Rise of Capital.* Sydney: Allen and Unwin.

Robison, R. (1997) 'Politics and markets in Indonesia's post-oil era', in G. Rodan, K. Hewison, and R. Robison (eds) *The Political Economy of Southeast Asia.* Oxford: Oxford University Press.

Robinson, R. and Gallagher, J. (1961) *Africa and the Victorians: The Official Mind of Imperialism.* London: Macmillan.

Robison, R. and Hadiz, V. (2004) *Reorganising Power in Indonesia: the Politics of Oligarchy in an Age of Markets.* London & New York: RoutledgeCurzon.

Robison, R. and Rosser, C. (2000) 'Surviving the meltdown: liberal reform and political oligarchy in Indonesia', in R. Robison, M. Beeson, K. Jayasuriya, and H.-R. Kim, *Politics and Markets in the Wake of the East Asian Crisis.* London: Routledge.

Rock, D. (2002) 'Racking Argentina', *New Left Review,* **17** (September–October), 55–86, available at http://newleftreview.org/PDFarticles/NLR25104.pdf accessed 11 April 2006).
Rock, M.T. (1999) 'Reassessing the effectiveness of industrial policy in Indonesia: can the neo-liberals be wrong?' *World Development* **27** (4), 691–704.
Rodrik, D. (1996) 'Understanding economic policy reform', *Journal of Economic Literature,* **34** (1).
Rodrik, D. (1990) 'Stabilisation and structural adjustment', *World Development,* **18.**
Rodrik, D. (1999) *The New Political Economy and Developing Countries: Making Openness Work.* Policy Essay 24, Washington, DC: Overseas Development Council.
Rodrik, D. (2006) 'Goodbye Washington consensus, hello Washington confusion? A review of the World Bank's economic growth in the 1990s: learning from a decade of reform', *Journal of Economic Literature,* **44,** 973–87.
Rodrik, D., Subramaniam, A., and. Trebbi, F. (2004) 'Institutions rule: the primacy of institutions over geography and integration in economic development', *Journal of Economic Growth,* **9,** 131–65.
Rogaly, B. (1996) 'Microfinance evangelism, "destitute women" and the hard selling of a new anti-poverty formula', *Development in Practice,* **6** (May), 100–12.
Rohrbach, D. (1988) *The Economics of Smallholder Maize Production in Zimbabwe: Implications for Food Security,* Michigan State University: MSU International Development Paper No. 11.
Rousseau, J.-J. (1762/1968) *The Social Contract: or, Principles of Political Right.* Harmondsworth: Penguin.
Rowntree, B.S. (1901) *Poverty: A Study of Town Life.* London: Macmillan.
Rowntree, B. Seebohm (1901) *Poverty: a Study of Town Life.* London: Macmillan.
Russian Federal Statistics Service (Rosstat) (2007a) *Russia in Figures.* 2007 edition.
Russian Federal Statistics Service (Rosstat) (2007b) *Dokhodi, Raskhodi i Potreblenie Domashnikh Khoziaistva* (Incomes, Expenditures and Consumption of Domestic Households), June 2007.
Sachs, J. (2005) *The End of Poverty: How We Can Make it Happen in Our Lifetime.* London: Penguin Books.
Sachs, J. (2007) *Reith Lectures 2007: Bursting at the Seams. Economic Solidarity for a Crowded Planet.* http://www.bbc.co.uk/print/radio4/reith2007/.
Sachs, J. and Warner, A. (1995) 'Economic reform and the process of global integration', *Brookings Papers on Economic Activity,* (1), 1–117.
Sachs, J., McArthur, J.W., Schmidt-Traub, G., et al. (2004) 'Ending Africa's poverty trap', *Brookings Papers on Economic Activity,* **1,** 117–241.
Saith, A. (2006) 'From universal values to Millennium Development Goals: lost in translation?' *Development and Change,* **37,** 1167–99.
Sala-i-Martin, X. (1997) 'I just ran two million regressions', *American Economic Review Papers and Proceedings,* **84** (2), 178–83.
Sala-i-Martin, X. and M. Pinkovskiy (2010) '*African poverty is falling... much faster than you think!*' Cambridge, MA: National Bureau of Economic Research, Working Paper 15775.
Schadler, S.,. Bennett, A., Carkovic, M., et al. (1995) *IMF Conditionality: experience under stand-by and extended arrangements, part I: Key issues and findings,* Washington, DC: IMF, occasional paper 128.
Schwarz, A. (1999) *A Nation in Waiting: Indonesia's Search for Stability.* Westview: Boulder.
Sen, A.K. (1957) *Choice of Techniques.* Cambridge: Cambridge University Press.
Sen, A.K. (1982) *Poverty and Famines.* Oxford: Oxford University Press.
Sen, A.K. (2009) *The Idea of Justice.* London: Allen Lane.
Serova, E. and Khramova, I. (2001) 'Market transactions in Russia's agriculture'. Paper presented at Golitsino II Conference: 'Framework for investigating issues in factor

markets and economic organisation of Russian agriculture'. Golitsino, Russian Federation: 6–7 July 2001.

Service, R. (2003) *A History of Modern Russia.* London: Penguin.

Service, R. (1997) *A History of Modern Russia.* London: Penguin.

Shamsul (1987) 'The battle royal: the UMNO election of 1987', *Southeast Asian Affairs* 1988. Singapore, Institute for Southeast Asian Studies.

Sherraden, M. (1991) *Assets and the poor: a new American welfare policy.* New York: M.E. Sharpe.

Shevtsova, L. (2007) 'Post-communist Russia: a historic opportunity missed', *International Affairs,* **83**, 891–912.

Sidel, J. (2006) *Riots, Pogroms, Jihad: Religious Violence in Indonesia.* Ithaca: Cornell University Press.

Simmons, B. and Elkins, Z. (2004) 'The globalisation of liberalisation: policy diffusion in the international political economy', *American Political Science Review,* **98** (February), 171–88.

Singh, I. (1990) *The Great Ascent.* Baltimore: Johns Hopkins University Press.

Skidelsky, R. (2000) *John Maynard Keynes, vol 2: The Economist as Saviour.* London: Macmillan.

Slater, D. (2004) 'Indonesia's accountability trap: party cartels and presidential power after demographic transition', *Indonesia,* **78**, 61–92.

Smillie, I. (2009) *Freedom from Want: the Remarkable Success Story of BRAC.* West Hartford, Connecticut: Kumarian Press.

Smith, W.C. (1990) 'Democracy, distributional conflicts, and macroeconomic policymaking in Argentina 1983–89', *Journal of Inter-American Studies and World Affairs,* **32** (2), 1–42.

Ssewanyana, S. and Younger, S.D. (2007) 'Infant mortality in Uganda: determinants, trends and the Millennium Development Goals', *Journal of African Economies,* **17**, 34–61.

Steffek, J. (2003) 'The legitimation of international governance: a discourse approach?' *European Journal of International Relations,* **9** (2), 249–75.

Steinbeck, J. (1947) *A Russian Journal.* Harmondsworth: Penguin.

Stern, N. (2006) *The Economics of Climate Change: the Stern Review.* Cambridge: Cambridge University Press.

Stewart, F. (1993) 'The economics of conflict', annual conference of Development Studies Association, Swansea.

Stewart, F., and Wang, M. (2006) 'Do PRSPs empower poor countries and disempower the World Bank, or is it the other way round?', chapter 11 in G. Ranis, J.R. Vreeland, and S. Kosack (eds) *Globalisation and the Nation State: The Impact of the IMF and World Bank.* London: Routledge.

Stiglitz, J. (1976) 'The efficiency wage hypothesis, surplus labour and the distribution of income in LDCs', *Oxford Economic Papers,* **28**, 185–207.

Stiglitz, J. (1998) *More Instruments and Broader Goals: Moving Towards the Post-Washington Consensus.* WIDER Annual Lectures 2. Helsinki: World Institute for Development Economics Research.

Stiglitz, J. (2003) *Globalisation and its Discontents.* New York: Norton.

Stiles, K. (1995) *Negotiating Debt: the IMF Lending Process.* Boulder: Westview Press.

Stillman, S. and Thomas, D. (2008) 'Nutritional status during an economic crisis: evidence from Russia', *Economic Journal,* **118**, 1385–418.

Stone, R. (2002) *Lending Credibility: the International Monetary Fund and the Post-Communist Transition.* Princeton: Princeton University Press.

Strange, S. (1973) 'The IMF: monetary managers' in R. Cox and H. Jacobson (eds) *The Anatomy of Influence: Decision Making in International Organizations.* New Haven: Yale University Press, 263–97.

Strange, S. (1998) *Mad Money*. Ann Arbor: University of Michigan Press.

Strauss, J., Beegle, K., Dwiyanto, A., et al. (2004) *Indonesian Living Standards: Before and After the Financial Crisis*. Singapore: ISEAS.

Streeten, P., Burki, S., ul Haq, M., Hicks, N., and Stewart, F. (1981) *First Things First: Meeting Basic Human Needs in Developing Countries*. Oxford: Oxford University Press.

Suarez, H.J. (2003) *Una semana fundamental: 10–18 octubre 2003*. La Paz: Muela del Diablo Editores.

Svensson, J. (2000a) 'Foreign aid and rent-seeking', *Journal of International Economics*, **51**, 437–61.

Svensson, J. (2000b) 'When is foreign aid policy credible? Aid dependence and conditionality,' *Journal of Development Economics*, **61**, 61–84.

Svensson, J. (2003) 'Why conditional aid does not work and what can be done about it', *Journal of Development Economics*, **70**, 381–402.

Swinnen, J. and Heinegg, A. (2002) 'On the political economy of land reforms in the former Soviet Union', *Journal of International Development*, **14**, 1019–33.

Tchetvernina, T., Moskovskaya, A., Soboleva, I., and Stepantchikova, N. (2001) *Labour Market Flexibility and Employment Security: Russian Federation*. Geneva: International Labour Office (ILO), Employment Sector.

Teal, F. (2006) 'Consumption and welfare in Ghana', *Journal of Development Studies*, **42** (October), 1252–69.

Teera, J., and Hudson, J. (2004) 'Tax performance: a comparative study'. *Journal of International Development*, **16**, 785–803.

Teorell, J., Charron, N., Samanni, M., Holmberg, S., and Rothstein, B. (2009) The Quality of Government Dataset, version 17 June 2009. University of Gothenburg, The Quality of Government Institute (www.qog.pol.gu.se).

Teubal, M. (2001) 'Rise and collapse of neoliberalism in Argentina: the role of economic groups', *Journal of Developing Societies*, **20** (3–4), 173–88.

Thacker, S. (1999) 'The high politics of IMF lending', *World Politics*, **52** (1), 38–75.

Thacker, S. (2006) 'The high politics of IMF lending', chapter 5 in G. Ranis, J.R. Vreeland, and S. Kosack (eds) *Globalisation and the Nation State: The Impact of the IMF and World Bank*. London: Routledge.

Therkildsen, O. (2008) *Taxation and State-building with a (more) Human Face*. Policy Brief, October, Danish Institute for International Studies, www.diis.dk/oth.

Theroux, P. (2003) *Dark Star Safari: Overland from Cairo to Cape Town*. London: Penguin.

Thirkell-White, B. (2003) 'The IMF, good governance and middle-income countries', *European Journal of Development Studies*, **15**, 99–125.

Thirkell-White, B. (2004) 'The International Monetary Fund and civil society', *New Political Economy*, **9**, 251–70.

Thirkell-White, B. (2005a) *The IMF and the Politics of Financial Globalisation: From the Asian Crisis to a New International Financial Architecture*. Basingstoke: Palgrave Macmillan.

Thirkell-White, B. (2005b) 'The Wall-Street-Treasury-IMF complex after Asia: neoliberalism in decline?' in R. Robison (ed.) *The Neo-liberal Revolution: Forging the Market State*. Basingstoke, Palgrave.

Thirkell-White, B. (2007a) 'The political economy of financial crisis in Malaysia and Indonesia', paper presented at International Studies Association Annual Convention, Chicago, February.

Thirkell-White, B. (2007b) 'Indonesia and Malaysia; the persistence of domestic state-business relationships', in J. Robertson (ed.) *Power and Politics After Financial Crisis: Rethinking Foreign Opportunism in Emerging Markets*. Basingstoke: Palgrave Macmillan.

Thirtle, C., Lin, L., and Piesse, J. (2002) *The Impact of Research-led Agricultural Productivity Growth on Poverty Reduction in Africa, Asia and Latin America*. King's College London: Management Centre Research Paper 016.

Tignor, R. (2005) *W. Arthur Lewis and the Birth of Development Economics.* Princeton NJ: Princeton University Press.

Timmer, P. (1975) 'The political economy of rice in Asia: Indonesia', *Food Research Institute Studies,* **14**, 197–231.

Timmer, P. (2004a) 'The road to pro-poor growth: the Indonesian experience in regional perspective', *Bulletin of Indonesian Economic Studies,* **40**, 173–203.

Timmer, P. (2004b) 'Operationalising pro-poor growth: Indonesia'. Working paper produced for UK Department of International Development, available at www.dfid.gov.uk.

Timmer, P. (2007) 'How Indonesia connected the poor to rapid economic growth', Chapter 2 in T. Besley and L. Cord (2007), *Delivering on the Promise of Pro-poor Growth: Insights and Lessons From Country Experiences.* Washington and London: World Bank and Palgrave Macmillan.

Timmins, N. (1995) *The Five Giants.* London: HarperCollins.

Tiwari, M. (2015) 'Looking back to move forward: the MDGs and the road to post 2015: introduction to JID special issue on reflections on the post 2015 debate' *Journal of International Development,* **27** (April).

Tornquist, O. (2006) 'Assessing democracy from below: a framework and Indonesian pilot study', *Democratization,* **13** (2).

Toye, J. (1993) *Dilemmas of Development: Reflections on the Counter-revolution in Development Theory and Practice.* Oxford: Blackwell.

Toye, J. (1995) 'Ghana', Chapter 14 in P. Mosley, J. Harrigan, and J. Toye (eds) *Aid and Power: The World Bank and Policy-based Lending.* London: Routledge. 2 vols.

Toye, J. and Toye, R. (2004) *The UN and Global Political Economy: Trade, Finance and Development.* Bloomington: Indiana University Press.

Treisman, D. (1999) *After the Deluge: Regional Crises and Political Consolidation in Russia.* Ann Arbor: University of Michigan Press.

Treisman, D. and Gimpelson, V. (2001) 'Political business cycles and Russian elections, or the manipulations of "Chudar" ', *British Journal of Political Science,* **31**, 225–46.

Tripp, R. and Marfo, K. (1997) 'Maize technology development in Ghana during economic decline and recovery', Chapter 7 in D. Byerlee and C.K. Eicher (eds), *Africa's Emerging Maize Revolution,* Boulder, Colorado: Lynne Rienner.

Uganda Government, Ministry of Finance (2007) *Moving out of Poverty: Understanding Freedom, Democracy and Growth From the Bottom Up.* Available at www.finance.go.ug/uppap.

UNDP (United Nations Development Programme) (2014) *The Millennium Development Goals Report 2014,* www.undp.org/content/dam/undp/library/MDG/UNDP_MDG Reports_ SP_2014Final1.pdf.

UNICEF (2002) *Chicos y Chicas en Riesgo Educativo: El Trabajo Infantil en la Argentina* (Children's education at risk: child labour in Argentina). Buenos Aires: UNICEF.

United Kingdom, Ministry of Overseas Development (1975) *Overseas Development. The Changing Emphasis in British Aid Policies: More Help for the Poorest.* London: HMSO (Cmnd 6270).

United Kingdom, Department for International Development (2000) *Eliminating World Poverty: Making Globalisation Work for the Poor.* London, HMSO.

United Kingdom, Department for International Development, Foreign and Commonwealth Office, and HM Treasury (2005) *Partnerships for Poverty Reduction: Rethinking Conditionality.* London: HMSO.

United Kingdom, House of Commons (2002) *Fifth Report from the International Development Committee. Session 2001–2:* HC-785-II. Pages 70–84 on Tobin tax variants.

United Kingdom Treasury (2004) *The International Finance Facility.* Treasury Public Affairs Department, London: Stationery Office.

United Nations (1951) *Measures for the Economic Development of Underdeveloped Countries.* New York: United Nations Economic and Social Council.

United States Treasury (2000a) *Report on IMF reforms (report to Congress in accordance with sections 610(a) and 613(a) of the Foreign Operations Appropriation Act, 1999) March 2000 version.*

United States Treasury (2000b) *Response to the report of the International Financial Institution Advisory Commission 8th June 2000.*

Unsworth, S. (2009) 'What's politics got to do with it? Why donors find it so hard to come to terms with politics, and why this matters', *Journal of International Development,* **21**, 883–94.

Valente, C. (2008) *Land Transfers in South Africa: what Impact on Beneficiary Welfare?* PhD thesis, University of Sheffield.

Valente, C. (2009) 'The food (in) security impact of land redistribution in South Africa: microeconometric evidence from national data', *World Development,* **37**, 1540–53.

Van Cott, D.L. (2003) 'From exclusion to inclusion', Bolivia's 2002 elections', *Journal of Latin American Studies,* **35**, 751–75.

van de Laar, A. (1980) *The World Bank and the Poor.* The Hague: Martinus Nijhoff Publishing.

van de Walle, N. (2001) *African Economies and the Politics of Permanent Crisis 1979–1999.* Cambridge: Cambridge University Press.

van de Walle, N. (2005) *Overcoming Stagnation in Aid-dependent Countries.* Washington, DC: Center for Global Development.

van Zyl, J. (1996) 'The farm size-efficiency relationship' in J. van Zyl, J. Kirsten, and H. Binswanger (eds) *Agricultural Land Reform in South Africa.* Cape Town: Oxford University Press.

Varangis, P. and Schreiber, G. (2002) 'Cocoa market reforms in West Africa', in T. Akiyama, J. Baffes, D. Larson, and P. Varangis (eds) *Lessons from Market Reforms Over the Last Two Decades.* Washington, DC: World Bank.

Verschoor, A. (2007) 'The Trojan-horse principle in development assistance: a reading of Uganda's experience with aid', *Review of Development Economics,* **11**, 78–92.

Vines, D. and Gilbert, C. (2004) *The IMF and its Critics: Reform of Global Financial Architecture.* Cambridge: Cambridge University Press.

Wade, R. (1996) 'Japan, the World Bank and the art of paradigm maintenance: the East Asian miracle in political perspective', *New Left Review,* **217**, 3–37.

Weeks, J. (1973) 'Uneven sectoral development and the role of the state', *IDS Bulletin,* **5** (October), 76–82.

Weeks, J. (1992) *Development Strategy and the Economy of Sierra Leone.* Basingstoke: Macmillan and New York: St Martin's Press.

Wegren, S. (2002) 'Rural orientations to land privatisation in Russia', *Journal of International Development,* **14**, 1033–45.

Weisbrot, W. and Sandoval, L. (2007) 'Bolivia's economy: an update', Issue Brief, Center for Economic and Policy Research, available at http://www.cepr.net.

Wells, J. (1974) 'Distribution of earnings, growth and the structure of demand in Brazil during the 1960s', *World Development,* **2** (January), 9–24.

Whaites, A. (2008) 'States in development: understanding state-building', unpublished working paper, Department for International Development, London.

Whiteley, P. (2000) 'Economic growth and social capital', *Political Studies,* **48**, 443–66.

Whitfield, L. (2008) 'State elites and the "new poverty agenda" in Ghana', unpublished paper, Danish Institute of International Studies.

Whitfield, L. (ed.) (2009a) *The Politics of Aid: African Strategies for Dealing With Donors.* Oxford: Oxford University Press.

Whitfield, L. (2009b) 'Ghana: breaking out of aid dependence? Economic and political barriers to ownership', Chapter in Whitfield (ed.) (2009a).

Whitfield, L. (2009c) 'Ghana since 1993: a successful democratic experiment', Chapter 4 in A.R. Mustapha and L. Whitfield (eds) *Elites and Poverty in Africa.* Oxford: Oxford University Press.

Wiggins, S. (1985) 'The planning and management of integrated rural development in drylands: early lessons from Kenya's arid and semi-arid lands programmes', *Public Administration and Development,* 5, 91–109.

Wilkie, J. (1967) *The Mexican Revolution: Federal Expenditure and Social Change Since 1910.* Berkeley: University of California Press.

Willett, T. (2003) 'The IMF and capital account crises: the case for separate lender of last resort and conditionality functions'. Chapter 13 in G. Ranis, J. Vreeland, and S. Kosack (eds) *Globalisation and the Nation State; the Impact of the IMF and World Bank.* London: Routledge.

Williams, D. and Young, T. (1994) 'Governance, the World Bank and liberal theory', *Political Studies,* **42**, 84–100.

Wilson, F. (1972) *Labour in the South African Gold Mines 1911–1969.* Cambridge: Cambridge University Press, African Studies Series 6.

Wimmer, A., de Soysa, I., and Wagner, C. (2002) 'Political science tools for assessing feasibility and sustainability of reforms'. Washington, DC: unpublished paper for Independent Evaluation Office of the IMF.

Winters, J.A. (1996) *Power in Motion: Capital Mobility and the Indonesian State.* Ithaca NY: Cornell University Press.

Wolff, J. (2007) '(De-)mobilising the marginalised: a comparison of the Argentine *piqueteros* and Ecuador's indigenous movement', *Journal of Latin American Studies,* **39**, 1–29.

Woods, N. (1998). *Governance in International Organizations: the Case for Reform in the Bretton Woods Institutions. International Monetary and Financial Issues in the 1990s.* UNCTAD/G24. Geneva, United Nations.

Woods, N. (2000) 'The challenge of good governance for the IMF and the World Bank themselves', *World Development,* **28** (5).

Wood, G. (2003) 'Staying secure, staying poor: the Faustian bargain', *World Development,* **31** (April), 455–71.

Woods, N. (2006) *The Globalizers: The IMF, the World Bank and their Borrowers.* Ithaca, New York: Cornell University Press.

Woolcock, M. (1998) 'Social capital and economic development: toward a theoretical synthesis and policy framework', *Theory and Society,* **27**, 151–208.

Woolcock, M. and Narayan, D. (2000) 'Social capital: implications for development theory, research and policy', *World Bank Research Observer,* **15** (August), 225–49.

World Bank (1983) *Focus on Poverty: a Report by a Task Force of the World Bank,* Washington, DC: World Bank.

World Bank (1989) *Sub-saharan Africa: from Crisis to Sustainable Growth: a Long Term Perspective.* Cambridge, Cambridge University Press.

World Bank (1990) *World Development Report 1990: Poverty.* Washington, DC: World Bank.

World Bank (1991) *World Development Report 1991: the Challenge of Development,* Washington, DC: World Bank.

World Bank (1993) *The East Asian miracle: Economic Growth and Public Policy.* Washington, DC: World Bank.

World Bank (1994) *Adjustment in Africa.* Oxford and New York: Oxford University Press.

World Bank (1997) *World Development Report 1997: the State in a Changing World.* Washington, DC: World Bank.

World Bank (2000) *World Development Report 2000: Attacking Poverty*. Washington, DC: World Bank.

World Bank (2003) Report No. 26127, *Argentina. Crisis and Poverty 2003 A Poverty Assessment*, Volume I: Main Report, PREM (Washington, DC: The World Bank).

World Bank (2004) *Russian Federation: Poverty Assessment*. Report 28923-RU. 28 June. Washington DC: World Bank Poverty Reduction and Economic Management Unit.

World Bank and IMF (2005a) '2005 review of the PRS approach: balancing accountabilities and scaling up results'. http://go.worldbank.org/815EOPWMZO.

World Bank (2005b) *Well-being and Poverty in Ethiopia; the Role of Agriculture and Agency*, report 29468-ET, Washington, DC, 18, July.

World Bank (2006a) *World Development Report 2006: Equity and Development*, Washington, DC: World Bank.

World Bank (2006b) *Indonesia: Making the New Indonesia Work for the Poor*. Washington, DC: World Bank.

World Bank (2007) *World Development Report 2007: Agriculture for Development*. Washington, DC: World Bank.

World Bank (2010) *The World Bank in Russia: Russian Economic Report*. At www.worldbank.org.ru.

Wraith, R. (1967) *Guggisberg*. Oxford: Oxford University Press.

Yemtsov, R. (2003) *Quo vadis? Inequality and Poverty Dynamics Across Russian Regions*. Helsinki: WIDER discussion paper.

Index

Material appearing in the footnotes is suffixed 'n', e.g. 201 n. 15 = page 201, footnote 15.

The manufacturer's authorised representative in the EU for product safety is Oxford University Press España S.A. of El Parque Empresarial San Fernando de Henares, Avenida de Castilla, 2 - 28830 Madrid (www.oup.es/en or product.safety@oup.com). OUP España S.A. also acts as importer into Spain of products made by the manufacturer.
Printed and bound by CPI Group (UK) Ltd, Croydon, CR0 4YY
14/09/2026
02216293-0013